BLACK THEOLOGY:
A DOCUMENTARY HISTORY,
1966–1979

BLACK THEOLOGY:
A DOCUMENTARY HISTORY,
1966–1979

Edited by
Gayraud S. Wilmore and James H. Cone

ORBIS BOOKS
Maryknoll, New York 10545

The Catholic Foreign Mission Society of America (Maryknoll) recruits and trains people for overseas missionary service. Through Orbis Books Maryknoll aims to foster the international dialogue that is essential to mission. The books published, however, reflect the opinions of their authors and are not meant to represent the official position of the society.

Library of Congress Cataloging in Publication Data

Main entry under title:

Black Theology.

    Bibliography: p.
    1.   Black theology—Addresses, essays, lectures.
2.   Afro-Americans—Religion—Addresses, essays, lectures.
3.   Black power—Addresses, essays, lectures.
I.   Wilmore, Gayraud S.   II.   Cone, James H.
BT82.7.B56   230   79-12747
ISBN 0-88344-041-5
ISBN 0-88344-042-3 pbk.

Second Printing, April 1980

CONTENTS

PART III
BLACK THEOLOGY AND THE RESPONSE OF WHITE THEOLOGIANS

PART IV
BLACK THEOLOGY AND THE BLACK CHURCH

PART V
BLACK THEOLOGY AND BLACK WOMEN

PART VI
BLACK THEOLOGY AND THIRD WORLD THEOLOGIES

Acknowledgment is gratefully extended for permission to reprint the following:

"Black Power and the American Christ" by Vincent Harding. Copyright 1967 Christian Century Foundation. Reprinted by permission from the January 4, 1967, issue of *The Christian Century*.

"Black Power: A Religious Opportunity." Reprinted by permission of Hawthorn Books, Inc., from *Black Power and Urban Unrest* by Nathan Wright, Jr. Copyright © 1967 Nathan Wright, Jr. All rights reserved.

"Black Theology of Liberation" from *The Radical Imperative* by John C. Bennett. Copyright © 1975, The Westminster Press. Used by permission.

"Currents and Crosscurrents in South African Black Theology" by David J. Bosch. Reprinted from *Journal of Religion in Africa*, vol. 6, no. 1 (1974). Reprinted by permission of E. J. Brill.

"Toward a Black Catholic Theology" by Edward K. Braxton, from *Freeing the Spirit* vol. 5, no. 2 (1977), pp. 3–6. Reprinted with permission.

"Let's Not Waste the Holy Spirit" from *Black Christian Nationalism* by Albert B. Cleage, Jr. Copyright © 1972 by Albert B. Cleage, Jr. By permission of William Morrow & Company.

"Black Women and the Churches: Triple Jeopardy" by Theressa Hoover, from *Sexist Religion and Women in the Church* by A. Hageman, copyright © 1974. Used by permission of Follett Publishing Company.

"Black Theology and Feminist Theology: A Comparative View" by Pauli Murray, from the January 1978 *Anglican Theological Review* (600 Haven Street, Evanston, Ill. 60201). Used by permission.

"In Search of Our Mothers' Gardens" by Alice Walker, from *Ms.* magazine, vol. 2, no. 11, May 1974. Reprinted with permission.

"An African Views American Black Theology" by John Mbiti. Reprinted from *Worldview*, August 1974. Used by permission of *Worldview*.

GENERAL INTRODUCTION

A few years ago James H. Cone asked me if I had considered editing a book for seminary students that would collect and appraise the various sources for Black Theology embedded in the history and culture of our people in the Americas and West Africa. As intrigued as I was with the idea, my work at Boston University School of Theology during that period would not permit me to get on with it. This book is, in a way, a much less ambitious version of what Professor Cone proposed and, observing the maxim that "the one who has a good idea gets appointed to the committee," I have enlisted him in its preparation.

The process we have followed here is different from what is usually found in a work prepared by two authors. Except for consultation about the content of the essays each of us has written, we did not attempt to blend our individual voices into a single harmonious sound. In other words, we collaborated in the compilation of the work as a whole, but made no effort to present a uniform approach to the material or to flatten out the peaks and promontories of conceptual and stylistic differences. For that reason each of us has initialed his own contributions in order that the reader may know precisely who should be blamed for what!

This kind of collaboration commended itself to us because it would present to the reader the topic from two different approaches which cohere within the same school of thought, but take their departures from different academic disciplines—systematic theology and history.

But more needs to be said on this point. Relative to my own generation of teachers, James H. Cone belongs to that younger group whose books and articles first began to appear in the late 1960s. Moreover, Cone was born and received his undergraduate education in the South. I was born several years earlier and educated in the North. Although both of us were converted and "brought up" in Black churches, his home congregation was a part of a historic Black denomination while mine was a Black congregation of a predominantly White denomination. Further, his career has been almost exclusively academic, as a college and seminary professor, with a brief appointment as a local pastor. More than half of mine has been as a pastor and social activist on the staffs of national agencies of my church. Since 1969 Cone and I have worked together to give Black theological leadership a voice both in the United States and overseas. There is much that we hold in common, but we have our differences.

1

In the Introduction to Part II I have written about what the work of James H. Cone has meant to my ministry over the past ten years. But this is probably enough to indicate a certain variance and complementarity between us which, if our assumption is correct, should help the introductions to the material represent some important and interesting perspectives on the current discussion about Black Theology within the Black Christian community.

Our purpose is threefold. First, we wanted to gather together the most significant documents of the Black churches and church-related movements which would present the origin and development of Black Theology. The theological renaissance we have witnessed and participated in over these last ten years did not fall from the sky, nor was it born in the minds of scholars. It arose out of what Ralph Ellison has described in another context as a "concert of sensibilities" among leaders within the institutional Black Church as they sought to respond to events in the secular society. From the beginning it had an institutional base, first within the churches themselves, and then within interdenominational organizations such as the National Conference of Black Churchmen (NCBC),* the Southern Christian Leadership Conference (SCLC),[1] the Interreligious Foundation for Community Organization (IFCO), the Alamo Black Clergy of the San Francisco Bay Area, the Philadelphia Council of Black Clergy, and other local and regional caucuses. We have reprinted here those documents we considered most important in terms of chronology and subject matter. It was around these statements by Black churchmen that a movement was mobilized within and alongside religious institutions as a counterpoise to secular groups such as the National Association for the Advancement of Colored People (NAACP), the National Urban League and the Congress of Racial Equality. Black Theology was, in a sense, the intellectual spark that flew from the anvil of oppression upon which the Black religious groups were hammered into existence.

Second, we wanted to fill out the picture with articles and essays that presented the program of Black Theology, or played a significant role in setting Black preachers and scholars in motion. Here the selection process became more difficult. Other observers will surely contest our choices and some will want to add more than we found practicable to include. The literature on Black Theology is voluminous. It comprises not only what has been written in the United States, but also in Africa and the Caribbean. We have deliberately avoided material from influential books in this vast area, but have instead concentrated on journal articles that made an impact at the time of their publication even if, as is so often the case in a revolutionary situation, they faded from view as time went on.

*The NCBC was orginally the National Committee of Negro Churchmen (NCNC). The name was changed to the National Committee of Black Churchmen in 1967. After 1972 it became the National Conference of Black Churchmen. The NCBC includes both men and women and there is now a proposal to rename it the National Conference of Black Christians. To avoid confusion, the organization is usually termed the National Conference of Black Churchmen in this book except in the original documents.

Finally, it was our intention to write the kind of critical commentaries that would reflect our own personal experience as participants in what transpired. The personal factor is crucial in this connection. Both Black religion and theological reflection are characteristically biographical and experiential. This is, perhaps, one of the features which sets them apart from the mainline White Church. Black people have done theology out of their guts, out of individual and collective experiences of struggle. The message of the Bible did not come to us in monasteries, in theological libraries, or in debates with philosophers and kings, but in "hush-arbor" meetings out of earshot of the patrollers, under the lash of plantation overseers, and in the dilapidated, impoverished ghettos of a hundred cities that continue to be concentration camps for an exploited racial group.

In contrast to most of White theological writing, a strong personal note runs through what Cone and I have written here. We have, in a sense, "testified." Without what we would consider an undue strain for "objectivity," we have sought to share ourselves freely, and sometimes intimately, in reflection upon the meaning of the events that have shaped our minds over the past few years and, indeed, mark the course of our own public and private struggles. Whether or not the essays introductory to each part of the book clarify how this remarkable movement developed, and whether or not we have been faithful to the truth, the reader must decide. In both the text and in notes we have indicated the sources of opinions that vary from our own. But for those who would plead that they have no basis for evaluation, we have no apology. As Paul said to Festus, ". . . this thing was not done in a corner." To those scholars and church leaders who closed their eyes or looked away in another direction, we can only say what Paul might have said to Festus: "You obviously didn't understand the situation."

Theological students, pastors, and thoughtful laypeople have had some difficulty understanding the origin, development, and significance of Black Theology in the United States and the Third World. It has been our purpose, when the failure of leadership in Washington, the retrenchment of the Bakke decision, and the escalation of the struggle in Southern Africa reveal ominous clouds on the horizon, to get into their hands a documentary history of what a small, vocal minority of Black Christians made of survival and liberation through Jesus Christ.

In the Black community news about Jesus is habitually read between the lines, or as a transparent overlay, of the text that history writes in the public media. Karl Barth may not have realized it, but what he is alleged to have said about Christians reading the Bible in one hand and the newspaper in the other is precisely what we have been doing for years. From the beginning Black Theology and Black History have been inseparable. Our interpretation of history, its triumphs and tragedies, has come out of an encounter with the God of history. The world has been a stage, and the slaves and masters—the Black underclass and the White establishment—have supplied the *dramatis personae* for God's struggle in behalf of his oppressed Black children. Black History, therefore, must be understood as sacred history and Black theological thought as eventful theology.

This is not to say that Black Christians have been involved in an impulsive response to the flux of circumstance. Black Theology is not an unsophisticated, anti-intellectual reaction to whatever is happening at any moment in time—a mixture of emotion and pious propaganda. It is, rather, a hardheaded, practical, and passionate reading of the signs of the times in the White community as well as the Black. It is an elucidation of what we have understood God to be about in our history, particularly in the history of our struggle against racist oppression. This book will demonstrate that Black Theology was formulated by Christian activists in response to events—events which had the unmistakable sign that God is saying and doing something about Black people in White America.

Part I deals with the evolution of theological reflection out of the church-related civil rights movement and the quasi-religious movement of Black Power in the late 1960s. The White establishment came to regard the first with suspicion and the second with fear. The documents show that Black churchmen rejected both the conservatism and the liberalism which were behind these reactions. The decisions they made launched the first attempt since Garveyism to separate mainline Black Christianity from the theology of the White churches and conceive liberation in the context of the legitimate use of ethnic consciousness and power.

We turn in Part II to the attack upon White religion that characterized the Black Manifesto crisis and the theology that flowed from it. Here Nathan Wright's pithy comment about the role of secular powers in relation to the forces of organized religion seems especially prophetic.

> In some sense of the word, all channels for the operation of cosmic purposes are woefully unworthy of their task. . . . If the devil himself had raised in these recent months the issue of power, it could hardly be less grace-laden for us and for our world.[2]

Clearly the material in Part II shows that the death of "Christian race relations" occasioned by the Black Manifesto not only deepened the crisis, but brought about a theological shift far distant from the social Christianity and integrationism of the statement that forty-eight prominent church leaders signed on July 31, 1966. Nothing illustrates more dramatically the eventful nature of Black Theology than the Atlanta statement of 1969. Black theologians were saying that God himself, through the boisterous and sometimes bumbling tactics of James Forman, opened the door for a new theological interpretation legitimating the disruption of White church services and the demand for reparations.

The documents and articles in Parts I and II belong to the first developmental stage of contemporary Black Theology.[3] They signaled the end of the subordination of the Black Church to the norms of White Protestantism. We no longer trusted one another. Black Christians could not trust White church leaders really to understand and appreciate the power nature and radicality of the gospel in the postintegration period. White church leaders could not trust Black Christians to make a theological interpretation of Black pride and power without betraying the transcendence and colorlessness of the gospel.

Some of this emerges in the articles we have included in Part III, which deals with the response of White theologians. But not all White theologians misunderstood or mistrusted what we were about. We have tried to be stringently fair about that and to include those articles constructive for Black Theology as well as those that bear out our contention about the moral failure of White Christianity.

Part III opens up a second stage in Black Theology. It was becoming more of an academic affair among a relatively small group of schoolmen, Black and White. It is no accident, for example, that in this period the Society for the Study of Black Religion was organized under the leadership of C. Shelby Rooks, of the Fund for Theological Education in Princeton, New Jersey. Composed mainly of Black seminary professors (there were many more than in the previous decade), this group inherited the scholarly interests of the waning National Conference of Black Churchmen (NCBC) and during the early 1970s gave a rather decorous respectability to Black Theology. It encouraged the reading of papers and fostered a dialogue with scholars working on indigenous theologies in Africa and the Caribbean. A Third World perspective was developing in Black Theology in the United States. Recalling how Black artists were rarely appreciated at home until they received attention abroad, this may have had something to do with the increasing attention we received from White American theologians.

In any case, it should be emphasized that this second stage was not merely one of jousting with White academicians while the discussion of Black Theology went begging for an audience in the Black churches. What has already been said about the pressure of events upon theological reflection holds firm. With few exceptions the documents in Part IV belong to this stage of development and represent the growing response of the historic Black churches and sects to Black Theology and its ability rightly to divide the word of truth in the confusion of a rapidly changing historical situation.

Richard Nixon assumed the presidency on January 20, 1969. He was just in time to deal with the new militancy in the Black community. By the next year his Southern strategy of law and order and "benign neglect" of the poor disparaged the self-interests of Black people. He set about to reverse the War on Poverty begun by Lyndon Johnson and, with a viciousness bordering on genocide, began a systematic and clandestine elimination of Black radicalism. Soon after the Nixon era began, the White denominations broke away from their Black caucuses, and the Interreligious Foundation for Community Organization floundered in disuse. Local congregations and judicatories fumed over such improprieties as Black Christian support for Angela Davis. Contributions to national denominational budgets fell off as Whites complained that money was still being funneled to Black militants. By the time of the humiliating denouement of Nixon's Watergate administration in August 1974, what had been known as the "church civil rights coalition" was dead. From that time to the present the Black Theology movement has been regarded with dismay by the White Church, Protestant and Roman Catholic.

The material in Part IV will show, however, that these national developments helped to push the official leadership of the Black denominations toward some of the emphases of the younger theologians, even though many Black Christians continued to be ignorant of what they were writing. With one notable exception all the major Black churches that had anything at all to say about theology in the 1970s gave open or tacit approbation to the main concepts of Black Theology. This little-known fact, well demonstrated by the documents, disproves the frequent allegation that the movement has no credibility in the Black Church.

Thus the second stage of Black Theology in the United States was much more complex than the first. Its reformulation in the NCBC statements was a reaction to the attempt of most White theologians to see it as a mere fad and appendage to Black Power. Both the NCBC and church documents represent the disillusionment and defiance of Black Christians over the retrenchment of the Republican years—a retrenchment paralleled in the national religious institutions of the White Christian middle class. In such a climate it is not surprising that the historic Black churches spoke out against the conservatism that was leading the American and European churches away from the confrontation with racism and imperialism that characterized the 1960s. And it was appropriate that scholarly Black preachers and seminary professors would seek to disprove the argument that Black Theology was nothing more than pious sociology and had no place in the world of religious thought.

In the spring of 1976 the *Journal of Religious Thought* of Howard University's School of Religion published a new statement on Black Theology, which indicated that an important transition was in process. Although the statement reaffirmed the position taken in 1969 it was scrupulous in its avoidance of identification with either the Hartford or the Boston statements in which two different groups of White theologians sought to define the faith for the times. They were speaking to a difficult period of the mid-1970s when mounting conservatism on one hand, and the vitality of Eastern cults on the other, challenged the White denominations.

The angle of its attack on racism, individualism, and the materialism of the American economic system shows that the 1976 statement reflected the increasing influence of Latin American and other Third World theologies on the Black theologians. With this statement, coming near the end of Part IV, we are beginning to run out of the usefulness of the way we had organized the book up to that point. On the threshold of a new and final stage of theological development it appeared that the chronological pattern of the book should now yield to topical considerations which would permit us to deal with two developments that actually span the entire history of the movement—Black women and the dialogue with African theologians. It may be helpful for the reader to keep things in perspective by skipping to Parts V and VI after reading the 1976 statement on Black Theology and then coming back to the 1977 statement and Cone's Atlanta address at the end. For with those two pieces we enter upon the third and present phase of this theological odyssey.

Part V, we willingly concede, is something of an embarrassment. Why should essays written by Black women be consigned to a separate section? The articles themselves, introduced by James Cone, who has experienced the burden of representing the men before conferences of Black women theological students, defines the problem. Black Theology has been a Black-male-dominated enterprise and to the extent that it continues to be so, our sisters say quite clearly, it cannot be an authentic means of liberation.

The overwhelming predominance of Black women in our churches makes this situation all the more ironical. From the beginning of the movement women have been involved, but the very fact that we have gathered their contributions in one of the closing sections of the book is as much a testimony to institutional chauvinism as it is to their marginality. That is one of the changes we are likely to see in the third phase of Black Theology. The few essays we have chosen for this section are eloquent reminders that this glaring deficiency in the Black Church, and therefore in its theology, is more obvious and more inexcusable there than in the secular Black community. Judgment begins, once again, in the household of God.

We come finally to Part VI and the relationship between our work in the United States and theological work in the Third World. From one viewpoint this discussion might well have come earlier in the book. The National Conference of Black Churchmen began its dialogue with African theologians in 1969. But from another viewpoint we have placed it where it belongs, for 1977 was something of a watershed for our encounter with Third World theologies and the real beginning of a deepened awareness of the need to "internationalize" Black Theology in the United States. In December of that year the second Ecumenical Conference of Third World Theologians was held in Ghana, where both Black men and women from the United States participated. Equally important was the August 1977 conference of the Black Theology Project of Theology in the Americas in Atlanta, Georgia, where the involvement of people from the Third World and a focus on the situation in Southern Africa significantly influenced the substance and tone of the conference's "Message to the Black Church and Community." Some concluding comments need to be made about the political and economic climate in which these two historic events took place. Once again the leverage of history on theology becomes evident—a leverage which in 1977 lifted Black Theology in America into the third and present stage of its development.

When Jimmy Carter took office in January 1977 the bleak statistics on the economic condition of Black Americans was his legacy from the Nixon-Ford years. The unemployment rate was 13.2 percent as compared with 6.1 percent for Whites. Black teenagers were experiencing 39 percent unemployment, with figures running as high as 45 percent in some inner-city areas. Although Blacks were earning their highest wages in history in 1977, almost a third of all Black families were beneath the $5,500 poverty line for an urban family of four. Only 8.9 percent of White families were in that category. In the meantime, the cities were stagnating with the loss of more than a million jobs to the suburbs since 1969. They festered with widespread physical decay, inferior and segregated public schools, and Black-on-Black crime. Black people looked expectantly toward Washington where Carter, who would not have been there without our large majorities at the polls, faced the challenge of a conservative Supreme Court and an apathetic Congress.

By the time of the annual conventions of the National Urban League and the NAACP that summer it was clear to Vernon Jordan and other Black leaders that Carter's appointment of Andrew Young and Patricia Harris to high offices should not be allowed to disguise his failure to move quickly to amend disastrous conditions in the Black community. The coincidence of a presidential election year with the national bicentennial celebration had made patriotic rhetoric the common commodity of both church and state for several tedious months. But when the memory of God and the Rights of Man faded into the past with the campaign slogans of Gerald Ford and Jimmy Carter, White America returned to its customary indifference about the plight of the poor and the minorities. The gap continued to widen between the rising middle class of both colors plus the eight to ten million destitute Americans, predominantly Black, Native American, and Hispanic. Monsignor Geno Baroni, the erstwhile champion of the "White ethnics," warned that this unmeltable underclass "presents our most dangerous crisis, more dangerous than the Depression of 1929, and more complex."[4]

An equally complex and dangerous situation existed in Southern Africa which, since the late 1960s, had become an urgent concern for increasing numbers of Black Americans. The stalemate in Zimbabwe and Namibia under White minority rule had grown steadily more explosive. In June 1976 a rebellion broke out between thousands of Black students and the police in the segregated township of Soweto in South Africa. This precipitated the most serious crisis for the Vorster government since Sharpeville.

Carter appointed Andrew Young ambassador to the United Nations and broke the long-standing American estrangment from the front-line African states by inviting President Julius K. Nyerere to Washington. It was an uncertain gesture. Many Blacks regarded these motions toward Africa as a calculated move to prevent Soviet incursion and to mollify the outrage of Black citizens who were beginning to be sensitive to the linkages between American-supported racism in Africa and their own treatment in the United States. The Soweto crisis continued to fan the flames of revolution during 1977 even as Vice-President Mondale and Ambassador Young made unprecedented diplomatic journeys to the continent in behalf of negotiated settlements in Salisbury and Pretoria.

It was in this charged atmosphere of disappointments at home and anxieties about the situation in Africa that the first national conference on Black Theology met for five days in Atlanta in August 1977. Unlike any previous meeting since the Detroit IFCO conference in 1969, the Atlanta conference included not only the familiar church leaders and theologians, but the so-called "street people" and representatives of left-wing political organizations. It was less dominated by professional theologians and less concerned simply to react to what was or was not happening in the White churches. This meeting was more political and more international than any previous conference of either the Black churchmen's group or the Society for the Study of Black Religion. And it was under the sponsorship of neither of those two organizations. Theology in the Americas (TIA), a new interracial and predominantly Roman Catholic agency that organized the first engagement between North American and Latin American theologians in Detroit in 1975, had been authorized by the participants to continue with a series of conferences to promote the formulation of a North American theology of liberation. Under the leadership of Sergio Torres, an exiled Chilean priest and executive secretary of TIA, and the staff work of two Christian activists who headed the Black Theology Project, Muhammad Kenyatta, a Baptist minister, and Sister M. Shawn Copeland, O.P., a national planning committee was set up. The Atlanta conference was chaired by Charles Spivey, a Black pastor from Chicago.

It is possible to exaggerate the importance of keynote addresses, but it is safe to say that James H. Cone's paper, which opened the Atlanta conference, did what keynotes are supposed to do. It defined the basic issues and pointed the direction of the future. In my opinion, this paper (reprinted as the last document in Part IV) marks the beginning of the third stage of Black Theology in the United States. Cone was critical of conservative tendencies in the Black denominations and called for the application of "the most severe scientific analysis to our church communities in terms of economics and politics." He stressed the need for the churches to deal with their "credibility problem" and questioned whether their dreams of a new heaven and a new earth embraced Western capitalism, or "a radically new way of life more consistent with African socialism as expressed in the Arusha Declaration in Tanzania."

These were not entirely unprecedented ideas. They are certainly adumbrated in some of the earlier documents of the NCBC. But they are ideas that Cone's writings had not emphasized. In opening the door to the contribution of Marxism in shaping a praxis for Black Theology, however, Cone was not uncritical of its deficiencies in the North American situation. He firmly rejected Marxist dogma, for example, which neglected the problem of racism in favor of a class analysis. In that connection he quoted approvingly Mao Tse-tung's comment, "There are people who think that Marxism is a kind of magic truth with which one can cure any disease. We should tell them that dogmas are more useless than cow dung. Dung can be used as fertilizer."

Cone also raised in this address, more sharply than ever before, the African identity of Black Americans. It is even more significant that this Pan-African thesis was balanced with his insistence that "liberation knows no color bar." The universal nature of the gospel connects the liberation of Black people with the liberation of all people from a "world-wide system of oppression." This appraisal of a carefully considered Marxist analysis of capitalism and the emphasis on the common ground which Black Theology shares with other theologies of liberation represents an important turning point in the movement. It set the tone in Altanta for the discussions that followed and the conference message reflects its influence upon the Black Theology Project after 1977.

Whether or not these new emphases can provide the substance for the recruitment and educational tasks of the movement in the 1980s is not yet certain. What seems certain is that the effort to penetrate Black Christianity with a theological and political perspective consistent with Black spirituality, the historic themes of Black folk religion, and the vicissitudes of history made a decisive turn toward the Third World. The earlier stages of Black Theology only glanced in that direction. Since Atlanta, Black theologians have insisted that they are Third World theologians as well.

It is not to be doubted that Black Theology in the United States, particularly as it is done in the Black Theology Project, has been influenced by the work of the Latin American liberation theologians. The very existence of the Black Theology Project, as a continuation of the debate with the Latin Americans that began with the Detroit conference of 1975, is testimony to that fact. But the subterranean radicalism of the nineteenth-century Black churches and the incipient Liberation Theology of the Garvey movement of the twentieth-century have worked their silent magnetism upon an important segment of Black Christianity in America. The future is still open for more light, and the effort of Black theologians and activist preachers in the United States to make the Black Church more relevant to the struggle of oppressed peoples everywhere is by no means played out.

One final word of explanation to the reader is necessary. It may seem strange to compile writings on Black Theology without including significant extracts from the major books that have defined and debated the pivotal theological issues over the last few years. But this book is primarily about the movement aspect of Black Theology. For that reason it focuses on the documents and shorter writings that gave shape to the effort made by many people, within and outside the churches, to advance the witness of Black religion in the arena of politics and social action. The longer contributions of writers such as J. Deotis Roberts, Jr., William R. Jones, Joseph R. Washington, Jr., Major J. Jones, Cecil W. Cone and Joseph A. Johnson, Jr., belong to the more academic side of the movement where professional theologians argued with one another over the biblical and theological basis of the confrontation with White Theology.

There can be no adequate understanding of the full meaning of Black Theology without grappling with those issues, but that was not our primary intention. Nevertheless, some of them are discussed in the parts introduced by James H. Cone. In the concluding essay of this volume he reviews the theological debates from his vantage point as one of the principal contenders. We have also included an annotated bibliography prepared by Vaughn Eason, who has been the executive director of the Black Theology Project since 1978. The reader will find most of the important books and articles necessary for further study in that listing.

We would like to acknowledge the interest and support of many people in the preparation of this book, but the list is too long. A few names, however, should be mentioned: Bishop John Adams of the A.M.E. Church, Bishop Herbert Bell Shaw of the A.M.E. Zion Church, Dr. Emmanuel McCall of the Southern Baptist Convention, Dr. William H. Bentley of the Black evangelicals. These persons supplied indispensable information. Delores Williams and Jacquelyn Grant gave valuable assistance on the topic of Black Theology and Black Women. Cornel West, Lester Scherer, and Vaughn Eason read parts of the final manuscript and made many useful suggestions. Whatever may be the deficiencies of the product must be assumed by ourselves alone. To all we express sincere thanks and beg their tolerance for what has not been done well enough, despite good counsel. We rest in the hope that this after all is only the beginning of setting the record straight. Many and better histories of Black Theology will surely follow in the years to come.

G.S.W.

Notes

1. Although Dr. Martin Luther King, Jr., never sought to draw the Southern Christian Leadership Conference into the Black Theology movement, many of his close associates did, including Ralph Abernathy, Bernard Lee, Wyatt T. Walker, Andrew Young, and Hosea Williams. At the Third Annual Convocation in Oakland, November 11-14, 1969, a national committee was organized representing the National Conference of Black Churchmen (NCBC), SCLC, IFCO, and the Black Economic Development Conference (BEDC). The stated purpose

was to "coordinate policies and programs, to do long-range planning for the politicization and empowerment of the Black community, and to confirm our mutual responsibility for and accountability to one another." From the *Minutes of the Third Annual Convocation*, NCBC.

2. Nathan Wright, Jr., *Black Power and Urban Unrest* (New York: Hawthorn Books, 1967), p. 67.

3. It should be noted that three important publications preceded the NCBC meetings in 1969 and helped to give shape to concepts that became central to Black Theology: Nathan Wright's *Black Power and Urban Unrest*, see pp. 66-69 especially; Vincent Harding's article, "The Religion of Black Power" in Donald R. Cutler, ed., *The Religious Situation: 1968* (Boston: Beacon Press, 1968), pp. 3-38; and Albert B. Cleage's *The Black Messiah* (New York: Sheed and Ward, 1968).

4. *Time* magazine, August 29, 1977, p. 15.

PART I

THE END OF AN ERA:
CIVIL RIGHTS TO BLACK POWER

INTRODUCTION

Mainline Black churches, however exclusive they may seem to outsiders, are usually located in the heart of the ghetto. All appearances to the contrary, they are ghetto institutions and are recognized as such by their pastors and members who may live in other parts of the city and by the "street people" on the block. During the Watts rebellion in Los Angeles when a gang from another vicinity marauded the neighborhood of a prestigious Black Presbyterian church, threatening to burn it down, the young toughs who lived around the church, most of whom had never been inside, protected the building. "If you wanna burn down some White folks' church, that's hip," they said to the outside gang leader, "but this is *our* church, and you ain't messing with it. Understand?" The other gang did. And the church was left unmolested.

Black pastors and church members, even while they may complain about burglaries, broken glass in the parking lot, and vandalism, understand that their churches belong to the neighborhood in which they stand and cannot but be identified with the weal and woe of the impoverished masses with whom many of them have little intercourse except, perhaps, on Sunday mornings. In the case of Black Baptist, African Methodist, and Pentecostal congregations, even those with a strong orientation to middle-class values, some of those masses are members of the church—mixing freely with physicians, lawyers, and schoolteachers at worship and weekday functions. Even the Black congregations of the predominantly White denominations, the Episcopal, United Presbyterian, Congregational, Lutheran, and Roman Catholic, often contain a mixture of the educated Black middle class who have moved out of the neighborhood and a sprinkling of the very poor whose dilapidated row houses and apartments are in the shadow of the church building. The Black Church, in other words, is inseparable from the ghetto. In the final analysis, whatever motivates the ghetto to peace-making or rebellion must motivate the Black Church.

This is one reason why the Black clergy who gathered in Harlem early in July 1966, during one of the "long, hot summers" of revolt and guerrilla warfare, broke with Dr. King's interpretation of Black Power as "a nihilistic philosophy born out of the conviction that the Negro can't win."[1] Under the leadership of Benjamin F. Payton, then executive director of the Commission on Religion and Race of the National Council of Churches and a Harvard-educated Baptist preacher, they affirmed the Black Power statement and derived from it a theological analysis that sets the stage for the emergence of Black Theology.

15

Some of the younger Black clergy had been deeply involved in the civil disorders that swept through the nation from the Harlem and Rochester rebellions in the summer of 1964 to the Chicago fire-bombing and looting in July 1966. They did not condone the violence and criminal behavior of some of the street people, but they understood its causes only too well and were caught up in it as leaders whose first impulse was to look to the safety and welfare of their people. They met secretly with underground leaders, articulated demands to the press, argued with the politicians, and diverted the police and national guard so that some of their folks could get out of the cordoned-off areas.

One A.M.E. Zion pastor in Brooklyn's Bedford-Stuyvesant area hid two boys and their gasoline cans in the trunk of his car and drove through a police blockade to prevent their arrest. In Los Angeles, during the Watts outbreak in 1965, Black preachers formed an armed guard of men from their congregations to repulse a White motorcycle gang trying to invade their neighborhood in retaliation for the burning. In Newark and Detroit Black clergy cooperated with the grassroots leaders of the rebellion in ways that would have made them vulnerable to prosecution even though they attempted to restrain the violence and turned their churches into shelters and feeding stations for those who had been burned out.

It was a time of great soul-searching and ambivalence for the Black Church in the more than 128 cities that erupted during the period 1963–1968.[2] Some of the ministers found themselves reading David Walker, Frantz Fanon, and Dietrich Bonhoeffer for the first time, seeking ethical guidelines for the unfamiliar situation into which they felt drawn by inexorable circumstance—or was it by the hand of God? What is the responsibility of the churches of the oppressed when the oppressed revolt? How much of the truth should one tell the police when the children of one's own parish are liable to police brutality and summary arrest? What should be the Christian position regarding violence against property as a tactic of insurrection in the face of extreme deprivation and exploitation by the White power structure —city hall, the banks, the landlords, the police?

These questions and others swirled around the places where Black preachers gathered daily to analyze the situation and plot their strategies. All of them knew that this was the most serious national crisis since the Civil War. They met it with courage and creativity.

Almost to a man these pastors had supported Dr. King's movement of nonviolent direct action, but by the height of the rebellion in 1967 many believed that following King meant to give more attention to loving the enemy than doing something about the suffering of brothers and sisters. The people were tired of waiting for the Supreme Court and the Congress. The celebration and congratulation which accompanied the passage of the 1964 Civil Rights and the 1965 Voting Rights Acts seemed gratuitous to ghetto-dwellers who did not have the price of dinner at a desegregated restaurant, whose children continued in abandoned, all-Black innercity schools twelve years after the Brown decision, and who were afraid to register and vote for fear of having name and address fall into the hands of creditors, police investigators, or the Internal Revenue Service.

The people were saying, "Enough!" The sacred right of the American people to overthrow a tyrannical government was being exercised—whether wisely or unwisely. The elastic band of violence, which had been stretched to extremity by White Power, was snapping back in the name of Black Power and would return ineluctably with a force equal to that which had been applied in the first place. For many it was not given to the Black Church to stand in judgment upon the oppressed and exploited people in whose midst it lived and carried out its mission—however shortsighted and class-conscious that mission may have been in the past. It was the destiny of the Black preachers and their churches to rise or fall with the masses. Those masses were hurting and were determined to bring an end to their misery by whatever means possible. They were demanding the imposition of power—coercive power—economic, political, raw physical power, if necessary, and there was justification enough in theological and ethical considerations for the Black Church to follow them. Perhaps in following it would, once again, earn the right to lead.

The Black Power Statement of the National Committeee of Negro Churchmen is the first document to deserve our attention (Document 1). It was written by a small committee headed by Dr. Payton, circulated for signatures among some of the most influential Black ministers in the United States, and published as a full-page advertisement in the July 31, 1966, edition of the *New York Times*. We have included the signatories of this historic document to show the support it received from a wide segment of Black church leadership across the nation. Despite its essentially integrationist tone, pointed out by Vincent Harding in a critical appraisal of NCBC documents,[3] it nevertheless represents the beginning of Black reflection on the racial situation in America independent of the White theologians and ethicists whose writings the liberal–neo-orthodox consensus on the race problem presented. It was the banner around which a new organization, the National Committeee of Negro Churchmen, was formed with Benjamin F. Payton as its first president—an organization which, while continuing to recognize Martin Luther King, Jr., as the titular leader of the Black revolution, sought to challenge his moderate, assimilationist position and apparent reluctance to concede that power was the name of the game—even among born-again Christians.

Although the primary emphases of Black Theology, as later developed by James H. Cone, were not extrapolated from the Black Power Statement of NCNC, this document was a turning-point in the history of Black Church involvement in the civil rights movement. Stokely Carmichael, the chief spokesman for Black Power, quoted freely from it in speeches across the nation. It was, in fact, the only philosophically cogent defense of Black Power to come out of the rebellions of 1963–1966 and it erected the ideological and the institutional bases upon which Black Theology was to build an alternative to the liberal and neo-orthodox theologies of the American religious establishment.

The NCNC issued its second pronouncement on November 6, 1966 (Document 2), after a solemn processional, in full vestments, to the Statue of Liberty. The statement was published in the *New York Times* as another full-page advertisement. Its purpose was to speak to the issue of racism and power on the eve of a congressional election threatened by White-backlash candidates seeking to exploit the civil disorders in Chicago, Cleveland, and other Northern cities that year.

A third statement, not included in this volume, was published by the NCNC in 1966. It focused upon the exclusion of Congressman Adam Clayton Powell from his seat as chairman of the powerful House Labor and Education Committee. The statement, entitled "The Powell Affair—A Crisis of Morals and Faith," pointed out the "precipitousness and harshness" of congressional action against Powell when Congress had refused to discipline Rep. Thomas Lane of Massachusetts after his widely publicized conviction for tax evasion. Indeed it found punitive action against Powell for his peccadillos with secretaries and expense accounts an example of the cynical use of White Power in opposition to Black political aspirations. It was, for NCNC, a repudiation of "the legitimate and necessary power of a racial minority to participate fully and effectively in political and economic decisions that affect the destiny of us all."

It is appropriate to follow these two documents from the NCNC with a provocative article by Vincent Harding (Document 3), which appeared in the *Christian Century* on January 4, 1967, and revealed some of the radical christological considerations that Black religionists were exploring in view of Black Power. Harding, a Mennonite historian and the director of the Institute of the Black World in Atlanta, was a perceptive critic of the early development of the NCNC and a lay theologian whose writings have had a profound impact upon those who tried to think theologically about the meaning of Black Power between 1966 and 1969. His finest contribution to the discussion was an essay published one year later,[4] but the *Christian Century* article reprinted in this compilation was one of the first scholarly reflections on the significance of Black Power in the context of the Christian faith.

Much of the early activity of the National Conference of Black Churchmen took place in the committee rooms and conference halls of the National Council of Churches (NCC). The elements of a new theological perspective for the representatives of the Black denominations in the NCC were formulated in confrontation with White churchmen at those meetings. This was the case for the document entitled "The Church and the Urban Crisis"(Document 4). Its historic significance is that it was promulgated at the time of the first open split between Black and White church leaders within a national interdenominational agency. The National Council of Churches provided the largest and most recognized forum for Black and White Christians to negotiate their differences and present a united front to the nation. When, on September 27, 1967, a national conference on urban problems sponsored by the NCC exploded into two caucuses, one Black and one White, it was apparent that the differences were acute and a new era of polarization had begun. The preamble of "The Church and the Urban Crisis" declared:

> We discovered that in order to learn the truth about ourselves and our situation, so successfully covered over by years of hypocrisy and dissimulation, we had to make a decision unprecedented in ecumenical conferences under the aegis of the National Council. We made the decision to divide the conference into a white caucus and a black caucus.

Actually the decision was forced by the younger Black clergy present who were angry and frustrated by the compromises necessary for ecumenism and interracial amity during one of the most riot-torn years in the nation's history. The ad hoc group, which called itself the National Committee of Negro Churchmen and had produced the Black Power statement of 1966, was well represented at the conference in Washington en route to the first meeting of the permanent organization in Dallas, Texas.[5] Tensions were running high. Some of the Black leaders felt that only disengagement in separate rooms would vindicate their commitment to Black Power and force the White delegates to make up their minds about the legitimacy of such a stance within American Christianity.

At one point, after the caucuses had retired to separate conferences, a small delegation from the White caucus appeared at the door of the room where the Blacks were meeting and requested admission. They explained that they had nothing in common with the other Whites and felt "lonely" and bereft of fellowship with the Blacks whose impatience and vehemence they understood and shared. It was a moment of quiet pathos and wistfulness. With equal earnestness the Black churchmen explained their position. The time had come, they said, for provisional separation. A part of the freedom they sought was the freedom not to be conditioned by the feelings of White brothers and sisters who needed them for the sake of their own injured consciences. Whites, rather, needed to experience the pain of the disjunction to which God's judgment had subjected the churches. Only so, they insisted, would it be possible for the two groups to reassemble on the final day of the conference and speak with one voice about the depth of the racial crisis in church and society. Permission for entrance was refused and the White splinter group returned to their meeting room.

The jointly worded preamble, which was composed by an interracial committee on September 30, is followed by the texts of the two separate statements developed by the caucuses. This is one of the most important documents in this part because it clearly indicates the direction in which Black church leaders and theologians were moving one year after the Black Power banner was raised and what it looked like when unfurled in the National Council of Churches. The brief statement of the White caucus shows the influence of the splinter group, which prevailed over their more conservative colleagues. The latter were shocked and offended by the demand for Black separatism, but in the end reluctantly agreed to endorse it, "knowing . . . that our separate work with blacks and whites is our common task and work together."[6]

One of the intellectual leaders of the Black Power movement and an Episcopal church executive in Newark, New Jersey, was Dr. Nathan Wright, Jr. Wright helped to organize and chaired the first National Black Power Conference, which was held in Newark while the city's Black ghetto still smoldered from the riots of July 1967. He was also one of the founders of the NCNC and a signatory of the statement that begins Part I. It was through Wright's insistence that the first Black Power conference included a working group on "Black Religion." This set the pattern for consideration of the role of religion in the revolution at subsequent conferences of nonchurch militants. Here we include his essay "Black Power: A Religious Opportunity" (Document 5) as an example of how certain Black religious scholars responded to the challenge of Black Power. His position cleaves to a more classical view of the Christian faith than Vincent Harding's, but Wright, from the perspective of a Northern ghetto, actually took a more activist posture than Harding, who at the time was teaching history at Spelman College in Atlanta.

This essay appeared in Wright's book *Black Power and Urban Unrest*[7] and was more in keeping with the disposition of the parish ministers in the NCNC. It shows how one of the Northern movement's key leaders understood Black Power in relation to worship, community outreach, and other aspects of the Christian life. There are also powerful theological ideas which Wright developed further in subsequent writings. For example, the glorification of Blackness in staking a claim for the worth of the degraded and oppressed. To glorify, he writes, "is to clarify, to make clear and plain and straight."

> All of life must be clarified in this sense. It must be given and seen in that dimension which sets it forth in terms of glory. . . . To see life as it truly is means to see it as God sees it, in its eternal dimension, in the glory appropriate to its involvement with and in the life of God.

The final document in this part was issued by the Board of Directors of NCBC on April 5, 1968, in Chicago. This statement on the "Urban Mission in a Time of Crisis" (Document 6), coming after the inaugural convocation in Dallas the previous fall, is the first forthright attack upon the White church establishment and calls for the resources of the affluent White denominations which sponsored "urban work" in the ghetto. It is, therefore, a forerunner of the Black Manifesto of the Black Economic Development Conference and, I suspect, influenced James Forman via his contact with members of the Interreligious Foundation for Community Organization (IFCO), which in turn was dominated by the NCNC directors who wrote this pronouncement. It insists that White churchmen come to the bargaining table and "surrender" their monetary and material resources for use by Black churchmen in the inner city. The Black Manifesto said the same thing the next year in more fervid language. The statement is also noteworthy by the fact that it calls for renewal of Black church life in terms of cultural heritage, liturgical practice, and theological interpretation. In this sense it anticipated some of the concepts of Black Theology which went beyond politicization and liberation to espouse cultural nationalism and the reclamation of the Black religious tradition.

By sheer coincidence this document was drafted on April 4, 1968 —the day Dr. King was assassinated. A great pall of sorrow and gloomy foreboding fell over the meeting of the Board of Directors in Chicago —the scene of his unpropitious introduction to the hard-nosed and irreverent secularity of the Northern urban ghetto. The meeting was abruptly adjourned (the statement was dated a day later by the editorial committee) and members shared taxis to O'Hare airport contemplating in silence the meaning of his life and the irredeemable viciousness of the racist conspiracy which even then, we were persuaded, had snatched it away.

The King of love was dead and with his death an era of interracial church social action and theological innocence came to an end. Everyone knew that the memory of his commitment and faithfulness would never be permitted to die in the Black Church, but for those church leaders and theologians retreating from a city ready to burst into a strange, elegiac violence, a new challenge to America had to be mounted, one more consonant with the pragmatic sensibilities of the religious experience and theological maturity of a proud Black people come of age.

G.S.W.

Notes

1. Martin Luther King, Jr., *Where Do We Go from Here: Chaos or Community?* (New York: Harper & Row, 1967), p. 44.

2. For a detailed analysis of the urban rebellions, see the *Report of the National Advisory Commission on Civil Disorders* (New York: Bantam Books, 1968), pp. 35-200.

3. Vincent Harding, in *Renewal*, vol. x, no. 7, October–November, 1970.

4. Harding, "The Religion of Black Power," in *The Religious Situation: 1968*, Donald R.

Cutler, ed. (Boston: Beacon Press, 1968), pp. 3-38. This is essential reading for understanding the deficiencies many Black religionists found in King's theology and some of the motifs that Cone, Cleage, Eichelberger, and others were to develop later.

5. For the early history of the NCBC, with a brief description of its several public statements, see Leon Watts, "The National Committee of Black Churchmen," *Christianity and Crisis*, vol. 30, no. 18 (November 1970), pp. 237-243. Also, my *Black Religion and Black Radicalism* (Garden City, N.Y.: Doubleday, 1972), pp. 262-306.

6. A similar development took place in the Student Non-Violent Coordinating Committee and other interracial activist groups where Whites were urged to return to their own communities to fight against racism at its source.

7. Nathan Wright, Jr., *Black Power and Urban Unrest* (New York: Hawthorn Books, 1967).

1

BLACK POWER

Statement by the National Committee of Negro Churchmen, July 31, 1966

We, an informal group of Negro churchmen in America, are deeply disturbed about the crisis brought upon our country by historic distortions of important human realities in the controversy about "black power." What we see shining through the variety of rhetoric is not anything new but the same old problem of power and race which has faced our beloved country since 1619.

We realize that neither the term "power" nor the term "Christian conscience" is an easy matter to talk about, especially in the context of race relations in America. The fundamental distortion facing us in the controversy about "black power" is rooted in a gross imbalance of power and conscience between Negroes and white Americans. It is this distortion, mainly, which is responsible for the widespread, though often inarticulate, assumption that white people are justified in getting what they want through the use of power, but that Negro Americans must, either by nature or by circumstance, make their appeal only through conscience. As a result, the power of white men and the conscience of black men have both been corrupted. The power of white men is corrupted because it meets little meaningful resistance from Negroes to temper it and keep white men from aping God. The conscience of black men is corrupted because, having no power to implement the demands of conscience, the concern for justice is transmuted into a distorted form of love, which, in the absence of justice, becomes chaotic self-surrender. Powerlessness breeds a race of beggars. We are faced now with a situation where

This statement was first published in the *New York Times,* July 31, 1966. At the time the organization was known as the National Committee of Negro Churchmen with headquarters in New York City. It is now the National Conference of Black Churchmen, headquartered in Atlanta, Ga.

conscienceless power meets powerless conscience, threatening the very foundations of our nation.

Therefore, we are impelled by conscience to address at least four groups of people in areas where clarification of the controversy is of the most urgent necessity. We do not claim to present the final word. It is our hope, however, to communicate meanings from our experience regarding power and certain elements of conscience to help interpret more adequately the dilemma in which we are all involved.

I. To the Leaders of America: Power and Freedom

It is of critical importance that the leaders of this nation listen also to a voice which says that the principal source of the threat to our nation comes neither from the riots erupting in our big cities, nor from the disagreements among the leaders of the civil rights movement, nor even from mere raising of the cry for "black power." These events, we believe, are but the expression of the judgment of God upon our nation for its failure to use its abundant resources to serve the real well-being of people, at home and abroad.

We give our full support to all civil rights leaders as they seek for basically American goals, for we are not convinced that their mutual reinforcement of one another in the past is bound to end in the future. We would hope that the public power of our nation will be used to strengthen the civil rights movement and not to manipulate or further fracture it.

We deplore the overt violence of riots, but we believe it is more important to focus on the real sources of the eruptions. These sources may be abetted inside the ghetto, but their basic causes lie in the silent and covert violence which white middle-class America inflicts upon the victims of the inner city. The hidden, smooth and often smiling decisions of American leaders which tie a white noose of suburbia around their necks, and which pin the backs of the masses of Negroes against the steaming ghetto walls—without jobs in a booming economy; with dilapidated and segregated educational systems in the full view of unenforced laws against it; in short: the failure of American leaders to use American power to create equal opportunity *in life* as well as *in law*—this is the real problem and not the anguished cry for "black power."

From the point of view of the Christian faith, there is nothing necessarily wrong with concern for power. At the heart of the Protestant reformation is the belief that ultimate power belongs to God alone and that men become most inhuman when concentrations of power lead to the conviction—overt or covert—that any nation, race or organization can rival God in this regard. At issue in the relations between whites and Negroes in America is the problem of inequality of power. Out of this imbalance grows the disrespect of white men for the Negro personality and community, and the disrespect of Negroes for themselves. This is a fundamental root of human injustice in

America. In one sense, the concept of "black power" reminds us of the need for and the possibility of authentic democracy in America.

We do *not* agree with those who say that we must cease expressing concern for the acquisition of power lest we endanger the "gains" already made by the civil rights movement. The fact of the matter is, there have been few substantive gains since about 1950 in this area. The gap has constantly widened between the incomes of non-whites relative to the whites. Since the Supreme Court decision of 1954, de facto segregation in every major city in our land has increased rather than decreased. Since the middle of the 1950s unemployment among Negroes has gone up rather than down while unemployment has decreased in the white community.

While there has been some progress in some areas for equality for Negroes, this progress has been limited mainly to middle-class Negroes who represent only a small minority of the larger Negro community.

These are the hard facts that we must all face together. Therefore we must not take the position that we can continue in the same old paths.

When American leaders decide to serve the real welfare of people instead of war and destruction; when American leaders are forced to make the rebuilding of our cities first priority on the nation's agenda; when American leaders are forced by the American people to quit misusing and abusing American power; then will the cry for "black power" become inaudible, for the framework in which all power in America operates would include the power and experience of black men as well as those of white men. In that way, the fear of the power of each group would be removed. America is our beloved homeland. But, America is not God. Only God can do everything. America and the other nations of the world must decide which among a number of alternatives they will choose.

II. To White Churchmen: Power and Love

As black men who were long ago forced out of the white church to create and to wield "black power," we fail to understand the emotional quality of the outcry of some clergy against the use of the term today. It is not enough to answer that "integration" is the solution. For it is precisely the nature of the operation of power under some forms of integration which is being challenged. The Negro Church was created as a result of the refusal to submit to the indignities of a false kind of "integration" in which all power was in the hands of white people. A more equal sharing of power is precisely what is required as the precondition of authentic human interaction. We understand the growing demand of Negro and white youth for a more honest kind of integration; one which increases rather than decreases the capacity of the disinherited to participate with power in all of the structures of our common life. Without this capacity to *participate with power*—i.e., to have some organized political and economic strength to really influence people with whom one interacts—integration is not meaningful. For the issue is not one of racial balance but of honest interracial interaction.

For this kind of interaction to take place, all people need power, whether black or white. We regard as sheer hypocrisy or as a blind and dangerous illusion the view that opposes love to power. Love should be a controlling element in power, not power itself. So long as white churchmen continue to moralize and misinterpret Christian love, so long will justice continue to be subverted in this land.

III. To Negro Citizens: Power and Justice

Both the anguished cry for "black power" and the confused emotional response to it can be understood if the whole controversy is put in the context of American history. Especially must we understand the irony involved in the pride of Americans regarding their ability to act as individuals on the one hand, and their tendency to act as members of ethnic groups on the other hand. In the tensions of this part of our history is revealed both the tragedy and the hope of human redemption in America.

America has asked its Negro citizens to fight for opportunity *as individuals* whereas at certain points in our history what we have needed most has been opportunity for the whole group, not just for selected and approved Negroes. Thus in 1863, the slaves were made legally free, as individuals, but the real question regarding personal and group power to maintain that freedom was pushed aside. Power at that time for a mainly rural people meant land and tools to work the land. In the words of Thaddeus Stevens, power meant "40 acres and a mule." But this power was not made available to the slaves and we see the results today in the pushing of a landless peasantry off the farms into big cities where they come in search mainly of the power to be free. What they find are only the formalities of unenforced legal freedom. So we must ask, "What is the nature of the power which we seek and need today?" Power today is essentially organizational power. It is not a thing lying about in the streets to be fought over. It is a thing which, in some measure, already belongs to Negroes and which must be developed by Negroes in relationship with the great resources of this nation.

Getting power necessarily involves reconciliation. We must first be reconciled to ourselves lest we fail to recognize the resources we already have and upon which we can build. We must be reconciled to ourselves as persons and to ourselves as an historical group. This means we must find our way to a new self-image in which we can feel a normal sense of pride in self, including our variety of skin color and the manifold textures of our hair. As long as we are filled with hatred for ourselves we will be unable to respect others.

At the same time, if we are seriously concerned about power then we must build upon that which we already have. "Black power" is already present to some extent in the Negro church, in Negro fraternities and sororities, in our professional associations, and in the opportunities afforded to Negroes who make decisions in some of the integrated organizations of our society.

We understand the reasons by which these limited forms of "black power" have been rejected by some of our people. Too often the Negro church has stirred its members away from the reign of God in *this world* to a distorted and complacent view of *an otherworldly* conception of God's power. We commit ourselves as churchmen to make more meaningful in the life of our institution our conviction that Jesus Christ reigns in the "here" and "now" as well as in the future he brings in upon us. We shall, therefore, use more of the resources of our churches in working for human justice in the places of social change and upheaval where our Master is already at work.

At the same time, we would urge that Negro social and professional organizations develop new roles for engaging the problem of equal opportunity and put less time into the frivolity of idle chatter and social waste.

We must not apologize for the existence of this form of group power, for we have been oppressed as a group, not as individuals. We will not find our way out of that oppression until both we and America accept the need for Negro Americans as well as for Jews, Italians, Poles and white Anglo-Saxon Protestants, among others, to have and to wield group power.

However, if power is sought merely as an end in itself, it tends to turn upon those who seek it. Negroes need power in order to participate more effectively at all levels of the life of our nation. We are glad that none of those civil rights leaders who have asked for "black power" have suggested that it means a new form of isolationism or a foolish effort at domination. But we must be clear about why we need to be reconciled with the white majority. It is *not* because we are only one-tenth of the population in America; for we do not need to be reminded of the awesome power wielded by the 90% majority. We see and feel that power every day in the destructions heaped upon our families and upon the nation's cities. We do not need to be threatened by such cold and heartless statements. For we are men, not children, and we are growing out of our fear of that power, which can hardly hurt us any more in the future than it does in the present or has in the past. Moreover, those bare figures conceal the potential political strength which is ours if we organize properly in the big cities and establish effective alliances.

Neither must we rest our concern for reconciliation with our white brothers on the fear that failure to do so would damage gains already made by the civil rights movement. If those gains are in fact real, they will withstand the claims of our people for power and justice, not just for a few select Negroes here and there, but for the masses of our citizens. We must rather rest our concern for reconciliation on the firm ground that we and all other Americans *are* one. Our history and destiny are indissolubly linked. If the future is to belong to any of us, it must be prepared for all of us whatever our racial or religious background. For in the final analysis, we are *persons* and the power of all groups must be wielded to make visible our common humanity.

The future of America will belong to neither white nor black unless all Americans work together at the task of rebuilding our cities. We must organize not only among ourselves but with other groups in order that we can, together, gain power sufficient to change this nation's sense of what is *now* important and what must be done *now*. We must work with the remainder of the nation to organize whole cities for the task of making the rebuilding of our cities first priority in the use of our resources. This is more important than who gets to the moon first or the war in Vietnam.

To accomplish this task we cannot expend our energies in spastic or ill-tempered explosions without meaningful goals. We must move from the politics of philanthropy to the politics of metropolitan development for equal opportunity. We must relate all groups of the city together in new ways in order that the truth of our cities might be laid bare and in order that, together, we can lay claim to the great resources of our nation to make truth more human.

IV. To the Mass Media: Power and Truth

The ability or inability of all people in America to understand the upheavals of our day depends greatly on the way power and truth operate in the mass media. During the Southern demonstrations for civil rights, you men of the communications industry performed an invaluable service for the entire country by revealing plainly to all ears and eyes, the ugly truth of a brutalizing system of overt discrimination and segregation. Many of you were mauled and injured, and it took courage for you to stick with the task. You were instruments of change and not merely purveyors of unrelated facts. You were able to do this by dint of personal courage and by reason of the power of national news agencies which supported you.

Today, however, your task and ours is more difficult. The truth that needs revealing today is not so clear-cut in its outlines, nor is there a national consensus to help you form relevant points of view. Therefore, nothing is now more important than that you look for a variety of sources of truth in order that the limited perspectives of all of us might be corrected. Just as you related to a broad spectrum of people in Mississippi instead of relying only on police records and establishment figures, so must you operate in New York City, Chicago and Cleveland.

The power to support you in this endeavor *is present* in our country. It must be searched out. We desire to use our limited influence to help relate you to the variety of experience in the Negro community so that limited controversies are not blown up into the final truth about us. The fate of this country is, to no small extent, dependent upon how you interpret the crises upon us, so that human truth is disclosed and human needs are met.

Signatories:

Bishop John D. Bright, Sr., A.M.E. Church, First Episcopal District, Philadelphia, Pennsylvania

The Rev. John Bryant, Connecticut Council of Churches, Hartford, Connecticut

Suffragan Bishop John M. Burgess, The Episcopal Church, Boston, Massachusetts

The Rev. W. Sterling Cary, Grace Congregational Church, New York, New York

The Rev. Charles E. Cobb, St. John Church (UCC), Springfield, Massachusetts

The Rev. Caesar D. Coleman, Christian Methodist Episcopal Church, Memphis, Tennessee

The Rev. Joseph C. Coles, Williams Institutional CME Church, New York, New York

The Rev. George A. Crawley, Jr., St. Paul Baptist Church, Baltimore, Maryland

The Rev. O. Herbert Edwards, Trinity Baptist Church, Baltimore, Maryland

The Rev. Bryant George, United Presbyterian Church in the U.S.A., New York, New York

Bishop Charles F. Golden, The Methodist Church, Nashville, Tennessee

The Rev. Quinland R. Gordon, The Episcopal Church, New York, New York

The Rev. James Hargett, Church of Christian Fellowship, U.C.C., Los Angeles, California

The Rev. Edler Hawkins, St. Augustine Presbyterian Church, New York, New York

The Rev. Reginald Hawkins, United Presbyterian Church, Charlotte, North Carolina

Dr. Anna Arnold Hedgeman, Commission on Religion and Race, National Council of Churches, New York, New York

The Rev. R. E. Hodd, Gary, Indiana

The Rev. H. R. Hughes, Bethel A.M.E. Church, New York, New York

The Rev. Kenneth Hughes, St. Bartholomew's Episcopal Church, Cambridge, Massachusetts

The Rev. Donald G. Jacobs, St. James A.M.E. Church, Cleveland, Ohio

The Rev. J. L. Joiner, Emanuel A.M.E. Church, New York, New York

The Rev. Arthur A. Jones, Metropolitan A.M.E. Church, Philadelphia, Pennsylvania

The Rev. Stanley King, Sabathini Baptist Church, Minneapolis, Minnesota

The Rev. Earl Wesley Lawson, Emanuel Baptist Church, Malden, Massachusetts

The Rev. David Licorish, Abyssinian Baptist Church, New York, New York

The Rev. Arthur B. Mack, St. Thomas A.M.E.Z. Church, Haverstraw, New York

The Rev. James W. Mack, South United Church of Christ, Chicago, Illinois

The Rev. O. Clay Maxwell, Jr., Baptist Ministers Conference of New York City and Vicinity, New York, New York

The Rev. Leon Modeste, The Episcopal Church, New York, New York

Bishop Noah W. Moore, Jr., The Methodist Church, Southwestern Area, Houston, Texas

The Rev. David Nickerson, Episcopal Society for Cultural and Racial Unity, Atlanta, Georgia

The Rev. LeRoy Patrick, Bethesda United Presbyterian Church, Pittsburgh, Pennsylvania

The Rev. Benjamin F. Payton, Commission on Religion and Race, National Council of Churches, New York, New York

The Rev. Isaiah P. Pogue, St. Mark's Presbyterian Church, Cleveland, Ohio

The Rev. Sandy F. Ray, Empire Baptist State Convention, Brooklyn, New York

Bishop Herbert B. Shaw, Presiding Bishop, Third Episcopal District, A.M.E.Z. Church, Wilmington, North Carolina

The Rev. Stephen P. Spottswood, Commission on Race and Cultural Relations, Detroit Council of Churches, Detroit, Michigan

The Rev. Henri A. Stines, Church of the Atonement, Washington, D.C.

Bishop James S. Thomas, Resident Bishop, Iowa Area, The Methodist Church, Des Moines, Iowa

The Rev. V. Simpson Turner, Mt. Carmel Baptist Church, Brooklyn, New York

The Rev. Edgar Ward, Grace Presbyterian Church, Chicago, Illinois

The Rev. Paul M. Washington, Church of the Advocate, Philadelphia, Pennsylvania

The Rev. Frank L. Williams, Methodist Church, Baltimore, Maryland

The Rev. John W. Williams, St. Stephen's Baptist Church, Kansas City, Missouri

The Rev. Gayraud Wilmore, United Presbyterian Church U.S.A., New York, New York

The Rev. M. L. Wilson, Covenant Baptist Church, New York, New York

The Rev. Robert H. Wilson, Corresponding Secretary, National Baptist Convention of America, Dallas, Texas

The Rev. Nathan Wright, Episcopal Diocese of Newark, Newark, New Jersey

2

RACISM AND THE ELECTIONS: THE AMERICAN DILEMMA, 1966

A Statement by the National Committee of Negro Churchmen

A few days ago the 80th anniversary of the Statue of Liberty was celebrated here on Liberty Island. On November 8, a so-called "white backlash" will confront the American people with a fateful choice in the elections across the country. We, an informal group of Negro churchmen, assembled from the four corners of this land, gather here today in order to highlight the critical moral issues which confront the American people in those elections—issues symbolized here in the Statue of Liberty.

Our purpose here is neither to beg nor to borrow, but to state the determination of black men in America to exact from this nation not one whit less than our full manhood rights. We will not be cowed nor intimidated in the land of our birth. We intend that the truth of this country, as experienced by black men, will be heard. We shall state this truth from the perspective of the Christian faith and in the light of our experience with the Lord of us all, in the bleakness of this racially idolatrous land.

The inscription inside the Statue of Liberty, entitled "The New Colossus," refers to America as the "Mother of Exiles." It concludes with these moving words:

> "Keep ancient land, your storied pomp!" cries she
> With silent lips. "Give me your tired, your poor,
> Your huddled masses yearning to breathe free.
> The wretched refuse of your teeming shore.
> Send these, the homeless, tempest-tost to me.
> I lift my lamp beside the Golden Door!"

This statement was issued November 3, 1966, at the Statue of Liberty, and was first published in the *New York Times*, November 6, 1966.

31

This poem focuses on the linked problems of identity and power which have been so tragically played out on the stage of this nation's history. "Mother of Exiles" and "The New Colossus"—these symbols capture both the variety of groups and experience out of which this nation has been hammered and the fervent hope of many early Americans that in this land the world would see a new and more human use of power, dedicated to the proposition that all men are created equal.

We remind Americans that in our beginnings we were all exiles, strangers sojourning in an unfamiliar land. Even the first black men who set foot on these shores came, as did most white men, in the role of pilgrims, not as slaves. Sharing common aspirations and hopes for a land where freedom could take root and live, for the briefest of moments black men and white men found each other in a community of trust and mutual acceptance.

However, if America became a "Mother of Exiles" for white men she became at the same time a cruel system of bondage and inhumanity to black men. Far from finding here a maternal acceptance, her black sons were thrust into the depth of despair, at times so hopeless that it wrung from their lips the sorrow song: "Sometimes I feel like a motherless child." What anguish is keener, what rejection more complete, or what alienation more poignant than this experience which called forth the metaphor, "motherless child"?

But that is only part of our story. For somewhere in the depth of their experience within this great land, those same black men and women found a ground of faith and hope on which to stand. Never accepting on the inside the identity forced upon them by a brutalizing white power, they also sang—even prior to emancipation—"Before I'll be a slave, I'll be buried in my grave and go home to my Lord and be free." A faith of this quality and integrity remains alive today.

There is, to be sure, a continuing dilemma of "crisis and commitment" in our country. But it is not the quarrels among the civil rights leaders, nor is it the debate about Black Power, nor is it the controversy surrounding the riots in our cities. The crisis is what it has always been since shortly after the first black Americans set foot upon these shores. It is not a crisis rooted in the Negro community. It is a "crisis of commitment" among white Americans who have consistently taken two steps forward toward becoming mature men on race and one and a half steps backward at the same time. The power of "The New Colossus" has never been fully committed to eliminating this monstrous racism from the life of the American people.

Look at the record of fitful and mincing steps forward and of cowardly steps away from the goal of racial justice. The slaves were freed in 1863, but the nation refused to give them land to make that emancipation meaningful. Simultaneously, the nation was giving away millions of acres in the midwest and west—a gift marked "for whites only." Thus an economic floor was placed under the new peasants from Europe but America's oldest peasantry was provided only an abstract freedom. In the words of Frederick Douglass, emancipation made the slaves "free to hunger; free to the winter and rains of heaven . . . free without roofs to cover them or bread to eat or land to cultivate. . . . We gave them freedom and famine at the same time. The marvel is that they still live."

We should, therefore, be neither shocked nor surprised that our slums today confront us with the bitter fruits of that ancient theft. Is it conceivable that the shrill cry "Burn, Baby, Burn" in Watts, Los Angeles, and across this country, could ever be invented by men with reasonable chances to make a living, to live in a decent neighborhood, to get an adequate education for their children? Is it conceivable that men with reasonable prospects for life, liberty and the pursuit of happiness for themselves and for their children could ever put the torch to their own main streets? The answer is obvious. These are the anguished, desperate acts of men, women and children who have been taught to hate themselves and who have been herded and confined like cattle in rat-infested slums.

Frederick Douglass is indeed correct when he suggests that "the marvel is that Negroes are still alive" not to mention sane. Look at the record. We submit that to pass a Civil Rights Bill as this nation did in 1875 and then refuse to enforce it; to pass another Civil Rights Bill (weaker this time) in 1964 and then refuse to enforce it; to begin an anti-poverty program with insufficient funds in the first place and then to put the lion's share of this miniscule budget into Head Start programs when unemployment among Negro men continues to skyrocket; to declare segregation in our schools unconstitutional as the Supreme Court did in 1954, and refuse to end it forthwith; to set up guidelines for desegregating hospitals and then refuse to appropriate moneys for the enforcement of these guidelines; to insist on civil rights legislation aimed at the south and then to defeat the first piece of such legislation relevant to areas outside the south; to preach "law and order" into the anguish of Negro slums in full view of the contributions of policemen to that anguish and then to insist that policemen be their own judges; to hear suburban politicians declaim against open occupancy in one breath and in the very next breath insist that they are not racists: these are the ironies which stare us in the face and make it all but impossible to talk about how much "progress" has been made. The fact of the matter is if black Americans are not accorded basic human and constitutional rights which white Americans gain immediately upon their entry into citizenship, then there really are no substantive gains of which to speak.

Therefore, we will not be intimidated by the so-called "white backlash," for white America has been "backlashing" on the fundamental human and constitutional rights of Negro Americans since the 18th century. The election of racists in November will merely be a continuation of this pattern.

But: Let us try to be very clear about one thing, America. Black Americans are determined to have all of their full human and constitutional rights. We will not cease to agitate this issue with every means available to men of faith and dignity until justice is done.

We are dealing at bottom with a question of relationship between black and white, between rich and poor, ultimately between believers in different gods. We support all of our civil rights leaders for we believe that they all have important insights to share with us on this critical question. For our part, we submit that our basic goal in this struggle is to make it possible for all persons and groups to participate with power at all levels of our society. Integration is not an aesthetic goal designed to add token bits of color to institutions controlled entirely by whites. Integration is a political goal with the objective of making it possible for Negroes and other Americans to express the vitality of their personal and group life in institutions which fundamentally belong to all Americans.

If the tremendous power of this nation—this "New Colossus"—begins to move "with conquering limbs astride from land to land," then we are bound to forget the tired, the poor, the "huddled masses yearning to be free." America is rich and powerful. But America is neither infinitely rich nor omnipotent. Even America must make choices.

We submit that the resolution of the crisis which is upon us requires a change in the nation's priorities. The welfare and dignity of all Americans is more important than the priorities being given to military expansion, space exploration or the production of supersonic jet airliners.

To this end, we of the Negro church call for a massive mobilization of the resources in the Negro community in order to give leadership in the fulfillment not only of our own destiny but in order to help produce a more sane white America.

We further call upon white churchmen to join us by endeavoring to mobilize the resources of the white community in completing with us the task at hand.

Finally, we say to the American people, white and black, there is no turning back of the clock of time. America cannot be America by electing "white blacklash" candidates in the November elections.

Again we say: America is at the crossroad. Either we become the democracy we can become, or we tread the path to self-destruction.

3

BLACK POWER AND
THE AMERICAN CHRIST

Vincent Harding

The mood among many social-action-oriented Christians today suggests that it is only a line thin as a razor blade that divides sentimental yearning over the civil rights activities of the past from present bitter recrimination against "Black Power." As is so often the case with reminiscences, the nostalgia may grow more out of a sense of frustration and powerlessness than out of any true appreciation of the meaning of the past. This at least is the impression one gets from those seemingly endless gatherings of old "true believers" which usually produce both the nostalgia and the recriminations. Generally the cast of characters at such meetings consists of well-dressed, well-fed Negroes and whites whose accents almost blend into a single voice as they recall the days "when we were all together, fighting for the same cause." The stories evoke again the heady atmosphere, mixed of smugness and self-sacrifice, that surrounded us in those heroic times when nonviolence was our watchword and integration our heavenly city. One can almost hear the strains of "our song" as men and women remember how they solemnly swayed in the aisles or around the charred remains of a church or in the dirty southern jails. Those were the days when Martin Luther King was the true prophet and when we were certain that the civil rights movement was God's message to the churches—and part of our smugness grew out of the fact that *we* knew it while all the rest of God's frozen people were asleep.

A Veil between Then and Now

But as the reminiscences continue a veil seems to descend between then and now. The tellers of the old tales label the veil Black Power, and pro-

Vincent Harding was the first Director of the Institute of the Black World, Atlanta, Georgia, and continues as Chairman of the Institute's Board of Directors. He has taught at Spelman College, Temple University, and the University of Pennsylvania. This article first appeared in the *Christian Century*, January 4, 1967.

nounce ritual curses on Stokely Carmichael and Floyd McKissick and their followers.

The trouble with these meetings is that they are indeed becoming ritual, cultic acts of memory that blind us to creative possibilities. Because that "veil" may be a wall, not primarily for separating but for writing on— both sides of it. Or it may be a great sheet "let down from heaven"; or a curtain before the next act can begin. Most of us appear totally incapable of realizing that there may be more light in blackness than we have yet begun to glimpse.

Such possibilities should be pondered especially by those of us who combine the terrible privileges of blackness and Christian commitment within a single life. We are driven to see not only what was happening in our warm, genteel days of common black-white struggle, but to grasp clearly what is happening now. We have no choice but to hold Black Power in our black arms and examine it, convinced that Christ is Lord of this too. Anyone who is black and claims to be a part of the company of Christ's people would be derelict if he failed to make such an examination and to proclaim with fear and trembling and intimations of great joy what he has discovered.

Perhaps the first and central discovery is also the most obvious: there is a strong and causative link between Black Power and American Christianity. Indeed one may say with confidence that whatever its other sources, the ideology of blackness surely grows out of the deep ambivalence of American Negroes to the Christ we have encountered here. This ambivalence is not new. It was ours from the beginning. For we first met the American Christ on slave ships. We heard his name sung in hymns of praise while we died in our thousands, chained in stinking holds beneath the decks, locked in with terror and disease and sad memories of our families and homes. When we leaped from the decks to be seized by sharks we saw his name carved on the ship's solid sides. When our women were raped in the cabins they must have noticed the great and holy books on the shelves. Our introduction to this Christ was not propitious. And the horrors continued on America's soil. So all through the nation's history many black men have rejected this Christ— indeed the miracle is that so many accepted him. In past times our disdain often had to be stifled and sullen, our anger silent and self-destructive. But now we speak out. Our anger is no longer silent; it has leaped onto the public stage, and demands to be seen and dealt with—a far more healthy state of affairs for all concerned.

If the American Christ and his followers have indeed helped to mold the Black Power movement, then might it not be that the God whom many of us insist on keeping alive is not only alive but just? May he not be attempting to break through to us with at least as much urgency as we once sensed at the height of the good old "We Shall Overcome"days? Perhaps he is writing on the wall, saying that we Christians, black and white, must choose between death with the American Christ and life with the Suffering Servant of God.

Who dares deny that God may have chosen once again the black sufferers for a new assault on the hard shell of indifference and fear that encases so many Americans?

If these things are difficult to believe perhaps we need to look more closely both at the American Christ and the black movement he has helped to create. From the outset, almost everywhere we blacks have met him in this land, this Christ was painted white and pink, blond and blue-eyed—and not only in white churches but in black churches as well. Millions of black children had the picture of this pseudo-Nazarene burned into their memory. The books, the windows, and paintings, the filmstrips all affirmed the same message—a message of shame. This Christ shamed us by his pigmentation, so obviously not our own. He condemned us for our blackness, for our flat noses, for our kinky hair, for our power, our strange power of expressing emotion in singing and shouting and dancing. He was sedate, so genteel, so white. And as soon as we were able, many of us tried to be like him.

Glad to Be Black

For a growing edge of bold young black people all that is past. They fling out their declaration: "No white Christ shall shame us again. We are glad to be black. We rejoice in the darkness of our skin, we celebrate the natural texture of our hair, we extol the rhythm and vigor of our songs and shouts and dances. And if your American Christ doesn't like that, you know what you can do with him." That is Black Power: a repudiation of the American culture-religion that helped to create it and a quest for a religious reality more faithful to our own experience.

These young people say to America: "We know your Christ and his attitude toward Africa. We remember how his white missionaries warned against Africa's darkness and heathenism, against its savagery and naked jungle heart. We are tired of all that. This Africa that you love and hate, but mostly fear—this is our homeland. We saw you exchange your Bibles for our land. We watched you pass out tracts and take in gold. We heard you teach hymns to get our diamonds, and you control them still. If this is what your Christ taught you, he is sharp, baby, he is shrewd; but he's no savior of ours. We affirm our homeland and its great black past, a past that was filled with wonder before your white scourge came. You can keep your Christ. We'll take our home." That is Black Power: a search for roots in a land that has denied us both a past and a future. And the American Christ who has blessed the denial earns nothing but scorn.

The advocates of Black Power know this Christ well. They see his people running breathlessly, cursing silently, exiting double-time from the cities with all their suffering people. They see this white throng fleeing before the strangled movement of the blacks out of the ghettos, leaving their stained-glass mausoleums behind them. This very exodus of the Christians from the places where the weak and powerless live has been one of the primary motivating forces of Black Power.

The seekers of Black Power, seeing their poorest, most miserable people deserted by the white American Christians, have come to stand with the forlorn in these very places of abandonment. Now they speak of Black Unity, and the old Christian buildings are filled with Negroes young and old studying African history. The new leaders in the ghettos tell them: "Whites now talk about joining forces, but who has ever wanted to join forces with you? They only want to use you—especially those white American Christian liars. They love you in theory only. They love only your middle-class incarnations. But they are afraid of you—you who are black and poor and filled with rage and despair. They talk about 'progress' for the Negro, but they don't mean *you*."

These young people whose names we old "true believers" intone in our nightly litanies of frustrated wrath have listened with the perception born of alienation to white Christians speaking to Negroes of "our people and your people, our churches and your churches, our community and your community, our schools and your schools." And they hear this hypocrisy crowned with the next words from bleeding Christian hearts: "Of course some of your most spiritual (and quiet) people may come to our churches, and your wealthiest (and cleanest) people may move into our communities, and your brightest children may come to our schools. But never forget: we expect regular hymns of gratitude for our condescension. Always remember that they are still ours and not yours—people and communities and schools and churches." And as an afterthought: "But of course we all love the same Christ."

Sensitized by Apprehension

To this the angry children of Malcolm X shout fiercely: "To hell with you and your Christ! If you cannot live where we live, if your children cannot grow where we grow, if you cannot suffer what we suffer, if you cannot learn what we learn, we have no use for you or your cringing Christ. If we must come to where you are to find quality and life, then this nation is no good and integration is irrelevant."

Then Black Power leaders turn to the people of the ghettos. "Let us use the separateness that the white Christians have imposed upon us," they say to the black brothers. "Let us together find our own dignity and our own power, so that one day we may stand and face even those who have rejected us, no longer begging to be accepted into their dying world, but showing them a world transformed, a world where we have shaped our own destiny. We shall build communities of our own, where men are truly brothers and goods are really shared. The American Christ is a Christ of separation and selfishness and relentless competition for an empty hole. We want no part of him."

Let there be no mistake. These evangels of a new movement are not deaf. They hear all the American words. They listen when good Christians ask: "Why should we pay our taxes to support those lazy deadbeats, those winos, those A.D.C. whores? Our money doesn't belong to them. Our money . . . our money . . ." Sensitized by long years of apprehension, the blacks need only look into the mirror to know who those "deadbeats" and "winos" are and what the "A.D.C. whores" look like. At the same time they wonder why the same white Christians sing no sad songs about tax rebates for General Motors' investments in South Africa's apartheid, and why they raise no complaints about the tax money given to farmers for planting nothing.

Groveling No More

They open that American family magazine the *Saturday Evening Post* and find an enlightened northern editor saying to rebellious blacks that all whites are Mississippians at heart. He adds: "We will do our best, in a half-hearted way, to correct old wrongs. [Our] hand may be extended grudgingly and patronizingly, but anyone who rejects that hand rejects his own best interests." To those who live in the realm of Black Consciousness this snarling voice is the voice of the people of the American Christ. Out of their anguished indignation the black rebels reply: "We reject your limp, bloodied hand and your half-hearted help. We shall use our own black hands and lives to build power. We shall love our own people. We shall lead them to a new justice, based on the kind of power that America respects—not nonviolence and forgiveness, but votes and money and violent retaliation. We shall beg no more. You shall define our best interests no longer. Take your Mississippi hand and your Cicero Christ and may both of them be damned." That is Black Power.

As black men they have long seen into the heart of American darkness. They have no patriotic illusions about this nation's benevolent intentions toward the oppressed nonwhite people of the world, no matter how often the name and compassion of divinity are invoked. With eyes cleared by pain they discern the arrogance beneath the pious protestations. The American Christ leads the Hiroshima-bound bomber, blesses the marines on their way to another in the long series of Latin American invasions, and blasphemously calls it peace when America destroys an entire Asian peninsula. And as black men they know from their own hard experience that these things can happen because this nation, led by an elder of the church, is determined to have its way in the world at any cost—to others. How often have the white-robed elders led the mob thirsting for the black man's blood!

Black people are not fooled by the churchly vestments of humility. They hear arrogant white pastors loudly counting dollars and members, and committees smugly announcing the cost of their new modern churches—hollow tombs for Christ. They hear the voices: "Negroes, oh Negroes, you must be humble, like Christ. You must be patient and long-suffering. Negroes, don't push so hard. Look at all we've given you so far." And the voices trail off: "Negroes, dear Negroes, remember our Lord taught how good it is to be meek and lowly." And then a whisper: "Cause if you don't, niggers, if you don't, we'll crush you."

So the Black Power advocates sanely shout, "Go to hell, you whited sepulchers, hypocrites. All you want is to cripple our will and prolong our agony, and you use your white Christ to do it." To the black people they say: "Don't grovel, don't scrape. Whether you are 1 percent or 50 percent or 100 percent black, you are men, and you must affirm this in the face of all the pious threats. You must proclaim your manhood just as the white Christians do—in arrogance, in strength and in power. But the arrogance must be black, and the strength must be black, and black must be the color of our power."

Christian Blasphemers

Then comes the sharpest of all moments of truth, when Christian voices are raised in hostility and fear, directing their missionary chorus to the young men drained of hope by the ghetto. "Black boys," they say, "rampaging, screaming, laughing black boys, you must love—like Christ and Doctor King. Black boys, please drop your firebombs. Violence never solved anything. You must love your enemies—if they're white and American and represent law and order. You must love them for your rotting houses and for your warped education. You must love them for your nonexistent jobs. Above all, you must love them for their riot guns, their billy clubs, their hatred and their white, white skin."

It would be terrifying enough if the voices stopped on that emasculating note. But they go on: "Just the same, black boys, if the enemies have been properly certified as such by our Christian leaders, and if they're poor and brown and 10,000 miles away, you must hate them. You must scream and rampage and kill them, black boys. Pick up the firebombs and char them good. We have no civilian jobs for you, of course, but we have guns and medals, and you must kill those gooks—even if some of them do resemble the image reflected in the night-black pool of your tears."

What can a nation expect in response to such vicious words? It gets the truth—far more than it deserves. For the black men reply: "Hypocrites, white hypocrites, you only want to save your skin and your piled-up treasure from the just envy-anger of your former slaves, your present serfs and your future victims. In the name of this Christ you deny our past, demean our present and promise us no future save that of black mercenaries in your assaults upon the world's dark and desperate poor."

Their rage cries out: "Give us no pink, two-faced Jesus who counsels love for you and flaming death for the children of Vietnam. Give us no blood-sucking savior who condemns brick-throwing rioters and praises dive-bombing killers. That Christ stinks. We want no black men to follow in *his* steps. Stop forcing our poor black boys into your legions of shame. We will not go."

"If we must fight," they say, "let it be on the streets where we have been humiliated. If we must burn down houses, let them be the homes and stores of our exploiters. If we must kill, let it be the fat, pious white Christians who guard their lawns and their daughters while engineering slow death for us. If we must die, let it be for a real cause, the cause of black men's freedom as black men define it. And may all the white elders die well in the causes they defend." This is Black Power—the response to the American Christ.

Unbelievable words? If any Christian dare call them blasphemous, let him remember that the speakers make no claims about Christ or God. Only we Christians—black and white—do that. If the just creator-father God is indeed alive, and if Jesus of Nazareth was his Christ, then we Christians are blasphemers. We are the ones who take his name in vain. We are the ones who follow the phony American Christ and in our every act declare our betrayal of the resurrected Lord.

If judgment stands sure it is not for Stokely Carmichael alone but for all of us. It is we Christians who made the universal Christ into an American mascot, a puppet blessing every mad American act, from the extermination of the original possessors of this land to the massacre of the Vietnamese on their own soil—even, perhaps, to the bombing of the Chinese mainland in the name of peace.

If judgment stands sure it is not primarily upon SNCC that it will fall, but upon those who have kidnapped the compassionate Jesus—the Jesus who shared all he had, even his life, with the poor—and made him into a profit-oriented, individualistic, pietistic cat who belongs to his own narrowly defined kind and begrudges the poor their humiliating subsistence budgets. These Christians are the ones who have taken away our Lord and buried him in a place unknown.

We shall not escape by way of nostalgia or recrimination. For if he whom we call the Christ is indeed the Suffering Servant of God and man, what excuse can there be for those who have turned him into a crossless puppet, running away from suffering with his flaxen locks flapping in the wind?

If God is yet alive we cannot afford time to reminisce about the good old days of the civil rights movement when everybody knew the words of the songs. The time of singing may be past. It may be that America must now stand under profound and damning judgment for having turned the redeeming lover of all men into a white, middle-class burner of children and destroyer of the revolutions of the oppressed.

Chance for Redemption

This may be God's message for the church—through Black Power. It is a message for all who claim to love the Lord of the church. If this reading is accurate, our tears over the demise of the civil rights movement may really be tears over the smashing of an image we created or the withdrawal of a sign we were no longer heeding. Therefore if we weep, let it not be for the sins of SNCC and CORE but for our own unfaithfulness and for our country's blasphemy. And let us begin to pray that time may be granted us to turn from blond dolls to the living, revolutionary Lord who proclaimed that the first shall be last and the last, first.

If this message can break the grip of self-pity and nostalgia on us, the power of blackness may yet become the power of light and resurrection for us all. Has it not been said that God moves in mysterious ways his wonders to perform? I can conceive of nothing more wonderful and mysterious than that the blackness of my captive People should become a gift of light for this undeserving nation—even a source of hope for a world that lives daily under the threat of white America's arrogant and bloody power. Is that too much to hope for? Or is the time for hoping now past? We may soon discover whether we have been watching a wall or a curtain—or both.

4

THE CHURCH AND THE URBAN CRISIS

Statements from Black and White Caucuses,
National Council of Churches Conference
on the Church and Urban Tensions,
Washington, D. C., September 27-30, 1967

PREAMBLE

More than 100 persons from seventeen denominations met in Washington, D. C., under the auspices of the National Council of Churches, from September 27 to 30.

We came together from all over the nation, after a summer of anguish and revolt, expectantly and fearfully.

We came in an hour of grave crisis in the cities of our country—a crisis of severe distrust and alienation between black and white both within and outside of the churches.

We came to wrestle once again with the problem of our disorder and disobedience as Christians and God's design for renewal and reconciliation in a time of world-wide revolution.

We came conscious of the context in which any meaningful conversation about church strategy for racial justice could take place among us. The context of Black Power—that mood and strategy of the black community which is transforming the civil rights movement into a movement for the identity, self-image and dignity of black people through the development of legitimate power in the arenas of political, social and economic decision-making in the United States.

The overarching question of our discussions was "Who really are we who seek in our various places to bear witness to the God of justice and reconciliation between white Americans and black Americans?" To put the matter another way, we were forced in Washington to ask of ourselves, "What are we required to face honestly about ourselves—about our whiteness and our blackness—before we are able to confront the world together in the name of Jesus Christ, in whom we were made One?"

As we struggled with these questions, which really have to do with the existential nature of the Church in the United States, we came face to face with our own delusions and pretensions. We discovered that in order to learn the truth about ourselves and our situation, so successfully covered over by years of hypocrisy and dissimulation, we had to make a decision unprecedented in ecumenical conferences under the aegis of the National Council. We made the decision to divide the conference into a white caucus and a black caucus.

Although we continued to meet together in plenary sessions, it was in these separate groups that some of us in Washington experienced more than ever before the scandal of our separateness in the two worlds and the two churches of America. We experienced also the most honest and intensive confrontation many of us have ever known with the tragic reality of American racism, the poverty of our own spirits and confessions and finally, the necessity of a strategic withdrawal into our own separate staging-areas before we could emerge together to do battle with a common enemy on a common battlefield.

Out of the two caucuses of this conference came the two statements which are reproduced below. They are neither definitive nor are they conclusive positions for white and black churchmen. They do mark the beginning of what some of us believe is a new and more relevant dialogue about the role of the church in the urban crisis. They also suggest some of the themes and commitments that we who were together in Washington wish to explore further as we plan together and separately for participation in the racial revolution.

Without pretending that we have spoken either the ultimate or the authoritative word, we make bold to commend this document to churchmen for whatever study and implementation they, by conscience and conviction, are guided to make.

A DECLARATION OF BLACK CHURCHMEN

We, Black Churchmen, meeting in caucus find ourselves profoundly distressed, disturbed, frustrated and in a state of utter disquietude about the nature and mission of the church in a time of revolution. We have come to realize that Black Power is an expression of the need for Black Authenticity in a white-dominated society, a society which has from its earliest beginnings displayed unadulterated racism. We affirm without fear of repudiation the meaningfulness of blackness and our identity as Black Churchmen. We confess the guilt which is ours for past actions and inaction in failing to be instruments for the expression of the will of God as Black Churchmen. We therefore propose now to speak and act, out of our own shame and guilt, concerning the lack of the Church's responsiveness to the needs of black people seeking to be free and human in a dehumanizing world.

White Churches

We call upon the white churches at this point in history to recognize that in spite of the many commendable contributions in the past to the struggle for social justice, we have come to a point when the very structures, forms and priorities are being seriously questioned, particularly by the Black Power Revolution. Racial Justice can no longer be considered just another cause pursued by a few while the rest of the church does business as usual. Moreover, it cannot simply be a cause alongside of other causes—to be used as a ploy to justify the existence of the Church, but must become the number one priority as it is the number one problem of the nation.

Therefore, we commend the belated action taken by the General Board of the National Council of Churches of Christ in the U.S.A. in its resolution "The Crisis within the Nation," September 14, 1967, wherein it pledges ten percent of its unrestricted capital funds for development in the Black community and calls upon its member constituents, among other things, to make available its resources for development in the Black community. It specifically states that "funds be used for the development of programs in ghetto communities which are planned and directed by representatives of those communities for maximum benefit of the communities." We recognize that this is an initial step in the right direction and call for its immediate implementation.

We further call upon the white churches to commit themselves to the following:

1. To join with us in affirming the legitimacy of the Black Power movement and to be open to the word that God is speaking to us through the issues it raises.
2. To turn in their distress to the leadership of the Black Church recognizing the insights borne out of a history of struggle against the exclusion and oppression of Black people in Church and Society; supporting the initiatives borne of these insights; and seeking the guidance, collaboration and support of the Black Churches in the formulation and implementation of all church policies and programs.
3. To declare a three-year moratorium on suburban new church development, and make the funds available from such work in people-centered ministries in the Black and White communities.

Black Churches

Historically the Black Church in America represented an authentic expression of Black Power. It grew out of the needs of Black People to glorify God and to affirm their own humanity, to find a sense of identity, to have something controlled by Black People, to form an institution whose express purpose would be to celebrate, preserve and enhance the integrity of Blackness under the Lordship of Christ, to be responsive to the needs of Black People and responsible to them. The historic step to separate from the White Church was the first clear call for Black Power.

However, we confess that in recent times we have not lived up to our heritage, for we have not celebrated, preserved and enhanced the integrity of Blackness. Rather we have fallen prey to the dominance of White Society and have allowed the truth, meaningfulness and authenticity of the Black Church to be defamed by our easy acceptance of its goals, objectives and criteria for success. Therefore, the Black Church has unwittingly become a tool for our oppression, providing an easy vehicle for escape from the harsh realities of our own existence. This of necessity makes it impossible for us to be instruments of liberation which is our calling as Christians and particularly Black Christians.

Since as Black Churchmen we find ourselves in the unenviable role of the oppressor, we are in real danger of losing our existence and our reason for being, if indeed we have not already lost them. We rejoice in the Black Power Movement, which is not only the renewed hope for Black People, but gives the Black Church once again, its reason for existing. We call upon Black Churchmen everywhere to embrace the Black Power Movement, to divest itself of the traditional churchly functions and goals which do not respond to the needs of a downtrodden, oppressed and alienated people.

We further call upon the Black Church to commit itself to the following:

1. To the establishment of freedom schools to offset the degradation and omission of a white-dominated public school system.
2. To workshops fostering Black family solidarity.
3. To training lay leadership in community organization and other relevant skills.
4. To massive efforts to support financially Black groups for self-determination.
5. To the removal of all images which suggest that God is white.

Having spoken to the Black Church and the White Church, we now speak specifically to Black Churchmen in Black Churches or Non-Black Churches.

On July 26, 1966, a group of Black Churchmen met to form a new movement in American Christendom—the National Committee of Negro Churchmen. The major purpose of this group was to declare that at this juncture of history, under the impetus of the Black Power Movement, Black Churchmen needed to consolidate their energies and resources in a consciously Black organization for the purpose of enhancing the self-image, dignity and power of the Black Community in America.

We support the National Committee of Negro Churchmen. We call upon Black Churchmen of the Black Church and Black Churchmen of the Non-Black Churches to participate in it. We call for support of the national committee by both the Black and Non-Black Churches.

Furthermore, we call upon the National Committee of Negro Churchmen to complete the process of organization by:

1. The establishment of a national headquarters with a paid secretariat.
2. To establish regional offices through which every Black Churchman can participate in the institutional and theological renewal of Black Religion enabling it to make its unique contribution to the universal church free from pernicious racism.
3. To divest itself of internal partisan politics and ecclesiastical gamesmanship.
4. To structure itself in such a way as to provide the kind of revolutionary impetus needed for these crucial times.
5. To call for a conference of Black theologians to consider the theological implications of Black Power.

Finally, we call upon Black Churchmen who find themselves in Non-Black Churches either to find ways of exercising a high degree of influence over structures of those churches or to return home to the Black expression of religion. We further call upon the Black Churchmen in Black Churches to insure the return of the Black Church to an expression of its original reason for being.

A DECLARATION OF WHITE CHURCHMEN

The problem of race in America is centered in white America.

The white church is a racist church.

The American black man did not create the ghettos of our sick cities. White America has enslaved him.

The American black, by and large, does not own the ghettos. They are owned by white men.

The American black does not control the ghettos. They are controlled by immoral structures of white men.

However, American blacks will transform the ghettos. Whites must seek a way to transform themselves, or we will constitute an *apartheid* society.

The body gathered in this caucus is determined to transform the white society. We are encouraged by the courage of the black American brother who has shown that he will create a new black society in America. Therefore, where it is possible, we will move together for the transformation of American society.

Where it is not possible to work together at present, we will work separately, knowing at the same time that our separate work with blacks and whites is our common task and work together.

5

BLACK POWER:
A RELIGIOUS OPPORTUNITY

Nathan Wright, Jr.

Fulfillment

Black Power, in its simplest terms, speaks to the nature of humanity. The greatest problem before the churches, and before every institution in our world, is some form of the human problem. What is the human goal? Toward what end should every aspect of human life be directed? The answer given by the current impetus toward Black Power is the one word *fulfillment*.

The black people of America want to fulfill their potential, for their own good and for the larger enrichment of the common store of all Americans. To become what one must be demands the presence, the building up, of power. Centuries ago Aristotle made what has since become the most classic expression of human destiny. He declared that what a thing will be, that it is, whether it be a horse or a man. The unstated ingredient which he assumed was the presence of power. All men need the power to *become*. Indeed, the Greek words for power (*bia*) and life (*bios*) reflect the essential interrelationship of power and life. Power is basic to life. Without power, life cannot become what it must be.

In order to respond effectively to the human problem, institutions concerned with ultimate social ends must be power-producing enterprises. They must be or become enablers, facilitating human growth into self-direction toward its appointed flower and fulfillment. Conversely, any agency which promotes dependency or which limits self-directed progress toward maturity and self-sufficiency complicates the human problem. It warps the human condition and subverts the divine purpose of human growth.

In religious terms, a God of power, of majesty and of might, who has made

Nathan Wright, Jr., is a member of the faculty of the State University of New York at Albany and an Episcopal priest. This essay is from his book *Black Power and Urban Unrest: Creative Possibilities,* New York: Hawthorn Books, 1967, pp. 135-155.

man to be in His own image and likeness, must will that His creation reflect in the immediacies of life, His power, His majesty and His might. Black Power raises, for the healing of humanity and for the renewal of a commitment to the creative religious purpose of growth, the far too long overlooked need for power, if life is to become what in the mind of its Creator it is destined to be.

So often in religious life in America we have tended to settle for less than ultimate goals. We have courted the illusory separate but equal despoiler of human growth. We have sought to do our level and most conscientious best within the frameworks of class and pseudo-caste which forbade the fulfill-ment of God's design for His creation. We have fed men lavishly, where a sense of the divine purpose of human growth should have prompted our teaching of men to feed themselves *and* our affording them the sustained and equitable opportunity for self-provision. Power is essential to life. Men may kill and destroy as wantonly by smothering, by too much uncritically-thought-out kindness, as by neglect. The Black Power issue here recalls the churches—and every institution concerned with the human condition—to the employment of critical judgment in every intention to facilitate human growth. We must worship God—and serve our fellow man—with our minds as well as with our hearts. The head and heart must be reunited in the religious enterprise. To feel kindly disposed may be lethal, if one's kindliness is not wedded to informed and tempered judgment.

The churches, then, must constantly keep before them the purpose of human growth. The programs and policies of the churches must be planned and re-examined continually from this perspective. Is human potential being thwarted in its effort to become what it must be? From such a perspective or frame of reference as this, a far more creative attitude would need to be developed in many areas of the life of our religious institutions. We could no longer effectively restrict the opportunities for service by clergy whose minds and hearts are formed for greatness and extensive service but whose skins are darker than what a racist-ridden secular culture might desire. For what ends are we to settle? Which gods, to put it more clearly, are we to worship? Not only would such a race-related question be asked. We would also need to raise new questions concerning the utilization of retired persons, the employment of female skills, the right incentives for Christian steward-ship, and the specifics of Christian service in the world. The power issue thus holds the key for the opening of many doors.

Every parish clergyman might measure the fruitfulness of his tasks by their relationship to the furtherance of power. Have I created dependency? Or have I facilitated self-directed growth? This is the root question as it relates to the human condition with our families, with friends and in every personal and corporate relationship in life. It is the enduring issue in our civic life in reference to the schools. It bears upon the kind of charity with which we face the condition of the aged. Every life yearns, or should yearn, for growth and for fulfillment. It should always be facilitated toward that very end.

It is crucial to understand the role of pain in the pattern of growth. "No pain, no progress" is a dictum of universal applicability. At the center of life, so the Christian contends, is a cross. It is "the emblem of suffering and shame." It may be painful to us to allow another to suffer in order for growth to be facilitated. But the mothers of infants, the teachers of adolescents and those associated with the medical arts all know just how essential pain is to human growth. We must often forgo apparent little kindnesses to do the larger and far kinder thing. We must even more often forego—aggressively, graciously and single-mindedly—the caprice of the unkind customs of the communities and of households of which we are a part, "lest we make the word of God to no effect through our traditions."

Life yearns for fulfillment. The churches of America—as they are attentive and attuned to the need for power on the part of all—must turn, in ways which are marks of religious regeneration, toward the central and most enduring task of human life. They may work, as God would will, for the empowerment of life to become what He would have it be.

Focus

The Black Power concept is startling. It brings into focus an apparent incongruity in associating power with those whom our culture conditions us to think of as powerless. Could there be anything more ludicrous than a powerful half-grown child? It is like speaking of vigorous laziness or discontented contentedness. It is hard for those conditioned by our American racist-ridden culture to accept blackness and power in one breath. Even many Negroes, who often out-hate their white fellow Americans when it comes to loathing blackness, think of it as unseemly to compound the term Black Power.

Yet our religious life should enable us to bring into new and more creative focus things which otherwise we might not see and understand. Our religious life should enable us to see all reality in the light of Ultimate Reality. In this sense, those who practice the presence of God and would "see God face to face" must inevitably grow in the capacity of seeing the face of God not beyond, but in and through, the face of every man. Nonetheless the most common American experience is for racial bigotry to increase as apparent religiosity increases. Witness the relation of whites in the Bible Belt to blacks of the almost identical area called the Black Belt. Fundamentalism and intolerance are more than incidentally related. There is no evidence of increased intermarriage—which historically is the most natural of all forms of human interchange—among "the Spirit-filled." Nor is there a greater evident commitment to human fulfillment and racial interchange among monastic or conventual communities. There is an evident inherent basic flaw in any religious experience which cannot unloose and move beyond a deadly cultural bind or limitation.

The seeming incongruity of blackness and power, in the face of the need for all men to appropriate power for human growth, reminds us of the vital need for a new focus to be brought to bear on human life. A possible clue to a resolution of our predicament lies in the glorification aspect of the Black Power emphasis. Blackness which includes by definition all shades and complexions of non-whiteness—has been degraded in our culture. The glorification of blackness implicit in the term Black Power is a conscious or unconscious effort to stake a claim for the worth of those in our nation who are termed non-white. Essentially it is a clarification. The root meaning of the term "glorify" is to clarify, to make clear and plain and straight.

All of life must be clarified in this sense. It must be given and seen in that dimension which sets it forth in terms of glory—now and forever. To see life as it truly is means to see it as God sees it, in its eternal dimension, in the glory appropriate to its involvement with and in the life of God. Is not another way of looking at the purpose of fulfillment to see as the end of all life its transfiguration, its glorification, its clarification for what it is in the mind and vision and will of the agency of its creation?

Our worship, for example, should be directed to this purpose. It should reflect life in its most clear and untarnished sense. The life of the ancient church, the church in its earlier centuries, tended to reflect this aspect of religious purpose far more than does the worship of the church today. The spirit of the ancient church in this regard must be recaptured. We may see this aspect of clarification or glory in several of the main features of the worship of the early church.

The worship of the early Christian church was familial in character. Its setting reflected this quality of its life. The worshipping congregation gathered around a family table. At the head of the table was the father of the family, who sat in the seat of Christ. Here he presided over what many other members of the family of God did in corporate worship. From his seat at the head of the table, that is, behind it and facing the family, the president or priest or bishop also taught the lessons of the faith to those of the household of faith. Worship took place in the atmosphere of an intimate family gathering. The church tended to sense a oneness in Christ, similar in spirit to the historical family oneness of the Jews, but transcending and enfolding the limits of physical lineage. It was St. Augustine who gave the classic expression to the early church's sense of being a family, and so of fashioning or welding all of human life into the oneness which the church realized in Christ. Writing of the undesirability of marriage between blood or close relatives, St. Augustine gave utterance to the early church's sense of relationship, either actual or potential, with all of human life. The church sensed a need, in the most deeply human terms, to make of the human race one blood-related family within the household of faith. St. Augustine explained:

> The first of all marriages was that between the man made out of dust and his mate who had issued from his side. After that, the continuance and

increase of the human race demanded births from the union of males and females, even though there were no other human beings except those born of the first two persons. That is why men took their sisters for wives.

But, of course, just as this is the best thing to do when natural necessity compels it, it becomes all the more wicked when moral obligation condemns it. This can be proved as follows. The human law is love and this law is best respected when men, who both desire and ought to live in harmony, so bind themselves by the bonds of social relationships that no one man monopolizes more than one relationship, and many different relationships are distributed as widely as possible, so that a common social life of the greatest number may best be fostered.[1]

St. Augustine takes his position a step further, indicating that the more diverse the population the more the faithful should choose in marriage those most distant from them in race, clan, province, culture or nation. In this way those of the church might express the oneness of the human family in Christ.

The religious institutions of America may make a saving reassessment—with the focus here afforded by the issue of Black Power—of the interrelated nature of human life. The assumption of the kind of oneness held by those in the early church is manifestly lacking in the church today. Our focus is not their focus. Yet the familial nature of the Christian life is consistent with their conception of the nature and destiny of human life.

The worship of the ancient church was marked by a hierarchical framework of relationships. There were different or specialized roles to perform. But the filling of these roles was open to all. Thus the Roman Pontiff at the time of the Peace of Constantine was a man of black African descent. Pope Melchiades led the Church at Rome through its last days of illegality into the period of its final legal recognition. Although slavery was accepted, it bore scarcely any more connotations of inferiority within the church, or outside of it, than did foreign citizenship. The ranks of the church were open to all and the inherent dynamics of the church tended to empty slavery of its low status. The focus of the church was upon life seen as it should be—and is eternally—and according to which pattern it must therefore be lived in the here and now.

The worship of the early church was marked by a depth of individual and corporate participation by many and by all which is lacking in the church today. The chief pastor presided over what others did singly and collectively. He was a facilitator, an enabler, rather than a star performer. All who desire the growth of others into their due fulfillment should be enablers. They should help others to grow in the self-directing power to become what they should be. All in the early church participated in the ministry to the sick and others. Today we must doubtless learn in the church that even the sick can minister, bringing healing to themselves as they engage in therapeutic acts on behalf of others. The aged too, or perhaps especially, have more time and more maturity for tasks in the church and outside of it calling for the skills and other gifts of the unhurried and the wise. The Black Power emphasis upon the maximum use of all human potential for the greater good of all suggests for the churches perhaps untapped human resources which are ripe for the church's harvesting.

The worship of the ancient church brought a further sense of clarity or focus upon the nature of the church's life through its use of sacred writings. The lessons from the Old and the New Testaments were read as family history. The Epistles were intimate letters of the family, alive with the feelings of those bound by close-knit ties. The Old Testament readings were lessons in family lore, a reminder of the family heritage of those who were spiritually, and so essentially, the sons of Abraham. The Scriptures reflected in this setting a life or inheritance into which one had already entered, rather than a system of beliefs to which one must give assent. The Scripture readings were experiences in being. Knowledge of Christ was not so much fact-knowledge as it was the knowledge of relationship, as in the knowing of one's wife or husband. It was life of one in another, in the sense in which St. Paul speaks of life "in Christ."

Finally, the worship of the early church brought a new sense of focus or of clarification in that its essential act of thanksgiving, or of Eucharist as it was called, involved the transfiguration or the lifting of life on to a plane where it befitted the purpose of God. Utilizing the earthy symbols of bread, water and wine, every aspect of life was symbolically reunited with its Originator, Sustainer and End. Life was glorified. Indeed, it always was and is so on the level of the eternal, which was and is the true; and so the church simply had to make Eucharist or to give thanks for the clarification or for the glory of life which is forever a constant in the mind, experience and sight of God. What *will be* on an eternal plane *is now* for those who, with thankfulness for God's doings, enter into the realities which are as yet to be revealed. The ancients may be said to have sensed that "It does not yet appear what we shall be, but when Christ who is our life shall appear, we shall appear with him in glory, for we shall see him as he is."[2] The mind of the early church was expressed when Tertullian wrote, *"Christianus alter Christus,"* the Christian is another Christ. Every Christian was a revelation of Christ. Can Christians denigrate or restrict or deface the life of Christ in their black brothers and still be called by the name of Christ?

By clear implication, the Black Power concept may both chasten and challenge the churches of America to at least focus upon the realities which they are called both to see and be. American religion needs to be regenerated. Black Power, as a concept emphasizing the need to bring a different focus to bear upon life itself and its possibilities, may open a pathway toward the renewal of American religious life.[3]

Self-Concept

No programs of renewal by themselves will lead to any re-creative trends in American religion. The churches of America must have a new self-concept and a firm determination to fulfill it. A self-concept is developed chiefly by one's secure alignment with power. This is true of children as their personalities are structured through the power dynamics of the home. This is true of young adults as they are Americanized and incorporate something of the force of the nation's life into their lives. This is the way that adults find identification in their communities and in every circle of relationships. They identify with power or create new blocs of power. It is through the tensions and coalescence of power that families are formed and shaped. The power of wives and husbands in creative tension and coalescence allows for adult growth and produces the atmosphere which determines the unique character of families and ultimately to a great degree the character of the nation itself.

The clergy and the churches of America are no exception to this rule. They either identify with existing power or they form new associations of power. Power is essential to institutional and professional being and performance. The fully evident need for a new type of power base by the black people of America has led logically to a reaching after the collective power of those whom racism in America has effectively disinherited. In this endeavor the churches have begun to play a unique and vital part. Potentially all the churches of America have much to gain from the current focus on Black Power.

Numbers of Negro clergy have seen in Black Power the means of restoring to themselves, as well as to the Negro churches, a new sense of integrity and self-respect. Thus the National Committee of Negro Churchmen has taken a leadership role across the nation both in promoting the positive aspects of Black Power and in encouraging its extensive development in every black community in the land. In this endeavor they have themselves been encouraged by growing numbers of white churchmen. Some of these have shared continually in thoughtful analyses of the social role of the churches in American life. Others are from among those who have found in the power issue an unexpected source of potential vitality and new meaning, perhaps as never before in their religious life. There has been a mounting realization that the self-concept not only of the Negro churchmen of America but also of the churches as a whole has been wanting. Indeed, what many see as the current crisis in American religion reflects the need for a new sense of wholeness, integrity, and common purpose on the part of all the churches of America.[4]

We have noted how the churches can benefit pastorally from the implications of Black Power which re-emphasize growth-producing mechanisms and goals. The churches have at least as much to gain in their prophetic role. It is always good to have a sense of purpose in one's life. But if one senses its affinity with cosmic purpose, it puts a spring in one's step and gives a tone to one's spirit which spells vibrancy and a quiet sense of confidence and command. Such has been the spirit of countless churchmen who through the recent raising of the issue of power have a new sense of purpose. One white clergyman told that, although he had not admitted it, he had yearned to leave the ministry until he experienced a sense of awakening with the raising of issues afforded by Black Power. He explained that the only way he could accomplish things in his ministry was by aligning himself with one form of power or another among the businessmen or among the matrons who had long assumed and exercised a kind of proprietary trust over every aspect of the parish life. These lords and ladies of the enterprise allowed him to preach whatever he wanted, within limits, and especially so long as no implementation of prophetic notions was expected. He had been well provided for, and no great demands were made upon him. But he saw himself increasingly as being under house arrest, as the kept person in a kind of illicit enterprise where religion was used, unconsciously perhaps but no less effectively, for something considerably less than the purposes of God.

The clergyman went on to explain that issues raised by the focus on Black Power had the effect of turning him on and of providing a new sense of both his being and his vocation. He saw in the Black Power idea, and in those persons associated with it, a new source of his own personal strength and a new avenue to significant relationships. He felt that he could now speak to his people with a new sense of integrity about race relations, as Black Power focused interest not upon what is due the Negro but upon what the black people of America are seeking to add in terms of the enrichment of American life. Who in his parish could object to the lesser taxes from a reduction of the high tariff now paid for relief? Who could object to the development on the part of any benighted segment of the community of the kind of impressive self-respect which commands the admiration and confidence of others? Who could object to the determination on the part of those representing hitherto overlooked resources to add their insights and services to the broad confrontation of issues in our local, national and international life? He felt, and sensed that his congregation would feel the same, that God knows that at this juncture in our corporate life we need the help of all. Black Power was, in his mind, a gift like grace to American life. In his teaching, preaching, and pastoral services, he saw for himself and his congregation new possibilities for a new and more dynamic self-awareness.

Essential to the operation of any institution is the lively and common recognition of its own nature and purpose. The literature of Christian witness is replete with how-to-do and what-has-been-done prescriptions. But most often overlooked is the recognition that only from the point of self-awareness—such as that to which Black Power addresses itself for American Negroes—can authentic self-directed and growth-producing activities be performed. The church in America has lacked self-awareness. It has failed to see itself in the same lively terms as did the ancient church. It was seen then as a living organism, extending the life of God in the world. Seen as an organism, it is clear that conscious growth toward the fulfillment of the purposes inherent in its life need to be fostered. It can be recognized that only by its own proper nurture can its functions outside its life be performed. Unless the church has a genuine inner life, it cannot have an authentic outer life. Those who are self-aware know that their basic goal is not to *go* somewhere but simply to *be* what they potentially are, in and through each present circumstance in life.

The clergyman who moved toward a new sense of self-awareness finally indicated that he felt that there were no more exciting prospects before him than in helping his people to ascertain new forms of outreach in the Negro community.

Service

Just how can white young people and adults assist in projects relating to the Negro community in ways consistent with the impetus toward Black Power?

For those in the churches, the most immediate recognition must be that any project is more an expression of one's being than it is of one's outreach. As it is true of the churches, so it is true of America as a whole: Bringing the kind of fulfillment to all of America to which Black Power addresses itself must be seen as a need inherent in the nation's being and that of its every citizen. The greatest area of need is in the conversion of every American to the idea of moving America toward its destiny by developing and utilizing the full potential of all. In this endeavor we must begin where we are. White Americans inevitably will find in their present primary associations and relationships in the white community plenty of opportunity for conversion and enlistment. The best forms of change are always those which begin among our personal or primary relationships in prompt and unobtrusive ways.

In the American culture it is well-nigh impossible for any of us to escape racist assumptions and involvements. Simply witness the way we marry, which indicates clearly that in basic human relationships involving the deepest mutuality and interchange white Americans do not choose to include non-whites, those whom we consider "something else." The same cannot be proved to be equally true of Negroes. It is not they who make the laws or define the taboos and customs of the land. A group-dynamics laboratory experience demonstrated the nature of the problem which we face. A member of the group, which comprised about eight Negroes and four white people, remarked that she had no racial prejudice and was very fond of Negroes. A training group laboratory standard is a thoroughgoing honesty, and in this spirit a white group trainer replied: "That's interesting. I hate Negroes. . . ." After a brief pause, he continued explaining: "My cultural

upbringing makes me that way. But I do my best to control and overcome it."
The woman who spoke of having no racial prejudice quickly got the message.
American life infects us all with its limitations. We must be honest with
ourselves, and be mindful of the subtle ways in which our upbringing—in the
light of the historical experience of our nation—will inevitably tend to make
us other than what our ideals decree. Before we can engage in activities
fruitfully with others, we must be mindful at least of the need to be self-aware
in this regard. In this way, we can generate or further stimulate our own
growth, and by our openness to our own limitations we can minimize the
possibility of undue offense to others.

Close to home still, we can serve the needs of the Negro community by
deliberately creating opportunities for black people to work in and relate to
our communities in ways perhaps hitherto untried. As school officials, as
clergymen, as professionals in other capacities, we may ask whether such
opportunities as these have been opened equitably to Negroes in the towns
or cities where we live. Correcting imbalances in an imbalanced culture must
always be done in arbitrary and calculated ways until the cultural pattern itself
is changed. Then again, we may ask some further questions. Do Negroes
belong to my country club or business or other group? And if not, why not?
In how many ways am I the beneficiary of opportunities arbitrarily denied to
others? Another way of putting this last question is: How do growth possibilities open to me limit unfairly the growth possibilities of others? Do I
unconsciously lessen the dignity or worth of any human life?

A pressing need, emphasized throughout this entire discussion of Black
Power and urban unrest, is for the creation of many forms of dialogue
designed to facilitate continuing and accelerating changes in every community. We can serve the needs in the Negro community by devising local
forums for white people, and encouraging Negroes and mixed groups to do
the same, for discussions concerning the myriad implications of the principles
of growth and fulfillment. We can do this in reference to our business life and
in regard to our social, religious and civic life. In this way, we may build
mechanisms for broader and continuing changes throughout the life of our
communities. Here it may be underscored once more that our confrontation
with the issue of Black Power may open up for us approaches long needed,
and doubtless more greatly needed for the future, to many problems which
might otherwise have been more difficult to treat.

In every community and institution in America, group laboratory
dynamics could profitably be taught. Those who teach always grow through
every teaching experience. The force of all that is said in these pages is that
here—in the Black Power issue—may be an unexpected once-in-a-lifetime
kind of opportunity for America, and all of its institutions, to face with the
greatest ease and effectiveness the growing needs and challenges presented
by a world of continuing change.

In devising service projects for work in the Negro community itself, we must be careful to work only as enablers. It is often far more difficult to recruit, train and stimulate others to do a task than it is to do it ourselves. Yet, when we perform a task in the stead of others, several limiting things happen. When our work stops, there is no self-generating agency to continue where we left off. Then again, when only our hands have been put to work, the multiplied resources which we might have equipped for self-generating or self-directed service do not produce their multiplied results. Enabling work should be done with those who will or should have the responsibility for the work's continuation. Thus we begin and end with would-be responsible adults. Effective ways of recruiting, stimulating, training and initially sustaining adults in new tasks which they should routinely assume need to be devised and taught to large numbers of those who wish to serve as enablers. Older young people, as well as adults, can do this. They can share in visiting with local people from door to door, and in other unobtrusive ways alerting, informing and encouraging those who need such support in their efforts toward common goals.

Negroes need to be assisted in efforts to organize themselves. There are enabling ways in which all may share in this kind of endeavor. The need for such organization is urgent. Divisiveness in any portion of a community works to the detriment of all. In every benighted community such division can be costly. The Negro community—the most long benighted in America—is no exception to this rule. Divisiveness in the Negro community creates waste for which all must pay. We may therefore choose whether we shall pay in a limited way for prevention or pay continually for effects. In reference to the need for organization in the Negro community, the late Dr. Adam Clayton Powell, Sr., wrote:

> The race was completely disorganized when the Emancipation Proclamation was issued. At the close of the Civil War, there were as many groups and factions as there were slave plantations. These groups were not only taught by their owners to mistrust and hate each other, but the members of each group also were encouraged to tattle on each other. This was necessary to maintain the institution of slavery.[5]

When others outside the Negro community see the need for organization among Negroes, they often tend to see no more than what the late Dr. Powell has related here. But the Powell statement goes on to speak of how the Negro people have been organized by the Negro churches and other agencies. These organizations need, however, to be brought together to serve the economic and civic purposes which can be achieved through Negro solidarity and self-respect. Organization for these purposes cannot be done directly by anyone other than Negroes themselves. In this vein Dr. Powell explained: "I do not consider the . . . NAACP and the National Urban League, Negro organizations. These organizations for the most part are supported by white people and largely dominated by them." Negroes definitely must belong to these organizations, bringing even greater resources to them than in the past. Still, by far the most basic and as yet unaccomplished task lies in the fact that Negroes must organize themselves. In this endeavor they must begin by utilizing substantial resources supplied by others, in terms of brain power, money, and quietly unobtrusive time-absorbing facilitating tasks. The very divisiveness of Negroes ironically makes massive financial and other support from the white community an initial catalyzing necessity. The important continuing ingredients are Negro leadership, self-determination and growing financial self-support of the organization designed for developing self-respect. Organization gives to the Negro an equitable power stance from which to treat with dignity those outside of his own community. All of America can benefit from this. Its tangible encouragement is an immediately vital necessity in every community in the land.

The churches of America have begun to encourage such organization among Negroes. Principles of the Community Organization for Development, or C.O.D., for the northeastern New Jersey Negro and Spanish-speaking communities, need to be widely disseminated and discussed. White people of all age groups and of all levels of influence may be involved in C.O.D.-type enterprise in many new forms of service, devised freshly to meet each need or situation as it may arise.

In whatever service the churches perform in regard to the Negro community, the churches may grow only as they are first willing to be changed themselves. Oppressors cannot truly help the oppressed in enduring and growth-producing ways. Our mind-set may be changed for an openness to truly creative service only as we first disavow and disassociate ourselves from the privileges of being white. We must make interraciality into a two-way street, facilitating the opportunity of those whom we would serve—and others like them—to have access to all the same advantages and to all the same relationships as are open and available to us. Otherwise we work in limited and self-defeating ways which frustrate our national purposes, and we as churchmen deny the basic realities of the church's inner life.

Sacred Possibilities

The concept of Black Power directly involves a forthright claim to the inherent dignity and worth of black people. Life does have worth, and that worth is realized when it has or appropriates the power to become what it should be. Such power as this is inherently religious, and it points to a neglected aspect of religious life in the churches of America.

The earliest Christian creed addressed itself to the issue of power. It simply spoke of Jesus as Lord. In the cultural context in which the first creed was uttered it was an affirmation and commitment to Jesus as the divine embodiment and expression of power. Power as God's breath, according to the

Genesis story of the creation, was infused into the life of man. Man was thereby given the potential likeness of his Creator. He was made to live in time as he would live in eternity.

In both symbolic and literal terms in the Hebrew-Christian religious experience, all that God's power touches is said to be sacred. To be sacred means to have an eternal dimension. It means to reflect the power, or to fulfill the purposes, of God. To the precise extent that Black Power affirms and extends God's truth and purposes, it is in that same degree possessed of a sacred and eternal nature. It is partially thus a sign of the presence of God's rule, which is what is meant by the term "the kingdom of God."

Philosophically, life does not move upward toward the end of time. Time and eternity are not time sequences. Life does not historically improve as time goes on. There is always conflict, and never in the broadest sense is there "enduring peace." Time and eternity are like two horizontal though infinitely unequal lines, which are close enough to be in a kind of tension. Wherever the power of the eternal is appropriated and realized in human life, at such precise points the lines of time and eternity converge and become as one. Thus God's power may always be appropriated. We may at any time enter into, accept, and fulfill our divine and eternal inheritance "in Christ." Life in the kingdom, under God's rule and in His power, is an ever-present immediate possibility. The sacred is anything which at any point in the time-eternity complex is God-empowered or God-possessed.

In a religious sense, then, the expression of human dignity, as in the term Black Power, speaks to immediately present possibilities, as one chooses to merge his life with the purposes and qualities of life lived on the level of the eternal. It is this sense of the presence of the eternal which the apocalyptic literature of the Old Testament sought to add to the judgmental sense of prophecy. So often in the churches our social concerns unhelpfully annoy, as those who teach of other-directed duties take on something of the demeanor of or are seen as God's angry men. There is an absence of a sense that there is always present the power to make sacred purposes immediate realities.

The apocalyptic literature is marked by involvement of the things of the eternal with the things of time. Time and eternity converge. The Prophet Elisha's experience of looking into the heavens and seeing the hosts of heaven coming to his rescue and prompting the observation that "they who are with us are more than they who are against us" (II Kings 6:16) is an example of the apocalyptic. The appearances of angelic or heavenly beings in the Genesis literature, the experience of Daniel in the lion's den, the deliverance at the Red Sea, and the deliverance from the fiery furnace—all, in a sense, are examples of at least the spirit of the apocalyptic.

The apocalyptic sees in immediate terms the vindication of the ultimate plans and programs and purposes of God. Its art or grace is the capacity to look through the mind's eye into the heavens and to see from heaven's perspective what we may recognize as being actualized on an eternal plane. What is to come to pass is, even now, on an eternal plane.

What the apocalyptic adds to the judgmental sense of prophecy is the dimension not simply of confidence of ultimate vindication. It adds, more significantly, the grace to seek to enter *in immediate terms* into the experience of the realities (or goals) which are yet to be. It either makes the so-called "art of the possible" obsolete or else redefines it to include the ultimate.

A prophetic concern allows for—and makes acceptable—the sounding of the trumpets. The apocalyptic adds the imperative—and the grace—to reshape our own involvement in present affairs as though the ultimate were either a present or proximate fact. Those who are concerned with human dignity or with any aspect of the divine purpose may here see how with quiet confidence we may boldly enter into new and sacred dimensions of life with immediacy, with graciousness and command. It is in this spirit that black men may walk, even now, revealing each day something of the power which comes from eternity. Seeing this, others doubtless will wish to appropriate this same power and walk with them . . . forever.

The Black Power concept presents itself as an opportunity for the churches of America. In many ways it may raise new questions and suggest possibilities for the quickening of a self-awareness in the churches of the land. This might be akin to the arousing of a giant possessed of infinite strength of which he had been unaware.

Notes

1. St. Augustine, *City of God,* Book XV, chap. 16.
2. This is a juxtaposition of two texts.
3. For a more complete discussion of the concept set forth here, see *One Bread, One Body* by Nathan Wright, Jr. (New York: Seabury Press, 1962).
4. See *The Trumpet Sounds* by Dr. Anna Arnold Hedgeman (New York: Holt, Rinehart and Winston, 1964).
5. Adam Clayton Powell, Sr., *Upon This Rock* (New York: Abyssinian Church, 1929), p. 107.

6

URBAN MISSION IN A TIME OF CRISIS

Statement by the National Committee of
Black Churchmen, April 5, 1968

The National Committee of Black Churchmen at the meeting of our Board of Directors in Chicago, Illinois, on April 5, 1968, took action to declare to the white religious establishment in the United States our conviction that the black church is the most viable and durable institution in the central cities of most of the major metropolitan areas of the nation.

We believe it would be a tragic mistake for predominately white denominations to choose to by-pass this institution in an effort to relate to and invest in the urban ghettos. The black church has a physical presence and a constituency already organized in these communities. It is available as a means by which the whole Christian community can deal substantively and effectively with the urban crisis, the sickness of body and spirit which we see in the metropolitan centers of America today.

We, therefore, call upon the white churches and churchmen to take with utmost seriousness the black church as the only, though imperfect, link with inner city life for the mission of the church and we insist that the mission structure of the national denominations must identify with and be led by the black churches if their efforts are to have either credibility or reality.

We, therefore, call upon the white churches and churchmen to re-appraise their strategies and expenditures so that the rich potential of the black churches can be fulfilled with the excellent by-products of mutual respect, comradeship and ecumenical development resulting therefrom.

It is in this connection that we call upon the white churches and churchmen of America to do the following:

1. Realize that the time is very late, perhaps too late and that they are severely limited in meaningful corrective action available to them in the

summer of 1968 and therefore should aim their strategies, programs and projects at the long-range target.

2. Be prepared to come to the bargaining table and sit across from black churchmen to negotiate.

   a. the surrender of white church resources which currently are being expended in irrelevant, non-productive and patronizing missions to black churches in order that the white church through true partnership with black churchmen can achieve what it has purported to be its missionary goals and lofty purposes in the cities.

   b. the confrontation of white racism, paternalism and indifferentism in white churches and white communities in order that black churchmen may have a greater facility, confidence and credibility in their own confrontation of incipient black racism and violence in the inner city.

3. The National Committee of Black Churchmen suggest the following program concepts:

   a. the allocation of a portion of finances and other resources presently available for evangelism and urban missions to a repository to be established by the National Committee of Black Churchmen. On its part, the NCBC would undertake to validate and finance proposals which have the purpose of planning and executing the mission to the inner city through the NCBC, the black denominations and the black caucuses of the white denominations.

   b. the further development of the Economic Development Corporation of the NCBC which could serve as a repository and economical development bank into which all ghetto-bound and other funds could be deposited for economic development projects brought forth by church groups, congregations or through the black caucuses of the several denominations.

4. Because of the depressed economic situation in most black communities the black church has seldom been adequately staffed to perform its task of Christian education and mission. Accordingly, priority must be given to providing the necessary staff, financial resources, equipment and property, educational materials and instrumentalities for use among black people. Both black and white denominations should reorder priorities and reallocate their resources, equipment and property for use among black people. Both black and white denominations should reorder priorities and reallocate their resources toward these ends.

   In the light of the above considerations and recommendations and in order to prepare black churches to better serve the communities in which they exist the National Committee of Black Churchmen commits itself to the development of a new and creative style of black churchmanship which will emphasize its distinctive task and opportunity. There are three interrelated dimensions for this new style of mission.

1. The renewal and enhancement of the black church in terms of its liturgical life, its theological interpretation, its understanding of its mission to itself, to the white church and to the nation.
2. The development of the black church, not only as a religious fellowship, but as a community organization, in the technical sense of the term, which uses its resources, influence and manpower to address the problems of estrangement, resignation and powerlessness in the political, cultural and economic life of the black community.
3. The projection of a new quality of church life which would equip and strengthen the church as custodian and interpreter of that cultural heritage which is rooted in the peculiar experience of black people in the United States and the faith that has sustained them for over two centuries.

PART II

THE ATTACK
ON WHITE RELIGION

INTRODUCTION

No one knows exactly when the term "Black Theology" originated. It is certain that the only *distinctively* Black theological reflection in written form that anyone was aware of prior to 1964 was produced by the religious teachers and leaders of the Nation of Islam—the so-called Black Muslims. Joseph R. Washington's unwarranted announcement that year that "the Negro knows no theology" and that "White Christians have damned Negro congregations to existence in a religion without faith [sic!] and therefore without theology"[1] may well have provoked the term as a repudiation of his position. But we are not sure if he was the first to use it. It does not appear in either of his first two books, although *The Politics of God* certainly makes a case for what may be called the first systematic Black theological statement since Garvey and McGuire, who founded the African Orthodox Church during the twenties. *The Politics of God* was Washington's ambivalent effort to correct the controversial allegation of his first book.

As far as I know no one has claimed to have used the term before the publication of James H. Cone's *Black Theology and Black Power.*[2] In all likelihood, however, it was in some use before that time—either by members of the NCBC Theological Commission or by Albert B. Cleage, Jr., and his followers. Cleage himself was greatly influenced by the Muslim minister Malcolm X and founded his Shrine of the Black Madonna as early as 1953, long before the term had come into vogue.[3] He may well have used it during the Detroit rebellion in 1967, if not much earlier. Cleage was also an active member of the NCBC almost from its inception and took part in the first theological discussions of that new movement of militant Black clergy in 1967.

In any case an embryonic Black Theology was gaining currency in the early days of the National Conference of Black Churchmen, a way of doing Christian theology that Cleage was later to denounce as a "Black schoolmen's theology . . . written for white acceptance."[4] It is my opinion, in contradiction of Cleage's position, that the Black Theology developed in the NCBC and given its first scholarly expression by James H. Cone was an attack on White religion and the White churches of the United States. Far from being a mere "schoolmen's theology," it began as an understanding of the relevance of the gospel for Black liberation conceived mainly by Black pastors and church executives who were struggling to define their faith vis-à-vis a White religious establishment which had betrayed them. A few theological professors participated in the movement from the beginning, but it was men like Albert B. Cleage, Jr., Lawrence Lucas (a Harlem Roman Catholic priest), and Calvin Marshall (an A.M.E. Zion minister in Brooklyn) who were preaching every Sunday in the ghettos of the nation and hammering out the first tenets of a Black Theology on the anvil of their experience. These men stormed the ramparts of White ecclesiastical and theological authority. They were the Black Jeremiahs who cried out to the White churches and synagogues of America:

> Thus says the Lord. . . . You recently repented and did what was right in my eyes by proclaiming liberty, each to his neighbor . . . but then you turned around and profaned my name (Jer. 34:13-17).

The prophetic message of the Black Theology of the 1960s was an attack on the White churches by mainline Black churchmen. That attack required, as in the Black Power statement of 1966, words of encouragement and explanation to Black Christians. This attempt to develop a catechesis for Black church members, caught in the crossfire between their own pastors and church executives on one side, and the White religious establishment on the other, is what gradually took shape as an understanding of the gospel as freedom for the oppressed and Jesus Christ as the Liberator. There should be no attempt to disguise the fact that Black Theology was also a polemic aimed at White church leaders and the theological traditions which supported the shallow religious liberalism of the day. It was not so much an appeal for White acceptance, as Cleage suggested, as a demand for White repentance and material reparation. But it should always be remembered that from the beginning Black Theology intended to speak to the Black Church and community about the ethnic pride, political realism, and religious radicalism hidden in the deepest recesses of the Black experience but almost forgotten by Black people in their rush to embrace White standards and values.

It could not have been otherwise for Christianity to have continued to be a viable option for the younger generation of the waning days of the civil rights period. It is important to understand the socioeconomic and political context in which all theological systems arise, particularly in their relationship to the survival of nationhood and the maintenance of institutions which integrate oppressed communities. In that sense even radical theological movements have what is essentially a conservative function. Black Theology was no exception. It arose partly as a survival mechanism for that part of the Black Church caught up in the changes occurring in American society in the mid-1960s, which had to be regulated so that a "moving equilibrium"[5] could be maintained against powerful centrifugal forces in the Black community.

The cry for Black Power frightened almost as many Black people as it did White people, but for the former it rang true. The strength of Black Muslim preaching against Christianity both before and after the assassination of Malcolm on February 21, 1965, was that it was not the natural religion of

Black people. It was a White religion which, since the beginning of slavery, had been used to emasculate the Black man. Although Martin Luther King, Jr., had demonstrated that it could also be an effective weapon in the struggle for the "full manhood rights of the Negro," his integrationist policy made him and most of the ministers in his movement stop short of the kind of Black political and cultural nationalism that had such an appeal in the ghetto. Black nationalism was one of the keystones of the Muslim philosophy and, when conjoined with the pragmatics of Black Power in a Stokely Carmichael or an H. Rap Brown, it had a powerful attraction for the young shock troops of the rebellion who always had been unreliable proponents of the doctrine of suffering love and nonviolence. Many Blacks, young and old, would not follow Malcolm into the Nation of Islam, but believed he spoke the truth about Christianity being a religion for White people. Once they were convinced of this, no traditional Negro Christian evangelicalism could satisfy their religious needs and hold them within the Black Christian church.

When the Student Non-Violent Coordinating Committee (SNCC) broke with Dr. King in 1966 and the Black Panther Party displayed uncommon courage in the face of arrogant White Power and contempt for the conventional processes of American justice upon which the older leadership had pinned its hopes, the weakness of the moderate centrism of the Black Church became evident. Thousands of young Blacks had already left the churches. More were leaving every day. A new Black Christian alternative was needed and it had to begin on two ideological and theological bases—the first would give clear sanction to Blackness, to Black pride and power; the second would sever theological and programmatic relationship with what had been so thoroughly discredited by Malcolm, Carmichael, and others.

The concern of the Black Church to speak to its youth out of the context of the revolution in order to stem the tide of dechristianization is illustrated by the following quotation from a study guide published by the General Board of Christian Education of the Christian Methodist Episcopal Church:

> The potential of the power of young Black Americans is tremendous. The Black Church should see to it that this power is used constructively. It must address itself to a realistic attitude toward "Black Power." The fact is, before any ethnic group can enter the open society it must first close ranks. . . . The Church must speak to young people about power, "Black Power." . . . Destiny demands that the gifts of blackness be used to renew society and not to destroy it; to make this a free and open society, not to indulge anger or appease vanity. Black Power must be used for these noble ends, and it is the responsibility of the Black Church to give youth the correct interpretation of power.[6]

National events from 1964 to the election of Richard Nixon in 1968 helped to reinforce the widespread opinion among Blacks that the White Christian guardians of American public morality had been discredited. The passage of the Civil Rights Act of 1964 had no effect on conditions in the ghetto. The Kerner Commission recommendations on how to prevent civil disorder and a fatal polarization of American society had been given wide publicity but were practically ignored by Washington. The rebellions of 1967 had left sprawling areas of severe property damage in cities like Newark and Detroit. The promises of public and private agencies to rebuild and correct the deplorable housing situation in the ghettos had been halfhearted and unfulfilled. The federal government's War on Poverty program had failed to make an impression on unemployment, health, and education, and with the election of Nixon, against the strong opposition of the Black electorate, there was the expectation that it would be totally dismantled. Add to this the empty victory of King in Chicago and his assassination in the spring of 1968, the refusal of Congress to take seriously the "Domestic Marshall Plan" of the National Urban League or the "Freedom Budget" of the A. Philip Randolph Institute, and the failure of Abernathy's Poor People's Campaign following the death of King, and you have a picture of almost unrelieved gloom, disillusionment, and frustration.

It is not precisely accurate to say that White religion had to be the scapegoat for this disastrous situation, but it was an excellent candidate. Robert Lecky and Elliott Wright express doubt that the attack could have occurred had the White churches not raised the expectations of the poor with highly publicized national social-action programs with plenty of money and a steady stream of anti-poverty rhetoric during 1968 and 1969.[7] It seems less than charitable to blame White religious groups for taking seriously the fact that they finally had come into the revolution and were trying to catch up. William Stringfellow is closer to the truth when he writes:

> The churches and synagogues, in a sense, volunteer as the initial targets for reparations because they claim a surrogate vocation in society as custodian of the conscience of the nation. An issue raised with the churches is thus raised symbolically for all institutions and persons in society and, presumably, it is raised in the place of the most mature moral sensitivity, experience and alertness. The congregations of white religion have no standing to complain. . . .[8]

In my opinion it is not that the White religious establishment stimulated a climate of unrealistic expectations, or even that its traditional role as custodian of public righteousness made it a perfect target, that explains the radical Black Church movement of the late 1960s and the attack on White religion mounted by the Black Manifesto and elucidated by Black Theology. The explanation, if it must be simplified, is more likely to be found in the failure of White religious leadership to understand that the Black Church was as alien to the ideological consensus of White Protestantism, Roman Catholicism, and Judaism as the Black masses were. They *were* the Black masses. The

National Council of Churches and the denominations seemed not to understand that their refusal to make room in the establishment for effective Black Power and its theological implications for American Christianity could explode into a potentially violent confrontation.

Not only did White ecclesiastical structures fail to understand and appreciate the history of Black religion in America, but they made the erroneous assumption that those Blacks who were members of White denominations or who represented the historic Black denominations in interchurch agencies were conventional middle-class church loyalists who were cut from the same cloth as themselves. They were, of course, never altogether comfortable with Black leadership because the latter were never really members of "the club." They came out of strange, "Native Son" backgrounds and attended theological schools most White people had never heard of. But the Whites were confident, too confident, that in a crisis these Black leaders and their churches would conform to the stipulations of White Protestantism. They were presumed to be "house niggers" who associated with the "field niggers" after office hours but did not share their sectarian biases and mistrust of White people. Thus White church leaders miscalculated the extent of solidarity of the mainline Black Church with the masses of Black people who were still marginal to American society and church life. No matter how middle class the Black Church leadership may have seemed, it was this marginated subsociety that the Black Church had always represented and from which it received the impetus to enter the struggle for liberation since the pre-Civil War period. The failure of White leaders to understand this made them oblivious to the heterodox and rebellious currents that ran through the ranks of Black Christians with whom they were associated. It was another failure of communication, a familiar phenomenon in interracial relations.

Two events illustrate the miscalculation of the liberal White establishment in the late 1960s. First, the sudden call for Black Power within the civil rights movement during the summer of 1966 and, second, the crisis over the Black Manifesto in 1969. In both instances the majority of the national leadership of the denominations, partly in reaction to the backlash in the White constituencies and partly because of its own fear of Black militancy, resisted the attempt of Black churchmen to marshal the policy-making apparatus and resources of Protestantism on the side of the new groups rising from the shambles of King's movement—the younger Blacks who were in alliance with the National Conference of Black Churchmen and the Interreligious Foundation for Community Organization. When the churches refused to recognize and fund the National Black Economic Development Conference, which had been created by IFCO and was the vehicle for the Black Manifesto, what could have been a moderate and negotiable transition to the empowerment of the Black Church and its allies turned into a bitter and forthright attack on White religion in general.[9]

The disengagement of what came to be known as Black Theology from the reigning theologies of liberalism and neo-orthodoxy came about as a rationalization of the ideological differences between White leadership and the older, more conservative officialdom of the Black churches on one hand, and, on the other hand, the radical Black cadre within the predominantly White structures and the younger, radical leadership emerging in the Black denominations. It was not possible for those influential within American Christianity, Protestant or Roman Catholic, to have anticipated this development. For White historians, theologians, and church bureaucrats were almost totally ignorant of the peregrinations of Black religion in America and the motifs of accommodation and protest which ebbed and flowed in its ambivalent relationship to White Christianity. Black Theology was the historic expression of discontent and protest elements within the Black religious tradition which transcended denominational affiliations and the Roman Catholic-Protestant split and broke through the surface of institutional Christianity in the Black community whenever the obstacles to dignity and power became intolerable.

The etiology of Black Theology is difficult. It is the intellectual reflex of the Black religious community to oppression, and all of the subtleties and complexities of White racism are involved. It has been an interpretation of the Christian religion for degraded and subordinated Blacks that surfaced from time to time throughout the history of the race in the New World. But the inability of White theologians to articulate an American perspective of the Christian faith that would encompass the distinctive perceptions of Black Christians and the failure of White church leaders to assimilate Black churchmen within the policy-making and programmatic structures of the establishment *with effective power* gave rise to Black Theology's radical revisitation in the mid-1960s.

As will be shown in a later part of this book, a few White scholars and churchmen understood what was going on. In discussing what he called "the new strategy" of the churches, Joseph C. Hough, Jr., picked up the basic emphasis of the late Robert Spike, executive director of the NCC Commission on Religion and Race in 1965, who stressed the importance of "para-church agencies" in opening lines of communication and collaboration between the White denominations and the alienated Black masses.[10] Hough made this the central focus of White Protestant strategy for dealing with the challenge of Black Power and "Negro Pluralism" from an enlightened Christian ethical standpoint. He conceded that it involved risks but was necessary for the churches to help shape Black institutions not subject to their control and the kind of public policy that could deal with the enormous problems of the urban ghetto.

This, then, is the general focus for the future white Protestant strategy in race relations. It is a focus upon church-related agencies which can be the tactical arm of the churches by participating in projects within the Negro community and by developing support for local, state and national government policies that deal creatively with the problems of the ghetto in the city. Moreover, these agencies can also be the institutional channels for interpreting the ghetto to the churches and for training laymen in the task of mission to the city.[11]

Unfortunately Hough's perception of the significance of what was happening in 1968 and his strategy for White Protestantism made no impression on the Interchurch Center in New York City. What he called for was what IFCO was organized to be in September 1967 and the purpose of the National Black Economic Development Conference. But IFCO was never taken seriously as a quasi-independent Black entity. When Black churchmen obtained the majority of the votes in its Board of Directors, the White Christian and Jewish funding sources began to divert most of their allocations to "designated projects" in order to maintain control of the agency's outreach into the Black community. This was precisely what Spike, Hough, and a few other White churchmen had warned against—another form of ecclesiastical colonialism. Black church leaders like Albert B. Cleage, Jr., Earl Allen, and Dr. Anna Arnold Hedgeman, who were members of the Black Churchmen's group and participated in the creation of IFCO, favored the direct funding of ghetto organizations with "no strings attached." They tried in vain to cut down on the support the churches wanted to give to inner-city projects that were missionary outposts of the denominations and under the control, for the most part, of White "urban specialists." Lucius Walker, the executive director of IFCO, shared this view but was effectively obstructed by the White denominational staffs to which he had to report.

This strategy of direct funding was, in fact, the main burden of the Black Manifesto, which concentrated on the empowerment of Black social, economic, and political institutions independent of White control and the base for the actualization of self-determination across the nation. But the Manifesto was presented not as an IFCO budget request but as a demand and an attack upon the recalcitrance of White religious institutions.

This historic document, issued from the IFCO-sponsored National Black Economic Development Conference on April 26, 1969, rightfully opens this part (Document 7). It was, in a sense, the scenario for the praxis of the theological movement which had begun two years earlier but received its driving force from the struggle between IFCO and the denominational mission bureaucracies. There is no need for an extended introduction to the Black Manifesto here, since we have included my own detailed analysis in the article entitled "A Black Churchman's Response to the Black Manifesto." This was originally a paper produced for the Department of Evangelism of the United Presbyterian Church and was subsequently published by one of the Black Methodist denominations.[12]

The response of the National Conference of Black Churchmen, which immediately follows the Manifesto in Part II, is brief but significant (Document 8). It expresses the dominant opinion in that organization less than two weeks after the document was issued from the conference at Wayne State University in Detroit. I have already suggested that the idea for a manifesto was stimulated a year earlier by the "Urban Mission" statement of the NCBC Board of Directors. Several members were in close contact with the Northern Student Movement and the remnant of SNCC, which had drifted into New York and other cities after the assassination of Dr. King. James Forman, the author of the introduction to the Manifesto and the one who placed it before the Detroit conference on April 26, had come to me that morning to share its contents and to ask my opinion about what he planned to do. Lucius Walker, Earl Allen, and other Black churchmen knew about it and may have participated, directly or indirectly, in its formulation. This is not to detract from the central importance of James Forman, the embattled freedom fighter and former director for International Affairs of the Student Non-Violent Coordinating Committee, for the Manifesto and its disruptive presentation to the White churches and synagogues depended primarily upon his personal charisma and daring. But it is to record for history that a group of Black preachers and church executives had already decided that the time had come for a showdown with the power structure of the White churches, and they stood squarely behind the substance if not the rhetoric of Forman's attack.

The NCBC document makes this clear in its salute to the controversial proposal which "troubled the waters of Siloam." Perhaps even more clearly than the Manifesto, it defines the culpability of White religious institutions and includes the foundations and "the private sector of the American economy" in the demand for reparations. This was the first religious response to Forman and it came swiftly to give notice to the ecclesiastical bureaucracies that, just as Black churchmen did not stand with them in the debate over Black Power, they would not stand with them in the cynical asphyxiation of IFCO. The Black caucuses that had recently emerged in all of the predominantly White churches in the NCC were called upon to accept responsibility for the Manifesto and the strategies necessary to implement its program. The Executive Committee action was, therefore, a formal adoption of the Manifesto by those who were most responsible for its appearance and were, perhaps, too cowardly to have promulgated it themselves. This was its churchly certification and invitation to the White churches, in the words of the April 5, 1968, "Urban Mission" statement, "to come to the bargaining table." Its theological interpretation in a broader context was to come later in the summer of 1969.

The next document selected for this part is, as a careful reading will show, a theological addendum to the Black Manifesto (Document 9). It was not consciously planned as such, but that is what it is. The first official statement of the meaning and purpose of Black Theology was issued on June 13,

1969, from Atlanta by the Theological Commission of NCBC (Document 10).[13] It has been analyzed by Preston N. Williams and others so that no further commentary is needed here.[14] The remainder of this book is, in a sense, an extended interpretation of and commentary on this basic explication of Black Theology. It is impossible to miss the significance of the Black Manifesto and the call for reparations in this statement. It makes unmistakably clear that what was termed "Black Theology" by those who gathered in Atlanta amid the storms of international controversy which broke out between Black and White churchmen was, from the beginning, rooted and grounded in the demand for the reparational empowerment of the Black community. That community of which the Black Church had been the spiritual and, in terms of property and dollars, the material core since slavery, would "not be turned from its course." In virtue of a radical Christian witness of confrontation with White power it would seek "complete fulfillment of the promises of the Gospel."

The next two documents are further indication of the growing estrangement of the National Conference of Black Churchmen from the mainstream of American Christianity. The attack upon the White churches continued well into the decade of the 1970s, but with waning effectiveness. Calvin Marshall, the A.M.E. Zion pastor in Brooklyn and a member of the NCBC Executive Committee, succeeded James Forman as chairman of the Black Economic Development Conference and, to all intents and purposes, the NCBC became the principal exponent of the programmatic goals of the Manifesto, sharing representation on the BEDC Steering Committee with the young non-church-related radicals who had followed Forman into Riverside Church and conducted sit-ins in the denominational offices at 475 Riverside Drive, New York City. By the end of 1969, the NCBC was as distant ideologically from the mainstream of both the Black and the White denominations as it would ever be. At the May meeting of its Board of Directors the president, A.M.E Zion Bishop Herbert Bell Shaw, had said that the NCBC's continued existence depended on relations with the Black Power movement and the street people as well as with such groups as the Consultation on Church Union. "We are here as islands," he said, "but like islands we must be connected by the water that flows in between."[15]

That connection was made with the radical community by representation on the Steering Committee of the BEDC and by the plans made for the Third Annual Convocation in Oakland, California, where the Alamo Black Clergy, a Bay Area caucus, arranged for the leaders of the Black Panther Party to attend and address the convocation.

The mood at Oakland in November was angry but undaunted. The demand for reparations had been rejected by almost all of the White churches. But even more serious was their refusal to give official recognition to the Black Economic Development Conference as a legitimate arm of the Black Church for implementing the actually moderate program of the Manifesto.

"Recommendations" for funding various projects as an alternative to the BEDC were made and a few carried out, but the only major grant related to the demand for reparations was made by the Special Program of the Episcopal General Convention. The grant, totaling $200,000, was allocated to the NCBC for transfer to the BEDC. IFCO never received the modest grant it sought from the NCC to set up administrative machinery for the BEDC, which could have "regularized" its operation across the nation and greatly reduced the growing resentment over the gamesmanship of the Whites in pretending to respond to the goals of the Manifesto while rejecting its means.

The "Message to the Churches from Oakland, California"(Document 11), is, therefore, one of the most belligerent pronouncements of prominent leaders of the Black Church in the United States to Black Christians—and obliquely, to the White Church. It is a carefully worded explication of the theological and political orientation of the NCBC at the close of a year of pitched battles. It was an attempt to expand upon the theological themes opened up by the Atlanta statement on Black Theology and to relate them to the history and culture of Black people as well as to their aspiration for political and economic liberation. But at Oakland for the first time the Black churchmen addressed themselves directly to "oppressed peoples . . . in the Third World." The Oakland Message represents a shift of emphasis from the parochial interests of Black nationalism to "racism, capitalism and imperialism" as demonic world powers with which the White churches and synagogues of America were in complicity. From Oakland went a wider challenge for the White religious institutions

> to divest themselves of their own great wealth—much of it ill-gotten—built upon the bodies of exploited races and classes wherever imperialistic political and economic influences have extended within and beyond national boundaries, and to make massive ecclesiastical resources of capital and technical assistance available to powerless people in Africa, Asia, Latin America and the United States.

The World Council of Churches had already been confronted by the BEDC representatives at Nottinghill in England. Although its Central Committee refused to atone for the guilt of slavery and other past injustices, it made an unprecedented decision on August 21, 1969, in allocating $200,000 to be distributed to "organizations of oppressed racial groups whose purposes are not inconsonant with the general purposes" of the WCC. Thus the action of Black Power advocates and churchmen in the United States persuaded the major world body of Protestantism and Orthodoxy to begin direct financial assistance to the oppressed which, notably, included the Southern African liberation movements—previously considered too hot to handle by the churches. It led directly to the action of the Central Committee at Canterbury in setting up the "Ecumenical Programme to Combat Racism."

This agency deserves the credit for being the most effective world church instrument involved in the struggle for the end of neocolonialism and racism in Africa.[16]

The Black Declaration of Independence (Document 12) follows the Oakland Message in this part. It was written by a small committee in New York and represents the last full-page advertisement NCBC was to publish in the *New York Times*—at the beginning of a new decade that witnessed the declining influence of the organization.

This document, issued on July 4, 1970, deserves to be included here not because of its originality, for it was written as close to the language and style of the Declaration of 1776 as possible, but because it appeared at the height of alienation and Black nationalist sentiment within a movement bitterly frustrated by the obduracy and insincerity of the White churches, the disunity which crept into the ranks as caucuses made their own accommodation with their denominations, and the weariness of the battle. That battle was not over, for it was to shift to other fronts and be waged by other troops. Looking back over the years it is possible now to say that the enduring contribution to come out of the National Conference's struggle, from the Black Power statement of 1966 to the Black Declaration of Independence of 1970, was the conceptualization of a theological basis for breaking the suffocating embrace of White liberalism and exposing the racism that continued, under siege and by no means vanquished, in the institutions that presumed to be the conscience of the nation.

Without consulting my collaborator, James H. Cone, I have chosen to conclude this section with the chapter on "The White Church and Black Power" from his book *Black Theology and Black Power* (Document 13). No collection of the literature of the Black Church movement of the 1960s and 1970s would be complete without a representative sample of his writing during that period. More than anyone else James H. Cone set the tone and described the content for Black Theology with the publication of his first book, *Black Theology and Black Power*, in 1969. The Atlanta statement on Black Theology that year bears the unmistakable stamp of his perspective and style. He was, of course, the key member of the NCBC Theological Commission which drafted it.

When *Black Theology and Black Power* appeared in 1969 very few of the leaders of NCBC, outside of the African Methodists, had heard of James Cone, a recent Ph.D. from Northwestern University and assistant professor of religion at Adrian College in Michigan. "What," I asked increduously, "is a Black theologian doing at a little White college in the boondocks of Michigan!"

I remember someone giving me a review of the book from the *Detroit Free Press* in an unguarded moment. I whooped for joy. Here was a mature and scholarly presentation, albeit ebullient with youth, of what we could not find words to say from the first day that Benjamin Payton and I sat down in his office to compose the draft of the Black Power statement. Who was this young professor who articulated the faith of the new breed of Black churchmen as if he had been present at every interminable committee meeting and midnight bull session that had taken place among the members of the NCBC from its inception? It was for me a moment of spiritual exultation and I went out to find the book, which I read through in one sitting.

Cone became, almost immediately, the "resident theologian" of the National Conference, whether he realized it or not. I remember how we excused him from the in-fighting and strategy meetings at the Interchurch Center and at the NCBC headquarters at 125 E. 125th Street, New York City, because he had more important work to do thinking through the theological meaning of what we were about. Older scholars such as George Kelsey, J. Deotis Roberts, and Preston N. Williams, not to mention the respected professors in the South, were not devalued by his relocation to Union Seminary (in New York) in the vortex of the struggle. But no one had severed the Gordian knot which tied us to the old theology more cleanly than he. Some recoiled at the vehemence with which he attacked White Christians, but many of us realized that this was precisely what we needed at that moment, for we had burned our theological bridges behind us and had nowhere to go except all the way home. That meant in the direction of the latent radicalism that had been harbored within the soul of Black Christianity since George Liele and David George cut their moorings in the late eighteenth century and set their faces like flint for Jamaica and Sierra Leone. The crisis over the Black Manifesto mandated a theological exodus from White Christianity that would match the Manifesto's clarion summons to Black pride, power, and self-determination. James Cone had supplied the first systematic statement of what that journey required in terms of a re-reading of the Scriptures and a reconstruction of the theology of the Black Church.

We have been examining in the documents of this section the attack made on the White Church by Black churchmen beginning roughly in April 1969—perhaps the most crucial year in the annals of Black religion in America since Marcus Garvey came to the United States looking for Booker T. Washington. This final contribution from James Cone raises the fundamental question that hovered above everything that Forman and the National Conference of Black Churchmen said that year: What is the true responsibility of the Church of Jesus Christ in the world? Cone writes:

> If the real Church is the people of God, whose primary task is that of being Christ to the world by proclaiming the message of the gospel (kerygma), by rendering services of liberation (diakonia), and by being itself a manifestation of the nature of the new society (koinonia), then the empirical institutionalized white church has failed on all counts.

As the 1960s drew to a close nothing was clearer to Black churchmen. The only thing they lacked was a vision of what the *Black* Church should be and the will to bring it into reality. Cone presented that vision in chapter 4 of *Black Theology and Black Power*, but it is in the chapter reprinted here that he recounts the history and analyzes the failure of White theology to prevent the White Church from continuing its "chaplaincy to the forces of oppression." Such an analysis was indispensable to the early development of a Black Theology and with it we can leave the agony of the NCBC in the 1960s and go on to the debate with the White theologians.

G.S.W.

Notes

1. Joseph R. Washington, *Black Religion, the Negro and Christianity in the United States* (Boston: Beacon Press, 1964), p. 142.

2. James H. Cone, *Black Theology and Black Power* (New York: Seabury Press, 1969). Cone's book is discussed later in this introductory essay.

3. Albert B. Cleage, Jr., *Black Christian Nationalism, New Directions for the Black Church* (New York: William Morrow, 1972), p. 223.

4. Ibid., p. xv.

5. Irwin T. Sanders, *The Community, an Introduction to a Social System* (New York: Ronald Press, 1958), p. 153.

6. Caesar D. Coleman, ed., *Beyond Blackness to Destiny* (Memphis: The Christian Methodist Episcopal Church, 1970), p. 119.

7. Robert S. Lecky and H. Elliott Wright, eds., *Black Manifesto: Religion, Racism and Reparations* (New York: Sheed and Ward, 1969), p. 6.

8. William Stringfellow, "Reparations: Repentance as a Necessity," in Lecky and Wright, ibid., p. 57.

9. For the critical role of IFCO in the attempt to make the National Black Economic Development Conference acceptable to the churches, see Lucius Walker, "IFCO and the Crisis of American Society," in Lecky and Wright, *Black Manifesto*, pp. 133-139.

10. Joseph C. Hough, Jr., *Black Power and White Protestants* (New York: Oxford University Press, 1968), p. 207.

11. Ibid., pp. 211-212.

12. Coleman, *Beyond Black to Destiny*, pp. 95-109.

13. This group was sometimes called the Committee on Theological Prospectus which, I am confident, was a misreading of "Perspective" in the original mandate for its formation in Dallas in 1967.

14. Preston N. Williams, "The Atlanta Document: An Interpretation," *Christian Century*, October 15, 1969.

15. *Minutes* of the Board of Directors, May 7, 1969, pp. 1-2.

16. See the report on the Nottinghill confrontation and the subsequent meeting of the Central Committee in John Vincent, *The Race Race* (New York: Friendship Press, 1970), pp. 39-48.

7

THE BLACK MANIFESTO

Introduction: Total Control as the Only Solution
to the Economic Problems of Black People

Brothers and Sisters:

We have come from all over the country burning with anger and despair not only with the miserable economic plight of our people but fully aware that the racism on which the Western World was built dominates our lives. There can be no separation of the problems of racism from the problems of our economic, political, and cultural degradation. To any black man, this is clear.

But there are still some of our people who are clinging to the rhetoric of the Negro, and we must separate ourselves from these Negroes who go around the country promoting all types of schemes for black capitalism.

Ironically, some of the most militant Black Nationalists, as they call themselves, have been the first to jump on the bandwagon of black capitalism. They are pimps, black power pimps and fraudulent leaders, and the people must be educated to understand that any black man or Negro who is advocating a perpetuation of capitalism inside the United States is in fact seeking not only his ultimate destruction and death but is contributing to the continuous exploitation of black people all around the world. For it is the power of the United States Government, this racist, imperialist government, that is choking the life of all people around the world.

We are an African people. We sit back and watch the Jews in this country make Israel a powerful conservative state in the Middle East, but we are concerned actively about the plight of our brothers in Africa. We are the most advanced technological group of black people in the world, and there are many skills that could be offered to Africa. At the same time, it must be publicly stated that many African leaders are in disarray themselves, having been duped into following the lines as laid out by the western imperialist

This document was presented by James Forman to the National Black Economic Development Conference in Detroit, Michigan, and adopted on April 26, 1969. On May 4, 1969, Forman presented it to the congregation of Riverside Church, New York City.

governments. Africans themselves succumbed to and are victims of the power of the United States. For instance, during the summer of 1967, as the representatives of SNCC, Howard Moore and I traveled extensively in Tanzania and Zambia. We talked to high, very high, government officials. We told them there were many black people in the United States who were willing to come and work in Africa. All these government officials, who were part of the leadership in their respective governments, said they wanted us to send as many skilled people as we could contact. But this program never came into fruition, and we do not know the exact reasons, for I assure you that we talked and were committed to making this a successful program. It is our guess that the United States put the squeeze on these countries, for such a program directed by SNCC would have been too dangerous to the international prestige of the United States. It is also possible that some of the wild statements by some black leaders frightened the Africans.

In Africa today there is a great suspicion of black people in this country. This is a correct suspicion since most of the Negroes who have left the States for work in Africa usually work for the Central Intelligence Agency (CIA) or the State Department. But the respect for us as a people continues to mount, and the day will come when we can return to our homeland as brothers and sisters. But we should not think of going back to Africa today, for we are located in a strategic position. We live inside the United States, which is the most barbaric country in the world, and we have a chance to help bring this government down.

Time is short, and we do not have much time and it is time we stop mincing words. Caution is fine, but no oppressed people ever gained their liberation until they were ready to fight, to use whatever means necessary, including the use of force and power of the gun to bring down the colonizer.

We have heard the rhetoric, but we have not heard the rhetoric which says that black people in this country must understand that we are the vanguard force. We shall liberate all the people in the United States, and we will be instrumental in the liberation of colored people the world around. We must understand this point very clearly so that we are not trapped into diversionary and reactionary movements. Any class analysis of the United States shows very clearly that black people are the most oppressed group of people inside the United States. We have suffered the most from racism and exploitation, cultural degradation and lack of political power. It follows from the laws of revolution that the most oppressed will make the revolution, but we are not talking about just making the revolution. All the parties on the left who consider themselves revolutionary will say that blacks are the vanguard, but we are saying that not only are we the vanguard, but we must assume leadership, total control, and we must exercise the humanity which is inherent in us. We are the most humane people within the United States. We have suffered and we understand suffering. Our hearts go out to the Vietnamese, for we know what it is to suffer under the domination of racist America. Our hearts, our soul and all the compassion we can mount go out to our brothers in Africa, Santo Domingo, Latin America and Asia who are being tricked by the power structure of the United States which is dominating the world today. These ruthless, barbaric men have systematically tried to kill all people and organizations opposed to its imperialism. We no longer can just get by with the use of the word "capitalism" to describe the United States, for it is an imperial power sending money, missionaries and the army throughout the world to protect this government and the few rich whites who control it. General Motors and all the major auto industries are operating in South Africa, yet the white dominated leadership of the United Auto Workers sees no relationship to the exploitation of the black people in South Africa and the exploitation of black people in the United States. If they understand it, they certainly do not put it into practice, which is the actual test. We as black people must be concerned with the total conditions of all black people in the world.

But while we talk of revolution, which will be an armed confrontation and long years of sustained guerrilla warfare inside this country, we must also talk of the type of world we want to live in. We must commit ourselves to a society where the total means of production are taken from the rich and placed into the hands of the state for the welfare of all the people. This is what we mean when we say total control. And we mean that black people who have suffered the most from exploitation and racism must move to protect their black interest by assuming leadership inside of the United States of everything that exists. The time has ceased when we are second in command and the white boy stands on top. This is especially true of the welfare agencies in this country, but it is not enough to say that a black man is on top. He must be committed to building the new society, to taking the wealth away from the rich people, such as General Motors, Ford, Chrysler, the DuPonts, the Rockefellers, the Mellons, and all the other rich white exploiters and racists who run this world.

Where do we begin? We have already started. We started the moment we were brought to this country. In fact, we started on the shores of Africa, for we have always resisted attempts to make us slaves, and now we must resist the attempts to make us capitalists. It is in the financial interest of the United States to make us capitalist, for this will be the same line as that of integration into the mainstream of American life. Therefore, brothers and sisters, there is no need to fall into the trap that we have to get an ideology. We HAVE an ideology. Our fight is against racism, capitalism and imperialism, and we are dedicated to building a socialist society inside the United States where the total means of production and distribution are in the hands of the State, and that must be led by black people, by revolutionary blacks who are concerned about the total humanity of this world. And, therefore, we obviously are different from some of those who seek a black nation in the United States, for there is no way for that nation to be viable if in fact the United States remains in the hands of white racists. Then too, let us deal with some arguments that we should share power with whites. We say that there must be a revolutionary black vanguard, and that white people in this country must be willing to accept black leadership, for that is the only protection that black people have to protect ourselves from racism rising again in this country.

Racism in the United States is so pervasive in the mentality of whites that only an armed, well-disciplined, black-controlled government can insure the stamping out of racism in this country. And that is why we plead with black people not to be talking about a few crumbs, a few thousand dollars for this cooperative, or a thousand dollars which splits black people into fighting over the dollar. That is the intention of the government. We say . . . think in terms of total control of the United States. Prepare ourselves to seize state power. Do not hedge, for time is short, and all around the world the forces of liberation are directing their attacks against the United States. It is a powerful country, but that power is not greater than that of black people. We work the chief industries in this country, and could cripple the economy while the brothers fought guerrilla warfare in the streets. This will take some long range planning, but whether it happens in a thousand years is of no consequence. It cannot happen unless we start. How then is all of this related to this conference?

First of all, this conference is called by a set of religious people, Christians, who have been involved in the exploitation and rape of black people since the country was founded. The missionary goes hand in hand with the power of the states. We must begin seizing power wherever we are, and we must say to the planners of this conference that you are no longer in charge. We the people who have assembled here thank you for getting us here, but we are going to assume power over the conference and determine from this moment on the direction which we want it to go. We are not saying that the conference was planned badly. The staff of the conference has worked hard and has done a magnificent job in bringing all of us together, and we must include them in the new membership which must surface from this point on. The conference is now the property of the people who are assembled here. This we proclaim as fact and not rhetoric, and there are demands that we are going to make and we insist that the planners of this conference help us implement them.

We maintain we have the revolutionary right to do this. We have the same rights, if you will, as the Christians had in going into Africa and raping our Motherland and bringing us away from our continent of peace and into this hostile and alien environment where we have been living in perpetual warfare since 1619.

Our seizure of power at this confernce is based on a program, and our program is contained in the following Manifesto:

We the black people assembled in Detroit, Michigan, for the National Black Economic Development Conference are fully aware that we have been forced to come together because racist white America has exploited our resources, our minds, our bodies, our labor. For centuries we have been forced to live as colonized people inside the United States, victimized by the most vicious, racist system in the world. We have helped to build the most industrial country in the world.

We are therefore demanding of the white Christian churches and Jewish synagogues, which are part and parcel of the system of capitalism, that they begin to pay reparations to black people in this country. We are demanding $500,000,000 from the Christian white churches and the Jewish synagogues. This total comes to 15 dollars per nigger. This is a low estimate for we maintain there are probably more than 30,000,000 black people in this country. $15 a nigger is not a large sum of money and we know that the churches and synagogues have a tremendous wealth, and its membership, white America, has profited and still exploits black people. We are also not unaware that the exploitation of colored peoples around the world is aided and abetted by the white Christian churches and synagogues. This demand for $500,000,000 is not an idle resolution or empty words. Fifteen dollars for every black brother and sister in the United States is only a beginning of the reparations due us as people who have been exploited and degraded, brutalized, killed and persecuted. Underneath all of this exploitation, the racism of this country has produced a psychological effect upon us that we are beginning to shake off. We are no longer afraid to demand our full rights as a people in this decadent society.

We are demanding $500,000,000 to be spent in the following way:

1. We call for the establishment of a Southern land bank to help our brothers and sisters who have to leave their land because of racist pressure on people who want to establish cooperative farms, but who have no funds. We have seen too many farmers evicted from their homes because they have dared to defy the white racism of this country. We need money for land. We must fight for massive sums of money for this Southern Land Bank. We call for $200,000,000 to implement this program.

2. We call for the establishment of four major publishing and printing industries in the United States to be funded with ten million dollars each. These publishing houses are to be located in Detroit, Atlanta, Los Angeles, and New York. They will help to generate capital for further cooperative investments in the black community, provide jobs and an alternative to the white-dominated and controlled printing field.

3. We call for the establishment of four of the most advanced scientific and futuristic audio-visual networks to be located in Detroit, Chicago, Cleveland, and Washington, D.C. These TV networks will provide an alternative to the racist propaganda that fills the current television networks. Each of these TV networks will be funded by ten million dollars each.

4. We call for a research skills center which will provide research on the problems of black people. This center must be funded with no less than 30 million dollars.

5. We call for the establishment of a training center for the teaching of skills in community organization, photography, movie making, television making and repair, radio building and repair and all other skills needed in communication. This training center shall be funded with no less than ten million dollars.

6. We recognize the role of the National Welfare Rights Organization and we intend to work with them. We call for ten million dollars to assist in the organization of welfare recipients. We want to organize the welfare workers in this country so that they may demand more money from the government and better administration of the welfare system of this country.

7. We call for $20,000,000 to establish a National Black Labor Strike and Defense Fund. This is necessary for the protection of black workers and their families who are fighting racist working conditions in this country.

*8. We call for the establishment of the International Black Appeal (IBA). This International Black Appeal will be funded with no less than $20,000,000. The IBA is charged with producing more capital for the establishment of cooperative businesses in the United States and in Africa, our Motherland. The International Black Appeal is one of the most important demands that we are making for we know that it can generate and raise funds throughout the United States and help our African brothers. The IBA is charged with three functions and shall be headed by James Forman:

  (a) Raising money for the program of the National Black Economic Development Conference
  (b) The development of cooperatives in African countries and support of African Liberation movements.
  (c) Establishment of a Black Anti-Defamation League which will protect our African image.

9. We call for the establishment of a Black University to be funded with $130,000,000 to be located in the South. Negotiations are presently under way with a Southern University.

10. We demand that IFCO allocate all unused funds in the planning budget to implement the demands of this conference.

In order to win our demands we are aware that we will have to have massive support, therefore:

(1) We call upon all black people throughout the United States to consider themselves as members of the National Black Economic Development Conference and to act in unity to help force the racist white Christian churches and Jewish synagogues to implement these demands.

(2) We call upon all the concerned black people across the country to contact black workers, black women, black students and the black unemployed, community groups, welfare organization, teacher organizations, church leaders and organizations explaining how these demands are vital to the black community of the U.S.

Pressure by whatever means necessary should be applied to the white power structure of the racist white Christian churches and Jewish synagogues. All black people should act boldly in confronting our white oppressors and demanding this modest reparation of 15 dollars per black man.

(3) Delegates and members of the National Black Economic Development Conference are urged to call press conferences in the cities and to attempt to get as many black organizations as possible to support the demands of the conference. The quick use of the press in the local areas will heighten the tension and these demands must be attempted to be won in a short period of time, although we are prepared for protracted and long-range struggle.

(4) We call for the total disruption of selected church-sponsored agencies operating anywhere in the U.S. and the world. Black workers, black women, black students, and the black unemployed are encouraged to seize the offices, telephones, and printing apparatus of all church-sponsored agencies and to hold these in trusteeship until our demands are met.

(5) We call upon all delegates and members of the National Black Economic Development Conference to stage sit-in demonstrations at selected black and white churches. This is not to be interpreted as a continuation of the sit-in movement of the early sixties but we know that active confrontation inside white churches is possible and will strengthen the possibility of meeting our demands. Such confrontation can take the form of reading the Black Manifesto instead of a sermon or passing it out to church members. The principle of self-defense should be applied if attacked.

(6) On May 4, 1969, or a date thereafter, depending upon local conditions, we call upon black people to commence the disruption of the racist churches and synagogues throughout the United States.

(7) We call upon IFCO to serve as a central staff to coordinate the mandate of the conference and to reproduce and distribute en masse literature, leaflets, news items, press releases, and other material.

(8) We call upon all delegates to find within the white community those forces which will work under the leadership of blacks to implement these demands by whatever means necessary. By taking such actions, white Americans will demonstrate concretely that they are willing to fight the white skin privilege and the white supremacy and racism which has forced us as black people to make these demands.

(9) We call upon all white Christians and Jews to practice patience, tolerance, understanding, and nonviolence as they have encouraged, advised, and demanded that we as black people should do throughout our entire enforced slavery in the United States. The true test of their faith and belief in the Cross and the words of the prophets will certainly be put to a test as we seek legitimate and extremely modest reparations for our role in developing the industrial base of the Western world through our slave labor. But we are no longer slaves, we are men and women, proud of our African heritage, determined to have our dignity.

(10) We are so proud of our African heritage and realize concretely that our struggle is not only to make revolution in the United States, but to protect our brothers and sisters in Africa and to help them rid themselves of racism, capitalism, and imperialism by whatever means necessary, including armed struggle. We are and must be willing to fight the defamation of our African image wherever it rears its ugly head. We are therefore charging the Steering Committee to create a Black Anti-Defamation League to be funded by money raised from the International Black Appeal.

(11) We fully recognize that revolution in the United States and Africa, our Motherland, is more than a one-dimensional operation. It will require the total integration of the political, economic, and military components and therefore, we call upon all our brothers and sisters who have acquired training and expertise in the fields of engineering, electronics, research, community organization, physics, biology, chemistry, mathematics, medicine, military science, and warfare to assist the National Black Economic Development Conference in the implementation of its program.

(12) To implement these demands we must have a fearless leadership. We must have a leadership which is willing to battle the church establishment to implement these demands. To win our demands we will have to declare war on the white Christian churches and synagogues and this means we may have to fight the total government structure of this country. Let no one here think that these demands will be met by our mere stating of them. For the sake of the churches and synagogues, we hope that they have the wisdom to understand that these demands are modest and reasonable. But if the white Christians and Jews are not willing to meet our demands through peace and good will, then we declare war and we are prepared to fight by whatever means necessary. We are, therefore, proposing the election of the following Steering Committee:

Lucius Walker	Mark Comfort
Renny Freeman	Earl Allen
Luke Tripp	Robert Browne
Howard Fuller	Vincent Harding
James Forman	Mike Hamlin
John Watson	Len Holt
Dan Aldridge	Peter Bernard
John Williams	Michael Wright
Ken Cockrel	Muhammad Kenyatta
Chuck Wooten	Mel Jackson
Fannie Lou Hamer	Howard Moore
Julian Bond	Harold Holmes

Brothers and sisters, we no longer are shuffling our feet and scratching our heads. We are tall, black and proud.

And we say to the white Christian churches and Jewish synagogues, to the government of this country, and to all the white racist imperialists who compose it, there is only one thing left that you can do to further degrade black people and that is to kill us. But we have been dying too long for this country. We have died in every war. We are dying in Vietnam today fighting the wrong enemy.

The new black man wants to live and to live means that we must not become static or merely believe in self-defense. We must boldly go out and attack the white Western world at its power centers. The white Christian churches are another form of government in this country and they are used by the government of this country to exploit the people of Latin America, Asia, and Africa, but the day is soon coming to an end. Therefore, brothers and sisters, the demands we make upon the white Christian churches and the Jewish synagogues are small demands. They represent 15 dollars per black person in these United States. We can legitimately demand this from the church power structure. We must demand more from the United States Government.

But to win our demands from the church which is linked up with the United States Government, we must not forget that it will ultimately be by force and power that we will win.

We are not threatening the churches. We are saying that we know the churches came with the military might of the colonizers and have been sustained by the military might of the colonizers. Hence, if the churches in colonial territories were established by military might, we know deep within our hearts that we must be prepared to use force to get our demands. We are not saying that this is the road we want to take. It is not, but let us be very clear that we are not opposed to force and we are not opposed to violence. We were captured in Africa by violence. We were kept in bondage and political servitude and forced to work as slaves by the military machinery and the Christian church working hand in hand.

We recognize that in issuing this manifesto we must prepare for a long-range educational campaign in all communities of this country, but we know that the Christian churches have contributed to our oppression in white America. We do not intend to abuse our black brothers and sisters in black churches who have uncritically accepted Christianity. We want them to understand how the racist white Christian church with its hypocritical declarations and doctrines of brotherhood has abused our trust and faith. An attack on the religious beliefs of black people is not our major objective, even though we know that we were not Christians when we were brought to this country, but that Christianity was used to help enslave us. Our objective in issuing this Manifesto is to force the racist white Christian church to begin the payment of reparations which are due to all black people, not only by the Church but also by private business and the U.S. government. We see this focus on the Christian church as an effort around which all black people can unite.

Our demands are negotiable, but they cannot be minimized; they can only be increased and the Church is asked to come up with larger sums of money than we are asking. Our slogans are:

ALL ROADS MUST LEAD TO REVOLUTION
UNITE WITH WHOMEVER YOU CAN UNITE
NEUTRALIZE WHEREVER POSSIBLE
FIGHT OUR ENEMIES RELENTLESSLY
VICTORY TO THE PEOPLE
LIFE AND GOOD HEALTH TO MANKIND
RESISTANCE TO DOMINATION BY THE WHITE CHRISTIAN CHURCHES AND THE
    JEWISH SYNAGOGUES
REVOLUTIONARY BLACK POWER
WE SHALL WIN WITHOUT A DOUBT

* Revised and approved by Steering Committee.

8

THE NATIONAL COMMITTEE OF BLACK CHURCHMEN'S RESPONSE TO THE BLACK MANIFESTO

Statement of the Board of Directors, NCBC

The Board of Directors of the National Committee of Black Churchmen meeting in Atlanta, Georgia, on May 7, 1969, has considered the Black Manifesto. We rise to salute the Interreligious Foundation for Community Organization, which sponsored the National Black Economic Development Conference, which, in turn became the channel through which James Forman could appear as a modern-day prophet to speak to the churches. We are mindful that the program proposed has troubled the waters of Siloam, yet we know that however much the churches may shake to the vibrations of its own cleansing the healing of Christ is working upon them.

We have taken action to support in principle the demands of the National Black Economic Development Conference upon the churches and synagogues of the United States, as a beginning.

There is no question but that the American religious establishment, along with almost every other institution in the society, was the conscious beneficiary of the enforced labor of one of the most inhuman forms of chattel slavery the world has ever known. Some churches actually owned slaves and many others thrived on the tithes and offerings of both Northern and Southern churchmen who profited directly and indirectly from the uncompensated labor of the slaves. The white churches and synagogues undeniably have been the moral cement of the structure of racism in this nation and the

At the time this statement was made, the NCBC was known as Committee rather than Conference.

vast majority of them continue to play that role today. They are capable, out of their enormous corporate assets, to make some reparation for their complicity in the exploitation of blacks. In so doing they will not only provide a significant contribution from the private sector to the solution of the present national crisis, but will demonstrate to other American institutions the authenticity of their frequently verbalized contrition and of their faith in the justice of God.

It must be clearly understood that the black church does not stand in the same dock as the white church before the bar of justice. Black churches were the victims rather than the guardians and perpetrators of racism in America. We do, nevertheless, accept the responsibility of the black churches to share in the remuneration of the black communities; for we recognize that it is these communities which have sustained our churches over the years. We urge the black caucuses and the black denominations to play major roles in interpreting the justness, humanness, and theological soundness of the demands of the Black Manifesto.

Therefore, we urge all of the religious black caucuses and our brethren within the predominantly black denominations to accept the responsibility to develop the strategies necessary to obtain the funds which are demanded. We further call upon them to assess the institutional assets of their respective denominations and to negotiate the specific amounts which are to be allocated through IFCO for the purposes outlined in the Manifesto.

In the pursuance of these ends, we appeal to the black caucuses and black denominations to unify their efforts of advocacy and implementation of the Manifesto through the coordination provided by the NCBC, and we instruct the Executive Director of the NCBC to immediately begin this coordinating activity.

Finally, we would insist that the great private foundations not be excluded from this vanguard of contributors from the private sector. Many of the foundations are the creatures of corporations whose founders and stockholders amassed incredibly huge fortunes from a capitalistic system which was rooted and grounded in the exploitation of our forefathers. While a few of them supported the civil rights movement, none of them have done what they ought to have done about the mounting crisis among "non-white" peoples in the urban and rural ghettos of the nation. We call upon the foundations as well as the churches and synagogues to provide millions of dollars for economic and social development in the black community.

The NCBC, through its Executive Director and its affiliates, is ready to participate in whatever conferences and negotiations may ensue from the demands of our brothers for the reparational relief of the suffering of black people. We urge the private sector of the American economy, particularly the churches, synagogues and foundations, to receive these demands with the utmost seriousness. The many warnings of the past went unheeded. They are now only echoes receding in the distance. It is too late to call for propriety and moderation. A radical challenge has been placed before us on the threshold of a summer of unmitigated discontent and crisis. That challenge must be met with an equally radical commitment to undo, as much as we are able, the injustices of the past and to eliminate the injustices of the present. The means are available. The will to use them now must not be withheld.

9

A BLACK CHURCHMAN'S RESPONSE TO THE BLACK MANIFESTO

Gayraud S. Wilmore

The Need for Clarification and Commitment

On Sunday, May 4, 1969, James Forman walked down the aisle of Riverside Church in New York City and hurled a series of demands at its minister and people. That dramatic confrontation with one of the historic symbols of White middle class Protestantism has precipitated perhaps the most serious crisis in the American religious establishment since the bitter polemics and antagonisms which divided it prior to the Civil War.

Actually the May 4 confrontation did not so much precipitate a crisis as it revealed a crisis which had already existed in the major denominations for at least three years prior to Forman's return from SNCC obscurity. This crisis had to do, first, with a lack of theological clarity about the depth and seriousness of Black Revolution in America. Second, it stems from an enervating battle fatigue among the liberal churches that had fought for civil rights. And third, the crisis relates to the fact that these churches, since 1966, had shown little enthusiasm for or commitment to the goals of the Black Power movement.

The physical and psychological distance of the ghetto from where most White churchgoers live and the superficial, often distorted, picture of what was going on there which Americans receive from the mass media contributed to their ignorance and, consequently, to their anxiety. Also affecting Whites was a rapid series of new developments: the expulsion of White liberals from the new Black movements; their inability quickly to discover

This article is an excerpt from a longer paper originally written for the Department of Evangelism, United Presbyterian Church. It was distributed to the staff of the denomination's Board of National Missions on June 30, 1969.

93

meaningful alternative lines; the escalation of looting, burning, and guerrilla tactics; the sudden emergence of Black caucuses within nine of the major denominations, including the Roman Catholic Church; the rapid decline of interest in integrating schools, fair housing, and in the customary political liberalism of the 1968 presidential election campaign. All these contributed to a gloomy sense of hopelessness on the part of many White Christians and Jews. This in turn triggered sometimes racist predispositions and ultimately caused a withdrawal of commitment to Black people.

Although the church bureaucracies attempted to arrest this defection by various devices such as study of the Report of the Kerner Commission, the Crisis in the Nation program, and the exaltation of the memory of Martin Luther King, Jr., the door had already been slammed shut on the kind of crusading church social action for racial justice that flowered after Birmingham and Selma. In the narthex of the White sanctuaries and around the dinner table in the polished homes of suburbia, the conversation (about whether to call Black people "Negroes" or "colored," about Black college students at Cornell carrying guns, or the decline in interracial coalitions and in the number of Blacks applying for membership in church or country club) is strained, guilty, frightened, and most of all confused.

When Forman entered Riverside Church and challenged the top leadership of the denominations by occupying their offices on May 15, he merely opened the gate behind which a flood of resentment, guilt, fear and confusion had been building up for several months within the various religious communions and in the White liberal community as a whole. That gate had to be opened sooner or later for the good of the church and the nation.

It is now more obvious than before that something must be done to help White churchmen and a large percentage of middle-class Black churchmen to understand what has been happening in the United States—and especially in the churches themselves—since the Black Power slogan gained currency. They need to understand *why* it has happened and to perceive that this is the time for a radical departure from what the church has known itself to be and do. This need is exposed and made all the more critical by the emergence of James Forman and the National Black Economic Development Conference, an event which is itself a kind of focusing of the contemporary history of the struggle for racial justice in the United States.

The Theological Meaning of the Present Crisis

There has always been, at least among Christians in the United States, a misapplication of theology to the concept of racial integration. From Liston Pope's *The Kingdom beyond Caste* to Joseph Washington's *Black Religion,* American theologians, both Black and White, have been interpreted as teaching that the Christian understanding of brotherly love, social progress and the unity of mankind in the family of God required the disappearance of all ethnic and racial identity and separateness. People thought that the closure of sociological and spiritual space between the races would bring about "nonsegregated churches and a nonsegregated society." Such a church and society, in which "all black cats would appear to be gray," were thought to be complementary and mutually reinforcing aspects of Western Christian democracy, the secularized image of the Kingdom of God on earth.

Since 1966 the new interest in "Black Theology" among Black churchmen is evidence that the theology which has been dominant in the American churches failed Black Christians. It found racial prejudice and discrimination to be denial of the sovereignty of God and the Christian doctrine of man, but it made no allowance for the Black experience of faith and life in the community of poverty and oppression.

Racial identity should be no bar to full fellowship and participation in the church and in society. That much White theologians and ethicists made clear. But they were in error to suppose that White perceptions of churchmanship and human reality in American society were the only Christian perceptions. And they were in error not to understand what role his or her own racial identity played in the perceptions of the White Christian—including those of the theologian!

Black humanity in America is formed in the matrix of psychological and physical suffering, segregation, discrimination and the ever-present remembrance of a previous condition of involuntary servitude. Out of this condition has come a type of person, a type of human being whose sensibilities and perceptions, religious and secular, are rarely identical with those who are "born White" in America. This does not, however, make such sensibilities and perceptions invalid. Indeed it may give them a certain depth and richness, a certain passion for justice that can discern in the truth about Jesus Christ that which modern White Christians have both forgotten and ignored.

Black Power and Black Theology are perspectives which move along this line to reclaim something of value in Black humanity and the Black Church. To the extent that American theology denigrated those values by presupposing that the themes and motifs of an "integrated" Christianity (read "desegregated, but White") were normative for all Christians, it disqualified Black religion just as Black humanity had been disqualified by the White politicians, labor leaders and businessmen.

Liberal theologians in the United States never calculated the extent to which the infusion of God's love for others is related to the freedom and ability to affirm and esteem oneself. They neglected to state the extent to which the achievement of authentic personhood (which is a prerequisite of discipleship) is related to the need for a positive sense of historic community and group experience. Such self-esteem based on group identity precedes and supersedes, at least for people who have known segregation, a satisfactory experience of koinonia in most interracial churches.

Do Churches Have Special Guilt?

If the involvement of the American churches in slavery and their subsequent exploitation of Blacks is demonstrably true, and if, despite the liberal
theology and ethics of integration, the White religious community was unable or unwilling to make integration work, then a most pernicious injury,
spiritually and materially, has been committed upon Black people in this
nation, and the White religious establishment cannot evade the fact of its
special burden of guilt. That is the message of the Black Manifesto, of the
May 7 statement of the National Conference of Black Churchmen, and of the
Black caucuses of several predominantly White denominations.

Certainly it is no secret that the White Church has been and is today deeply
entrenched in the system of White oppression. Many of the laypersons who
sit on the governing boards of wealthy White congregations are the absentee
owners and managers of the corporate and political structures which have
kept Black people in deprivation and powerless. Many of the homeowners
who refuse to sell to Black buyers and effectively keep them from moving
into White neighborhoods are members of fine suburban congregations.
Almost all of the great White denominations have huge investments in
hundreds of American firms which are reaping 19 percent profits from the
dehumanizing apartheid economics of the Republic of South Africa. Many
White churches own thousands of acres in the South where Black sharecroppers, desperately in need of land, are being forced into the already crowded
urban ghettos. White churches make purchases of thousands of dollars and
contract for the building of million-dollar sanctuaries from discriminatory
businesses and contractors and yet refuse to join Project Equality which uses
church purchasing power to open up jobs for Black folk.

What About Reparations?

The Manifesto goes on to call for the actually modest sum of 500 million
dollars in reparations from the White churches of the United States, as an
effective method of making some redress for their share in the institution of
slavery and the benefits of Black oppression which accrued to the White
society of which they are a part.

The concept of reparations has by no means been disallowed in modern
times, however unorthodox the Manifesto's particular usage may be. Reparations are a form of indemnity to repair or mend "that honor which by injury
was eclipsed" (in the words of the *Encyclopedia Americana*) and are usually
monetary in form, paid out of political interest or out of moral duty and
concern for the general welfare.

Great Britain, France, the Netherlands, and the United States received
reparations from Japan after the hostilities of 1864; Spain from Peru in 1869;
the United States from China in 1900. West Germany assumed the liability of
2 billion dollars for victims of the Nazi persecution. In 1953 the Federal

Republic of Germany undertook the payment of 820 million dollars (used to resettle 500,000 Jews) to indemnify individuals inside and outside of Hitler's Germany for their persecution. The United Nations laid upon Israel reparational obligations of 336 million dollars in land or movable property lost by Arab refugees during the war of 1948. Israel refused to acknowledge the exact sum but agreed to make compensation if it could receive a loan.

Professor Harvey Cox, in a recent article, notes that the U.S. government has made "sporadic and insufficient" reparations to American Indians; that it made inadequate repayments to Americans of Japanese ancestry for losses suffered during their internment during World War II. In another example, Cox mentions the G.I. Bill of Rights as reparational legislation.

Gordon C. Bjork, in the June 24, 1968, issue of *Christianity and Crisis,* writes:

> The estate of one generation in our society is passed to the next after the subtraction of liabilities incurred. By the same logic the debts incurred by our white forefathers in the deprivation of Negroes by slavery and discrimination calls for the repayment of debts from our massive inheritance. It is a repayment of accrued liabilities because part of our inheritance was accumulated by the systematic underpayment of a minority race that was suppressed by law and violence.

It is to his credit that Dr. Ernest Campell, minister of Riverside Church, was the first churchman since the publication of the Black Manifesto to point out the theological meaning of reparations. "From the beginning," he told his parishioners after the May 4 confrontation, "the Christian church has taught that restitution is an essential part of penitence. You don't simply say, 'I'm sorry' to a man you've robbed. You return what you stole or your apology takes on a hollow ring. . . ."

Penitence, in other words, is sorrow for sin as an offense against God and involves a purpose of amendment. It is clear that such amendment is related to the concept of reparations. The same idea is contained in the Christian doctrine of repentance:

> There is in repentance a certain quality of infinitude. With the penitent mood comes new insight, fresh illumination leading to an almost painful anxiety to make atonement to the person or persons wronged, to society, to the spiritual order which has been violated. The repentant man stands ready for any task, however great, for any service, however distasteful. Repentance is thus transformed into a moral dynamic.

No institution in American society has made more confessions of guilt for its involvement in the sin of slavery and in segregation and discrimination against Black people than has the Christian Church. No institution in America has issued more high-sounding pronouncements of the principles of a commitment to social justice. If reparations are truly an acceptable form of the concrete expression of repentance, then the White churches of the nation have a religious duty to demonstrate the seriousness and sincerity of the Christian conscience by repaying to oppressed minorities whatever reasonable portion can be calculated from the benefits which have accrued to them through slavery and Black subjugation.

Forman Speaks God's Judgment to the Church

Whatever one may think of James Forman's politics and tactics of disruptive confrontation, the church should recognize that this is not the first time that God has called upon the wrath of those outside the church to summon it to repentance and obedience. The great wealth that churches have accumulated may have become a spiritual liability. Rather than help men and women to destroy the dehumanizing, demonic structures which cripple them, most church funds have been used simply to enhance the welfare of the churches and their members.

The time may be at hand for the cleansing of the Temple as our Lord accomplished it. The time may be here, as the Scriptures warned, for "judgment to begin in the household of faith." It well may be that for all his vehemence and rudeness, James Forman is being used by God to declare to the churches, "This night your soul is required of you; and the things you have prepared, whose will they be?" (Luke 12:20).

The theological meaning of the present crisis of race relations in the United States is that Black Power, the legal concept of reparations, and the appearance of James Forman as a stringent and arrogant critic of the American religious establishment may be seen, through the eyes of faith, to be redemptive.

First, the theological defense of integration never took account of the painful deracination and dehumanization which Black people were called upon to suffer as the price of a powerless and humiliating assimilation into an essentially racist White Christian Church culture.

Second, the concept of reparations comes on the contemporary scene as a creative and altogether practical way to concretize the theological doctrine of repentance and break with the spiritual sterility of a church which is suffering from an excessive verbalization and deficient performance of theology. It is, in somewhat the same sense as the new interest in churches paying taxes, an appropriate form of servantship to the community of poverty and oppression, in the spirit of the kenosis or "self-emptying" work of Christ and his subjection to secular authority in obedience to God.

Finally, the Black militant and Spanish-American leaders who are confronting the churches and disrupting worship services, insofar as they speak the truth (where truth has often been withheld by the false prophets "who cry 'peace! peace!' when there is no peace"), render service to the church as unwitting instruments in God's hands for the burning and healing of his people. By the witness of men like James Forman and Eliezer Risco, the church as an institution is called to be renewed, to become the revolutionary vanguard of God's inbreaking Kingdom.

The bland, liberal theology and missionary posture of conventional American Christianity are exposed as inadequate for a world in which God is shaking the foundations. Something more is needed for today—a radical theology of revolution which can impel churchmen, beyond Black Power and White Power, to grasp the reality of the new being of humanity which Christ came to bring and which he made possible by the dethronement of all the principalities and powers of this world.

If it is the Black Manifesto which has revealed this crisis of theological clarity and ethical commitment within the churches and synagogues of America, churchmen ought to read it carefully and critically, but also joyously, giving God the praise. Instead of locking church doors, calling the police and sending personnel home from the denominational offices, churchmen should be listening to what the Black and Brown militants are saying, and engaging them in intensive dialogue. Open hearings should be held in local churches (as did one congregation in a wealthy suburb of Detroit) in order that church people can discuss the Manifesto, ask questions of the pastor, and assess the legitimacy of the reparations concept and the surplus resources of their congregations.

10

BLACK THEOLOGY

Statement by the National Committee of Black Churchmen, June 13, 1969

Why Black Theology?

Black people affirm their being. This affirmation is made in the whole experience of being black in the hostile American society. Black Theology is not a gift of the Christian gospel dispensed to slaves; rather it is an *appropriation* which black slaves made of the gospel given by their white oppressors. Black Theology has been nurtured, sustained and passed on in the black churches in their various ways of expression. Black Theology has dealt with all the ultimate and violent issues of life and death for a people despised and degraded.

The black church has not only nurtured black people but enabled them to survive brutalities that ought not to have been inflicted on any community of men. Black Theology is the product of black Christian experience and reflection. It comes out of the past. It is strong in the present. And we believe it is redemptive for the future.

This indigenous theological formation of faith emerged from the stark need of the fragmented black community to affirm itself as a part of the Kingdom of God. White theology sustained the American slave system and negated the humanity of blacks. This indigenous Black Theology, based on the imaginative black experience, was the best hope for the survival of black people. This is a way of saying that Black Theology was already present in the spirituals and slave songs and exhortations of slave preachers and their descendants.

All theologies arise out of communal experience with God. At this mo-

This statement, produced by the Committee on Theological Prospectus, NCBC, was issued at the Interdenominational Theological Center, Atlanta, Georgia. It was adopted at the NCBC 1969 annual convocation in Oakland, California.

ment in time, the black community seeks to express its theology in language that speaks to the contemporary mood of black people.

What Is Black Theology?

Black Theology is a theology of black liberation. It seeks to plumb the black condition in the light of God's revelation in Jesus Christ, so that the black community can see that the gospel is commensurate with the achievement of black humanity. Black Theology is a theology of "blackness." It is the affirmation of black humanity that emancipates black people from white racism, thus providing authentic freedom for both white and black people. It affirms the humanity of white people in that it says No to the encroachment of white oppression.

The message of liberation is the revelation of God as revealed in the incarnation of Jesus Christ. Freedom IS the gospel. Jesus is the Liberator! "He . . . hath sent me to preach deliverance to the captives" (Luke 4:18). Thus the black patriarchs and we ourselves know this reality despite all attempts of the white church to obscure it and to utilize Christianity as a means of enslaving blacks. The demand that Christ the Liberator imposes on all men *requires* all blacks to affirm their full dignity as persons and all whites to surrender their presumptions of superiority and abuses of power.

What Does This Mean?

It means that Black Theology must confront the issues which are a part of the reality of black oppression. We cannot ignore the powerlessness of the black community. Despite the *repeated requests* for significant programs of social change, the American people have refused to appropriate adequate sums of money for social reconstruction. White church bodies have often made promises only to follow with default. We must, therefore, once again call the attention of the nation and the church to the need for providing adequate resources of power (reparation).

Reparation is a part of the Gospel message. Zaccheus knew well the necessity for repayment as an essential ingredient in repentance. "If I have taken anything from any man by false accusation, I restore him fourfold" (Luke 19:8). The church which calls itself the servant church must, like its Lord, be willing to strip itself of possessions in order to build and restore that which has been destroyed by the compromising bureaucrats and conscienceless rich. While reparation cannot remove the guilt created by the despicable deed of slavery, it is, nonetheless, a positive response to the need for power in the black community. This nation, and, a people who have always related the value of the person to his possession of property, must recognize the necessity of restoring property in order to reconstitute personhood.

What Is The Cost?

Living is risk. We take it in confidence. The black community has been brutalized and victimized over the centuries. The recognition that comes from seeing Jesus as Liberator and the Gospel as freedom empowers black men to risk themselves for freedom and for faith. This faith we affirm in the midst of a hostile, disbelieving society. We intend to exist by this faith at all times and in all places.

In spite of brutal deprivation and denial the black community has appropriated the spurious form of Christianity imposed upon it and made it into an instrument for resisting the extreme demands of oppression. It has enabled the black community to live through unfulfilled promises, unnecessary risks, and inhuman relationships.

As black theologians address themselves to the issues of the black revolution, it is incumbent upon them to say that the black community will not be turned from its course, but will seek complete fulfillment of the promises of the Gospel. Black people have survived the terror. We now commit ourselves to the risks of affirming the dignity of black personhood. We do this as men and as black Christians. This is the message of Black Theology. In the words of Eldridge Cleaver:

> We shall have our manhood.
> We shall have it or the earth will be leveled by our efforts to gain it.

11

A MESSAGE TO THE CHURCHES
FROM OAKLAND, CALIFORNIA

Statement by the National Committee of Black Churchmen,
Third Annual Convocation, November 11-14, 1969

We came to Oakland as an act of faith. We came seeking a deeper experience of the mission of God in the contemporary world than has ever been provided by the denominations and local congregations to which some of us belong, from which some of us have fled in profound disillusionment, and which some of us have observed, but only with doubt and distrust.

In a time of the increasing institutionalization and bureaucratization of the Church we do not come to create a new institutional form of the Church. We are not here to invent a new denomination. Our primary and overreaching concern is to seek, through our common experience and consciousness of being black and powerless in a part of the world dominated by white racism and white power, a new religio-cultural, political and economic vocation which can relate to our own deep alienation from a religious, cultural, political and economic system which is not compatible with our own instincts and sensibilities but which has been commended to us and imposed upon us by white, bourgeois, European and American religious, political and economic institutions interlocking and conspiring with one another to whitenize and subordinate black people.

This new vocation to which we are called is *political* in the sense that it seeks radically to change, by whatever means are necessary, the racist structures which dominate our lives; *cultural* in the sense that it seeks to identify, recreate, unify and authenticate whatever traditions, values and styles of life are indigenous or distinctive to the black community; and *theological* in the sense that we believe that it is God—however He chooses to reveal Himself today to oppressed peoples in America and in the Third World—who has

103

chosen black humanity as a vanguard to resist the demonic powers of racism, capitalism and imperialism, and to so reform the structures of this world that they will more perfectly minister to the peace and power of all people as children of One God and brothers of one another.

We black people are a religious people. From the earliest recorded time we have acknowledged a Supreme Being. With the fullness of our physical bodies and emotions we have unabashedly worshipped Him with shouts of joy and in the tears of pain and anguish. We neither believe that God is dead, white, nor captive to some highly rationalistic and dogmatic formulations of the Christian faith which relate Him exclusively to the canons of the Old and New Testaments and accommodate Him to the reigning spirits of a sociotechnical age. Rather, we affirm that God is Liberator in the man Jesus Christ, that His message is Freedom, and that today He calls all men to be what they are in themselves, and among their own people, in the context of a pluralistic world-society of dignity and self-determination for all. We believe that in a special way God's favor rests today upon the poor and oppressed peoples of the world and that He calls them to be the ministering angels of His judgment and grace as His Kingdom of Freedom and Peace breaks in from the future upon a world shackled to ancient sins and virtues and upon the present inequalities, imperialistic wars, and ambitions of privileged nations, classes and power-groups.

This call of God which we in the NCBC hear in what we have been saying to one another in Oakland is a call to suffering and sacrifice. It is a call to identification with frustrated, emasculated, down-trodden men, women and children, most of them black, to share their anguish and their hope and to work for their enlightenment and empowerment, not that they might in turn become oppressors, but that through them the world might be saved from the selfishness, greed and subjugation which has characterized the centuries-old hegemony of the white, Anglo-Saxon, European civilizations of the West.

We therefore call upon the white, Christian churches of America and Europe, which have nurtured and sustained the systems of injustice that have driven the world to the present crisis, to submit themselves to radical reformation. We challenge them to psychologically and institutionally disengage themselves from the nations within whose boundaries they have so often baptized and sanctified racism, imperialism and economic selfishness, and take upon themselves the kind of revolutionary posture that can force the transfer of requisite countervailing power to oppressed peoples wherever they may be found. We challenge them to divest themselves of their own great wealth—much of it ill-gotten—built upon the bodies of exploited races and classes wherever imperialistic political and economic influences have extended within and beyond national boundaries, and to make massive ecclesiastical resources of capital and technical assistance available to powerless people in Africa, Asia, Latin America and the United States.

We believe that the Black Manifesto, which was issued this year to the churches of America and to several official church convocations in Europe by the Black Economic Development Conference, is a most significant and essentially accurate assessment of the guilt and reparational responsibility of white Christendom and the wealthy Jewish communions of the United States. We reaffirm our support of that document and particularly of its programmatic objectives with respect to the situation of black people in the United States, Africa and the Caribbean area.

The NCBC will not desist from calling the white religious establishment of the United States to the full and immediate implementation of the demands of the Manifesto. Nor will we excuse from participation in the achievement of its objectives the historic black churches of America which have left undone many of the things they ought to have done in the slums and rural ghettos of the United States, Africa and the West Indies.

We do not shrink from the revolutionary, anti-capitalistic implications of the Manifesto. While all of our members do not give unqualified endorsement to every strategy and tactic stated or implied in the original document issued in Detroit, the National Committee of Black Churchmen, as a body, is committed to the essential spirit and meaning of the analysis and proposals, and will continue to press them upon the churches and synagogues of America, upon the National Council of Churches in the U.S.A., and upon the World Council of Churches.

We demand that individual white church agencies and white brethren, who call themselves our allies, recognize the imperative nature and urgency of this task in light of the crisis that is upon us in the cities and depressed rural areas in this most affluent and powerful nation of the world.

By the faith of our fathers, by the faith of Nat Turner and Denmark Vesey, of Allen and Varick, of Delany, of Garvey and DuBois and Martin Luther King, Jr., and Malcolm X, and by the grace of God, the NCBC has undertaken, in cooperation with IFCO and BEDC, to call this nation, beginning with the white churches, which have a clear and acknowledged moral responsibility, to the conference table to negotiate in good faith the transfer of power to those segments of society which have been deprived of freedom, justice and self-determination. It *can* be done. It can be done peacefully. *It must be done* in any case, or peace, brotherhood and reconciliation will remain empty, mocking words in an American wasteland of racial hatred and strife. Now is the time to act, for as the words of Isaiah 42 sternly remind us in every nation and generation: "He will not rest nor be silent until He has established justice in the earth."

Having thus analyzed our situation, and being ready and determined to respond to the promptings of this same God, we have been made to recognize that it is not enough simply to call the white churches to the negotiation table. Long, agonizing months of fruitless negotiations with these churches, in efforts to lead them to recognize and to fund the Black Economic Development Conference, have forced us sadly to acknowledge the harsh reality that the white churches and church structures are not capable of positive responses to the considered opinions of their black peers. We accept the defiance of us which this exposes; but we intend to do several things about that defiance. We are unalterably committed to the effecting of a more equitable power balance "by whatever means are necessary." Means additional to negotiation are now necessary. The time has come for us to resort to the use of unusual forms of pressure upon the white church structures if we are ever to realize the legitimate goal of a literal transferral of power.

One of the chief symbols of white church power is the institution known as the National Council of Churches of Christ in the U.S.A. That institution—not unlike the World Council of Churches, the myriad regional and local councils of churches, and the white denominations themselves—is a sorry example of institutionalized white decision-making power. This is true notwithstanding the fact that it has token representation of blacks in executive capacity. The General Secretary is white; the Deputy General Secretary is white; all of the Associate General Secretaries are white; the heads of divisions which are of critical relevance to the black condition, such as the Division of Christian Life and Mission, the Division of Overseas Ministries, and the Division of Christian Education, are white. These are untenable and thoroughly unacceptable realities. They comprise an affront to black churchmen everywhere.

We, therefore, announce our dedication to a battle which must culminate in the appointment of a black General Secretary of the N.C.C., and in the designation of black churchmen, in significant numbers, at the level of Associate General Secretaries and division heads. These appointments must be black churchmen who come not only from the ranks of the white denominations, but who presently labor within the fold of the great, historical black communions. The day has passed when we can be played one against the other. The NCBC, therefore, in concert with black churchmen everywhere, will determine whom you shall appoint.

Time and circumstance have met in such a way as to place us, at this day, on the virtual eve of the convening of the General Assembly of the National Council of Churches. That assembly will meet in the city of Detroit during the first week of December, 1969. In the light of our deliberations in Oakland, and in view of the stance which we have been forced by white recalcitrance to take, we declare our intention to assure that that General Assembly is confronted with the serious issues which here we have raised. One way or another, that General Assembly shall deal with this aspect of the black agenda. We have neither the need nor the intention to divulge the means by which we shall accomplish this end. We simply announce that sufficient pressures shall be brought to bear upon the Assembly to cause it to deal with these issues. Whether it deals wisely or foolishly with them is for the Assembly to determine. We are persuaded that mere suggestions and reasonable arguments are lost in the mires of verbiage and committee referrals which are so readily spawned by white church institutions. To us "black empowerment" means, precisely, black empowerment; it does not mean endless dialogue with persons and institutions which have demonstrated a propensity for eternal, infernal dialogue.

When the N.C.C., in 1967, spoke of a "Crisis in the Nation," it was speaking of the black condition. It named that crisis as one of the two top priorities for programming and funding. Yet, as the N.C.C., and as every black churchman knows, little enough has been done by that institution literally to re-order its priorities in line with its eloquent statement. We are convinced that only the transfer of power, at significant levels, can help to bring progress in this area of alleged concern. Detroit must see the establishment of our efforts to accomplish this goal. The battle once begun, we pledge ourselves to the vigorous pursuit of these objectives, by whatever means are necessary, until victory is won. If it should be that racism and white negativism are, indeed, so vital a part of the reality of the N.C.C. that it would choose to destroy itself before acceding to these just insistences, then it is clear that the N.C.C. is incapable of becoming relevant to blacks, and, being thus irrelevant, would serve a more Christian purpose in its demise than it would in a continuation of its present disguise.

Let no white churches, church institutions or churchmen seek comfort in the fact that we place our present focus upon the National Council of Churches. It is only the accidental timing of the meeting of the General Assembly which directs us so to do. Let the World Council of Churches know, assuredly, that it is programmed into our agenda; let every regional and local council of churches across this land know, without doubt, that our intentions and our agenda speak to them all; let all national and regional denominations, judicatories, dioceses and what-have-you know that this day we are speaking to them in tones of clarion sound. Our agenda for the white church structures is all-embracing. Fidelity to Jesus Christ, the Lord of all, informs us that none may be allowed the deceptive comfort of respite.

Our deliberations in Oakland have led us to know that it was for the clarification of these purposes that we were brought to Oakland, and it is with these resolutions and determinations that, under God's guidance, we return to our individual places and ramparts to work, to strive, and to fight.

Let all of the church of God say, "Amen!"

12

THE BLACK DECLARATION
OF INDEPENDENCE,
JULY 4, 1970

National Committee of Black Churchmen

IN THE BLACK COMMUNITY, July 4, 1970 A DECLARATION by concerned Black Citizens of the United States of America in Black Churches, Schools, Homes, Community Organizations and Institutions assembled:

When in the course of Human Events, it becomes necessary for a People who were stolen from lands of their Fathers, transported under the most ruthless and brutal circumstances 5,000 miles to a strange land, sold into dehumanizing slavery, emasculated, subjugated, exploited, and discriminated against for 351 years, to call, with finality, a halt to such indignities and genocidal practices—by virtue of the Laws of Nature and of Nature's God, a decent respect to the Opinions of Mankind requires that they should declare their just grievances and the urgent and necessary redress thereof.

We hold these truths to be self-evident, that all Men are not *only* created equal and endowed by their Creator with certain unalienable rights among which are Life, Liberty and the Pursuit of Happiness, but that when this equality and these rights are deliberately and consistently refused, withheld or abnegated, men are bound by self-respect and honor to rise up in righteous indignation to secure them. Whenever any Form of Government, or any variety of established traditions and systems of the Majority becomes destructive of Freedom and of legitimate Human Rights, it is the Right of the Minorities to use every necessary and accessible means to protest and to disrupt the machinery of Oppression, and so to bring such general distress and discomfort upon the oppressor as to the offended Minorities shall seem most appropriate and most likely to effect a proper adjustment of the society.

Prudence, indeed, will dictate that such bold tactics should not be initiated for light and transient Causes; and, accordingly, the Experience of White America has been that the descendants of the African citizens brought

108

forcibly to these shores, and to the shores of the Caribbean Islands, as slaves, have been patient long past what can be expected of any human beings so affronted. But when a long train of Abuses and Violence, pursuing invariably the same Object, manifests a Design to reduce them under Absolute Racist Domination and Injustice, it is their Duty radically to confront such Government or system of traditions, and to provide, under the aegis of Legitimate Minority Power and Self Determination, for their present Relief and future Security. Such has been the patient Sufferance of Black People in the United States of America; and such is now the Necessity which constrains them to address this Declaration to Despotic White Power, and to give due notice of their determined refusal to be any longer silenced by fear or flattery, or to be denied justice. The history of the treatment of Black People in the United States is a history having in direct Object the Establishment and Maintenance of Racist Tyranny over this People. To prove this, let Facts be submitted to a candid World.

The United States has evaded Compliance to laws the most wholesome and necessary for our Children's education.

The United States has caused us to be isolated in the most dilapidated and unhealthful sections of all cities.

The United States has allowed election districts to be so gerrymandered that Black People find the right to Representation in the Legislatures almost impossible of attainment.

The United States has allowed the dissolution of school districts controlled by Blacks when Blacks opposed with manly Firmness the white man's Invasions on the Rights of our People.

The United States has erected a Multitude of Public Agencies and Offices, and sent into our ghettos Swarms of Social Workers, Officers and Investigators to harass our People, and eat out their Substance to feed the Bureaucracies.

The United States has kept in our ghettos, in Times of Peace, Standing Armies of Police, State Troopers and National Guardsmen, without the consent of our People.

The United States has imposed Taxes upon us without protecting our Constitutional Rights.

The United States has constrained our Black sons taken Captive in its Armies, to bear arms against their black, brown and yellow Brothers, to be the Executioners of these Friends and Brethren, or to fall themselves by their Hands.

The Exploitation and Injustice of the United States have incited domestic Insurrections among us, and the United States has endeavored to bring on the Inhabitants of our ghettos, the merciless Military Establishment, whose known Rule of control is an undistinguished shooting of all Ages, Sexes and Conditions of Black People:

For being lynched, burned, tortured, harried, harassed and imprisoned without Just Cause.

For being gunned down in the streets, in our churches, in our homes, in our apartments and on our campuses, by Policemen and Troops who are protected by a mock Trial, from Punishment for any Murders which they commit on the Inhabitants of our Communities.

For creating, through Racism and bigotry, an unrelenting Economic Depression in the Black Community which wreaks havoc upon our men and disheartens our youth.

For denying to most of us equal access to the better Housing and Education of the land.

For having desecrated and torn down our humblest dwelling places, under the Pretense of Urban Renewal, without replacing them at costs which we can afford.

The United States has denied our personhood by refusing to teach our heritage, and the magnificent contributions to the life, wealth and growth of this Nation which have been made by Black People.

In every stage of these Oppressions we have Petitioned for Redress in the most humble terms: Our repeated Petitions have been answered mainly by repeated Injury. A Nation, whose Character is thus marked by every act which may define a Racially Oppressive Regime, is unfit to receive the respect of a Free People.

Nor have we been wanting in attentions to our White Brethren. We have warned them from time to time of Attempts by their Structures of Power to extend an unwarranted, Repressive Control over us. We have reminded them of the Circumstances of our Captivity and Settlement here. We have appealed to their vaunted Justice and Magnanimity, and we have conjured them by the Ties of our Common Humanity to disavow these Injustices, which would inevitably interrupt our Connections and Correspondence. They have been deaf to the voice of Justice and of Humanity. We must, therefore, acquiesce in the Necessity, which hereby announces our Most Firm Commitment to the Liberation of Black People, and hold the Institutions, Traditions and Systems of the United States as we hold the rest of the societies of Mankind, Enemies when Unjust and Tyrannical; when Just and Free, Friends.

We, therefore, the Black People of the United States of America, in all parts of this Nation, appealing to the Supreme Judge of the World for the Rectitude of our Intentions, do, in the Name of our good People and our own

Black Heroes—Richard Allen, James Varick, Absalom Jones, Nat Turner, Frederick Douglass, Marcus Garvey, Malcolm X, Martin Luther King, Jr., and all Black People past and present, great and small—Solemnly Publish and Declare, that we shall be, and of Right ought to be, FREE AND INDEPEN-DENT FROM THE INJUSTICE, EXPLOITATIVE CONTROL, IN-STITUTIONALIZED VIOLENCE AND RACISM OF WHITE AMERICA, that unless we receive full Redress and Relief from these In-humanities we will move to renounce all Allegiance to this Nation, and will refuse, in every way, to cooperate with the Evil which is Perpetrated upon ourselves and our Communities. And for the support of this Declaration, with a firm Reliance on the Protection of divine Providence, we mutually pledge to each other our Lives, our Fortunes, and our sacred Honor.

Signed, by Order and in behalf of Black People . . .

13

THE WHITE CHURCH AND BLACK POWER

James H. Cone

Let the Church discover and identify itself with groups of
people that suffer because of unjust situations, and who have
no way of making themselves heard. The Church should be the
voice of those who have no one. The Church must discover
these groups and identify herself with them. Here is the
modern Way of the Cross, the way of Christian responsibility.

Emilio Castro

The meaning of Black Power and its relationship to Christianity has been
the focal point of our discussion thus far. It has been argued that Black Power
is the spirit of Christ himself in the black-white dialogue which makes
possible the emancipation of blacks from self-hatred and frees whites from
their racism. Through Black Power, blacks are becoming men of worth, and
whites are forced to confront them as human beings.

There is no other spirit in American life so challenging as the spirit of Black
Power. We can see it affecting every major aspect of American life—
economic, political, and social. In major white and black universities its spirit
is manifested in the demand for more emphasis on "black studies." Black
students have literally taken over some administration buildings in an effort
to make white authorities recognize the importance of their demands. In
politics, Stokely Carmichael and Charles Hamilton have given the political
implications of Black Power.[1] For them Black Power in politics means blacks

Reprinted from Cone, *Black Theology and Black Power* (New York: Seabury Press, 1969), pp.
62-90.

controlling their political destiny by voting for black people and perhaps eventually forming a coalition with poor whites against middle-class whites. For some others it means black nationalism. Economically it may mean boycotting, or building stores for black people. Religiously or philosophically it means an inner sense of freedom from the structures of white society which builds its economy on the labor of poor blacks and whites. It means that the slave now knows that he is a man, and thus resolves to make the enslaver recognize him. I contend that such a spirit is not merely compatible with Christianity; in America in the latter twentieth century it is Christianity.

Some critics of this thesis may ask about the place of the Church in my analysis. It may appear that its role as an agent of God in the world has been overlooked. This leads us to an investigation of the biblical understanding of the Church and its relationship to white denominational churches.

What Is the Church?

What is the Church and its relationship to Christ and Black Power? The Church is that people called into being by the power and love of God to share in his revolutionary activity for the liberation of man.

Mythically the interrelation of God, man, and the world is presented in the Genesis picture of the man and the woman in the garden. Man was created to share in God's creative (revolutionary) activity in the world (Gen. 1:27-28). But through sin man rejects his proper activity and destiny. He wants to be God, the creator of his destiny. This is the essence of sin, every man's desire to become "like God." But in his passion to become superhuman, man becomes subhuman, estranged from the source of his being, threatening and threatened by his neighbor, transforming a situation destined for intimate human fellowship into a spider web of conspiracy and violence. God, however, will not permit man thus to become less than the divine intention for him. He therefore undertakes a course of not-so-gentle persuasion for the liberation and restoration of his creatures.

The call of Abraham was the beginning of this revolutionary activity on behalf of man's liberation from his own sinful pride. This was followed by the exodus, the most significant revelatory act in the Old Testament, which demonstrated God's purposes for man. God showed thereby that he was the Lord of history, that his will for man is not to be thwarted by other human wills. And when Pharaoh said to Moses and Aaron, "The Lord is righteous, and I and my people are wicked" (Exod. 9:27), he was saying that even he recognized the righteousness of God in contrast to the wickedness of men.

The history of Israel is a history of God's election of a special, oppressed people to share in his creative involvement in the world on behalf of man. The call of this people at Sinai into a covenant relationship for a special task may be said to be the beginning of the Church.[2] In the Old Testament, Israel often refers to herself as the *qahal,* the assembly or people of God.[3] Israel is called into being as a people of the covenant in which Yahweh promises to be their God and they his people. Israel's task is to be a partner in God's revolutionary activity and thus to be an example to the whole world of what God intends for all men. By choosing Israel, the oppressed people among the nations, God reveals that his concern is not for the strong but for the weak, not for the enslaver but for the slave, not for whites but for blacks. To express the goal of her striving, Israel spoke of the Day of the Lord and the Kingdom of God, in which God would vindicate his people from oppression and the rule of his righteousness would be recognized by all. This would be the day when the lion would lie down with the lamb and men would beat their swords into plowshares.

In the New Testament, the coming of God in Christ means that the Kingdom of God expected in the Old Testament is now realized in Jesus of Nazareth. The Day of the Lord has come in the life, death, and resurrection of Jesus. This day is no longer future but present in the man Jesus. In him is embodied God's Kingdom in which men are liberated. He is, as Paul says, the "New Adam," who has done for man what man could not do for himself. His death and resurrection mean that the decisive battle has been fought and won, and man no longer has to be a slave to "principalities and powers."

With him also comes a new people which the New Testament calls the *ekklesia* (church). Like the people of Old Israel, they are called into being by God himself—to be his agent in this world until Christ's second coming. Like Old Israel, they are an oppressed people, created to cooperate in God's liberation of all men. Unlike Old Israel, their membership is not limited by ethnic or political boundaries, but includes all who respond in faith to the redemptive act of God in Christ with a willingness to share in God's creative activity in the world. Unlike Old Israel, they do not look forward to the coming of the Kingdom, but know that, in Christ, God's Kingdom has already come and their very existence is a manifestation of it. The Church merely waits for its full consummation in Christ's second coming. Therefore, its sole purpose for being is to be a visible manifestation of God's work in the affairs of men. The Church, then, consists of people who have been seized by the Holy Spirit and who have the determination to live as if all depends on God. It has no will of its own, only God's will; it has no duty of its own, only God's duty. Its existence is grounded in God.

The Church of Christ is not bounded by standards of race, class, or occupation. It is not a building or an institution. It is not determined by bishops, priests, or ministers as these terms are used in their contemporary sense. Rather, the Church is God's suffering people. It is that grouping of men who take seriously the words of Jesus: "Blessed are you when men revile you and persecute you and utter all kinds of evil against you falsely on my account" (Matt. 5:11). The call of God constitutes the Church, and it is a call to suffering. As Bonhoeffer put it:

Man is challenged to participate in the sufferings of God at the hands of a godless world.

He must plunge himself into the life of a godless world, without attempting to gloss over its ungodliness with a veneer of religion or trying to transfigure it. . . . To be a Christian does not mean to be religious in a particular way, to cultivate some particular form of asceticism, . . . but to be a man. It is not some religious act which makes a Christian what he is, but participation in the suffering of God in the life of the world.[4]

"Where Christ is, there is the Church." Christ is to be found, as always, where men are enslaved and trampled under foot; Christ is found suffering with the suffering; Christ is in the ghetto—there also is his Church.

The Church is not defined by those who faithfully attend and participate in the 11:00 A.M. Sunday worship. As Harvey Cox says: "The insistence by the Reformers that the church was 'where the word is rightly preached and the sacraments rightly administered' will simply not do today."[5] It may have been fine for distinguishing orthodoxy from heresy, but it is worthless as a vehicle against modern racism. We must therefore be reminded that Christ was not crucified on an altar between two candles, but on a cross between two thieves. He is not in our peaceful, quiet, comfortable suburban "churches," but in the ghetto fighting the racism of churchly white people.

In the New Testament perspective, the Church has essentially three functions: preaching *(kerygma),* service *(diakonia),* and fellowship *(koinonia).* Preaching means proclaiming to the world what God has done for man in Jesus Christ. The Church tells the world about Christ's victory over alien hostile forces. If we compare Christ's work on the cross with warfare, as Oscar Cullmann[6] and others do, then it is the task of the Church to tell the world that the decisive battle in the war has been fought and won by Christ. Freedom has come! The old tyrants have been displaced, and there is no need for anyone to obey evil powers. The Church, then, is men and women running through the streets announcing that freedom is a reality. This is easily translated into the context of modern racism. God in Christ has set men free from white power, and this means an end to ghettos and all they imply. The Church tells black people to shape up and act like free men because the old powers of white racism are writhing in final agony. The Good News of freedom is proclaimed also to the oppressor, but since he mistakes his enslaving power for life and health he does not easily recognize his own mortal illness or hear the healing word. But the revolution is on, and there is no turning back.

Modern kerygmatic preaching has little to do with white ministers admonishing their people to be nice to "Negroes" or "to obey the law of the land." Nor does it involve inviting a "good Negro" preacher to preach about race relations. Preaching in its truest sense tells the world about Christ's victory and thus invites people to act as if God has won the battle over racism. To preach in America today is to shout "Black Power! Black Freedom!"

It is important to remember that the preaching of the Word presents a crisis situation. The hearing of the news of freedom through the preaching of the Word always invites the hearer to take one of two sides: He must either side with the old rulers or the new one. "He that is not for me is against me." There is no neutral position in a war. Even in silence, one is automatically identified as being on the side of the oppressor. There is no place in this war of liberation for nice white people who want to avoid taking sides and remain friends with both the racists and the Negro. To hear the Word is to decide: Are you with us or against us? There is no time for conferences or talk of any sort. If the hearing of the Word and the encounter with the Spirit do not convict you, then talk will be of little avail.

The Church not only preaches the Word of liberation, it joins Christ in his work of liberation. This is *diakonia,* "service." Though the decisive battle has been fought and won over racism, the war is not over. There is still left what G. P. Lewis calls the "mopping-up operations."[7] Just as the war in Europe continued for months after it was "won" at Stalingrad and El Alamein, so the war against the principalities and powers continues after the decisive battle on the cross.[8] We still have to fight racism. The evil forces have been defeated but refuse to admit it. "Although defeated," writes William Hordern, "evil still has sufficient strength to fight a stubborn rear-guard action."[9] It is the task of the Church to join Christ in this fight against evil. Thomas Wieser puts it this way:

> The way of the church is related to the fact that the Kyrios Lord himself is on his way in the world, . . . and the church has no choice but to follow him who precedes. Consequently obedience and witness to the Kyrios require the discernment of the opening which he provides and the willingness to step into this opening.[10]

The opening has been made and the Church must follow. To follow means that the Church is more than a talking or a resolution-passing community. Its talk is backed up with relevant involvement in the world as a witness, through action, that what it says is in fact true.

Where is "the opening" that Christ provides? Where does he lead his people? Where indeed, if not in the ghetto. He meets the blacks where they are and becomes one of them. We see him there with his black face and big black hands lounging on a streetcorner. "Oh, but surely Christ is above race." But society is not raceless, any more than when God became a despised Jew. White liberal preference for a raceless Christ serves only to make official and orthodox the centuries-old portrayal of Christ as white. The "raceless" American Christ has a light skin, wavy brown hair, and sometimes—wonder of wonders—blue eyes. For whites to find him with big lips and kinky hair is as offensive as it was for the Pharisees to find him partying with tax-collectors. But whether whites want to hear it or not, *Christ is black, baby,* with all of the features which are so detestable to white society.

To suggest that Christ has taken on a black skin is not theological emotionalism. If the Church is a continuation of the Incarnation, and if the Church and Christ are where the oppressed are, then Christ and his Church must identify totally with the oppressed to the extent that they too suffer for the same reasons persons are enslaved. In America, blacks are oppressed because of their blackness. It would seem, then, that emancipation could only be realized by Christ and his Church becoming black. Thinking of Christ as nonblack in the twentieth century is as theologically impossible as thinking of him as non-Jewish in the first century. God's Word in Christ not only fulfills his purposes for man through his elected people, but also inaugurates a new age in which all oppressed people become his people. In America, that people is a black people. In order to remain faithful to his Word in Christ, his present manifestation must be the very essence of blackness.

It is the job of the Church to become black with him and accept the shame which white society places on blacks. But the Church knows that what is shame to the world is holiness to God. Black is holy, that is, it is a symbol of God's presence in history on behalf of the oppressed man. Where there is black, there is oppression; but blacks can be assured that where there is blackness, there is Christ who has taken on blackness so that what is evil in men's eyes might become good. Therefore Christ is black because he is oppressed, and oppressed because he is black. And if the Church is to join Christ by following his opening, it too must go where suffering is and become black also.

This is what the New Testament means by the service of reconciliation. It is not smoothing things over by ignoring the deep-seated racism in white society. It is freeing the racist of racism by making him confront blacks as men. Reconciliation has nothing to do with the "let's talk about it" attitude, or "it takes time" attitude. It merely says, "Look man, the revolution is on. Whose side are you on?"

The Church is also a fellowship *(koinonia).* This means that the Church must be in its own community what it preaches and what it seeks to accomplish in the world. Through the preaching of the Word, the Church calls the world to be responsible to God's act in Christ, and through its service it seeks to bring it about. But the Church's preaching and service are meaningful only insofar as the Church itself is a manifestation of the preached Word. As Harvey Cox puts it, *koinonia* is "that aspect of the church's responsibility . . . which calls for a visible demonstration of what the church is saying in its kerygma and pointing to in its diakonia."[11] Thus the Church, by definition, contains no trace of racism. Christ "has broken down the dividing walls of hostility" (Eph. 2:14). That is why Karl Barth describes the Church as "God's subjective realization of the atonement."[12]

It is this need to be the sign of the Kingdom in the world which impels the Church continually to ask: "Who in the community does not live according to the spirit of Christ?" This is the kind of question which was so important to the sixteenth-century Anabaptists, and it must be vital for the Church of any age. Speaking to this question, Barth says: "The church which is not deeply disturbed by it is not a Christian church."[13] It cannot be "Christ existing as community" or "Christ's presence in history," as Bonhoeffer would put it, without being seriously concerned about the holiness of its members.

It is true that this concern may cause the community to ask the wrong questions. It may focus on irrelevancies (smoking, dancing, drinking, etc.) rather than on the essential (racism). But it is only through the asking of the question, "What makes men Christians?" that the true Church is able to be Christ in the world. The true Church of Christ must define clearly through its members the meaning of God's act in Christ so that all may know what the Church is up to. There can be no doubt in the minds of its members regarding the nature of its community and its purpose in the world. It must be a community that has accepted Christ's acceptance of us, and in this sense, it must be holy. At all times and in all situations holy members of the holy church, and therefore Christians, were and are the men assembled in it who are thereto elected by the Lord, called by His Word, and constituted by His Spirit: just so many, no more and no less, these men and no others.[14]

The White Church and Black Power

If the real Church is the people of God, whose primary task is that of being Christ to the world by proclaiming the message of the gospel (*kerygma*), by rendering services of liberation *(diakonia)*, and by being itself a manifestation of the nature of the new society *(koinonia)*, then the empirical institution-alized white church has failed on all counts. It certainly has not rendered services of reconciliation to the poor. Rather, it illustrates the values of a sick society which oppresses the poor. Some present-day theologians, like Hamilton and Altizer, taking their cue from Nietzsche and the present irrelevancy of the Church to modern man, have announced the death of God. It seems, however, that their chief mistake lies in their apparent identification of God's reality with the signed-up Christians. If we were to identify the work of God with the white church, then, like Altizer, we must "will the death of God with a passion of faith." Or as Camus would say, "If God *did* exist, we should have to abolish him."

The white church has not merely failed to render services to the poor, but has failed miserably in being a visible manifestation to the world of God's intention for humanity and in proclaiming the gospel to the world. It seems that the white church is not God's redemptive agent but, rather, an agent of the old society. It fails to create an atmosphere of radical obedience to Christ. Most church fellowships are more concerned about drinking or new buildings or Sunday closing than about children who die of rat bites or men who are killed because they want to be treated like men. The society is falling apart for want of moral leadership and moral example, but the white church passes innocuously pious resolutions and waits to be congratulated.

It is a sad fact that the white church's involvement in slavery and racism in America simply cannot be overstated. It not only failed to preach the kerygmatic Word but maliciously contributed to the doctrine of white supremacy. Even today all of the Church's institutions—including its colleges and universities—reveal its white racist character. Racism has been a part of the life of the Church so long that it is virtually impossible for even the "good" members to recognize the bigotry perpetuated by the Church. Its morals are so immoral that even its most sensitive minds are unable to detect the inhumanity of the Church on the black people of America. This is at least one of the suggestions by Kyle Haselden, who was in most cases a very perceptive white southern churchman:

> We must ask whether our morality is itself immoral, whether our codes of righteousness are, when applied to the Negro, a violation and distortion of the Christian ethic. Do we not judge what is right and what is wrong in racial relationships by a righteousness which is itself unrighteous, by codes and creeds which are themselves immoral?[15]

The question is asked and the answer is obvious to the astute observer. The Church has been guilty of the gravest sin of all—"the enshrining of that which is immoral as the highest morality."[16] Jesus called this the sin against the Holy Spirit. It is unforgivable because it is never recognized.

Pierre Berton puts it mildly:

> In . . . the racial struggle, there is revealed the same pattern of tardiness, apathy, non-commitment, and outright opposition by the church. . . . Indeed, the history of the race struggle in the United States has been to a considerable extent the history of the Protestant rapport with the status quo. From the beginning, it was the church that put its blessing on slavery and sanctioned a caste system that continues to this day.[17]

As much as white churchmen may want to hedge on this issue, it is not possible. The issue is clear: Racism is a complete denial of the Incarnation and thus of Christianity. Therefore, the white denominational churches are unchristian. They are a manifestation of both a willingness to tolerate it and a desire to perpetuate it.

The old philosophical distinction between the primary and secondary qualities of objects provides an analogy here, where only the primary qualities pertain to the essence of the thing. Regarding the Church, are not fellowship and service primary qualities, without which the "church" is not the Church? Can we still speak of a community as being Christian if that body is racist through and through? It is my contention that the racism implies the absence of fellowship and service, which are primary qualities, indispensable marks of the Church. To be racist is to fall outside the definition of the Church. In our time, the issue of racism is analogous to the Arian Controversy of the fourth century. Athanasius perceived quite clearly that if Arius' views were tolerated, Christianity would be lost. But few white churchmen have questioned whether racism was a similar denial of Jesus Christ. Even Haselden, certainly one of the most sensitive of the white churchmen who have written on the subject, can speak of white Christian racists.

If there is any contemporary meaning of the Antichrist (or "the principalities and powers"), the white church seems to be a manifestation of it. It is the enemy of Christ. It was the white "Christian" church which took the lead in establishing slavery as an institution and segregation as a pattern in society by sanctioning all-white congregations. As Frank Loescher pointed out, its very existence as an institution is a symbol of the "philosophy of white supremacy."[18] "Long before the little signs—'White Only' and 'Colored'—appeared in the public utilities they had appeared in the church."[19] Haselden shows clearly the work of the Church in setting the pattern which later became general law for all of America:

> First came the segregation of the Negro within the church; then followed the separation of the churches by the "spontaneous" withdrawal of the Negro Christians; much later, the elaborate patterns of segregation were to arise in the church and in secular society.[20]

With its all-white congregations, it makes racism a respectable attitude. By remaining silent it creates an ethos which dehumanizes blacks. It is the Church which preaches that blacks are inferior to whites—if not by *word*, certainly by "moral" example.

In the old slavery days, the Church preached that slavery was a divine decree, and it used the Bible as the basis of its authority.

> Not only did the Christianity fail to offer the Negro hope of freedom in this world, but the manner in which Christianity was communicated to him tended to degrade him. The Negro was taught that his enslavement was due to the fact that he had been cursed by God. His very color was a sign of the curse which he had received as a descendant of Ham. Parts of the Bible were carefully selected to prove that God had intended that the Negro should be the servant of the white man and that he would always be a "hewer of wood and a drawer of water."[21]

Several ministers even wrote books justifying slavery. "It may be," wrote

George D. Armstrong in *The Christian Doctrine of Slavery,* "that *Christian* slavery is God's solution of the problem [relation of labor and capital] about which the wisest statesmen of Europe confess themselves at fault."[22] In another book, *Slavery Ordained of God*, Fred A. Ross wrote that "slavery is ordained of God, . . . to continue for the good of the slave, the good of the master, the good of the whole American family, until another and better destiny may be unfolded."[23]

Today that same Church sets the tone for the present inhumanity to blacks by remaining silent as blacks are killed for wanting to be treated like human beings. Like other segments of this society, the Church emphasizes obedience to the law of the land without asking whether the law is racist in character or without even questioning the everyday deadly violence which laws and law enforcers inflict on blacks in the ghetto. They are quick to condemn Black Power as a concept and the violence in the ghetto without saying a word about white power and its 350 years of constant violence against blacks. It was the Church which placed God's approval on slavery and today places his blessings on the racist structure of American society. As long as whites can be sure that God is on their side, there is potentially no limit to their violence against anyone who threatens the American racist way of life. Genocide is the logical conclusion of racism. It happened to the American Indian, and there is ample reason to believe that America is prepared to do the same to blacks.

Many writers have shown the Church's vested interest in slavery and racism in America.[24] At first the "white Christian" questioned the Christianizing of the slave because of the implications of equality in the Bible and because of the fear that education might cause the slave to fight for his freedom. Slave masters at first forbade the baptism of slaves on the ground that it was an invasion of their property rights. But the churchmen assured them that there was no relationship between Christianity and freedom in civil matters. In the words of the Bishop of London:

> Christianity, and the embracing of the Gospel, does not make the least Alteration in Civil property, or in any of the Duties which belong to Civil Relations; but in all these Respects, it continues Persons just in the same State as it found them. The Freedom which Christianity gives, is a Freedom from the Bondage of Sin and Satan, and from the Dominion of Men's Lust and Passions and inordinate Desires; but as to their outward Condition, whatever that was before, whether bond or free, their being baptized and becoming Christians, makes no matter of Change in it.[25]

In fact some churchmen argued that Christianity made blacks better slaves. When slaves began to get rebellious about their freedom, according to a Methodist missionary, "it was missionary influence that moderated their passions, kept them in the steady course of duty, and prevented them from

sinning against God by offending against the laws of man. Whatever out-
breaks or insurrections at any time occurred, no Methodist slave was ever
proved guilty of incendiarism or rebellion for more than seventy years,
namely from 1760 to 1833."[26]

Many ministers even owned slaves. In 1844, 200 Methodist traveling
preachers owned 1,600 slaves, and 1,000 local preachers owned 10,000
slaves. This fact alone indicates the white Methodist Church's tolerance and
propagation of the slave system. There is no evidence that it saw any real
contradiction between slavery and essential Christianity.

Some northern white Methodist churchmen would probably remind me
that the Church split precisely over that issue in 1844. This seems to suggest
that at least the north was against slavery. If the north was against slavery, it
nevertheless had no intention of viewing blacks as men. Northern churchmen are reminded that it was in their section of the country that "free
Negroes" seceded from various white churches because of intolerable
humiliation by whites. It was northerners who pulled Richard Allen and his
companions from their knees as they knelt at prayer at St. George's
Methodist Episcopal Church in Philadelphia. "We all went out of the church
in a body," wrote Allen, "and they were no more plagued with us in the
church."[27] There is no evidence at all that the north was more humane than
the south in its treatment of blacks in the churches. The north could appear to
be more concerned about the blacks because of their work toward the
abolition of slavery. But the reason is clear: Slavery was not as vital to their
economy as it was to the south's.

Some southern churchmen might argue that the Church in the pre-civil
War days was indeed a real expression of their concern for blacks. It was an
integrated Church! Surprisingly, H. Richard Niebuhr suggests that the worship of white and black people together was an indication that the great
revival and the democratic doctrines of the Revolution which fostered the
sense of equality had "pricked the conscience of the churches on the subject
of slavery."[28]

> White and black worshipped together and, at their best, sought to
> realize the brotherhood Jesus had practiced and Paul had preached.
> There were many significant exceptions, it is true. But the general rule
> was that the two races should be united in religion. . . . In the Methodist
> and Baptist churches, . . . it was the conviction of the essential equality
> of all souls before God which inspired the white missionary and an
> occasional master to share the benefits of the common gospel in a
> common church with members of the other race.[29]

Apparently, Niebuhr's identity with the oppressor got the best of his theological and sociological analysis. For it is clear that "integration" was a practice
in the southern churches because, as Niebuhr himself says, it was "the
less of two evils." It was dangerous to the slave system to allow slaves to

have independent uncontrolled churches. The abolitionist activity in the northern black churches and the Nat Turner revolt of 1831 reaffirmed this fear. Laws were even passed which prevented the education of blacks and the assembly of more than five blacks without white supervision. Rather than being a demonstration of brotherhood or equality, the "integration" in the churches was a means of keeping a close watch on blacks. Haselden is right about the Church. It was and is the "mother of racial patterns," the "purveyor of arrant sedatives," and the "teacher of immoral moralities."

The Quakers were the only denominational group which showed any signs of radical obedience to Christ. Its leaders, George Fox and George Keith, declared clearly the contradiction between slavery and the gospel of Christ. An example of the Quaker view of slavery is illustrated by the resolution of 1688, passed in Germantown:

> Now tho' they are black, we cannot conceive there is more liberty to have them slaves, as it is to have other white ones. There is a saying, that we shall doe to all men, like as we will be done our selves: macking no difference of what generation, descent, or Colour they are. And those who steal or robb men, and those who buy or purchase them, are they not all alicke? Here is liberty of Conscience, wch is right and reasonable, here ought to be lickewise liberty of the body, except of evildoers, wch is an other case. But to bring men hither, or to robb and sell them against their will, we stand against.[30]

It is unfortunate that such men were in the minority even among the Quakers. There was the temptation to let economics, rather than religion, determine one's actions. The Quakers, like most groups who could afford it, owned slaves. But the spirit of freedom and liberty in civil matters was at least the concern of some Quakers, which is more than can be said of others.

In light of this history it is not surprising that the white churchmen have either condemned Black Power, or, as is more often the case, joined the other silent intellectuals in our colleges and universities. They have never championed black freedom. During the most fervent period of lynching,[31] the Church scarcely said a word against it. Loetscher's study of the twenty-five major denominations comprising the Federal Council of Churches of Christ in America shows that until 1929 most churches scarcely uttered a word about white inhumanity toward blacks. In fact, Gunnar Myrdal pointed out, "Methodist and Baptist preachers were active in reviving the Ku Klux Klan after the First World War."[32] There is little question that the Church has been and is a racist institution, and there is little sign that she even cares about it.

> So far as the major denominations are concerned, it is the story of indifference, vacillation, and duplicity. . . . It is a history in which the church not only compromised its ethic to the mood and practice of the

times but was itself actively unethical, sanctioning the enslavement of human beings, producing the patterns of segregation, urging upon the oppressed Negro the extracted sedatives of the Gospel, and promulgating a doctrine of interracial morality which is itself immoral.[33]

Some churchmen probably would want to point out their "unselfish involvement" in the civil rights struggle of the 1950's and 1960's. It was a black man, Martin Luther King, Jr., who challenged the conscience of this nation by his unselfish giving of his time and eventually his life for the poor blacks and whites of America. During the initial stages of his civil-disobedience campaign, most white churchmen stood silently by and criticized with their political cohorts. And most who eventually joined him in his work were "Johnnies-come-lately." Even here their participation reminds one of the white churchmen of the pre-Civil War era. As long as the south was the target, northern churchmen could assure themselves that it was a southern problem, totally unrelated to their own northern parishes. Most thus came to think of themselves as missionaries for Christ in a foreign land. But when King brought his work north, many retreated and complained that he was confusing politics with religion. King only regained his popularity among northern churchmen after the emergence of the concept of Black Power. They came to view King's nonviolence as the less of two evils. I am convinced that King's death was due to an ethos created by the white church, which permits whites to kill blacks at will without any fear of reprisal. Few white men have been convicted and imprisoned for slaying a black or a white involved in civil rights.

Since the emergence of the recent rebellion in the cities, it seems that the most the white churches do is to tell blacks to obey the law of the land. Occasionally, a church body passes a harmless resolution. Imagine, men dying of hunger, children maimed from rat bites, women dying of despair—and the Church passes a resolution. Perhaps it is impossible to prevent riots, but one can fight against the conditions which cause them. The white church is placed in question because of its contribution to a structure which produces riots. Some churchmen may reply: "We do condemn the deplorable conditions which produce urban riots. We do condemn racism and all the evils arising from it." But to the extent that this is true, the Church, with the exception of a few isolated individuals, voices its condemnation in the style of resolutions that are usually equivocal and almost totally unproductive. If the condemnation was voiced, it was not understood! The Church should speak in a style which avoids abstractions. Its language must be backed up with relevant involvement in the affairs of people who suffer. It must be a grouping whose community life and personal involvement are coherent with its language about the gospel.

The Church does not appear to be a community willing to pay up personally. It is not a community which views every command of Jesus as a call to the cross. It appears, instead, as an institution whose existence depends on the evils which produce the riots in the cities. With this in mind, we must say that when a minister condemns the rioters and blesses by silence the conditions which produce the riots, he gives up his credentials as a Christian minister and becomes inhuman. He is an animal, just like those who, backed by an ideology of racism, order the structure of this society on the basis of white supremacy. We need men who refuse to be animals and are resolved to pay the price, so that all men can be something more than animals.

Whether Black Power advocates are that grouping, we will have to wait and see. But the Church has shown many times that it loves life and is not prepared to die for others. It has not really gone where the action is with a willingness to die for the neighbor, but has remained aloof from the sufferings of men. It is a chaplaincy to sick middle-class egos. It stands (or sits) condemned by its very whiteness.

This leads one to conclude that Christ is operating outside the denominational white church. The real Church of Christ is that grouping which identifies with the suffering of the poor by becoming one with them. While we should be careful in drawing the line, the line must nevertheless be drawn. The Church includes not only the Black Power community but all men who view their humanity as inextricably related to every man. It is that grouping with a demonstrated willingness to die for the prevention of the torture of others, saying with Bonhoeffer, "When Christ calls a man, he bids him come and die."

Is there any hope for the white church? Hope is dependent upon whether it will ask from the depths of its being with God: "What must I do to be saved?" The person who seriously asks that question is a person capable of receiving God's forgiveness. It is time for the white church to ask that question with a willingness to do all for Christ. Like the Philippian jailers who put the question to St. Paul, the answer is the same for the white church as it was to them: *Repent*, and believe on the Lord and Saviour Jesus Christ! There is no other way. It must own that it has been and is a racist institution whose primary purpose is the perpetuation of white supremacy. But it is not enough to be sorry or to admit wrong. To repent involves change in one's whole being. In the Christian perspective, it means conversion.

Speaking of Jesus' understanding of repentance, Bornkamm says: It means "to lay hold on the salvation which is already at hand, and to give up everything for it."[34] This involves a willingness to renounce self and the world and to grasp the gift of salvation now here in Jesus Christ. But there is no repentance without obedience and there is no obedience without action. And this is always action in the world with Christ fighting the evils which hold men captive.

For the white churches this means a radical reorientation of their style in the world toward blacks. It means that they must change sides, giving up all claims to lofty neutrality. It means that they will identify utterly with the oppressed, thus inevitably tasting the sting of oppression themselves. It means that they will no longer "stand silently or march weakly protesting" but will join the advocates of Black Power in their unambiguous identification "with the oppressed and with the revolutions made by the oppressed."[35] A racist pattern has been set, and the Church has been a contributor to the pattern. Now it must break that pattern by placing its life at stake.

Black Power and American Theology

In a culture which rewards "patriots" and punishes "dissenters," it is difficult to be prophetic and easy to perform one's duties in the light of the objectives of the nation as a whole. This was true for the state church of Germany during the Third Reich, and it is true now of the white church in America as blacks begin to question seriously their place in this society. It is always much easier to point to the good amid the evil as a means of rationalizing one's failure to call into question the evil itself. It is easier to identify with the oppressor as he throws sops to the poor than to align oneself with the problems of the poor as he endures oppression. Moreover, the moral and religious implications of any act of risk are always sufficiently cloudy to make it impossible to be certain of right action. Because man is finite, he can never reach that state of security in which he is free of anxiety when he makes moral decisions. This allows the irresponsible religious man to grasp a false kind of religious and political security by equating law and order with Christian morality. If someone calls his attention to the inhumanity of the political system toward others, he can always explain his loyalty to the state by suggesting that this system is the least evil of any other existing political state. He can also point to the lack of clarity regarding the issues, whether they concern race relations or the war in Vietnam. This will enable him to compartmentalize the various segments of the societal powers so that he can rely on other disciplines to give the word on the appropriate course of action. This seems to characterize the style of many religious thinkers as they respond to the race problem in America.

Therefore, it is not surprising that the sickness of the Church in America is also found in the main stream of American religious thought. As with the Church as a whole, theology remains conspicuously silent regarding the place of the black man in American society. In the history of modern American theology, there are few dissenters on black slavery and the current black oppression among the teachers and writers of theology. And those who do speak are usually unclear. Too often their comments are but a replica of the current cultural ethos, drawing frequently from nontheological disciplines for the right word on race relations.

More often, however, theologians simply ignore the problem of color in America. Any theologian involved in professional societies can observe that few have attempted to deal seriously with the problem of racism in America.

It is much easier to deal with the textual problems associated with some biblical book or to deal "objectively" with a religious phenomenon than it is to ask about the task of theology in the current disintegration of society. It would seem that it is time for theology to make a radical break with its identity with the world by seeking to bring to the problem of color the revolutionary implications of the gospel of Christ. It is time for theology to leave its ivory tower and join the real issues, which deal with dehumanization of blacks in America. It is time for theologians to relate their work to life-and-death issues, and in so doing to execute its function of bringing the Church to a recognition of its task in the world.

For the sickness of the Church in America is intimately involved with the bankruptcy of American theology. When the Church fails to live up to its appointed mission, it means that theology is partly responsible. Therefore, it is impossible to criticize the Church and its lack of relevancy without criticizing theology for its failure to perform its function.

Theology functions within the Church. Its task is to make sure that the "church" is the Church. The mission of the Church is to announce and to act out the gospel it has received. When the Church fails in its appointed task by seeking to glorify itself rather than Jesus Christ, it is the job of theology to remind her what the true Church is, for theology is that discipline which has the responsibility of continually examining the proclamation of the Church in the light of Jesus Christ. "Dogmatic theology is the scientific test to which the Christian church puts herself regarding the language about God which is peculiar to her."[36] The task of theology, then, is to criticize and revise the language of the Church. This includes not only language as uttered speech but the language of radical involvement in the world. The Church not only speaks of God in "worship" but as it encounters the world with the gospel of Jesus Christ. It is the task of theology to make sure that the Church's thoroughly human speech, whether word or deed, agrees with the essence of the Church, that is, with Jesus Christ who is "God in his gracious approach to man in revelation and reconciliation."[37]

The Church cannot remain aloof from the world because Christ is in the world. Theology, then, if it is to serve the need of the Church must become "worldly theology." This means that it must make sure that the Church is in the world and that its word and deed are harmonious with Jesus Christ. It must make sure that the Church's language about God is relevant to every new generation and its problems. It is for this reason that the definitive theological treatise can never be written. Every generation has its own problems, as does every nation. Theology is not, then, an intellectual exercise but a worldly risk.

American theology has failed to take that worldly risk. It has largely ignored its domestic problems on race. It has not called the Church to be involved in confronting this society with the meaning of the Kingdom in the light of Christ. Even though it says, with Tillich, that theology "is supposed to satisfy two basic needs: the statement of the truth of the Christian message and the interpretation of this truth for every new generation,"[38] it has virtually ignored the task of relating the truth of the gospel to the problem of race in America. The lack of a relevant, risky theological statement suggests that theologians, like others, are unable to free themselves from the structures of this society.

The close identity of American theology with the structures of society may also account for the failure to produce theologians comparable in stature to Europeans like Bultmann, Barth, and Bonhoeffer. Some try to account for this by pointing to the youth of America; but that seems an insufficient explanation, since other disciplines appear to hold their own. The real reasons are immensely complex. But one cogent explanation is that most American theologians are too closely tied to the American structure to respond creatively to the life situation of the Church in this society. Instead of seeking to respond to the problems which are unique to this country, most Americans look to Europe for the newest word worth theologizing about. Most graduate students in theology feel that they must go to Germany or somewhere else in Europe because that is where things are happening in the area of theology. Little wonder that American theology is predominantly "footnotes on the Germans." Theology here is largely an intellectual game unrelated to the issues of life and death. It is impossible to respond creatively and prophetically to the life-situational problems of society without identifying with the problems of the disinherited and unwanted in society. Few American theologians have made that identification with the poor blacks in America but have themselves contributed to the system which enslaves black people. The seminaries in America are probably the most obvious sign of the irrelevance of theology to life. Their initiative in responding to the crisis of black people in America is virtually unnoticeable. Their curriculum generally is designed for young white men and women who are preparing to serve all-white churches. Only recently have seminaries sought to respond to the black revolution by reorganizing their curriculum to include courses in "black studies" and inner-city involvements; and this is due almost exclusively to the insistence of black students. Most seminaries still have no courses in black church history and their faculties and administrators are largely white. This alone gives support to the racist assumption that blacks are unimportant.

In Europe the situation seems to be somewhat different. Karl Barth's theology was born in response to the political and economic crisis of Germany. He began his career as a liberal theologian; he believed that the Kingdom of God would soon be achieved through the establishment of a socialist society. He put his confidence in the latent resources of humanity; and this meant that Barth, along with many liberal theologians of his day, believed in the adequacy of the religious man, the adequacy of religion, and the security of the culture and civilization. The First World War shattered his hope of the Kingdom of God on earth. The "civilized man" who was supposed to be moving steadily, even rapidly, toward perfection had cast himself into an orgy of destruction. In the wake of the war came Communism and Fascism, both of which denied Christian values. As a result of the war and its aftermath, Barth felt that the problem of man was much more desperate than most people realized and would not be solved simply by changing the economic structure. For a while Barth was in a state of shock. In particular he was burdened with the task of declaring the Christian message to his congregation every Sunday. What could he say? People did not want to hear, he was quite sure, his own man-made philosophy or his own opinions.

In due time Barth was led from his anthropocentric conception of Christianity to a thoroughgoing theocentric conception. He was led from trust in man to complete trust in God alone. He was convinced that he could not identify God's Word with man's word. No human righteousness can be equated with divine righteousness; no human act can be synonymous with God's act. Even the so-called good which man does in this world counts as nothing in God's eyes. To identify God's righteousness with human righteousness is to fail to see the "infinite qualitative distinction" between God and man, the distinction between what is human and what is divine.

This radical change in Barth's theological perspective had nothing to do with abstract theological thinking but with his confrontation with the political, economic, and social situation of Germany. It was the rise of a new political order that caused Barth to launch a devastating and relentless attack on natural theology. When American theologians picked up the problem, they apparently did so without really knowing that for Barth and his sympathizers the natural theology issue was not merely an intellectual debate but an event, an event about the life and death of men. Observing the rise of Hitler during the 1930's, Barth saw clearly the danger of identifying man's word with God's Word. To say that God's Word is wholly unlike man's word means that God stands in judgment against all political systems. The work of the state can never be identified or confused with God's Word. In Hitler's campaign against the Jews, an alien god dominated Germany; men were being slaughtered on his altar. It was no time for caution or lofty "objectivity." When Barth said "Nein!"—no natural theology, no blending of the Word of God and the word of man—the *political* implication was clear: Hitler is the Antichrist; God has set his face against the Third Reich.

Americans have generally agreed that Barth's rejection of natural theology was a mistake. Is that because American theologians still see a close relationship between the structures of this society and Christianity? As long as there is no absolute difference between God and man, it is possible to view America as the "land of the free and the home of the brave," despite the oppression of blacks. As long as theology is identified with the system, it is impossible to criticize it by bringing the judgment of God's righteousness upon it.

Barth's theology may serve as an example of how to relate theology to life. The whole of his theology represents a constant attempt to engage the Church in life situations. Its notable development (compare *Romans* with *The Humanity of God*) is clearly a response to the new problems which men face in worldly involvement.

If American theology is going to serve the needs of the Church by relating the gospel to the political, economic, and social situation of America, it must cut its adoring dependence upon Europe as the place to tell us what theology ought to be talking about. Some European theologians, like Barth and Bonhoeffer, may serve as examples of how to relate theology to life, but not in defining *our* major issues.

There is a need for a theology of revolution, a theology which radically encounters the problems of the disinherited black people in America in particular and the oppressed people of color throughout the world in general. As Joseph Washington puts it:

> In the twentieth century white Protestantism has concentrated its personnel, time, energy, and finances on issues that it has deemed more significant than the "American Dilemma": pacifism, politics, liberal versus conservative controversies, prohibition, socialism, Marxism, labor and management aspects of economic justice, civil liberties, totalitarianism, overseas mission, fascism, war and peace, reorganization of ecclesiastical structures, and ecumenical issues.[39]

It has overlooked the unique problem of the powerless blacks.

In this new era of Black Power, the era in which blacks are sick of white power and are prepared to do anything and give everything for freedom now, theology cannot afford to be silent. Not to speak, not to "do theology" around this critical problem, is to say that the black predicament is not crucial to Christian faith. At a moment when blacks are determined to stand up as human beings even if they are shot down, the Word of the cross certainly is focused upon them. Will no one speak that Word to the dead and dying? Theologians confronted by this question may distinguish three possible responses. Some will, timidly or passionately, continue to appeal (mistakenly) to Paul's dictum about the "powers that be." We will have law-and-order theologians as we have law-and-order pastors and laymen. Others will insist that theology as such is necessarily unrelated to social upheaval. These men will continue as in a vacuum, writing footnotes on the Aramaic substratum of Mark's Gospel or on the authorship of the *Theologia Germanica* or on the "phenomenon" of faith. Could a black man hope that there are still others who, *as theologians*, will join the oppressed in their fight for freedom? These theologians will speak unequivocally of revelation, Scripture, God, Christ, grace, faith, Church, ministry, and hope, so that the message comes through loud and clear: *The black revolution is the work of Christ.*

If theology fails to re-evaluate its task in the light of Black Power, the emphasis on the death of God will not add the needed dimension. This will mean that the white church and white theology are dead, not God. It will mean that God will choose another means of implementing his word of righteousness in the world. It will mean also that the burden of the gospel is placed solely on the shoulders of the oppressed, without any clear word from the "church." This leads us to our last concern, the black church. It is indeed possible that the only redemptive forces left in the denominational churches are to be found in the segregated black churches.

The white response so far, in and out of the Church, is, "Not yet," which in the twisted rhetoric of the land of the free means, "Never!" "Law and order" is the sacred incantation of the priests of the old order; and the faithful respond with votes, higher police budgets, and Gestapo legislation. Private and public arsenals of incredible destructive force testify to the determination of a sick and brutal people to put an end to black revolution and indeed to black people. The black man has violated the conditions under which he is permitted to breathe, and the air is heavy with the potential for genocide. The confrontation of black people as real persons is so strange and out of harmony with the normal pattern of white behavior that most whites cannot even begin to understand the meaning of black humanity.

In this situation of revolution and reaction, the Church must decide where its identity lies. Will it continue its chaplaincy to the forces of oppression, or will it embrace the cause of liberation, proclaiming in word and deed the gospel of Christ?

Notes

1. See their *Black Power: The Politics of Liberation in America* (New York: Random House, 1967).

2. Some biblical scholars identify the call of Abraham as the beginning of the Church, but this involves critical-historical problems that are not pertinent here. As far as Israel's awareness of herself as an elect people is concerned, few authorities would fail to place the beginning at the exodus and wilderness experiences.

3. For an analysis of the relationship between *qahal* and *ekklesia* see J. Robert Nelson, *The Realm of Redemption* (New York: Seabury Press, 1951), pp. 3–19.

4. Bonhoeffer, *Prisoner for God*, ed. Eberhard Bethge, trans. R. H. Fuller (New York: Macmillan Co., 1953), pp. 166–167. Used with permission.

5. Cox, *The Secular City* (New York: Macmillan Co., 1965), p. 145.

6. Cullmann, *Christ and Time*, trans. F. V. Filson (Philadelphia: Westminster Press, 1949).

7. Lewis, *The Johannine Epistles* (London: Epworth Press, 1961), p. 84.

8. Ibid.

9. Hordern, *Christianity, Communism and History* (London: Lutterworth Press, 1957), p. 27.

10. Quoted in Cox, *Secular City*, p. 126.

11. Ibid., p. 144.

12. Barth, *Church Dogmatics*, Vol. IV, Part I, trans. G. Bromiley (Edinburgh: T. & T. Clark, 1956), p. 643.

13. Ibid., p. 695.

14. Ibid., p. 696.

15. Haselden, *The Racial Problem in Christian Perspective* (New York: Harper & Row, 1959), p. 48.

16. Ibid.

17. Berton, *The Comfortable Pew* (Philadelphia: J. B. Lippincott Co., 1965), pp. 28–29.

18. Loescher, *The Protestant Church and the Negro, a Pattern of Segregation* (New York: Association Press, 1948), p. 9.

19. Haselden, *The Racial Problem,* p. 29.

20. Ibid.

21. E. Franklin Frazier, *Black Bourgeoisie* (New York: Collier Books, 1965), p. 115. Used with permission.

22. Quoted in ibid., p. 115.

23. Ibid.

24. See Washington, *Black Religion* (1964) and *Politics of God* (1967), both published by Beacon Press; H. Richard Niebuhr, *The Social Sources of Denominationalism* (Cleveland: Meridian Books, 1929); Haselden, *The Racial Problem;* E. Franklin Frazier, *The Negro Church in America* (New York: Schocken Books, 1963).

25. Quoted in Niebuhr, *Social Sources of Denominationalism,* p. 249.

26. Ibid., p. 251.

27. Ibid., p. 260.

28. Ibid., p. 244.

29. Ibid., pp. 247–248.

30. Shelton Smith, Robert Handy, and Lefferts Loetscher, *American Christianity,* Vol. I (New York: Charles Scribner's Sons, 1960), p. 181.

31. See Ralph Ginzburg, *One Hundred Years of Lynching* (New York: Lancer Books, 1962).

32. Myrdal, *An American Dilemma: The Negro Problem and Modern Democracy* (New York: Harper & Brothers, 1944), p. 563.

33. Haselden, *The Racial Problem,* p. 63. Used with permission.

34. Bornkamm, *Jesus of Nazareth,* p. 82.

35. Harding, "The Religion of Black Power," in *Religious Situation,* p. 12.

36. Barth, *Church Dogmatics,* Vol. I, Part 1, p. 1.

37. Ibid., p. 3.

38. Tillich, *Systematic Theology,* Vol. I (Chicago: University of Chicago Press, 1951).

39. J. Washington, *Black Religion,* p. 228.

PART III

BLACK THEOLOGY
AND THE RESPONSE
OF WHITE THEOLOGIANS

INTRODUCTION

Since the publication of *Black Theology and Black Power* (1969) and other books and articles on Black Theology arising out of the civil rights and Black Power movements, North American white theologians have found it increasingly more difficult to ignore the question, "What has the gospel to do with oppressed Blacks in their struggle for liberation?" Before the emergence of the literature of Black Theology, Black people's invisibility in White theological deliberation was not challenged. Whether one speaks of liberal or conservative, neo-orthodox or secular theologians, the oppression of Black people did not represent a high priority on their theological agenda. Even when these White theologians spoke of "social salvation" (John Bennett)[1] and the "politics of God" (Paul Lehmann)[2] in the social environment of lynchings, legal segregation, and the civil rights movement (all of which were preceded by 250 years of legal slavery), they remained either conspicuously silent about the oppression of Black people or mentioned it only as an incidental theological comment. In no case did they seek to engage in a meaningful dialogue with Black history and religion on the assumption that Black people might provide some theological insight into the search for a contemporary understanding of the gospel. They apparently assumed that all new theological ideas came from Europe (especially Germany!), because that is where they concentrated most of their intellectual endeavors.

White seminary and university professors seldom used books written by Black people as required reading or even referred to Black religious history as an appropriate object for serious intellectual study. This failure is especially surprising since Martin Luther King, Jr., and the civil rights movement occupied such a visible place in the news media. Black students often raised the issue about the *theological* silence on the Black struggle for freedom and were usually rebuffed gently but firmly. Most White professors seemed surprised that Black students thought the Black experience worthy of serious theological inquiry.

The theological blindness of White professors in relation to the Black experience did not mean that they were consciously and intentionally racist. Only a few were blatantly racists; most were cordial and considerate. Some were even genuinely sympathetic to this Black concern but confused about what to do concerning it. But the issue, from the perspective of Black students, was not whether White professors were concerned about the political plight of Black people. Rather, it was whether they were prepared to

135

rethink the assumptions that defined their understanding of the theological task. Most White professors were not prepared to entertain that kind of radical questioning.

For whatever reason, it is a sad fact that all White seminaries ignored the Black experience as a serious object of theological reflection and neglected to define the theological task in terms supportive of justice and equality for Black people. One of the best indicators of this blindness of White professional theologians in relation to the Black experience was their failure to encourage and support Black doctoral students and to invite the best ones to return to their faculties. Only a few Black students could expect to be accepted into a doctoral program, and almost none could have any hope of becoming a professor at a major White seminary. George Kelsey (Drew), Charles Long (University of Chicago), Grant Shockely (Garrett), and Nathan Scott (University of Chicago) were exceptions.

The failure of White professional theologians to respond to the Black struggle for justice is even more surprising when one considers the involvement of the White Church. As early as the 1950s many White churches could no longer remain indifferent to Black oppression, because Martin Luther King, Jr., and other Black ministers reminded them that the 11:00 A.M. Sunday hour was still the most segregated hour of the nation. The civil rights movement, with sit-ins, marches, and other public demonstrations (sometimes in White churches), made it very difficult for White pastors and their congregations to ignore the implication of the gospel for Black people's struggle for justice. But White theologians tended to remain in the ivory tower of their scholarly research and seldom tried to relate it to oppressed Black people.

The White theological establishment began to respond to the Black struggle for justice in the late 1960s and early 1970s, after many of their seminaries were taken over by Black students in the context of urban insurrections, Black Power, and James Forman's Black Manifesto. With an increasing body of literature on Black Theology (including such authors as J. Deotis Roberts, Gayraud Wilmore, and William Jones), it became difficult for White professors to ignore the theological relevance of the Black experience. Slowly some White theologians began to respond to Black Theology in their writings. But the majority remained adamant in their silence, because they contended that theology is concerned with the *universal* dimension in the gospel, which transcends the particularities of the Black experience. The particular concerns of Black people, they contended, were at best an *ethical* problem or even a *pastoral* problem and thus more appropriately belonged in the "practical" department.

One of the first persons to challenge this assumption in a White theological context was J. Deotis Roberts. In an essay ("The Black Caucus and the Failure of Christian Theology"[3]) presented at the October 1968 meeting of the American Academy of Religion, Roberts defined his task as that of analyzing the "Black Caucus" trend in White churches as a *theological* issue. Most were not prepared to take Roberts seriously. But Roberts refused to be dismissed so easily and thus insisted on the *theological* relevance of the Black experience.

Because White theologians were unprepared for the appearance of Black Theology, most needed to be reeducated on how to deal with it in their classrooms. This task was undertaken by a committee of Black theologians, under the leadership of Charles Shelby Rooks, and was sponsored by the American Association of Theological Schools. After an extended period of study by this committee and a conference at Howard University with White seminary deans and professors, the results of both were published by *Theological Education* (1971).[4] At the Howard University conference, there was much resistance by White theologians when we insisted that the Black experience was relevant for theological education. Their resistance is partly the reason why this event did not produce as many changes in theological education as we had hoped and also why it has seldom been referred to in theological seminaries.

The change in attitude of most White professors regarding the relevance of Black Theology has been slow and due largely to the presence of a significant group of Black students and faculty in the seminary community. When no Black person served on the seminary faculty, Black students often insisted that they hire one or suffer the consequences of a disrupted seminary life.[5] After encountering the hostility of Black students, most seminary administrators began to realize that hiring a Black professor was not nearly as risky as they had previously envisioned.

My dialogue with White theologians on Black Theology has occurred in several professional societies, as well as in many seminary and university contexts. Initially many White theologians took refuge in my highly publicized comment to Whites: "Keep your damn mouth closed. . . ."[6] Even though I understand better now why White theologians often retreated after hearing that remark, I make no apologies for having made it or for having made several other so-called intemperate remarks about White theologians, because I still think that the insurrections of Watts, Newark, and Detroit demanded it. I admit that I was an angry Black theologian who tended to be intemperate in my argument when measured by the reasoned style of White university and seminary professors. But I strongly felt that the reality of Black suffering did not provide the context for such reasoned arguments.

The reasoned and calm approaches to Black Theology by J. Deotis Roberts, Major Jones, and Gayraud Wilmore did not end the silence of White theologians. If some White theologians were put off by my militancy, why did they not engage in dialogue with Black theologians whose language was more congenial to their theological etiquette? The absence of any substantive dialogue of White theologians with other Black theologians seemed to suggest that my militancy was not the chief reason for their silence.

It is fortunate that some White theologians did not retreat in the face of Black militancy, but accepted it as a theological challenge. Why? Peter C. Hodgson gives this reason. "There is an authentic role [in the creation of Black Theology] only if white theologians sense their own survival to be at stake as well. I believe this to be the case, for American democracy cannot survive if liberation of blacks and other ethnic minorities is not completed."[7] Therefore Hodgson engages the themes of Black Theology in a book-length treatise, entitled *Children of Freedom* (1974). In a subsequent, larger volume entitled *New Birth of Freedom: A Theology of Bondage and Liberation*,[8] he develops further his dialogue with Black Theology.

One of the first White theologians to go on record regarding the importance of Black Theology for theology generally was Frederick Herzog. In his life and his writings, Herzog made it clear that Black Theology had something to say to White Theology which the latter dared not ignore if it wished to encounter the Word of God for our times. He suffered much isolation for his stand, because of the uncompromising way in which he stood his ground. His best-known work in this area is *Liberation Theology: Liberation in the Light of the Fourth Gospel* (Seabury, 1972). In addition to this book, he has written numerous articles[9] and was responsible for putting together a symposium on Black Theology which was published first in Germany (*Evangelische Theologie*, January–February 1974) and then in North America (*Union Seminary Quarterly Review*, Fall 1975).

Other North American White theologians who have written on the subject of Black Theology include Paul Lehmann,[10] Benjamin Reist,[11] G. Clarke Chapman, Jr.,[12] Glenn R. Bucher,[13] Rosemary Ruether,[14] and John Carey.[15] In addition to the so-called liberal theological response to Black Theology, a more conservative response is found in the May–June 1974 issue of *The Other Side*.

I have especially appreciated the dialogues with my colleagues at Union Seminary. I have participated in many jointly taught courses, and we have debated the differences in our theological perspectives. What I appreciated the most was our capacity to disagree on serious theological issues and still retain a respect for each other. In this context, I remember well the many public debates that occurred between Paul Lehmann and me. Some sense of our debates is reflected in his *Transfiguration of Politics*, my *God of the Oppressed*, and his article included in this volume.

Black Theology's dialogue with European theologians has occurred in the context of the World Council of Churches and especially in the Faith and Order Commission, where Gayraud Wilmore has made a major contribution. Deserving special mention was a consultation organized by the Faith and Order Commission and the Program to Combat Racism. Wilmore chaired the consultation and played a major role in writing the report that was published under the title *Racism in Theology and Theology against Racism*.[16] But even before this consultation, a theological symposium on Black Theology and Latin American Liberation Theology was held at the Ecumenical Centre at Geneva (May 1973) under the sponsorship of Unit III (Education and Renewal) and under the leadership of Archie LeMone, who then served as the youth coordinator. The intention of this symposium was to introduce Black and Latin American theologies of liberation to the European theological establishment. This symposium was later published in *Risk*[17] under the title "Incommunication." The incommunication was not so much between Black Theology and Latin Theology, as has been suggested, because the symposium was not designed for a dialogue between Latin and Black theologies. The incommunication happened between European theologians and the representatives of both Latin and Black theologies. Their difficulties with Black Theology were very similar to those expressed by White North Americans.

Fortunately, there were other European theologians who took Black Theology seriously. They include Jürgen Moltmann,[18] Henry Mottu,[19] Helmut Gollwitzer,[20] Bruno Chenu,[21] and George Casalis.[22] This dialogue has enabled Black theologians to broaden their perspectives and to challenge the global presuppositions of European theology.

The basic differences between Black and White theologians, in North America and Europe, stem from a radical difference in the economic, social, and political power of the communities from which our theologies arise. The initial move of White theologians was to minimize this point about the social determination of theological knowledge by appealing to the Bible, divine revelation, or a common humanity. Therefore our discussions centered on such topics as ideology, love and reconciliation, violence, and the place of reason in theology. I have learned much from these discussions and remain ever more firmly convinced that one's praxis in life inevitably shapes one's theological perceptions.

The articles included in this section represent some of the most serious responses to Black Theology by white theologians to appear in print. The articles by Lehmann, "Black Theology and 'Christian' Theology" (Document 14), and Gollwitzer, "Why Black Theology?" (Document 15), were written in response to an essay of mine entitled "Black Theology on Revolution, Violence and Reconciliation" and first appeared in the context of a symposium on Black Theology in *Evangelische Theologie* and the *Union Seminary Quarterly Review*. Jürgen Moltmann wrote the introduction for this dialogue, and other persons participating in it included C. Eric Lincoln and Herbert O. Edwards. This symposium is important because it represents the most significant conversation between White and Black theologians to appear in print. Gollwitzer's "Why Black Theology?" is perhaps the most substantial response that any European theologian has given to Black Theology. To my knowledge, the only possible exceptions are the articles by Henry Mottu and a book, *Dieu est Noir*, by Bruno Chenu.[23] While Gollwitzer's concern is similar to other White theologians (i.e., ideology, violence, etc.), he has carried them to such a deep level of theological analysis that no Black theologian can afford to ignore his challenge.

Paul Lehmann's "Black Theology and 'Christian' Theology" provides a similar challenge from the North American context. Similar questions are raised about violence and ideology. For persons interested in my response to Lehmann as well as to Gollwitzer, I refer them to my "Black Theology and Ideology: A Response to My Respondents," which is found in both *Evangelische Theologie* (January–February 1974) and the *Union Seminary Quarterly Review* (Fall 1975).

To understand the concerns of Lehmann and Gollwitzer, it is necessary to keep in mind the Barthian influence on their theological perspectives, especially at the point of ideology. I understand this concern because I too was influenced by Barth, a point that still troubles some of my Black colleagues in theology. But Lehmann and Gollwitzer are not narrow-minded Barthians and that is why I have learned much from their analyses. The way in which I identified God's revelation so unqualifiedly with Black people's struggle for freedom seemed to overlook the provisional identity of God's revelation with any political movement. Furthermore, my comments, on the one hand that "The fact that I am Black is my ultimate reality" and, on the other, that "Christianity begins and ends with the man Jesus" seemed to contradict each other. My starting point certainly needed clarification. My *God of the Oppressed* is an attempt to clarify some of these concerns. Of course, I knew the dangers involved and agreed with much of what Lehmann and Gollwitzer expressed in their analyses. But even more important to me at the time was the suffering of my community and the need to develop a theological perspective that took seriously God's empowerment of them for struggle. To caution them about the dangers of ideology as found in Nazism or North American White racism seemed inappropriate, especially in view of the powerlessness of the Black community and the social and political privilege of most White theologians. What gives White theologians the right to question Black people about the dangers of identifying God with a particular race of people? The sensitivity of Gollwitzer and Lehmann at this point enabled their dialogue with Black Theology to move to a much deeper level than usual among White theologians.

A similar comment could apply to other White theologians, especially John Bennett. His essay "Black Theology of Liberation" (Document 16) is included in his book entitled *The Radical Imperative* (1975). Aside from Reinhold Niebuhr and Paul Tillich, no North American theologian has made a greater impact on theological and ethical thinking than John Bennett. He was the president of Union Seminary when I was invited to teach there in 1969. Although he was sometimes bothered by militancy and my tendency to lump all White theologians into a racist category, he always encouraged my theological development and defended my right to speak according to the depths of my theological convictions. While his article reveals some of his concerns about Black Theology, it also shows his openness to listen to Black Theology and to learn from its perspective.

Paul Holmer has given one of the most provocative responses to Black Theology to have appeared in print. As a White liberal theologian, who was not prepared to define his scholarly interests in the light of Black people's struggle for justice, no one has been more critical of Black Theology than Paul Holmer. Despite his apparent insensitivity to racism in White theology, he is to be commended for speaking his mind. He represents a perspective that is widely held but seldom expressed. In an early essay, "Remarks Excerpted from 'The Crisis in Rhetoric,' " he suggested that Black theologians "are not free to violate the canon of exact reflection, careful weighing of evidence, and apt argument, if they want to make a case for other intellectually responsible listeners."[24] My *God of the Oppressed* was written partly in response to this type of criticism of Black Theology.[25] Apparently my response did not satisfy Holmer because he has extended his criticism in his more recent article entitled "About Black Theology" (see Document 17 of this volume).

In this introductory essay, my concern is not to respond to the criticisms Paul Holmer directs against Black Theology. I only wish to say that I know of no Black theologian who argues for what Holmer is against. Because Holmer cites no source to substantiate what he designates as Black Theology, it is difficult to know which Black theologians represent the perspective he wishes to critique. With the absence of specific references, it is easy to conclude that Holmer's perspective on Black Theology was derived from his personal and unpleasant encounters with radical Black students at Yale Divinity School. If this is the case, then something more is involved in his response than an intellectual critique of Black Theology. While I am sympathetic to the preservation of an atmosphere of debate in an academic community, it is not always possible to do that when the issues involve justice and liberation. If Black students deeply believe that academic structures in the seminary itself represent the oppressive structures against which they are fighting, then it is not likely that they will respect them. However much one may disagree with the "disorder" created by such students, it is not sound scholarly research to use these personal experiences as the primary source for a definition of Black Theology. Personal experience is important in any scholarly activity, but it cannot serve as a substitute for scientific research. While Holmer may be widely read in Black history and theology, there is little in his essay that reflects it. Because the issues he raises are important and deserve the attention of Black theologians, it is really unfortunate that he does not provide specific literary sources as the context for his criticisms.

Another important essay is G. Clarke Chapman, Jr.'s "Black Theology and Theology of Hope" (Document 18). He compares Black Theology with the

Theology of Hope as represented in the writings of Jürgen Moltmann. It is a careful assessment and shows an extensive knowledge of both theological movements.

The last essay, "Currents and Crosscurrents in South African Black Theology" (Document 19) is by David Bosch, a White South African who teaches at the University of South Africa. This essay is important because it compares Black Theology in the United States with Black Theology in South Africa from the perspective of a White South African theologian.

J.H.C.

Notes

1. See his *Social Salvation* (New York: Charles Scribner's Sons, 1935).
2. See his *Ethics in a Christian Context* (New York: Harper & Row, 1963).
3. *Journal of Religious Thought*, vol. 26, no. 2 (Summer Supplement, 1969).
4. For an account of the conference at Howard University, see *Theological Education*, vol. 6, no. 3 (Spring 1970). For the Report of the Special AATS Committee on "The Black Religious Experience and Theological Education for the Seventies," see *Theological Education*, vol. 6, no. 3 (Spring 1970, Supplement).
5. Two of the most publicized takeovers happened at Colgate Rochester Divinity School in Rochester, New York (1969) and Union Theological Seminary in New York (1969). Black students at Colgate were concerned about the failure of the seminary faculty and administrators to hire a Black faculty after nearly two years of discussing this issue. Three Black faculty were hired after the takeover. With regard to Union, the takeover was not for the purpose of hiring Black faculty. (Lawrence Jones and Eric Lincoln were already teaching at Union and I was expected to arrive in September 1969). The takeover occurred in the context of James Forman's Black Manifesto and for the purpose of addressing the economic development of the Black community at large. The Board of Directors, faculty, and students made a substantial contribution toward that goal.
6. Cone, *A Black Theology of Liberation* (Philadelphia: J. B. Lippincott, 1970), p. 194.
7. *Children of Freedom* (Philadelphia: Fortress Press, 1974), p. 2.
8. Philadelphia: Fortress Press, 1976.
9. Some of his other writings include "Theology of Liberation," *Continuum*, vol. 7, no. 4 (Winter 1970); "Political Theology," *Christian Century*, July 23, 1969; "Liberation: Hermeneutic as Ideology Critique," *Interpretation*, vol. 28, no. 4 (October 1974).
10. See his article included in this volume (Document 14) and his *Transfiguration of Politics* (New York, Harper & Row, 1975).
11. See his *Theology in Red, White, and Black* (Philadelphia: Westminster Press, 1975).
12. See his article included in this volume (Document 18) and also his "American Theology in Black, James H. Cone," *Cross Currents*, vol. 22, no. 2 (Spring 1972).
13. See his "Liberation in the Church: Black and White," *Union Seminary Quarterly Review*, vol. 29, no. 2 (Winter 1974).
14. See her "Black Theology and Black Church," *Journal of Religious Thought*, vol. 26, no. 2 (Summer Supplement, 1969); "Is There a Black Theology? The Validity and the Limits of a Racist Perspective," in *Liberation Theology* (New York: Paulist Press, 1972); "The Black Theology of James Cone," *Catholic World*, October 1973; "Crisis in Sex and Race: Black Theology vs. Feminist Theology," *Christianity and Crisis*, vol. 34, no. 6 (April 15, 1974).
15. See his "Black Theology: An Appraisal of the Internal and External Issues," *Theological Studies*, 1972. Another article that should be mentioned is Robert Osborn, "White Need for Black Theology," *Journal of the Interdenominational Theological Center*, vol. 4, no. 1 (Fall 1977). Regarding the dialogue with Black Theology, I regret that the important volumes, *Black Theology II*, edited by Calvin Bruce and William Jones (Lewisburg: Bucknell University Press, 1978), and Schubert Ogden, *Faith and Freedom: Toward a Liberation Theology* (Nashville: Abingdon, 1979)

came to my attention too late for consideration in this volume. In *Black Theology II,* Edward Leroy Long, Clyde Holbrook, Letty Russell, Randolph Miller, and William Becker address the issues of Black Theology directly.

16. Geneva: World Council of Churches, 1975.

17. Vol. 9, no. 2, 1973. The major representatives of Black and Latin theologies were Hugo Assmann, Paulo Freire, Eduardo Bodipo-Malumba, and myself. Of special interest are the news reports of this event and the comments by many European participants which are included in this *Risk* issue, along with the major presentations by Assmann, Bodipo-Malumba, Freire, and myself. It was very clear that the Europeans resented what we had to say and they expressed their feelings with passion.

18. Although Moltmann has not written extensively on Black Theology, he has done much to put it on the theological agenda in Europe through his teaching and speaking. See his "Introduction" to the symposium on Black Theology in *Evangelische Theologie* (January–February 1974) and *Union Seminary Quarterly Review* (Fall 1975).

19. Mottu and I began our teaching at Union Seminary about the same time (1969). Rubem Alves joined us about a year later. The three of us had many conversations together. After leaving Union to return to his home in Geneva, Mottu came back to Union as the Harry Emerson Fosdick Professor for one year. See especially "Noirs d'Amérique et opprimés du Tiers Monde à la recherche d'une théologie de la libération (James Cone et Rubem Alves)," *Bulletin du Centre Protestant d'Etudes*, Geneva, March 1972; "Le context historique et culturel de la théologie noire" *Lumière et Vie*, Lyon, November–December 1974.

20. See his important article included in this part, Document 15.

21. The only full-length book manuscript to be published in Europe on the specific subject of Black Theology is Chenu's *Dieu est Noir* (Edition du Cenurion, 1977). It is an excellent interpretation of Black Theology. See also his "Point de vue d'un théologien européen," *Lumière et Vie,* November–December 1974.

22. Georges Casalis was present at the WCC May 1973 symposium on Black and Latin Theology. See his interpretation of it: "Un Colloque insolite ou: 'la non-communication,' " in *Parole et Société* (Paris, 1973).

23. An important German dissertation is Wilhelm Otto Deutsch, *Schwarze Theologie in den USA: Grundzüg einer Theologie de Befreiung*, Inauguraldissertation zur Erlangung der Würde eines Doktors de Theologie der Abtielung für Evangelische Theologie der Ruhr—Universität Bochum.

24. See his "Remarks Excerpted from 'The Crisis in Rhetoric;" in *Theological Education*, vol. 7, no. 3 (Spring 1971), p. 211.

25. See *God of the Oppressed* (New York: Seabury Press, 1975), pp. 7, 247n, for references to Paul Holmer.

14

BLACK THEOLOGY
AND "CHRISTIAN" THEOLOGY

Paul L. Lehmann

It would be presumptuous in the extreme for a theologian, whose formation has been shaped almost exclusively by membership in the white community of the United States, to undertake a *reply* to Professor Cone's trenchant statement of the central reality and significance of black theology. The burden of guilt, which membership in the white community makes at once grievous and inescapable, requires silence and listening before the long overdue claims of the black revolution. Perhaps in retrospect, the textual circumstance that my own discussion of "the politics of God" (to which Professor Cone has referred) sets out from the imaginative remark of a young Muganda woman, may have been a proleptic clue to our present and ongoing conversation with one another. Nevertheless, Cone has rightly brought me up short on the omission of specific attention to black Americans in *Ethics in a Christian Context.*[1] In view of that tiny proleptic clue and our ongoing conversation, as also in view of Professor Cone's invitation to take part in the present symposium, I wish seriously to acknowledge both previous guilt and previous theological deficiency through a *response* that is a footnote, not a reply, to what he has written. Just as Frantz Fanon, whom Cone rightly and approvingly cites, defined the destiny and task of black people in broader terms than those confined to black Americans, so I venture to hope that it may be possible, in assent to Fanon's vision, for Europeans and Americans, including theologians, to break out of their social, cultural, and ideological

Paul L. Lehmann, Charles A. Briggs Professor Emeritus of Systematic Theology, Union Theological Seminary, is best known for his *Ethics in a Christian Context* and *The Transfiguration of Politics.* This essay was written in response to an essay by James H. Cone, entitled "Black Theology on Revolution, Violence and Reconciliation." Both essays appeared in the *Union Seminary Quarterly Review* (Fall 1975) as part of a symposium on Black Theology.

parochialisms, and join black people in *their* present calling to "work out new concepts, and to try to set afoot a new man". Admittedly, it is easier to show a "willingness to take the risk to create a new humanity" in a verbal exchange than in concrete acts. Since this limitation applies also (though in lesser degree) to Professor Cone, it may, perhaps, be suspended in the interest of the present conversation.

The distinction between black theology and "Christian" theology, under which this response to Professor Cone is being attempted, does not mean that black theology is not Christian theology. Nor does the distinction intend to assert or to suggest that black theology and Christian theology are incompatible. On the contrary! The distinction is intended to affirm with Professor Cone that in the United States today, black theology—in Cone's sense—is the point of departure for exploring "the truth" of "Christian" theology. At the same time, the distinction seeks to take account of the possibility—which Professor Cone does not always seem to do—that "the truth" to which "Christian" theology is open and obedient is not unqualifiedly identical with the concrete reality of blackness or any other concrete reality of the human condition and the human story.

If I understand Professor Cone aright, black theology is an "analysis of the gospel of Jesus, the point of departure [for which is] black liberation." "Liberation" is the word which, in Cone's view, accurately conjoins the biblical account of what is most characteristic of God's way of being God in the world and the realities of black experience in the United States. The distinction, familiar since Harnack, between the "gospel *of* Jesus" and the "gospel *about* Jesus" is obviously neither expressed nor implied in Cone's formulation. On the contrary, Cone is concerned about two conditions fundamental to theological thinking in the light of Christian revelation, faith, and experience.

Sociological Concreteness

The first of these conditions is the human reality and meaning of God's self-disclosing activity in the world as described in the Bible and expressed in the central Christian doctrines of incarnation, atonement, redemption, and reconciliation. The second condition is the insistence upon the *concreteness* of theological conception and analysis. In this insistence, Cone is in line with Irenaeus and Athanasius, with Augustine and Aquinas, with Luther and Calvin, Schleiermacher and Ritschl; and very much on the point at issue between Karl Barth and Dietrich Bonhoeffer. These are the theologians who wrestled in a primary way with the question of the relation between theology and truth, in the biblical sense. Hence, in their thought, the integrity of theology is defined by the congruence of faithfulness with concreteness in dealing with "the great deeds done by God" in such a way as to "express knowledge on our part," in Albrecht Ritschl's phrase.[2] In so doing, Cone is firmly in the tradition which gives priority to the *fides qua creditur* over the *fides quae creditur*.

It follows from the above, that the concreteness with which Cone's theology is concerned is *sociological*. It is the experience of black people in the United States, whose history is a movement from slavery to liberation, from powerlessness to power—power being the freedom to be who one is and to participate as one is able, and without dehumanizing restrictions, in the humanization of "the whole human running race" (Sister Corita). The congruence of this sociological reality with the biblical experience of God makes the adjective "black" in Cone's theology a *socio-theological* designation, not an exclusively *chromatic* one. Cone is often misunderstood in this matter, with the result that his theology is simplistically misread as a sanctification of a reverse racist ideology. Of course, there is a color factor in the phrase, "black theology." But the chromatic sense of the phrase is only the point of entry into the primary socio-theological reality of blackness in America required by the concreteness toward which all "Christian theology" must strive. Thus Cone correctly declares that if God's election of the Israelites

> means anything for our times, it means that God's revelation is found in black liberation. God has chosen what is black in America to shame the whites. In a society where white is equated with good and black is defined as bad, humanity and divinity mean an unqualified identification with blackness. The divine election of the oppressed means that black people are given the power of judgment over the high and mighty whites.

Cone alludes to 1 Corinthians 1:26ff. But one could add also the Magnificat (Luke 1:46ff.).

Nevertheless, although black theology is Christian theology, "Christian" theology is not black theology. The quotation marks around the adjective "Christian" underline the *distance* between any given theology and "the truth" to which every theology is bound. The quotation marks underline also the *tentativeness* with which the self-disclosure of God—in election and incarnation, in crucifixion and resurrection, in a new humanity and a new creation on their way to fulfillment—lends itself to theological description and conceptualization. Just as the God who elects Israel hides his identity in disclosing his name; as the child in the manger is the human, yet hidden, presence of the creator and redeemer of the world in the life-time and death-time of Jesus of Nazareth (including his humiliation and exaltation); as the new humanity and the new creation are at once promise and experience, hope and assurance—so the "Christian" character of theology is attested, not by definition, but by the room which such a theology makes for the freedom and priority of "the truth" by which it is claimed over thoughts which take the shape of words. The signs of this freedom and priority are the "listeningness" and humor with which these words are said. In short, "Christian" theology is a compound of transcendence and humility. The transcendence for which such theology makes room signals the freedom of God in and over every theology. The humility, which breathes in and out of such a theology, signals a due awareness of the ambiguity and frailty of having the truth "as not having it" (2 Cor. 6:8), of holding the truth "in earthen vessels" (2 Cor. 4:7). This is why Calvin urged that the proscription of images set down in the second commandment includes also mental images. This is also why the pursuit of "Christian" theology under that proscription preserves for theology the transcendence and humility, the distance and tentativeness which mark the difference between theology and ideology. Professor Cone has made it plain that in the United States today, Christian theology cannot be "Christian" except as black theology. But it must also be made plain that black theology cannot not be "Christian" theology except as the liberation which it proclaims includes also the transcendence and humility which set free black theology, as indeed every theology, from the temptation and practice of ideology and the idolatry implicit in them.

Is Dialogue with Black Theology Possible at All

The foregoing statement, however, itself belongs in quotation marks. That is, the statement can only be set down if at the same time it is suspended. Devoid of quotation marks, the statement would come under Professor Cone's stricture that "no white theologian has taken the oppression of black people as a point of departure for analyzing the meaning of the gospel today." Devoid of quotation marks, the statement is uncomfortably close to—if not another expression of—"the unverbalized white assumption that Christ is white, or that being Christian means that black people ought to turn the other cheek—as if we blacks have no moral right to defend ourselves from the encroachments of white people." As such, Professor Cone could only and rightly reject the statement as "an untruth." Devoid of quotation marks, the statement puts us, with respect to the possibility of theological conversation, in the same corner as are those whom Cone correctly criticizes for thinking and talking about violence and nonviolence in total disregard of the question: "Whose violence?" Devoid of quotation marks, conversations between white theologians and black theologians about black theology are *ab initio* excluded. Indeed, so forcefully has Cone put the case for black theology as to raise the question whether conversation between white theologians and black theologians about black theology is possible at all. It is this impossibility which must be faced and overcome, certainly in the United States, and since Fanon, also in the European "West," if the truth which alone makes any theology "Christian" is not to be imprisoned by the unacknowledged rhetoric of a white ideology masking as theology.

The suggestion made above that black theology is the point of departure for apprehending and exploring the "truth" of "Christian" theology does not mean that dogmatics has been transposed from its proper milieu in the community of Word and Sacrament which is the church to a prevailing social milieu which currently is *de facto* black. Jesus Christ is the same, yesterday, today and forever (Heb. 13:8). For black theology, as for white theology, and for any theology that seeks and finds its "Christian" identity, He is Himself the center and the criterion of the "truth" by which theology is claimed. But just as Calvin opened his *Institutio religionis christiana* with the admission that the exposition of Christian doctrine could start from either end of the polar relation between God and man, so Cone, in contrast to Calvin, insists that the present time requires that theology begin with man, specifically with man in the concrete reality and matrix of black experience.

One need not proceed at once to the revision of all existing dogmatic efforts in the frenetic attempt at a *Te deum nigrum*. But the integrity of dogmatics today requires that at whatsoever point one begins the exploration of Christian doctrine, a "Christian" theology must, from the beginning and throughout, take account, in its talk about Jesus Christ, or about God, or about sin and salvation, of the concrete realities of black experience. Only in this way, can black theologians and white theologians be honest about the sociological reality which reminds them at once of their own vulnerability to ideological distortion and of the wisdom of the dogmatic tradition which reserves omniscience for God alone. Only as black theologians and white theologians together take primary account of the concrete realities of black experience, can they reciprocally correct one another in the truth and grace that in Jesus Christ *are* the reality of the human condition. In this way, the commitment to "Christian" theology liberates black theology and white theology for the transcendence and listening which "break down the middle wall of partition" (Eph. 2:14) between them and bind both to the "truth that makes us free" (John 8:32). One must agree with Cone's agreement with Moltmann that "truth is revolutionary" and that truth involves "discovering that the world can be changed and that nothing has to remain as it has been."

Professor Cone has identified three factors in such a reciprocally correctional theological dialogue which severely strain its viability. The test by which the possibility of a "Christian" theology beyond black theology and white theology stands or falls is provided by the critical tension between revolution and violence, on the one hand, and reconciliation, on the other. Here I find it most difficult to keep clearly in view the line of demarcation between Cone's proper correction of the ideological taint in my own white theologizing, and a seemingly fierce rejection of the possibility of a "Christian" theology as open to any theologian whose "white past" virtually excludes him from the "black future" affirmed by the "black revolution." Cone carefully says that the "black revolution involves tension between the actual and the possible, the 'white past,' and the 'black future.' " Yet when he goes on to say that "the black revolution involves . . . the black community accepting the responsibility of defining the world according to its 'open possibilities,' " I find myself troubled. If the "open possibilities" before "the black community" include the transcendence and listening which signal the transformation of black theology and white theology into "Christian" theology, I think it must be recognized that these "open possibilities" at the same time define the boundary between a white theology similarly inclusive of transcendence and listening and a white theology which fails to challenge and thus sanctifies white oppression. I agree with Professor Cone that it is "incumbent upon us as black people to become 'revolutionaries for blackness,' rebelling against all who enslave us." But the fierce remark of Marcus Garvey, cited by Cone, raises as critical a problem as it is designed to settle. "Any sane man, race or nation that desires freedom must first of all think in terms of blood" will surely strike the ear of Germans, including Christians, with an uncertain, if not dismaying sound. This trumpet blast requires the correction and also the awakening of American memories as well. In Germany as elsewhere, many still remember the bitter struggle for a "Christian" theology against a theology of "blood and soil" in the German experience of National Socialism.

There is another and suppressed memory which Christians in America will need to awaken, both for themselves and for their countrymen. This is the memory that Marcus Garvey was identifying; the memory of a black struggle against white oppression which had closed all open possibilities to the black community save one: "resistance unto blood." When Garvey is read in the light of the Letter to the Hebrews (e.g., 12:4) rather than in the light of the fanaticism of Adolf Hitler, his dictum does indeed become a test at once of the liberation of white theology from ideological corruption and of the white community for a "Christian" theology through the open possibilities of the black community. However much Cone may be unaware (or seem to be) of the ideological temptations and corruptions of black theology, his case for the revolutionary thrust of black theology cannot on that account be dismissed. Only as a white theology does this kind of listening can it hope to join a black theology in a dialogue of reciprocal correction en route to the freedom and integrity of a "Christian" theology. Such a movement could also mean the liberation of American and European theology from the chauvinistic parochialism which has too frequently and too long alienated and isolated each from the other. And in this event, black theology would have been the catalyst for a genuine theology of the Church for the world, to which European and American theology for the past two centuries have aspired "in principle" without achieving "in fact."

Whose Violence?—Whose Reconciliation?

The reality of black experience in the United States and under European colonialism makes it inevitable that the prospect of such a fully church dogmatics is far from a tranquil one. It is the child of the revolutionary travail of a new birth. Not least significant in Professor Cone's forceful and unmasking essay is his readiness to face the ultimate issue of the revolutionary relation between violence and reconciliation which no "Christian" theology can escape. Indeed, the refusal of black theology to circumvent this question may be its major catalytic contribution to the emergence of a "Christian" theology. In his insistence upon the questions "Whose violence?" and "Whose reconciliation?" Cone has rightly unmasked the disobedience which has made "Christians, unfortunately, . . . not known for their revolutionary actions." In so doing, he has also exposed the facile self-deception with which Christians are wont to press the distinction between violence and nonviolence, with insufficient attention to the sociological reality which by this logic foredooms the victims of oppression both to condemnation and to their oppression.

In pressing the questions: "Whose violence?" and "Whose reconciliation?" Professor Cone has brought that question to a point from which it is possible to make a theological move which regrettably he does not make. The theological move is that the questions: "Whose violence?" and "Whose reconciliation?" lead directly to the recognition of the fundamental human reality of violence as man's radical inhumanity to man which only God's reconciliation can prevent and heal. The gospel is that people can be reconciled with one another only as they are reconciled to God; and when people are thus reconciled to God they give themselves in thought and word and deed to the empowerment of the poor, to the liberation of the oppressed, to the struggle against every dehumanizing dimension of human existence. Cone rightly declares that "reconciliation means that people cannot be human . . . unless the creatures of God are liberated from that which enslaves and is dehumanizing." In this same sentence, Cone writes that "God cannot be God" unless the creature is liberated. But putting it this way involves Cone in an imprecision as regards the gospel which is analogous to the imprecision which Professor Moltmann expresses as regards violence and nonviolence. The gospel is that God *refuses* to be God without being reconciled to man and in this empowerment man is to be reconciled to his fellowman. Similarly, Moltmann, whom Cone quotes, rightly declares that "the problem of violence and non-violence is an illusory problem." But one cannot say, as Moltmann then does, that "there is only the question of the justified and unjustified use of force and the question of whether the means are proportionate to the ends."[3] It is because the gospel transposes the question of violence from the ethical to the apocalyptic sphere that it also deprives force of every justification, not least the one which illusorily seeks a proportionate relation of means to ends.

It is understandable that Cone should reject white answers to the questions: "Whose violence?" and "Whose reconciliation?" But there is a dimension of the gospel of special significance for that ultimate confrontation between violence and reconciliation toward which the fallen condition of human affairs inevitably tends. The gospel is the good news of a God who heals as He liberates and liberates as He heals. It is He, therefore, who judges the oppressor and empowers the oppressed; and in so doing, He sustains those whom He condemns with the mercy of hope and restrains those whom He empowers with the mercy of compassion. Meanwhile, under the gospel, oppressors and the victims of oppression can and must continually pray that they may be forgiven as they forgive.

The revolutionary thrust of black theology rightly focusses attention upon the question: "Whose?" and makes black theology the bearer of this ultimate dimension of the gospel in its terrifying and liberating concreteness. But I do not find in Professor Cone's account of black theology an indication of this dimension of the gospel. I do not find an indication of this dimension in white theology either, except as an a-revolutionary avoidance of the question: "Whose?" by addressing the question "to blacks by whites." Thus, in pressing upon Professor Cone the question of the missing dimension of the gospel in black theology, I find myself bound to press the same question upon white theology. In so doing, a risk of faith at another and deeper level than "being completely sure what Jesus did or would do" is involved. At this deeper level, the risk of faith is the risk of obedience to what Jesus *did* and is still doing today. This is to invite men and women, in the power of their humanity for which He has set them free, to engage in the struggle for the liberation of any and all who are oppressed and enslaved; and thereby sharing in the saving risk of creating a new humanity. What Jesus is really about is the possibility and the power of bringing freedom and justice and forgiveness together.

In concluding this response in this way, I venture to join with the risk of faith and the risk of obedience, a risk of hope. This risk is that Professor Cone might find it possible to regard the exploration of the missing dimension of the gospel, common alike to black theology and to white theology, a paradigmatic foretaste of the reciprocal conversation and correction through which black theology and white theology endeavor to make "Christian" theology concrete.

Notes

1. Paul Lehmann, *Ethics in a Christian Context* (New York: Harper & Row, 1963). See especially pp. 81ff.
2. Albrecht Ritschl, *Justification and Reconciliation*, Vol. 3, trans. Macintosh (Edinburgh: T. and T. Clark, 1902), p. 34. The original is in *Rechtfertigunund Versachnung*, Vol. 3 (Bonn: Adolf Marcus, 1883), p. 32.
3. See Jürgen Moltmann, *Religion, Revolution and the Future* (New York: Charles Scribner's Sons, 1969), p. 143.

15

WHY BLACK THEOLOGY?

Helmut Gollwitzer

Black theology as distinguished from white theology—this phenomenon exists because colonialism and slave trade existed. Not a theme of mere historical retrospection, it deals with a factor that through its efforts determines our present-day reality. Whoever belongs to the camp of "white theology," as soon as he is confronted by "black theology," has every reason to become conscious of the specific historical and societal conditioning of his theology and his view of the Christian message. Although he did not deny the conditioning thus far, since probably he was aware of the historicity of his thought for some time, it now receives—on account of the negative characterization through black theology—a terrifying relevance. Ideology critique as self-criticism is now required of him, but not merely as an individual; the tradition itself in which he stands and which he tries to develop further is being questioned as a whole. This is happening not just in the programmatic sense in which, under the aegis of the scripture principle, tradition-criticism has long been part of the theology evolving from the Reformation, but through the rejection which reaches his whole world, the world of the white man, from another segment of humankind. It is a rejection on theological grounds in the name of the Gospel. As a member of his world he appears under a spell which falsifies not merely isolated theological statements, but church and theology as a whole, which he can break only in giving up his hitherto uncritical solidarity with the other world and trying to "become black." This is the concrete form of the *metanoia* by which he sees himself challenged—cutting deeper into his lifestyle than any *metanoia* he had previously imagined. He may comfort himself in the thought that the major

Helmut Gollwitzer is Professor of Systematic Theology with the Faculty in Philosophy at the Free University of Berlin. This essay was written in response to an essay by James Cone entitled "Black Theology on Revolution, Violence and Reconciliation." Both essays appeared in the *Union Seminary Quarterly Review* (Fall 1975) as part of a symposium on Black Theology.

spokesman of black theology, James H. Cone, himself gratefully recurs to instruction he received from white theology, so that the rejection does not qualify as counterfeit or useless everything white theology has produced in the course of centuries. This response resembles Luther's referral to those voices in the early church which are in accord with the Gospel in order to answer the question, where under the papacy the one holy Catholic church had existed. But this does not change anything in regard to the dilemma of the white theologian's situation and his tradition, which becomes uncovered through the rejection. Nothing is changed in the urgency of the challenge to zero in, not only on the Christian as historically determined in general, but especially also on the counterfeiting influence of this fact in Christian thought. The naiveté in which the theologian has hitherto accepted theological thought and the context of the tradition in which it takes place—as universally addressed to all men, valid, accessible, and useful for all men in the same way—breaks to pieces. He suddenly sees himself together with the world to which he belongs from the outside, as it were, from the perspective of another community and another historical fate. And he must ask himself to what extent his theology and its tradition were perhaps merely a reflection of his world, the world of the dominant race. To what extent it might be more would have to prove itself insofar as it liberates him from the unquestioned interdependence with his world, so that it brings him into critical opposition to it.

A Sketch of White Guilt-History

The factors we need to consider first are colonialism and slave trade. Two far-reaching transformations shaped the history of the church in its early stage. The first is the step from the Jews to the Gentiles, the liquidation of Jewish Christianity—the transformation of the church into the Gentile church whose relationship to Israel, the Hebrew Bible, and the ongoing life of the Jewish community now becomes a persistent problem. Now the Jews live as "the others" in the midst of Christian societies, as the dark foil of the Christian self-awareness, and they are paying for their otherness with a long history of unbelievable suffering. All present rejections of antisemitism have not led to the determined desire of a contrite heart to face the history of the effects of Christian antisemitism and thus also the radical critique of the Gentile thought traditions by Judaism—a parallel to the critique of our white theology by black theology.

The other transformation is the Constantinian takeover in the church. Earlier the church was a social and ethnic mixture reflecting the ethnic pluralism of the hellenistic world. Now it turns into the church of the white nations, of the Christian Occident and Orient, especially after the church in North Africa and Asia Minor disappeared under the assault of Islam. Christianization offered white people, endowed with the mobility and activity characteristic of the temperate zones and especially of that peculiar continent called Europe, an unheard of self-confidence which first proved itself in the struggle against Islam and in the crusades, but then reached out over the entire globe in the age of the great discoveries "empowering" the Europeans to regard all non-Christian peoples as destined by God for domination and exploitation. So the coasts of Africa and India were plundered by the Portuguese. The Pope divided up the New World between the Spanish and the Portuguese. The Aztec and Inca peoples were destroyed in a manifold Auschwitz. The lonely Las Casas to whom persistent historical legend imputes the guilt of the substitution of black slaves for the enslaved Indians not only protested the turn of events, but in remarkable radicalism proclaimed that God was now taking sides with the abandoned pagans against the corrupt Christian church and its members devoured by greed, and that God was the partner of the Indian who in ever new uprisings stood against the white masters—a pristine unacknowledged theology of liberation and revolution.[1]

The theological reason for the western self-understanding that doomed the non-white peoples to slavery lies in the so-called absoluteness of Christianity together with the specific form it assumed in medieval sacramental piety:[2] whoever did not share in the sacraments had no part in eternal bliss and God was his enemy. Theology and proclamation are not only responsible for that which they *mean*, but also for what they *effect*. What has been said becomes historically effective not in terms of the meaning which it has in the self-understanding of the preachers, but in terms of the meaning in which—with reductions and reinterpretations—it is perceived and appropriated. The claim that it was meant differently does not amount to a hill of beans as long as the "differently" is not directed (with all one's might and in unmistakable clarity) against the distorted view. The Reformation rightly protested that this was the problem with the proclamation of the medieval church. The distortion belongs to the guilt-history of the church (which according to Carl Amery is its success-history). For "not the reaching of original goals and intentions is the acceptable criterion of success, but the efficiency in prevailing over against other forces. Christianity—as consciousness-condition or consciousness-component of a large and active segment of humankind—has changed the world, or, rather, helped to change it. That was its effectiveness which reaches beyond the boundaries of the Christian church-oriented self-understanding."[3] In a time which usually interpreted human life in the coordinate system of a religious *Weltanschauung* (that is, in regard to the exercise of the divine sovereignty over the world, judgment day, and life after death) the guarantee of salvation offered in the sacramental faith could almost automatically induce the consciousness of predestination holding the non-elect in contempt. Even though this guarantee as inculcated by theology was not absolute, since religious and moral achievements were also demanded in order for man to stand on judgment day, the deep chasm between Christian and non-Christian mankind consisted in the fact that in Christian mankind one at least had the chance to get hold of salvation offered, whereas in the non-Christian part the offer was not even extended. Christian missions endeavored to carry the offer there too. We cannot here reflect at length on its history, rich in courage, but also weighted with difficulties. In any case, where paganism was not reached by missions or where it resisted conversion to Christianity, divine judgment seemed apparent. As long as salvation in Jesus Christ was understood as merely *offered* until it was realized in definite demonstrable conditions—participation in the sacrament or (in Protestantism) in faith (which unawares was identified with the right doctrine of faith)—the proclamation of Jesus Christ as Savior and Lord of the universe turns inevitably into Christianity's claim of absoluteness. And whoever has the privilege of belonging to this Christianity is climbing far above the rest of humankind. If through the societal domination of the church this consciousness of being privileged becomes the consciousness of an entire culture, it can express itself in particular individuals and groups as a sense of obligation toward those who thus far did not share the privilege. That is, it can show itself in missionary and charitable activity (even though, as the history of missions shows, often permeated by the superiority-consciousness of the privileged who regards himself as a model, which, of course, is nothing less than cultural imperialism). In the historical reality of nations and states there is only a small step from the consciousness of religious privilege to political and economic imperialism. Whenever the religious consciousness as pervasive consciousness in culture begins to dwindle in due course, the consciousness of privilege, which meanwhile has become quite ingrown and advantageous, does not disappear at all.[4]

This is what happened among the European nations during the age of the great discoveries. The Spanish and Portuguese established their colonial empires on "Christian" grounds. The new understanding of the Gospel in the Reformation at first pulled out the rug from underneath this particular justification. But the replacement of sacramental piety by the inward piety of faith unflinchingly retained the consciousness of privilege. The Reformation did not change a thing in the fate white people prepared for the colored peoples of the world.[5] Whether Rome, Wittenberg, or Geneva prevailed, whether justification before God occurred through works or through faith, whether *est* or *significat* was correct, whether the Canons of Dort or the declarations of the Remonstrants became accepted church doctrine, whether Cromwell or Charles I won—for the red, the yellow, and the black all this was irrelevant. It did not change their condition. For the white confessors of the faith, regardless of their particular Christian hue, the people of color were all destined for bondage; "oneness in Christ" might pertain to heaven, but certainly not to this earth. Only Pietism offered another impetus. That is, at least a few of its marginal figures (especially the groups around Zinzendorf) tried to establish community between whites and colored people. But on the whole, far from entering into a more Christian relationship to the non-

Christian world, those peoples having turned Protestant wrested from the Latin peoples part of their empires and spread colonialism over the globe—with a vengeance. The capitalist revolution as the revolution of the white, christianized, Protestant peoples began its worldwide victory and opened up a new age of slavery that even today—although in changed forms of enslavement—has not as yet been terminated. Millions of people were treated first as animals to be hunted and then as beasts of toil. Even until the beginnings of the nineteenth century in certain regions of the United States it was unlawful to offer them a minimal education, Christian instruction, or to baptize them. In fulfillment of the Old Testament word that the sins of the fathers would be visited upon the third and fourth generation, the United States have inherited a problem which they will not be able to solve in their present societal and spiritual mood, so that it will continue to poison and brutalize American society. Big fleets were engaged in the slave trade, entire regions of Africa were depopulated while Europe and the European immigrants of the New World were waxing rich. Here emerged—in a much more literal sense than with the free wageslave of the European proletariat—"a class in radical chains," victims of "no particular injustice, but of injustice in principle," a class "which in a word reflects the complete loss of humanity."[6] Not only were the streets of Liverpool paved with Negro skulls—as the saying goes—but the whole development of the wealth of the white nations (which one has in mind when with a sense of shame one speaks of the industrial nations today) derives from these two sources: (1) the surplus of the poor rural population in the European nations themselves, which was increasing by the widespread expropriation of the peasants, who, as the proletariat, became the human base for the new industry, and (2) the exploitation of other continents for raw materials, which, in the case of Africa, meant human raw materials. Karl Marx has described the situation—the so-called primitive accumulation—quite adequately in chapter twenty-four of the first volume of his *Capital*, using the evidence of his day. Every theologian should know this chapter, since quite intentionally Marx speaks here derisively of the "Christian character of primitive accumulation."[7]

That these are sins of the past which in our progressive stage of capitalism in the age of decolonization have been overcome is understandably no more than an apologetic illusion promulgated for our peace of mind. Not only in the United States' racial crisis and in South African apartheid do we experience this past as present; it is also present in the following factors: (1) The economical and political "headstart" of the white world-center over the irreparably damaged development of the Third World nations which cannot catch up. The "headstart" we white Christians daily enjoy is due to the sins of the past and is an irreversible historical development. The sins of our fathers are still our advantage today. (2) Humankind today is still very much shaped by white racism. "Imperialism" is not a demagogic catchword, but a reality. And this imperialism is white. This may well also relate to the strange fact which has been repeatedly pointed out by Arnold Toynbee: that besides Jews and gypsies the North Germanic peoples show the most exclusive race-consciousness and therefore prove—as demonstrated in the United States, South Africa, and Rhodesia—especially neurotic in keeping their distance from race-mixing. The Protestant Northgermanic peoples, the English, and the Dutch were also the promoters of capitalist evolution. In any case, the upper rungs of contemporary world society—if one disregards for a moment the special case of Japan and the maverick nations that have bolted away from the capitalist world system—are occupied by the upper strata of the white nations. And even the upper strata of the Third World nations have no hopes of reaching these top rungs that dominate the scene.

> It is a well-known fact that ethnic homogeneity increases the higher one climbs in the managerial hierarchy. On the lower strata there is a great pluralism of nationalities. But the composition of the upper strata becomes increasingly more homogeneous. This is partly due to the different degree of qualification among the various nationalities. More important, however, is the fact that mutual understanding and unconstrained communication becomes increasingly important the higher one climbs in the decision making process. A common background is of central importance[8]—

that is, the background of white Western culture. This is especially confirmed by the phenomenon of the multinational conglomerates that begin to dominate Western society more and more. Colored individuals such as Ralph Bunche who have reached the top change that as little as the emergence of a few black banks in the United States. Even today in Marxist theory the interdependence between class domination and race domination has been too little recognized and analyzed, since it too is being developed by white theorists. The perspective from the bottom of the totem pole, from the disadvantaged races, sees clearly "the facts . . . namely that most people are colored and that whites are a minority; that everywhere the colored are poor while the whites are rich; that therefore the colored are kept in bondage to the whites, and that all underdeveloped nations are colored and very poor at the same time," and that "the colored nations [find] all white nations united in one camp against them if they should demand sanctions against a particularly vicious exercise of white domination."[9]

Thus in identifying Christianity with the christianized peoples and with what they made of Christianity one can very well claim: "An unbiased non-European (or extraterrestrial) observer . . . will view Christianity as part of a very aggressive, irresistible force which with missionaries and gunboats, factories and medical stations, banks, napalm, and peace corps workers since several centuries has taken possession of the rest of the planet."[10] And how did Christian theology, the theology of these white nations and especially of the white Protestant nations, react? How did it take note of and respond to this crusade of conquest and exploitation over other continents, the enslavement of the blacks, the extermination of the Indians and the Australian aborigines? How did it fulfill its mandate as a guardian?

There is no reason, none whatsoever, to deny James Cone's observation that the black does not appear in white theology. Calvinists and Arminians in Holland hassled over predestination. It did not have any arresting influence on the election-consciousness of their slave traders. In England the Anglicans and the Puritans were fighting it out with each other; as to their attitudes toward Indians and blacks there was no difference. One engaged in anti-Catholic polemics; the desire to lighten the Spaniards and the Portuguese of their colored booty was at best increased thereby. However carefully one pursues the theological tomes and tracts of the seventeenth and eighteenth centuries one will hardly find references to the fate of the colored peoples exposed to white power, although the money which flowed into the country through their exploitation also benefited churches and the theological schools in their material needs. The Gospel which proclaims liberation to the captives and good news to the poor apparently did not remind them of the colonial misery. And it apparently had no practical consequences that in the body of Christ, Jews, Greeks, barbarians, and masters and slaves are one. It is characteristic for our academic enterprise in which the most remote figures of church history are made subjects of ever new dissertations that assertions such as mine have to appear as "guesstimates" without scholarly documentation, since it is non-existent. When finally owing to the renewal of English Protestantism the slavery issue entered the Christian consciousness, opponents as well as partisans of slavery offered theological arguments[11] similar to what is still happening in South Africa in our time. Theology seemed available for the issue at hand. But to the best of my knowledge no one as yet has examined to what extent this twofold theological argumentation had been prepared for the *loci* of Protestant Orthodoxy, and which schema of the old theologians were usable for the issue in one way or other, although what was at stake here was the responsibility of the church for millions of human beings, for the agents as well as their victims, and the practical effect of church doctrine and proclamations among its hearers as well.

In white theology, as Cone repeatedly indicates, the black person does not appear—very similar, by the way (and the parallel is worth pondering), to the animals (whose absence Albert Schweitzer noted).[12] What offered itself as justification of slavery was fundamentalism (for example, the curse of Ham, Gen. 9:20-27) and the primitive Christian reticence in matters of slavery.[13] Causes for disquietude over slavery, however, are not discernible in the affirmations of the Christian confession. The anti-slavery movement, which, at least beginning with the eighteenth century (with the exception of the Quakers who had a headstart), commenced in the American churches, and was argued on grounds of ethical precepts from the New Testament, especially the love commandment and the golden rule.[14] But what significance did the core doctrines of the Reformation confessions have? For example, what about justification by faith when the white Christian encountered the African black? Or what about God's decrees of election which were not, as one was well aware of in Calvinism, commensurate with the color of a man's skin? What about the thesis Lutherans pitted against the Calvinist doctrine of the eternal decree of predestination, namely that God's saving will *serie et univer-salis* pertains without qualification to *all* men? Also, what about the sacraments which supposedly unify the "great multitude . . . from every nation, from all tribes and peoples and tongues" (Rev. 7:9) in the one church (Gal. 3:28)? From all this doctrine, to the best of my knowledge, no uneasiness evolved in regard to colonial exploitation, manhunt, shipment of humans across the Atlantic, and the degradation of human beings to beasts of burden, a million times over, systematically and with a vengeance.

This problem area cannot be shrugged off by appealing to the historical limitations of all theology. For here a modern humanism is not the criterion, but the biblical texts themselves and the resulting dogmatic assertions. In that the blacks did not appear in the theology of the church, remaining an "invisible man" relative to its dogmatic claims, this whole theological tradition covering centuries of the church—mark it well, covering centuries in which the black very much appeared in white economics and politics—is subject to the question whether the human problems negotiated were ever *more* than the problems of the privileged part of mankind, the problems of Western subjectivity to which the originally ecumenically comprehensive Christian message was reduced and in keeping with which Western Christian man turned inward. This new inwardness became the means which proved necessary not only as cover-up of the existing inner European structures of power against a critique on grounds of the Christian message (which appeared for the last time in the peasant uprisings of the sixteenth century), but also to keep the horrible fate of the black out of sight—at best to be disquieted by him in human pity, but not in Christian brotherhood.

German theology was confronted with these questions only by the time the world had been nearly divided up and open slave trade was prohibited, that is, when the *status quo* established by colonialism and slave trade had been perfected. This made it easier for her to accept European imperialism (in which the German Reich now was caught up, too) as a would-be calling of Christian Europe for ordering the world and to exploit it for its own missionary aspirations. On account of German colonial politics, arising historically rather late and the Scandinavian countries being dissociated from imperialistic competition, Lutheran theology even more easily than the theologies of other denominations could ignore slavery and racist colonialism.[15]

Werner Elert, the author of *Morphologie des Luthertums*, entitled the second volume of this work "Social Teachings and Social Effects of Lutheranism."[16]

In the description of the social dynamics of Lutheranism the black does not even appear at those points where Lutheranism had entered a slave-holder society. From Elert we learn something about the attitudes of the Lutherans in the American Civil War.[17] But that in the war the slavery question was a central issue, is not even mentioned by Elert. And in the chapter on Lutheran missions[18] there is much ado—in keeping with the general interest of the time when the book was written—about the relationship between missions and "foreign nationality," but not a word about colonialism. Elert to his satisfaction, however, can observe about the Lutheran Salzburgers, settled in the South since 1734, "how the employ of slaves from the outset was contrary to their convictions and how they constantly wrestled with the ethical aspect of the issue."[19] These Salzburgers, different from the dominant Anglo-Saxon population, were intent upon the conversion of blacks and the amelioration of the slave trade, never forgetting "that here too is a man." The patriarchal stance ameliorated slavery, but did not transcend it. Thus during the Civil War the Lutherans usually remained neutral, that is, they were never active on the side of the abolitionists.[20] The "social effects of Lutheranism" thus became tangible for blacks only in rather small measure.[21] With considerable certainty one can state furthermore that the white proclamation in the Lutheran churches addressed to the blacks was hardly different from what blacks would hear in other denominations: "The deeper the piety of the slave the more valuable will he be in every respect."[22] The increase of his value as a slave, not his elevation from slavery to brotherhood was the motive for permitting the Christian instruction of the slaves which, by the way, was attained only in the eighteenth century. That was at a time when theology supported the devaluation of baptism. The right insight that baptism and enslavement of a human being are mutually exclusive had caused the earlier prohibition of instruction. It was rescinded only when a hairsplitting theology offered the way out "that the conferring of baptism doth not alter the condition of the person as to his bondage or freedom; that diverse masters, freed from this doubt, may more carefully endeavour the propagating of Christianity by permitting children, though slaves, or those of greater growth if capable, to be admitted to that sacrament."[23]

This does not prevent the illusions one can encounter in theological literature in regard to slavery, whenever it is mentioned. Occasion for reference arises when persons who desire the change of societal structures begin to appeal to the New Testament. To hold against it the fact that the literal word of the New Testament does not furnish prooftexts for slavery and that primitive Christianity was not a socio-revolutionary movement seems to the theological critics of such appeals finally too meager. And one does not wish to speak of the sheer indifference of the New Testament toward miserable social conditions. Since the debate over Franz Overbeck's claim[24] that the Stoa was a much more effective anti-slavery force than primitive Christianity and that "the victory of Christianity" had once more propped up slavery close before its abolition, an effort has been made to ascribe to Christianity the direct or at least the indirect merit for the overcoming of slavery.[25] The New Testament view of "the unconditional acknowledgment of the actual equality of all men before God and each other" and "the admission of slaves as fully equal members of the churches would sooner or later lead to the abolition of slavery. The timing depended on the economic and cultural development of the nations and the inculcation of the principles of Christianity among the Christianized peoples."[26] These principles—this should no longer be denied by appealing to an alleged New Testament indifference in these matters—are indeed opposed to the enslavement of human beings. But the fact that their inculcation did not take place during the time of the greatest political influence of the Christian churches should at least be worthy of theological analysis. This question, and together with it, centuries of horrifying human misery and Christian guilt are being skipped over in the view of Hans Schulze as to the time after the end of the immediate Parousia expectation (which still determines St. Paul's attitude toward the slavery issue): "Now the mandate for the shaping of society becomes important; it becomes inescapable. Meanwhile [! H.G.] the incompatibility of the slave status—taking up again the example of slavery—with the image of man oriented in Christ becomes manifest; this incommensurability has become a moral and social factor. From here a new beginning must be made."[27] Or take Helmut Thielicke:

> In that St. Paul reviews the slave Onesimus in terms of such qualities and commends him to his former masters as "brother" he indirectly attacks the structure of slavery and undermines it. The most extreme paradox, desired by St. Paul, is that Onesimus now returns to slavery only because of one motive, the motive of freedom. . . . Thus an explosive is smuggled into the structural form of slavery which can change this order and must make it ready for an abolition of the structure.[28]

Must? That took in fact nineteen hundred years! Who constantly lengthened the cord of the fuse? If the automatism of the sequence from a "conversion of the human heart" to the change of the structure is in good order, as Thielicke claims, this question is worthy of the most intensive examination.[29] "This transformed heart is the germ cell of world transformation;" with this formula Thielicke and many others make the conversion of the heart the precondition of the societal revolution. The formula proves its truth in that without a revolution of the inner perspective the external change remains empty and thus soon reverts to the old misery. But it overlooks the kernel of truth in the Lutheran doctrine of the two kingdoms which stresses that the conversion of the heart and structural change appear on two different levels. It also disregards the insight of Karl Marx (in the third thesis on Feuerbach) that the inner change comes to pass in practical labor over external change. That no automatism exists which guarantees the peaceful transition from the inner to the outer change is proved by the history of the United States in that a bloody Civil War was necessary in order to provide the slaves with at least legal liberation. The neutral attitude of the Lutherans in this war is another proof. If one keeps this in mind, the ideological consolation-character of such formulas stands exposed: the slaves which are supposed to wait for the "changed heart" of their white masters instead of taking control of their own fate would be waiting in vain until this very day.

Other social and spiritual developments had to be added to the conversion of the heart in order to ignite the explosive actually contained in the Gospel which stands in opposition to societal impediments increasingly interjected in Christianity. As in antiquity the rational humanism of the Stoics, in modernity the rational humanism of the Enlightenment, putting the church Christians to shame has demanded the application of human rights also for the slaves.[30] It belongs to the "strategy of God" mentioned by Thielicke[31] that the conversion of the heart proves to be dependent on the partnership with the rationalists and (let us not forget!) with material interests, "so that no human being might boast" (I Cor. 1:29). Such a partnership together with its praxis is apparently necessary in order for Christians to be freed from their religious ideology into which they have transformed the New Testament faith in regard to submission to God's will and the preference of inner over outer freedom.

Metanoia, Reconciliation, and Violence

Thus, it takes a long road of self-critical historical reflection before white theology will be able to respond to the challenge of black theology. The danger lies too close that the genuine questions would evolve into a topic of merely theoretical discussion among tenured university professors in the white "affluence-ghetto," and that reservations would function merely as an effort of shielding oneself against the indictment. The latter leaves us only one chance within which a dialogue will be possible that would afford us the opportunity of warnings and reservations. This chance lies in Cone's invitation for white theology to "become black," i.e., to undergo a practical *metanoia* wherein first of all guilt is confessed as shared with our white Christian ancestors and is exposed and also examined as to its causes; wherein, secondly, we recognize that with our affluence including the material status of our divinity schools and seminaries we are daily beneficiaries of white imperialism as the major factor in the present world situation; and wherein, thirdly, solidarity with the exploited masses of the colored world (who today no less than in former times are deprived of their rights) becomes real in the anti-imperialist struggle. Only in this practical solidarity can credible Christian theology, in keeping with its mandate, be done today. In this respect, black theology, as George Casalis rightly states, determines the basic relationship between the battle for the future of mankind and the Gospel which causes the battle and bears witness to it. From now on a theological ivory tower no longer is possible, only a praxis and a reflection which prove that one has taken sides in the planetary class struggle, the side of God for the liberation of all men who are victims of oppressive systems and profit-hungry men. Theology must ask each church, each Christian: On which side do you take your stand in the decisive struggle in the first, second, and third world?[32]

This challenge of taking sides, which appears because of black theology, sounds terrifying only to him who is blind to the fact that the empirical church has actually always taken sides. Its ethics of the state and its social ethics meant taking sides for the status quo, insofar as the church tried to improve it while not wanting to recognize a Christian mandate fundamentally to change it or even—with different theological arguments—basically to deny it. For black theology, the mild liberal reformism white social ethics has agreed upon by and large no longer makes sense. It invites white theology, finally to become revolutionary and thus truly Christian.[33]

Here the *metanoia* to which black theology's call to repentance challenges and invites white theology comes close to the radicalness of Jesus' call to *metanoia*. And here thanks to black theology we notice that Jesus' call reaches into the politico-social dimension, and that, as long as we shrink from revolutionizing it, we have not really heard it. "These are the true forms of dying which do not occur in the desert outside human society [thus also not only in the realm of inwardness! H.G.], but in economics and politics."[34] "Only the person converted also in his wallet is truly converted" is a good old Pietist saying which of course meant only the "giving" *within* existing property relations, but which now must be expanded to these themselves, to freedom over against them and the willingness to give them up. This does not happen in the aforementioned reformism. It persists in staying within the foundational structures of the bourgeois system and does not relate *metanoia* thereto.[35] Only a theology which reflects its solidarity with the victims of this system and serves present-day Christian praxis can discuss the theological problems in Cone's project[36] in such a way that it does not secretly serve the reformist tendency to secure itself against revolutionary *metanoia*, but rather serves the common progress in a common task. Let me lift out a few points.

Context and Conflicts. Paul Lehmann[37] rightly indicates that black theology is contextual, which is an important hermeneutical perspective for the exclusion of unjust criticism demanding of a theological project of timeless accuracy and indiscriminate applicability for all seasons and places. Black theology shares its contextualism with every theology insofar as all thought is conditioned, formed, and limited by everything that makes up our situation. The point is not to get rid of our dependency on the context, but to reflect it critically, so that our thought is not just a reflex of our situation and controlled by it, but that it is controlled by God's Word and thus becomes an act of freedom over against our situation. Whether or not this liberation of our thought is achieved through the hearing of the Word of God will prove itself in its critical relationship to our contextualized interest, and in reaching beyond our situation preparing the appearance of new situations and beginning to be of service to other situations.

This also pertains to *(a)* Cone's language about God. If Herbert O. Edwards asks whether or not with Cone we have a "more or less functional . . . definition of God" this question places Cone near several forms of existentialist God-talk in which "God" is merely the expression for interpersonal functions or merely the supplier of our affluence—a God-talk no longer capable of objecting to Feuerbach's suspicion of religious projection and in which the doxological dimension of the worship of God for God's sake, energetically introduced by Karl Barth against the neo-Protestant functionalization of God, has been completely lost again. Here it is determined on grounds of human interests who God must be, if he wishes to be worshipped by us. For this one does not—just because also his God-talk is contextual— dare to reproach Cone offhand. One is entitled, however, to call his attention to the negative examples from the history of theology. We might often turn to the Gospel on the existential level of our needs, and our believing affirmation of the Gospel may find its initial motive often enough in the fact that we discover our needs affirmed in the Gospel. But theology has no right to make this route her law. It influences theology as a whole if it either moves from our needs to God or from God's revelation to our needs. The latter is the biblical route. Here all utterances about God's relationship to us, about his knowledge (Mt. 6:8,32) of what we need and his affirmation and fulfillment thereof become statements about his free grace and only on these grounds statements about our right—our right to ask him for it as well as our right to work and battle for it. Not that we dream up for ourselves a divine covenant partner and, for example, as black theologians, join this dream to the political liberation struggle, as comfort, in the end, however superfluous and merely decorative. It is rather that the promise of grace in which the eternal God makes the condition of us temporal human beings his condition sends us to our brethren in prison, to participate in their struggle for the discovery of new impulses and new criteria in the struggle.

In view of grace one can say that "God chose what is weak in the world to shame the strong" (I Cor. 1:27); therefore also that he chose what is black; therefore also that he defines himself in his action: that he is weak and that he is black. This not, however, because the weak and the black were better in his eyes than the strong and the white. That "all have sinned and fall short of the glory of God" (Rom. 3:23) remains true and proves itself in that the inner crippling inflicted by the societal condition is no less strong in blacks than in whites. Even though the balance of guilt may weight whites more than blacks, that does not change the fact that the *metanoia* to which God's grace calls all men is no smaller and no easier with blacks than with whites, although its concrete form may be different. God's partisanship for the oppressed is not a "Yes" to everything they do in various enterprises. It is a critical "Yes" leading to transformation and thus to new methods of the class struggle from below instead of a mere repetition of the class struggle from above.

This pertains also to *(b)* Cone's talk about reconciliation. He is justified in his rejection of a proclamation of reconciliation from the white side which aims at demobilization of the blacks, at cessation of their battle. He stands against an ideological pacifism of reconciliation which seeks the embrace of the combatants without elimination of the causes of the battle, so that it unilaterally profits those on the top of the ladder. This was the proclamation blacks had to listen to as slaves when they were finally permitted to attend the worship services of the whites. This prostitution of the reconciling message in "reconcilism" (as Lenin contemptuously called it) confronts us, however, with the task to speak of the reconciliation of God with *all* men and of the reconciliation between men evoked in such a way that the inexorableness of the revolutionary struggle is not crippled, but receives a new quality. When Nat Turner with his band rose up—empowered by the reading of the Bible and divine visions—in order to kill whichever white person got in their way,[38] it was a sheer reaction to white crimes, not a struggle which would take into account the white wrongdoers as sinners reconciled to God.

How does God's reconciliation in his self-sacrifice in Jesus Christ affect the human conflicts in which Jesus' disciples are enmeshed in this eon? *(a)* In any case, in that way that we cannot think of ourselves as the righteous against the unrighteous, the guiltless against the guilty, however much right there may be on our side and however much guilt there may be on the other side. Self-justification and condemnation are no longer possible. Newly added guilt on one's own side, as it results from the conflict, will no longer be denied by us and taken lightly. *(b)* In any case, the goal is peace with the enemy and not his destruction or oppression. The conflict is no longer for vengeance's sake, but for the sake of greater justice. *(c)* In any case, in that conflict the enemy is viewed as the man already loved and sought by God. Also the enemy has been deformed by the unjust conditions he has created, from which he has profited and for the continuance of which he is fighting. He is a prisoner of his own prison. Martin Luther King's main contention that in the battle of the blacks also the liberation of the whites is at stake dare not get lost even in the more violent forms of the battle. *(d)* In any case, we finally are forbidden neutrality and invited to take sides where injustice and oppression are obvious. We are to take sides—often enough against our own interests —with the oppressed. Since not only change of heart, but also change of the social structure—which happens through laws and thus with the support of political power—is the issue, it follows that in principle we cannot get out from under political partisanship and participation including direct or indirect employment of violent means (the mark of every political struggle!).[39] This taking sides of Jesus' disciples impelled by the Gospel is a challenge addressed to all hearers of the Gospel, also to those on the side of the opposition, to join in the battle against oppression.

Freedom in the Concrete. What I just got through saying does not intend a reduction of reconciliation to inwardness or merely individual relationships—a way out occasionally used by the theological ethics of war in order to reconcile the "faith in reconciliation" with the realism of the law of war. To the contrary, the point is to discover the actual effects of the "faith in reconciliation" on the conflict situation, as long as and to the extent that we cannot escape it. This inevitable relationship between the message of reconciliation and the political battle, points out a particular aspect of truth in black theology: the rejection of the separation of spiritual salvation from earthly welfare. In the tradition of the church this separation has not only served the comfort of the believer in inescapable external need, but also as opium for the oppressed in order to derail them from their rage over unjust conditions, and thus as a rotten reconciliation. Against such a misunderstanding of the New Testament stands the Old Testament view of *shalom*: wholeness of salvation involving body and soul, liberation from conditions destroying both body and soul. Slaves who experienced such conditions most devastatingly cannot divide up liberation and hold external liberation in such low esteem as it was expected of them by the white theology of segregation.[40] Their experience has been branded by bondage and freedom. From experience they know the correspondence between temporal and eternal freedom. They called upon God as *liberator* (as Buber translates instead of Luther's "redeemer") in their spirituals and after the Civil War experienced him concretely. "I never forget the day we was set free! . . . It was the fourth day of June 1865 I begins to live, and I gwine take the picture of that old man in the big black hat and long whiskers, sitting on the gallery and talking kind to us, clean into my grave with me."[41] "There is something 'bout being free, and that makes up for all the hardships, I's been both slave and free, and I knows."[42] "For black slaves who were condemned to live in human imprisonment heaven meant that the eternal God had made a decision concerning their lives which could not be destroyed by their white slave masters."[43]

With division between the spiritual and the secular also, the other division falls by the wayside which equally reflects the interests of the white masters, the division between God's action and our own action in regard to salvation and freedom: "When I starts preaching I couldn't read or write and had to preach what Master told me, and he say tell them niggers iffen they obeys the master they goes to Heaven; but I knowed there's something better for them, but daren't tell them 'cept on the sly. That I done lots. I tells 'em iffen they keeps praying, the Lord will set 'em free."[44] Praying, however, is not only looking forward to God's action. It is also at the same time the beginning of our own action. "Can a serious prayer in the long run remain without corresponding action? Can one ask God for something which one is not at the same moment willing and determined within the limits of one's own possibilities to bring about?"[45] Thus "Christianity did not weaken the desire for liberation among the slaves. . . . Rather, there are many evidences that the slaves applied the Gospel to the most varied forms of resistance. . . . In fact, many believed that the only hands God has were their own, and that without the risk of escape and rebellion slavery would never end."[46] The Gospel as "explosive" also proved itself in the other areas of white oppression. If Thielicke in his use of this metaphor characteristically anticipated only an (to be expected, but never actually occurring) abolition of slavery the actual explosion took place among the slaves: their desire for freedom was stimulated by the Gospel and realized by its power. They were Christian Ovambos who in December 1970 dared the first strike in Namibia, strengthening themselves through prayers and the singing of hymns. The event was summed up in a terse remark: "Pagans do not strike."[47] The reconsideration (so inevitable for contemporary political theology) of the interdependence of divine and human action, of God's kingdom and active *metanoia* toward freedom, belongs to the instruction black theology is imparting to white theology.

Avoiding Pride. Cone's use of biblical motifs is selective. That is the case with all of us. Whether in such a selection the use of the Bible serves only for retroactive legitimation and illustration of a concept earlier and otherwise conceived, or whether this concept was found in listening to the biblical message will be decided in the determining role played by the central biblical themes. Exodus, covenant, election, and God's partisanship with the lowly are certainly such themes. Biblically, however, these are indissolubly united with the event of cross and resurrection. What Cone has to say about cross and resurrection is certainly still inadequate. We will more fully do justice to his reticence in this regard, if we do not forget that he functions as spokesman of a suffering segment of humanity which exactly through the message of the crucified has found comfort and hope in its crucifixions. Therefore theological hairsplitting is not in order here as it may be practiced by a white divinity faculty on the dissertation of a doctoral candidate who, in reflections on Jesus' death of torture, may be advancing his academic career. If God's election is considered in reference to Jesus' cross, any election-consciousness with its inevitable *hybris* becomes subject to the critique of the cross. Thus the covenant is not only the promise that God is with us, but it turns into the question whether or not we (and our battling) are with God. As a result the Pharisaism of the oppressed as well as that of the oppressor crumbles. This entails that the necessary awakening of racial consciousness—black is beautiful—is kept from becoming mere resentment (in Nietzsche's sense) or mere repetition of white contempt for different skin color. The recent white warnings against black racism and nationalism obviously also belong to the chapter of white hypocrisy. The internationalization of capital in the age of transnational conglomerates tries to replace the national ideology of the middle class by an international one. Therefore everything that, for example, was produced by German Lutheran theology in regard to fatherland and folk ideology in the first half of this century for us today takes on the character of antiquated comicality. For the peoples and races, however, whose backbone was broken by white racism, the healing of this backbone is of decisive importance.[48]

> When I was young, for example, it was an insult to be called black. The blacks have now taken over this once pejorative term and made of it a rallying cry and a badge of honor, and are teaching their children to be proud that they are black. . . . Black is a tremendous spiritual condition, one of the greatest challenges anyone alive can face. . . . Nothing is easier, nor, for the guiltridden American, more inevitable, than to discuss this as chauvinism in reverse. But, in this, white Americans are being—it is in part their fate—inaccurate. To be liberated from the stigma of blackness by embracing it is to cease, forever, one's interior agreement and collaboration with the authors of one's degradation.[49]

But if Baldwin says at another point that the "powerless, by definition, can never be 'racists,' for they can never make the world pay for what they feel or fear,"[50] this is valid only for the time of powerlessness.

What is at stake in the anti-imperialist struggle as a (not only, but also) political struggle is power, the redistribution of power—to put it more accurately in terms of the anti-racism program of the World Council of Churches. Theology has the task of reflecting on the temptations of power. Under the promise of God's covenant and election it may not only reinforce the—quite legitimate—courage to be oneself, the courage of identity. Under the aegis of a proper interpretation of *God's* election it must also prepare against the transformation of pride in one's identity into the *hybris* of an election consciousness which makes election its own end and thus does not view election as mission to service. If election is, however, understood as such a mission, it finds its basic models in the election of Israel as a blessing for all the nations of the earth (Gen. 12:3) and in the obedience of the Son of God who takes the road of the cross. Thus it can prepare for that readiness to suffer which he needs who rises from the passivity of suffering and its humiliation to do battle against it, thereby taking upon himself new sufferings. Thus it can give hope in defeat. The pain-shy white activism is not replaced by a corresponding black activism. The profound black experience of the not only dehumanizing, but also humanizing power of suffering is drawn into that time when all sufferings of humiliation will have been terminated. This cannot be preached to suffering and battling colored humanity from the outside, from the side of whites; they can only be suspected of ideology. But the black Christians who are battling along with colored humanity, equipped with the message of Jesus' cross and resurrection, are sent to their brothers and sisters in order to help them stay clear of the repetition of white sins.

In this way black theology keeps itself from becoming a rationalization or acculturation-ideology as it so often happened in white theology. The critical power of the message of the cross makes us respect the difference between God's liberation struggle and our liberation struggles. If our motive in the political liberation battle is the obedience to the Gospel of God's liberation struggle on the political level, and if we ask God for his blessing, that is, that he identify himself with our struggle and through it pursue his work, it still makes for a difference if God identifies himself with us or we identify with him. In that we arrogate the latter to ourselves we prevent the former. What we ask *of him* we do not seek to undertake ourselves.

Whose Violence? To the extent that Cone deals with the issue of violence (which always presents an important question for a Christian theology of the political), understanding cannot be reached without difficulty. Human history is the history of violence. Also all present societies are sustained by violence, by the threat and use of increasingly perfectionized, terrifying means of violence. The history of civilization is not, as it might appear from the abolition of torture and the humanization of the penal code in a few countries, a history of the elimination of violence. The progressive factors are more than compensated for, however, by the reappearance and spread of torture in our century and the horrors of modern military technology. In view of the impossibility of the abolition of war the church has exercised itself in the attempt of mitigating the horrors of war. But as the church of the ruling classes it has neither contributed much to the abolition of torture (the enlightenment was more effective here) nor has it resisted the military development. It distinguished between just and unjust wars, but its simultaneous rationalization of the non-application of this distinction served in making the citizens morally available for the wars of the ruling classes without any distinction. Whereby it needs to be added in this context that the rules developed in regard to modern warfare become effective only for wars between white nations, never for colonial wars. In view of all these facts the demand of nonviolence directed by members of the white ruling class to colored revolutionaries is pure hypocrisy, whether conscious or unconscious, and needs no further comment.

The problem of violence arises, however, anew *within* the revolutionary movement to which Cone, occupied only with refutation of the insinuations of white hypocrisy, seems to pay too little attention.[51] Violence brutalizes, even though the oppressed cannot avoid it in their struggle. Limiting violence to a last resort and humanizing the methods of violence as much as possible are in the interest of the revolutionary movement, not only for reasons of expediency, but for retention of the humane freedom-loving character of the movement itself. The corrective task of the Christians participating in it consists in resisting the allegedly necessary education in hatred and the brutalizing reverse effect of violence upon those that exercise it. Thus the *problem* of violence becomes a challenge for black theology within the revolutionary movement of the colored peoples in regard to which it can learn some pros and cons from the *history* of the problem in white theology.

Notes

1. In the years of Hitler's regime of bondage, it was Reinhold Schneider who brought to life again the figure of the first protest against colonialist perversion of Christianity in his book, *Las Casas vor Karl V* (1938). The thoroughly radical dimension and importance of this forgotten battle has been described for the first time in the dissertation by Claudia Lange, *Kolonialismus das Zeugnis von Las Casas* (Free University of Berlin, 1972).

2. This sacramental piety spelled doom for the Jews in Europe (cf. Karl Kupisch, "Das christliche Zeitalter" in *Der ungekundigte Bund,* Stuttgart, 1962, p. 83). The same pertains to the conduct of the invaders from the West in other continents. An eloquent example is the report of the Italian world traveller Francesco Carlotti, *Reise um die Welt 1594* (Herrenalb, 1966). He recounts the outstanding religiosity and ethics of the Indians of Goa: they view their religion as superior to all others, but do not therefore damn the religion of the Christians. "On the contrary, one of my best friends, an exceedingly cultured and intelligent person, often said to me, 'Even the Christians could save their souls if they only would live in a moral and civilized way.' He held it would be enough if one does for others what one wishes to have done for oneself. In this respect, religion does not make any difference. The Golden Rule suffices in order to secure a resting place for oneself after death. I have tried as far as I was able, to convince him of the opposite, that is, that baptism is the only way for us if we wish to partake of God's glory in the next life" (p. 254).

3. Carl Amery, *Das Ende der Vorsehung: Die gnadenlosen Folgen des Christentums* (Reinbeck, 1972), p.11.

4. Max Weber's proposition that the Protestant ethic, especially the Calvinist doctrine of predestination, contributed to the development of capitalism, is right at least in observing that modes of cultural conduct die hard even if their religious presuppositions are no longer alive.

5. "It was the Germanic-Protestant culture in contrast to the Roman Catholic which promoted this development [of abolishing slavery]." This self-satisfied observation by E. von Dobschutz ("Sklaverei und Christentum," *Die Religion in Geschichte und Gegenwart*—hereafter, RGG—3rd ed., vol. 18, p. 433) is correct in regard to the abolition movement during the transition from the eighteenth to the nineteenth century, but it ignores the fact that this "Germanic-Protestant culture" earlier had continued and expanded slavery eagerly and that it is psychologically much more geared to racist *apartheid* than the "Roman Catholic culture."

6. Karl Marx, "Einleitung zur Kritik der Hegelschen Rechtsphilosophie," in *Fruhschriften,* ed. S. Landshut (Stuttgart: Alfred Kroner, 1953). pp. 222f.

7. Karl Marx and Freidrich Engels, *Werke* (Berlin: Dietz, 1972), vol. 23, p. 781.

8. Steven Hymer, "Multinationale Konzerne und das Gesetz der ungleichen Entwicklung," in *Imperialismus und strukturelle Gewalt: Analysen uber abhangige Reproduktion*, ed. Dieter Senghaas (Frankfurt, 1972), p. 225.

9. Gunnar Myrdal, "Rolle un Realitat der Rasse," *Aufsätze und Reden* (Frankfurt, 1971), pp. 101, 103. For Latin America: Sven Lindqvist, *Lateinamerika: Der geplünderte Kontinent* (Hamburg, 1971), pp. 85-89.

10. Carl Amery, op. cit., p. 13.

11. Cf. Manfred Linz, "Sklaverei als 'ethischer Modellfall'," *Evangelische Theologie*, 1959, pp. 569-584; Adolf Lotz, *Sklaverei, Staatskirche und Freikirche: Die englische Bekenntnisse im Kampf um die Aufhebung von Sklavenhandel und Sklaverei,* vol. 9 in *Kolner Anglistische Arbeiten* (Leipzig, 1929). As regards John Wesley, his "Thoughts on Slavery" (1774) have to be mentioned with appreciation. His disciple John Wilberforce drew out this line of thought.

12. Albert Schweitzer, *Kultur und Ethik* (Bern: P. Haupt, 1923). "Just like the housewife who has cleaned the living room is careful that the door is closed and no dog can enter to disfigure her accomplishments with the traces of his paws, similarly European thinkers take great care that no animals run around in their ethics" (p.225).

13. M. Linz, op. cit. Linz describes the way from apology for slavery to the "positive-good theory" or sheer ideology according to which slavery is no longer tolerated as a necessary evil, but defended as a "divine blessing for whites and negroes" (p. 573). Linz also sketches in outline the material interests behind this development.

14. Cf. M. Linz, op. cit., pp. 575ff. But Linz can also say: "For the opponents of slavery the whole Bible spoke eloquently against this institution" (p. 575).

15. How stubbornly this stance of ignoring the issue continues can be learned from the fact that the editors of the third edition of RGG in 1959 substituted Carl Mirbt's article in the second edition on "Kolonialpolitik und Mission"—which was found no longer acceptable—with a no less naive article by L. B. Greaves (see RGG, III, pp. 1147ff.). See also Mirbt's book, *Mission und Kolonialpolitik in den deutschen Schutzgebieten* (Tubingen: Mohr, 1910), written in the same style.

16. Werner Elert, *Morphologie des Luthertums*, vol. 2, *Soziallehren und Sozialwirkungen des Luthertums* (Munich: Beck, 1932). In regard to the stance of the North American churches in matters of slavery cf. Emanuel Hirsch, *Geschichte der neueren evangelischen Theologie* (Gütersloh: C. Bertelsmann, 1951), vol. III, pp. 363ff.

17. Werner Elert, ibid., pp. 261ff., p. 277.

18. Ibid., pp. 278-290.

19. Ibid., pp. 458f.

20. The "apolitical" stance of the Lutherans also mentioned by Elert (ibid., p. 258) was in fact as M. Linz correctly states (op. cit., p. 579) a political decision to support the existing order. Linz quotes a sentence from the *Lutheran Observer* of 1860, one year before the Civil War, which recalls familiar statements in our time: "Up to this day our church has not been confused because we have excluded the topic of slavery, as is proper, from our church gatherings."

21. It should nevertheless be mentioned that, as Elert proudly reports (*Morphologie*, p. 460), the Lutheran Denmark was the first country to prohibit the slave trade in 1792. In 1794 the French National Convent followed; in 1806/07, the British crown. Pope Gregory XVI belatedly declared the trading of black slaves prohibited in 1839.

22. Quoted by James H. Cone, *The Spirituals and the Blues: An Interpretation* (New York: Seabury, 1972), p. 23. See this page also for the quote from a slave catechism. In a similar way, former slaves report about the sermons they listened to in their youth. See B. A. Botkin, *Lay My Burden Down* (Chicago: University of Chicago Press, 1945), pp. 25ff., and the opposite example, p. 65.

23. Thus the English law of 1667 which abolished the previous order of enfranchising a slave who had been christened or baptized. See Theo Lehmann, *Negro Spirituals: Geschichte und Theologie* (Berlin, 1965), p. 65. Lehmann quotes the English original as follows: "That the conferring of baptisme doth not alter the condition of the person as to his bondage or freedome; that diverse masters, freed from this doubt, may more carefully endeavour the propagation of Christianity by permitting children, though slaves, or those of greater growth if capable, to be admitted to that sacrament."

24. Franz Overbeck, "Über das Verhaltnis der alten Kirche zur Sklaverei in römischen Reiche," in *Studien zur Geschichte der alten Kirche* (Erlangen und Leipzig, 1898[2]), pp. 116-159. Alphons Steinmann, *Sklavenlos und alte Kirche* (Munich-Gladbach: Volksverein, 1910, 1922[3]), and by the same author, *Paulus und die Sklaven von Korinth* (Braunsberg, 1911).

25. In the most uninhibited way by Leo XIII in his Encyclical of May 5, 1888. This at least caused Cardinal Lavigerie to attempt founding an international movement for the abolishment of the slave trade (see RGG[2], V, p. 579).

26. Thus J. Witte in RGG[2], V, p. 577 (article on "Sklaverei und Christentum"). In the corresponding article in the third edition of RGG, vol. VI, p. 102, H. D. Wendland holds against this "sooner or later" formulation that the New Testament ethic of the Christian community "had not made questionable the social institution of slavery" (the expression "questionable" is questionable here). He also adds the strange empiricist argument that "slavery has existed in numerous ways in America, Africa, and Asia until the nineteenth century without being principally opposed by the churches."

27. Hans Schulze, *Gottesoffenbarung und Gesellschaftsordnung: Untersuchungen zur Prinzipienlehre der Gesellschaftstheologie* (Munich: C. Kaiser, 1968), pp. 172f.

28. Helmut Thielicke, "Konnen sich Strukturen bekehren?" in *Zeitschrift für Theologie und Kirche*, 66, 1969, pp. 112f. Such an apologetic maneuver of skipping the facts of church history is old. It can be found already, for example, in Ch. E. Luthardt, *Apologetische Vortrage: Uber die Grundwahrheiten des Christentums* (Leipzig: Dorffling and Franke, 1883[10]), p. 225: Christianity

has not "immediately and outwardly annulled slavery, but it taught people to recognize the person, the Christian brother in the slave and thereby broke down the abominable institution from inside."

29. Thielicke not only neglects this research, but without any proof charges those who undertake it, and who therefore represent a "theology of revolution," with the "mistake" that they onesidedly promote a "project of world change" concentrating on structures only and overlooking the necessity of a change of heart.

30. David Friedrich Strauss, *Der alte und der neue Glaube* (Bonn: E. Strauss, 1903[15]), p. 56: "To respect the human being even in the slave" was learned not from Christianity, but from Stoicism. "The abolition of slavery was not an achievement of the Christian church, but of the much maligned Enlightenment. Human rights is not a Christian, but a philosophical concept." This type of polemic reminds us of Overbeck and of Joachim Kahl's presentation of "the church as slave-holder" (in *Das Elend des Christentums*, rororo aktuell, 1968, pp. 18-27). It is no less onesided than the opposite Christian apologetic which appeals to the humanism of the Gospel without mentioning church history. The much needed book by Siegfried Schultz, *Gott ist kein Sklavenhalter: Die Geschichte einer verspateten Revolution* (Hamburg, 1972) is free of both mistakes, although I feel that the harsh criticism of the Apostle Paul needs correction. Cf. the reactions to S. Schultz's article "Hat Christus die Sklaven befreit?": Helmut Cron, *Evangelische Kommentare*, 1972, 1, pp. 13-18; Peter Stuhlmacher, ibid., pp. 297ff.; Eduard Schweizer, *Evangelische Theologie*, 1972, 5, pp. 502-506.

31. Thielicke, "Konnen sich Strukturen bekehren?" p. 114.

32. George Casalis, "Die theologischen Prioritäten des nächsten Jahrzehnts," in *Theol. Practica*, 1971, p. 323.

33. The history of the United States since the emancipation of the slaves in 1865 proved to the blacks that true emancipation can only be realized through a revolution of the whole society. Therefore they are no longer content with reformism. Marx's opposition to Lasalle is still valid today: "It is as if among slaves, who finally discovered the secret of slavery and began a rebellion, one slave still caught in outmoded views would write on the program of rebellion: slavery has to be abolished because the feeding of slaves within the system of slavery cannot exceed a certain low maximum." ("Kritik des Gothaer Programs," 1875, II, in Marx/Engels, *Ausgewahlte Schriften*, II [Berlin: Dietz, 1968], p. 22). How much catching up there is to be done in white theology in its approach toward revolution becomes clear in a remark by Arnold A. T. Ehrhardt in his *Politische Metaphysik von Solon bis Augustin*, vol. 2, *Die christliche Revolution* (Tübingen: Mohr, 1959), p.19: "This attitude toward slavery also affords us a criterion for the way in which Christianity has to be considered as revolutionary. For it is a fact which has often been overlooked in political theories that revolutions should not be judged by the terror they spread or the destruction they cause but by the question whether or not they offer a political alternative to the system they oppose. A movement is truly revolutionary if the new political principles cannot be fit into the existing system they oppose, if they at best can be balanced with it only temporarily, if every single principle of the ruling order (even the most benevolent one) is exposed to intensive criticism by representatives of a new order, because no principle of the old system could, or should, be valid in view of the revolutionary principles. In this sense Christianity during the first centuries was the radical revolution—and should be the same today, even though emotionally its voice might be divided when current political opinion is at stake."

34. Martin Luther, *Complete Works of Martin Luther* (*Weimarer Ausgabe* 43, p. 214) (Genesis lecture): *Hae sunt verae mortificationes, quae non fiunt in desertis locis extra societatem hominum, sed in ipsa oeconomia et politia.*

35. James Baldwin, referring to a piece by William Faulkner, set in the time of slavery, indicates what pertains to the social ethics of white theology (with the exception of religious socialism): "He is seeking to exorcise a history which is also a curse. He wants the old order, which came into existence through unchecked greed and wanton murder, to redeem itself without further bloodshed—without, that is, any further menacing itself—and without coercion. This old orders never do, less because they would not than because they cannot. They cannot because they have always existed in relation to a force which they have had to subdue. This subjugation is the key to their identity and the triumph and justification of their history, and it is also on this continued subjugation that their material well-being depends. One may see that the history, which is now indivisible from oneself, has been full of errors and excesses; but this is not the same thing as seeing that, for millions of people, this history—oneself—has been nothing but an intolerable yoke, a stinking prison, shrieking grave. It is not so easy to see that, for millions of

people, life itself depends on the speediest possible demolition of this history, even if this means the leveling, or the destruction of its heirs," James Baldwin, *No Name in the Street* (New York: Dial Press, 1972), pp. 46f.

36. It is a matter of much regret that a translation of Cone's second volume, *A Black Theology of Liberation* (New York: Lippincott, 1970) has not as yet found a German publisher.

37. This reference and the one to Herbert O. Edwards (p.164) are to other articles in the *Union Seminary Quarterly Review* (Fall 1975) symposium, of which my article is a part. H.G.

38. For the confessions offered in prison by this leader of a slave rebellion, see Herbert Apteker, *Nat Turner's Slave Rebellion* (New York: Humanities Press, 1966).

39. Violent means are part and parcel of every political battle because even within a parliamentary system where it is initially fought peacefully by ballots it takes place within the framework of government power guaranteeing law and order and aims at gaining the power, that is, the competency for legislation and the enforcing of laws by the power of the state.

40. Cf. James H. Cone, *The Spirituals and the Blues* (New York: Seabury, 1972), p. 16.

41. See James H. Cone's interpretation of Spirituals in "Singend mit dem Schwert in der Hand," *Evangelische Kommentare*, 1971, pp. 442-447.

42. See, besides many others, the words of two former slaves, whom B. A. Botkin quotes in his moving book, *Lay My Burden Down* (Chicago: University of Chicago Press, 1945), pp. 107, 109, 267.

43. See James H. Cone, "Singend mit dem Schwert in der Hand," p. 447.

44. B. A. Botkin, op. cit., p. 26.

45. Thus Karl Barth in 1938 in view of the vast prison of the criminal Nazi state in *Rechtfertigung und Recht*, reprint in *Theologische Studien*, Heft 104, 1970, pp. 44f.

46. James H. Cone, "Singend mit dem Schwert in der Hand," p. 445.

47. Cf. H. L. Althaus, "Die Heiden streiken nicht," in *Lutherische Monatshefte*, 1974, 4, and the reports about the Ovambo strike, published by the Vereinigte Evangelische Mission under the titles, "Evangelium und Menschenrecht" and "Kirchliches Handeln oder politische Aktion," in *Dokumentationsreihe der Vereinigten Evangelischen Mission*, Heft 1 and 2 (Wuppertal, 1972).

48. If such formulations remind the German reader of similar utterances by the "German Christians" under Hitler, he has to realize how inappropriate this comparison is.

49. James Baldwin, *No Name in the Street*, pp. 189f.

50. James Baldwin, ibid., pp. 93f.

51. The same pertains to the passionate utterances by James Baldwin which are quite understandable—and as such valid—but do not look beyond the present situation: "It is not necessary for a black man to hate a white man, or to have any particular feelings about him at all, in order to realize that he must kill him. Yes, we have come, or are coming to this, and there is no point in flinching before the prospect of this exceedingly cool species of fratricide—which prospect white people, after all, have brought on themselves. Of course, whenever a black man discusses violence he is said to be advocating it. This is very far indeed from my intention, if only because I have no desire whatever to see a generation perish in the streets. But the shape and extent of whatever violence may come is not in the hands of people like myself, but in the hands of the American people, who are at present among the most dishonorable and violent people in the world. I am merely trying to face certain blunt, human facts. I do not carry a gun and do not consider myself to be a violent man: but my life has more than once depended on the gun in a brother's holster. I know that when certain powerful and blatant enemies of black people are shoveled, at last, into the ground I may feel a certain pity that they spent their lives so badly, but I certainly do not mourn their passing, nor, when I hear that they are ailing, do I pray for their recovery. I know what I would do if I had a gun and someone had a gun pointed at my brother, and I would not count ten to do it and there would be no hatred in it, not any remorse. People who treat other people as less than human must not be surprised when the bread they have cast on the waters comes floating back to them, poisoned." (Op. cit., pp. 191f.)

16

BLACK THEOLOGY OF LIBERATION

John C. Bennett

James Cone is the chief systematic exponent of a "black theology" of liberation. He states one reason for a new black theology: "No white theologian has ever taken the oppression of black people as a point of departure for analyzing God's activity in comtemporary America."[1] I am sure he is right. One could say more than that: The predominantly white churches and their white theologians did not face the full depth of the wrong done by our country to blacks since its beginning until after they were prodded by a new generation of blacks in the 1950's.

As critics look back upon the theologians of the social gospel movement they charge them with neglecting the problem of black oppression, with showing almost no awareness of what was happening to blacks in their own time. This was true of Walter Rauschenbusch, the greatest of them. In the case of Josiah Strong, one of the most popular writers connected with the movement, there was a tendency to think of the global supremacy of Anglo-Saxons. Strong was also concerned about the effect of the great influx of non-Anglo-Saxon immigrants upon our cities. This was a kind of racism that is shocking to us, but it was congenial to the flamboyant belief in world progress under the leadership of "advanced" peoples that was common in the "progressive era" around 1900.

Explanations of this neglect in the case of many leaders of the social gospel include the idea that they were Northerners who regarded oppression of blacks as a Southern problem. Their culure-affirming optimism kept them from perceiving the malignancy and pervasiveness of this evil in their culture.[2]

John C. Bennett is President Emeritus of Union Theological Seminary, New York City. This article is an excerpt from his book *The Radical Imperative* (Philadelphia: Westminster Press, 1975), pp. 119-131.

I have been surprised in rereading my first book, *Social Salvation*, in which I dealt with many social evils that had priority for me in 1935, that the evil of racial injustice was not one of them. I was concerned chiefly about the human consequences of the economic depression and about the threat of war.

Rauschenbusch and others were aware of the horror of episodes of lynching and he included them as one of the marks of "the Kingdom of Evil." He traced the origin of the lynching spirit to "our fathers" who "created the conditions of sin by the African slave trade and by the unearned wealth they gathered from slave labour for generations."[3]

One major reason for the neglect of black oppression was preoccupation with economic issues. Racial injustice has a most important economic aspect, but what concerned Rauschenbusch and his generation was the rapacity of untamed business, the lack of power of the industrial workers, and the poverty in Northern cities, which they knew firsthand. My book was a case in point. While that is no defense of my own limited awareness, it does give some explanation of my priorities at the time.

The famous "Social Creed of the Churches," adopted by the Federal Council of Churches in 1908, dealt only with economic issues and did not mention race. It is more remarkable that when the creed was expanded and revised in 1932 there was the same neglect of race. That expanded statement began: "The Churches Should Stand For:" There followed seventeen articles, thirteen of which dealt with economic objectives. One dealt with the treatment of offenders; another with the repudiation of war, calling for the peaceable settlement of all controversies; a third dealt with freedom of speech and assembly and the press and freedom of communication of mind with mind. There was also the following article: "Justice, opportunity and equal rights for all; mutual goodwill and cooperation among racial, economic and religious groups." This was the only reference to race in a document that was called "The Social Ideals of the Churches" and that, after four years of preparation, was adopted by a full meeting of the representatives of the denominations that were members of the Federal Council of Churches—in matters of social policy the chief predecessor of the National Council of Churches.

I want to put beside that total neglect of the oppression of black Americans the testimony of one of the most admired black leaders of the last generation, Dr. Benjamin E. Mays, president for many years of Morehouse College. Dr. Mays is not a militant, and he is quite free from the more recent antiwhite attitudes. Indeed I would be surprised if he did not have great difficulty with the idea of "black theology." Yet in his autobiography entitled *Born to Rebel* (1971) he describes the plight of black people before and after the appearance of that statement of "The Social Ideals of the Churches" in words that are as devastating in their criticism of white oppressors as any the most militant blacks use today. He writes as follows: "Not only in major areas—the right to vote, the right to economic security, the right to education, the right

to decent housing—was the Negro deprived. But these basic denials prolifer-
ated also in countless ways to guarantee that every Negro should be consistently subjected to humiliating injustices and insults calculated to destroy his
self-respect, his pride, and his sense of manhood."[4] This moderate leader,
who was himself highly honored by the churches, having been a vice-
president of the Federal Council of Churches in 1948, and who late in life
became president of the Atlanta Board of Education, makes this judgment
about the churches: "I believe that throughout my lifetime, the local white
church has been society's most conservative and hypocritical institution in
the area of White-Negro relations."[5] Such words from a contemporary
militant might be regarded as coming out of hostility toward the white
church, but Benjamin Mays has no such hostility. His book is full of reports
of experiences that he himself suffered that illustrate all that he says about the
systematic efforts to humiliate his race. It is out of this bitter experience that
black theology has come. White people have nothing in their experience that
enables them fully to understand it. Martin Luther King, Jr., who embodied
all that was most persuasive in the civil rights movement, did more than
anyone else to bring about a change in the outlook of a great many persons in
the white churches. He had trouble until the very end with the idea of "black
power," even though he organized black power with great effect. I doubt if he
would ever have chosen to put together the words "black theology." Yet
without that early civil rights movement which he represented, I wonder if
black theology today would not be an unheeded voice in a white wilderness.

I realize that many readers may regard this as a one-sided picture of the role
of white people both in the North and in the South between the 1920's and
the 1950's. There were many efforts to deal with specific issues as they arose.
For example, it was the practice of church groups to avoid meeting in any
place where there might be discrimination against blacks, and this was a
matter of great symbolic importance. There were also pioneering activities by
many institutions, such as the student Christian movements and especially
the Y.W.C.A., in arranging interracial events. White leaders in the North
gave strong support to the Fellowship (later Committee) of Southern
Churchmen, which was involved in considerable costly pioneering in the
South. Much spadework was done by Southern moderates to counteract the
venom of race prejudice. This side of the story, however, does not cancel out
the massive support by most churches of discrimination against and segregation of the black minority.

A leading African theologian, John Mbiti, a professor from Uganda who is
now the director of the Ecumenical Institute of the World Council of
Churches, has warned that black theology is an American phenomenon and
not representative of black Africa. He says: "It was forced into existence by
the particularities of American history." He says that in southern Africa black
theology deserves a hearing. But he makes the interesting comment that
blacks in southern Africa, unlike those in the United States, are not free to

talk about black liberation; they need first to be liberated. He says that African theology "grows out of our joy in the experience of the Christian faith, whereas Black theology emerges from the pains of oppression." This also must be a partial view because there is oppression in black Africa, not least in Mbiti's own country, Uganda, where it is often oppression of blacks by blacks. Mbiti does not deny the validity of black theology in the United States and he does underline its special strategic role here.[6]

Black theology belongs to the stage of the black struggle for liberation that has followed the early spring of the civil rights movement when it was a cause with clear objectives that aroused great enthusiasm in the white liberal community both religious and secular. During that period many gains were made in overcoming legal barriers to desegregation and also in enabling blacks to secure the right to vote where it had been denied them, a right that they have used. The political power that blacks are gaining now may well be the most important result of the legislation passed in that period.

Black theology belongs to a later period, one in which blacks are disillusioned about the substance of the early gains, in which integration is seen as token entrance into the white world on terms set by whites, in which voluntary separatism in place of imposed segregation has considerable attraction. The gains of the civil rights movement created more hopeful changes in the South than in the North. The Northern backlash against efforts to integrate schools became as ugly and as stubborn as the earlier Southern backlash. The most frustrating aspect of the continuing oppression of blacks is in the increase of the economic deprivation of the majority of them. Urban ghetto communities are cursed by unemployment rates of 30 to 40 percent of their young people, and the national rate of black unemployment is more than double that of whites. Also, the gap between incomes of blacks and whites has widened even though many blacks with training have better opportunities than before. Many cities have black mayors, but too often their task is to preside over urban deterioration and inhuman conditions for their own race. On the other side I think it should be said that the efforts of educational institutions on all levels to include blacks and to counteract the effects of their exclusion from educational opportunities in the past has been considerable. Also, there is much less of the deliberate humiliation of black people by the white majority in both North and South.

I confess it is difficult for me as a white man to write about black theology. I am in danger of doing one of two things in any given case. It is easy to say an uncritical "yes" to all that is said against white people, out of a sense of guilt for the past. It is also easy to become defensive against what may seem to be unfair attacks upon whites. If I were to follow James Cone's advice literally, I would be silent on the subject. He says: "If whites were really serious about their radicalism in regard to the black revolution and its theological implications in America, they would keep silent and take instructions from black people."[7] Yet if I were to write about other movements for liberation and neglect black liberation, this would suggest indifference, a sure sign of white racism.

Both white and black critics may think that I give too much attention to James Cone's version of black theology, which they may be inclined to regard as an ephemeral explosion. I do not doubt that it, like most white theologies, will soon be dated. But Cone is the most systematic black theologian today and his thought is reflected in corporate statements of the National Committee of Black Churchmen. It is taken seriously by Gayraud S. Wilmore, author of the recent and much-admired comprehensive statement of black religious thinking, *Black Religion and Black Radicalism* (Doubleday, 1972).

Cone's black theology at its center is an affirmation of the liberating work of God for all oppressed peoples. The exodus is seen as the original liberating event, which reveals that God "is the God of the oppressed, involved in their history, liberating them from bondage."[8] Cone says: "The resurrection event means that God's liberating work is not only for the house of Israel but for all who are enslaved by the principalities and powers."[9] Cone regards his theology as centered in Jesus Christ and he stresses as I have done the identification of Christ with the poor and oppressed. He begins his first book, *Black Theology and Black Power*, by saying that "Black Power" is "Christ's central message to twentieth-century America."[10] He comes to this conclusion because faithfulness to Jesus Christ as the liberator of black people requires, in his view, the use of black power to effect that liberation. He has no patience at all with those who draw pacifist implications from the teachings of Jesus. He is disdainful of white people who preach nonviolence to black people while in their own interests they control the many forms of institutionalized coercion or violence that keep blacks in their position of inferiority and deprivation. I have no quarrel with the conclusion that faithfulness to Jesus Christ does not involve a law of nonviolence applicable to all situations, but I think that Cone too easily reduces the tension between violence and the teachings of Jesus; however, I am more interested in emphasizing that tension in addressing oppressors than I am in addressing the oppressed. Cone speaks much of Christ as black or as a black event. He says that "thinking of Christ as non-black in the twentieth century is as theologically impossible as thinking of him as non-Jewish in the first century."[11] He is using "black" symbolically and not literally as, I think, Albert Cleage, Jr., does in his book *The Black Messiah*.[12]

The casual reader can be thrown off by Cone's use of the words "black" and "white." He is responsible for a natural misinterpretation because he does not explain what he is doing with the words except in two footnotes in *A Black Theology of Liberation*.[13] I think that he must intentionally preserve this ambiguity because he wants all white people, in the first instance at least, to feel the lash of his rhetoric against whiteness as such. And he wants to keep the emphasis on those who are literally black because they are the largest oppressed community in the United States.

In his footnotes Cone does say that "white" may refer to an attitude rather than to a color in the literal sense. He is aware that after his wholesale criticism of all white theology he may be taunted for depending as much as he does on Karl Barth and Paul Tillich. Also, "black" may refer to all suffering and oppressed people. Cone does speak of this in the text of his book (pp. 27, 28). This would be his answer to those who wonder where the Indians and the Chicanos and impoverished and oppressed white people come in. It would be his answer also in the ecumenical context to those who wonder at the provincialism of his books in their neglect of yellow and brown peoples. Had Cone been more careful about this use of words, his books might too quickly have provided an "out" for his white readers; attention might have been so diverted toward a global context for liberation that the intensity of his concern for the black victims of American white people would have been lost. The following two sentences represent many others: "American white theology is a theology of the Antichrist, insofar as it arises from an identification with the white community, thereby placing God's approval on white oppression of black existence."[14] The words "insofar as" enable Cone to make exceptions, though he would not want this to become a habit. "He [God] is not color blind in the black-white struggle, but has made an unqualified identification with black people."[15]

The narrowness of Cone's focus may be seen in the way in which he deals with the Vietnam war. He questions the "authenticity" of the white opposition to the war, since "the destruction of black humanity began long before the Vietnam war and few white people got upset about it."[16] He asks: "Is it because white boys are dying in the war that whites get so upset?" The direct, deliberate, and massive destruction of Vietnamese, who are not white, by our Government was not paralleled by comparable direct, deliberate, and massive destructions of blacks by our Government. There was an emergency aspect of the officially initiated and guided destruction in Vietnam that makes Cone's remarks on this subject an indication of a blind spot of his own. Also, there was a disproportionate use of American blacks in the war because of the deferments that were readily open to many more whites. They were sent to kill yellow people and became victims themselves. I was always sorry that more black leaders did not share the outrage of Martin Luther King, Jr., about the war, for—in spite of all inherited deprivations and handicaps—articulate blacks could have had considerable influence on public opinion and on the Federal Government.

All theologies are to some extent strategic theologies. They give emphasis to the questions of a particular time and place and they seek to counteract what are believed to be the errors that are most tempting at the time of writing. Cone's black theology is so much a strategic theology that, especially in its doctrine of sin, it will surely be misleading as new situations develop. In the context of this book at this time I understand his statement, "Because sin is a concept that is meaningful only for an oppressed community as it reflects on liberation, it is not possible to make a universal analysis that is meaningful for both black and white people."[17] The strategic nature of this theology is seen in his statement that while black theology does not deny that all men are sinners, "what it denies is white reflections on the sin of black people."[18] I am not interested in white reflections on the sin of black people. I do think that it is important that black theology show some signs that it is preparing black people for the discovery of their own sins, for their own self-criticism. I fail to see that this is yet one of Cone's interests. His use of "white," ambiguous as it is, according to two footnotes, does easily give the impression that the destruction of white sources of sin and error would liberate all humanity. Such a sentence as the following may easily mislead whites and blacks alike: "What we need is the destruction of whiteness, which is the source of human misery in the world."[19] I think that it would be good if Cone were to put a theological message in a sealed envelope to be read at some future time when black people gain more power, when blacks are seen to be oppressors of other blacks or of whites. This is especially important because black theology is a call to revolution, and revolutionaries, whatever form the revolution may take, are greatly tempted to a passionate self-righteousness which distorts the mind and the spirit. I am not concerned about threats of black violence that Cone engages in, because I agree with him that the greater violence today is the violence of "the system" against blacks.

I think that there is an element of unreality in Cone's tendency to regard white racism as monolithic and unchanging with all whites save those who are "black" in spirit. I realize that it is easier to see this element of unreality when one sees the world from a white perspective, and I cannot avoid doing that. Cone's writings are intended to be polemical, and he paints with a broad brush, but it would be desirable to relate black theology to a more empirical effort to diagnose the phenomenon of racism. I am not the one to do that, but there are a few considerations that I should like to raise for discussion. This is a racist culture. Racism is embedded in institutions as varied as racially slanted intelligence tests, the habits of police, and practices in the sale of real estate. The deposit of centuries of an imposed state of inferiority has left its mark on what black people expect for themselves and on what white people expect of them.

Some results of a Harris poll taken among American blacks show the terrible consequences that remain of the centuries of oppression. "More than four out of five blacks think that whites consider Negroes inferior. Two thirds of blacks believe whites to be afraid that blacks are better people than they are. Nearly the same number—63%—feel that whites regret having abolished slavery" (*Time*, April 6, 1970). That last statement I find incredible, but even if it is exaggerated it reveals a great deal about what blacks see as present-day racism.

Yet there have been significant changes in law, and to a considerable extent law has been an educator. Blacks in the South, as I have said, seem now to be more hopeful than are blacks in the North. For this both federal law and Southern black power have a good deal of the responsibility. The old-fashioned political racist demagogues are dying out and the constituency to which they have appealed is narrowing. The election of black sheriffs in Southern counties is regarded as having special importance for the day-to-day welfare of black people. I think that the election by a whole state of high black officials such as Wilson Riles, the chief education officer of California, is a sign of the diminution of prejudice. Also, fortunate blacks who are well trained are in great demand for employment by many institutions, including universities, church bureaucracies, and private business. However, I should not do much celebrating of gains for blacks until the walls that surround ghettos are leveled and until the statistics concerning black unemployment and black incomes change radically for the better.

If we think of conscious attitudes of white people, it seems to me that more emphasis should be put on diversity. There is a wide spectrum of attitudes. On the one hand there are the hostile racists who seek to keep blacks in positions of inferiority. On the other hand there are those who tend to treat blacks as objects, or who show awkwardness in their relations with them, but who sincerely support black causes. If you call the latter group "racists," it makes a difference that on most issues they can be persuaded to be allies of black power and that their votes add up as well as black votes. Black liberation depends on black power, but not on isolated black power. It must have allies, but Cone's polemics leave little space for them.

Also, it should be recognized that many whites are first- or second-generation Americans and their ancestors had no part in the slave system or in the establishment and hardening of the institutions of discrimination and segregation. Often they were Europe's poor, and they are not won to the black cause by rhetoric that associates them with those sins of American history. The language of reparations, while justified in many contexts, makes little sense to them. Today they should be helped to see that it is superficial for them to compare their winning of their way as white people in spite of initial ethnic disadvantages in this country with the situation of blacks who have handicaps growing out of centuries of an imposed status of inferiority. There is here a human problem that is not helped by wholesale denunciations.

The tension between blacks and Jews, seen in the issue of quotas, in confrontations in the ghetto between blacks and Jews (the latter as landlords, shopkeepers, teachers, and social workers), and in the common black identification with Arabs as part of the Third World, is one of the most tragic aspects of the racial conflict in America. This is a unique problem in itself and calls for careful thought. It is not helped by undiscriminating polemics based upon our nation's history of black oppression.

Cone would regard it as a diversion, but I think that in the long run we should see the white American attitude toward blacks as part of a more comprehensive racism that does not easily accept the humanity of nonwhite people on other continents. It is not a static attitude. We have seen the Japanese become accepted as human after they were hated as subhuman yellow creatures during the Second World War. The Chinese, who were "yellow hordes" for so long, are much admired for their achievements in transforming their country. I hope that a similar change will come in the American attitude toward the people of Indochina, whose racial difference made it possible for Americans to treat them as "gooks" who could easily be made victims of atrocities on land and targets of relentless bombing from the air. I have referred to an Anglo-Saxon and northern European racism that has in the past controlled the attitude of Americans to "lesser breeds without the Law." It dominated immigration policies until recently. It is no longer often defended, but it remains a strong influence and clouds the vision of large parts of the population.

I have no zeal for these criticisms of Cone's black theology because I believe that it appeared at the right time and that it has important work to do. It has deepened my own awareness of the blind spots of white theologians, beginning with myself.

Notes

1.   James H. Cone, *A Black Theology of Liberation* (J. B. Lippincott Company, 1970), p. 31.
2.   There is a very helpful article on "Social Gospel Christianity and Racism" by Glenn R. Bucher in *The Union Seminary Quarterly Review*, Winter 1973.
3.   Rauschenbusch, *A Theology for the Social Gospel* (The Macmillan Company, 1971), p. 79.
4.   Benjamin E. Mays, *Born to Rebel: An Autobiography* (Charles Scribner's Sons, 1971), p. 75.
5.   Ibid., p. 241.
6.   John Mbiti, "An African Views American Black Theology," *Worldview*, August 1974.
7.   Cone, *A Black Theology of Liberation*, p. 119.
8.   Ibid., p. 19.
9.   Ibid., p. 21.
10.   James H. Cone, *Black Theology and Black Power* (The Seabury Press, Inc., 1969), p. 1.
11.   Ibid., p. 69.
12.   Albert B. Cleage, Jr., *The Black Messiah* (Sheed & Ward, Inc., 1969).
13.   Cone, *A Black Theology of Liberation*, pp. 28 and 32.
14.   Ibid., p. 25.
15.   Ibid., p. 26.
16.   Ibid., p. 174.
17.   Ibid., p. 190.
18.   Ibid., p. 100.
19.   Ibid., p. 193.

17

ABOUT BLACK THEOLOGY

Paul Holmer

No one could live this past decade without being troubled by the shrill demands for relevance. These have come from a variety of sources and with differing intensities. Perhaps nothing has shaken confidence in the universities and other educational institutions as much as the almost complete capitulation of administrative staffs and the faculty to the sundry and demanding spirits of the day. For in one situation after another, educational leadership also tended to follow, rather than to lead or even to discipline, the vagaries of social pressures and indefinite demands. Besides, there was a new intellectual force buttressing this educational adaptation. It was a kind of "ad hoc" historicism, a vague explanatory thesis, which, in effect, told us as we went along, about the psychology of the alienated, the sociology of the distressed, the ethics of the oppressed and the politics of minorities.

All this quasi-knowledge of groups was also centered in and voiced by a new breed of relevant professors, who had made contemporaneity their field, albeit their disciplines were many. The upshot was that from within the educational confines, not just from men of affairs, there came a strong and insistent voice that was always closing the gap between what is and what ought to be. For the new field-concerns celebrated relevance. Suddenly there was a pressure for "new" everything, including a kind of new "academism." For it looked as though that very general explanation and justification of past policies, that once was tortured out of stubborn material by scholarship, was now being provided by a new kind of "ad hoc" teacher-scholar, who was both explaining "why" present people were the way they were and also proposing the policy by which to fructify expectations and also to heal the wrongs. It looked for a while as if we were, with this new socialized learning, going to get

Paul Holmer teaches theology at Yale Divinity School. This essay first appeared in the *Lutheran Quarterly*, vol. 28, no. 3 (1976), pp. 231-239.

a few sureties, not just about the dead past but for the living present and the aborning future.

It might be no surprise to say that higher education began to look, very briefly, as though it would fulfill the liberals' political dreams. Most of us in the universities these past few decades have drunk rather deeply from that ideological cup. We have learned to want everything—convenience, comfort, mobility, status, style, perhaps a little religion thrown in—and we have also shared the popular political morality—that we could get these "goods" if we could only change the wretched social arrangements and educate ourselves and others properly. The new "academism," coupled with the popular demands and affluence and a host of other things, gave an optimistic and quasi-moral set of reasons for both the rising expectations and for meeting a whole set of demands rising up for new freedoms, for no war, for equality, for all kinds of socially relevant studies.

I refer to these things mostly because I bear the opprobrium of not fighting them more cogently, more courageously and with firmer insight. I take slight consolation in the notions that are so general among faint-hearted academics, namely that time educates all of us or that we had no alternative. For if the first is true, the rationale for academic learning itself is badly eroded; and the second is not only false but is precisely like the rationalization one has read for every capitulation to dictatorship. It is strangely similar to what I thought were flatulent and egregious moral mistakes when I heard them from the lips of colleagues in Germany when they explained why they did nothing about the vanquishing of the Jews in the mid-1930's.

More than this, I also found that something new, Black Theology, began to obtrude itself in one of the fields where I seek competence. Above all, it was a novelty, and like all novelties it was not easily assimilable. But, it was the way that it obtruded itself that made things difficult. I was told that I "must" be threatened by it, for being white, I could be nothing else; that it was "black" and could only be understood by blacks and that they were the only jury; that it all had to do with black revolution and that revolution was its touchstone as well as the one thing needful. I began to hear that there was a black logic, a black experience and a black morality. When all of that was put together with talk of a black Virgin and a black God, there was the strong temptation to let it all slip by as a kind of intellectual wantonness.

Once more a kind of sociology of learning, born both of vague theory and the new academic lore on the one side, and of a condescending kindness on the other, began to manifest itself in the universities and seminaries. For academic people have been loathe to criticize thoughts lately, mostly because they seem to be convinced by an outrageously mistaken theory. It suggests that most thoughts are only ways of adaptation, subtle ways of behaving, and that we have to accept and to respect them for what they are, just as we accept and respect a group's customary ways of eating, sleeping, talking and, for example, courting one another. So, Black Theology was not so much examined and listened to as it was blanketed by an ambiguous expressionist theory. Once more the accommodating manner of the modern ethos seemed to me to render dignity neither to the professors on the one side nor to Black Theology and blacks on the other.

At this juncture I am not at all content with (*a*) the strangely tolerant air of the modern university where criteria of sense/nonsense, truth/falsity, reasonable/unreasonable, good/bad, right/wrong, have lost much of their governing force and authority. Where everything, including ideas and convictions, even standards and logical criteria, is treated as an anthropological and sociological by-product, then we are in for a time when non-intellectual criteria, which are infinitely more dangerous, come to have full sway. But, (*b*) I continue to share misgivings about Black Theology, mostly because it seems to share the weaknesses and fundamentally non-intellectual ethos of our day. Theology, even in its most austere and long-standing academic mode, has difficulties enough, for it often lacks an identifiable structure and aim. But Black Theology shares the difficulties of theology in general, plus those engendered by its complicity in the new academism already noted.

In what follows, I will, therefore, isolate some issues which arise in Black Theology, but which obviously do not have their origin there—they are also wider difficulties. Unless I am very wrong, indeed, Black Theology is too important to be treated by neglect or by condescending kindness; instead, I want to bring criteria to bear upon it, so that its difficulties will not isolate its proponents and so that its merits will not be hidden from honest inquirers.

II

Imagine my consternation when facing in 1967 a class of advanced students, gathered ostensibly to discuss Kierkegaard's literature, to be met by the flat demand—"Before I sign up for this course, what does Kierkegaard have to do with the Black movement?" An isolated instance would be tolerable enough; but there was and still is something else operative. For when I said, trying to be sympathetic if for no other reason than that unflinching opposition seemed so empty and futile, "On the one hand, nothing; on the other everything," I was told with unapologetic indignation that I had better get with the "movement" or else. I know it is fashionable to excuse impoliteness and threats on the grounds of "they have the right to be angry," or "how would you feel if. . . ." However, right here is another kind of issue altogether.

The Black Theology movement has been part of the new "academism" and the new "puritanism." And I think it is intellectually deprived because of it. What it contained in urgency and thrust at the moment, it has lost in authority and quality. Of course, I do not mean to imply that "puritanism" might, in this instance, or others for that matter, be associated exclusively with purity in the specifically sexual sense of chastity. If the Black Movement were, it might be refreshing for all of us. But recent puritan types, both academic and religious, seem to be very far from worrying anybody about such notions. Rather, puritanism and the novel academism of these recent years has evinced an all-or-nothing attitude, a marked reluctance to compromise and a tendency to bring everything to judgment by a single standard. This strikes me as a feature of Black Theology, as if the fate of the Blacks, even to Blacks, were the one thing needful. The unfortunate feature of Black Theology, as I have been reading it, is that it shares this passion to override everything else; and then, besides, it adds a note as if it is not only backed by a relentless imperative, but that it ought to do so.

Of course, Black Theology, as part of the social movements and the new academic fever, acquired a certain importance simply because it was exclusive, shrill and demanding. It fed the need for drama and histrionics. It gave a kind of religious sanction for those who wanted to prove themselves by attacking something powerful. Christian theology is, after all, a huge and almost oppressively weighty tradition, fed often by genius and insinuated into all kinds of practices and ethical decisions. Clearly enough, too, our generation has been taught to see the corruptions of the earlier generation and to feel the need for sweeping away anything that kept the world from getting better. And many of the moral thrusts in all of this are laudable. Insofar as Black Theology gave these voice and discipline, one can probably praise it. For a while, it gave rationale to the notion that gladiatorial talk was going to get an equitous moral order finally established.

But I think there was a near-fatal flaw in all of this. The much good that was promised by the vision and the wounding of consciences was undone by the false idea that puritanic academism and religiosity invariably fosters. That is, plainly, that the present cause, this demanding and overpowering need, was sealed off, unique and ordinarily unreachable. The cause of the Blacks in the Black Theology became over-simplified, singular, and so important that it muzzled the wide range of Blacks, it silenced all challenges of others, it avoided modification, complexity and conversation. It became a privilege of the elected, not a right of all who seek understanding.

This is, of course, also the way with ideologies. In the world in which we live where dangers are everywhere and securities only temporary, we must remember that mountains are moved in very odd ways. I, for one, and I suspect other theologians and philosophers, too, are grateful to that small number of good men whose criteria for the conduct of their lives are plainly social and moral, who want social justice, a world given to the concerns of majority, and an end to the plight of the hapless, the helpless, the defrauded and the poor. And, indeed, from Black leaders those criteria came forth, levelled against our plans, our smugness, our institutions and our every-day judgments. But with Black consciousness and theology there came also a restriction upon discussion, upon give-and-take. True to form, also, was the notion developed that discussion, argumentation, and plain and unhurried talk was "white," irresponsible and plainly again, a luxury one cannot afford if the enormity of the cause is truly felt.

This, I say again, is the failure of the recent academic posture and also, in great part, of Black Theology. It proposes itself both as a privilege of the Blacks, whose experience is said to be unique and self-authenticating, and yet an obligation to be recognized and responded to by everybody else, who, in the nature of the case, progressively are stripped of the means to respond in any meaningful way. The consequence of all this is that Black Theology was treated and is being treated with what I think was and is a denigrating tolerance. I think it still goes on and is still denigrating. I am not arguing for intolerance; but I am suggesting that theology, be it Black or anything else, must not be policed as if examination of it were forbidden; nor must it be simplified for the sake of revolution, liberation or unity of people, for that will only lead to an avoidance of challenge and its use as a cover for failure. We have had enough, too, of the cult of extreme statement, for, at best, this only attracts attention and does not cultivate understanding. Obviously, this is to say that one must make a choice. If we are going to incite and to raise alarms, then we must address an audience in one way and expect a limited response; but if we are going to do theology (or philosophy, or history, or any science one pleases), then our language has to have nuances and we forsake the notion that the audience is deaf to everything except superlatives and loud threats.

This is said not because Black Theology is exclusively that way. On the contrary; but much of it is and it shares that feature with the ardent "academism" and the puritanical fevers of our day. But there is another serious issue at stake: namely, the isolation to which Black Theology speaks and then the despairing isolation that it creates by the extremity of attitude and statement with which it is enveloped. I want, therefore, to address this matter herewith.

III

In religious matters we do want to recognize an intimate connection between the quality of men's lives and the qualitative thrust of their speech. There is, after all, a language of faith. It is not different from other languages in either syntax or vocabulary. But there is such a thing as so living that certain words will be forced to one's lips. One's evaluations and judgments, one's views of the world and oneself, will be distinctively in an "of" mood. And what the words become "of" may well be the same factors that make one's deeds "of," too. So, a person who speaks out "of" great conviction may also act out "of" the same great conviction.

But religion does not involve only convictions. After a while a life that is religiously cultivated—by hymns, by preaching, by churches, by admonitions, by examples, by hopes, fears and expectations—that life gets a definitive form. And from such a formed life also comes forth songs and laments, dirges and joys, ways of summing up one's experience, and a definitive grasp of the world one is in. When one put God, Jesus Christ, gospel songs and a hortatory panoply into the ecology, the human plant certainly can and does respond to all of it. If we thought it were all conditioning, then we would not want to listen to the words that were said, but probably only measure their intensity. Maybe, then, they would all be treated as if they were yelps and interesting noises, significant only if they were loud. Or they might indeed be signs of ecstasy and be in the family of cries and sighs, exclamations and interjections.

Personal religion certainly can be a conditional response, and it can be a matter of a-rational and inchoate reaction. Surely religion among Blacks is no different here than religion among other groups. There is plenty of this kind of primitive immediacy in certain contexts and times. But then there is, also, a veritable well-spring of the language of faith bursting forth too. And this language of faith I find to be exceedingly worth listening to, for it "says" something and it is not only a noise. It must be attended to with great care. The spirituals are truly like the Psalms and seem to me to share a starkness, a pathos and the very form of life with them, across the gulf of centuries and cultures. This language of faith also tumbles out through Black preaching; and that preaching often shares in its hectic eloquence and histrionic fervor a great deal with the New Testament and other long stretches of faithful speech.

For reasons which are deep and have to do with exigencies of the human spirit, there is a logic to this language, a logic which ties up a form of life, a way of speaking, a set of emotions, and which taken altogether makes for the very meaning of faith itself. Insofar as there is no logic like that, we can also say that this language makes for a basic knowledge of God. This is theology in the briefest and most elemental sense. One can say, with a great deal of confidence, that in order to know God one must learn to sing, to speak, to feel, in that manner commensurate to, and productive of, such a surge of speech. And I see every reason to suggest that the experience of the Blacks, like the experience of the Hebrews, like the experience of others too, sometimes is so felt, conceived and understood that it leads to knowledge of God and the language of faith.

All of us are debtors to the Hebrews in this respect, to the first Christians surely, and I would suppose that many have discovered also the literature of the Blacks. One can call this stream of speech, which is faithful and also "of" the ethos, strivings and sufferings of Blacks, "theology" because it turns out that it is not an index only to Black psychology but also it is about God. Now this latter comment is what has to be teased into shape and made more amenable by the academic study that is also called "theology."

But here is where the difficulties abound. Because of the strenuous pressures of our time, internal and external, many Black theologians have stressed the indigenous sources of the knowledge of God in Black religion to mean that knowledge can not be anything but Black and private. This is both intellectually wrong and socially debilitating. Black Theology, if it wishes to make something manifest, needs to join in the many-sided and wide-ranging and subtly-hued interchange between present and past. This is what academic life is always about. Those people who think we cannot afford such a luxury because of the strenuousness of our time are not aware of the fact that without it, we doom ourselves to converting everything only to ideologies —where tones become more strident as the listeners get weary and turn it all off.

The point of the seminary and the university is not to act simply as a conduit for points of view. They must also be arenas where people and ideas meet each other in a variety of ways. That academic theologian who wants to be responsible to the deepest pathos and overwhelming insightfulness of witness in Black religion, can do little for it if he converts it only to a battle-cry which must compete with all other such cries in the weary world. Instead, he must, again like all scholars and teachers, take what is unique in origin and idiosyncratic in expression, and bring it into the reach of others. Just as great historical writing shows us that there is no past so different that it is unreachable and completely sealed-off, so academic theology must always show us that the validity of past thoughts is not limited to any one time and place. However, Black theologians, like the modern academics who live in stress, are in another self-created predicament. They have been speaking as if the problems of the present were so devastating and so peculiar, that they were unrecognizable by anything that went before. But this is twaddle. Black theologians of the academic sort have a glorious prospect of linking Blacks, their thoughts and lives, with thoughts of God and man of the past, in the confidence that no one is quite beyond the reach of the past. By this means, we also gain a little more understanding of ourselves and God.

But more particularly, there has been something wrong with the notion that Blacks are their own jury, just as it is downright silly to think Whites are their own jury. The notion of the Blacks being a society which alone can judge its own thoughts, its own theology, can make mockery of reasoning itself. To say that Black travail produced a Black language of faith is to declare a plain fact; but this is not to suggest that Black Theology is only a descant upon the crying of the people. It is and it is not; and the senses in which it is not are the ones that academicians can properly deploy. Here we have to make a plea for rationality itself which teases out of the juxtaposition of past and present, this group and that, precisely those criteria and standards in virtue of which something is said that makes sense. That sense is recognizable across immense differences, across injustices, inequities, temporal gaps and cultural chasms.

This is, then, a difference between an ideology—which demands immediate response, seeks strident simplification, and produces an exclusive band of ideologues—and a theology, which is content with considerate attention, a many-faceted statement, and a group of people who seek understanding but seldom, therefore, claim it. I am suggesting that even the Black causes will stand to gain considerably among at least the educated people by moving always from the former and into the latter. That it shares this fate with so many other recent causes and movements seems to me to be obvious enough. But, in addition, in contexts of the modern universities, I want to see the thought of Blacks, on Christian things as well as in all kinds of other issues, now fully articulated and made tangible. I think it deplorable if the effort to understand should be thwarted by what I can only assume to be a mistaken bit of epistemology and misplaced rhetoric—namely, that that thought can only be understood from within.

IV

There is one final point. For a long while now a debate has been going on in moral theory about whether or not an action is still moral if we justify it in non-moral terms. So, Immanuel Kant thought that if you acted out of truly moral motives, because you ought to do something, that being attracted to that action by the pleasure it would bring would make your action non-moral. Or to put it in another way, if one is of the view that non-moral reasons can be advanced as grounds for moral actions, then it has seemed to many moralists that morality itself is vitiated and denied. An example might be that if one says that happiness, here conceived as a non-moral end, is being proposed as the reason for being just, then being just begins to lose its point. In these circumstances, one could become happy in all kinds of ways other than by being just, and they all might serve as well. Morality and its strenuousness would disappear.

That is, then, that if morality plays a role in a game that is not that of morality itself, then morality itself has a vanishing significance. So if you do good because it impresses your neighbor, soon you can learn to impress your neighbor without bothering about being good at all. One of the features that seems wrong to me about some Black Theology is the ease with which that theology has been fed into the Black revolution and the raising of Black consciousness. However laudable these ends may be, it does seem to me reprehensible, again on intellectual grounds, when the same is done with Christianity and Black Theology. Of course, one can say, easily enough, that this has been done before and by emperors, kings, popes and slaveowners. All of that may be true. But this is no defense against the charge that this is to make of religion in itself an ideology. But this was said earlier and in another context; here we are intent upon another point.

That point is, simply, that the Christian faith is such that believing it and practising it must depend upon doing these for intrinsically Christian reasons.

If one does Christian things, even hymn-singing, preaching and theology, in order to raise black consciousness and to foment social change, one is no longer doing them for the glory of God. This way of thinking finally leads one to the recognition that religious practises and beliefs are finally a matter of indifference. If other things will get one those same ends, then one might as well evaporate the religious stream right now. For if the reason for religious living is in something non-religious, then it follows that the religious allegiance, enthusiasm and distinctive Black religious experience is, in a devastating sense, a matter of indifference.

This is why religion which becomes a kind of backing for a political order becomes such a mean and ignoble thing. One can also see easily enough why there is a trivialization of religion that takes place when it is justified because it will produce peace of mind and generally improve one's chances for success. Any kind of talk that surrounded such views as these noted above do not seem to ever have been instances of theology. For when religious discourse becomes a rationale for kingship, that rationale is not theology any longer. That is why we call it something else—an ideology or even a rationalization. But Black Theology, which now is coming forth from the seminaries, seems to present a strange and ambiguous appearance.

On the one hand, it is precisely "theology" which is the discipline in which distinctions like the one we have drawn are laid bare. Theology also has this disinterested and logical-like force about it. It is that band of reflection that allows us the access by which to criticize a religion which becomes an ideology and a faith which serves ignoble and lesser ends. Black theology certainly has done, and ought to do, this in continuing and subtle ways, for and in white religion too. But to see so much of Black Theology almost become a means only of inspiring a Black revolt or social change seems to admit a deep fault. This is not a fault because there is no time or place for revolt or radical change. Rather it is, again, the fact that this very way of thinking and writing entails an exploitative use of religion, which can have as its end only the demise of the hold of religion upon one. But if that is the aim, then it ought to be assayed directly.

Furthermore, there is the other delicate matter of what this means on the part of those who engineer these things. When morality is taught as if it will obviously pay you to pursue it, then one might also be taking advantage of the susceptible en route. If religious sensibilities are being praised for being Black and indigenous, all might be well and good; but if they are being praised and then used for non-religious ends, it does follow that some moral ineptitudes and intellectual lapses are being combined. The unsuspecting ones, whose lives are nurtured in faith, do not need that kind of exploitation. For it is exploitation, of a very subtle sort, to propose moral conduct for non-moral ends, and religious conduct and belief for non-religious ends.

Black theology cannot afford to confuse these matters. And if there is any point to reading history at all, it can be profitable right here. For the misshapen character of Christian religion and belief is nowhere more graphically illustrated than on this very issue. Slavery itself is an example of anxious men suborning the faith for the sake of profit, order and a host of other ends, ignoble and noble. It is in conversation with the painfully achieved theological clarity that has come and gone on this issue through history that we continually order ourselves to a more pristine and adequate life. This conversation is also the one into which Black theologians must plunge, not only to save the faith of all of us but also to save themselves from the errors that are not otherwise discernible.

18

BLACK THEOLOGY AND THEOLOGY OF HOPE: WHAT HAVE THEY TO SAY TO EACH OTHER?

G. Clarke Chapman, Jr.

Within the last decade, two theological movements stirring both excitement and misapprehension have been Black Theology and the Theology of Hope. As contemporaneous movements, have they something in common? Although emphatically separate in origin and program, a comparison is nonetheless invited by certain structural parallels and occasional cross-references. For purposes of this essay, Jürgen Moltmann will represent the Theology of Hope, except where other references are explicit, and generalizations concerning Black Theology will derive from several leading black American theologians, but especially from James H. Cone.

In the late 1960's, Cone and other black theologians found in Moltmann one of their most useful sources for citation; since then, there has been widespread reaction against reliance on any white theologian. In the same period, Moltmann spent a sabbatical year at Duke University, traveled widely, experienced the German student unrest beginning in 1967, and his own writings shifted into a phase of social activity and "political theology." Moltmann's interest in Cone rests partly on personal acquaintance with him, and at Tübingen, he has held a seminar on Cone's theology. But he has never offered a formal critique; in fact, he has rarely expressed himself in print on the topic of Black Theology. Of course, both Black Theology and Theology of Hope are still dynamic, unfinished movements, but perhaps by now some tentative comparisons have become possible.

G. Clarke Chapman, Jr., is Associate Professor of Religion at Moravian College, Bethlehem, Pennsylvania. This essay first appeared in the *Union Seminary Quarterly Review*, vol. 29, no. 2 (Winter 1974).

A Comparison of Origins, Cultural Contexts, and Central Themes

It is important first of all to note how different the two schools are in origin, development, and cultural context. A hasty syncretism under superficial rubrics can only distort the integrity of each. It is obvious, but nonetheless of profound consequence, that Black Theology is thoroughly Afro-American, while the Theology of Hope is just as thoroughly dependent on its Germanic heritage. Black Theology rests upon continual remembrance of centuries of oppression, extending up to the present, and so its sources are the great preachers and anonymous singers of slavery days, as well as the towering contributions of more recent minds like W. E. B. DuBois, Langston Hughes, and Henry M. Turner. By contrast, Moltmann's theology is consciously rooted in centuries of Europe's intellectual tradition, including Luther, seventeenth-century Calvinism and Federal Theology, the philosophy of Hegel and the leftward branch of its development through Marx to Ernst Bloch, and finally, twentieth-century dialectical theology and Karl Barth. The mission of Black Theology is located within the distinct consciousness of a physically marked minority group, struggling for new status within a wider hostile society. But Theology of Hope is rooted in the consciousness of the lost majority status of Christians within an older and now complacently secularized Europe, a consciousness that must now compete with powerful ideologies (such as Marxism) and technological challenges. The responsibility felt by Black Theology is towards its ethnic-racial group, including the often poorly educated masses of blacks isolated from the mainstream of American prosperity. Theology of Hope is related more to certain educational and confessional enclaves in an indifferent society, especially the gathered elite of the universities and the diminishing faithful inside the church walls. If the black ghetto and the dispirited unemployed form the context of the one movement, the lecture hall and the socialist factory worker suggest the context of the other.

Considering these major differences, it is all the more surprising that there are also some similarities. Indeed, both Moltmann and Cone make a number of parallel points, although this is rarely with any evidence of direct dependence upon one another, and neither has settled into a consistent, definable theological stance as such. For example, both men share the basic assumption that God is presently at work in and through general history. This immediately sets Cone and Moltmann apart from theological existentialism, as well as the whole heritage of Schleiermacher and pietism. Revelation comes through history, as anticipated and pioneered in Jesus Christ.[1] Both reject "natural theology," particularly in the form of civil religion which gives religious sanction to the ties and values of the nation. Moltmann's polemic, however, is theologically rooted in the Second Commandment and in the political overtones of the crucifixion,[2] while Cone's is experientially grounded in the daily outrage of a minority's insight into how a majority manipulates idealism for its self-confirmation. And both insist that the future is fluid and not simply to be dictated by the past, although for neither is it very clear just how the future *is* determined, or by what combination of divine and human agency.

Liberation, violence, and salvation. Thematically, the broadest area of agreement is liberation. It is interesting that both Moltmann and Cone make brief but favorable references to Marcion, the second-century heretic, although for somewhat dissimilar reasons.[3] For Moltmann, Marcion retained the insight, later lost by the church, into the unprecedented *novum* of what happened in Christ. Cone, meanwhile, sees Marcion as preserving austere righteousness, at least in one god, before the later unification of divine attributes favoring a wrathless, sentimentalized love. Both Marcion references, however, have an indirect bearing on the hope of a coming liberation for oppressed humanity. And both agree in bringing the traditional concept of love much closer to the urgencies of justice and to an impassioned resolution to stand for the freedom and happiness of the other person.[4]

In the liberation struggle today, just as in the Exodus and the Magnificat, God is no impartial observer, but is identified and present among the poor and the humiliated. Moltmann affirms a "Messianism of the oppressed," among whom God "tabernacles"; and in similar fashion, Cone speaks of Christ's liberating work in the black movement today.[5] Therefore, the church cannot abstain from the struggle, but like her Master must take sides with the disinherited; in the American context, for instance, this would mean the willingness to "become black" through selfless solidarity with the black-skinned dispossessed.[6] This divine partnership is not intended to raise social class or race to idolatrous status, but rather to utilize dialectically the harsh realities of the present in attaining the final goal of a Christian universalism. Thereby the rich, the white, and the oppressor will also be saved from a social relationship that ironically imprisons master as well as slave.[7] The only point at which Moltmann and Cone would disagree here is the issue of whether or not ultimate reconciliation will actually transcend racial identity.[8]

To what, then, is man liberated? Freedom by its very nature is a comprehensive totality, not compartmentalized, with spiritual freedom being played off against secular, or moral freedom against political.[9] Moltmann says there is no *liberation* in the singular, but instead there are *liberations* in the plural, corresponding to the cumulative levels and vicious circles of man's estrangements.[10] In similar fashion, Cone has referred to freedom as having both an historical (socio-economic and political) dimension and a non-quantifiable dimension beyond history.[11] That is, for black Americans freedom is not a negation, a mere absence of restraints, oppression, or discrimination, but also an affirmation of being, an opening into self-fulfillment and joyful development of latent powers.[12] The paradoxical transcendence implicit in a holistic view of freedom is well illustrated in the words and music of the spirituals and the blues. It is significant that Cone's book, *The Spirituals and the Blues* (1972) is devoted to just that subject, at the same time that Moltmann also has seen the need to go beyond social liberation to a new emphasis on freedom as eschatological spontaneity, play, and affirmative joy in the present.[13]

Any discussion of liberation sooner or later must grapple with the provocative issue of violence. It is dangerous to generalize and to discuss the justifiability of violence in the abstract; yet to foresee every possible combination of particular circumstances, especially from the viewpoint of the victims, is an almost impossible task. Understandably then, neither Black Theology nor Moltmann have unequivocal positions on this question. Nevertheless, they diverge in tendency. Although Black Theology does not categorically endorse violence, it frequently does leave the door open to tactical violence as at times the lesser of two evils in a covertly violent society. Sometimes Cone's rhetoric goes even further; but typically, as also in the controversial preamble to the Black Manifesto, such militant statements are qualified by the disclaimer "that this is not the road we want to take" unless forced to it by white intransigence.[14] Moltmann, speaking under quite different circumstances, is predictably more cautious, although it is true that in an essay written in 1968 he states that the issue of violence *vs.* non-violence is an illusory problem, and the question should instead be which uses of force are justifiable and proportionate to humane goals.[15] But this is immediately followed with an appeal to use means better than those of the opponent, as did Martin Luther King, Jr. As we shall see, Moltmann's later writings are increasingly critical of social revolutionaries, whom he sees as only perpetuating vicious circles of antagonism and coercion.

Both Black Theology and Moltmann would agree in regarding those groups active for human liberation as embodying divine transcendence. Moltmann seems to derive this position from his earlier study of Dietrich Bonhoeffer, who saw transcendence not as an epistemological barrier but an ethical/social one, the "otherness" of the divine Thou coming through the strangeness of human encounter. Moltmann has developed this view in light of situations of oppression, where revolutionary groups can offer jaded modern man fresh glimpses of a transcendence mediated by the crunch of historical abrasion.[16] Parallels to this can be seen in many statements by Cone, linking manifestations of God to acts of black liberation.[17] A point of difference, however, would be Moltmann's view of Christians as joyous revolutionaries, never obsessed with a program or ideology, and ready to laugh about it all in the light of the greater, eschatological revolution still to come.[18] For Black Theology, this degree of self-distancing from the historical struggle would dangerously relativize its urgency.

A final topic of comparison is the concept of salvation. For blacks, the context of this theme is the dehumanization and loss of identity caused by the peculiar conditions of Anglo-American slavery and the veiled racism which followed.[19] This alienation of racial and personal identity, and the corresponding dilemmas, is perceived by Moltmann more sympathetically than by many Europeans.[20] Especially in recent writings, he insists that, although ultimate salvation is an eschatological event, its proleptic anticipation here and now must embody a reciprocal interaction of both personal transformation and structural change of society.[21] In other words, *Emanzipation* and *Erlösung* are not isolated, but are dialectically related as the immanent and transcendent aspects of genuine freedom.[22] Black Theology would also acknowledge the dual aspect of pre-eschaton salvation; however, it must insist that, after centuries of over-emphasis on personal piety, the social dimension of liberation is a non-negotiable prerequisite to any further talk of reconciliation, conversion—or even of the divine role in effecting redemption.[23]

Criticism of Moltmann by Black Theology

Leaving undiscussed the many points at which Black Theology and Moltmann's theology simply have no relationship to each other, negative or positive, because of divergent interests, we now examine the criticisms made or implied by each side of the other. The following discussion is indebted to a number of interviews, conducted in the summer and fall of 1972 with several black theologians and with Moltmann, which have been of great value in supplementing the fragmentary written references.

Of the Theology of Hope, there are two major criticisms expressed by black theologians: it is said to be both too oriented towards the future and to be set in a context too alien to the black experience. We will discuss them in this order.

Theology of Hope is too futuristic. The first charge is not one that Cone himself has emphasized, aside from asking briefly, "How seriously does he [Moltmann] take history?" In fact, in his first two books, Cone praises Moltmann for having a balance of present and future in his eschatology which energized criticism of and alert responsibility for current conditions.[24] But among several other black theologians, Moltmann's thrust is seen as too futuristic.

An emphasis on the future is suspect because, for blacks in contemporary America, the tasks of the present day should demand all human attention. Deotis Roberts comments, "his [Moltmann's] view of revelation is too narrow. Eschatology . . . [must] be 'a realizable eschatology' in the here and now in order to be hopeful to black Christians."[25] Elsewhere, Roberts discusses Rubem Alves' *A Theology of Human Hope*, calling it the most helpful book for blacks on eschatology, yet criticizing it soundly nonetheless as "too futuristic."[26] Now if even Alves can be faulted for this—even though ironically he himself levels the same charge at Moltmann, preferring instead a much more phenomenological, anti-transcendental approach—then surely black distrust of future-talk is great! Roberts maintains that to theorize about the future may be possible for whites, who have a security and a certain degree of assured status in the present, but for blacks facing a day-to-day struggle for sheer existence, not to mention human dignity, such abstraction is an impermissible luxury. Roberts speaks for many when he concludes:

> Instead of moving from the future to the present, we move from the present to the future—at least to begin. Only after we are aware of what God is doing in this world to make life more human for blacks may we speak of God's future breaking into our present and look forward to the new age.[27]

Indeed, comments C. Shelby Rooks, Black Theology may have more to contribute than to receive, in restoring a theological balance here.[28]

Another reason for suspicion of a future-orientation is that it would detract from a recovery of the long suppressed past.

> The most terrifying act of cruelty that America perpetrated on its Black citizens was to write them out of history books and at the same time to refuse them access to this life. This was done deliberately in order to salve American conscience about slavery and to maintain that evil system. But, for the Black man, these twin acts denied him his true past, thus making him rootless, and refused him any future, thus making him hopeless as well as powerless.[29]

A clear rediscovery of the past, restoring both a sense of identity for blacks and a realism open to explicitly reciprocal negotiation with whites, is the indispensable foundation for any future hopes. How may one hope for tomorrow, if he does not know who he is today, and why yesterday made him that way?[30] And how can relations between white and black be set aright before both have faced their joint history with ruthless honesty and have prepared by costly atonement for a common future?

> Reparations means to look back at the past and see what I must do to repair the damage I've done there in order for reconciliation to happen. Reparations, reconciliation, and forgiveness belong together, and the white church will have to face up to it. It cannot "leap" into the future without dealing with the demands the blacks are making on the white man to "stand still long enough to look at what you've done to me, what has happened to me, and out of your tremendous resources make some amends, that I might stand with you and go into the future together with you."[31]

Still another reason for mistrusting a hope-theology is one shared with many white critics, namely the conviction that not theology, but instead, that science and technology are the only disciplines equipped to deal with the future. "Theology is not a futuristic discipline. It has no methodology to deal with the future. Its stuff is the stuff of the past and the present."[32] After all, theology is rooted in historic revelation from the past, and (as hermeneutic) it tries to mediate it into the present. The implication is that the future is quite indeterminate, and that the only way it can be humanly influenced is by the insertion of new physical factors supplied by the applied sciences. Behind this view lies the familiar Cartesian-Kantian division of outer/physical and inner/moral realms. "Reality," it would seem, must be present or material—if not both.

Theology of Hope is provincially European. The second major objection to Theology of Hope is one made by every black theologian surveyed, namely that it is too alien to black experience to be of real use in the formative tasks of Black Theology. Moltmann's thought "ignores" black psychology and the need to combine subjective experience with what is objectively given. "It does not . . . ring true to the black experience. Like many other 'transport' theological movements, it belongs to another 'situation.' "[33] In his latest book, this has become the main criticism by Cone against Moltmann and others: "the future about which they speak is too abstract and too unrelated to the history and culture of black people. . . . As a black theologian, I believe that authentic Christian hope must be defined by the oppressed's vision of the expectant future and not by philosophical abstractions."[34] In Cone's earlier writings this charge had been levelled against many white theologians, but not yet against Moltmann; however, he received at that time much criticism for his heavy reliance on arguments from Euro-American theologians.[35] *The Spirituals and the Blues* is a quite different book, probing and interpreting the very sources of black folk religion, virtually without citation from contemporary white theologians. In recent conversation, Cone made it clear that, although Moltmann's writings interest him as an academic exercise in theology, he must maintain his own independence as a theologian. This means not worrying about how his thought may correspond or disagree with that of others, but working to take seriously his own task and his own distinctive situation in America and the black community.[36]

In other words, every effective theology must be indigenous, and this is no less true for twentieth-century Afro-Americans than it was for sixteenth-century Germans or first-century Gentiles. Around the world as well, there is a new awakening to the fact that the tradition of Western Christendom is after all not the only perspective available for Christian faith. Hence, most, if not all, black theologians now discourage interest in contemporary white theology, until such time as the largely untapped rich sources of black folk religious expression have at least been explored and brought to light. For too long, whites have dictated the theological agenda for non-whites. The door to eventual dialogue may not be tightly shut, but for the foreseeable future Black Theology, as a fledgling, "neoteric" discipline,[37] must develop internally and establish more firmly what its alternatives are to those (white) norms formerly considered universal and ultimate. Furthermore, there is the suggestion that Theology of Hope might be assisted out of its European provincialism if it had more dialogue with the variegated world-views of the vast non-white populations of the globe!

Criticism of Black Theology by Moltmann

Now the other side. Concerning Black Theology there are two, possibly three, critical questions which Moltmann would raise. The indefinite number reflects the fact that, despite his personal interest, Moltmann seldom mentions Black Theology in his writings, and still more rarely criticizes it when he does. To some extent (but only as explicitly noted in the following), it is possible to elaborate these references by extrapolation from the context of his discussions of European ideologies of revolution.

The problem of evil. His first major question is whether the essence of evil has been sufficiently analyzed and grasped by Black Theology. The radical and totalitarian embrace of human perversity should not be restricted to a single context. "A human emancipation of man, even racial identity itself, is not actualized if one overlooks the economic and political circumstances. Racism is too closely bound with social injustice and political incapacitation. . . . In the underestimation of these connections lies the limitation of anti-racist liberation movements and theologies."[38] Racism is not the source of all evil, but one of a number of its interrelated expressions.

This helps explain why the black movement finds it difficult to cooperate with other liberation movements.[39] Instead of cooperation, there is feuding and hostility among advocates of Black Power, the Marxists, Women's Liberation, etc., because each movement traces the origin of sin to a different source: racism, capitalism, sexism, etc. But ought there not to be cooperation towards the common goal of human liberation? And how would Cone's exclusive attention to white racism explain the self-seeking of the black bourgeoisie, or bloodshed among African tribes? The insidious evil of racism is by no means to be excused or relativized, but neither ought it to be seen in isolation from the demonic subtleties spanning the whole spectrum of man's estrangement from God.

The possibility for reconciliation. Secondly, Moltmann would question whether reconciliation among former enemies is at last possible, following the militant type of Black Theology which Cone represents. Certainly they both agree that partisanship and solidarity with the oppressed is the only path to future justice and unity, even "reconciliation." The point of contention, for Moltmann, is whether this goal is really attainable, in the framework of Cone's insistence on liberation as self-determination. Latent in this question is the influence of Martin Luther King, Jr., whose assassination occurred at the climax of Moltmann's year in America, and to whom Moltmann dedicated his first book of essays published in English.[40] Accordingly, he feels that partisanship must be seen more explicitly as a concern for eventual redemption of black and white alike from racial hate. If liberation movements are to avoid becoming new terrorisms, in which the victims merely exchange places with the former victimizers, then the victims also need to confess their own guilt as they struggle for freedom.[41] Of course *their* guilt is not oppression; that is the crime only of those holding power. Rather, apathy is the characteristic failing of the oppressed. Thus they also share in the common human estrangement, "sin," and must not permit themselves the luxury of claiming to be guiltless.

Thus, for Moltmann love is not only to be defined as empathy and a passion for justice. It includes also a critical trust in the eventual transformability of one's opponent, and a permanent self-criticism concerning the presumed righteousness of one's own position.[42] Any rigid schema of "friend *vs.* enemy" thinking is a vicious circle that itself derives from man's alienation. Such schemes must be overcome in those proximate goals attainable in history which Moltmann calls "concrete utopias." Indeed, he goes further in one passage, and apparently wishes a trans-racial or supra-racial community:

> Only in a humane society where man no longer identifies and differentiates himself racially, where each group receives and assumes an equal share of responsibility for the whole, can the future be attained. The concrete utopia must, in this instance, envisage a new identity of man which overcomes, relativizes, and destroys all racial identifications. The present deadly antagonisms must at the very least be transformed into no-longer-deadly, i.e., productive antagonisms.[43]

If the goal is indeed reconciliation, the methods and entire perspective of a liberation theology will be affected. But unfortunately, few today take reconciliation seriously. Accordingly, Moltmann is wary of the tendency, in European movements of social change such as Marxism, to deify or idolize man. To be sure, he has not specifically charged Black Theology with this danger, but at least the warning could be considered implicit; liberationists are often tempted to elevate man to a status of omnicompetence. Ironically, such an ideology makes man not more, but actually less than, human; it demands impossible achievements of him, as if he were a total, self-identical (and therefore infinite) being.[44] But man's eccentric position, his inner tension between finitude and self-transcendence, and his eschatologically unfinished quality indicate that true liberation can only be found within the context of man's creatureliness and his response to the prevenient guidance of the one sovereign God. Only, when deification of man is excluded, is reconciliation of man thus enabled.

The loss of eschatological freedom. To be fair, it must be noted that Moltmann has never explicitly directed the following criticism at the American scene. But it is easily extrapolated from his general writings as at least potentially a critical question, applicable to the more radical wing of Black Theology. Increasingly in recent years, Moltmann has warned of the loss of eschatological freedom in revolutionary movements. On the European scene, this loss occurs in at least two forms. One is the activism of the "adventurous heart," the glorification of sheer power and will which, like Alexander the Great, dramatically cuts the Gordian knot.[45] Salvation is through spontaneous action and vigorous decision, which impatiently bypasses the interminable discussions and compromises of democracy. An example in Germany was the fascination of power for its own sake, apart from program or policies, by many intellectuals in 1914 and 1933. But "decisionism" brings its own self-imprisonment, both by its loss of love and by its distrust of all norms which, since they are inescapable even when ignored, exercise an insidious and unobserved tyranny.

Another mode in activism of the loss of eschatological freedom is found in the more ideological freedom movements, including the Marxists and some leftist student leaders of Germany's university unrest since 1967. Since then, Moltmann has become increasingly concerned about the legalism implicit in revolutionary as well as counter-revolutionary positions. A direct result is his engaging essay, "The First Liberated Men in Creation," with the German subtitle, "Endeavors about Joy in Freedom and Delight in Play." Against the unrelenting, even totalitarian claims made for ethics, utilitarianism, and immediate social productivity, Moltmann reminds us of the divine sanction for aesthetics, enjoyment of created things as ends in themselves, and unfettered affirmation of being. Just as God created the world, guides it, and became incarnate in it, not out of duty or necessity, but rather out of His good pleasure and love, so man also ought to share in the struggle for human destiny without sacrificing the quality of eschatological freedom here and now, the joy in the sheer beauty and worth of existence.

The paradigmatic example of eschatological freedom in contrast to revolutionary legalism is found in Jesus' relationship to the Zealots. Much has been written lately about this theme, but most evidence indicates that Jesus differed at decisive points from the Jewish liberation movement of the first century. To be sure, the freedom fighters appeal to the "political theology" of many parts of the Hebrew Scriptures and had genuine religious grounds for waging a guerrilla-style Holy War against the blasphemies of a foreign occupation regime.[46] But despite what he held in common with the Zealots and the Pharisees, Jesus decisively countered God's righteousness to all their legalism, breaking through the cycle of revenge and the careful alignments of friend/foe identifications.[47] He refused to coerce the Kingdom of God into appearing, but instead represented it proleptically with the joy of one offering a wedding feast. "This liberation from legalism, which has to and repeatedly does lead to retaliation, can well be called the 'humane revolt' of Jesus, if one wants to apply modern revolutionary terminology at all—which is possible only with reservation."[48] For this eschatological freedom, Jesus was then feared and hated by all factions, revolutionary as well as colonialist, patriot as well as imperialist. The cross was the result, but the new life of Easter was and is ever anew the vindication.

This illumines Moltmann's growing suspicion of strategies of violence. Unless a new humanity begins to emerge, the overthrow of a regime would simply mean that the oppressed become the new oppressors. Martin Luther King, Jr., was an example of this new humanity, withstanding the anxieties and temptations of power, and refusing to use the methods chosen by opponents. In this way, at least in industrial nations where non-violent means are still possible, a genuine revolutionary would break with the whole cycle of coercion and bloodshed, and find a new freedom to choose better means. Unfortunately, self-conscious "theologies of revolution" lapse back into legalism." Radical Christianity will have a revolutionary *effect*, but a revolutionary program would be just the way to neutralize it. The title 'revolutionary' must, if at all, be given from the outside; one cannot claim it for himself."[49] Perhaps under some conditions prevailing in the Third World, violent resistance to tyranny may be the only responsible (but nonetheless guilt-producing!) path open to love. But the short-term gains, however desirable, envisaged by any liberationist must not be purchased at the cost of that distinctive quality of radical freedom in the present, which is received from God's future.

Replies and Evaluation: Moltmann's Response

These, then are the major criticisms that Black Theology and Moltmann would make of each other. Now, inferring how each side would reply to the critiques, let us discuss and evaluate their implications. First, the response to the black criticisms of the Theology of Hope.

The charge that the Theology of Hope is too future-oriented. This objection is not peculiar to Black Theology, but has been common among whites on both sides of the Atlantic. Often it verges on the superficial, decrying a "one-sided futurism" and calling for "more balance" between past-present-future, perhaps under the illusion that the golden mean is somehow a theological criterion, and that truth is gained by giving equal weight to all contenders.[50] Harvey Cox, for instance, wants "a theology of juxtaposition," winning surrealistic insights by playing off the tensions of all three time dimensions against one another by a "collage principle."[51] But can a theology aligned toward and obedient to the resurrected Christ survive the leveling crush of the common denominator? Another and more defensible way to criticize eschatological theology is the semi-mystical "presentism" of Michael Novak,[52] who maintains that for today, thinking of the future is dehumanizing because it sacrifices life now for the sake of distant ideological projections. Hence, "my dream for the future—at least in America—is that humans will taste their present more, and love their future less. Fewer people will get killed that way."[53]

It should be noted that Moltmann himself would quite agree with such warnings against the misuses of ideological futurology, as his "The First Liberated Man in Creation" makes clear, or indeed against any Comtean "technological chiliasm" and utopian scientism.[54] But a dehumanized futurology assumes an emphatically non-eschatological, immanental unfolding of history, which omits what Moltmann sees as precisely the attracting power of the qualitatively new.[55] Furthermore, to shrink back into fixation on the present moment is to accommodate oneself too conveniently to the prevailing social structures, and to sink from the eschatological longings and self-sacrifice of agape-love into a protective apathy towards the suffering creation. We may add that it remains to be seen whether in fact Novak's latest writings honoring white ethnic America may not indeed have this effect.

From the viewpoint of Black Theology, it is at least understandable why Moltmann might be seen as too wrapped up in the future. But it is also ironic that at the same time some black theologians press the opposite charge, i.e., of being too submerged in the present, against the thought of the late Reinhold Niebuhr.[56] It is said the weakness of the later Niebuhr was that he saw political alternatives solely in terms of present history and "what is possible now." This led him to rely on middle-axioms and a "realism" which —especially on the race issue—was a pragmatic conservatism. By his too hasty rejection of Marxism, Niebuhr also lost "the *positive* dimensions of utopianism," remarks James Cone; by contrast, Black Theology should emphasize "utopias, dreams, and imagination," to keep people from being solely determined by present history.[57] Now these objections to (especially the later) Niebuhr are certainly well taken, even though it is doubtful that Niebuhrian thought is beyond resuscitation in a new and leftward form.[58] But then ought Moltmann to be criticized for supplying the very emphasis found lacking in Niebuhr? Aside from other points on which either or both men could be faulted, is it consistent for Black Theology[59] without further distinctions to criticize a present-pragmatic emphasis because it is not future-utopian, and a future-utopian emphasis because it is not present-pragmatic?

More important however is the intrinsic viability of an eschatological theology such as Moltmann's. This should indeed be questioned and carefully analyzed. In doing so, however, it seems there is widespread misunderstanding on both sides of the Atlantic as to just what Moltmann intends by "the future." It is more than just one of several temporal dimensions; rather it is the mode of God's being, who is both ground and transformer of whatever fraction of reality we experience as "world." The word *Zukunft* (future) covers two traditions of conceptualization.[60] One is the future as *futurum*, the future participle of *fuo* and ultimately deriving from the Greek work *physis*. *Physis* is the eternally begetting, productive womb of all existent things; it is the extension of the material world in the broad sense, and so—after the pattern of the natural sciences—is known by extrapolation from past and present factors. It is this naturalistic-technological sense of "future" that a majority of Moltmann's critics continue to take for granted. But the second word-tradition behind *Zukunft* is the future as *adventus* (or *parousia*), meaning the coming or arrival of persons or events, and used messianically by the prophets and apostles—that is, never of Jesus' incarnation or a coming "again," but rather of the universal advent of Christ at the Endtime. The *novum* that is coming is in principle new and radically transforming, not just quantitatively better. Thus it can*not* be extrapolated from what is already at hand, but can only in faith be "anticipated"[61] when announced. What is so difficult for most moderns to understand in reading Moltmann is precisely this point: the future as *adventus* cannot be (epistemologically) extrapolated from present or past experience, not even from the revelation in Christ, *except* and insofar as it is already (ontically) grounded in God's being. For God is the mode of being which we can perceive only as "future," but which is nonetheless "real" because of that—*more* "real" in fact than our transient experiences of what we ordinarily call "reality" in history.

Moltmann's entire enterprise is thus more radical than it might first appear. What is at stake is nothing less than the ontological framework behind theology itself. This is why it is so fatuous to call for "a bit more balance" between Moltmann's concept of the future and the other time dimensions. The fundamental challenge attempted by Moltmann is this: is the future (as *adventus*) the basic ontic reality (God's self-presentation and promise), or not? Such primal matters are not simply or immediately resolved, of course, and no one can deny that Moltmann may be quite mistaken in his whole monumental assertion. But the challenge ought to be faced for what it is, for it confronts the primordial perception of time—both of western civilization (that the present is the ultimate reality—"I'm thinking right *now*, therefore I am"), as well as of traditional African civilization (*Zamani*, the vast sea of past generations, is the ultimately real time, and *Sasa*, the "now-ness" and fleeting span of this generation, is a dependent reflection of it).[62] There can be no compromise, no 50/50 "divvying up." Either Moltmann is right, and eschatology is the magnetic core of reality (both in its attracting and repelling power), or Shelby Rooks and Michael Novak are right, and the future is to be abandoned to the custodial grip of technology. The ontic decision is basic!

The role of Moltmann's eschatological ontology. Argumentation cannot be attempted here, but it may be asked whether this eschatological ontology, if accepted, would then offer any real support for the concerns of Black Theology. I believe it would, in at least two ways. First of all, Black Theology insists that the urgent tasks of the present demand man's full attention. So they do. But if this were the only focus, and if after bone-grinding, exhaustive effort the problems of the present do not yield, the result is despair and desperation. The liberation struggle has had both successes and many stalemates or failures. What has theology to say, in those instances when the present seems utterly intractable? Must it only exhort further and apparently futile attempts from broken flesh and broken spirits? Surely black Americans, of all peoples, know just how perverse and demonically unrelenting the present circumstances sometimes can be; they know all too well the depths of racism, depths which we whites only begin to glimpse, and which will surely persist in some form for years to come. Against such odds, hope is no evasion or opiate. Rather, a theologically articulated hope can restrain despair and enable tomorrow to yield resources for yet another assault against the walls.

Moltmann's later writings generally give increased emphasis to the responsibilities and tensions of the present which result from the impending *adventus*. Indeed, his latest book, *Der gekreuzigte Gott*, develops some ideas that appear significant for oppressed peoples. There he restates Theology of Hope as the obverse side of an *eschatologia crucis*. The God-forsakenness of Jesus on the cross is the clue to the suffering and voluntary self-negation of God Himself, which not only gave rise to the later doctrine of the Trinity, but which injects in history a ceaseless dialectic, a cosmic fermentation that will continue until the consummation of the Endtime. This recent turn in Moltmann's thinking undermines the aloofness and impassibility of a theistic framework, offering tantalizing, if only partially articulated, glimpses of what a genuinely Christian concept of God would be. These suggestions in Christology give little comfort to defenders of any status quo, and certainly some resources for its challengers.

The second way in which a new eschatological ontology might undergird a Black Theology has to do with preserving the past—a concern often considered hostile to a "future-orientation." Black and other critics (such as Rubem Alves) have indeed some grounds for criticizing Moltmann's view of "history" as tending toward a sort of docetism, for he sometimes expresses himself quite negatively, if loosely, towards "history."[63] These puzzling statements are perhaps attributable to the Platonic remnants clinging to early dialectical theology, in which Moltmann is schooled, and also to his eagerness to demonstrate the tensions and dynamic fluidity of the historical process. At any rate, such passages are quite outnumbered by others that insist on the reality of history and the impossibility of evading that reality.

But more important than such statistical bookkeeping is the basic position of Moltmann and other hope theologians that the past is not only important, it is also unfinished and therefore redeemable! Like the pieces of a kaleidoscope, its meaning is still ambiguous, fragmentary, and filled with agonizing waste and incompletion; that is precisely why man longs for the eschaton, to heal the brokenness and fix the significance glimpsed in the precious past. Hope does not deaden, but awakens this sensitivity to the past, and it does so by illuminating the distinction between those parts of the past in which the future (as *adventus*) has already begun and is still to be sought, and those parts where it has been blocked and aborted. The Gospel does not beckon us to escapist dreams or forgetfulness, but cuts deep into "the provisional past," separating Promise from Law, and the anticipation of what is to come from the clinging to what is futile and decaying. The *novum* thereby creates an historical continuity in the midst of discontinuity, promises that the broken pieces will come together, and generates *ex nihilo* new possibilities for the apparently ruined or aborted hopes of earlier generations.[64] The future which awaits the present moment is also the future of innumerable past moments, and the destiny of millennia of humanity will stand or fall upon that denouement.

This view of the past as not yet finished, but drawing towards its climax, seems congruent with the thrust of Black Theology. Among American slaves alone, there is the wreckage of millions of anonymous and forgotten lives whose blood cries up from the ground. If the Theology of Hope is right, these lives have not been wasted, no matter how much it may appear so in the present provisional stage of history, but will be gathered up and vindicated by the future. As J. B. Metz has said, challenging our implicitly Darwinian view of history, "'meaning' is not a category reserved for the winners," for because of the remembrance of Christ's passion we can anticipate a revolution not only in favor of the living, but of the dead, silenced, and forgotten ones.[65] To take but a single example, in the Denmark Vesey slave insurrection, planned in Charleston in 1822, 131 persons were arrested, and thirty-seven were executed; one of the leaders told the others, "Do not open your lips; die silent as you shall see me do."[66] But is silence before the executioner the "last word"? Or is a "new" and decisive word still to be spoken over these unfinished lives, in the common future ahead? Is the past—not just the heroic or well-known past, but the countless lives endured and wasted in obscurity—finally redeemable? Only hope can reply, Yes!

This conservation of the past, by the way, is typical also of other hope theologians. J. B. Metz has already been quoted, and he is fond of citing Herbert Marcuse on the "dangerous insights" and "subversive contents" of memory.[67] According to Wolfhart Pannenberg, not only does the "openness to the world" inherent in many require a resurrection for its completion, but the necessarily *social* realization of human destiny means that *every* human individual must be present to participate; to attain the completed number of persons from every era demands a concept of general resurrection of the dead.[68] By utilizing such theology, the agony of the black past is not discarded or relativized, but is lifted up for impending vindication and consolation in the divine Advent, and this without lapsing into the twin dangers of enervating present moral action or of glorifying only the successful past and its heroes. Thus, can it be so simply asserted that, for Black Theology, Moltmann's theology is "too future-oriented"? Black theologians must judge for themselves, but the question deserves reopening.

The question of Moltmann's provincialism. The second major objection by Black Theology to Moltmann, it may be remembered, is that the Theology of Hope is too alien to the black experience. How may this criticism be evaluated? Again, whites ought not to reply for blacks. But to further the discussion, I would venture a hearty Yes as well as a qualified No.

First, as a school of theological reflection, the Theology of Hope is indeed alien to black culture and mentality; the critics are right. As we have seen, the backgrounds of the two movements are quite diverse, and it is a disservice to both to mix them in a careless syncretism. Further, Cone and others are justified in asserting the need for an independent Black Theology. Just as white American theologians have felt obliged to act as footnotes to the awesome thinkers of Europe, so black theologians have for too long felt subservient to the issues, concepts, and debates of Euro-American theology. But as all factions of Black Theology vigorously agree, from Roberts to Wilmore to Cone, theology must become indigenous if it is to reach its own people. This does not entail permanent isolation from other traditions, or an arrogant rejection of dialogue. It simply means that for a number of years Black Theology will have an enormous task ahead of itself, in belatedly recultivating and analyzing its own distinctive resources, and that as a "neoteric" discipline just entering its critical-expansive stage it is not interested for the time being in criticism from outside sources.[69] For most outsiders still retain and would reimpose those older ("white") standards of ultimacy from which Black Theology itself is only now painfully emerging.

Under these sensitive conditions, should Moltmann even venture to speak to Black Theology? It is a dilemma, and one shared by many whites. If he did discuss Black Theology, his motives as a non-black critic would always be open to challenge. A parallel example is seen in Cone's intemperate remarks about two white authors, Joseph Hough and Freeman Sleeper, both of whom of course could justly be criticized on more substantive grounds.[70] On the other hand, to refuse to discuss Black Theology may also appear condescending or irresponsible. For example, Deotis Roberts relates that at Duke University, on the night of the assassination of Martin Luther King, Moltmann preferred not to answer a question as to how his European theology might speak to that tragic event; in Roberts' opinion this seemed at the time an evasion.[71] Probably, in the present circumstances, it is better for now that non-blacks remain at a respectful distance from Black Theology's discussions, and this Moltmann does. True, he does express the wish that at a future time white and black theologians may jointly work toward a more "*Christian* theology."[72] But this comment ought not to mean nostalgia for the old integrationist (i.e., whites-holding-the-cards) approach, but hope for a genuine inter-cultural, intergroup dialogue within Christianity.

However, to grant that as a school, the Theology of Hope is alien to Black Theology does not imply that the future or hope as such are irrelevant bases on which to construct a theology for black people. More than a century ago, Frederick Douglass noted the enormous driving power of hope:

> Temporal wants supplied, the spirit puts in its claims. Beat and cuff your slave, keep him hungry and spiritless, and he will follow the chain of his master like a dog; but, feed and clothe him well,—work him moder-

ately—surround him with physical comfort—and dreams of freedom intrude. Give him a *bad* master, and he aspires to a *good* master; give him a good master, and he wishes to become his *own* master. Such is human nature. You may hurl a man so low, beneath the level of his kind, that he loses all just ideas of his natural position; but elevate him a little, and the clear conception of rights rises to life and power, and leads him onward.[73]

Another example: in discussing the psychological pressures of Anglo-American slavery, Stanley Elkins draws the controversial parallel of Nazi concentration camps, and notes carefully the thoroughly disintegrative effects on personal identity of a belief that there was no future, nothing but a limitless extension of the present and its dehumanizing prison roles.[74] Psychologically, hope plainly supplies the possibility of preserving one's humanity.

Furthermore, ideas of the future ought to be theologically based on the dimension of the transcendent, and thus have at least some approximation to what Moltmann describes as *adventus*. This is in contrast to much of the talk of hope in Black Theology, which seems to be simply hortatory, a goad and reinforcement for ethical imperatives in the present. As such, that hope has no ontic basis, except the indirect one of a Pelagian anthropology. But, as Roberts says in criticism of Cone, "an eschatology without a future dimension is only partially complete."[75] As discussed earlier, to urge ethical action against great odds and without a transcendent reference point beyond the announced hopes, is to invite a disillusionment which in turn can lead to terrorism or apocalyptic despair. Yet a transcendent base need not conflict with vigorous social commitments, as the highly ontologically-based imperatives of Marxism or early Puritanism have shown. Hope must have an ontic status, and the clarification of this is the task of theology. But as to whether Moltmann's Germanic thought offers any helpful resource or not for Black Theology in articulating this base is an issue to be decided entirely by black theologians themselves.

Replies and Evaluations: Black Theology's Response

Secondly, let us examine Moltmann's critical questions for Black Theology, to the extent such can be inferred, and the viability of his comments.

Understanding evil. The first of three critical issues raised was whether Black Theology has sufficiently thought through the profound nature of evil. To this must be replied: No—and Yes! No, in one sense evil is not seen broadly enough. That is, racism is indeed too often isolated as the only sin worthy of the name, rather than seen in its interlocking complexity, involving economic and political structures as well as psychological anxieties and projections, as Moltmann notes. Indeed, one might go further and ask just why modern racism developed at the beginning of the modern era, concurrently with Europe's great surge of capitalism, nationalism, and expansionism. What common factors or interrelationships lie behind this massive, aggressive confluence which now so characteristically determines modern man, and the distinctively western pattern of his alienation from God? Little analysis has been written about racism in this light.

On the other hand, however, the "Yes": Black Theology *has* grasped the profound nature of evil, in a way which Moltmann and most of us whites find difficult to comprehend. For "racism" is sin seen in its irrational and bitter radicality, if not always in its breadth. Black Theology may well ask in reply: why is white racism so resistant, so very resilient, in the face of other changing social factors? Not just in collusion with politico-economic interests, but even when these tides flow against it, racism endures and breeds again. For example, by every economic criterion the Populist movement at the end of the last century, and even today in the rural South, should have allied poor whites and poor blacks; the opposite was the actual result. How can the "broad view" of sin come to grips with the many-headed Hydra of racism? As for the lack of cooperation with other liberation movements—is it not striking how frequently in the past, when there has been cooperation with other interest groups, that *black* liberation is co-opted, relativized into a secondary position? Black Power reflects a legitimate disillusionment with the policy of alliances. The extreme opposite position, ethnic isolation, brings its own difficulties, of course, and at present seems also out of favor with leaders of the Black Panthers, for instance. But the tactical dilemma still remains, since black interests cannot be *reduced* to those of other liberation movements: to what extent can there be cooperation against a common foe, without vitiating black interests and identity?

Racism must not be defined in compartmentalized seclusion. But in its depths and savagery the concept does come close to touching the very essence of human sin, combining as it does the irrational yet total scope of sinful inclinations, their self-destructive power and futility, and the delicate combination of anxiety, merging into sublimated lust for power. Augustine would have understood it all quite well. And within Black Theology, much of the creative power of James Cone's thought is related to his use of "black" (and conversely, "white") as both a physiological-historical fact and as an ontological condition—i.e., symbolizing any and all humanity that suffers and resists oppression in solidarity with its victims.[76] Certainly racism has ontological dimensions, to say the least.

On reconciliation. The second major query by Moltmann concerns the nature of reconciliation and how it could be made possible. Since James Cone and Martin Luther King, Jr., are the two black theologians with whom Moltmann is familiar, some contrast between them seems implicit in his mind. However, between Cone and King there is no fundamental disagreement on this one point: reconciliation is the final goal sought by all (including black) theology.[77] In fact most black theologians, from Roberts to Wilmore (excluding, however, the religious black nationalism represented by Albert Cleage)[78] would also agree on that goal—although Shelby Rooks, for instance, would prefer the term "co-existence."[79] What *is* very much at issue, however, is the burning question of *on what terms* reconciliation is possible! Here a hard realism, refined by three hundred fifty years of the American experience, intrudes. Lofty phrases, such as "brotherhood" or "a just and honorable peace" are notoriously susceptible to ideological manipulation, and always to the benefit of him who holds the most (veiled or naked) power.

The basis and precondition for reconciliation, as all leaders of Black Theology firmly agree, must be liberation.[80] They will of course need to continue to reflect on what forms and means of liberation are consistent with the goal. But whites also need to be cautious and humble in discussing this; above all, they dare not *demand* reconciliation with blacks, any more than modern Germans, with Jews. The guilt is too great for that. From the side of oppressors and former slaveholders, reconciliation must be preceded by atonement and recompense. And despite some oratory, this has never really been undertaken by American society. Of course atonement ultimately derives from the Cross and God's once-for-all self-sacrifice; but in the present situation, white Americans as the offending part must take the initiative to demonstrate and actualize for today this atonement for the fellowman. Without a self-abasement by the powerful and the (however "well-intentioned") brutalizers, at the feet of the weak and victimized, Christ's atonement has not yet reached either side. For our time and place, before reconciliation can be further discussed, the agenda must be headed by that concrete and abrasive word, "reparations."

Brief note may also be taken of a passing remark by Moltmann concerning future racial identity within reconciliation. To what extent will reconciliation require this identity to be transformed or surmounted? This is a very sensitive and necessarily remote issue, in the present state of affairs, and may wisely be deferred. As a neoteric discipline, Black Theology has no need to speak to that point now, and as a largely integrationist (i.e., one-way!) perspective, white theology has no right to speak of that yet.

The question of eschatological freedom. The third major critical question posed by Moltmann, this one however directed towards European liberation movements, concerns the danger of losing eschatological freedom through revolutionary legalism. This is a distinctively Christian query, and pertinent for many other areas of twentieth-century life as well. But it is problematic, as Moltmann himself realizes, as to how appropriate it is as a challenge to Black Theology—especially since that rubric covers a range of distinctive individual thinkers. Albert Cleage, for instance, would be far more vulnerable to this criticism than Deotis Roberts. However, since Black Theology is widely supposed by whites to be a mere religious cover for revolution, and since James Cone (the black with whom we are most concerned) has sometimes used that idiom (especially in *A Black Theology of Liberation*), the question does deserve some attention.

At the outset, it should be said that "revolutionary legalism" is a dangerously easy accusation to level, by those who are already firmly in power and whose own forms of legalism and loss of eschatological freedom is covert, both cushioned and veiled by the social structures. Theologically, "Freedom and Legalism" is an issue of the highest importance. But socio-politically, it is fair to discuss it only if whites are equally willing to risk standing under the same possible indictment. Only with this prior agreement, can discussion then proceed.

One form of revolutionist discussed by Moltmann is obviously prone to legalism, and that is the ideological type, especially the Marxist. But this is only marginally relevant here. Some secular black militants are in varying degrees influenced by Marxism, but—aside from a few phrases now accepted as common currency—one hardly finds many avowed Marxists among black theologians.

Another form of revolutionist described by Moltmann is more pertinent: the "decisionist," glorifying bold and normless action. As German intellectual history shows, decisionism is not at all limited to the deprived classes, the "have-nots." It may attract ultra-rightist groups and the affluent. But it is understandable why a relatively powerless minority group, impatient with centuries of broken promises and racist rationalizations, would try to maximize whatever power they do possess by mobilizing sheer resolve to the utmost. But is Black Theology really a form of decisionism? Some language used by Cone and several others may suggest that it is, but may also be understood as attempts to evolve a non-Euro-American rhetoric, one which embraces the whole nature of man and not simply his logical faculties. Moreover, black words are finally to be judged in light of black actions, and on the whole it is clear that these actions have *not* been the spontaneous violence typical of decisionism. One has only to look at the careful strategies and realism of groups such as IFCO, People United to Save Humanity (PUSH), and NCBC, to see that black leadership has generally been more enlightened and patient than white society has reason to hope for.

Nevertheless, to the modest extent that decisionism does accurately describe some modes of Black Theology, Moltmann's warnings are theologically sound and noteworthy.[81] Norms, for instance, cannot be dispensed with, for every action is in fact predicated on goals and assumptions, however inarticulate. Nor can Christian activism omit a love which trusts in the transformability of the enemy. The mystique of martial music is indeed compelling, but is of doubtful compatibility with the Lordship of the crucified Son of Man.

Any use of revolutionary language also opens up the question of violence. Moltmann's growing mistrust of violent action in some respects seems to approach the perspective (but not the resulting social passivity) of Jacques

Ellul, who sees violence as inherently and irrevocably legalistic, a natural part of the fallen realm of "necessity" which stands in utter contrast to freedom.[82] And it is true that violence parallels legalism, by perpetuating itself as one strategy to the continuing exclusion of others, by its reciprocity-cycle inviting retaliation in kind, and by the stereotyping needed for its continuing ruse of legitimation. As such, violence in all its manifestations—the covert forms preferred by the privileged and those in power, and the overt forms which are all that remain for the oppressed and those out of power—is to be seen theologically as allied with the Law, never with Grace, and thus standing as an instrument of condemnation and guilt under God. But, as Moltmann sees more than does Ellul, this theological judgment still does not extricate the Christian from the practical reality of his involvement, passive or active, in the relentless machinery of this world. The particularities of those conditions under which violent resistance may or may not serve universal human rights is a subject still untouched by the simple identification of violence with legalism.

Surely a wider theological discussion on the theme of violence is necessary. But the need for such discussion cannot as such imply that Black Theology necessarily falls under this general theme. A careful reading will show that justifications for violence are not nearly as characteristic for Black Theology as many whites suppose. Interesting, but not appropriate here, would be a psycho-theological investigation into why for three hundred fifty years white Americans have had such compelling and, history indicates, highly exaggerated fears of black violence. This is not to deny that Cone and others allude sometimes to liberation associated with violence, nor to exclude the critical questions which still need to be directed frankly towards such statements. But rather it is to set such allusions in their proper context as relatively infrequent statements from thinkers who, by every criterion, have demonstrated responsible leadership, and who are surrounded daily by massive and uncriticized covert violence in a white society.

But if the fearsome overtones of revolution are admitted to be tangential, the heart of Moltmann's third critical question would still be this: does Black Theology sacrifice eschatological freedom, as the price for direct liberation from social and physical oppression? This is a serious danger found in every liberation movement, of course, from the early labor struggles to Women's Liberation. And especially in Cone's earlier writings, one often finds "freedom" used synonymously with socio-political group self-determination. This is indeed basic, but it is an overly narrow definition and has been criticized as such by some other black theologians. It neglects the broader economic, sociological, and even spiritual network of interrelationships upon which human self-fulfillment depends. In fact, it seems to be a mirror image of the restrictive (white) American vision of freedom as mere absence of governmental constraints, laissez faire: as long as we be emancipated from King George III and his modern bureaucratic counterparts, we are supposedly "free"—regardless of encroaching economic monopolies, environmental pollution, social conformism, and spiritual apathy.

But never did Cone consistently equate liberation with simply group self-determination. One need only recall his statements on the "freedom to be," i.e., to actualize all human potentialities.[83] Freedom has two dimensions, the second going beyond historical self-determination and into the realm of the non-quantifiably human. And here Cone's latest book makes a special contribution. For in *The Spirituals and the Blues*, he demonstrates the magnificent resources of black religion and music to sustain exactly that quality so often lacking in the white descendants of Puritan Christianity, namely, eschatological freedom! The spirituals actualized a dimension of freedom in and under the conditions of slavery, which the slavemaster himself is forever deprived of. For instance, the concept of "heaven" (and similarly, of "home" in the blues) served to parry the thrust of both white values and misery from surrounding society, and to irradiate a quality of transcendence into the present, giving hope for the future.[84] This analysis resembles Moltmann's own descriptions of hope in both its present and eschatologically liberating aspects. In fact, the black idiom "soul," elusive as it is of precise definition, but suggestive of triumph over impossible odds, a flash of joy untrampled by hostile reality, is the only authentically American equivalent of what in Europe is discussed more ponderously as "realized eschatology," and "eschatological existence *dennoch*." Perhaps some Black Theology in the late 1960's tended to restrict freedom to a narrow, all-too-American view of political unconstraint. But on the whole, any charge of eschatological freedom being lost in revolutionary legalism seems to fall wide of the mark. To the contrary: the "soul" of black religion offers, to a legalistic society that does not deserve it, the richest indigenous source of praise and self-expression of eschatological freedom—a life of joy in the midst of pain, hope, and striving to receive the future.

Conclusion

Have, then, Black Theology and the Theology of Hope anything to say to each other? With all due precautions for observing the integrity of each and the great cultural and theological differences separating them, I think the answer still must by Yes. They do share certain problems which must be considered if either movement is to retain its vitality. For example, both insist God is at work in transforming history and the present into the future, but both are deficient in criteria for identifying just where God is to be detected in the swirl and ambiguity of onrushing events. As a second example, each has its own difficulties in creating a new and appropriate mode of theological language. Black Theology, aware that both whites and blacks will be its readers, combines a defensiveness and an extravagance in its reaction to Euro-American language habits, and Moltmann utilizes both a simplified biblical theology (offensive to analysts, e.g., James Barr) and a sophisticated dialectic from left-wing Hegelianism (puzzling to laymen). In each movement, it would seem that language, audience, and subject matter must be more carefully aligned. Both examples show the interminable problem of struggling for theological conceptualization which, in obedience to God's self-offering, can best unite clarity with comprehensiveness, and universality with versatility.

But perhaps it is in this struggle that the two movements have the most to contribute to each other, and thereby jointly to a jaded and cynical theological readership. For both have a vision of the future divine Kingdom of justice and freedom on earth, and both seek to show how this is to be realized within and despite this world, the present and the past, and the actions and sufferings of real persons. For this vision and its actualization, however, neither school is quite adequate. The strength of Moltmann is his study of the ontological priority of the future as the mode of God's being, opening the way for eschatology to be more than empty poetic words, but rather to be the active basis for thinking about man and God, and about man and man. The strength of Black Theology is both its realism, grounded firmly in the daily experience of a people sojourning in a strange land, and its "soul," the ability to enact joy and celebration in the face of demonic powers. This may not be the propitious time, but perhaps in some eventual dialogue, the one can provide a breadth of vision and some conceptual resources for viewing the present in light of the future, and the other can provide the toughness of concrete experience and the range of emotional presence for viewing the future in the tensions of the present.

Notes

1. Here, however, Cone is more Christocentric, even Barthian, than most black theologians. For instance, Deotis Roberts prefers a more general, Tillichian approach (*Liberation and Reconciliation* [Philadelphia: Westminster, 1971]), and Gayraud Wilmore, in his *Black Religion and Black Radicalism* (New York: Doubleday, 1972) joins John S. Mbiti (*African Religions and Philosophy* [New York, Doubleday, 1969]) in emphasizing an inherent African spirituality.

2. See especially Jürgen Moltmann, "Theologische Kritik der politischen Religion," in *Kirche im Prozess der Aufklärung* (Munich-Mainz: Kaiser Grünewald, 1970), pp. 11-51; Cone is referred to on p. 34. Similarly, Moltmann, "Political Theology," *Theology Today*, XXVIII (April, 1971), 6-23. And in "Christian Theology and the Afro-American Revolution," *Christianity and Crisis*, XXX (June 8, 1970), 124, Cone grants that Moltmann is among the few exceptions to the usual Christian identification with the power structure.

3. James H. Cone, *A Black Theology of Liberation* (Philadelphia: Lippincott, 1970), pp. 126-28, and Moltmann, *Religion, Revolution, and the Future* (New York: Scribner's, 1969), pp. 13-15.

4. Moltmann, *Umkehr zur Zukunft* (Munich: Siebenstern, 1970), pp. 53-54, and Cone, *Black Theology and Black Power* (New York: Seabury, 1969), pp. 47-56.

5. Moltmann, "Theologische Kritik," pp. 47-48 (where he also endorses Cone's statement that for the twentieth century, Christ is to be seen as "black"); *Der gekreuzigte Gott* (Munich: Kaiser, 1972), pp. 261-63. Cf. Cone, *Black Theology*, pp. 38-42, 57-61, 118-21.

6. Cone, *Black Theology*, pp. 151-52, "Christian Theology," p. 124. See also his "Black Theology and Black Liberation," Christian Century, LXXXVII (September 16, 1970), 1087. Cf. Moltmann, *Religion*, pp. 140-43.

7. Moltmann, *Religion*, pp. 142-43; Martin Luther King, Jr., is here cited. Cf. Cone, *Black Theology*, pp. 41, 145; *Liberation*, pp. 185-86.

8. Moltmann, *Religion*, p. 40; Deotis Roberts (op. cit., pp. 24, 140, 152, 177), on the more conservative end of Black Theology, may tend to agree. Some black theologians, such as Shelby Rooks ("Toward the Promised Land," mimeographed lecture, Texas Christian University, Feb. 15, 1972, p. 13), refuse to advocate either revolution or reconciliation, but foresee instead a "co-existence."

9. Moltmann, "Theologische Kritik," p. 45. Cf. Cone, *Liberation*, pp. 160-64, 168-70; cf. also Joseph R. Washington, Jr., "How Black is Black Religion?" in *Quest for a Black Theology*, ed. James J. Gardiner and J. Deotis Roberts (Philadelphia: Pilgrim, 1971), pp. 40-41.

10. Moltmann, *Religion*, pp. 37-41; *Der gekreuzigte Gott*, pp. 306-12. Cf. his "Gemeinschaft in einer geteilten Welt," *Evangelische Kommentare*, V (September 1972), 527-28.

11. Cone, interview (June 12, 1972); cf. *The Spirituals and the Blues* (New York: Seabury, 1972), pp. 91-102, 142. Similar holistic perspectives on freedom occur in most black theologians. An excellent example is Gayraud Wilmore, op. cit., p. 298:

> Although political emancipation was the concrete expression of that freedom, it did not exhaust its meaning. The freedom toward which the Afro-American religious experience and early Black theology tended was freedom as existential deliverance, as liberation from every power or force that restrains the full, spontaneous release of body, mind and spirit from every bondage which does not contribute to the proper development of the whole person in community. Not simply political freedom, but the freedom of the human being as a child of God, to be himself; to realize the deepest and highest potentialities of his psychosomatic nature.

12. See Cone, *Black Theology*, p. 39: "Freedom is *not doing what I will but becoming what I should. A man is freed when he sees clearly the fulfillment of his being and is thus capable of making the envisioned self a reality*." See also, *Spirituals*, pp. 91, 95, and his "Black Power, Black Theology, and the Study of Theology and Ethics," *Theological Education*, VI (Spring, 1970), 213. Cf. Major J. Jones, *Black Awareness: A Theology of Hope* (Nashville: Abingdon, 1971), p. 83.

13. Moltmann, "The First Liberated Men in Creation," *The Theology of Play* (New York: Harper & Row, 1972).

14. Cone, *Black Theology*, pp. 20, 29-30, 138-43; *Liberation*, pp. 56-57; and his "Response to Lochman," *Christianity and Crisis*, XXXII (July 10, 1972), 167. On the Manifesto, cf. Wilmore, op. cit., p. 279.

15. "God in Revolution," *Religion*, pp. 143-45. Similar are the statements within "Gewalt und Liebe," *Umkehr*, pp. 45-55, and his "Rassismus und das Recht auf Widerstand," *Evangelische Kommentare*, IV (May, 1971), 253-57.

16. "The Lordship of Christ and Human Society," in *Two Studies in the Theology of Bonhoeffer*, by Jürgen Moltmann and Jürgen Weissbach (New York: Scribner's, 1967; original German essay in 1959), pp. 21-94, especially pp. 29-35. Cf. "The Future as New Paradigm of Transcendence," *Religion*, pp. 177-99; "Theologische Kritik," p. 48; and his "Antwort auf die Kritik der Theologie der Hoffnung," in *Diskussion über die "Theologie der Hoffnung" von Jürgen Moltmann*, ed. Wolf-Dieter Marsch (Munich: Kaiser, 1967), p. 237. A striking parallel is expressed by Charles H. Long, "The Black Reality: Toward a Theology of Freedom," *Criterion*, VIII (Spring-Summer, 1969), 5-6, who says that blacks now offer America the opportunity of experiencing the mystery and "otherness" of the *mysterium tremendum*.

17. See Cone, *Black Theology*, p. 38: "Black rebellion is a manifestation of God himself actively involved in the present-day affairs of men for the purpose of liberating a people." Cf. pp. 63, 99, 118, 150.

18. Moltmann, *Religion*, p. 146; *Theology of Play*, pp. vii, 12-14, 45-53, 66-72.

19. "Racism" refers to attitudes derived from the conviction of the superiority of one's own racial-ethnic group, together with physical or psychological domination exercised, conscious or not, over other groups. Cf. the definition given by Uppsala, 1968 (quoted by Moltmann, "Rassismus," p. 253).

20. Moltmann, *Der gekreuzigte Gott*, pp. 48–52, 307; Cone is cited in both passages.

21. Moltmann, *Umkehr*, pp. 34-35; *Theology of Play*, pp. 51-53; also his *Mensch: Christliche Anthropologie in den Konflikten der Gegenwart* (Stuttgart: Kreuz, 1971), p. 167.

22. Moltmann, *Religion*, p. 79.

23. Even Deotis Roberts, for instance, who is relatively traditional among black theologians,

is adamant that liberation is the necessary precondition to reconciliation (*Liberation and Reconciliation*, pp. 24, 32-34, 138-140, 177).

24. The brief remark comes from the interview with Cone, June 12, 1972; cf. *Black Theology*, pp. 37, 101-103; *Liberation*, pp. 211, 244-45.

25. Roberts, "Black Consciousness in Theological Perspective," *Quest for a Black Theology*, p. 81.

26. Rubem Alves, *A Theology of Human Hope* (Washington: Corpus, 1969); his own criticisms of Moltmann are elaborated on pp. 55-68, 94, 130. Roberts' discussion of Alves is in *Liberation and Reconciliation*, pp. 157-60.

27. Roberts, *Liberation and Reconciliation*, p. 157.

28. C. Shelby Rooks, interview, June 7, 1972.

29. Rooks, "Toward the Promised Land," p. 9.

30. Accordingly, Roberts criticizes Alves, who speaks from a Brazilian, anti-colonialistic perspective of a people eager to forsake a bitter past, rather than to rediscover its roots (*Liberation and Reconciliation*, p. 159)! Also, a white theologian from quite a different school of thought has raised the same criticism of hope theology's inability to cope with the modern questing for the "self": Walter H. Capps, *Time Invades the Cathedral* (Philadelphia. Fortress, 1972), pp. 137-39.

31. Gayraud Wilmore, interview, June 12, 1972.

32. Rooks, interview, June 7, 1972.

33. Roberts, *Liberation and Reconciliation*, p. 156; cf. "Black Consciousness," p. 81. Cf. Jones (*Black Awareness*, pp. 12, 88-89), who however does not always understand Moltmann correctly (e.g., p. 134).

34. Cone, *Spirituals*, p. 106; cf. also p. 107.

35. E.g., Wilmore, *Black Religion and Black Radicalism*, pp. 295-96, 300-301.

36. Cone, interview, June 12, 1972.

37. William Jones, "Toward an Interim Assessment of Black Theology," *Christian Century*, LXXXIX (May 3, 1972), 513-17. This is an excellent summary and evaluation, which deserves the widest possible readership.

38. Moltmann, *Der gekreuzigte Gott*, p. 313.

39. Moltmann, interview, Dec. 6, 1972.

40. See Moltmann, *Religion*, for references to King on pp. v, xvi, 142, 145, and Moltmann's "Man and the Son of Man," in *No Man is Alien*, ed. J. Robert Nelson (Leiden: Brill, 1971), p. 203.

41. Moltmann, interview, Dec. 6, 1972.

42. Moltmann, *Umkehr*, pp. 103-104.

43. Moltmann, *Religion*, p. 40.

44. Moltmann, *Mensch*, pp. 84, 154-55, 165.

45. Ibid., pp. 140-51.

46. Cf., the incisive discussions by Martin Hengel, *Was Jesus a Revolutionist?* (Philadelphia: Fortress, 1971), and *Gewalt und Gewaltlosigkeit: Zur "politischen Theologie" in neutestamentlicher Zeit* (Stuttgart: Calwer, 1971). Moltmann's comment on Hengel's research is summed up in *Der gekreuzigte Gott*, p. 135, n. 59.

47. Moltmann, *Der gekreuzigte Gott*, pp. 132-38.

48. Ibid., p. 135.

49. Moltmann, *Religion*, p. 137; cf. p. 145. Under circumstances of gross violation of human rights, resistance by force to tyranny may be a responsible duty and perhaps the only way to express love, but it is still not theologically justifiable in a programmatic way; cf. "Rassismus," pp. 255-57.

50. See, e.g., Ralph G. Wilburn, "Some Questions on Moltmann's Theology of Hope," *Religion in Life*, XXXVIII (Winter, 1969), 586-87, 593-94. Here Moltmann is accused of selecting only several of many biblical eschatologies, but it seems incredible to claim he combines Luke and Hebrews, omitting the balanced vision of Paul! Just the reverse is closer to the truth.

51. Harvey Cox, *The Feast of Fools* (New York: Harper & Row, 1970), pp. 121-38.

52. Novak, "Editorial: Future-Hating," *Journal of Ecumenical Studies*, VIII (Summer, 1971), 622-26. Cf. the final point of John J. Vincent, "Some Hesitations on Hope," *Religion in Life*, XL (Spring, 1971), 64-73.

53. Novak, op. cit., p. 626.

54. Moltmann, *Mensch*, pp. 38-58, especially 47-50; also his *Hope and Planning* (New York:

Harper & Row, 1971), especially pp. 178-223.

55. Moltmann, *Theology of Hope* (New York: Harper & Row, 1967), pp. 230-65.

56. Cf. in particular the brilliant and scathing article by H. O. Edwards, "Racism and Christian Ethics," *Katallegete* (Winter, 1971), pp. 15-24, which lifts up a number of statements by Niebuhr that today many Niebuhrians would rather forget.

57. Cone, interview, June 12, 1972. In *Liberation*, most of Cone's half dozen references to Niebuhr are quite favorable, but then they are also referring to the "early Niebuhr" of *Moral Man and Immoral Society*.

58. Dale Patrick, "Opening Niebuhrian Thought to the Left," *Christianity and Crisis,* XXX (October 19, 1970), 212-15.

59. It should be noted, however, that Cone himself is consistent, as his main objection to Moltmann is not the issue of future-orientation.

60. Moltmann, "Antwort," pp. 210-13; much of this is also given in English, in his "Theology as Eschatology," in *The Future of Hope*, ed. Frederick Herzog (New York: Herder & Herder, 1970), pp. 10-15. Cf. *Der gekreuzigte Gott*, pp. 171-74.

61. Moltmann's key word "anticipation" and the related vision of "concrete utopias" seem at least partly derived from Bonhoeffer's view of "the penultimate" which prepares for the revelation of Christ, by shaping the present in light of what is to come (cf. "Lordship of Christ," p. 80).

62. Mbiti, op. cit., pp. 15-28.

63. For example, Christ's resurrection is said to free us, not only from tyranny within history, but "from the tyranny of history itself" (*Uumkehr*, pp. 127-28, 141: the English revision of the former reference, *Religion*, p. 37, is softened). History is experienced in the *difference* between reality (which presumably thus must be something other than history) and the future (*Religion*, p. 28). And in *Theology of Play* (p. 37) there is an awkward passage that tries to identify "eternity" with the experience of joy, and "time" with the experience of pain.

64. Moltmann, "Antwort," pp. 202-203, 218-21; *Religion*, pp. 6-9, 28-32, 210-12; *Theology of Hope*, p. 103. In *Perspektiven der Theologie: Gesammelte Aufsatze* (Munich: Kaiser, 1968), pp. 114-16, 112-24, Moltmann defends the thesis that historical science (*Historie*) both depends on living, unfinished memory (*Geschichte*) and yet is in fatal estrangement from it, since only "dead facts" are objective and capable of manipulation. Real "remembering" is thus possible only with the unmastered past, the unfulfilled anticipations of the historical process. In the recent *Der gekreuzigte Gott* (pp. 287-90), in the context of dialogue with Freudian psychology, Moltmann says that moments of dreaming regression into the past enrich the total man, who in his maturity lives not only towards the future or in the momentary present, but also in continuity with the past. God's suffering enables sympathy in all dimensions, including openness towards the past.

65. Metz, "Erinnerung des Leidens als Kritik eines teleologisch-technologischen Zukunfts-begriffs," *Evangelische Theologie*, XXXII (July-August, 1972), 350. Cf. Moltmann, *Theology of Hope*, p. 268.

66. Wilmore, op. cit., p. 86.

67. Metz, op. cit., p. 347; cf. Moltmann, "Man," p. 205.

68. Wolfhart Pannenberg, "Zukunft und Einheit der Menscheit," *Evangelische Theologie*, XXXII (July-August, 1972), 395. Cf. his *What is Man?* (Philadelphia: Fortress, 1970), pp. 79-81; *Jesus: God and Man* (Philadelphia: Westminster, 1968), pp. 83-88, 193, 391. Even Ernst Bloch, according to Walter Capps, op. cit., pp. 37-39, believes in a sort of transmigration of souls, for some of the above reasons (however, Gerald O'Collins contests this interpretation of Bloch, *Interpretation*, XXVI [October 1972] 475).

69. William Jones, op. cit.

70. Cone, *Liberation*, pp. 194-96. However, Cone earlier gives courteous credit to several other white authors on race or Black Power, notably Joseph Barndt's *Why Black Power?* (New York: Friendship, 1968). Cf. *Black Theology*, p. 155, n.l.

71. Roberts, interview, May 24, 1972.

72. Moltmann, interview, Dec. 6, 1972.

73. Frederick Douglass, *My Bondage and My Freedom* (New York: Arno and New York Times, 1968), pp. 263-64. Also somewhat parallel to Moltmann is Douglass' description of the bewilderment of an escaped slave for the first time in a northern city, as he is caught between his powerful memories of slavery and the first dream-like glimpses of a freedom that, in fact, is already reality for those who recognize it (pp. 339-40).

74. Stanley Elkins, *Slavery*, second edition (Chicago: University of Chicago, 1968), pp. 107-108.

75. Roberts, *Liberation and Reconciliation*, p. 162. Cf. Moltmann, *Mensch*, pp. 55-58. Joseph R. Washington's *The Politics of God* (Boston: Beacon, 1967) is an example of black eschatology which retains the transcendent, in traditional biblical categories (cf. pp. 153-77).

76. Cone, *Liberation*, p. 32 n.: see also pp. 11-12, 27-29, 124, 183; *Black Theology*, pp. 150-51. Important is the clarification made in a letter to John Lawrence (editorial, *Frontier*, XIII [June, 1970, 81]), explaining the choice of "blackness" as a symbol for "the oppressed." Cone's Tillichian symbolism here is in sharp distinction to the straightforward racial distinction made by Albert Cleage, for instance. Cf. G. Clarke Chapman, Jr., "American Theology in Black: James H. Cone," *Cross Currents*, XXII (Spring, 1972), 139-57, especially pp. 143-44.

77. See e.g., Cone, "Theological Reflection on Reconciliation," *Christianity and Crisis*, XXXII (January 22, 1973), 303-308.

78. Albert Cleage, *The Black Messiah* (New York: Sheed and Ward, 1968).

79. Rooks, interview, June 7, 1972, "Toward the Promised Land," p. 13.

80. Roberts, for instance, insists that both words in his title *Liberation and Reconciliation* be taken equally seriously, and that the former is the prerequisite for the latter (cf. especially chapter 2). Also cf. n. 31, above.

81. Moltmann, *Mensch*, pp. 150-51.

82. Jacques Ellul, *Violence* (New York: Seabury, 1969), especially pp. 84-108, 127-31.

83. Cf. nn. 11 and 12, above.

84. Cone, *Spirituals*, pp. 86-107, 142.

19

CURRENTS AND CROSSCURRENTS
IN SOUTH AFRICAN BLACK THEOLOGY

David J. Bosch

The Background of South African Black Theology

As far as the continent of Africa is concerned, Black Theology was born some 270 years ago, near the mouth of the Congo River in present-day Angola. In about the year 1700 a Congolese girl, Kimpa Vita, with the baptismal name of Béatrice, began appearing in public as a prophetess. She claimed to have had several visions and to have experienced death and resurrection. She said that Saint Anthony had taken possession of her and had commanded her to preach and to teach. She, like Saint Francis of Assisi, first gave away all her possessions; she then launched a protest movement against the Roman Catholic Church. She forbade her followers to keep the times of fasting, to participate in the many church ceremonies and to sing the *Ave Maria* and the *Salve Regina*. She probably did so because she saw these practices as a meaningless, parrot-like expression of Christianity. Crosses and crucifixes had to be destroyed, as they were nothing but new fetishes which had replaced the old ones.

Of greater importance however, is the fact that Béatrice taught that Christ appeared as a black man in São Salvador and that all his apostles were black. He was a Christ who identified himself with the Africans, who threw in his lot with that of the suffering, oppressed blacks, as opposed to the white exploiters and oppressors. Therefore Christ would, according to her teachings, restore the old Congolese kingdom and establish a paradise on earth.

Béatrice's public ministry lasted for only a short period. In the year 1706 she was arrested and condemned to death. Like Joan of Arc she died at the stake, with the name of Jesus on her lips.[1]

David J. Bosch, a South African theologian, teaches at the University of South Africa and is Editor of *Missionalia*. This essay first appeared in the *Journal of Religion in Africa*, vol. 6, no. 1 (1974).

It is possible to argue the case for viewing Donna Béatrice's teachings as the first manifestation of Black Theology in Africa. This is especially true if we compare her intentions with the most pronounced characteristic of modern Black Theology, namely that it is pre-eminently a protest movement. It is a protest against an interpretation of the gospel which has been channelled according to white intentions. The *name* "Black Theology" is, however, of very recent origin. In South Africa it appeared only about three years ago, in 1970. Both the name and the specific shape Black Theology is taking in South Africa derive, of course, from the United States of America. It is nevertheless in many respects developing some local characteristics on South African soil, as we hope to show. In spite of the differences between South African and American Black Theology it will be necessary to take a look, very briefly, at the American manifestations of Black Theology before we consider this phenomenon in the South African context. Naturally we cannot hope to do justice to the scope and complexities of American Black Theology in a single paper. Only a few tendencies which influenced the development of Black Theology in South Africa will receive attention.

To some extent American Black Theology can be described as the Negro Christians' response to the challenge posed by the Black Muslims in the U.S.A. In the early' sixties the Black Muslims declared openly: "The Christian religion is incompatible with the Negroes' aspirations for dignity and equality in the U.S.A. Christian love has proved to be the white man's love for himself and his race. For the black man Islam offers the only hope for justice and equality in the world we must build for tomorrow." In contrast to this challenge the Black Theology of the late sixties has proclaimed that the Christian gospel, if preached correctly, truly aims at the dignity and salvation of the black man.

This does not mean, however, that there is but one uniform expression of Black Theology in the U.S.A. On the contrary, there are already different trends which may mutually differ to a considerable degree. The most militant form of Black Theology in the U.S.A. is to be found in the school for which James Cone is the main exponent. We shall have to draw attention to his important views, especially because it was mainly through the publications of Cone that Black Theology entered South Africa. For Cone, God's act of "liberation" stands in the centre. Because of this "hermeneutic key" he lays heavy emphasis on the Exodus and on being identified with Israel as God's chosen people. With reference to the liberation of Israel from Egypt he writes, for example: "Yahweh is the God of the oppressed and downtrodden and his revelation is made known *only* through the liberation of the oppressed."[2]

Other utterances of Cone include the following: "People who want to know who God is and what he is doing, must know who black people are and what they are doing. This does not mean lending a helping hand to the poor and unfortunate blacks of the society. It does not mean joining the war on poverty! Such acts are sin offerings that represent a white way of assuring themselves that they are basically a 'good' people. Knowing God means being on the side of the oppressed, becoming one with them and participating in the goal of liberation. We must become black with God!"[3] Elsewhere he refers to "the failure to see that blackness or salvation (the two are synonymous) is the work of God and not of man."[4] Black Theology, he declares, "cannot accept a view of God which does not represent him as being for blacks and thus against whites. Living in a world of white oppressors, black people have no time for a neutral God. . . . There is no use for a God who loves whites the same as blacks. . . . What we need is the divine love as expressed in Black Power which is the power to destroy their oppressors, here and now, by any means at their disposal. Unless God is participating in this holy activity, we must reject his love."[5] "Black Theology will accept only a love of God which participates in the destruction of the white enemy."[6] Therefore Black Theology takes literally Jesus' statement that "the last will be first and the first last." It is the task of Black Power to put this sentence into practice.

Cone attributes sin essentially to the white community only. As far as blacks are concerned, sin means the desire to be white instead of black; the refusal to be what they are; the loss of identity. Blackness is, as a matter of fact, synonymous with God's will. "God is black because he loves us, and he loves us because we are black."[7] Therefore, to love "is to make a decision against white people. Since love is that God meets our needs, God's love for white people could only mean wrath, that is, a destruction of their whiteness and a creation of blackness."[8]

It is therefore completely understandable that Cone, in his views on the Jesus of history, would follow the interpretation of those who contend that Jesus was, in actual fact, a revolutionary. Because Jesus was poor and oppressed, he must have been black. More than that: Jesus chose sides. He "was not for and against the poor, for and against the rich. He was for the poor and against the rich, for the weak and against the strong."[9] And if this applied to the Jesus of history, it applies to a much greater degree to the contemporary Christ. "He must be where men are enslaved. To speak of him is to speak of the liberation of the oppressed."[10] The choice before which the black man stands, is not a choice between violence and non-violence but merely between two forms of violence. "Concretely, ours is a situation in which the only option we have is that of deciding whose violence we will support—that of the oppressors or the oppressed, whites or blacks. Either we side with oppressed blacks and other unwanted minorities as they try to redefine the meaning of their existence in a dehumanized society, or we take a stand with Richard Nixon and Spiro Agnew whose interests are expressed in police clubs and night sticks, tear gas and machine guns. There is no possibility of neutrality. . . . Neither Nixon nor black people will allow that! . . . We must ask and answer the question, 'whose actions are consistent with God's work in history?' Either we believe that God's will is revealed in the status quo of America or in the actions of those who seek to change it."[11]

According to Cone, whites are definitely not allowed to participate in this whole discussion. Even liberally minded whites may not express any opinion or risk any interpretation of Black Power and related phenomena. He inveighs against two whites who had the audacity to write on Black Power: "Who do they think they are, pontificating about their brutality against us as if they have a relevant word about black humanity? They should know that the long history of white silence on black liberation renders their ideas irrelevant for both black and white people."[12]

American Black Theology is therefore not only interested in the black community; it is committed to a restructuring of the total American society, economics, politics, etc. It also touches the nerve centre of the whole American ecclesiastical life, so much so that Frederick Herzog, one of the few white theologians to grapple in earnest with Black Theology, has said that the crucial issue in the theology of the 'seventies will not be whether God is dead or alive, but whether he is black or white.[13]

Not all American proponents of Black Theology, however, agree on all issues. Albert Cleage could probably be grouped with Cone, in more than one respect. Both could be characterized as exponents of a "theology of revolution," in one way or another. Deotis Roberts, Major Jones and Joseph Washington, on the other hand, are much more cautious. Roberts and Jones, especially, have warned that the more strident forms of Black Theology run the risk of becoming mere black chauvinism, with little capacity for self-criticism. The sin which Cone and Cleage see rampant in white society so dominates their range of vision that it becomes impossible for them to interpret sin as a universal human problem which is also applicable to blacks.[14] Cone, for instance, tends to reduce every issue to one aspect only, and to offer partial solutions for all problems. An example of this is his view on the relationship between "liberation" and "reconciliation." To him the two are essentially synonymous. "To be reconciled is to be set free."[15] The question of an eventual reconciliation with the white man is therefore, in Cone's view, an irrelevant one. Power must be confronted with power, in order to liberate the black man; this is what reconciliation is all about.

Five Currents in the South African Context

It has been necessary to discuss briefly the situation in American Black Theology and especially the contribution of James Cone. It was, after all, via Cone that Black Theology in its present form reached South Africa. At one of the very first South African seminars on Black Theology, held at Roodepoort in March 1971, participants listened to a tape-recording by Cone on "Black Theology and Black Liberation."[16] This seminar and the other seminars held in 1971 were clearly profoundly influenced by Cone's thinking. In his introduction to the *Essays on Black Theology* Motlhabi writes: "We feel . . . what Cone says in our bones."

Since the name Black Theology appeared in South Africa and became popular (especially among the younger theological generation), several tendencies have become evident. Various interpretations of what Black Theology is or ought to be are being offered today. The most important of these interpretations are the following:

1. The first current in South African Black Theology shows essential agreement with the American model. This is, to some extent, the result of the intervention of a white theologian, Basil Moore, whose own views seem to coincide almost completely with those of James Cone. As leader of the multi-racial University Christian Movement, Moore organized the first seminars on Black Theology. He also prepared several papers for these seminars. The internal consistencies of the American model in the style of James Cone, however, found the multi-racial character of an organization like UCM in the long run unbearable. The logical result of this was the complete dissolution of UCM in 1972. The radical American model of Black Theology therefore today finds its authentic continuation in the exclusively black South African Students' Organization (SASO). The view that "Black consciousness" is a secular movement and "Black Theology" a religious one, is being rejected in these circles.[17] The two movements are in fact synonymous, for both are concerned with the total liberation of the black man. "Black Theology means taking resolute and decisive steps to free Black people not only from estrangement from God but also from slave mentality, inferiority complex, distrust of themselves and continued dependence on others culminating in self-hate."[18]

Those who follow the American model do not, however, necessarily agree on all points. One of the most able spokesmen in this category is the Lutheran pastor, Dr. Manas Buthelezi, a man who has already left his stamp on the whole debate. He distinguishes sharply between "African Theology" (to which I will refer in the next section) and "Black Theology." African Theology has, according to him, an ethnological point of departure, Black Theology on the other hand has an anthropological point of departure ("anthropological" in the theological, not the cultural sense). African Theology is concerned with Africanization, Black Theology with liberation—liberation also from one's own cultural heritage. "To be theologically honest, one need not reconstruct first the situation in which our grandfathers lived."[19] Moreover, in the South African situation an African Theology tied to a past tradition will always smack of something similar to the white Government's attempt to link the political future of the black man to past traditional institutions like the chieftainship.[20]

In "African Theology," Buthelezi maintains, nostalgia plays a more important role than theology. As a matter of fact, he sees a great deal of this kind of nostalgia also in the zeal of many white missionaries for an African theology of indigenization. After all, the older-generation missionary has lost his spiritual "home base" in Europe. He feels ill at ease in modern, secularized

Europe with its liberal theology. He is a stranger in his own home. He therefore throws himself with doubled zeal on agrarian Africa, trying to make his dream come true here. And the task of the formation of an African indigenous theology provides the possibility of realizing his romantic ideal. The missionary passionately desires to "marry" Africa, after Europe has proved "unfaithful in her love." African theology seems to offer the theme for the new "love poetry" which will, it is hoped, prove more satisfying than the new "adulterous love poetry" of modern Europe.[21]

Black Theology, on the other hand, finds its point of departure not in a romanticization of the past but in the dehumanization of the black man today. The existential situation of the black *anthropos* serves as point of orientation. In this context blackness acquires—as is the case in Cone's thinking—a theological meaning and dimension. "Blackness is a life category that embraces the totality of my daily existence. It determined the circumstances of my growth as a child and the life possibilities open to me. It now determines where I live, worship, minister, and the range of my closest life associates. Can you think of a more decisive factor in life? The totality of the only life I know has unfolded itself to me within the limits and range of black situational possibilities."[22]

2. There is also, however, a second trend, according to which Black Theology is interpreted as essentially the same as African Theology. A representative of this trend is Buthelezi's fellow Lutheran, Douglas Makhathini, lecturer at the Lutheran Theological College at Mapumulo in Zululand.[23] What Makhathini and others understand as African Theology is, however, not the same as "indigenization" as it used to be understood in Western missiology. The problem about the old mission policy of indigenization is that it was usually the missionaries who dictated to the younger churches the way in which they were supposed to become indigenous and autonomous. They decided which traditional elements could remain and be adopted in the church and which had to be discarded. However, at the Abidjan meeting of the All Africa Conference of Churches, held in 1969, William Eteki-Mboumoua of Cameroon argued in favour of a completely new approach in this respect.[24] He points to the difficulties in a purposive return to traditional cultural elements in Africa. Cultural elements which have been bottled up and vegetating since the colonial period in Africa are now suddenly being given new values in an artificial way. The traditional culture is, however, not rethought, remade or refuelled from within. During the past centuries the indigenous culture has been mummified. If we now, in the modern period, attempt a revival of archaic patterns of life, we run the risk of merely creating disembodied caricatures of once significant and functional institutions. We would then be producing "zombis" (a zombi being a man robbed of his spirit and reason and left with only his physical strength).

Many well-intentioned Western attempts at indigenization have, according to Eteki-Mboumoua and others, led to such a "Zombi" Christianity. Black

Theology in the form of African Theology, however, aims at something entirely different. The Abidjan meeting formulated this in the following way: "African Theology is a theology based on the biblical faith and speaking to the African soul. It is expressed in categories of thought which arise out of the philosophy of the African people."

From the above it is clear that people like Douglas Makhathini and others travel a path different from that of Manas Buthelezi in their expositions of Black Theology. According to Buthelezi, the difference between the black man and the white man is essentially sociological; according to Makhathini, Gabriel Setiloane and others the difference is not only sociological, but also cultural and philosophical. The African differs from the white man and this "otherness" comprises more than "the experience of being black," as Buthelezi puts it.

For this very reason it is understandable that Makhathini and Setiloane have but little time for the speculative character of European theology and for its inevitable dependence on Western culture and civilization. The Greek-Roman thought-forms and modes of expression of Western theology are the "swaddling clothes" that we need to tear open in order to get to Christ. Setiloane therefore says: "We are smothered to death by Western theologies which to us are human fabrications, changing fashion daily . . . so, if we find we cannot use the tools of Western theology, we have consciously to seek others."[25]

Whereas Buthelezi, like James Cone, borrows freely from modern Western theology (for instance from Jürgen Moltmann and Paul Tillich, as well as from the Theology of Revolution), Makhathini and others display very little interest in these Western schools of theology.

3. A third current in South African Black Theology is to be discerned among those black churchmen who see a close relationship between Black Theology and the traditional religions of Africa, thus excluding the uniqueness of the Christian gospel to a greater or lesser degree. We must, of course, remember that the African religions in this respect differ considerably from the religions of Asia. In the case of the latter we often encounter a powerful revival of the religion in a new form, as it were an aggressive response of these religions to the challenge of Christianity and the West. Islam, for instance, has its Baha'i and Ahmadiyya movements; Soka Gakkai emerged from Buddhism, and in modern Hinduism we find the Ramakrishna Order. So far there have been very few indications of a similarly militant missionary movement in Africa which would attempt to present the traditional religions in revived form as an alternative to Christianity. There are, however, some individual attempts in this direction; for instance, that of Okot p'Bitek of the University of Nairobi, whose booklet on *African Religions in Western Scholarship*, is in fact a passionate plea for a return to the traditional religions as these are, according to p'Bitek, in every respect superior to Christianity.[26] In Southern Africa there are very few indications of such a frank standpoint on this matter.

P'Bitek is, moreover, consciously and expressedly non-Christian. In South Africa we find instead a tendency towards a kind of compromise on this matter: Black Theology, which in origin is essentially a Christian theology, is being presented as basically in harmony with the traditional religions of Africa. Supporters of this approach do not—as p'Bitek does—reject Christianity openly and out of hand. They tend rather to create the impression that Christianity actually brought nothing which had not already been present in Africa. As a matter of fact, it is often plainly stated that Christianity contains harmful and unacceptable elements. Christianity is, according to Mokgethi Motlhabi, past director of the Black Theology programme of the University Christian Movement, responsible for an "almost insanely pessimistic view of man."[27] Steve Biko, first president of SASO, refers to the "cold and cruel religion" imported from Europe which "scared our people with stories of hell."[28]

The Rev. Solomon Lediga, until recently co-director of the Department of Studies and Communications of the South African Council of Churches, now director of IDAMASA (Inter-denominational African Ministers' Association of South Africa) sees a very close relationship between Black Theology and traditional African religions. There exists, according to him, practically no tension between the two. Black Theology, he says, "originates in the very existence of a religion pertaining to Africa. Perhaps Black Theology was dormant and covered in the mystery and taboo that pervades primitive religions the world over." Just as God spoke to Moses by means of the burning bush and the Sinai volcano, he still speaks to Africa today, in lightning and thunder; he speaks to Africa from the snow-capped Kilimanjaro, from all natural phenomena. "On the horns of the sacrificial beast is laid the altar of atonement (at-one-ment) with the Creator. . . . The flesh and blood of the goat cleans and unites. Those who partake of the feast of redemption live forever and those who do not eat of the meat and wash in the blood of the lamb are outcasts and they are doomed." Therefore, he says, "we shall sing praises unto this God [viz. of Africa: *Modimo, Nkulunkulu, Thixo* or *Qamatha*—D.J.B.] and tell the spirits of our forefathers who dwell in his courtyard to mediate for us. We shall commune with Him and the spirits in the sacrificial feast and offer to Him and His spirits beast and beer brewed from the granary He has secured for us." It is, after all, *this* God who is overflowing in love, not the sectarian and selfish God of the white man. It is the task of Black Theology to reveal anew this God to Africa.[29]

4. A fourth current in the present South African interpretation of Black Theology is to be found in the conviction that Black Theology found its earliest and most authentic interpretation in the widespread movement of the African Independent Churches. We have actually already alluded to this in our introduction when we described the movement of Donna Béatrice at the beginning of the eighteenth century as being the first bud on the tree of Black Theology. Especially in the so-called Ethiopian movement which started to

spread all over Southern Africa towards the end of the last century we may encounter elements strongly reminiscent of developments in modern Black Theology. White supremacy and opposition to that were, after all, among the first causes of the formation of these churches.

The expression "Black Theology" had, of course, until a few years ago, never been used in connection with these movements. In recent years, however, a clear connection is becoming increasingly evident between the Independent Churches and Black Theology. Victor Mayatula, a young, exceptionally energetic and gifted minister of the Bantu Bethlehem Christian Apostolic Church of South Africa, is one of those who are convinced that an authentic expression of what Black Theology is really about is to be found precisely in these churches. Black Theology is concerned with liberation; this is also the concern of the Independent Churches. In the Ethiopian and Messianic Churches, he says, the emphasis is on physical liberation, in the Zionist Churches it is on psychological liberation. He therefore sees a miracle taking place today: a large group of young black intellectuals are placing their hope in the Independent Churches. They are the young black philosophers and advocates of black consciousness, black solidarity and black communalism. As far as the exponents of American Black Theology are concerned, Mayatula seems to experience a special affinity with Albert Cleage and his theology of the Black Messiah.[30]

Looking at Mayatula and others, we may get the impression that there is indeed much to be said for interpreting the Independent Churches movement as a manifestation of Black Theology, especially if we regard opposition to white guardianship as a constitutive element in the development of Black Theology. It is, on the other hand, seriously to be doubted whether there are any prospects of the majority of the spokesmen of the Independent Churches ever summarizing what they campaign for under the heading "Black Theology." Black Theology appears to be pre-eminently a movement within the so-called *historical* churches, *inter alia* the Anglican, Methodist, Roman Catholic, Lutheran and Congregational Churches. It also seems very unlikely that black theologians in these churches would break away from their churches to join the Independent Churches. It is, of course, undoubtedly true that, during the past decade, black and white members of the historical churches have adopted an increasingly positive and tolerant attitude towards the independent churches. It is, however, improbable that this rapprochement can be atrributed to the influence of Black Theology. The rapprochement is rather to be regarded as a result of the sympathetic research of Sundkler and many others, and of the activities of the Christian Institute of Southern Africa, AICA (African Independent Churches' Association) and similar organizations.

5. The fifth and last current in the South African interpretation of Black Theology we could perhaps describe as a combination of the first and second currents outlined earlier. It may well be that the real future and lasting

contribution of South African Black Theology lies in this direction: that it will, so to speak, form the bridge or link between American Black Theology and the African Theology of the rest of the African continent. Motlhabi had spotted this already in 1971 and wrote in the introduction to the volume *Essays on Black Theology*: "Black Theology in South Africa, as this collection of essays shows clearly, is a unique combination of the theology of disinheritance and oppression and the theology of culture. It is North America's Black Theology and independent Africa's African Theology in which politics and 'culture' are deeply and inextricably intertwined."[31]

In an important contribution on the relationship between American Black Theology and African Theology, James Cone and Gayraud Wilmore[32] point out the similarities and differences, drawing attention to the peculiar fact that Black Theology exerts influence upon African Theology but that the reverse is not necessarily true.[33] This is indeed so. Africa—and especially Southern Africa—borrows from America in this field, but America adopts virtually nothing from Africa. The reason for this is obvious: the American Negro lacks the real cultural context in which African Theology is taking shape. He is, religio-culturally, simply not an African any more. Cone and Wilmore do indeed refer to "survivals of African religiosity" still to be found among the Negro inhabitants of the Sea Islands off the coast of South Carolina,[34] but it is very doubtful whether these "survivals" will prove to be adequate to serve as a basis for a meaningful incorporation of elements from African Theology. The traditional kinship system of the West African Negroes who were shipped to America centuries ago as slaves was in this process totally destroyed. Their American descendants of today can find no real anchor any more in that cultural past.

Contrary to this, it seems as though in South Africa the two theological trends of Black Theology and African Theology can indeed merge into a meaningful symbiosis. From a sociological and psychological viewpoint the position of the black man in Southern Africa is in many respects comparable with that of the Negro in the U.S.A.: this offers him fertile soil for a Black Theology very similar to that of the U.S.A. Culturally and philosophically, however, the South African black man is an African: this offers him the substratum for an *African* Theology. A genuine, sincere South African Black Theology will not be able to ignore any of these two elements. In the urban areas and among the black intellectuals, this specifically South African Theology will certainly show many similarities with its American counterpart; in this Manas Buthelezi is probably correct. In the rural areas and "homelands," however, there will be more similarities to theological developments elsewhere in Africa. Because of the interaction between sociological and cultural elements peculiar to the South African situation, general theological developments in South Africa will, however, neither coincide with the American model nor with the model we find elsewhere in Africa.

Some Elements in South African Black Theology

I should now like to discuss briefly some of the major elements in South African Black Theology. I shall concentrate on the last of the five "models," but must emphasize that some of the elements are present—in some instances very explicitly—in the other models.

1. Black Theology is an appeal to the black man to overcome his slave mentality. This challenge reverberates like an echo in the *Essays on Black Theology*, for instance in the contributions of Adam Small, Steve Biko, James Cone, Nyameko Pityana and Manas Buthelezi. The most potent weapon in the hands of the oppressor is the mind of the oppressed.[35] The black man is enslaved by his own thinking and attitudes even more effectively than by his enslavement to any power outside himself. He has been taught to think "white" and to equate "white" with "valuable." He has been accepted as human only insofar as he has rejected "black" ideals and accepted "white" ideals. This inexorably led to the black man's developing a "colonized" mentality and becoming the victim of a "masochistic complex," the victim of self-hatred and self-loathing.[36] However, all this has now altered radically, a change at least partially due to Black Theology. The black man has discovered his "somebodiness" (Martin Luther King). He is no longer willing to live according to white definitions of his humanity. The appeal to him therefore rings clearly: Let us claim and affirm those things which we cannot change (such as our blackness) and acknowledge those things we can change (such as our attitudes to our blackness).[37] Here Black Theology borders on "Black consciousness."

2. A second element in South African Black Theology, related to the first, is the rejection of what is called white "tokenism," in other words, the habit of many white South Africans of trying to impress blacks by a condescending friendliness and benevolence towards them. Ernest Baartman (in spite of his Dutch-sounding name, a pure Zulu) says in this respect: "A 'non-white' is an existence with a coloured . . . pigmentation but wasting his life trying to be white. This existence crawls on its belly to whites and plays important among its own people. This existence feels honoured when invited to dinner by whites—and allowed to enter through the front door and referred to as Mr. So-and-so."[38]

It is clear that this is a castigation of the so-called "liberal" whites, those whites who plead for "integration" . . . but, of course, on their own (white) conditions! It is an attack on those whites who claim to be speaking for the blacks. Steve Biko says that even those whites who condemn the whole South African system often make it their business to control the response of the blacks to provocation. "Though whites are our problem, it is still other whites who want to tell us how to deal with that problem."[39] And the SASO commission on Black Theology lashes out against the Christian Churches in

South Africa with "their over-emphasis of racial fraternization as a solution to the problems of this country, whereas they are fully aware that the basic problem is that of land distribution, economic deprivation and consequently the disinheritance of the Black people."[40]

Integration is therefore rejected with just as much contempt as segregation—after all, both take place on the conditions of the white man. "The concept of integration, whose virtues are often extolled in white liberal circles, is full of unquestioned assumptions that embrace white values. It is a concept long defined by whites and never examined by blacks."[41] Therefore even the liberal student organizations NUSAS and UCM were not good enough: "black visibility" on committees does not necessarily imply "black participation." The idea of a really integrated church is also being rejected as "unpractical" and "farcical."[42]

3. The discussion on the previous two elements may perhaps create the impression that South African Black Theology is identical on these points with its American counterpart, especially as propagated by James Cone. On closer examination, however, this does not seem to be the case. We find that even some of the most severe critics of white "tokenism" and of integration, people like Baartman and Buthelezi, also say things that seem to be absent from Cone's writings. Baartman for instance writes: "This is the difficult demand . . . 'TO LOVE THE WHITE MAN.' We cannot hate our fellow man. God created us in love because He loved us, He so loved us that He chose the way of love that goes through bitterness, sweat and blood. He chose death. It is difficult to love whites. It is costly to love whites, yet the black man must. The life that the whites seek to destroy through hatred must be rebuilt in love. . . . The Gospel directs us all to unity. Those in Christ must be one in Christ. This was Christ's own prayer. . . . Today those who work for unity among the blacks do so in the face of growing opposition. The majority of those in the church still speak of unity but this majority is slowly but surely being whittled away. We constantly pray that the day must never come when every black man will say, 'I shall have nothing to do with the white man.' "[43] Manas Buthelezi writes in the same vein: "What is it that is unique in the Christian gospel? It is the love of God in Jesus Christ that transforms strange neighbours into loving brothers. It is very often said that points of racial contact are points of friction. What is unique about the Gospel is that it changes points of contact into points of fellowship."[44]

In this context it is also important to draw attention to the fact that a man like Buthelezi reveals a genuine concern for the white man. He pleads, for example, for a missionary endeavour in South Africa which would, for a change, go in an opposite direction: from black to white. If white people are lost, the black man may be held responsible by God for this. "Does it ever occur to black people that they have an evangelistic duty of getting the white man out of the spiritual darkness which has prevented him from seeing that the black is his daily life brother? God will ask: 'Black man, where were you when the white man abandoned my Gospel and went to destruction?' When the black man answers, 'I was only a kaffir, how could I dare to preach to my baas?' God will say: 'Was Christ's resurrection not sufficient to liberate you, black man, from that kind of spiritual and psychological death? Go to eternal condemnation, black man, for you did not muster courage to save your white brother.' "[45] The aim of such a black mission to whites is therefore "to preach love to the white man so that he may have the courage to see . . . that his security is not necessarily tied to his rejection of the black man."[46]

4. There is, fourthly, an *ecumenical* element in Black Theology in South Africa. Baartman reminds us of the fact that for many blacks it is merely an accident of history that they belong to their specific denomination. "I have no deep emotional ties to or differences from any of the imported denominations in this country. I have no forefather who was persecuted. . . ."[47] Black Theology is challenged to transcend all artificial and imported denominational differences. Black Christians in South Africa must be de-denominationalized. Black Theology must offer the black man a new spiritual home, as well as a new identity. All black and brown Christians are called upon to draw nearer to one another. At this stage this does not yet mean the formation of a single powerful black church, but at least that the emphasis must be put elsewhere than is the case at present; there must be the realization that black Christians of different churches have more things in common than things which keep them apart.

5. Black Theology is, in the fifth place, an *anti-pietistic* theology. The traditional theology of Western missionaries in Africa, Protestants and Roman Catholics alike, was in essence pietistic. It is, however, important to note that their theology of mission was pietistic not merely because of their own inner convictions, but also because of the immensity of the task facing them in Africa. The early Western missionary in Africa was confronted by a world of which he understood very little. To proclaim the Gospel in this world in such a way that all spheres of life of the Africans would be affected—spheres of life which the missionary himself did not understand—was extremely difficult. The missionary therefore, whether he wished to or not, usually limited himself to the "salvation of the souls" of Africans, urging them to comply with specific church regulations and some outward norms of respectability. Even the missionary whose own theological position was anything but pietistic, in actual practice often preached an attenuated version of the Gospel, emphasizing mainly the relationship between a specific "soul" and God. As a result of this, black converts were often not taught the implications of being a Christian in all areas of one's ordinary daily life. This static, one-sided type of religion, Lawrence Zulu says, was "solely centred on the individual, . . . stressing the role of the institution—the church building, Sunday worship and sacraments. With these things duly performed, what else was needed?"[48]

This whole attenuated, pietistic version of the Gospel is being rejected radically by the spokesmen of Black Theology. The Gospel is concerned with the whole man and his total need, and with liberating him from social malconditions which dehumanize and debilitate him.

Evaluation

An evaluation of South African Black Theology is at this stage extremely difficult, not least because of the different and opposing currents we encounter in the movement. If I nevertheless risk an evaluation, such an evaluation will of necessity be merely provisional. What I do say here, is said with great circumspection:

1. In the first place, the majority of spokesmen for a Black Theology do themselves admit that their theological statements are *situational*. Douglas Makhathini, for instance, says plainly that Black Theology claims no permanence beyond its present validity. It may only claim a hearing as long as it is functional and relevant, and will sooner or later have to give way to another approach.[49] Its relevance is being determined by the sociological position in which the black man finds himself today. If this situation changes drastically, Black Theology in its present form will become obsolete.

Theo Sundermeier is therefore correct when he asserts that Black Theology does not belong among the theological disciplines of Systematic Theology or Exegesis, but in that of *Hermeneutics*. Black Theology has an apologetic-pastoral and socio-ethical purpose. It aims at influencing and changing people's consciousness. It intends to be proclaimed and experienced. As far as its intention is concerned, Black Theology therefore finds its nearest equivalent in the hermeneutics of Gerhard Ebeling: the Biblical text is not the object I have to interpret, but the subject that interprets me. In a similar vein Black Theology intends to interpret the experience of the black man with the aid of the Bible *coram Deo*. Black Theology, as hermeneutic key, focuses the light of Scripture on the black man's experience of reality.[50]

The same, of course, holds true of the American versions of Black Theology. In his book on *A Black Theology of Liberation*, James Cone attempts to cover all major Christian doctrines, treating them from a Black Theology perspective. This book thus pretends to be a publication in the field of systematic theology; in reality, it is entirely a book on hermeneutics. It offers a systematic treatment of the Gospel in the light of the experiences of the black man in the U.S.A. Black Theology, in both the United States and South Africa, finds its *leitmotiv* in Luke 4:18-19. These words, spoken by Jesus in the synagogue in Nazareth, have for Black Theology the same central significance as the words of Rom. 1:17 ("The just shall live by faith") had for the Reformers.

2. In a critical evaluation of Black Theology the critical remarks coming from the ranks of black theologians themselves are of far greater significance than the value judgments of whites. In this connection I should like to draw

your attention to two such critical voices, both of black Anglicans: Ephraim Mosothoane, a young lecturer at the Anglican Seminary St. Bede's in Umtata (Transkei), and Bishop Alpheus Zulu, bishop of the diocese of Zululand and one of the vice-presidents of the·World Council of Churches.

In a paper read at the missiological Institute at Mapumulo in September 1972, Mosothoane said that it was undoubtedly true that Africa was to be enriched by the Gospel. "But if it is to be enriched it must also be judged by the Gospel."[51] "Do not think that just because you are an African all is well with you. Do not conclude that your black skin automatically puts you on God's side."[52] In South Africa, Mosothoane argues, it is not only the black man who is oppressed and treated as outcast. No, within the ranks of black people themselves there are other blacks who are despised and ostracised by their fellow-blacks: those who are accused of witchcraft, the illiterate, the unmarried mothers, and others belonging to similar categories. They are, in the language of the New Testament, the *ptochoi*, the "poor." The blacks will also be called to account by God with regard to these unfortunate people.

Bishop Zulu, in a paper on "Whither Black Theology?" likewise voices his uneasiness about some points: "Black Theology . . . will not make every black man Christian. Like all theology it can give rise to numerous heresies and is therefore a dangerous exercise. Some exponents of Black Theology give the impression that theology should be the handmaid of black revolution and that this revolution necessarily must be violent. There is also the ambiguity of phrases which describe God as being 'for blacks and therefore against whites.' Another difficult expression is that 'blacks are oppressed *because* they are black.' . . . Black theologians however, need to guard against equating 'God being on the side of the oppressed' with 'the oppressed being on the side of God.' *According to the Bible, there is no merit in being oppressed or poor.* It is by God's gracious love that he takes their side and acts for their liberation. God's righteousness denies everybody the prerogative of assuming the role of God's agent punishing the wicked. No theology can give sanction for a freedom which allows people to do what they please. If it did, it would bless tyranny. . . . Some black theologians seem to equate human love with God's. They say if God is on the side of the oppressed he cannot at the same time love the oppressor. At this point, the black man is in danger of exalting one sin—that of oppressive discrimination—as above all others, and sending to heaven those who do not commit it and to hell those who do."[53]

We must understand clearly that it demands unusual courage in men like Mosothoane and Zulu to say these things. They run the risk of being rejected by their fellow-blacks; as far as Bishop Zulu is concerned, this is already beginning to happen. I myself refrain from giving a value judgment of their viewpoints; I should merely like to draw your attention to the fact that this kind of attitude is totally absent in the Black Theology of the American James Cone. His approach lacks entirely any element of self-criticism.

3. Finally: what ought my attitude as a white theologian to be with regard to Black Theology? According to some blacks the white man has no right at

all to say anything whatsoever on this subject, because, according to James Cone, "the very essence of whiteness [is] an antithesis of the gospel of Christ."[54] If, however, theology is what it ought to be, namely an ecumenical science, we shall not be able to accept this point of departure. One thing is true, however: whatever whites have to say about Black theology must be said in subdued tones. They will have to learn especially to submit their unquestioned assumptions to a severely critical test. And a study of Black Theology with an honest, open mind cannot but create in the white student an ever increasing understanding of its deepest intentions. The white theologian will not be able simply to ignore Black Theology—that is the easy way out. But in his evaluation of Black Theology he will also have to guard against simply labelling Black Theology as a "Communist front organization" or as a neo-Marxist ideology inspired by the thoughts of Mao Tse-Tung, Fidel Castro and Ché Guevara.[55] For the white theologian Black Theology must first and foremost serve as an occasion for sincere self-examination. Does Black Theology really imply—as many whites tend to judge at first sight—a rejection of the very heart of the Gospel? Or do we here perhaps encounter a rejection of the way in which white Christians expressed the Gospel?

I have the impression that Black Theology is one of many factors forcing Western Christianity to reorder its theological priorities and to retest many of its axiomatic assumptions. We shall have to learn to read the Bible with new eyes and new hearts. Frederick Herzog has in this respect shown us *one* possible way, by writing a commentary on St. John's Gospel from the perspective of Black Theology, under the title *Liberation Theology*.[56] His point of departure is that, unless we turn our theological attention to the oppressed, we will never understand the Gospel.[57] In the line of Descartes' *Cogito, ergo sum*, Herzog says that we in Western theology are actually still engaged in theological "navel-gazing," in turning in upon ourselves. Camus wants to replace Descartes' *Cogito, ergo sum* with "I rebel, therefore we exist." Herzog thinks that a more adequate corrective, from the Christian perspective, would be *Compatior, ergo sum*: "I suffer with others, therefore I am."[58]

The challenge before which Black Theology places us, is articulated in this *Compatior, ergo sum*. It is at this stage not at all clear how this is going to work out in actual practice. It would, of course, be repulsive if whites were to try to outblack the blacks[59]—that would simply amount to a new form of refined paternalism. One thing is, however, very clear: Nothing less than a new *metanoia* is expected of us, a new and radical conversion.

Notes

1. Cf, Marie-Louis Martin, *Kirche ohne Weisse, Simon Kimbangu und seine Millionenkirche im Kongo* (Basel: Friedrich Reinhardt, 1971), pp. 31–35.
2. James Cone, "Black Theology on Revolution, Violence and Reconciliation," *Dialog*, 12, Spring 1973, p. 130.
3. Cone, *A Black Theology of Liberation* (Philadelphia and New York, 1970), p. 124.
4. Cone, ibid., p. 125.

5. Cone, ibid., pp. 131, 132.
6. Cone, ibid., p. 136.
7. Cone, ibid., p. 137.
8. Cone, ibid., p. 138.
9. Cone, ibid., p. 214.
10. Cone, ibid., p. 215.
11. Cone, *Dialog*, Spring 1973, pp. 131, 132.
12. Cone, *A Black Theology of Liberation*, p. 195.
13. Cf. John J. Carey, "Black Theology: An Appraisal of the Internal and External Issues," *Theological Studies* 33 (4) 1972, p. 688.
14. Cf. Carey, ibid., pp. 684–697. See also J. Deotis Roberts, *Liberation and Reconciliation: A Black Theology* (Philadelphia, 1971); Major J. Jones, *Black Awareness. A Theology of Hope* (Nashville and New York, 1971); J. J. Gardiner and J. D. Roberts (eds.), *Quest for a Black Theology* (Philadelphia, 1971).
15. Cone, *Dialog*, p. 133.
16. Included in M. Motlhabi (ed.), *Essays on Black Theology* (Johannesburg: University Christian Movement, 1972), pp. 28–36.
17. Cf. Motlhabi, ibid., p. 53.
18. Resolution of SASO, "Commission on Black Theology," *SASO Newsletter*, August 1971, p. 17.
19. Buthelezi, "An African or a Black Theology?" in Motlhabi, op. cit., p. 8.
20. Cf. M. Buthelezi "African Theology and Black Theology: A Search for a Theological Method," in H.-J. Becken (ed.), *Relevant Theology for Africa* (Durban: Lutheran Publishing House, 1973), p. 20.
21. Cf. Buthelezi, in Motlhabi, op. cit., p. 7.
22. Buthelezi, in Motlhabi, op. cit., p. 7.
23. Cf. Douglas Makhathini, "Black Theology," in H.-J. Becken, op. cit., pp. 8–17. Cf. also Gabriel Setiloane, "Black Theology," *South African Outlook*, February 1971.
24. Cf. W. Eteki-Mboumoua, "Africa's Cultural Revolution," *South African Outlook*, October 1969, pp. 156–160, 166.
25. Setiloane, op. cit., p. 30.
26. Nairobi, Kampala and Dar-es-Salaam: East African Literature Bureau, n.d. [1971].
27. Cf. Motlhabi, op. cit., p. 96; see also p. 98. Cf. also Ananias-Mpunzi, in Motlhabi, op. cit., p. 110.
28. Cf. S. Biko, "Black Consciousness and the Quest for a True Humanity," in Motlhabi, op. cit., pp. 22, 23.
29. Cf. Solomon Lediga, "A Relevant Theology for Africa," in H.-J. Becken, op. cit., pp. 25–33.
30. Cf. Victor Mayatula, "African Independent Churches' Contribution to a Relevant Theology," in H.-J. Becken, op. cit., pp. 174–177.
31. Motlhabi, op. cit., p. 1.
32. James Cone and Gayraud Wilmore, "African Theology," *Pro Veritate*, January 1972, pp. 2–4; February 1972, pp. 18–21, 24.
33. Cf. Cone and Wilmore, *Pro Veritate*, February 1972, p. 20.
34. Op. cit., p. 18.
35. Cf. Steve Biko in Motlhabi, op. cit., p. 21.
36. Cf. M. Buthelezi, "The Theological Meaning of True Humanity," in Motlhabi, op. cit., pp. 78, 79.
37. Cf. Ananias Mpunzi, "Black Theology as Liberation Theology," in Motlhabi, op. cit., p. 110.
38. E. Baartman, "Black Consciousness," *Pro Veritate*, March 1973, p. 4.
39. S. Biko, in Motlhabi, op. cit., p. 19.
40. Cf. *SASO Newsletter*, August 1971, p. 17.
41. Biko, in Motlhabi, op. cit., p. 20.
42. Bonganjalo Goba, *Pro Veritate*, September 1971, pp. 9–10.
43. Baartman, *Pro Veritate*, March 1971, pp. 5, 6.
44. M. Buthelezi, "Christianity in South Africa," *Pro Veritate*, June 1973, p. 4.
45. Buthelezi, ibid., p. 6.
46. Buthelezi, ibid.

47. Ernest Baartman, "The Black Man and the Church," *Pro Veritate*, April 1973, p. 5.

48. L. B. Zulu, "Nineteenth Century Missionaries in South Africa," in Motlhabi, op. cit., p. 87.

49. Cf. Makhathini, op. cit., p. 12.

50. Cf. Theo Sundermeier, "Schwarze Theologie in Südafrika," *Die Brücke*, June 1973, p. 5.

51. E. Mosothoane, "The Message of the New Testament Seen in African Perspective," in H.-J. Becken, op. cit., p. 62.

52. Mosothoane, ibid., pp. 66, 67.

53. Alpheus Zulu, "Whither Black Theology?" *Pro Veritate*, March 1973, p. 13.

54. Cf. James Cone, *A Black Theology of Liberation*, pp. 195, 196.

55. So e.g. Adriaan Pont, "Black Theology—voorbereiding vir die rewolusie?" *In die Skriflig*, March 1973, pp. 14–30.

56. Frederick Herzog, *Liberation Theology: Liberation in the Light of the Fourth Gospel* (New York: Seabury, 1972).

57. Cf. Herzog, ibid., p. viii.

58. Cf. Herzog, ibid., p. 15.

59. Cf. Herzog, ibid., p. ix.

PART IV

BLACK THEOLOGY
AND THE BLACK CHURCH

INTRODUCTION

An impressive literature on the Black Church has accumulated in recent years, but the term still carries a certain ambiguity. Usually it refers to that institution or group of Christian denominations "owned and operated" by people of African descent. In such cases Black congregations within the predominantly White communions are excluded, although this is a questionable practice because almost 90 percent of these Christians also "own and operate" their churches and are in contact with one another in various informal networks and ethnic caucuses which preserve a historical continuity and a measure of separate identity. Taking these two factors into account it is probably more accurate to speak of the Black Church as almost 18 million Christians in the United States who claim and are recognized to have some degree of African ancestry and who are organized in congregations and other religious institutions in which the Afro-American membership predominates and is in control, at least on the local level.

The other definition of "Black Church" is ideological and, some would claim, theological. It is weighted toward cultural and attitudinal factors and values descriptive of those who claim membership in such a church. This usage of the term came into vogue in the mid-1960s when the designations "Negro" and "Colored" went out of fashion—especially among the urbanized middle classes—and "Black" began to connote ethnic pride, affirmation of the history and culture of Afro-America, and solidarity and militancy in the struggle against all forms of White domination and racism. As applied to religious institutions Blackness meant the renewal and enhancement of the most esteemed values of Afro-American spirituality, the search for the distinctive norms and characteristics of African and Afro-American religion, the refusal to accept Euro-American theology and church structures as normative. These predispositions toward the blackenization of religion and theology were usually linked with Pan-African and Black Power activism.

One or the other of these two basic meanings of the term "Black Church" should be called to mind where it appears in this essay. It should be clear that where we speak of the "Negro Church" a contrast is being made with the Black Church of the second definition. We shall, however, often speak of the Black Church with nothing more in mind than those congregations and denominations in which people of African descent are in the majority. The context should clarify the meaning intended. The terminological confusion

241

which habitually arises in any discussion of the Afro-American group in the United States points to the significance of the problem of identity in almost every period of Black history and, in relationship to Black Theology, suggests why questions of faith or ultimate concern are just beneath the surface of the issue of ethnicity.

The Black Power movement and the rise of Black Theology in the late 1960s brought about a crisis of identity among all shades of Afro-Americans —from the "light, bright and damn near white" and the "high yellers" to "cold black" brothers and sisters whose blood line could be traced back without deviation through the genetic pool of the White race to an African progenitor. Everyone had to decide if, and to what degree, his or her self-understanding was going to be reconditioned by the new definitions of Blackness arising from the political radicalism and cultural renaissance that followed in the wake of the "long, hot summers."

To be sure, "Black is beautiful" had something to do with skin color and was a complete reversal of color preferences that had dominated many prestigious Negro clubs, fraternities, sororities, and even churches for years. But it would take only a glance at some of the leaders of the revolution—for example, Adam Clayton Powell, Jr., and Albert B. Cleage—to know that Blackness had to do with far more than that. It had also to do with culture and consciousness, with a new fearlessness, a sense of power and a new appreciation of everything that belonged to the Afro-American experience:

> slappin five
> throwing yr head back and laughin loudly
> getting excited talking bout somethin excitin
> hip slick
> talking with yr whole body
> be-boppin
> rhythm
> soulfood
> rappin and rappin and more rappin
> corn-rowin plattin
> being fraid of ghosts
> dashikis
> preachin without a manuscript for an hour
> bushes naturals fros
> prayin without a prayerbook
> cappin
> shoutin
> tall tales
> the boogaloo soul train
> Mahalia B.B. King Aretha Coltrane![1]

Blackness had to do with the revalorization of all of these meanings and modes of Black life in America. It emphasized the freedom, integrity, and charism that originated in Africa, survived genocide and miscegenation in the Deep South, flowered in the Harlem of Claude McKay and Langston Hughes, and erupted in the flaunted boldness of the Black Panther Party and the violence of Newark, Watts, and Detroit. That eruption of the 1960s, unlike the stages preceding it, shattered most of the connections with White bohemianism and classical liberalism. Celebrating total alienation from the culture and traditions of White America, it forced a crisis of personal and group identity upon millions of Negroes who only months before had marched arm-in-arm with White comrades toward an integrated utopia. In the religious language of the times, toward: "a nonsegregated church in a nonsegregated society."

I have written elsewhere that "an identity crisis is a critical event in the self-development of a person or a group when a decision must be made either to affirm or deny an historical individuality."[2] The existence and development of a subculture within a larger system does not necessarily mean that such a crisis has already occurred and a self-conscious identity has been established, for the differentiation assumed on both sides can be based simply upon the recognition and legitimation of subordination and superiority. That is not a decision about the identity of the self, but about its lack of identity. A true crisis of identity on the part of a subordinated person or group involves an existential choice of selfhood—a naming of the self. It is a self-election to be whom one chooses to be. What is involved, first of all, is tearing oneself out of the enveloping husk of an other being with whom a fraudulent coalescence, imposed and legitimated, has stifled individuality and self-consciousness. Such a tearing is always a painful process and the more slowly it proceeds, like taking off a scab, the more painful it is. A part of the crisis today is that many Negroes and Negro institutions, having made only a tentative decision about Blackness, are going through a slow and painful process of psychological individuation and liberation.[3]

C. Eric Lincoln assumes that this process has already taken place in the Black churches, although he recognizes a certain cultural lag before its completion. He argues that "the Negro Church died in the 1960s to give birth to a new Black Church which rejects the spiritual humiliation and ethical limitations of Negro-ness. . . . Yet the Negro Church which died lives on in the Black Church that is born of its loins and is flesh inseparable from and continuous with an earlier version of Afro-American religion."[4] From this angle it is possible to see large segments of the Black Church in America as still unwilling to accept the full implications of Blackness and yet reluctant to avow the norms and presuppositions of the White Protestant evangelicalism which "structured and conditioned it [but] are not the norms and presuppositions to which contemporary Blacks . . . can give their assertation and support."[5] The Black Church, in other words, is still in the throes of a crisis of identity and the primary emphasis of Black Theology, viz., that the Black Christian struggle for liberation unconceals (Herzog) the essence of the gospel and is therefore confirmed by it, lies on the other side of the crisis which most Black Christians today find to be a slow and painful transition.

The debate over the retention of the term "African" in the names of the two earliest Black Methodist churches—the African Methodist Episcopal Church of Richard Allen and the African Methodist Episcopal Zion Church of James Varick and Christopher Rush—illustrates the anguish over identity experienced by Black Christians in the nineteenth century. Bishop Benjamin Tucker Tanner of the A.M.E. Church believed that theological considerations were involved in holding on to "African" in the title of the denomination. What was at stake for him was the humanity of this new Afro-American people whom God had called into existence for freedom and who had received from him the ministry of witnessing to human liberation. He explained his preference for the name "African":

> What then is the intended force of the title African? Is it doctrinal or national? It is first doctrinal and secondarily national. The doctrinal goal to which the A.M.E. church aspired was the humanity of the Negro. . . . It sought to become a church wherein the claim to humanity of this despised class would be practically recognized. The sublime truth means only that men of African descent are found to be there, and found as men, not slaves; as equals, not inferiors.[6]

The Black Church of the nineteenth century, despite its "client" relationship to White churches, was clearer about its identity than many of us are today. It knew itself to be God's judgment upon the inhumanity of racism. Its Blackness was, therefore, an expression of its sense of cultural vocation. By every measure it was an amazing institution. Led for the most part by illiterate preachers, many of whom were slaves or recently freedmen, poverty-stricken and repressed by custom and law, this church converted thousands, stabilized family life, established insurance and burial societies, founded schools and colleges, commissioned missionaries to the far corners of the world, and *at the same time* agitated for the abolition of slavery, supported illegal actions in behalf of fugitives, organized the Underground Railroad, fomented slave uprisings, promoted the Civil War, developed community political education and action in behalf of civil rights, and provided the social, economic, political, and cultural base of the entire Black community in the United States. This was a church that had a way of identifying itself which symbolized its calling to serve the broad needs of Black humanity. Its identity and vocation went hand and hand. The term "African," which had the same force as the term "Black" has for some Black Christians today, was avowed by Baptists, Methodists, Presbyterians, and Episcopalians alike as a badge of pride in origin and in a cultural vocation to vindicate Black humanity and the dignity of their life together through the power of the gospel of Jesus Christ.

Sometime between the end of Reconstruction and the beginning of the modern civil rights movement the identity of the Afro-American Church as an institution with the specific cultural vocation of liberation for all facets of Black life faded into desuetude in the face of the enervating forces of the Northern migration. What Tucker discovered about the Black churches of Memphis during the first half of the twentieth century could be said about Black churches in many cities across the nation when the traditional institution was shattered and splintered against the hard realities and despair of the urban ghetto.

> The ministry lagged so far behind black business and professional groups in supporting labor unionism and civil rights, that by the end of the thirties a black scholar, Ralph Bunche, could profile the leadership in Memphis without mentioning the clergy, except to criticise their inertia. "The Negro preachers of Memphis as a whole have avoided social questions. . . . They have preached thunder and lightning, fire and brimstone, and Moses out of the bullrushes, but about the economic and political exploitation of the Negro of Memphis they have remained silent."[7]

There are important exceptions to this melancholy description of the Black Church after the turn of the century, but it is close to the truth about the institution as a whole. It was not simply the triumph of Bookerite accommodationism. The identity of the church as an agent of Black solidarity and liberation collapsed under the weight of a ghettoized version of American fundamentalism. Shorn of roots in the militant Black Church of the mid-nineteenth century, Black Christians turned inward to find a White, Americanized Jesus—the image of their psychic void—and traditional spirituality became uncoupled from a sense of the historic cultural vocation of the Black Church to transform the whole of Black life.

The central purpose of the new Black Theology movement in the United States, as well in the Caribbean and in South Africa, was not to glorify Black skin color and promote a new form of Black racism, but to impel a crisis of identity which could reawaken in Black people a belief in their historical individuality as providential and bind the spiritual power generated by that renewed sense of peoplehood to the vocation of cultural decolonization and political liberation. The history of God's liberating acts, from the Exodus to the mission of Jesus, provided a paradigm of a gathered nation, a people "who were no people," often faithless and disobedient, but called through their suffering and sacrifice to demonstrate that God delivers the oppressed and "to him who has no might increases strength" (Isa. 40:29).

Whether Lincoln is correct in his allegation that "the Negro Church is dead" because its old self-image and norms are not those which prevail in the contemporary Black community, it is certain that the ghost of the culturally irrelevant, fundamentalistic "Negro" church of the early twentieth century still haunts the leadership of the Black Church today. If Emmanuel L. McCall is correct that Black theologians speak mostly to themselves and that we are mistaken if we assume "that black liberation theologians represent the thinking and attitudes of the 'rank and file,'"[8] it is not because Black Theology is obscure, unbiblical, or has no doctrine of the Church, but because the majority of Black preachers confuse themselves with Billy Graham and the most unenlightened versions of White evangelicalism. Because they do not know the rock from which they were hewn, they and their people do not know who they are and the inheritance that was passed on to them by men like Benjamin Tucker Tanner, William W. Colley, and Alexander Walters. Because their sense of sin is personal and individualistic they have an understanding of redemption that cannot admit the sanctification of secular conflict and struggle. Because they are willing to accept what Lincoln calls "Americanity"[9] as normative Christianity, they are unable to see how their own ethnic experience in the United States authenticates the truth of God's revelation in Scripture and how the gospel then illuminates and gives meaning to the most profound symbol of that experience—the symbol of Blackness.[10]

It would be a gross error to assume that the first document in Part IV (Document 20), written by Joseph H. Jackson, represents the thinking of all of the clergy and laity of the six-million-member National Baptist Convention, U.S.A., Inc. of which he is president. It was, however, placed in the Record of the 91st Annual Session of the Convention in Cleveland, Ohio, September 7-12, 1971, as the official position of the denomination and it represents the thinking of many Negro Christians who reject Black Theology. We may regard this document as the voice of that "Negro Church" which, according to Lincoln, died in the 1960s but "lives on in the Black Church that is born of its loins and is flesh of its flesh. . . ." Surprisingly, in several places it pays appreciative compliments to James H. Cone. It speaks of his "brilliant theological work" and acknowledges the biblical basis of his interpretation of Christian doctrine. But in the end Cone and Black Theology are condemned, not so much because—it is important to note—they do not cohere with the evangelical tenets that are explicated in Part I of the document, but because Black Theology threatens the harmonious relationship between Blacks and Whites in the United States. It polarizes the races, gives comfort to those who desire confrontation and neglects the experiences of Negroes which are not full of "bitterness or hatred against people of other races and groups."

This negative appraisal of Black Theology is not, strictly speaking, a theological disputation, a reasoned argument against its doctrinal substance as set forth in Cone's *A Black Theology of Liberation*. There is in this document a tacit acknowledgment of "hermeneutical space" within the Black religious experience, the recognition of and respect for the freedom within the Black Church when it attempts to remain faithful to "the sources and norms of theology" and, most significantly, relates the faith "to a specific historic struggle." This curious toleration of an avowedly unacceptable theological position, attacked on essentially nontheological grounds, may give sanction to the observation that the crisis of identity is a perennial characteristic of Black Christianity and that the "Negro Church" is in a constant state of disequilibrium. It "lives on," but is always in transition to a more authentic expression of its historic identity and, therefore, its ineluctable vocation in American society.[11]

It is appropriate to follow this statement from the president of the National Baptist Convention, U.S.A., Inc. with one adopted by the Progressive National Baptist Convention, Inc. (Document 21). Gardner C. Taylor, pastor of the Concord Baptist Church of Brooklyn, New York, was president of the Progressive Convention in 1968. His memorable address to the 7th Annual Session in Washington, D.C., is reprinted to illustrate the posture of those who left the National Baptist Convention in 1961 and brought Black Theology and liberation to many Black Baptist congregations.

The third and fourth documents in this section represent the contribution of Black caucuses to the early discussions which produced the first glimmerings of Black Theology in the late 1960s.[12] During this period Black caucuses were organized in at least ten of the largest predominantly White Protestant church bodies, and Black priests, nuns, and laity were organized within the Roman Catholic Church.[13] There has been no scholarly investigation of this remarkable phenomenon in American Christianity, but we will not fully understand the religious history of the twentieth century until this movement has been carefully analyzed and its impact upon American denominations assessed. Within the space of a few years, roughly from 1965 to 1970, Black clergy and laity who had been thought to be securely "integrated" in the White Church reconstituted themselves in separate Black enclaves and declared war on the White establishment and its theology.

This was not, of course, the first time the predominantly White denominations produced militant religious leadership in the Black community. The same thing had happened in the 1840s and '50s when Black ministers in White denominations, like Charles B. Ray, Theodore S. Wright, and Henry Highland Garnet, swung toward radical abolitionism and played a leading role in the organization of the American and Foreign Anti-slavery Society. The clergy of the Black denominations, having already rid themselves of White control, could not experience the ravages of racism in church and society more keenly than their brothers who found that neither ordination in the White churches nor a seminary degree protected them against discrimination and humiliating dependency. In the 1960s it was the members of the Black caucuses who were most humiliated by the reluctance of the White churches to join the struggle for liberation and who first experienced a crisis of identity—the need to define themselves and the faith they professed over against the White institutions to which they belonged. It is with no offense to those who led the caucuses and Black Theology movements to recall that history is replete with instances of the crusading teetotaler who used to be the biggest drunk in town. And here I do not exclude myself.

In any case, the caucuses played an important role in decolonizing the minds and spirits of Black Christians in both the White and the Black denominations. Most of them issued pronouncements which may be found in the official records of their respective denominations. We include here an influential statement (Document 22) from the most powerful—Black Methodists for Church Renewal—representing more than 300,000 Black United Methodists, the largest group of Blacks in any predominantly White Protestant church. The second statement is not from a denominational but an interdenominational and "regional" caucus, many of which sprang up in metropolitan areas across the nation.

Philadelphia had long been a center of Black church action against racial oppression, from Richard Allen and Absalom Jones to Leon Sullivan. The Philadelphia Council of Black Clergy continued that tradition with this position paper on the meaning and role of Black religion in American society (Document 23). Neither of these two caucus documents is strictly "theological" in the sense given to that term in White church circles. They are, nevertheless, prolegomena to the Black theological reflection which they helped to provoke. The texts suggest why Black Theology cannot be separated from active secular engagement and how it challenges the traditional understanding of the universality of the Church.[14]

The assumption that contemporary Black Theology is purely an academic enterprise and has made no positive impression upon the Black denominations is erroneous. The documents presented here from the Progressive National Baptist Convention, Inc.(Document 20), the Christian Methodist Episcopal Church (C.M.E.) (Document 24), and the African Methodist Episcopal Church (A.M.E.) (Document 25) prove that the leadership of those major Black churches agrees with the basic interpretations of Cone, Roberts, Joseph A. Johnson, and other Black theologians. Whether these official positions have filtered down to the people in the pews is another matter which is no more uncertain than whether the works of Reinhold Niebuhr, Paul Tillich, and the process theologians are familiar and acceptable to the rank and file of the White denominations.

The main point is that for the first time in many years the historic Black churches are not depending upon the confessional standards of the White denominations or upon the writings of White theologians to provide their theological orientation. Particularly in the case of the Black Methodist denominations one notes the increasingly high level of theological education and interest within the episcopacy itself, and the seriousness with which the bishops and executive officers of the churches are promoting theological study among the clergy and exposing themselves to workshops and lectures by professional Black theologians.[15]

The document in this section from the Board of Bishops of the African Methodist Episcopal Zion Church is of particular interest, not only because Zion has long held the reputation of being "the Freedom Church" among Black denominations, but also because in recent years its clergy have been in the forefront of the movement which promoted Black Theology. In the late 1960s a caucus of younger Zionite ministers, who called themselves the "Sons of Varick," began to challenge the church to take a more active role in the Black revolution. Among them was the Yale Divinity School theologian Leon Watts; Calvin Marshall, the pastor of the Varick Memorial A.M.E.Z. Church in Brooklyn and successor to James Forman as chairman of the Black Economic Development Conference; and Vaughn Eason, the founder of the Philadelphia Council of Black Clergy. Bishop Herbert Bell Shaw was not one of the "Sons of Varick" activists but, as chairman of the Board of Directors of the NCBC, Shaw was more than a titular leader of that interdenominational movement and represented the institutional base of Black Theology within Black Methodism in the United States and England.

The statement included here, from the 40th General Conference of the A.M.E. Zion Church, was written by Bishop Shaw (Document 26). Its emphasis on the African origin of Black religion and the solidarity of Afro-American Christians with the Third World is the mode of such Black theologians as Albert B. Cleage and George Thomas, a Zionite professor at the Interdenominational Theological Center in Atlanta.[16]

It was important to include among these selections from the literature of the Black Church two representative statements from the Black Evangelical group. Much has been written about the "New Evangelicals" in the White churches and their departure from the political conservatism of the standard brand of Protestant fundamentalism.[17] But outside of Evangelical circles little attention has been given to the emergence in recent years of a group of Black Evangelical preachers and scholars who were developing their own version of Black Theology within smaller denominations such as the Church of God in Christ, the Church of Christ–Holiness, and other Black Pentecostal and Holiness bodies. During the early years of the Black Theology movement some attempt was made by the NCBC through Black Evangelical activists such as Herbert Daughtry, Columbus Salley, and C. Herbert Oliver—all leaders of the National Black Evangelical Association (NBEA) —to bring the two movements together in a united front for Black liberation. That attempt was unsuccessful, partly because of the different kinds of institutional structures out of which the two groups operated.

In any case the Black Evangelicals represent a variant form of Black theological reflection and action no less discontinuous from the mainstream of White Evangelical theology than the historic Black denominations are from neo-orthodoxy and liberal theology in the White Protestant establishment.[18] We present here two essays: one by a younger Black Evangelical theologian, Ronald Potter (Document 27), and the second by the Evangelical scholar William Bentley, considered by many to be the spokesman of the Black movement within White Evangelicalism (Document 28). These two contributions are representative of a new mood among the younger clergy of Black Pentecostal and Holiness churches,[19] and indicate the extent to which Black Evangelicals have been responsive to the Black Theology movement and are participating in the development of its distinctive biblical perspective. Bentley has been particularly insistent about Black Theology maintaining a central focus upon Scripture and Evangelical spirituality.[20] Many Black Pentecostals do not share his confidence in the work of "non-Evangelical" Black theologians and are drawn more to the position taken by the National Baptist Convention, U.S.A., Inc. But many clergy and laity in the smaller and more conservative Black churches are convinced that "Christian theology is a theology of liberation," and are finding it possible to accept the main emphases of Black Theology.[21]

It is possible that the concept of Blackness as a category for theological interpretation presents the most serious difficulty for Black Christians in the Evangelical and more conservative camps who are otherwise ready for Liberation Theology. This is evidently not the case with the caucuses of Black Roman Catholics which have developed since 1968. The adaptation of Roman Catholicism in Africa to traditional African culture in catechetical and liturgical practices and the deference of the church in the United States to the folk traditions of White immigrant groups have opened the eyes of many Black Roman Catholic priests and nuns. Paul VI during his visit to Africa told the Ugandan Catholics to "let your Blackness beautify the Church" and fostered the indigenization of Roman Catholicism on the continent. Black Catholics in the United States, after years of neglect and subordination within their church, could not pretend that developments following Vatican II had nothing to do with them. Black nuns had shown signs of their radicalization in the early 1960s and when the Black Catholic Clergy Caucus met on a national basis for the first time in April 1968, the hierarchy was advised that "the Catholic Church is primarily a white racist institution" and that "immediate, effective and total reversal of present practices is called for."[22] Within two years the National Office for Black Catholics (NOBC) was established in Washington, D.C., and has since been the coordinating agency for Black theological discussion among almost one million Black Catholics in the United States. The historic document which launched this unprecedented development within American Catholicism, the statement of the Black Catholic Clergy Caucus of April 18, 1968, is included in this part (Document 29).

One of the first books reflecting the change in attitude among Black priests appeared in 1970: *Black Priest/White Church*, by Father Lawrence Lucas, pastor of Resurrection Parish in the New York Archdiocese.[23] Lucas was an active member of the Theological Commission of the NCBC and helped to close the gap between Black Catholics and Black Protestants in the Black Theology movement. We are still waiting for a book by a Black Roman Catholic theologian which will present the direction of the thought of the three caucuses in a more systematic fashion. In the meantime several priests and nuns have published articles on rapprochement with Protestants on Black preaching and liturgical traditions, the relevance of the African heritage, and other topics relating to the indigenization of the Church in Afro-American culture.[24]

As a second contribution from Black Catholics we are reprinting Edward K. Braxton's "Toward a Black Catholic Theology" (Document 30). While it is by no means a radical departure from the classical tradition, it nevertheless indicates the influence Black Theology has had upon Black Catholic theologians and the general perspective of the caucuses. Father Edward K. Braxton is the leading Black theologian of the American church and has taught ecumenics at Harvard Divinity School. His leadership in collaborative work between Black Catholic and Protestant theologians could produce a movement of ecumenism among Black Christians that could make efforts toward Catholic-Protestant unity in the White community look pale by comparison. Roman Catholicism is the dominant form of Christianity among the Black people of the world. Afro-Americans, although overwhelmingly Protestant at the moment, are not inseverably bound to the traditions of the Reformation and a truly ecumenical Black Theology could bring a surprising unity in the future. The opening of the Vatican toward adaptation to indigenous cultures and the rapid development of Africanization and Latin American Liberation Theology suggest that Roman Catholicism may prove more congenial to a theological and ecclesial movement across faith barriers among Black Americans than is the North Atlantic White Protestant establishment. Thus the caucus movement among Black Catholics is of signal importance and we welcome the possibilities it augurs.

By far the most radical development of Black Theology has occurred in the Black Christian Nationalist (BCN) movement under the leadership of the Detroit pastor, Albert B. Cleage.[25] As indicated in the introduction to Part I, Albert B. Cleage was one of the leading figures in the early days of the Interreligious Foundation for Community Organization and the National Committee of Negro Churchmen. Later he broke with NCBC because of the latter's refusal to concur with his rejection of the New Testament canon and to follow him in a schismatic movement out of the institutional Black Church. I have personally wanted to see and have tried to encourage a reconciliation with Cleage, but there has been no intimation that he is interested. He has been, on all counts, the most consistent thinker among us. Cleage may have gone too far, but no one made a greater contribution to the decolonization of the minds of Black Christians, and no institution has sought more seriously to demonstrate the implications of Black Theology for local congregations than his Shrine of the Black Madonna. I have often wondered what Cleage and Roman Catholic theologians might be able to do in collaboration on a new Black theological agenda.

The two statements from the Black Christian Nationalists in this section, "What Black Christian Nationalism Teaches and Its Program" (Document 31), which describes what Cleage's followers believe, and "Let's Not Waste the Holy Spirit" (Document 32), make it difficult to imagine any joint theological effort between the Shrine of the Black Madonna and Black Roman Catholicism. It is nevertheless true that Cleage's movement, like most prophet-led movements, will some day have to go on without its charismatic founder. There are presently young men and women who are loyal followers of Cleage, but who are able to think for themselves and have, on at least one occasion, cooperated with the Black Theology Project—probably with the tacit approval of their leader.

The Black Christian Nationalist movement may not be the most exemplary model of a Black caucus, for, although it has shrines in several cities, it is not growing significantly. The masses of Black church members are not likely to support any radical revision of the Scriptures or a mass exodus out of the historic Black denominations. Garvey, Elijah Muhammad, and Malcolm X were not able to lead them in that direction and it is doubtful that Cleage will be able to do so. On the other hand, neither the Black Theology movement nor more radical religious movements can expect or need to be mass movements. Middle and lower-class Blacks are no longer the joiners they were in the 1920s and 1930s, but they will respond to judicious leadership that does not attack the base of Black folk religion and make shambles of customs and conventions that have been the means of their survival.

The final three documents in this part bring us back to the movement of Black preachers, church executives, and theologians who began to develop a new theological perspective within the historic Black denominations and the Black caucuses of the major White denominations. The first one, "Black Theology in 1976" (Document 33) is a statement of the Theological Commission of the National Conference of Black Churchmen, the first draft of which was written by J. Deotis Roberts, Roy Morrison, John Satterwhite, James H. Cone, and myself. It was later revised and approved in its present form by the full commission. It received wide distribution in *Liberation and Unity*, the Lenten booklet "for Meditation and Action." This booklet has been one of the most effective means of getting Black Theology to "the people in the pews." Since 1975 more than 300,000 copies of *Liberation and Unity* have been distributed, containing official statements on Black Theology accompanied by meditations for Lent written by Black churchmen and women around the themes of Black liberation and unity viewed from the perspective of the cross. This project is sponsored by the three Black Methodist denominations, the National Conference of Black Churchmen, and the Consultation on Church Union. It is the result of the emphasis on

Black ecumenism of the NCBC and is the only interdenominational resource for the laity that the Black Church has produced in many years.

The 1976 statement on Black Theology is the first official statement by the NCBC after the Atlanta document of 1969. It reconfirms the earlier statement and breaks new ground in its affirmation of Jesus Christ as the Black Messiah and the declaration that "some forms of socialism which stress humanism and cooperation are more Christian and more contributive to justice and morality than American capitalism." This new note is taken up again in the "Message to the Black Church and Community" issued from the National Conference of the Black Theology Project of "Theology in the Americas" held in Atlanta during the summer of 1977 (Document 34).

The Atlanta conference was designed to be a recapitulation of the famous conference sponsored by IFCO in 1969, when the Black Manifesto was first promulgated. Under the staff work of Muhammad Kenyatta, a Baptist clergyman, and M. Shawn Copeland, a Roman Catholic nun, the conference attracted a group of activists almost as large and diverse as the gathering at Wayne State University in April 1969. Methodist bishops, prominent Baptist preachers of the three major conventions, Pentecostalists, and members of the predominantly White churches joined with secular activists, Black Christian Nationalists, and Marxists to discuss the relevance of Black religion to the community and the struggle for liberation in Africa and the Caribbean. Presiding over this volatile mixture was Charles S. Spivey. He and I put together the final draft of the "Message" from the reports of the many working groups and it was adopted upon first reading with a standing ovation. In my opinion this was the most significant statement on Black Theology since 1969. Its content did not come out of a debate among professional theologians, but from the deliberations of lay people from all parts of the United States who had labored with the problem of religion and Black liberation and whose ideas were melded into a single pronouncement of faith and commitment to struggle in the name of Jesus Christ, the Liberator.

Charles Cobb, the president of the NCBC and national executive of the Commission on Racial Justice of the United Church of Christ, raised sharp questions about the authority of the conference and its relationship to the National Conference at one point during the meeting. Had the Black Theology Project under Spivey, Kenyatta, and Copeland usurped the role of the NCBC in sponsoring a national conference on Black Theology? Was the conference prepared to combine its activities with NCBC and avoid splintering the movement into two camps, one in close partnership with the Black Church, the other under the parental custody of the interracial "Theology in the Americas"? These questions were not out of order at this juncture of the movement's history and I regret that they were not fully answered at the Atlanta meeting, nor at NCBC's annual convocation later that year. But the significance of the conference and its message could not be gainsaid. We had reunited men and women, church-based and community-based elements, separated and out of contact for eight years. An interpretation of Black Theology had been agreed upon by church and grass-roots leadership which turned a corner from American economic liberalism to a forthright attack upon capitalism, and from nationalism to identification with the Third World. The movement had enunciated a theology of liberation that made sense for the times. It had come into a new maturity at Atlanta. As M. Shawn Copeland said in her *Cross Currents* article, the message to the Black Church and community from Atlanta "offers a pair of shoulders on which all Black theological reflection must stand in reaching toward the Messiah's kingdom of justice and truth, peace and love."[26]

The keynote address of James H. Cone at the Atlanta conference deserves republication here because its ideas and spirit pervaded the conference (Document 35). I have written in the introduction to this volume (see pp. 9–10) of new directions in Cone's theology and will not comment here except to say that it is a historic document in its own right and makes a fitting epilogue for this section on Black Theology and the Black Church.

At this writing it is not certain what will be the future of the Black Theology Project. There has been a division in the ranks over the resignation of Muhammad Kenyatta as executive director. The flame flickers but is not extinguished. The hostility of some centers of the Black Church to this way of thinking about the message of Christ within the Black experience of America has abated and preparations are being made in several denominations for opening up these themes and motifs to youth and adults in church schools and study groups. Paul Calvin Payne, the United Presbyterian Christian educator used to say, "If it doesn't happen in the local church, it doesn't happen." That is not altogether true because we have seen some things happen to Black Christianity in this country which were *extra ecclesia* on both the local and national levels. God still works in a mysterious way. But there is enough truth in Payne's adage for Black theologians to be forewarned. Black Theology began in the "invisible institution" of the slave church. If it is to have enduring value for the whole Church of Christ in what it has to say about liberation through the Black Messiah, it must remain with the people who gather within the visible institution where his Blackness is manifest in the suffering and triumph of their struggle to know and to be what they are—human beings, redeemed, redemptive, Black and free.

G.S.W.

Notes

1. "Blackness Is," unpublished poem by Fred Lucas, Jr., pastor of the Agape A.M.E. Church of Buffalo, New York.

2. "Identity Crisis: Blacks in Predominantly White Denominations," published lectures from the Colloquium on Black Religion of the Reformed Church in America, 1976, p. 3.

3. William E. Cross has described the stages of this process by which Negro adults move from Euro-American determinants to an anxiety-free, constructive commitment to Blackness. "The

Negro to Black Conversion Experience," *Black World*, vol. 20, no. 9 (July 1971), pp. 13-27. Cecil W. Cone has discussed the problem of an identity crisis in somewhat different but related terms in his book *The Identity Crisis in Black Theology* (Nashville: AMEC Press, 1975). Unlike Cross, who understands the crisis in psychological terms, Cone perceives it as an epistemological and methodological problem. Black theologians do not know who they are, not because they have rejected the pre-Civil War Black religious traditions, but because they misunderstand them and have mistakenly assumed that the secular and apologetic principles of interpretation which they appropriate from White theologians and the Black Power theorists can give them a point of departure for doing Black Theology. Only Black religion, properly understood as a transcendent, personal experience of the Almighty Sovereign God, can provide the data for an authentic Black Theology. So far, I am in agreement with Cecil Cone, but would contend that his search for the "essence" of Black religion has truncated what Black people know of God and the richness of the Black Church's worship, theology, and action. In my view the crisis is not in Black Theology but in the contemporary Black Church. I have presented this position more fully in "The Crisis of the Black Church in America," *The Lott Carey Herald*, vol. 46, no.7 (July 1978), pp. 3-11.

4. C. Eric Lincoln, *The Black Church since Frazier* (New York: Schocken Books, 1974), pp. 106-107.

5. Ibid.

6. Benjamin Tucker Tanner, *An Apology for African Methodism* (Baltimore: n.p., 1967), pp. 115-116. Tanner's position was that the word "African" could unite all Black people. Thus the theological significance of the term justified its nationalistic implications. See Daniel A. Payne, *Recollections of Seventy Years* (New York: Arno Press and the New York Times Books, 1968), p. 261.

7. David M. Tucker, *Black Pastors and Leaders: Memphis, 1819-1972* (Memphis: Memphis State University Press, 1975), p. 102.

8. Emmanuel L. McCall, in a review of Allan A. Boesak's *Farewell to Innocence*, in *Occasional Bulletin of Missionary Research*, vol. 2, no. 3 (July 1978), p. 110.

9. C. Eric Lincoln, "Black Sects and Cults and Public Policy," in Joseph R. Washington, Jr., ed., *Black Religion and Public Policy, Ethical and Historical Perspectives*, a University of Pennsylvania Afro-American Studies Program publication (1978), p. 2.

10. My own thinking about the symbolic meaning of Blackness and how its theological significance comes to light under a mythico-historical interpretation has been greatly influenced by the writings of Charles H. Long. See, for example, his "Perspectives for a Study of Afro-American Religion in the United States," *History of Religions*, vol. 2 (August 1971), especially pp. 58-61, and "Structural Similarities and Dissimilarities in Black and African Theologies," *Journal of Religious Thought*, vol. 32, no. 2 (Fall-Winter 1975), pp. 9-24. For a provocative discussion of the color symbolism of Western society and a transvaluation of Blackness in process terms, see also, Eulalio P. Balthazar, *The Dark Center, A Process Theology of Blackness* (New York: Paulist Press, 1973).

11. That the theological and social thought of Joseph H. Jackson is by no means discontinuous with some of the generic themes of Black religion in the United States is brought out in a study by Peter J. Paris, *Black Leaders in Conflict* (New York: Pilgrim Press, 1978). See especially pp. 58-64, 218-221.

12. These are excerpts from the original documents, the full texts of which may be found in Warner R. Traynham, *Christian Faith in Black and White, a Primer in Theology from the Black Perspective* (Wakefield, Mass.: Parameter Press, 1973), pp. 96-109.

13. The Protestant churches which experienced the emergence of new or revitalized Black caucuses include the American Baptist Convention; Disciples of Christ; Episcopal; Lutheran (Missouri Synod); Presbyterian, U.S.; Reformed Church in America; United Church of Christ; United Presbyterian, U.S.A.; Unitarian Universalist; and United Methodist.

14. In this connection see also Robert C. Chapman, "The Black Church Now," *The Black Church*, vol. 1, no. 1 (1972), pp. 45-57; Charles Shelby Rooks, "Toward the Promised Land" in the same issue, pp. 1-48; J. Deotis Roberts, "The Black Caucus and the Failure of Christian Theology," *Journal of Religious Thought*, vol. 26, no. 2 (Summer Supplement, 1969), pp. 15-33. For a different perspective on the Black Church and Black Theology see William L. Banks, *The Black Church in the U.S.* (Chicago: Moody Press, 1972), pp. 74-100, and *Black Theology and the Black Experience* by Anthony T. Evans, a pamphlet of the Black Evangelistic Enterprise, Inc., Dallas, published in 1977.

15. Bishop Joseph A. Johnson, Jr., who wrote the statement of the College of Bishops of the

C.M.E. Church which appears in this section, holds two doctorates in theology and is one of the seminal exponents of Black Theology. His list of publications on the subject is impressive. Johnson's latest work, *Proclamation Theology* (Shreveport: Fourth Episcopal District Press, 1977), is the first volume in a projected three-volume systematization of Christian theology from the Black perspective. Herbert Bell Shaw, presiding bishop of the A.M.E. Zion Church, is one of the founders of the Black Theology movement. No church official has given greater encouragement to the study of Black Theology within both NCBC and Black Methodism than Shaw. In January 1976 the bishops of the A.M.E. Church invited James H. Cone, himself a minister of that denomination, to lead them in a theological workshop which produced the "Black Position Papers." A.M.E. Bishop John H. Adams, who is also a scholar of Black Theology, had major responsibility for the research and preparation of these papers, excerpts of which we present here as the present theological position of the A.M.E. Church.

16. George Thomas, associate professor of Church and Society and director of the Religious Heritage of the Black World at ITC, was a missionary in Zaire and one of the Black theologians of the A.M.E. Zion Church who has related Black Theology to its roots in African religions. See his "Black Theology: Vanguard of Pan-African Christianity in America," *The Journal of the Interdenominational Theological Center*, vol. 1, no. 2 (Spring 1974), pp. 69-77.

17. See Richard Quebedeaux, *The Young Evangelicals* (New York: Harper & Row, 1974); Ronald Nash, *The New Evangelicalism* (Grand Rapids: Zondervan Press, 1963); Donald G. Bloesch, *The Evangelical Renaissance* (Grand Rapids: Wm. B. Eerdmans Publishing Co., 1973); and David F. Wells and John D. Woodbridge, *The Evangelicals* (Nashville: Abingdon Press, 1975).

18. For a picture of Black Evangelicals drawn by Black writers see the July-August 1975 issue of *The Other Side*, vol. 2, no. 4, entitled "The New Black Evangelicals."

19. See *Spirit, a Journal of Issues Incident to Black Pentecostalism*, published three times a year since 1977 by the Pentecostal community at Howard University in Washington, D.C.

20. The influence of Bentley's leadership in this respect may be seen in "Growing Together: A Conversation with Seven New Black Evangelicals," *The Other Side*, vol. 2, no. 4(1975), pp. 31-46.

21. Walter J. Hollenweger reports that members of the House of the Lord, a rapidly growing Pentecostal denomination, believe that political and social action is one of the gifts of the Holy spirit. *Concept*, Papers from the Department on Studies in Evangelism, WCC, special issue, no. 30 (June 1970), p. 19.

22. Joseph M. Davis, S.M., "Reflections on a Central Office for Black Catholicism," *Freeing the Spirit*, vol. 1, no. 3 (Summer 1972), p. 32.

23. Lawrence Lucas, *Black Priest/White Church: Catholics and Racism* (New York: Random House, 1970).

24. For examples, see Edward K. Braxton, "Reflections from a Theological Perspective," *This Far by Faith* (Washington, D.C.: National Office for Black Catholics, 1977), pp. 58-67; James P. Lyke, "Application of Black Cultural Considerations to Catholic Worship," ibid., pp. 50-57; Toinette Eugene, "Training Religious Leaders for a New Black Generation," *Freeing the Spirit*, vol. 2, no. 1 (1973), pp. 52-55. Sister M. Shawn Copeland, O.P., has been one of the major links between Black Catholics and Protestants in her post as co-director of the Black Theology Project in 1975-1977. See her article on the Atlanta Statement of the Project, *Cross Currents*, vol. 27, no. 2 (Summer 1977), pp. 144-146. A spirited response to an attack on Black Theology by Giabattista Modin, dean of the philosophy department of Rome's Pontifical Urban University, was written by Augustus R. Taylor, a Pittsburgh priest who teaches Black Theology at Duquesne University, published in the *National Catholic Reporter*, September 1, 1978. It gives notice to Vatican circles of the theological independence of the Black Catholic clergy of the United States and their refusal to be intimidated by European scholasticism.

25. Cleage's major writings are *The Black Messiah* (New York: Sheed and Ward, 1968) and *Black Christian Nationalism: New Directions for the Black Church* (New York: William Morrow & Co., 1972). See also Hiley H. Ward, *Prophet of the Black Nation* (Philadelphia: 1969).

26. M. Shawn Copeland, "The Atlanta Statement: Some Background and Comment," *Cross Currents*, vol. 27, no. 2 (Summer 1977), p. 146.

20

THE BASIC THEOLOGICAL POSITION OF THE NATIONAL BAPTIST CONVENTION, U.S.A., INC.

Part I

We begin with this statement of faith: "God is a spirit; and they that worship Him must worship Him in spirit and in truth" (St. John 4:24). We do not know all the qualities of things spiritual, and we cannot analyze the spirit into component parts. However, we know that spirit cannot be weighed in scales made by human hands or measured in terms of inches or feet. Neither can spirit be defined in terms of any material substances, and the most gifted artists cannot put on canvas a true picture of what spirit is. Whatever is spirit must be approached by the power of spirit or the soul forces in man. Our concept of God is spirit, and our approach to Him must be in spirit and in truth.

Jesus revealed God as spirit and as creative force, and as life-giving and life-sustaining power; and because of His all-inclusive nature, God to us is Father.

Our acceptance of Jesus Christ as our personal Savior is based on His message from the Sermon on the Mount, His personality and life force that He sheds in the gospel writings and through the revelation of truth that comes to us in all of the epistles of the New Testament.

We are drawn to Him by His divine character and by His redemptive love and mercy, and the goodness and justice through which and by which His kingdom is built—and by His sacrificial life, death, and resurrection, all sinners are invited and made welcome into His eternal kingdom.

In the light of these facts the invitation that He extends for salvation is to all men. That is why we preach "Whosoever Will Let Him Come."

This statement by President Joseph H. Jackson of Chicago was placed in the Record of the 91st Annual Session, National Baptist Convention, U.S.A., Inc., September 3-8, 1971. Dr. Jackson is pastor of the Olivet Baptist Church of Chicago.

257

The Need for the Universality of the Gospel

The need for the universality of the gospel grows out of the universality of the sins of all mankind.

> But now the righteousness of God without the law is manifested, being witnessed by the law and the prophets;
> Even the righteousness of God which is by faith in Jesus Christ unto all and upon all them that believe for there is no difference:
> For all have sinned and come short of the glory of God;
> Being justified freely by His grace through the redemption that is in Christ Jesus;
> Whom God hath set forth to be propitiation through faith in his blood, to declare his righteousness for the remission of sins that are passed through the forbearance of God.
> To declare, I say, at this time his righteousness: that he might be just, and the justifier of him which believeth in Jesus (Romans 3:21-26).

In the light of the truth revealed above, there are no pure races and no superior nations in the sight of God. There are no individuals who can by their wisdom, their knowledge, their rank, and their possessions win for themselves salvation or liberation from the sins that do so easily beset all the children of men.

The Universality of God's Plan of Redemption

God's knowledge of this universal imperfection of man, and God's concern for all are some of the reasons why He included all men in the plan of salvation and in the scheme of redemption. The writer of the Fourth Gospel gives to us the divine motivation for human redemption:

> For God so loved the world, that he gave his only begotten son, that whosoever believeth in him should not perish, but have everlasting life (St. John 3:16).

The mission of Jesus Christ into the world was not to condemn the world or to set one race over against another, or to liberate one race by leaving another in chains:

> For God sent not his son into the world to condemn the world; but that the world through him might be saved (St. John 3:17).

Only those who refuse Him, only those who reject Him, fall under the shadow of condemnation by their own choice and by their own acts.

The Theology That We Reject

Any theology that denies or negates the above principles falls outside of the theological tradition of the National Baptist Convention, U.S.A., Inc. Any theologian, be he black or white, that limits the redemptive effort of Jesus Christ to any race, to any color, to any nationality or any rank or group in society denies and negates the positive principles of redemption as discussed above.

Racial discrimination and any form of racial segregation cannot be supported in the light of the principles of redemption as stated above. There is no revealed truth that teaches us that God is white or black. God is a spirit. National Baptists was founded and organized by Negro Christian leaders, and they themselves refused to restrict their message to their own race and their own nationality. They have not written a creed of exclusiveness against other races or nationalities. What we say against white segregationists by the gospel of Christ we must also say against members of our own race who insist on interpreting the gospel of Christ on a strictly anti-white and pro-black foundation.

National Baptists' Theological Position and Civil Rights

Our idea of God inspires us to work for the establishment of social justice for all the citizens of the nation. We participate in the struggle for first-class citizenship under the guidance of the supreme law of the land. From the teachings of the eighth-century prophets and the message of Jesus, we believe God is on the side of the right, the just and the good. Our faith encourages us and our theological position allows us to feel a sense of obligation to help break the chains of all those who are oppressed.

Part II

An Appraisal of A Black Theology of Liberation, *by Professor James H. Cone, Associate Professor of Theology, Union Theological Seminary, New York, New York.*

Professor Cone has dedicated two hundred and forty-nine pages to his thesis that he seeks to prove, and to his conviction that he most positively and clearly shares. The author displays a wide range of acquaintance and a profound knowledge of theological thought. He has not willfully sought to leave out the great themes of Christian theology. He has included them. He has not embraced naturalism or humanism.

In the very first chapter he begins with the content of theology and speaks the truth when he says:

Christian theology is a theology of liberation (p. 1).

He embraces the sources and norms of theology and deals with revelation with clarity.

He makes no attempt to bypass the subject of God or to render man less than a creature who needs salvation.

Christ is also a conspicuous part of his moving discussion, and the Christ of his theology recognizes and gives due regard to the historical Jesus.

It is further significant that the author here relates all of the great Christian themes to a specific historic struggle.

Some Weaknesses

The outstanding weakness of this brilliant theological work on the part of Professor James H. Cone is his attempt to relate divine concern, and to reduce all of the great historic theological truths of the Christian religion, to the historic conflict between blacks and whites.

The author's thesis and his purpose both circumscribe him and render all of his basic conclusions too narrow to accommodate and to properly appreciate and appraise the universality of the Christian gospel of liberation.

For him liberation means simply the liberation of blacks from the oppression of whites. One would assume from the author's argument that if the day ever comes when blacks are totally liberated from the oppressive deeds of whites, the Kingdom of God would be at hand.

The author overlooks that aspect of liberation that has to do with the individual's victory over the temptation and the demoniac forces within man that must be conquered before he can be considered totally liberated.

With his thesis and his commitment to the revolt of blacks against whites—or the black revolution, he reduces, and maybe he is forced to reduce, revelation, Jesus Christ, and God Himself to a level of blackness, although the author admits that the only way to have Christian theology is that it must be Christ-centered. But when one needs *A Black Theology of Liberation,* one must conclude that the entire document is black-centered. But the author seems to avoid this pitfall by making or reducing both Jesus Christ and God to blackness. At one point he says:

> People who want to know who God is and what He is doing must know what black people are and what they are doing. . . . Knowing God means being on the side of the oppressed, becoming one with them and participating in the goal of liberation. We must become black with God (p. 124).

The author does not at all times use black or blackness as a symbol. Sometimes he means physical blackness. He says in another place:

> Even some black people will find this view of God hard to handle. Having been enslaved by the God of white racism so long, they will

have difficulty believing that God is identified with their struggle for freedom. Becoming one of his disciples means rejecting whiteness and accepting themselves as they are in all their physical blackness. This is what the Christian view of God means for black people (p. 125).

Some Personal Reflections

1. *A Black Theology of Liberation* can easily be interpreted as a gospel of hate of blacks against whites.

2. It could become required reading for those who wish to crusade in a violent manner against the so-called white establishment. The author says:

> Speaking for the black community, black theology says with Eldridge Cleaver "we shall have our manhood. We shall have it, or the earth will be leveled by our attempt to get it" (p. 34).

3. Professor Cone in his conclusion could well defeat all of the constructive efforts in better race relations in America, and could write off the past achievements in civil rights as of little or no value.

4. He not only polarizes blacks and whites in this country, but he freezes the polarization and leaves little or no latitude for future harmony to be achieved.

5. To assume that the total so-called black experience deals only with the confrontation with whites overlooks many other areas of that experience, part of which has accounted for the great institutions of the Negro church and other achievements by Negroes without bitterness or hatred against people of other races and groups.

If the Negro church accepts the point of view and the leadership of *A Black Theology of Liberation,* then black people will become the outstanding proponents of racial segregation in the United States of America.

21

THE PRESIDENT'S MESSAGE TO THE PROGRESSIVE NATIONAL BAPTIST CONVENTION, INC., SEPTEMBER 1968

Comrades in the Cause of Christ, assembled here in Washington, D.C., a number of considerations impress themselves indelibly upon our minds and clamor insistently for our attention. One feels here in Washington that he stands close to the nerve-center of the political arrangements of the whole earth. The ancients once said that all roads lead to Rome; so today all roads seem to lead to Washington as the governmental leaders of the world shuttle in and out of this Capital of the mightiest land since Rome spread her Pax Romana over almost all of the known earth.

One feels immediately here in Washington the memories and influences of the men of our nation's founding who so conceived and so dedicated this land to freedom's purposes, though like all mortals, they were themselves infected with the foibles and failures which belong to our common humanity. What names out of other eras this city summons to memory—Washington, Jefferson, Lincoln and Douglas to name but a few.

Those of us who see the nation as yet unfulfilled in its historic purpose are moved by other memories and thoughts when we come to this city. We think of that historic day in August, 1963 when a number which it seemed no man could number gathered beneath the likeness of Lincoln and heard our communal leaders issue to the nation in its very Capital the anguished cry of the disinherited, the pained pleading of Democracy's forgotten people: Who can ever forget the ringing words of the only authentic spiritual genius America has produced, Martin King, as he thundered a paean of hope in his immortal "I Have a Dream" address? Who can forget the deafening crescendos of assent as they rose up out of the innumerable host of Americans of all races and classes and colors and creeds gathered here.

From the *Minutes* of the 7th Session of the Progressive National Baptist Convention, Inc., held in Washington, D.C., September 3-8, 1968. It was written by Gardner C. Taylor, then president of the Convention. He is pastor of the Concord Baptist Church of Brooklyn, N.Y.

As we come back to Washington, we of the Progressive National Baptist Convention are poignantly and painfully aware that our brave, young standard bearer is no longer among us. His gallant heart, his gifted mind, his eloquent voice are denied to us at a time of greatest need. Looking out upon the unfulfilled dream, the wasted years, the broken promises, the moral ambiguity, the puzzled uncertainty of the nation, a memorable apostrophe from Literature floods the mind. One thinks of Wordsworth lamenting the passing of the author of "Paradise Lost" from English society at a time of great national crisis:

> Milton, thou should'st be living at this hour
> England hath need of thee.

Ah, Martin King, we mourn for you, but even more
we long for your leadership.

As we remember Dr. Martin King's trials and triumphs, we remember our part in them. Progressive Baptists may take justifiable pride in the unassailable fact which must now forever be true, that, when he had no spiritual home among black Baptists, cast out from the house of his Fathers, Progressive Baptists gave him a black Baptist residence. You provided him with an address in the community of black Baptists. Let angels record that truth and let succeeding generations bring their gratitude to your tentdoor.

True to Martin King's labors and hopes, we must face forward. Here in Washington we see more than the shrines of a Nation's memories; we remember Resurrection City as the shrine of the Nation's shame in its callous disregard of the cries of hunger and deprivation rising from millions of black, brown, Puerto Rican and white throats. America, what madness is upon you that hearing the anguished cries of hunger from your own children you could be so unmoved, so insolent, so hard-hearted! You do not remember that Jesus said, "Even evil souls know . . . how to give good to your own children." The cry of the poor must not be stifled. The indictment by the disinherited must not be silenced or else the God of history will act with summary judgment upon a Nation which had so much and would do so little.

How long will we persist in our madness in Viet Nam? Can you not hear our gallant young leader pleading in that mournful eloquence of his, last year, in Cincinnati, asking the leaders of the nation to confess and repent of our wrong in Viet Nam and so to save the nation the judgment of history and history's God? What an amalgam of destructive results has flowed from our futile commitment in that land so far away. Our boys die; our nation is divided; our young people despise us; our poor are unfed; our postal service must be curtailed; the world condemns us; our police are made the suppressers of legitimate protest and all our instrumentalities of Law are made the ugly tools of an evil National policy, thus rendering them enemies of peace, foes of Christian idealism and servants of sin and wrong. Ah, Brash Young Republic, hear from their graves the pleading of Robert Kennedy and Martin

King and thousands of our slain young men begging for the end of war and carnage!

Progressive Baptists, we must ask ourselves where we are going and why. It would be improper for me, as I pass on the standard of this host of the Lord to other hands, to command the direction in which we are to move. However, I make bold to throw out some hints of what it seems to me God is saying to us.

The division of Baptists into so many factions along racial and other lines must shame and pain us all. I know that we Progressive Baptists represent a new aspect of that division. I believe that God has called us out for a purpose. We have already extended a hand to other Baptists. Conversation has begun with American Baptists looking to closer cooperation. National Baptists of America have extended a hand of Christian friendliness to us. I preached for them in February. Through a delay in correspondence, we did not receive their acceptance in time to have one of their preachers open to us here the things of God. I hope that you will see to this another year. Likewise, our outstretched hand must be offered to others. We are sufficiently fluid, sufficiently fresh, sufficiently unencumbered and, I trust, sufficiently inspired of God to initiate the work of reconciliation which at last will make of our Baptist witness in this land one grand, united fellowship, to the glory of God and to the honor of Christ and to the healing of the nation.

I rejoice that our Christian Education Congress goes forward under the leadership of Dr. William Upshaw of Akron. We all take enormous pleasure in the progress of Progressive Women under the guidance of Mrs. Minnie Bruce, ably aided by our first Women's President, Mrs. Uvee Arbouin. I plead for support of our Laymen now headed by Mr. Roy Riser. Likewise, our Ushers Convention merits our interest and encouragement as they move under the Presidency of Mrs. Annie M. Serrano. Dr. R. A. Cromwell continues to guide our Foreign Mission Bureau with dedication and discernment. We must enlarge our support of our Foreign Mission enterprise. We must likewise continue our interest in Christian Education.

I shall not dwell upon our desire to secure property. The issue is very much alive, and it may be that God is even now opening before us a fresh possibility. Better to take our time and buy wisely than to rush and purchase blindly and foolishly. We still must secure land and we will.

I have recently attended the Baptist World Alliance Executive Committee as your representative, along with Dr. L. V. Booth, our Executive Secretary. You will be gratified to know that Progressive Baptists enjoy a very great regard and confidence in our World Baptist family. Also we have assisted some of our young people in their trip to the World Baptist Youth Conference at Berne, Switzerland.

I do not know how to assess the contribution and consecration of L. V. Booth to our Progressive Baptist Work. I have found him thorough and thoughtful, filled with vision and vigor. Indeed, I count the friendship which has grown between us one of the rich rewards of my tenure. He has put aside personal preference and opportunity more than once, as you know, in order to serve our Convention. I pray and hope that the Convention will remain aware of his spirit of devotion to our cause.

Progressive Baptists cannot live apart from the heady ferment now occurring in the land among our own people. The winds of change are blowing in the thinking of many people about our present stance and future direction in this land. We who minister to people must listen carefully to hear what is being said, to catch the words of truth being uttered in the excessive rhetoric of violence of so many of our best young minds. Those of us who are thirty-five and over came forward in an integrationist generation. We are startled and sometimes angered by younger people as they talk about separatism. Much of this talk is angry, petulant, pointless. We need not abandon the dream of an integrated society, but we need to hear what is real in much current comment.

To the amazement of some and the anger of others young black people have evolved a whole new thing about integration and separatism. At a memorial service at Oberlin College (whose child I proudly am) following Dr. King's martyrdom, white people were shocked to see the first rows of venerable old Finney Chapel reserved for blacks. Preaching in Chicago this past year, I was astonished to learn that black students had demanded segregated housing. At Colgate Rochester Divinity School, I was steered to a separate section of the cafeteria by black students who wanted to be among themselves. In Dearborn, Michigan, a minister announced that he would leave that community where he is the only black family, to return, he said, "to be with my own people."

I find it illuminating that Jesus called his disciples apart as it is recorded in the ninth Chapter of Luke. Jesus must have seen that every group must at some time or the other get with itself, find itself.

I have come to see that a Church needs to separate from the world every so often. It must carry on its own ceremonies of identification, its own acts of worship and praise when and where there are people of the same conversion, who love the same Lord and march under the same banner.

The same applies to a race such as ours. Not in isolation, but in retreat and communion among ourselves we must find our true selves in terms of those shaping events which have formed our peculiar and singular historical experience in this land.

The Scriptures suggest that the "Apartness" into which Jesus led his disciples was redemptive, cleansing, creative, restoring, preparatory. He called them apart that they might be empowered. "He gave them power and authority." Is this the valid word in the pained shrieks and the angry screams of the young "black-power" men? He gave them power. Something must stir inside of us if we are going to be adequate. That theme of power recurs like a symphonic theme through Holy Writ. I count one hundred fifty-five times it is used. The stranger who certified Jacob's new relationship spoke of power, "Thy name shall be called no more Jacob, but Israel, for as a Prince hast thou power with God and with men." In the magnificent, singing Fortieth of Isaiah the promise about enablement is clear, "He giveth power to the faint. Even the youth shall faint and be weary, and the young men shall utterly fall, but they that wait upon the Lord shall renew their 'power.' They shall mount up with wings as eagles, they shall run and not be weary and they shall walk and not faint." Of Jesus it was said, "As many as received him, to them gave he power to become the Sons of God."

There is a power growing out of our experience of blackness in this land. There is much that is wrong, distorted, disfigured, crippled about us, but there are gifts and powers in the very limp which is our history here. There is a quality of rapture among black people which is authentically Christian. There is a sense of optimism which sees the threatening clouds of life but sees them shot through with the light of God. "Over my head I see trouble in the air, there must be a God somewhere." Black people have been forced to be "three-world people," inhabitants of white America, inhabitants of Black America, inhabitants of that strange land of the amalgam of their racial dreams and what was beheld in the haunting report: "Looked over Jordan, and what did I see? A band of angels coming after me." There is the gift and power of black people as members of the "disestablishment" to see the society in its splendor and in its shame. There is the power of a rhythmic beat orchestrated by trouble and mourning and hope and which one hears in the strange, sad music of the black preacher when he moves honestly within the cultic setting. There is an apocalypticism, a Christian anticipation in vivid imagery of new structures produced out of cutting moral judgment, a beholding born of still-born societal aspirations and aided by the bitter mid-wifery of rejection and scorn.

When Jesus had empowered his disciples, he sent them back into the world. So finding ourselves as black Christians with a peculiar experience in this nation, we must return to the nation bearing in Christ's Name the gifts of our blackness.

We must take our stand in this ugly, sorrowing, sinning world. We must lift the hope of life in the colony of death even as Moses lifted the serpent in the wilderness. We must tell men that God loves this world—this angry, ailing world—unto Calvary. We must bear the tidings of redemption to earth's darkest places.

As we serve we must ever tell men who sent us. We are not among men of ourselves, of or by our own choice. We must tell men who sent us. We are not placed among men as a gimmick or a gesture. We must ever remind men to whom we bring a cup of cold water, a visit in sickness, a concern in nakedness and imprisonment as to who sent us.

We bear the Crown Seal of Jesus Christ. We are sent by One who loved the world so intensely that hate could not remould his love into its own likeness. We are sent by One who confronted evil with a character so clear and a purpose so pure that the hitherto unconquerable powers of wickedness were powerless before him. We are sent by a God who actually came where we are in Jesus of Nazareth in order that we might get where He is. He came here, being born in Bethlehem, reared in Nazareth, tempted in the wilderness, preached in Galilee, arrested in Gethsemane, tried in Caesar's court, died on Calvary's Cross and rose from Joseph's tomb. We must tell the world such a God has credentials of identification with us and certificates of care.

And now as I prepare to pass the standard of leadership on to other and more capable hands and turn to take my place loyally again in the ranks among Progressive Baptists "To Jesus Christ be glory and honor and thanksgiving and power and might forever and ever."

22

THE BLACK PAPER, 1968

Statement by Black Methodists for Church Renewal

I. Our Confession

We, a group of black Methodists in America, are deeply disturbed about the crisis of racism in America. We are equally concerned about the failure of a number of black people, including black Methodists to respond appropriately to the roots and forces of racism and the current Black Revolution.

We, as black Methodists, must first respond in a state of confession because it is only as we confront ourselves that we are able to deal with the evils and forces which seek to deny our humanity.

We confess our failure to be reconciled with ourselves as black men. We have too often denied our blackness (hair texture, color and other God-given physical characteristics) rather than embrace it in all its black beauty.

We confess that we have not always been relevant in service and ministry to our black brothers, and in so doing we have alienated ourselves from many of them.

We confess that we have not always been honest with ourselves and with our white brothers. We have not encountered them with truth but often with deception. We have not said in bold language and forceful action that, "You have used 'white power' in and outside of the church to keep us in a subordinate position." We have failed to tell our white brothers "like it is!" Instead, we have told our white brothers what we thought they would like to hear.

We confess that we have not become significantly involved in the Black Revolution because, for the most part, white men have defined it as "bad," for the other part, we have been too comfortable in our "little world," too

This document is a part of a report entitled "Findings of Black Methodists for Church Renewal" delivered to the United Methodist Church in February 1968 by the BMCR Caucus.

pleased with our lot as second-class citizens and second-class members of The Methodist Church.

We confess that we have accepted too long the philosophy of racism. This has created a relationship in which white people have always defined the "terms," and, in fact, defined when and how black people would exist.

We confess that we have accepted a "false kind of integration" in which all power remained in the hands of white men.

II. The Black Revolution

"The Black Revolution is a fact! It is a call for black people throughout the nation and the world to stand on their feet and declare their independence from white domination and exploitation. The mood of the day is for black people to throw off the crippling myths of white superiority and black inferiority. The old myths are being replaced by black pride, self-development, self-awareness, self-respect, self-determination and black solidarity."[1]

We are new men—the old man, "nigger," is dead. The "boy" is now a man!

We now stand as proud black men prepared to embrace our blackness and committed to address ourselves unequivocally and forcefully to racism wherever we find it, in and outside the church.

III. Black Power

How then do we respond forcefully and responsibly to racism in America and racism in The United Methodist Church?

"It is abundantly clear to many Americans that power is basic to all human dynamics. The fundamental distortion facing us in a controversy about 'black power' is rooted in a gross imbalance of power and conscience between Negroes and white Americans. It is this distortion, mainly, which is responsible for the widespread, though often inarticulate, assumption that white people are justified in getting what they want through the use of power, but that Negro Americans must, either by nature or by circumstance, make their appeal only through conscience. As a result, the power of white men and the conscience of black men have both been corrupted."[2]

Black power provides the means by which black people do for themselves that which no other group can do for them.

". . . Black power speaks to the need for black people to move from the stands of humble, dependent and impotent beggars to the stature of men who will take again into their own hands, as all men must, the fashioning of their own destiny for their own growth into self-development and self-respect."[3]

Black power is a call for black people in this country to unite, to recognize their heritage, and to build a sense of community. It is a call for us to take the initiative, to build the kind of community which crosses all class lines and geographical lines, in order that the resources and leadership of all black people may be used.

Black power means the development and utilization of the gifts of black men for the good of black men and the whole nation.

Finally, it is a call for us to respond to God's action in history which is to make and keep human life human.

IV. Black Power and the United Methodist Church

We, as black Methodists, affirm the search for black identity. When we affirm and embrace our blackness we are acknowledging what God has done and we no longer wear our blackness as a stigma, but as a blessing.

"In religious terms, a God of power, of majesty and of might, who has made man to be in His own image and likeness, must will that His creation reflect in the immediacies of life His power, His majesty and His might. Black power raises, for the healing of humanity and for the renewal of commitment to the creative religious purpose of growth, the far too long overlooked need for power, if life is to become what in the mind of its Creator it is destined to be."[4]

Therefore, as black Methodists, if we are obedient to God's creation, we have a responsibility to ourselves, the white community and to white Methodists to relate from a position of power.

The Methodist Church has failed institutionally and spiritually to be the church. It has refused to take seriously its mission to redeem all mankind. It has denied the black man's right to self-determination because it has frustrated his quest for self-realization. It has failed in every respect to see the black man as a child of God. The reality has been that the black man is denied full membership in the institutional church.

We as black Methodists reaffirm our belief in God and His church. We believe that all men are brothers and that God is our Father. However, we see the possibility that "white" Christians in general, and white Methodists in particular, may not be seriously committed to the church or the concept of the brotherhood of man under the fatherhood of God. We therefore have a responsibility under God to bring about renewal in the church at all levels of its existence. The thrust of "black power" in this context is to awaken black and white Methodists so they might come to see and carry out the mission of the church as it relates to all men. The United Methodist Church ought to be sensitive to every segment of society. It should minister realistically and effectively to the total needs of men—especially those who have been dispossessed by society and the church. Black power seeks to be the moving force behind the black man's effort to get the church to see and recognize him. A second aim of black power in The United Methodist Church is to help the dispossessed, especially the black man, to establish his selfhood in society and in the church.

To do this we propose that black and white Methodists across the country mobilize their spiritual, intellectual, economic, social and political resources in order to exert the necessary influence and/or pressure upon the power structures of The United Methodist Church on all levels to bring about change and renewal in order that it might unconditionally include all Methodists in its total Life. At the same time we propose to preach the Gospel of the "somebodiness" of the black man so that those who have not "identified" themselves as men might find that identity and exert their manhood.

We hope that this can be done within the new framework of the United Methodist Church. As for black Methodists, we are determined to serve God by redeeming our brothers, which in turn redeems us.

The Role of the Local Church

The local church in the black community must immediately redefine its own structure and life in terms of its ability to minister to the black community. If necessary, the local church should not hesitate to restructure itself in order to minister to its community, whether or not the restructuring reflects existing Methodist policy. In order that the totality of man's existence (for which the local church is concerned) may be seen as the arena for local church involvement, any redefinition plans should include an examination of all current movements and organizations such as those related to civil rights, social and economic justice, peace and general welfare.

I. Principles Regarding Local Church Staff Financing

A. It is necessary to have more direct "benevolent" giving from the black church to salaries of church staffs in order to compete effectively with agencies in and outside of the church for the best black leadership available.

B. Churches in a given area (parish, district, conference) should develop salary equalization plans, thus making it possible for church staffs to be assigned and utilized where need is apparent without undergoing financial jeopardy.

II. Local Church and Black Culture

The local church should undertake a program of creative teaching about the black man's contributions to the building of America, and nations throughout the world. This effort would include the collection of books and periodicals, contemporary and otherwise, written about African and Afro-

American accomplishments, thus making the local church a resource and surveyor of black culture.

III. *The Local Church Community*

The local church must look upon its task in the black community to be so crucial that the church initiates plans to establish team ministries in every congregation in the community. Such teams composed of clergy and laity, should be organized on the task force basis, providing special functions as legal services, employment counseling, cooperative buying, extra-educational programs, and community organization.

IV. *Effective Educational Programming*

A. The following educational styles should be introduced to local congregations:

1. establish courses of study on the black church to be used in schools of mission and other educational settings (e.g., E. Franklin Frazier, *The Negro Church in America;* Joseph R. Washington, *Black Religion: The Negro and Christianity in the United States*).
2. educate churchmen relative to the role of the church in the midst of violence.
3. educate for the redefinition of ministry in the black community to include concern for the totality of man's existence and the community's needs.
4. establish programs of political action using pertinent community issues, such as inadequate schools, sanitation problems, election, etc.

B. Educational innovations for local church staffs should include:

1. establishing training programs for effective staff efforts in the black community.
2. establishing courses in urban and rural sociology, each in its appropriate setting; and courses in administration for mission.
3. establishing programs linking pastors and laymen of different churches ("partners in learning") to utilize a variety of experiences and resources.
4. supporting mandatory "refresher-educational" opportunities for all local church staff, no less than one opportunity each quadrennium.

V. *The Local Church—Creative Power*

A. Programs and policies of all general boards and agencies of The United Methodist Church must be designed and/or implemented to insure the placement of black men at all levels of involvement in those agencies. Local churches can indicate this concern to the Methodist Publishing House and its affiliates, for example, through their support and purchases of church school materials, hymnals, clerical vestments, etc.

B. Utilizing this purchasing power, local churches must also insist that Methodist literature present a more composite account of black people, especially of their participation in The United Methodist Church.

VI. The Local Church and Economic Independence—"Action Toward the Transformation of the System"—Recommendations for Black Methodists

A. Pooling of financial resources for specific tasks which take priority in the black community. Such action might involve the following methods:

1. channeling a percentage of, or all of, the benevolence apportionment of a local church to local communal projects undertaken in alliance with other black congregations in a local community.
2. establishing a national fund (a portion of the above to be channeled to a national fund) in order to assist in those communities where personal involvement in situations has been threatened; and in order to aid communal projects in any of the nation deemed in need of national support.

B. Establish the means of initiating and responding to measures employed by "the system." Insure communal responsibility by seeing that:

1. each local church assesses its own situation and undertake such actions as suggested in VI, A, only after having communicated a declaration of intention to appropriate representatives of "the system," and to the continuing body, Black Methodists for Church Renewal.
2. each church agrees upon means of accountability. When action suggested in VI, A and B, is undertaken, each church should consent to answer for those actions in the name of the black community.
3. responses to measures employed by the system be developed out of the black community's self-interest and strengths. It is in the black community's self-interest to survive in and for its chosen purposes; to realize its own peace and order; to protect itself.

Therefore, let all responses of the system be assessed by the black brothers in the community. Let him whose individual actions jeopardize the community, and whose actions were without the consensus of the brothers, be liable to the judgement of the brothers.

Notes

1. Archie Rich, "The Black Methodists' Response to Black Power" (a mimeographed paper prepared for the National Conference of Negro Methodists, Cincinnati, Ohio, February 6-9, 1968).

2. "Statement of Black Power" (a mimeographed paper developed by the National Committee of Negro Churchmen, July 31, 1966).

3. Nathan Wright, Jr., *Black Power and Urban Unrest* (New York: Hawthorn Books, Inc., 1967), p. 60.

4. Ibid., p. 136.

23

BLACK RELIGION—
PAST, PRESENT AND FUTURE

From Position Paper by
Philadelphia Council of Black Clergy, 1968

Introductory Statement

Each of the world's cultures has at least one religious expression, barring a few exceptions. Consequently, it is natural that in the development of the American culture, several religious expressions won the acceptance of many Americans. However, it is the Christian religion that was and is the dominant religious expression of the American people.

When one describes the Christian religious expression of the United States of America, he has to take into account its several different religious slants. These are as varied as there are blends of the American way of life. According to Robert Williams' study of the *American Society,*[1] religious freedom prevailed in early America even though nobody intended it.

The task with which this paper is concerned is to establish a position for the Christian expression as it relates to American Black people.

One is not overstating the case by indicating the Christian religious expression has won the acceptance of the great majority of Black people. It is also true that the Christian religion, as it is practiced among white and Black people, is currently under great criticism. Much of this criticism is justified. Some of it is due to an inadequate analysis of the American social system and the significant role the Christian religion has played among Black people in their struggle to survive. Because of several legitimate frustrations with many of the alleged humanizing institutions in American society, the Christian religion being one, that failed to function in a manner to challenge the racial oppression of Black people, many are now wanting "to throw the baby out with the bath water." This is unfortunate but understandable.

275

The honest fact about the American Christian religion is that it is a "creation" of white society. This religion has been promulgated to the advantage of white society both in the good it has secured for whites as well as the inhuman acts it has rendered against Black people since 1619. However, the reality of the Christian religion has been contrary to the teachings of its source, Jesus Christ. His life symbolizes what the Christian expression is supposed to be. His ministry was almost a complete contrast to the practice of the Christian religion in the Western world following the second century. He served the poor, alienated, dejected, rejected, and the oppressed people of His society. Jesus was a beautiful human being. The gospels, which record His acts among men, clearly show Jesus to be against any force that denied to any man the full expression of life. In fact, the gospels show Jesus confronting the establishment in the interest of the rejected and the oppressed.

It is true that Black Christian leaders were taught the Christian religious expression by the white man. This version was biased in support of white society. It should also be noted that many Black ministers of the Christian religion and its followers were even denied the privilege of reading the Bible. As a result, it was difficult for Black men to learn first-hand about Jesus and His ministry; however, there were both freedmen and freemen who became learned leaders. Many of these persons were Christian ministers, among whom were Peter Williams, Jr., and Nathaniel Paul.[2] Nathaniel Paul understood the Christian religion and used it to strike hard against slavery. He stated in a speech delivered in 1827: "It [slavery] is so contrary to the laws which the God of nature has laid down as the rule of action by which the conduct of man is to be regulated towards his fellow man, which binds him to love his neighbor as himself, that it ever has, and ever will meet the decided disapprobation of heaven."[3]

Another example of this kind of courageous witness was when the Reverend Absalom Jones, a Black clergyman in Philadelphia, shortly after the turn of the 19th century led a delegation presenting a petition to the President of the United States demanding the freedom of slaves.

One of the most articulate Christian leaders of the 19th century was Henry Highland Garnet. Garnet and other leaders like him used the Christian religious expression and its principles to encourage Black people to stand against the forces of oppression. In an address given to "Slaves of the United States," these thoughts were expressed:

> The bleeding captive pled his innocence, and pointed to Christianity which stood weeping at the Cross. Jehovah frowned upon the nefarious institution, and thunderbolts, red with vengeance, struggled to leap forth to blast the guilty wretches who maintained it. But all was in vain. Slavery had stretched its dark wings of death over the land, the church stood silently by—the priests prophesied falsely, and the people love to have it so. . . .

It is in your power so to torment the God-cursed slaveholders that they will let you go free. . . . Yes, the tyrants would meet with plagues more terrible than those of Pharaoh. But you are a patient people. . . . In the name of God, we ask, are you men? Where is the blood of your fathers? . . . Your dead fathers speak to you from their graves. Heaven, as with a voice of thunder, calls on you to arise from the dust.[4]

There is abundant documentation that many religious leaders have taken strong positions against the oppression of Black people because of their faith in Jesus Christ. This indicates that the Black man has never bought totally the white man's view of what the Christian religious expression should be. History also indicates, unfortunately, that many Black leaders did follow the biased white concept of the Christian religion.

Jesus Christ's ministry was clearly identified with the alienated and the oppressed of His society. This points up a key characteristic of the substance of the Christian religious expression. It finds its meaning and source in the life and teachings of Jesus Christ. Jesus did not depend on the status quo for sustenance and identity. In fact, He attacked it. He got His support from the humanizing acts He performed for the despised and oppressed. The Christian religion, institutionalized in American society, has nurtured an oppressive white racism which is clearly not what Jesus was all about. When men like Henry H. Garnet spoke, they were the voices of Jesus.

Since the Christian religious expression has increasingly become the religion of the status quo, and since God is personified in Jesus Christ, Jesus as symbolized in white society presents a problem. White society is the oppressor of black people and it has "caucasianized" its God to fit its image. This is the white man's creation because the fact is that historically and anthropologically speaking Jesus was not a "white man." This kind of information has not been presented to the Black Christian religious community.

It is well to establish that the white Christian religious expression is status-quo oriented. The Black expression has an opportunity to be the religious arm of Black people that reflects the source of the Christian religion. Black people are the oppressed and alienated of American society. This is where the Black church and Black churchmen must stand to be representative of Jesus Christ and His teachings.

. . . .

The Promise of Black Nationalism

When one views the contemporary Black church it becomes abundantly clear that its main purposes, with one exception, do not serve the needs of the people who attend these churches; but quite the contrary, they serve the needs of the larger exploitative society. Since this is the case, the Black church can be easily indicted for having failed to meet its institutional responsibility to the Black community. The function of an institution is to organize in as effective a pattern as possible, those customs and practices of a community that aid it in its survival and stimulate it in its growth. Therefore, the function of the religious force is to organize those customs, practices and understandings that the community has embodied as its most important reality. This reality must define and clarify this particular community's reason for remaining as a group. It must strengthen the individual's reasons for living as a positive and creative part of that society. Religious force should be instrumental in enabling the people of the society to live together in trust and confidence toward and between each other. The religious institution should make it possible for the wisdom of one generation to be passed on to the next. It should embody truths and experiences that clarify the pitfalls that cause the breakdowns in human relationships. It should warn about the frailty and fright of the human heart as it inappropriately seeks to satisfy itself through greed and ignorance, thereby helping to decrease the possibility of this evil phenomenon occurring in the society in which the institution is functioning. The truth about the history concerning Black people in America is the tragic irony that institutions functioned in the Black community not for the needs of Black people but rather for the needs of white people; and the religious institution, together with other Black institutions, failed in its responsibility to develop a viable culture.

Now that the movement of Black people is clearly in the direction of forming a cohesive group, the Black church as well as other Black organizations are awakening to their task of helping to accomplish the needed unity of Black people. The Black church sees, more than ever, the awesome responsibility of helping to strengthen a people in a revolutionary situation with the moral fiber and muscle that will enable them to keep their eye on the good, as they viciously fight to rid the world of the reign of evil that has terrorized the vast majority of human beings for the past 400 years. For a fully human society, the Black religious force has the responsibility of inculcating and sustaining an authentic morality.

It will be no simple task to build a Black religious institution, any more than it will be easy to build any institution in the Black community. The novelty of the idea of strengthening the culture that will serve our needs will demand integrity and creativity. Our tendency will be to fall back on those institutional patterns that have been controlling us ever since we can remember, and to use them as models for the kinds of institution that we feel that we will need. The Black community must be frank and honest in its tacit admission that for all intents and purposes most of the institutional patterns surrounding us will be of no use to us whatsoever, for they are built on the very principle we are fighting against. The Black religious force will, in all likelihood, be devoid of denominationalism, sectarianism and any of the kind of religious traditions that we are used to in America. Unlike the present-day Black church, it will have to be authentically Black and Afro-American. It is our position that there is no such entity presently existing in the Black community; an entity that is authentically Black. We must be cautious not to mistake thoughtless emotionalism or empty intellectualism as authentic marks of the Black church; but rather we will have to use for a model our authentic prototype that existed in the slave church. When we analyze the Afro-American religious force as it was experienced in the slave community, we discover, as we have already indicated in this paper, that it was committed to the liberation of Black people; and it embodied all of its spiritual strength toward that end. Similarly, the emerging Black religious institution must also encourage and strengthen the Black community toward this holy goal of liberation.

It is our hope that Black clergy and Black theological students continue to awaken to this task. It is our intention that Black clergy and Black theological students commit themselves to the liberation of Black people in the same manner that we have committed ourselves to the faith of Jesus Christ. We hope that our brothers and sisters in the Black community will be able to understand that in most cases our commitment is to Christ and not to Christianity. For us there must be no difficulty in viewing Christ and the other founders of the world's great religions as clearly prototypes and examples of revolutionary figures that were committed to the eradication of evil systems. Since the leader we profess to follow was unshakeably committed to this cause, it is therefore clear that we have no choice but to have the same kind of commitment.

Notes

1. Robert M. Williams, Jr., *American Society: A Sociological Interpretation* (New York: Alfred A. Knopf, Inc., 1960), pp. 340-344.

2. Peter Williams, Jr., was the son of Peter Williams, one of the founders of the African Methodist Episcopal Zion Church in New York City. The son became an Episcopalian, was educated for the ministry and served at St. Philip's church in New York City. Nathaniel Paul was pastor of the African Baptist Society of Albany, New York.

3. Carter G. Woodson, *The Negro Orators and Their Orations* (Washington, D.C., 1925), p. 65.

4. Ibid., pp. 151-152, 157.

24

THE EPISCOPAL ADDRESS TO THE 27TH GENERAL CONFERENCE OF THE CHRISTIAN METHODIST EPISCOPAL CHURCH (EXCERPT)

The New Issue: White Racism and the American Society

1. White Racism

If one is to know the agony and the ecstasy in the struggle for social justice for black Americans, he must understand that there are some forces in America which are used to perpetuate poverty, racism, and oppression. White racism is the most explosive problem facing the nation today. Racism has deep roots in our society. It has shaped and determined many of the forms and structures of the basic institutions in America—local and national government, judicial systems, schools, church and family life. White racism is a cancer eating away at the very heart of this nation. Racism is rooted systematically in the political practices, value norms, and standards of American society, and its role in the shaping of America's economic, political, and cultural institutions has been of central importance. Racism in America is no marginal or isolated phenomenon. It is intrinsic to the American way of life.

When we use the term "white racism" we mean the conscious or unconscious belief in the inherent superiority of persons of European ancestry, especially those of northern European origin, which entitled these persons and all white persons to a position of power, dominance, and special privilege. The white racists believe that all black people, especially those of African ancestry, are innately inferior and this justifies the subordination and exploitation of the black man by the white man. Centuries of exploitation and oppression of people of color have created an ideology to justify, rationalize, and explain this behavior. Simply stated, the culture of the United States, in addition to whatever else it might be, is white supremacist. Racism is a

This document is an excerpt from the address of Joseph A. Johnson, Bishop of the Fourth Episcopal District of the C.M.E. Church held in Memphis, Tenn., May 6-17, 1970.

national product of the history, culture, and sociological-political and economic structure of the United States.

Racism cannot be dealt with fairly in terms of legal enactments and legislative programs because those who deal with white racism purely from the legal aspect fail to take into account its cumulative effects. These effects are the systematic destruction of family life and cultural unity, the ruthless assault on personality structure, the denial of manhood and womanhood, the disruption of family and community life, the crippling experience of exclusion from educational and technical training and employment, and the destruction of personality by the brutalized climate of force and violence designed to maintain racist structures intact.

The history of the black man in America has been one of endless struggle against the forces of racism, oppression, and exploitation. After four hundred years of the enslavement of our fathers, the black man today still remains on the fringe of society, deprived and decitizenized. We are no longer held in physical bondage but we are nonetheless bound by a history of social, economic, and cultural oppression which has been more damaging in its effects than physical enslavement. The black man in America has used a variety of strategies and programs. We have tried the vocational education programs of Booker T. Washington, the legal persuasionism of the NAACP, the emigrationism of Marcus Garvey, and the moral and ethical persuasionism of Martin Luther King, Jr. However, we are still oppressed. Even though some progress has been made, yet we remain on the fringe of American society. We are politically, socially, economically, and culturally enslaved.

The situation of the black man in America is desperate and baffling. Our situation is radical, unique, and complicated. It requires new strategies, new programs, new philosophies, and new interpreters. It requires a new orientation of the black man's thinking, about the society in which he lives and about himself. It demands a new understanding of the black man. It has forced the black man to draw on those resources, spiritual and moral, deeply imbedded in the black tradition and in the black religious experience.

Your Brothers in Christ know that racism is contrary to the basic beliefs of the Christian faith, and we cannot avoid recognition of the fact that we are witnessing God's judgement upon a civilization which has violated the law of love and the essential unity of mankind by denying the common humanity of some men and women. The humanity of all of those who have lived under the yoke of racism—whether black, white, or brown— has been distorted and all but destroyed. We must bear in mind that racism is an extreme form of departure from Christ's mandate that in the Kingdom of Heaven there is neither Jew nor Greek, male nor female.

We further believe that there is a need for massive repentance on the part of blacks and whites in order that our society may be made whole and that the cross of continual racial conflict may be lifted from man's shoulders.

Christians, we believe, are called upon to play a vital role in the midst of disunity, discontinuity, disorder, and violence. We are called upon to bring a gospel of hope, love, and promise of redemption. Above all, we are called upon to act in fulfillment of our Christian mission to find new creative ways of thinking about racism and to help build new structures out of which reconciliation can develop.

However, a large segment of the black community's reaction to racism precedes under the caption, "the quest for dignity, identity, and liberation." This thrust has expressed itself in five movements which have originated in certain sections of the black community and are labeled: "Black Power," "Black Theology," "Black Manifesto," "Black History," and "Black Studies."

Your Brothers in Christ believe that the Church must address itself to these trusts, critically evaluate them, suggest their limitations, and emphasize both their promises and their dangers.

2. Black Power

The advocates of this position define Black Power as a strategy of self-determination which is philosophically rooted in the unique psycho-social condition of the black man and in the collective black consciousness. Black Power is a call to black people to rediscover the richness of their own possibilities and to open themselves spiritually, morally, and psychologically to the true meaning of their lives as expressed in the black man's own unique, historically-evolving culture.

The National Committee of Black Churchmen, we are reminded, issued a statement on Black Power, July, 1966. That statement justifies the need and the use of black power by defining the powerlessness of the black man on the one hand and the powerfulness of the white man on the other hand. The situation actually exists in America where consciousless power meets powerless conscience.

The exponents of Black Power insist that we will never discover the solution for racism in America until a twofold ministry takes place: The powerful must discover conscience and the powerless must discover power. The Civil Rights movement during the last decade spend most of its efforts attempting to awaken the conscience of consciousless power. Black Power advocates contend that the next step is necessary; namely, the developing of power for powerless conscience that is black power. Thus Black Power is not only an inevitable response to powerlessness but also a logical development of the Civil Rights movement.

According to these interpreters of Black Power, black men have relied too much on the goodwill and moral consciousness of white America in their fight for a better life. In doing this, they have discovered that only a small amount of progress has been "permitted" and even this at the expense of the black man's identity and sense of worth. In too many instances in order for the black men to move ahead and gain acceptance in the large white society, many Black Americans have been forced to deny and reject their own racial and cultural heritage and accept the implied superiority of the white man's culture and way of doing things. The resulting pattern of self-hatred abetted by white racism has served to destroy the social cohesion of the black community.

Your Brothers in Christ believe that there can be no justice without equitable distribution of power. We think that it is ironical that when the powerless become interested in power, the powerful view both the demand and the concept of power with suspicion. We know that God has revealed Himself time after time as on the side of the powerless, not to endorse their powerlessness but to secure justice. The freedom which Black Power advocates as a legitimate goal is good, but it must be freedom with responsibility; freedom to determine one's own existence; and freedom to embrace one's own heritage. The concept, Black Power, as your Brothers in Christ understand it, is not a complete and full solution to the manifold problems that confront the black man today. Other powers are needed; namely, the power of love, truth, goodness, beauty, character, and soul. The black man in America must also utilize the power of the ballot, economics, skills, and general intelligence. These are the powers that when rightly used will determine the destiny of all men.

We further believe that the greatest power in the world has been made available to us in God's revelation through Jesus Christ our Lord. It is only when this power is appropriated in the life of man that he will be able to realize his unique destiny as a son of God.

3. The Emergence of Black Theologians

There has arisen in America a group of theological thinkers who refer to themselves as "Black Theologians." These Theologians are interested in the development of what they have chosen to call "Black Theology." This "Theology," according to its exponents, is a systematic interpretation of the meaning and significance of the Christian Faith for the worshipping, witnessing and proclaiming Black Christian community. "Black Theology" seeks to interpret the condition of the black man in the light of God's revelation in Jesus Christ. These "Black Theologians" are attempting to interpret the Christian Faith so as to make it commensurate with the black man's quest for freedom and liberation. These "Black Theologians" are determined to present a new understanding of the dignity of black men and women as children of God. "Black Theology" is Christian Theology precisely because it utilizes God's revelation in Jesus Christ as its point of departure.

These Black Theologians viewed with a sense of disgust the slow pace of the reformatory processes of "white theology" in the life of the white church establishment. Many believed that "white theology" has accommodated itself to a situation in which the broken brotherhood of man was perpetuated. It had failed to provide an effective ministry of reconciliation which could overcome the estrangement and the alienation in our land. Black Theologians who lean heavily on and are committed thoroughly to "Black Theology" insist that the white church establishment had presented the blacks of this country a religion of contentment in the state of life in which they find themselves. Such an interpretation of the Christian faith avoided questions about personal dignity, collective power, freedom, equality, and self-determination.

As we, your Brothers in Christ, view the rise of "Black Theology" we conceive it as a legitimate reaction on the part of impatient black scholars who will not accept second-class citizenship in the Kingdom of God and insist that the Christian Faith as experienced and expressed by the black, witnessing, worshipping community is legitimate. The movement is designed, if rightfully used, to correct one serious error which many hold concerning the Kingdom of God; namely, that membership in this Kingdom presupposes the elimination of all racial traits and characteristics which each racial group brings into the fellowship. In the Kingdom of God there is neither Jew nor Greek, bondman nor freeman, male nor female because there is a unity which transcends all diversities possessed by those who are a part of this rich fellowship. Every man brings to God the gifts which God has given him, and no gift should be absolutized and declared to be normative for the entire Christian fellowship. Advocates of "Black Theology" therefore must be warned that God's revelation in Jesus Christ is the absolute norm and all other gifts, traditions, and ideologies are judged by this norm.

4. The Black Manifesto

The Black Manifesto must be mentioned in that it represents a single thrust by a black man at the white church establishment which provoked an almost endless form of controversy. There is no need to go into detail on this matter here because your Brothers in Christ are aware of your familiarity with this issue.

We, your Brothers in Christ, request that white and black Christians, Jews, and all men of goodwill look beyond the rhetoric of the Black Manifesto, beyond the manner of presentation, beyond the controversy commonly associated with it, and face the basic issues raised; namely, the restoration of the human dignity of the black man, the elimination of white racism and the removal of the economic pressures that cause black people to live in a constant state of frustration.

We further believe that the Christian Church is also challenged by the Manifesto to reaffirm its discipleship to Jesus Christ, as He is being revealed to us again through the perspectives of the Black Experience and the resources of the emerging Theology, to the end that the Christian Church will take its rightful place, if it so please God, in the vanguard of the revolution for freedom, dignity, and the power to participate in the making of a new nation and in the God-given destiny of oppressed peoples throughout the world.

5. *Black Studies and Black History*

The Black Studies movement is an uprising against the oppression which confronts Blacks living in a white-oriented world. It represents the mood and attitude on the part of many black students that they have been mis-educated in both white and black colleges and universities. Many of the youth feel that the education which they are receiving is not preparing them to cope with the difficulties and problems of everyday existence. According to the young Blacks, the problems faced today are: the assaults on his personhood, police brutality and hostility, racial identity, white racism, freedom and responsibility, and the mastery of technical skills that will enable him to participate in this competitive American society. The Black youth of the nation want to live lives of freedom, responsibility, dignity, and self-respect. On the other hand, these young Blacks contend that they are confronted with the suffocating effects of a white racist culture which is determined to keep him "in his place."

Blacks today are made painfully aware of the fact that history can be manipulated in such a way to be used either as an instrument of oppression or an instrument of liberation. There is a growing feeling that the Blacks have not been told the truth about their history. He knows now that, insofar as the textbooks on history used in many of the high schools and colleges relate them, the contributions of the black man are invisible. All of this, the young Blacks contend, must be corrected. Possibly James Baldwin put it rather succinctly when he said:

> It is not really a "Negro revolution" that is upsetting the country. What is upsetting the country is a sense of its own identity. If, for example, one managed to change the curriculum in all the schools so that Negroes learned more about themselves and their real contributions to this culture, you would be liberating not only Negroes, you'd be liberating white people who know nothing about their own history. And the reason is that if you are compelled to lie about one aspect of anybody's history, you must lie about it all. If you have to lie about my real role here, if you have to pretend that I hoed all that cotton just because I loved you, then you have done something to yourself. You are mad.

The Black Studies program is also a cry for justice from the disinherited. The exploiting white racist society calls for law and order knowing that law and order as interpreted by many whites never serves the disinherited, only themselves. The quest for Black Studies in the colleges and universities of this nation shows that when law and order serves for purposes of exploitation the cry for justice may demand disorder.

The main argument for Black Studies has been presented, and your Brothers in Christ insist that the quest for freedom, identity, self-respect, and human dignity is a noble one. Further, we are justly proud of the young men and women who make up our fellowship and we share with them all of the legitimate goals which are presented under the head of Black Studies.

Black Studies can be so narrowly defined that it will be self-defeating and self-destructive, and this is one of the major dangers. Our youth must be warned so as not to permit its understanding of Black Studies to become a pseudo power and substitute for essential skills which are needed for the race's survival. We must not permit our understanding of blackness to create a new cult of incompetence. Blackness is not a substitute for nobility and must not be used to develop false illusions.

Our Church believes that the race needs black physicists as well as black philosophers: black politicians as well as black poets; black engineers as well as black writers; black business as well as black blues. Yes, if the *race is to do its thing* it must have these and more—black chemists, black inventors, black astronauts, black senators, secretaries, vice presidents and presidents. The revolutionist black man must be free to pursue his legitimate personal goals, secure in the dignity of his manhood, respecting those structures which make his freedom secure.

The quest for human dignity, identity, and liberation has stirred the hearts and minds of the youth of all lands. Those who have made the quest have sought to understand themselves and their position in the world in terms of economics, government, history, science, philosophy, sociology, music, and literature. These are legitimate avenues through which the pursuit of dignity, identity, and liberation may be sought, but the youth of our land must be warned that when these avenues or approaches have been exhausted the deeper and more fundamental questions will remain unanswered.

The Christian faith teaches us that the concept of man, of human nature, of dignity, identity, and liberation is derived from the nature of one particular man, Jesus Christ. Jesus Christ is the revealed Word of God and because He is God's Word and lived in absolute obedience to the will of God He is for us the true man. It is in Jesus Christ that man discovers his true self. Man, therefore, cannot on the basis of the study of the phenomena of the human in general nor the exact science of man in particular stumble upon the true word about himself.

The true word about man is revealed to us in Jesus Christ and proclaimed in the Hebraic-Christian tradition: "Man is made in the image of God," says the Old Testament prophet; and, "Seek ye first the Kingdom of God and His righteousness, and all these things shall be added to you," says Jesus of Nazareth. The exact sciences of man, be it sociology, biology, psychology, or history, are concerned with man only insofar as he represents one of the phenomena of the cosmos. These sciences can only show how a man is but they can never give the full answer to what man is. We Christians believe that what man is, how he ought to live, where he came from, and where he is going is given to us in God's revelation in Jesus Christ. The true understanding of man, his dignity and identity, is given to us in the Christian faith and more particularly in God's revelation in Jesus Christ. It is in Jesus, we believe, that the full and complete destinies of all men are discovered and realized, and that He gives to each believer the power of self-transcendence enabling all men to become sons of God. Those who are involved in the quest for human dignity, identity, and liberation ought to hear again the words of Jesus, "I am the way, the truth, and the life."

25

LIBERATION MOVEMENTS: A CRITICAL ASSESSMENT AND A REAFFIRMATION

Position Paper of the African Methodist Episcopal Church

I. Introduction

African Methodism came into being as a liberation movement and a protest against segregation and racism in the Christian Church and the world. Over one hundred eighty-nine years ago, Richard Allen and his followers were laboring to prevent Christianity in America from developing the racial stratification as evidenced today. The Episcopal Fathers reaffirmed their faith in our motto: "God our Father; Christ our Redeemer; Man our Brother," and, at the 38th Quadrennial Session of the General Conference in 1964, made the following pronouncement: "We unreservedly welcome into our fellowship without regard to race, nationality or social distinction all who will share the faith of Jesus Christ as Redeemer and Lord. . . ."

In November, 1787, the colored people belonging to the Methodist Society of Philadelphia convened together in order to take into consideration the evils under which they labored arising from the unkind treatment of their white brethren. The colored people were considered a nuisance in the house of worship and were frequently pulled off their knees while in the act of prayer and ordered to the back seats. From these and various other acts of unchristian conduct, they considered it their duty to devise a plan in order to build a house of their own in which they could worship God.

The formation of the Free African Society, organized in 1787, constituted the first serious attempt of oppressed black people in the United States of

This document is one of the Black Position Papers of the 40th Session of the General Conference of the African Methodist Episcopal Church, June 16–27, 1976, in Atlanta, Ga.

America to organize for the purpose of liberating their souls, minds and bodies from the oppressive and dehumanizing effects of chattel slavery. The Free African Societies, analogous to the cellular movement of the early church, provided the survival shelter for oppressed people in a strange and alien land. The same liberating spirit that motivated black people in and around Philadelphia, Delaware, New York and Maryland to unite in forming the African Methodist Episcopal Church was not an isolated event but was part of a universal movement of freedom and liberation which, like an idea whose time had come, could not be stopped.

In 1816 the African Methodist Episcopal Church made a formal response to the liberation movement and became a corporate entity for religious purposes. This act affirmed the self-determination process by which a people could, of their own volition, worship God under their own vine and fig tree in spirit and in truth, hold property and chart their own political and economic destiny.

II. The Black Experience in America

It is self-evident that the lack of racial justice in American society both is and has been a problem. It is a problem which has existed before the founding of this nation. It was a problem for the writers of the Constitution of the United States who legitimized the existence of slavery by providing that for purposes of taxation and congressional representation each slave would count as three-fifths of a person. Congress was prohibited from stopping the slave trade before 1808. It bound states to assist in returning fugitive slaves to their masters.

Although the Emancipation Proclamation was issued in 1863, forty years later, W. E. B. DuBois could write in *The Souls of Black Folk*, "The problem of the twentieth century is the problem of the color line." DuBois also noted that "the whites, North and South, [have tended] to shift the burden of the Negro problem to the Negro's shoulders and stand aside as critical and rather pessimistic spectators when, in fact, the burden belongs to the nation and the hands of none of us are clean if we bend not our energies to righting these wrongs."

The absence of racial justice is a crucial problem . . . one which lies . . . not at the periphery of American society but at its very heart. Gunnar Myrdal, in his *An American Dilemma*, claims that ". . . the treatment of the Negro is America's greatest and most conspicuous scandal." That the problem still remains is attested to in a multitude of ways, among them being the basic "conclusion" of the Kerner Commission: "Our nation is moving toward two societies, one black, one white—separate and unequal." This report, written some one hundred years later, following the assassination of Dr. Martin Luther King, Jr., makes it plain: ". . . white, moderate, responsible America is where the trouble lies. . . . White society is deeply implicated in the ghetto.

White institutions created it, white institutions maintained it, and white society condones it."

The Black Experience is a constant confrontation with racism which subordinates on the basis of color, one group to another, assigning inferior status to one and superior status to the other. For the Black man in America, racism is not a word but a fact; it is a ghetto; it is poverty; it is an event—demeaning in all of its ramifications. It is economic deprivation; it is red-lining which curtails the flow of financial aid to the inner city where the Black population is located. It is benign neglect; it is police brutality; it is inferior education; it is blatant disregard for the health, welfare and safety of the Black community. It is the denial of employment opportunities.

Justice is the ultimate goal because it promotes, as no other single goal, the realization of societies, social systems and institutions which both allow and encourage individuals to realize their full potential as unique persons. This is the end of the liberation movement and to this end the African Methodist Episcopal Church is irrevocably committed.

III. The Meaning of Liberation for the Church

The White Anglo-Saxon Protestant Churches in America are deeply involved in the oppression and racism which exists in America. They have condoned the spread of racism throughout the world. Their missionary emphasis was to carry the gospel to the heathens in foreign parts. The task was enshrouded with a benevolent despotism that brought on 18th and 19th century colonialism—a handmaiden of racism and economic exploitation.

Every white pulpit in America admonished slaves to obey their masters. After the Nat Turner revolt of 1837, many church denominations which opposed slavery vacillated. Many dropped the subject altogether.

As far back as 1775, Thomas Paine denounced the slave trade and indicted the WASP Church for its complicity in the slave trade:

> TO AMERICANS: That some desperate wretches should be willing to steal and enslave men by violence and murder for gain, is rather lamentable than strange. But that many civilized, nay christianized people should approve, and be concerned in the savage practice, is surprising and still persists, though it has been so often proved contrary to the light of nature, to every principle of justice and humanity. . . .
>
> Most shocking of all is alleging the sacred scriptures to favor this wicked practice. The plea is, in a great measure, false; they had no permission to catch and enslave people who never injured them.
>
> Such arguments ill become us, since the time of reformation came, under gospel light. All distinctions of nations, and privileges of one

above others, are ceased; Christians are taught to account all men their neighbors; and love their neighbors as themselves; and do to all men as they would be done by; to do good to all men; and man-stealing is ranked with enormous crimes.

After America had achieved her liberation and became a free and independent nation, the African Methodist Episcopal Church became the voice of God and the conscience of America.

The Black Free Church reminded America that a righteous God could not smile upon their new-won freedom when blacks, stolen from their native sod, were being held in bondage. A new interpretation and theological frame of reference was established: "God our Father; Christ our Redeemer; Man our Brother." This became the cutting edge and the "balance" in which America was weighed and found wanting.

God's work of salvation in Jesus Christ is human liberation. Jesus Christ becomes the point of departure for oppressed people to analyze the meaning of liberation. The Christological implications are implicit in the prophetic tradition. Jesus applies this tradition to himself:

> The Spirit of the Lord is upon me, because he hath anointed me to preach the gospel to the poor; he hath sent me to heal the broken-hearted, to preach deliverance to the captives, and recovering of sight to the blind, to set at liberty them that are bruised. To preach the acceptable year of the Lord.

The analogy becomes clear after Jesus' resurrection. The struggle for liberation and freedom continues with a new mandate and a new promise of power. It is God's will that all oppressive forces will be done away with. This is the meaning of the Exodus and the Incarnation. It is also the meaning of the Crucifixion and the Resurrection.

The struggle for liberation addresses the "now" and the "not yet" of the Gospel. God's Kingdom is breaking in on oppression, tearing down oppressive cruelty systems.

The Church is that community that participates in Christ's liberating work in history; it can never endorse unjust laws for the sake of order. The Church must say "no" to structures of oppression.

The historical liberation of God is the defining characteristic of the Church:

a) The Church proclaims the reality of divine liberation.
b) The Church actively shares in the liberation struggle. The Church lives on the basis of the radical demands of the gospel and makes the gospel message a social, economic and political reality.

c) The Church cannot be in isolation from the concrete realities of human suffering. It must share the suffering of oppressed people, bear the reproach of its enemies and struggle to bring about a new order.

> The eschatological implications for liberation are to speak of the promise of God's Word of liberation, disclosed in his future breaking into our present and overthrowing the powers of evil that hold people in captivity. (James H. Cone, *God of the Oppressed*.)

IV. Liberation Movements in the Black Community

The liberation movement had its origin in the formation of the Black Church. Much of the post-Emancipation leadership for the liberation movement came from the Black Church.

The cruelty and violence of the post Civil War oppression, especially below the Mason-Dixon line, encouraged and, in most instances, demanded the urban centers of the North. Uprooted and frightened, these dispossessed and powerless Black people set out in quest of the "promised land" and its new opportunities. They did not find the promised land overflowing with milk, honey and opportunities but they found New York, Chicago, Philadelphia and other similar urban centers to be desolate wildernesses of cultural, political, social and economic exile.

Unfortunately, the Black Church was not prepared to confront this resulting crisis; therefore, destiny and necessity demanded the birth of new organizations which could effectively share in the fight to liberate and empower the disfranchised Black masses. Out of this chaotic bewilderment and against this racist system called America came into being new social liberation movements. The National Association for the Advancement of Colored People (NAACP) and the National Urban League were among the first such groups to appear and, later, The Southern Christian Leadership Conference (SCLC), Congress on Racial Equality (CORE), Student Non-Violent Coordinating Committee (SNCC) and People United to Save Humanity (PUSH). Each of these movements has served and made a contribution to the liberation of Black and other oppressed peoples. Each has sought to fight and resist racist oppression and to advance the cause of liberation. Each group has worked separately as well as collectively in the interest of the mobilization and organization of the Black community for total liberation and self-determination.

The liberation movement in America during the early 1900's was advanced by the NAACP and the Urban League. Through the leadership provided by these organizations, there existed an "era of legalism" in America. Historian August Meier, in *Black Protest Thought in the Twentieth Century* states that during the First World War the NAACP won its first two cases before the Supreme Court and enjoyed an expanded membership as a result. The

NAACP pursued the legal struggle for the civil rights of Black Americans to insure their liberation while the Urban League assisted Black families in adjusting to city life. The Great Migration and the serious problems which resulted from the swelling numbers of urban dwellers presented organizations like the NAACP and the National Urban League with ever increasing responsibilities.

The era of non-violent, direct action was born during the Montgomery Bus Boycott in 1965. Our own sainted Rosa Parks, a deaconess in the African Methodist Episcopal Church, in the spirit of Allen, took a seat for justice by refusing to acquiesce to the racist dehumanization of the South. She found that the walk to the back of the bus was much farther than she had ever realized so she took the first seat she saw.

This era was characterized by a struggle for an interracial society with justice and equality as the motivating principles. The style of SCLC and Dr. Martin Luther King, Jr., SNCC and CORE was non-violent direct action as they pursued these noble objectives for what was still a disfranchised Black community. Operation PUSH, born out of Operation Breadbasket, an offspring of SCLC, has sought to move the liberation struggle into the arena of economic and political self-determination. The seeds of this struggle are vivid in the pages of history for they describe the intensity of the suffering patience of Black people. The history of this struggle is an epic in American culture characterized by sit-ins, paddy wagons, fire hoses, bombed churches, lynchings, police dogs, pray-ins, and a second march on Washington.

An historical assessment reveals that while these foregoing organizations and movements are distinctive in style, methods and orientation, yet they are inextricably one in their quest for the liberation and empowerment of the Black masses. Dr. James Cone, in his book *A Black Theology of Liberation*, states that the hand of God is "unreservedly with those who are humiliated and abused." The same has been evidenced in the liberation and accomplishments of those communal liberation groups.

V. Moral and Ethical Rationale for a Strategy of Liberation

The Church of Allen followed the Federal troops into the heart of the South, gathered together the scattered sheep of Africa who had been dispersed by the ravages of war and human exploitation, fed and clothed them and provided a means of education for over three million disfranchised, unlettered Blacks. Black bishops and preachers of African Methodism came into the South proclaiming the "gospel of liberation," declaring that the spirit of the living Christ was loose in the world—tearing down oppressive systems and ministering to the needs of the dispossessed and providing for the social, political and economic rehabilitation of our wounded race and our wounded nation.

Our quest for the liberation ethic and strategy can be realized only through radical identification with the dispossessed Black masses. This ethic of radical identification must provide for us a framework which enables us to fight with the victims of apartheid in South Africa against racist oppression. This ethic of radical identification helps us to fight for the liberation of the Black masses in Rhodesia. This ethic of radical identification was the raison d'etre of our Lord and Saviour who, like many of the Black and poor masses, proclaimed that "He had nowhere to lay His head." It was this ethic that motivated our sainted founder to minister to the sick and dying during the yellow fever epidemic. Through this dispositional ethic we reaffirm and recommit ourselves and our resources to the cause of justice, equality and freedom everywhere. We, therefore, unequivocally and unreservedly, in the spirit of Allen and Turner, oppose racism, oppression and tyranny everywhere but especially in Africa, South America and the Caribbean. We vehemently oppose the abuses of the Federal Bureau of Investigation and the Central Intelligence Agency in their several attempts to disdain and debunk Black leaders and Black organizations in their quest and struggle for freedom in America. We call for an immediate cessation to these atrocities. We support the struggles of the oppressed in their quest for liberation. We, therefore, call upon all humankind everywhere to join in the fight to end racism and oppression now, henceforth and forever more.

This interim ethic of radical identification demands that we search for an adequate and appropriate alternative to violence—an alternative which empowers the powerless with the Christian techniques of peace for the righting of injustice and the solution of conflict. We see in the present world-wide revolution and struggles the providential hand of Almighty God pulling down all structures and cultures that dehumanize and enslave, and establishing upon the earth new structures and cultures and societies founded upon justice wherein individuals are able and encouraged to realize their full potential as unique and authentic persons to the end that we all ". . . shall beat our swords into plowshares, and our spears into pruninghooks . . . and study war no more . . . ," and to the end that the kingdoms of this world will become the kingdom of our Lord and of His Christ.

VI. Recommendations

In 1976, at the Quadrennial Session of the General Conference, the Church of Allen, founded as a liberation movement, reaffirmed its position as a liberating influence in the world and made the following recommendations:

1. That the Committee on Position Papers be authorized to study, analyze and type liberation movements world-wide as to nature, function and purpose and to make recommendations to the Council of Bishops as to which movements would most appropriately correspond with our position on liberation. (While we support liberation movements, in principle, we should primarily concern ourselves with those which are consistent with the libera-

tion theology and which characterize the life and teachings of the African Methodist Episcopal Church.)

2. That the 40th Session of the General Conference of the African Methodist Episcopal Church direct the Council of Bishops in their next session to petition the United Nations for Non-Governmental Status.

3. That the African Methodist Episcopal Church convene other Black church bodies world-wide to address the question of Africa, its liberation and development.

4. That the 40th Session of the General Conference of the African Methodist Episcopal Church take a position in favor of the liberation and in support of liberation movements in South Africa and Rhodesia.

26

THE EPISCOPAL ADDRESS TO THE 40th QUADRENNIAL GENERAL CONFERENCE OF THE AFRICAN METHODIST EPISCOPAL ZION CHURCH (EXCERPT)

The Church and Racism

Racial hatred is an old and persistent disease in the blood stream of human society. It divided the Jew and the Samaritan, Greek and Barbarian, the Black American and the White American; and racial hatred is not a one-way-street type of infection, because it infects equally the one who harbors it as well as the one against whom it is directed; because invariably the one who is the object of racial hatred learns to hate the one who has made him a victim.

The Church's supreme consideration must be concerned with the fact that the hatred that arises between human beings for any reason, and most especially when based upon physical differences, offends heaven and shuts such people out from fellowship with God. This is the ultimate danger of all sin, and the sin of racism is so deep-seated and rampant that it should be of urgent consideration and concern within the Church. The Church should not and cannot be silent in this critical hour of mounting racism.

The voice of the Christian Church has been too weak in addressing itself to the task of solving the problem of racial hatred, for whether the Church wishes to be or not, it is still a definite part of the racial crisis. The Christian Church must speak outwardly with a fresh message of hope from God, or, by remaining silent, it will proclaim to one and all that Our God is inadequate for solving the racial problem.

Historically the voice of the Christian Church has been heard speaking out on matters that were thought to be important. It has been quick and ready to defend a theological heritage which has been handed down from generation

This document is an excerpt from the address of Herbert Bell Shaw, former chairman of the Board of Directors of NCBC and Bishop of the First Episcopal District of the A.M.E.Z. Church. The 40th Quadrennial General Conference was held in Chicago, May 5–15, 1976.

to generation, for the Church dares not allow its theological heritage to become tainted. But the Church has failed to become sufficiently involved in the racial crisis, which is actually the greatest crisis to rock our nation. While the Christian Church has been only half-heartedly involved in the battle against racism, some of the leaders in other areas of the American national life have spoken out definitely and boldly on the question of racism, and have acted decisively in behalf of minority groups.

We call upon its leaders to make the Church a powerful force in solving the racial problem. The pulpits of this land must point out that hatred—the deep, angry, bitter animosity which we call racial prejudice—warps the thinking in the United States, and is a sin cancer eating at the nations vitals and dooming the nation to failure. The acts of hatred directed towards Black people in this country are well known and of long duration, but there are depths of hatred and bitterness directed from the Black community towards white America that would shock and shake this land if they could be fully exposed.

The Church must assume that it is not too late for America to solve its racial problem, and it must begin to make its voice to be heard. It is a frightening truth that too often various agencies of the government, and some agents of commerce, have acted in closer harmony with the teachings of Jesus on justice and mercy than has the Christian Church. . . .

The Christian Church and the Third World

During many critical periods of human history, men are called upon to rise up and proclaim a new faith, establish a new religion and build a new civilization. Western civilization is rapidly declining, it is decaying from within. As it now exists it is incapable of serving as a proper vehicle of human progress. The kind of world in which we live now has rendered all present forms of organized society obsolete. This is not only true of western civilization, but of other civilizations as well. The time has come for mankind to rise up and create a new civilization.

Because of their detachment and youthful dynamism, third world people possess the kind of freedom from vested interest in both capitalistic and socialistic societies that are pre-requisites for this task. Both the capitalistic and socialistic societies are so involved in the preservation of the status quo that they are blinded to the urgent need of a new civilization.

The time has come for the third world people to rise up and build a new order. The African Methodist Episcopal Zion Church represents the third world people of the Black diaspora as well as the continent of Africa. Because of its ethnic origin and social economic history, Zion Methodism is aware of its identity with the people of the third world. God is preparing to build a new heaven and a new earth. He is calling upon the third world people to lead the way. If this sounds ridiculous or as wishful thinking, I call your attention to the Scripture that says:

Remove the diadem and take off the crown, this shall be the same; exalt him that is low, and abase him that is high. I will overturn and overturn and overturn it and it shall be no more, until he comes whose right it is; and I will give it him (Ezek. 21:26-27).

Human civilization is ordained of God as an instrument of human progress. When it no longer serves its purpose it is discarded by Divine Providence, and is replaced by a new civilization that is more relevant to the needs of the time.

In the book of Nehemiah, we see God preparing to restore a heritage, and build a new civilization. When God gets ready to build a civilization, redeem a nation, or restore a heritage the first thing He does is to find a man.

When God decided to save human nature from the flood . . . He found Noah. When He wanted to establish a new religion, He found Abraham. When He decided to liberate a people, He found Moses. When He got ready to make Israel a great nation, He found David. When God wanted to redeem mankind, He found Jesus Christ. When God's man and God's time meet, something new is the inevitable result. In Andrew Cartwright, God's man and God's time met, and Zion Methodism was planted in Africa.

Also in prophet Nehemiah, God's man and God's time met. Nehemiah was able to understand that the greatness of Israel depended upon the restoration of Jerusalem. Jerusalem was Israel's turf. It was Israel's place in the sun. The fortunes of the people of Israel were entwined with the destiny of the city of Jerusalem. The prophet understood this. The Israelites with whom he talked understood this. Therefore, they replied, "Let us rise up and build." The men of Israel who accepted the prophet's challenge were those who shared his faith.

This historic truth applies not only to Israel, but to the third world, to Black Africa and to Black men throughout the world as well. It has a peculiar application to this historic moment of world civilization. We would do well to ask ourselves, "What is the Black man's role in the world today?"

Like Israel of old the Black man has endured the affliction of slavery, exploitation, oppression and humiliation. God is moving to restore the heritage of the Black man. Africa is the Black man's Jerusalem. It is the Black man's turf. It is the symbol and focal point of his heritage. This heritage will never be restored as long as Africa is raped, exploited and oppressed. The reproach of the Black man throughout the world is directly related to the plight of Africa. The third world is made up of a multiplicity of ethnic groups and a complexity of religions and cultures. So is Africa. For this reason, we have chosen to view the plight of third world people through the African perspective.

Like Israel of old, if the Black man is to regain his lost domain, he must rebuild the walls of his Jerusalem, and establish a new civilization. He must build anew. The challenge of the Black man is to rise and build.

There is a continuity in history. The new is always built upon the foundation of the old. Therefore, the Black man must know his heritage. He must be proud of his ancient culture. He must believe that this heritage is worth restoring.

When we speak of restoring our heritage, we do not mean that we shall attempt to turn back the clock to pre-colonial days. We will use this heritage as a foundation, the fiber, out of which we shall weave a new culture. Our glorious past will serve as the foundation of this new civilization. It must be one which is based upon Black solidarity, pan-Africanism, and universal fraternity.

To believe in Blackness is not to despise whiteness. To work for Black liberation is not synonymous with white alienation. We believe that it is God's will that all men should live together in a state of harmonious mutuality and creative good will. The only guarantee of such an existence is to possess the power to protect ourselves against the demonic encroachment of those who would enslave or exploit us.

Historical Foundation

If we are to restore our heritage and build a new civilization we must first know our past history. We must know what we are and what we want to be. We must let no one else decide this for us. The African must decide for himself what his self-image is to be. This decision is crucial.

> A man's self perception is vital to what he does. His self-perception is still largely the result of his view of history. If African history is to provide the African with his self-perception and thus play an effective role in the building of an independent Africa, it has to correct the distortion and bridge the gap created by the colonial experience in the African historical tradition. African history must evolve its own identity independent of western historiography, the shackles of outside acceptability notwithstanding. (*Daedalus*, Spring 1974, p. 131.)

The Black man's history goes back beyond the horizons of dim antiquity. Africa is the cradle of humanity. Our history goes back before the Sahara was a desert and before the Semites ever swept down from the Arabian desert and from other parts of Asia.

It was in Africa that the early man developed the use of tools. This was more than a million years ago. Sixty thousand years ago the Black man discovered the use of fire. Egypt is the cradle of civilizations. The earliest of Egyptian civilizations was of Black African origin.

We must study the great empires of Ancient Africa: Ghana, Mali, Kanem-Bornu, Songhay, Benin, and many others. We must learn what made the empires great, and why they disappeared.

Men make history and history makes men. Man's historical experience determines his self-image. As we study the history of pre-colonial Africa we meet a people who had developed a strong historical tradition that contributed to a wholesome self-image. For thousands of years Black Africa had its conquerors and its heroes. It had experienced change that was gradual or rapid, peaceful and tragic, local and universal, superficial and fundamental. The African historical tradition enabled him to see and view both decay and renewal as a part of human growth and development. He saw the past, present and future linked together by the continuous flow of history. Continuity and stability were the essential ingredients in the African philosophy that enabled him to understand his historical experience. This does not mean that the African had a static view of life, but that his sense of historic continuity was keen and comprehensive.

Speaking of pre-colonial Africa, E. J. Alagoa says:

> Yet in spite of his conceptualization of a prosaic recent past and a glorious remote past a sense of continuity was maintained. The living identified themselves with the founding ancestors, and each man's self-confidence derived largely from his pride in them. He faced odds and tribulation in the knowledge that they continued to care about what happened to them. The youth were taught to revere and know their ancestors. The elders who were seen as drawing closer to the ancestors were regarded as potential recruits to their ranks and deemed to possess similar powers to influence the actions and fortunes of future generations. (*Daedalus*, Spring 1974, p. 126.)

The African emphasized the solidarity and uniqueness of each community. This gave him a strength and resilence that enabled him to evolve his own brand of Christianity, Judaism and Islam. Founded upon the belief of the intercommunication of past, present and future, the concept of the extended family and reverence for ancestors, the solidarity of African society and the continuity of African tradition was secured. African empires rose and fell, conquerors came and went, there were good times and bad, but African culture continued to grow from strength to strength.

> European colonization interrupted this continual flow of African tradition. It produced a traumatic effect upon African life by imposing on the African a gross distortion of its historical tradition. Having conquered through the technological superiority of their armaments, Europeans sought to maintain control over Africans, not only through technology, but also psychological defeatism. (Ibid., p. 126.)

Slavery, exploitation, racism, tribal strife were used as instruments of oppression and annihilation. The colonial masters made use of the big lie.

They declared that there was no such thing as African history and African Civilization; that the African had done nothing worthy of historical attention; that they were passive recipients and mere spectators of the march of human developments. This caused the Africans themselves to experience shock, widespread disorientation and loss of identity. This tragedy, as traumatic as it was, was by no means totally successful, neither on the African continent nor among Africans of the diaspora. Notwithstanding, much damage has been done. The African fell behind in many phases of human development.

The walls of African culture have been torn down. The gates of African dignity have been destroyed by white European exploitation, oppression, tribal strife, and the lack of technological advancement. Our task is clear. Out of the ruins of yesterday we must build our new Jerusalem.

> You see the distress we are in, how Jerusalem lieth waste and the gates thereof are burned with fire; come, let us build up the walls of Jerusalem that we be no more a reproach.

Black Africa is not entirely free. Economic servitude, technological dependence and neo-colonialism conspire to make us half slave. The nations of Black Africa must make greater strides toward economic and technological self-sufficiency. The nations of Africa are aware of these needs. "Operation Feed Yourself" in Ghana and similar projects in other African countries are attempts to free Africa from the clutches of neo-colonialism. Armed with a full knowledge of Africa's past glory, we must rise up and build. As our ancestors built civilizations in the past, so must we in the present and future.

27

THE NEW BLACK EVANGELICALS

Ronald C. Potter

Without doubt evangelical Christianity is the fastest growing religious movement in the United States today. Several religious observers note that, while the historic mainline Protestant denominations are losing members at a frightening pace, Evangelical churches, seminaries, and publishing houses are experiencing unprecedented growth.[1]

Spearheading this growing Christian movement is an emerging Evangelical "left." Though this radical wing is a small minority of the estimated forty million "born again" Christians, its influence is rising, even among more conservative Evangelicals. Richard Quebedeaux, a keen observer of the movement, has written:

> The vanguard of the evangelical left is centered on a small, highly literate, and generally younger elite. . . . Evangelicals of the left range from moderate Republicans to democratic socialists, if not Marxists.[2]

Unlike their more conservative elders, radical Evangelicals are seriously attempting to relate their faith to the social ills of society.

From all appearances, however, this radical Evangelicalism is essentially a White religious phenomenon. Though there have been recent journalistic efforts made to include the unique Black contribution to the movement the net result has been token at best.[3] To date little if anything has been written about the history, theology, and current debate taking place among the new breed of Black Evangelicals.

Before the new Black Evangelical movement can be further analyzed,

Ronald C. Potter is an Associate with *The Other Side* magazine and author of Sunday School curricula for Urban Ministries based in Chicago. He is presently Co-chairperson of the Theological Commission of the National Black Evangelical Association and also serves on the Planning Committee of the National Black Christian Students Conference. His essay is published here for the first time.

perhaps a clear definition of American Evangelicalism would be in order. Historically, several American religious movements claim an Evangelical heritage. The eighteenth- and nineteenth-century Great Awakenings, the revivalism of Dwight L. Moody, the conservative "old Princeton theology," and the sociotheological conservatism which grew out of the famous fundamentalist–modernist controversy of the 1920s are all variants of American Evangelicalism. Today's Evangelicals are basically conventional Protestants who hold staunchly to the authority of the Bible in all matters and adhere to orthodox Christian doctrine. They believe in making a conscious personal commitment to Christ, a spiritual encounter, gradual or instantaneous, known as the "born again" experience.

If attempting to arrive at a coherent definition of American Evangelicalism is difficult then the task is even more problematic when trying to define *Black* Evangelicalism. Theologically most mainline Black churches (especially Baptist and Pentecostal) are Evangelical if one means adherence to orthodox Christian doctrine. But within that broad group are those that adhere not just to doctrine but to a mentality, a subculture, a lifestyle. This distinct group consists of what I refer to as Black Evangelicals.

Black Evangelicalism is essentially a post-World War II phenomenon. It is a direct outgrowth of the "Bible School" and "Christian College" movement of the 1950s. Blacks educated in these institutions were given a White reactionary world-view. One Black Christian in describing his experiences in the fundamentalist world, has said:

> We were taught to shun the world, to be separate from it, and while I am sure the interest was right, the result of such instruction developed a negative and defensive mentality. I found myself viewing people as the enemy, especially if they smoked or cursed. They were to be saved, of course, but not necessarily to be loved as they were. Imperceptibly, I came to be more doctrine and program centered than people centered. . . . I became a fundamentalist.[4]

A prevailing belief, in the recent past, among most Black Evangelicals was that the Black community had very few "biblically sound" churches. This erroneous belief was popularized by Tom Skinner's *Black and Free.* In 1968 Skinner concluded that "The kind of religion usually found in the Negro churches is highly emotional, often superstitious and has little biblical foundation."[5]

Wittingly or unwittingly, Skinner left the unfortunate impression that most Black choirs are entertainers and performers and that most Black ministers are con artists and immoral preacher pimps. To be sure, it is doubtful whether a significant number of mainstream Black Evangelicals have moved from this position. Dr. William Bentley, former president of the National Black Evangelical Association, has suggested that the Black

Evangelical movement "remains for the most part, outside the mainstream of black Christianity. With the possible exception of black Pentecostals black evangelicalism is distinctly a middle-class religious phenomenon and has much more in common with its white counterpart than with the black."[6] In short, mainline Black Evangelicalism has tended to see Black Church/Black Christianity through White eyes.

II

During most of the turbulent sixties, Black Evangelicals remained conspicuously quiet. While Malcolm X, Stokely Carmichael, H. Rap Brown, and the Black Panthers attempted to define and defend Black personhood, most Evangelicals mouthed "pious irrelevancies and sanctimonious trivialities." Before the close of the decade, however, a vocal minority of militant Black Evangelicals came on the scene. Shortly after the assassination of Martin Luther King, Jr., the most militant critique to date from a Black Christian perspective was published—William Pannell's *My Friend the Enemy*. Pannell expressed the mood of militant Black Evangelicals when he wrote:

> The white man must learn to listen. I am bored beyond words with the white man's assessment of me—how I ought to think; how I, in fact, do think; how I should feel as a Christian. What you must learn is how I think, how I really feel.[7]

Pannell's colleague, Tom Skinner, who was previously tagged as the "Black Billy Graham," began to reverse that image in the late 1960s and early 1970s. As the new "Stokely Carmichael of the evangelical world" Skinner unleashed a vehement attack on White evangelical racism, militarism, and American civil religion. Without doubt, Tom's famous address to the Ninth Inter-Varsity Missionary Convention in 1970 made him the foremost evangelist of the gospel of holistic liberation.[8] By addressing crucial social issues, Skinner found himself *persona non grata* at several "Christian" colleges and churches. The famous Moody Bible Institute, for example, took him off their radio station because his messages were "too political." Skinner's prophetic challenges soon made him a "bad nigger" in many Evangelical circles.

During the late sixties the militant mood permeated what was then known as the National Negro Evangelical Association (now the National Black Evangelical Association). A major cleavage erupted at the 1969 NNEA convention between the older traditional Evangelicals and the younger militants. This cleavage was intensified at the following year's convention held in New York. Younger Black Evangelicals forced the convention to address itself to the unholy Graham-Nixon alliance and to support John Perkins, a Black Evangelical social activist who had been jailed and severely beaten for his involvement in social issues in Mississippi. The apex of the convention was a keynote address by perhaps the most articulate speaker at that time for militant Black Evangelicals, Columbus Salley.

In 1970 Salley, along with a White liberal Evangelical, co-authored a book entitled, *Your God Is Too White*. The book hit the Evangelical community like a bombshell. Its excoriation of White American Christianity was a bitter pill for many to swallow. Like Vincent Harding's *Black Power and the American Christ* and Albert Cleage's *Black Messiah*, Salley attempted to strip "Christianity" of its Whiteness and oppressive nature. In many respects *Your God Is Too White* was the handbook for militant Black Evangelicals.

Dr. William H. Bentley, the "godfather" of militant Black Evangelicals, was attempting to raise the social and ethnic consciousness of Black Christians years before Black Power was in vogue. Bentley, perhaps more than anyone else, has contributed to a distinct Black Evangelical nationalist school of thought.[9] Both a theologian and an astute church historian, Dr. Bentley is attempting to develop a truly liberating Black Evangelical theology. Without doubt New Black Evangelicals have come into their own.

III

Is there a relationship between the White Evangelical "left" and radical Black Evangelicals? To better understand the question one must examine the antecedent of the White "young Evangelicals," namely neo-evangelicalism.

Neo-evangelicalism was a reaction to "cultic fundamentalism" twenty-five years ago. It was characterized by a renaissance in evangelical theology and apologetics. In the area of social ethics, however, the new movement left much to be desired. Indeed, neo-evangelicalism, like most White religious movements, capitulated to White racism. E. J. Carnell, probably the greatest theologian of the movement, once wrote:

> Too much stress on racial injustice will divert the sinner's attention from the need to repent of his totally self-centered life. . . . If we let the Negro buy a house in a fashionable suburb we do an injustice to vested property interests.[10]

To be sure, this type of theologizing would fit perfectly in the antebellum South or in the racist society of South Africa.

Carnell, it must be said, at least was honest about his racism. The truth remains, however, that the colonizer, whether Christian or pagan, liberal or conservative, will not automatically seek the best interests of the colonized. The oppressors will never interpret the gospel correctly because it calls for the liberation of a people they hold in bondage.

New Black Evangelicals have the same distrust for the White Evangelical "left" as their elders had for neo-evangelicalism twenty-five years ago. Over the recent past there have been several confrontations between radical Black

Christians and "leftist" White Evangelicals. Since its inception Evangelicals for Social Action (a group which is attempting to link Evangelical faith with social action) has had serious problems in recruiting and keeping a significant Black presence.[11] Many former Black members feel that while ESA is to be commended for its fight against racial injustice, its onslaught against racism is still not strong enough. While militant Black Evangelicals certainly do not minimize the importance of other social issues, they affirm with W. E. B. DuBois that "the problem of the twentieth century is the problem of the color line."

Perhaps the greatest disillusionment of radical Black Christians is with the most radical element of the Evangelical "left." This radical segment tends to lean heavily on the Anabaptist tradition insofar as its social ethics and lifestyle are concerned. Such figures as Jim Wallis (editor of *Sojourners*), John Howard Yoder, William Stringfellow, and Jacques Ellul are representative of the movement. Their mood "tends to renounce political action and coercive power in favor of a more countercultural witness of non-violence and pacifism, exemplifying a whole new order based on Christian values."[12]

While the establishing of Christian countercultural values and lifestyles are certainly important, new Black Evangelicals feel that the seeming political withdrawal by radical White Christians is strangely reminiscent of the other-worldliness of fundamentalism.

Many New Black Evangelicals see the White Evangelical "left" to be as irrelevant to them as neo-evangelicalism was to their predecessors in the fifties. The new Blacks feel that White Evangelicals as a group, no matter how radical or young, will never come to grips with the demon of racism embedded within them.[13]

IV

Lerone Bennett, Jr., once wrote concerning the need for Black intellectual autonomy:

> The overriding need of the moment is for us to think with our own mind and to see with our own eyes. . . . We must create a new rationality, a new way of seeing, a new way of reasoning, a new way of thinking. . . . We see now through a glass whitely, and there can be no more desperate and dangerous task than the task which faces us now of trying to see with our own eyes.[14]

Unfortunately most militant Black Evangelicals have merely reacted against White Evangelicalism without clearly defining *their* alternative. This fallacy is partially due to their inability to develop a distinctly *Black* intellectual and spiritual frame of reference. Indeed, most radical Black Evangelicals still "see through a glass whitely." The overriding need for Black Evangelicals is the theological decolonization of their minds. This process, however, will not take place overnight.

First, new Black Evangelicals must begin to rethink those conclusions previously believed to be of God. They will have to raise the question "Hath God said?" in relation to what Evangelical theology has taught them. This will mean taking a fresh look at Scripture, devoid of White Evangelical hermeneutics and exegesis.

Black radical Christians must not avoid the task of theologizing for themselves by saying that White Evangelicals are *doctrinally* correct though *ethically* bankrupt. What is being suggested is that perhaps there is something fundamentally wrong with White Evangelical theology. Dr. James Cone correctly understood that "if concern for social action does not flow smoothly from the present theology, [you should] see what its weaknesses are, and then you will know better how to behave in the world in light of your relationship with God."[15]

The notion that White Evangelicals are not involved in liberating social action because they are racist is true as far as it goes. How then does one explain the same social paralysis on the part of *Black* Evangelicals? It is impossible for an individualistic, dispensationalist theology to be a liberating force for any oppressed people.

Second, given this reality, it is imperative that New Black Evangelicals construct *their own* liberating theology. Such an endeavor will be fallacious if Black Christians merely blackenize the theologies of E. J. Carnell, Carl F. H. Henry, Francis Schaeffer, and other White Evangelical "saints." Black Evangelicals must construct a theology out of their *own* social context. They must realize that all theology is contextual, including White American Evangelical theology.

The theological methodology of New Black Evangelicals must be dialectical in nature. That is, the theological starting point is both human and divine. Contrary to most evangelical theologizing, God does not eradicate concrete sociopolitical realities when he reveals himself to his people. Conversely, Black Evangelicals must hold that theology must be epistemologically valid. That is, while God uses the human/social context to reveal himself, it is indeed *God* who is doing the revealing and not merely human projections.

Therefore New Black Evangelical theology must be biblical, that is, it must be grounded primarily in the witness of Holy Scripture. Without the Scriptures as a norm, all God-talk drops to the level of humanism and anthropology. In essence New Black Evangelicals must construct a biblically liberating and prophetic theology which will speak meaningfully to the plight of Black people all over the world.

Third, radical Black Evangelicals must redefine the concept of mission. Clarence Hilliard, a New Black Evangelical, introduced such a redefinition at the 1974 Lausanne Congress on World Evangelization by way of a protest paper. Hilliard contended that evangelism must include the redemption of both the individual and the social order.

One of the best New Black Evangelical missions to date, especially to Black youth, is the National Black Christian Students Conference. NBCSC was conceived in 1974 by Dr. Ruth Lewis Bentley, a psychologist at the University of Illinois Medical School, and Ms. Wyn Wright Potter, director of Black Christian Education for the Reformed Church in America. This Black Christian nationalist organization is attempting to politicize, theologize, and organize Black Christian students to bring holistic liberation into oppressed Black communities. The NBCSC is by far one of the most radical endeavors by New Black Evangelicals to date.

Finally, there needs to be a coalition between New Black Evangelicals and radical Black Pentecostals. Such a coalition could be mutually helpful. Black Evangelicals need the spiritual vitality and grass-roots organization of the Pentecostals. The Pentecostals, on the other hand, need the systematic theological methodology that the Evangelicals can offer. Together, these two movements could become the most dynamic liberating force to take place in the Black community in twenty years.

Radical Black Pentecostals by themselves have effected positive change within the black community. The Rev. Herbert Daughtry, a militant Black nationalist Pentecostal, is in the forefront of the Black liberation struggle in Brooklyn, New York, Chairperson of Brooklyn's militant Black United Front and pastor of House of the Lord Pentecostal Church, Daughtry has in every respect preached and practiced a Black political theology. Other radical Pentecostals, too numerous to mention, are following suit.

In summary, New Black Evangelicals must meet the challenge of the times by preaching and practicing a prophetic and liberating gospel of liberation. Their faith must be able to speak meaningfully to the social, economic, spiritual, and political powerlessness in America's Black communities. Developing a holistic theology and gospel will not be easy. There are no simple solutions. But under the guidance of the Holy Spirit and the Lordship of Christ the Liberator, Black radical Evangelicals can become God's agents of change.

Notes

1. Several periodicals have covered the Evangelical resurgence over the past two years. One of the more comprehensive coverages was in *Time*, vol. 110, no. 26 (December 26, 1977), pp. 52-58.

2. Richard Quebedeaux, *The Worldly Evangelicals* (New York: Harper & Row, 1978), p. 84.

3. Quebedeaux's *Worldy Evangelicals* and *The Young Evangelicals* (New York: Harper & Row, 1974) as well as David F. Wells and John D. Woodbridge's *The Evangelicals* (Nashville: Abingdon Press, 1975) have given minimal coverage to Black Evangelicals.

4. William Pannell, *My Friend the Enemy* (Waco, Texas: Word Books, 1968), p. 50.

5. Tom Skinner, *Black and Free* (Grand Rapids: Zondervan, 1968), p. 148.

6. Wells and Woodbridge, *The Evangelicals*, p. 111.

7. Pannell, *My Friend the Enemy*, p. 123.

8. Several hundred young Black Evangelicals came to the Inter-Varsity Missionary convention in 1970. Skinner, perhaps more than anyone else in the convention, captured the militant, revolutionary mood of these Black student radicals in his address "The Liberator Has Come."

9. Without doubt, William Bentley is the main theorist of Black Evangelical nationalism. Part of his thinking appeared as "Black Christian Nationalism: An Evangelical Perspective," *Black Books Bulletin*, vol. 4, no. 1 (Spring 1976), pp. 26-31.

10. E. J. Carnell, *The Case for Biblical Christianity*, ed. Ronald Nash (Grand Rapids: Wm. B. Eerdmans Publishing Company, 1969), pp. 90-91.

11. The last major confrontation between radical Black Evangelicals and White Evangelical "leftists" came at the 1975 ESA convention in Chicago. William Bentley and Wyn Wright Potter were the major Black "dissidents" at the conference; *Eternity* (November 1975), pp. 8-9.

12. Donald Dayton, "Where Now, Young Evangelicals?" *The Other Side*, vol. 11, no. 2 (March–April 1975), p. 55.

13. It is the opinion of many Black Evangelicals that White Christians, irrespective of political ideology, will continue to sidestep the crucial issue of racism in America. For a history of the failure of White reformist groups significantly to address the race question in America, see Robert Allen, with the collaboration of Pamela P. Allen, *Reluctant Reformer: Racism and Social Reform Movements in the United States* (Garden City, N.Y.: Doubleday Anchor Books, 1975).

14. Lerone Bennett, Jr., *The Challenge of Blackness* (Chicago: Johnson Publishing Company, 1972), p. 36.

15. "Interview with James H. Cone," *The Other Side*, vol. 10, no. 3 (May–June 1974), p. 10.

28

FACTORS IN THE ORIGIN AND FOCUS OF THE NATIONAL BLACK EVANGELICAL ASSOCIATION

William H. Bentley

From its inception in Los Angeles in 1963, the National Black Evangelical Association has, in the language of the streets "gone through many changes." Growing out of a deeply felt need for meaningful fellowship among Blacks of evangelical persuasion across denominational lines, NBEA soon expanded its horizons and its self-conception to include ministry. Fellowship and Ministry—these are the poles around which the Association revolves.

At first we were not certain as to whom we should direct our ministry, which seems strange in view of the statement above. Should we concentrate on our Black community exclusively, or should we attempt an "a-race" approach (which everyone said was *the* Gospel Way)? And if racial identity should play a part, a seemingly superfluous question in view of the conscious choice of our name, how could we reconcile ethnic consciousness with Christian witness? Were we any different from white Christians in whose institutions of the time we were for the most part not welcome? Such ambiguities and considerations underlay our soul searching.

But these and other uncertainties shortly received at least initial clarification when the existing racial realities within white evangelicalism confronted our expanding self-consciousness. It was then that we were convinced that our major, concentrated field of service would be, and rightly so, the community which both birthed and nurtured us—Afro-America! Later this initial dedication to reaching our people was to receive more positive reenforce-

This essay is from William H. Bentley, *National Black Evangelical Association: Evolution of a Concept of Ministry* (Chicago: published by author, 1979), chapters 1 and 7.

ment as we progressively came to see that as a distinct people we had peculiar needs which whites as a group were not able to deal with—because of the fact of our distinctiveness.

Even a cursory glance at our programs of the first five conventions (Los Angeles, Philadelphia, Baltimore, Detroit, and Cleveland)[1] will show how pervasive was the idea among us that the "best" and "proper" methods for reaching our people—indeed all people—were those we had learned in the Bible Schools and theological seminaries of white evangelicalism. The author remembers, somewhat humorously, the reception his early dissenting from this tradition received when he daringly suggested that Black people, particularly their leaders, needed to understand their own people before they could effectively minister to them. Considering the background of the situation, perhaps such a revolutionary challenge to the exclusivity of white evangelical models should have been expected. Nevertheless, the subsequent history of the Association has shown how revolutionary that unintended challenge was.

In this respect, at least initially, we were not particularly clear in our vision, and were far from prophetic in our insights. Theological education, then as largely now,[2] was for the most part oblivious (due to its often unconscious, and therefore seldom questioned, preoccupation with its own ethnic consciousness) to the specific group needs of Afro-Americans. Since we were trained in such institutions it was virtually unavoidable that we would as unconsciously absorb the same views as those who taught us. Accordingly, there was little or no serious thought given to the development of viable strategies of an indigenous nature for reaching Black America.[3]

The closest we came to anything remotely akin to developing indigenous strategies was in a paper read at the Philadelphia Convention on "The Nature and Manifestation of Race Prejudice" (a title not original with the author), in which an attempt was made to explore the origins and contemporary development of racism within American culture in general, and within white American Christianity in particular. The paper sought to address the question of how white American religious culture has affected the nature of the Black religious experience. Today, there are many who are attempting to deal with the question,[4] but in 1964 and 65, neither Black nor white evangelicals seemed aware of the extent to which this was true. Nevertheless, there were some who had some sensitivity to the issues involved in a consideration of this valid query.

At the time, though unknown to us, a few of us were antedating many Black secularists in our rudimentary beginnings of coming to grips with the cruciality of ethnic self-acceptance. Thus, though unknown outside the parochialism of our endemic Black evangelicalism, NBEA early manifested the potential of becoming a pace-setter. Before "Black Power" became the rallying cry it later did, some Black evangelicals among us were thinking seriously in terms of group consciousness.

As indicated above, this essay on the origins of race prejudice within white

American Christianity, and how this has affected both form and content of the Black religious tradition, created some small furor. But because at that time our priorities were elsewhere, the ideas expressed and explored gathered dust and were filed away in that shadowy place where all ideas go when their time has not come. Little hope was expressed that these ideas would experience a resurrection. For then, as now,[5] a searching analysis of the roots of racism in Christian context was a major no-no! It was, and is, almost as unpopular with some Blacks as with many white brethren.

Some of the reasons for this reticence were related to our philosophy of economic support. Few of us within our organization were able to believe that sufficient financial support could be obtained from other sources than the standard white institutions to which we as Black evangelicals together with those who shared our separatist stance [6] were tied. It was from these same white institutions that we drew our role models and standards of leadership. The idea that traditional Black Christianity has for the most part been functionally and very often financially independent of white Christianity never seemed to occur to us.

Here was a strange thing! We were seeking to reach people, our people, but we had little awareness of the resources to be found within our own religious tradition, resources that had been forged in the fires of affliction and had not been exhausted by the mere passage of time. We could not draw on these because we hardly recognized their existence.[7] This is a rock upon which all white-based Black organizations eventually founder. The resulting cycle of dependency is so complete that those caught in its coils are virtually unable to escape. The will to self-discovery is paralyzed and Blacks caught in this situation are doomed to look at themselves through the eyes of others. It is no wonder that appreciation for Black institutions and Black resources is so infrequent, and—even then—so inadequate. And even less frequently drawn upon!

This is no blanket condemnation of white support, providing that no dehumanizing or paternalistic strings are attached to it. The history of the Black church has shown that substantial support from white Christians has played a more than respectable role in its welfare. Nevertheless, the Black church, especially the Black church in Black structures,[8] has for the most part remained financially independent in spite of its often precarious economic backing. This is a fact not sufficiently appreciated by many detractors of the Black church. Because of its independence, the Black community expects and demands that all religious interests and institutions minister effectively to community needs.

This is a major key to in-depth evangelization of Black Americans. It lies with the Black focus on Black community needs. In saying this no intent is made to deny or invalidate efforts by whites to reach Black Americans either in the past or contemporarily. But we wish to stress the point that the major efforts to accomplish the in-depth evangelization of Black Americans must be the work of Black leadership, with indigenous methods, and with the concept of total needs of the Black community in mind. Why this is so will be discussed in other places throughout the body of this essay.

* * *

The theology of James Cone,[9] and others who are in the same or similar theological bag, has had an effect, salutary or otherwise, upon the doing of theology in this country. Cone in particular, is also enjoying considerable exposure across the water in a number of European theological schools.

Primarily, Black Theology has a wider currency among white theologians who are not known to be evangelical. White evangelical theologians are not exactly unaware of the existence of Black Theology, since a few Black evangelicals have had minimal input into these sacred precincts via academia,[10] but for the most part, they are far more comfortable dealing with Latin American liberation theology than with this home-grown variety. Which is one of the endemic conceptual as well as structural weaknesses of much of American theology—a chronic myopia in matters pertaining to the interaction of the American social context with the doing of theology. On the whole, therefore, there has been next to nothing done to recognize the existence of Black Theology as a viable contribution, or even a critique to American evangelical theology.[11] It is at least arguable that what we shall have to await is the go-ahead signal from Basel, Heidelberg, Cambridge, Oxford, or the Sorbonne, before conceding even its conditional existence. As Blacks, however, we need not be dependent upon the outcome of that verdict, whether it comes or not. Within NBEA, its existence and its right to existence is acknowledged. What remains to be done is to construct a Black evangelical approach to it.

Nevertheless, not even white evangelical theology can entirely and forever escape from at least an acknowledgment of Black Theology's presence. And the credit, or blame, for much of the little contact they have had with it, and probably will have with it, has come from a tiny group of Blacks, mostly centrally located within the theological discussions which take place within NBEA theology workshops.

As yet, there is no real Black evangelical Black Theology. This is so for several reasons. Very few Black evangelicals are even conversant with the work James Cone and others are doing. The names Shelby Rooks, Henry Mitchell, Gayraud Wilmore, Cecil Cone, Deotis Roberts strike no familiar chord and call forth no recognition from the majority of us. And of the few who are aware of the existence of these and others, numbers of us prematurely reject what we little understand. Still others quickly condemn James Cone, the recognized leader of the movement, as a "radical" who is attempting to institutionalize Black racism as an antidote to white racism.[12] But perhaps the most telling indictment of all is, in the eyes of a considerable

number, the "brazenness" of postulating "an ethnic brand of theology." For
as a group, Black evangelicals believe that theology should be color blind.
Black theology is therefore "divisive"!

When we look at the ranks of those who are at least rudimentarily aware of
what is happening in the realm of Black Theology, we discover that reaction
rather than action is the most familiar response. Nevertheless, there have
been some scattered, sporadic, and impressionistic attempts on the part of a
few to suggest elements of what a Black Theology should be.[13] Specific plans
are now underway at the forthcoming Atlanta III Convention of NBEA, to
address this very need and to get such a project at least ready for the
launching pad. The project will be the joint product of Anthony Evans,
doctoral student at Dallas Theological Seminary and Chairman of the Commission on Theology, this author, and perhaps several younger theologues
who have already made some contributions to the development of an
evangelical viewpoint.[14]

The very intense interest shown in this new aspect of NBEA ministry is an
indication that we are becoming less and less dependent upon taking our first
cues from our white preceptors before we ourselves decide upon the discussion of issues crucial to our experience as Blacks and Christians in this
country. What Blacks need most, in the eyes of this writer, as well as a
number of others of similar persuasion, is a theological interpretation and
exposition of our collective experience, the Black Agenda as perceived by
those of us who are committed to the Lordship of Jesus Christ and who
believe that contained within the essence of the liberative Gospel of Jesus is
the revealed rationale for prosecuting the total deliverance of Black people
here in America.

We are, therefore, proclaiming our Declaration of Independence from
uncritical dependence upon white evangelical theologians who would attempt to tell us what the content of our efforts at liberation should be. In
an effort to make clear that our Declaration is not from theology per se, it will
be made more and more evident that our starting point will be as much the
doctrine of God and his attributes as the most staunch evangelical theological
system. In fleeing from the lion we seek to make certain that we do not fall
into the arms of the subjective bear.[15] We see no necessity of freeing
ourselves from our own evangelicalism. We do seek to free ourselves from
the *implied norms* of white theologians' exclusivisms! Simply stated, we will
think for ourselves and will no longer submit, even if that "enforcement" has
been the product of our own collective minds, to the compulsion to *first* seek
others' opinions before we formulate our own.

As stated above, we are aware, as are traditional white theologians, that the
doctrine of God is virtually determinant of the type of theology one comes up
with, but we are equally aware of the fact that merely starting with the idea of
God does not necessarily lead to a humane doctrine of Man! Had this been
automatically so, then the history of Christianity in America would have been

singularly free from theologically supported and derived systems and etiquettes or racism—something which a study of such history shows was decidedly not the case.

Black Theology, then, as some of us as Black evangelicals see it, in its present form, boldly addresses itself to this very issue. Its chief affirmation, at least in the view of James Cone, its leading exponent, is that God is active in the struggles of the oppressed in a special way in order to effect their liberation. The same view comes forth, with different emphases, in the work of Deotis Roberts, Cecil W. Cone, Henry Mitchell, Shelby Rooks, and others. In these and other writings, it is made clear that God's sovereign intervention gives the struggle a transcendent dignity, and justifies the unconquerable tenacity with which Black people in this country have continued the struggle.

As Biblical rationale for this principle of liberation, Cone proposes the Exodus Model. According to this model, God's intervention on the side of the oppressed hinges solely upon divine election and not through real or supposed virtues possessed by Black folk. Thus we are rendered free from the necessity of making ourselves to be qualitatively, in an absolute sense, "better" or "worse" than other ethnics, whether comprising the majority or minority population.

Cone, Mitchell, Roberts, and some others see parallels between the experience of Israel of the Old Testament, and that of Black Americans within America. But the Exodus Model is not the only one made use of by other Black theologians. For instance, Shelby Rooks (of the University of Chicago Divinity School) critiques the Exodus Model and sees it as inadequate for explaining major aspects of Black experience. Instead, he opts for what, to him, more satisfactorily accounts for our experience. To him, Blacks should be viewed as in exile (another biblical idea) and he proposes to call his model, the "Diaspora Model."[16] And there is the view of William Jones. To him, neither the Exodus Model nor the Diaspora Model have substance. If there is divine intervention at all, it is so ambiguous as to be irrelevant. To base the case on the Exodus Model gains nothing, for even in the case of Israel, it has historically proven nothing. Israel has suffered at least as much at the hands of the nations as she has experienced deliverance at God's hand. Thus Jones injects the problems of theodicy into the discussion and tentatively resolves the issue by coming up with, if not a limited God, one who is not sure on which side to intervene. In true William Jones fashion, he comes up with the idea that if Black people or any other people depend solely upon the supposed will of a God, limited or otherwise, for their deliverance, they will exhibit the same ambiguous collective experience as did the Jews, Afro-Americans, and any other oppressed and powerless group. The best, and safest, thing to do is to get on the battlefield and assist God in gaining the victory! Thus Jones' model is called the "Humanocentric,"[17] in distinction to the others, which are "theocentric."

It ought to be obvious from what has been said: the Black evangelicals are not remotely as advanced in Black theological thought as are the men whose views have been briefly and inadequately given above. It is partly in recognition of this fact that our Commission on Theology evolved. Long before the idea was accepted, the need was recognized. For if there are, and there are, substantive bases for recognition of common ground with the *idea* of a Black Theology, there are areas of concern upon which Black evangelicals, as a group, come to some differences in conclusions than some of our less than evangelical brethren come to. Thus we see our task, among other things, as a coming to grips with *both* theological traditions. Not that we expect, or even aspire, to come up with *the* truth. But we certainly hope to learn much more about the theological dimensions of our collective experience than the knowledge we thus far have in our grasp.

Within the Association itself, our interest in Black Theology grew naturally out of the Black awareness movements of the sixties. It has already been indicated that our first rudimentary contact came at the Chicago Convention of 1968. In Atlanta, despite the radical color of the Convention, there was no reference made to it.

Following Jackson, Mississippi, however, interest in it began to grow. In the same period Black writers like Howard Jones (*Shall We Overcome?*), James Earl Massey (at the time his unpublished article was in a manuscript edited by this author), William Pannell *(My Friend the Enemy)*, Bobby Harrison *(When God Was Black)*, Columbus Salley and Ron Behm (Behm is white and co-author with Salley of the important book *Your God Is Too White*), and the later books of Tom Skinner *(How Black Is the Gospel,* etc.) discussed aspects of it.

In addition, a conference involving both Blacks and whites was held in Boston, Massachusetts, which sought to discuss the issues raised by the Black consciousness ferment. Among the leaders who addressed themselves to this cluster of issues was Roxbury pastor, politician, and educator, Michael Haynes, Ron Potter, Carl Ellis (now a student a Westminster Theological Seminary), and others. The results of this conference, which was not held under the auspices of NBEA, were written up and became the substance of an entire issue of *Freedom Now*, which later was to be transmuted into *The Other Side*.

At the second New York Convention, there was little emphasis placed upon Black awareness per se. But of significance at that meeting was a series of off-the-cuff interviews conducted by John Alexander of *The Other Side*. The interview involved several members of an intra-NBEA Black Caucus,[18] which became the basis of another special issue under the heading of "The New Black Evangelicals."[19] Ron Potter, one of the better informed and articulate younger Black theologues, was special editor of the issue, which featured articles by Tom Skinner, Potter, Clarence Hilliard, Randy Jones (Philadelphia pastor and one of the more advanced exponents of an economic critique of the role of evangelicalism within the American social system, etc.), and this author. It also included a major discussion of some distinctives of the Black evangelical movement, in which Wyn Wright Potter (cochairperson of the National Black Christian Students Conference, and now a coordinator of Christian Education activities within the Office of the Black Council of the Reformed Church of America), and Debbie Scott (she has since adopted an African name—Asabi Yakini), together with others participated.

The issue likewise presented an interview with James Cone, though from another connection, and it was generally assumed that our contribution was intended to present some sort of interaction, though perhaps very basic, with the views of Cone. My article, together with the co-authored bibliographical one, was a quick sortie into the area of suggesting some principles, hermeneutical and otherwise, which could go into gathering materials for discussing a Black evangelical approach to a Black theology.

It was at the second Chicago Convention, however, where a consciously Black awareness emphasis was present, and where NBEA initiated the format of a theological workshop, so that the issues inherent in construction of such a theology could be debated. Discussants were three of our younger theological students: Anthony Evans, of Dallas Seminary, Ronald Potter, of Rutgers University, and John Skinner, at that time of Union Theological Seminary in New York. To observers, this was a major highlight of the Convention, attracting overflow crowds and productive of some very enlightening interaction between the discussants.

The format initiated here was repeated at San Francisco the following year, and this time Anthony Evans, now Chairman of the Commission on Theology, presided. In the absence of Potter, co-chairman of the Commission, Lem Tucker of Westminster Seminary, Professor Henry Mitchell of Claremont and Fuller Seminaries, and this author engaged in dialogue.

Again at Atlanta II, the format was expanded to include a paper read by Professor Noel Erskine, of Emory University and Candler School of Theology. The results of this meeting included a less strident emphasis than those that preceded this one, with all participants and observers agreeing that perhaps the meeting was the crucial one in which all ground was cleared and the laying of a foundation for a viable Black evangelical theology could commence.[20]

This rather extended treatment of the expanding role of theology, and Black theology in particular, as it has developed within NBEA, has several purposes.

One is to show how the emergence of this activity has broadened the scope of how the entire Association conceives its mission of how to reach Black America with the Gospel. Two, it suggests that we are evolving guiding principles which are pertinent to developing indigenous strategies for the areas of missions, evangelism, Christian education, higher education, social action, children and youth ministries, community outreach, political education and involvement, and economic issues involving the collective lives of

Afro-Americans. Thirdly, we are coming to be more convinced that programs of social action must be first undergirded with clear understanding of the issues involved and be capable of developing strategies, and not merely reacting, which can effectively enable us to cope with social reality and to build in spite of it.

Because as evangelicals, we have been taught—often without adequate appreciation of our own social, political, economic, and religious realities, or with insufficient understanding of our capabilities and gifts—to see ourselves as others see us, the first step toward answering the question of who we really are must come from the awareness of the frame of reference we are to locate within in order to know ourselves. In this we do not deny the correctness, within limits, of the view of ourselves others have of us. We cannot see ourselves as others see us. But the point made is that we cannot allow the *determination* of who we are to be placed into, or remain as the case may be, outside ourselves and in the hands of others, no matter who they are. The Delphian oracle long ago gave good advice: "Know thyself!"

Again, because an historical and contemporary characteristic of evangelicalism is to dichotomize too artificially "social" and "sacred"—in its extreme form we believe this to be more cultural than Gospel—we Blacks who have come to be called "evangelicals" (and so identify ourselves), having been nurtured under this world view from which the dichotomy comes, have need to be more critical of the extent to which the dichotomy is valid and actually reflective of biblical truth. The outcome of our evaluation should bring new knowledge not only of who we are, but also a deeper appreciation of the cultural realities which are indigenous to us as a distinct people.

A very important part of our cultural heritage is a tendency which may be regarded as the very opposite of the dichotomy. Unchecked, and uncritically accepted, it can lead us to that other extreme—which is just as incomplete and only partially reflective of Gospel truth. Our tendency to social perception, carried to the extreme, can lead to an equally unbiblical blurring of distinctions, where distinctions ought to and do exist. In either case, we will be left with a truncated Gospel. Either it will be so severely individualistic, that it is for all practical purposes societally blind. Or, and this is the other horn of the dilemma, we can be so blinded by some elements of our cultural heritage, that we in effect identify the Gospel with our Black culture. Caring for the whole, we must not minimize care for the soul! Our escape from the dilemma consists in our critical adoption of the more realistic "Both-And!"

All this boils down to the fact that we must be anchored to the Rock even while geared to the times! Both extremes must be carefully avoided, in the interest of full truth. Both extremes express important aspects of it.

Perhaps as good a note to end this part of our exploration as any other is to call all of us, Black and white, evangelical, fundamentalist, "Bible believing," or whatever, to the Scripture found in Luke 4:18: "The Gospel IS liberation!"

Notes

1. A complete listing of all national conventions to date, through 1979, appears in an appendix at the end of the book. Also dates and locations of future conventions will appear in specific places in the body of the history.

2. Black Theology, especially in the works of James Cone, but in a very rudimentary sense also to be found in the works of a few Black evangelicals (see the Bibiography), has introduced some unwanted leaven into the theological lump. It is true that such theological leadership, evangelical or otherwise, hardly trembles in its boots at the appearance of this immature upstart. Nevertheless, even in its admittedly incomplete form, the theological upstart has addressed itself to the interpretation of the entire Black American experience, something white traditional theological exponents never did. Black Theology has raised some very grave moral and ethical questions and has injected them into the establishment theological debate—questions which cannot be ignored or brushed aside with the time-serving remark that Black people are subsumed under the rubric of the universal. The rationale, however, for this particular ethnic approach is not based solely on response to the negation or ignoring of the Black ethnic experience. As noted above, its basic reason for being is to expound the Black experience in the light of the Biblical revelation.

3. The sole exception consisted in some brief remarks which the author addressed to an opening session of the first Los Angeles meeting in 1963. The biblical passage Ezekiel 3 was the basis of the remarks, and through them the message of the need for empathy rather than mere sympathy was expressed.

4. We are now in the post-sixties era, when such topics are regarded by many younger Black Christians, and by some whites, as irrelevant and passé. The gains made possible by Civil Rights and Liberation activists, in spite of the large element of bombast and rhetoric associated with both movements, are so taken for granted by the present generation "which knows not struggle" that it is as though the struggle never had been. Great effort, therefore, is required to cause the present generation, particularly those whose parents were peers to the activists, to think of racism within American culture as endemic and self-perpetuating, and therefore very much present in basically undiminished form. This is especially noteworthy, since present-day social analysis in this area places far more emphasis on the factor of class than race.

5. Resistance to in-depth analyses of racism comes from an array of sources and will not be entered into here. We are concerned to make the point that there is resistance and it is as alive and well as it was in the sixties. To date the only contemporary attempt to make such an analysis occurred a decade ago, but the majority culture did not accept the results then, and does not now. The Kerner Report was never accepted and made palatable to white America, and that is where the real roots of the problem originate. The problem is far deeper, however, than even the Kerner Report was able to demonstrate, and goes far back into the social, psychological, economic, and religious past of the nation. There are some unresolved basic antinomies enshrined in the political philosophy of the ruling documents of this country, and the ethical practices which historically have grown out of them, which keeps the racial pot boiling without ever cooking anything to mutual satisfaction. It is this author's view that such analyses must continue to be made so long as racism within American culture remains undealt with to the extent that little meaningful and measurable systemic change results. Ironically, an increasing number of Blacks of all ages (but not all classes) oppose such analyses almost as much as do many whites. Their view seems to be, "Why rub salt in old wounds?" A valid point—*if* that is all that is involved.

6. See my article in *The Evangelicals* . . . "Bible Believers in the Black Community." *Black evangelicalism as a distinct phenomenon*—and so identified—is of very recent origin, and developed out of the same forces which reacted with a new burst of orthodoxy to the issues of the unresolved "Fundamentalist-Liberal" controversy of the late 1920's and '30's. In its earliest form, Black evangelicalism (as a distinct movement outside the traditional mainline Black church) was most influenced by the Scofield Bible and the Bible school movement, which itself was heavily influenced by elements of the Dallas Theological Seminary faculty, notably the Lewis Sperry Chafer theology. It adopted, therefore, the same stance toward the traditional Black

church in Black structures, which it regarded as empty of Gospel proclamation, and the Black church within white structures—which it regarded as apostate—as white fundamentalism did toward the major white denominations. Until this day there is much in Black evangelicalism which consciously stands outside the mainstream of the Black church, which it adjudges to be apostate and therefore pathological. Black evangelicalism nevertheless as a belief system though not necessarily identifying itself by that name has historically been the position of Black Christianity and contemporarily exists in major dimensions within mainline Black denominations in both Black and white structures.

7. Special mention is made of the fact that the Black church survived the "Great Depression" years because Black people believed in their institution as having been raised up by God as a shelter in the midst of their experiences of storm and stress. Long before the days when we had a significant middle class, our congregations were made up for the most part of laborers and domestics and others of severely limited income. Still we kept our churches open with beyond sacrificial giving both of our money and ourselves. It is somewhat ironic that in contemporary Black America, when the income of our middle class has risen to the highest level in our entire history, there is a higher incidence of church closings due to inability to maintain them than there was during the leanest years of the Depression. Values and not mere financial ability have a lot to do with performance in this area. The writer is most personally and intimately familiar with Black Pentecostalism, where this phenomenon was observed by him.

8. The term is used to describe the institutional identity of ethnic Black Christianity historically and contemporarily. See "Bible Believers in the Black Community," and also the First B. Moses James Lectures (the joint product of this author and Dr. Noel Erskine of the Candler School of Theology) held at New Brunswick Theological Seminary and sponsored by the Office of the Black Council of the Reformed Church of America. The specific contribution of this author was "An Historical Overview and Interpretation of the Black Church in America."

9. Cone is the unrivaled progenitor of contemporary expressions of Black Theology. As an accomplished academic, he has within that context continued to place before his peers theological works which have provoked both heat and light. Although others have written on the subject, he more than others has commanded the critical attention of the professional community. His first book, *Black Theology and Black Power*, was a preliminary statement of the relationship of the Black liberation struggle, then carried on almost exclusively by secularists who were hostile to the Black church, to Christian theology in a Black perspective. It also was revelatory of the historical and contemporary inability, or unwillingness, or both, of traditional white theology to deal humanely with the Black experience. Its record has shown that it had been unable to extricate itself from participation in the climate of racial oppression which the white church, for the most part, had been more than a silent partner to. His second book, *A Black Theology of Liberation*, went a step further and built on the thesis that Black Theology was God's contemporary message of deliverance to the Oppressed, actualized and paradigmed by Blacks, as the most oppressed group in America. The third book, *The Spirituals and the Blues*, dealt with the substratum of materials, or at least some of them, which are a fruitful source of Black Theology. His fourth book, *God of the Oppressed*, is his most positive statement to date, although it is likewise a medium of dealing with his accumulation of critics, Black and white. It is his most ambitious struggle to relate his theology to the doctrine of God, and to show how it derives therefrom.

10. The author has had several fairly substantive contacts with some of the leading white evangelical theologians in a professional capacity, and in each case they were unable to see any validity in the case for a separate branch of theology called "Black." To a man, their feeling was that the Black experience, indeed all experience could well and adequately be subsumed under the rubric of traditional theology as practiced in its classical form in European and American theological seminaries. The same men were willing, however, to concede at least for purposes of debate, some conditional validity to Latin American liberation theology.

11. See, for example, the July-August 1975 issue of *The Other Side*, and also the papers written by Randy Jones and Ron Potter which were read at the Dallas Convention of NBEA. These papers were a part of an informal discussion with Dr. John Walvoord of Dallas Theological Seminary on the possibility of a Black Theology.

12. Elridge Cleaver in his *Soul on Fire* assumes that there is no discernible difference between Black ethnocentrism and white. Both are equally productive of negative response to outsiders. Formally, he is right, of course. Black hearts are as evil as are white ones. And yet, although there is much more to it than we can take time here to explicate, the question of who possesses and

continues to possess the power in the entire society to make its definitions "stick" lifts the discussion to another level than the formal. What Blacks *might* do *if* they were in power is strictly an a priori, which while valid, is not a final or complete answer to the question. Some Black apologists seek to make a distinction between "white racism" and "Black response." And while there is a good deal of truth there, yet the possible danger to drift off into semantics needs to likewise be guarded against. Sometimes it just might not be possible to clearly distinguish between the two.

13. Witness the ensuing debates within NBEA beginning with Chicago II and running through Atlanta II. See in addition a paper read at a ministers division meeting of Operation PUSH, included in the bibliographical listing.

14. At present Anthony Evans is scheduled to treat "The Biblical Foundation for an Evangelical Black Theology," and the author will deal with "The Contextual Basis for an Evangelical Black Theology " (the titles are subject to revision prior to Convention). It is to be hoped that some in-depth interaction will be possible with some of the sharper young thinkers such as Carl Ellis and Ron Potter, and others.

15. Dr. Francis Schaeffer expressed himself some time ago in an article in *Christianity Today* as having some concern that certain younger Black scholars were in danger of succumbing to the wiles of Barthianism in their pursuit of the varieties of Black Theology. Some of the same fears were expressed in a dialogue which took place at a conference which featured Dr. Schaeffer and in which this author was a respondent. As it is remembered, the view was expressed by Dr. Schaeffer that reaction to the failures of traditional white evangelical theology to deal satisfactorily with racism in American society could lead younger Black scholars into the mazes of neo-orthodoxy—as though such a theology was needed to give substance to Black theological protest and formulation. The fact of the matter is, neo-orthodoxy is as white as is evangelical theology. It relates even less, in a nonacademic way, to the every-day struggles of Blacks.

16. The concept is developed in a rather well-reasoned article by Rooks which appeared in *The Black Church*: Quarterly Journal of the Black Ecumenical Commission of Massachusetts, vol. 2, no. 1. The title of the article was "Toward the Promised Land."

17. William Jones, for a time, was a member of the history department at Yale University and identifies himself as Unitarian-Universalist. Jones, an avowed humanist, sees little validity to either the Exodus Model or the Diaspora Model. Theodicy is to him the crucial determinant. How can there be a good and just God if he allows his chosen people to suffer as much as the God of the Bible allows his people the Jews to suffer. These views and others are found in his book *Is God a White Racist?*

18. Because some felt that this Convention down-played and markedly deemphasized Black awareness in Christian context, the interview with John Alexander provided a forum for airing concerns that NBEA might be drifting from its ethnic-conscious base. We somewhat uneasily referred to our interview session as an "intra-NBEA Black Caucus."

19. The lead article in this issue (July-August 1975), probably the most important one, was written by Ron. It set the stage for a better understanding of all others. The central theme expressed by Potter was the affirmation that Blacks would think for themselves. He likewise gave a concise overview of the development of the Black evangelical movement and traces its origin to a more recent time than does this author. Theodore Moran, dean of students at Payne Theological Seminary and assistant professor of Church and Society at the same institution, should be mentioned at this point since his name was not included in the references made above. He has written a perceptive article in the issue also.

20. This is the substance of a personal communication by Tony Evans to the author. All parties to the most recent discussions agree that while the earlier sessions were hot and heavy, they were probably necessary to clear the air and lay the foundation for a more positive statement of the substance of an evangelical Black Theology. Of particularly helpful assistance was Noel Erskine. His acute and sensitive mind forced all of us to clarify our conception and articulation. Carl Ellis also made valuable contributions. Plans are being made for the production of printed essays which will be the substance of the theological conversations to be held at Atlanta III in 1979.

29

A STATEMENT OF THE BLACK CATHOLIC CLERGY CAUCUS, APRIL 18, 1968

The Catholic Church in the United States, primarily a white racist institution, has addressed itself primarily to white society and is definitely a part of that society. On the contrary, we feel that her primary, though not exclusive work, should be in the area of institutional, attitudinal and societal change. Within the ghetto, the role of the Church is no longer that of spokesman and leader. Apart from a more direct spiritual role, the Church's part must now be that of supporter and learner. This is a role that white priests in the black community have not been accustomed to playing and are not psychologically prepared to play.

The Catholic Church apparently is not cognizant of changing attitudes in the black community and is not making the necessary, realistic adjustments. The present attitude of the black community demands that black people control their own affairs and make decisions for themselves. This does not mean, however, that black leadership is to be exercised only in the black community, but must function throughout the entire gamut of ecclesial society.

It is imperative that the Church recognize this change. White persons working in the black community must be educated to these changing attitudes, and must be prepared to accept and function in conjunction with the prevailing attitudes of the black community.

One of these changes must be a re-evaluation of present attitudes towards black militancy. The violence occurring in the black communities has been *categorically* condemned and has called forth a wide variety of response, from "shoot to kill" to the recommendation of the Kerner Report. Such violence has even been specified as "Negro violence," as though there were a substantial or significant difference between violence in the black community and that which has occurred consistently throughout the history of the United

This document was first published by the National Office of Black Catholics in its magazine of Black liturgy, *Freeing the Spirit*, vol. 1, no. 3, Summer 1972.

States and of the world. Black people are fully aware that violence has been consciously and purposely used by America from its fight for independence to its maintenance of white supremacy. Since the black man is encouraged to fight abroad for white America's freedom and liberty, we are now asking why it is not moral for him to fight for his liberty at home. We go on record as recognizing:

1. the reality of militant protest;
2. that non-violence in the sense of black non-violence hoping for concessions after white brutality is dead;
3. that the same principles on which we justify legitimate self-defense and just warfare must be applied to violence when it represents black response to white violence;
4. the appropriateness of responsible, positive militancy against racism is the only Christian attitude against this or any other social evil.

Because of its past complicity with and active support of prevailing attitudes and institutions of America, the Church is now in an extremely weak position in the black community. In fact, the Catholic Church is rapidly dying in the black community. In many areas, there is a serious defection especially on the part of black Catholic youth. The black community no longer looks to the Catholic Church with hope. And unless the Church, by an immediate, effective and total reversing of its present practices, rejects and denounces *all* forms of racism within its ranks and institutions and in the society of which she is a part, she will become unacceptable in the black community.

We, **The Black Catholic Clergy Caucus**, strongly and deeply believe that there are few choices left to the Catholic Church, and unless it is to remain an enclave speaking to itself, it must begin to consult the black members of the Church, clerical, religious and lay. It must also begin to utilize the personnel resources of black Catholics in leadership and advisory positions in the whole Church and allow them to direct, for the most part, the mission of the Church in the black community. It is especially important that the financial resources channelled into the work of the Church in the black community be allocated and administered by black Catholic leadership.

To this end, in charity, we demand:

1. That there be black priests in decision-making positions on the diocesan level, and above all in the black community.
2. That a more effective utilization of black priests be made. That the situation where the majority of black priests are in institutions be changed; that black priests be given a choice of assignment on the basis of inclination and talent.
3. That where no black priests belong to the diocese, efforts be made to get them in, or at least consultation with black priests or black-thinking white priests be made.

4. That special efforts be made to recruit black men for the priesthood. Black priests themselves are better qualified for this recruitment at a time when the Catholic Church is almost irrelevant to the young black men.
5. That dioceses provide centers of training for white priests intending to survive in black communities.
6. That within the framework of the United States Catholic Conference, a black-directed department be set up to deal with the Church's role in the struggle of black people for freedom.
7. That in all of these areas black religious be utilized as much as possible.
8. That black men, married as well as single, be ordained permanent deacons to aid in this work of the Church.
9. That each diocese allocate a substantial fund to be used in establishing and supporting permanent programs for black leadership training.

30

TOWARD A BLACK
CATHOLIC THEOLOGY

Edward K. Braxton

There is an old saying that if you scratch the surface of one who thinks about life you will uncover a philosopher. In a similar way if you scratch the surface of one who thinks about religion you will uncover a theologian. Can it therefore be argued that if you scratch the surface of a Black Catholic who is thinking about religion in his or her context you have a Black Catholic theologian and that the product of his/her reflections constitutes a Black theology?

Theology can be defined in a host of ways. Theology may be technical philosophical reflection on the foundational questions of religion in the context of a university. By employing the methods of the academy it seeks to disclose the fundamental intelligibility of theological discourse. This may be termed foundational theology. Theology may also be technical philosophical reflection on the central themes, symbols, values of a particular church tradition in a church context. This brand of theology seeks to integrate, reinterpret and pass on the tradition that constitutes the self-concept of a religious group such as Roman Catholicism. This enterprise, sometimes apologetic in stance, may be termed systematic theology. There is yet a third possibility. Theology may be a reflection on the concrete experiential world and the wide-spread experience of oppression of various individuals and groups. In this context theology looks to the symbols of freedom and liberation that are a part of its tradition because they may provide the necessary catalysts for transforming the concrete social order. This may be called practical or pastoral theology. Very few Catholic lay persons of any hue know

This article first appeared in *Freeing the Spirit*, vol. 5, no. 2 (1977), pp. 3-6. Edward K. Braxton is a priest of the Archdiocese of Chicago who has taught at the Harvard Divinity School and Notre Dame. He is presently vicar for Theological Renewal of the diocese of Cleveland.

very much about academic or foundational theology. They simply do not have the technical skills for such an enterprise.

Most, however, do know something of practical or pastoral theology. From Sunday sermons, Catholic newspapers and periodicals they glean a conglomerate of ideas which they come to think of as "the Church view" on such issues as God, Jesus, the Church, morality, the fate of the dead, etc. Further they may be aware of the "social teachings of the Church" on war, racism, respect for life, etc., as expressed in papal encyclicals and Bishop's pastoral letters. It is no secret however that in spite of what they may be "supposed to think as Catholics" many people hold private views on almost every topic that are quite different from official teachings. Nor is this anything new. It's just being talked about more openly these days and the tensions which result from it are being exacerbated because we are in an unprecedented era of diversity and transition.

Fundamental theology has the high and distant goal of establishing a public language for discoursing about ultimate reality. Such an activity seeks to prescind from such particulars as race, sex, ethnicity, credal tradition, educational, economic and social situations. However, as you move into church or systematic theology and even more as you move into practical and pastoral theology these particulars play a very significant implicit or explicit function. Unfortunately in the Church in the past Western European, or more particularly German or Italian, theology and religious customs have been imposed on peoples of other rich heritages as if there were no room for diversity in the Catholic (i.e., open to all) Church.

Black theology is a relatively new phenomenon on the American theological scene—at least as a formal corpus. Yet its origins are as ancient as the rich religious culture of Africa and its roots are found in the free and post-Civil War experiences of slaves. It found beautiful expression in spirituals, sermons, blues, and stories of an oppressed people. Its contemporary spokesmen are a group of creative Protestant scholars who, as Deotis Roberts declared, "are not restrained by Catholic dogma."

While Martin Luther King, Jr., might be the admired patriarch of the present generation of Black theologians, his tempered views are not dominant in the writings of those on the scene today. In summary, they and their central themes are: *a*) Joseph Washington—the oppressed Blacks are God's chosen people; *b*) Albert Cleage—Jesus is, indeed, the Black messiah; *c*) J. Deotis Roberts—there is a compatibility and reconciliation with the thrust of Black liberation theology in a universal Christian vision; *d*) Eulalio Balthazar—White, Western theology sustains racism by supporting a color symbolism that sees white as good and black as evil; *e*) Major Jones—enriching Black liberation theology by constructing a Christian ethic of freedom based on agape; *f*) William Jones—the problem of evil framed in the compelling question, "Is God a White racist?"; *g*) Cecil W. Cone—an identity crisis in Black theology due to neglect of the experience of an almighty sovereign God as the point of departure for all Black theology; *b*) and, finally, James H. Cone, whose central theme is the joining of Black power with the biblical depiction of the God of the Exodus and the New Testament Jesus, who proclaims good news to the poor, release to captives, for the construction of a radical Black theology of liberation.

James Cone's work is probably the most systematic and he has produced the largest corpus. He insists that there are certain questions that emerge in classical Western, White theology which he considers not to be on the Black agenda. Such questions as rational arguments for the existence or non-existence of God, the christological questions of the early councils, meta-physical explanations for the problem of evil, questions about the cognitive content of biblical texts, the relationship of the assertions of religion to the advances of science—these are White questions, in Cone's view, while Black questions are those necessary for the existential survival of a people, for their liberation, their uplifting, their transformation.

I believe that this dichotomy is unfortunate. The question that must be asked is this: For which Blacks are these non-questions? Obviously those involved in the immediate struggle for survival, in past or present, are not likely to entertain metaphysical speculations. Nor are these questions for White people whose material existence is threatened. These are questions, I suggest, which in different formulations may be questions for some Black Christians in the pews, some Black college students, some Black ministers, and some Black scholars. A key unanswered question for me is this one: What constitutes an authentic Black experience? Who constitutes the accrediting agency for genuine Blackness? Who gives the stamp of approval, if you will, to someone's postures, attitudes, points of view, as being genuinely Black?

Much as one may applaud Alex Haley's brilliant achievement in *Roots*, it remains a fact that in most cases the contemporary Black American is a peculiar hybrid of both African and European cultures. While a good case—and an urgent case—may be made that the one must be reappropriated, by what necessity do we argue that the other must be cast off, and by what process is this to be done? These and other questions must be answered if Black theology is to mature.

Such a mature enterprise might enrich the Catholic Church with a new classic. It is evident that great classics in our secular as well as our religious traditions are at once deeply personal and particular in their origins and expressions, while being at the same time public and universal in their power to transform the human spirit. Paradoxically, the profound penetration of a specific cultural, social, or religious heritage may result in an expression that is universal in its power to illuminate the human spirit. Louis Armstrong and Billie Holiday produced very particularized music forms in American jazz and blues. Yet their works are acclaimed as classics in the same manner that the symphonies of Beethoven are classics, because they have the singular capacity to touch and transform the spirit of any attentive listener.

In our culture we have a great need to experience the classic in every context, both secular and theological. Otherwise, we will have a generation of people who know nothing of Melville's *Moby Dick*, the classic story of the menacing and seductive presence of evil that can be symbolized by the sea and the sea beasts. We will have a generation that thinks Peter Benchley's *Jaws* is the best sea story ever. Remarkably, and this is important, one need not have had the experience in order to be touched and transformed by the illuminating insights presented in a classic, *if* one has an attentive spirit. One need not be a member of a problem-laden Irish-American family in order to be stunned and challenged by an experience of Eugene O'Neill's *Long Day's Journey into Night*, nor need one have personal experience of the special pains and tragedies of Black urban tenement dwellers in order to participate fully in the catharsis of Lorraine Hansberry's classic play *A Raisin in the Sun*. These examples are in stark contrast to the vulgar, exploitative sensationalism found in such works as *Superfly*.

Currently there is emerging a vanguard of articulate Black Catholic priests, sisters, brothers, permanent deacons, and active lay persons. Surely if these individuals begin to record their reflections on their experience of the meaning of God, Jesus, Church, worship, social responsibility and community, the whole Church would be enriched. For American Black Catholics represent a unique and often overlooked population in the Church. Because of a unique history as sons and daughters of former slaves, as converts in many cases, as pioneers on the road to full liberation in America, the reflections of Black Catholics might focus the Church anew on the meaning and purpose of religion with telling and, yes, classic urgency.

31

WHAT BLACK CHRISTIAN NATIONALISM TEACHES AND ITS PROGRAM

Statement from the
Black Christian Nationalist Church, Inc., 1976

1. Nothing is more sacred than the Liberation of Black people.
2. The dream of "integration" reflects our acceptance of the myth of Black inferiority, and serves as the basis for our continuing enslavement.
3. Even within the framework of a correct analysis, philosophy, and program projection, it is impossible to build an effective organization without loyalty, discipline, and a clearly defined chain of command.
4. Individualism is a beast within each of us. We must fight the beast within as well as the beast without.
5. Black people are separate in every way and we must use our separateness as a basis for achieving power.
6. Black people had a rich and glorious history and culture long before the white man emerged from the caves.
7. The spirituality of African people encompassed the totality of life. Politics and economics are sacred because they offer programmatic mechanisms for our struggle against white oppression.
8. Properly interpreted, the Bible is a history of God's relationship with the African Nation, Israel, and the Black Messiah, Jesus. Without a correct BCN interpretation, the Bible has served to confuse and enslave a powerless Black people who have waited in vain for deliverance here on earth, and for transportation to a mythical heaven in the sky after death.
9. The "Latter Days" foretold by the Prophets ended almost 2,000 years ago. The end was climaxed by the fall of Jerusalem and the Fort of Masada, and the dispersion of the Black Nation Israel throughout the world. The prophecies from the Bible cannot be applied literally to the problems and realities of today. Biblical prophecy voiced the will of God for the African Nation Israel at a particular time and place.

Only the ignorant wait for the fulfillment of the prophecies addressed to a past which is dead and finished.

BCN is the living prophetic voice of God for African people in this day, and our prophecies will come to pass when Black people totally commit their lives to the struggle against white oppression.

10. God has historically chosen to work through groups and nations rather than through individuals. As shown in the Bible, the God of the Black Nation works through the power of the group experience to transform individuals and to bring into being a communal Black Nation.

The BCN Program

I. The Black Church must seriously work for the liberation of Black people through the realization of concrete and attainable goals here on earth as defined by the Black Christian Nationalist Movement.

II. BCN understands the vicious power reality of the white man's imperialistic, capitalistic, and individualistic society, and fights to free Black men from it by giving a revolutionary programmatic structure and direction to the Black Church by re-affirming the African origins of Christianity and the historic Blackness of the biblical Nation Israel and the Black Messiah, Jesus, as the basis of our struggle for African Redemption and the Liberation of Black people everywhere.

III. Realizing that power resides in institutions and not in individuals, BCN works to establish and develop counter institutions essential to a Pan-African Communal Black Society:

1. BCN works to build a revolutionary Black Church with a new Black Theology to serve the interests of Black people.
2. BCN works to build new Black schools which can re-affirm the Black man's original African identity, build a new commitment to African communal living, and teach the skills necessary for life in a highly technical, industrial society.
3. BCN works to build a complex of urban rural communes within which Black people can receive many of the advantages of African communal living in the satisfaction of everyday needs.
4. BCN works to create and implement a new Black economics which will enable many Black people to labor within a communal environment which places top priority upon service to the Black community.
5. BCN works to create a new independent Black political structure capable of focusing maximum political power in support of the interests of the Black community as defined by BCN.
6. BCN works to establish Black hospitals and social agencies to serve the Black community.
7. BCN works to establish a Pan-African communications network uniting African people and Black Liberation movements throughout the world.

8. BCN works to support Separatist Black Liberation movements everywhere.
9. BCN works for African Redemption (the Liberation, Unification, and Industrialization of our Motherland, Africa), as the cornerstone of the BCN Position.
10. Even as we work to build a world-wide institutional base for Pan-Africanism, we commit our lives and our resources to defend and protect Black communities and institutions functioning within the framework of the BCN Position.

32

LET'S NOT WASTE
THE HOLY SPIRIT

Albert B. Cleage

When Jesus came down from Nazareth and was baptized by John in the Jordan River, the heavens opened and the Holy Spirit descended upon him in the form of a dove and he received power. After spending forty days in the wilderness he walked by the Sea of Galilee and called his Disciples, who left their nets and fishing boats and followed him. He went into the synagogue at Capernaum and the people were astonished, because he taught them as one who had authority and not as the scribes. When John was in prison he sent his disciples to ask, "Are you the Messiah who is to lead the movement or shall we look for another?" Jesus could reply, "Tell John what you see and hear." The Holy Spirit is the revolutionary power which comes to an exploited people as they struggle to escape from powerlessness and to end the institutional oppression forced upon them by an enemy.

At Pentecost the Disciples were together as usual, eating, drinking, talking, and trying to remember and to understand the things Jesus had said and the things he had done. Suddenly it seemed that the room was filled with the rush of a mighty wind. It seemed as though tongues of fire came and rested over each head. The writer was trying to describe a deeply moving inner experience. Another person might have described the experience in a different way. There need not necessarily have been tongues of fire and the rush of a mighty wind, but there was the feeling that some great power was there, and that the Disciples had suddenly been caught up and were being acted upon by a force outside themselves. Each individual was touched and they began to talk. Galileans could not understand what they were saying. Yet

This article is from Albert B. Cleage's book *Black Christian Nationalism* (New York: William Morrow, 1972), pp. 249-260. Cleage, a former minister of the United Church of Christ, is the founder of the Shrine of the Black Madonna in Detroit, Mich.

visitors from other countries could understand them. Here again we have the symbolic language of the Bible. Suddenly caught up in the power of the Holy Spirit, they began to speak in such a way that people from everywhere except Galilee could understand them. Whether they were speaking strange languages in a literal sense, or whether the simple message of the Black Messiah calling men to struggle against oppression could be understood by the exploited and despised from every land, we do not know. This is the same simple message that oppressed nonwhite peoples understand everywhere in today's world.

You don't have to speak Swahili to understand the struggle of the people of Africa. You didn't have to speak French to understand *The Battle of Algiers*. You didn't have to speak Chinese to understand the suffering that created the revolution in China. In a sense, the common experience of suffering and misery creates a universal language of rebellion, struggle, and revolution, and in our kind of world the language of the Holy Spirit cannot but be the language of revolt. This is true in Vietnam. We do not speak Vietnamese, but we can clearly understand the voices of suffering and defiance. We can understand the words of a Vietnamese mother who sees her children consumed by napalm dropped from American bombers. We can understand the words of a Vietnamese man who sees his entire food supply being destroyed by flame-throwers in the hands of American soldiers. We can understand the words of Vietnamese children being tortured by American interrogation teams. The Holy Spirit gives us a sense of identification with the rage of suffering oppressed people everywhere, and so at Pentecost the remnant of the Nation Israel, so soon to be humiliated and dispersed by the fall of Jerusalem and Masada, could be understood by all. It is rage, anger, hatred, commitment. It is divine discontent. It is the mystery of a magic moment when we are touched by a power which we cannot understand.

Only a people can feel the Holy Spirit. God does not speak to individuals. Ordinary Black men and women came together in Montgomery, Alabama, and decided that they could no longer sit in the back of the bus. We wonder what at that moment made the back of the bus so much more irksome than it was a week before or a decade before. Why did Black people suddenly decide to walk? What happened? The most reasonable explanation is the simple one. In this time and in this place, these Black people were touched by the Holy Spirit. The conviction that God had created them equal gave them a new sense of dignity. They were no longer able to ride in the back of the bus. They had been touched by the Holy Spirit. They were forced to walk, and so they walked for more than a year. How can we say what touched a Black mother, whose child had been going to an inferior segregated school, who suddenly decided that she would take her child to an integrated school where the child could get a decent education? Where did she get the courage to face a mob? It was the Holy Spirit. How can we explain the rage of Black people in cities all across America in 1965, '66 and '67, Black people who were accustomed to being oppressed and exploited, who had grown calloused to brutality by white police officers, to injustice in white courts, to misinterpretations by white newspapers and the mass-communications media, and who were accustomed to the hostility of white people? Why did all these things suddenly become unbearable? Black people in city after city rose up against oppression, saying, "We will no longer tolerate these conditions." Why the sudden violence and the upheaval which still shakes America? It was as though the cities were filled with the rush of a mighty wind and tongues of fire rested over each Black head. We can't say it any better than the Bible says it. Why have Black college students suddenly decided that college is not a place to play and prepare for the exploitation of their Black brothers and sisters, but a place to prepare for participation in the Black Revolution? Why now? Why are students willing to face tanks and guns? We saw the pictures of the invasion of a campus in North Carolina: a handful of students practically unarmed, facing all the armed might of America on a Black college campus. Why are students in this day different? The power of the Holy Spirit. Why, at Howard University, would those who traditionally have been middle-class individuals trying to escape from their Black heritage and their Black identity, trying to absorb the life style of white people, suddenly decide that the university belonged to the Black community and ought to serve Black people?

When the power of the Holy Spirit came at Pentecost, a little group of Black Israelites who were disorganized, who had recently been discouraged, despondent, and separated because of the failure of Jesus, were together in one place. What did this little group do when the Holy Spirit came? It is not enough just to say that they suddenly felt as though the rush of a mighty wind had filled the room, and tongues of fire rested over each head. Everyone in the room felt that somehow life had new meaning and a new sense of direction. But what did they do? Sometimes you feel that the Holy Spirit has touched you. You feel power that you didn't know you had; you feel a commitment to do something that you didn't know you could feel. You want to move into areas of risk and sacrifice you didn't realize you had the courage even to dream of. These are moments when you have felt the Holy Spirit. The basic question is, What is your response to the Holy Spirit? If God can touch us, how do we respond? How did the Disciples respond two thousand years ago? It is not enough to say that one day a little handful of those who followed Jesus suddenly felt the power of God and went out into the world to change it. We cannot but ask, What did they do? It is not enough to say that they built the church, because to that we can simply reply, So what? The church has become the protector of oppression and institutional racism which constitutes the white man's world. The church has become a part of the machinery of oppression. If the church as we know it resulted from the Pentecostal experience, we can seriously question whether or not God had anything to do with it. The church of history does not commend itself to us as an act of God.

We accept Jesus as the Black Messiah sent by God to lead men in a revolutionary struggle for liberation because his life testifies to the validity of our faith. We can accept the beautiful mythology with which men have surrounded his birth because we can believe that the advent of a man like this, obviously sent by God, must have been attended by miraculous signs and wonders. Of course the heavens sang and a star came to rest over the lowly stable in which he lay. But we find it difficult to associate God with the church which bears the name of Jesus Christ. The institutional Christian church has never spoken for God nor mediated His spirit. Certainly God has tried through the person and teachings of Jesus and through the Holy Spirit made manifest at Pentecost. God was willing to become incarnate in the group of Disciples at Pentecost as He had become incarnate in Jesus at the moment of his baptism by John the Baptist in the Jordan River, as recorded in Mark, the oldest Gospel. Following the Crucifixion, the incarnation was to have been a group experience, as Jesus had suggested. The arrogant Catholic position that God is incarnate in the Church is Biblically and theologically correct, as opposed to the traditional Protestant heresy that salvation is an individual act accomplished by God on a one-to-one basis without the mediation of the church as Nation. The Catholic position is sound. The spirit of God came to followers of Jesus, *the church potential*, at Pentecost with power but found them apostate. They had lost contact with the life and teachings of Jesus. They wasted the Holy Spirit. To understand, we have but to turn back to the Disciples' own account of Pentecost and ask, What did the Disciples do with the Holy Spirit? They tell you, "We began to speak in tongues." They talked. "People listened so we told them about Jesus." Then what did you do? "We devoted ourselves to the Apostles' teaching and fellowship." That sounds like the church! They sat down together, listened to the Disciples preach, and enjoyed a beautiful fellowship. They wasted the Holy Spirit! They didn't really harness it to any kind of constructive program. The Holy Spirit comes. All God can do is give us a sense of togetherness, a sense of power, and a sense of commitment. If we waste it, it is gone.

Recently I spoke in Harlem at a mass meeting honoring Brother Malcolm. All through the meeting I was conscious of the fact that we were wasting the Holy Spirit. It was a beautiful program. It was one of those spectaculars which can only be gotten together in Harlem, which is still the artistic capital of Black America. There are so many talented people doing so many things and they come together once in a while for a spectacular, and this was that kind of occasion. There were people from Broadway; John O. Killens was there, John Henrik Clarke spoke, and Ossie Davis spoke. It was a beautiful program. There was a phenomenal dance group, with drummers who could jump seven feet in the air and never miss a beat going up or coming down. The Holy Spirit was there. The Disciples at Pentecost had no more spirit than we had that night in Harlem. Everybody was responsive. When the brother jumped and hit the drum, everyone was hitting it all the way up and all the way down with him. The spirit was there. It was beautiful. A group sang as an angelic choir might wish that it could sing. It was church! The National Black Theater put on a play. They had been rehearsing for a year, getting together, training people. It was beautifully done. The spirit was there. Let me describe their presentation.

A brother came out and walked down the aisle toward an empty stage, very dramatically. Music was coming through the amplifier right out of the Black experience: jazz, gospel, blues, and rock. They really had a soundtrack. Everyone's mind was blown before the actor reached the stage. It was beautiful. There he was, walking down the aisle ever so coolly and up onto the stage. The spotlight followed him. He faced the audience, took off his coat, and carefully folded it over his arms. His voice cracked like a machine gun. "Damn niggers! Damn niggers! Damn niggers! Damn niggers!" And then "damn niggers" came from every direction. He said, "This is some garbage we picked up in Harlem." That's what he said. A "nigger" came down the aisle, beating a woman all the way. She'd stop and he would knock her down. He dragged her up on the stage. They came with dope and liquor, cussing, screaming, loving, fighting. Every Black stereotype known to white racist America was personified. It was beautifully done, like a scene from Dante's *Inferno*. The self-hate was frightening in its intensity. The National Black Theater is experimenting with a new kind of theater which has the blood-curdling power of Voodoo. Finally a woman ran up on the stage and stabbed someone. He died for an eternity. In the middle of all of this, the back curtain opened and Brother Malcolm walked on the stage. The spotlight picked him up. He began to teach. "Don't be niggers, don't bring your dirt out into the street. Keep it at home. Lock your doors and get your business together." Everyone changed! The "niggers" faded into the shadows. Malcolm was talking and they were with him. He played his part well. He walked about talking about what Black people must do. While he was talking they were all huddled up in the shadows, and then they came out with their Muslim clothes on as though he had cleansed them by his words. Beautiful! Then more "niggers" ran down the aisle and shot him down on the stage. Sister Betty Shabazz was sitting near me in the front row. I don't know how she stood it. Then he fell down and died for another eternity. A new bedlam of grief rocked the theater. Everyone was crying and screaming. There must have been a hundred in the cast. People were standing, crying and screaming. The spirit was really there. People who weren't in the play were suddenly a part of the cast. They had just seen Malcolm killed before their eyes. Pallbearers came down the aisle carrying a casket. The spirit was there. They picked him up and put him in the casket and walked around with him, sobbing, crying, and screaming. A thousand people completely spirit-filled. Then suddenly Malcolm sat up in the casket. It was the Second Coming. People screamed, "He lives. He lives." He stood up and began to teach again as the lights were extinguished. We were not yet finished. There were poems about how beautiful it is to be Black, and how the time of the white devil is drawing to an end. Finally they said, "We will now hear from Reverend Albert Cleage from the Shrine of the Black Madonna in Detroit." I wondered what anyone could say after the two hours of emotional frenzy we had been through. We had wasted the Holy Spirit!

Everything had been beautiful, but we had wasted the Holy Spirit just as the early Christians had wasted it. We had gone through empty motions. We had not even recruited for the Black Muslims. No one had said anything about the problem. No one had identified the enemy. No one had mentioned a program. We had enjoyed the Holy Spirit. We had enjoyed ecstasy. No one had said anything about putting the Holy Spirit to work. We had burned it all up right there! There seemed nothing left to do but get drunk. Neither program nor direction had been either suggested or implied. It had been exactly like a Sunday-morning service of worship in a Black church. I said, "You are a funny people here in Harlem. I always thought I'd love to participate in a Malcolm memorial, here where you understood him best and loved him most. But I fear that you have forgotten the things he taught and the meaning of his life."

"This program has been all in honor of Brother Malcolm. Brother Malcolm taught us that the white man is the enemy. It is the white man's system of oppression that is destroying us. While we are here screaming that Black is beautiful, our brothers are starving to death in Mississippi and being driven off farms in Georgia and Alabama. Black people are being beaten to death in Detroit, and Black children are being denied a decent education all over this land. We are 'niggers' because the white man has deliberately and systematically 'niggerized' us. Let's not waste the Holy Spirit in a poem, a song, or a dance of self-hate. The day of the 'nigger' is drawing to a close. The era of the Black man has already begun to dawn. Let us look not backward but forward into our new day. Black culture must be an expression of our Liberation Struggle. It must express our hope and determination in poem, song, dance, and drama. It must express our total commitment to the liberation of Black people. There can be no Black art apart from the revolution in which we are engaged. Everything in the Black community must serve the Black Liberation Struggle. The white man is the enemy, yet everything we buy we buy from him. Black farmers in Georgia, Alabama, and Mississippi can't sell their produce because the white man is determined to drive them off the land. All we need is a truck and a driver to bring the food from Mississippi, Georgia, and Alabama to the people of Harlem. But we must know who the enemy is and we must develop a program and an organization designed to confront him."

"We can't use power until we get it, and we can't get it until we become a people. We must build a movement with power. Every organization we had has fallen apart because it had no program designed to meet our basic problem. BCN is building an organization which can unite Black people and secure the power necessary to deal with our oppression. A restructured national Black church could raise enough money on any single Sunday to save Black southern farmers. Black people would contribute for Black liberation if they had leadership. The African liberation movements are fighting to liberate our motherland, Africa! They are fighting white racists in Guinea, Zimbabwe, South Africa, Mozambique, and Angola, but they need support. A restructured national Black church could raise enough money on any Sunday to support the present African liberation movements for a month. There are critical battlefronts in America. The Cairo United Front and the Black struggle in North Carolina need support. A restructured national Black church could raise the funds necessary to support these critical battlefronts. BCN calls Black people to join such a movement. Today we train. Tomorrow we mobilize the power necessary to liberate Black people everywhere in the world."

"The revolution is about confronting an enemy and destroying his system of oppression. If the white man is oppressing you, then you must deal with him. We ought to be figuring out the things that have to be done. James Forman's Black Manifesto points out a direction for a national program. White people will never provide the money. But if white people refuse to pay reparations, the money still must be secured from somewhere! Two hundred million dollars for a land bank in the South is necessary. If white people don't put it up, we still need two hundred million dollars for a land bank in the South. We still need publishing houses, television stations, and everything else that James Forman suggested will enable a people to live. If we don't get it from one source, we must get it from another. That is what we ought to be talking about. That ought to be our agenda. That ought to be our top priority. We cannot afford the luxury of just having a good time. Black folks can enjoy being together better than anyone else in the world, but we waste the feeling of togetherness. Just think how many Black churches waste the Holy Spirit every Sunday morning, because they fail to tie it to any real, down-to-earth program. Salvation is saying, 'I believe in the revolutionary struggle which Jesus, the Black Messiah, inaugurated. I believe in the sacrifice he was willing to make. I believe that it is necessary for me to involve my total life in the struggle of Black people against the oppression of a white enemy establishment. I believe that I must become totally immersed in that struggle.' There is no other way to be saved."

"As Black people we live in an eternal Pentecost. Every moment of every day our ears are filled with the rush of a mighty wind until we almost cannot bear it, and we cannot rest for the tongues of flame which scorch us and drive us and will not let us be, until at last we lie bleeding and still and free."

BCN COVENANT

Declaring ourselves to be God's Chosen People, created in His image, the living remnant of the lost Black Nation, Israel, we come together as brothers and sisters in the Black Christian Nationalist movement. We are disciples of the Black Messiah, Jesus of Nazareth, who by his life, and by his death upon the cross, teaches us that nothing is more sacred than the liberation of Black people.

We covenant together, and pledge our total commitment to the task of rebuilding a Black Nation with power, here on earth. We will do whatever is necessary to achieve self-determination for Black people. We will fight the injustice, oppression, and exploitation of all Black people. As members of the Black Nation, we are bound together in an inseparable sacred brotherhood. To the service of his sacred brotherhood, we pledge our lives.

33

BLACK THEOLOGY IN 1976

Statement by the Theological Commission
of the National Conference of Black Churchmen

Introduction

On June 13, 1969 the first statement on Black Theology was issued from Atlanta by a group of Black religious scholars, churchmen and theologians. It heralded a new beginning for a movement in Afro-American Christianity that was at least as old as the first murmur of protest against slavery and oppression among Christian slaves in the United States. Its restatement at the end of the turbulent 1960's served notice to the world that the faith of the posterity of the slaves was expressed by a qualitatively different interpretation of Christianity than that of the posterity of the slavemasters.

From the beginning, our ancestors reflected theologically upon the meaning of their condition in relation to the revelation of God in Jesus Christ and the Scriptures. Jesus was for them the Liberator. They interpreted his Person and Work in spiritual songs, sermons and prayers as the promise and the assurance of liberation in both this life and in the life to come.

In concise theological language the 1969 Statement on Black Theology reiterated the persistent theme of liberation in Black Christianity and declared that the function of theological reflection in the Black church is to show that the gospel of Jesus Christ, the Liberator, is consonant with the aggressive effort to achieve and preserve the humanity of Black people. Further, the 1969 Statement called for "significant programs of social change" on the part of White Christians to abolish Black oppression. It affirmed that nothing less than White repentance and reparation could constitute a new beginning for shared power and responsibility.

The following statement is another explication of major themes in contemporary Black Theology by the Theological Commission of NCBC. It

340

reaffirms the historic Statement of 1969 and seeks to illumine issues of urgent theological import that face the Black Church in 1976: Black Theology's independence from both White Christian liberalism and the new conservatism, Black Theology as the theology of Black Ecumenism, Black Theology as the theology of the Black Messiah and Black Theology as a political theology.

I. Black Theology Affirms Black Spirituality

Black Theological reflection takes place in the context of the authentic experience of God in the Black worshipping community. That worship is, and has always been, about freedom under the reign of God—the freedom to suffer without self-pity, to struggle without despair, to win victories without vindictiveness and to celebrate worldly pleasures and happiness without anxiety and guilt. It is the freedom and blessedness promised to the poor and oppressed in the promise that theirs is the Kingdom of heaven.

But the worship of the Black Church cannot be separated from its life and ethical praxis. It is in the struggle against racism and oppression that the Black Church creates and recreates its theological understanding of the faith and expresses it in shouts of praise and sounds of struggle for the liberation of the oppressed.

Black Theology is open to critical examination and dialogue with all who come to it in sincerity. But Black Theology does not belong to White theologians. It will not be dictated to by those who want to enlighten the outmoded spirituality of the Black Church with the utilitarian reasonableness of the liberal democratic civil religion or the abstractions of the modern scientific world view. Nor will Black Theology be authenticated as legitimate Christian theology only when it agrees with those White theologians who presume to define heresy by carefully balanced declarations that avoid taking sides in the struggle for justice.

Black Theology is ultimately corrected and authenticated by the inseparable life and worship of the Black Church. It is rooted in neither American liberalism nor conservatism, but in Black spirituality and Black struggle. Its appropriation of the Christian faith and the ethical imperatives of the Gospel is grounded in the revelation of God contained in the inspired preaching, prayer and praise of Black worship informed by the Holy Scriptures. It is controlled by the revelation of God in the history of Black people that gives purpose, meaning and transforming power to the Black struggle for humanity and liberation.

II. Black Theology Affirms Black Ecumenism

Black Theology is the theology of the Black Church. It seeks the reunion of all Black Christians, Protestant and Roman Catholic, in one Church encompassing the totality of the Black religious experience and the history and destiny of all Black people. All efforts to reunite and renew the Black Church serve the ultimate purpose of confirming the catholicity, apostolicity and holiness of the whole church of Jesus Christ in which every race and nation joined together, each contributing properly and equally, upbuilds the One Church of Christ in love and justice. Black Theology does not deny the importance of interdenominational and ecumenical efforts toward church unity with White and other Christians. Rather it asserts the operational unity of all Black Christians as the first step toward a wider unity in which the restructuring of power relations in church and society and the liberation of the poor and oppressed will be recognized as the first priority of mission.

Jesus Christ reveals himself to Black people as the Liberator of the Black people of Africa, the Caribbean and Latin America as well as those of North America. The Gospel was known among African people by the end of the 2nd century, long before it finally extended north and east beyond the Mediterranean basin. But even if the earliest religious traditions of Black Africa cannot be shown to have been penetrated by elements of Christian belief, Black Theology affirms that God did not leave himself without a witness in Africa before the arrival of Christian missionaries. God shows no partiality. His eternal power and deity was shown to all mankind from the creation of the world and his wrath and mercy have fallen upon every race and nation because of universal sin and disobedience in the face of his revealed truth in Jesus Christ.

This truth of God was hidden in the traditional religions of Africa which awaited their fulfillment in the revelation of Jesus, the Liberator. It is within the ancient substructure of Black Religion and in the struggle for freedom and independence experienced by Black churches everywhere that Black Theology seeks evidence of divine revelation, suppressed on both sides of the Atlantic, and retained in the earliest expressions of slave religion in North America and the Caribbean.

The rediscovery of truth revealed to Africa by the indigenization of Christian theology in African culture and the unity of Black and African Christianity with its common experience of white racism and oppression, are basic goals of a Black ecumenism shaped by Black theologians in America working with colleagues on the African continent. Black Theology is an ecumenical theology which seeks to justify and enhance the search for unity among Black denominations in the United States and among Black Christians everywhere as one aspect of obedience to the will of God that all may be unified and liberated in Jesus Christ.

III. Black Theology Affirms the Black Messiah

Black Theology symbolizes Jesus Christ as the Black Messiah to remind Black people, in the most forceful manner, that God, through Christ, takes upon himself the badge of their suffering humiliation and struggle, transforming it by the triumph of his resurrection.

Blackness is a symbol of the Being, the humanity of Black people. In the context of the experience African and Afro-American people have had with Europe and America Blackness has meant inferiority and oppression. Insofar as Jesus Christ was subjugated and humiliated without cause, to save the world, he is recognized by Black Theology as the Oppressed Man of God who took upon himself the undeserved suffering of all oppressed people. Insofar as he is the conqueror of death and all the principalities and powers he is the Black Messiah who was raised from the dead to liberate the oppressed by the power of the God who delivered Israel from the hand of Pharaoh and revealed himself as a Strong Deliverer and Liberator from every oppression of human existence.

Blackness in these terms is more than skin color. Even though it is a symbol that rises from the historic meaning attached to black skin color in Western civilization, it points beyond mere color to the solidarity in suffering and struggle of the descendants of all enslaved and colonized people. The identification and affirmation of blackness by Black Theology is the affirmation of a mystery about a particular people and history that have an affinity to the mystery of the Cross. As the oppression and crucifixion of Jesus Christ is the mystery of Blackness that proleptically encompasses the whole history of Black people, so the dethronement of the powers of evil and the victory of the resurrection is the eschatological destiny of Blackness that gives meaning and a provisional foretaste of victory in the historic struggle of the oppressed.

Black Theology affirms this double meaning of Blackness and seeks to interpret it theologically, homiletically and liturgically in the life and worship of the Black Church. By so doing it unveils and gives a symbolic reference to a mysterious reality in which sin and suffering, grace and liberation are inexplicably conjoined in the experience of the oppressed and in all existence that is truly human.

IV. Black Theology Affirms a Political Program

Black Theology is a political theology. The encounter of Black people with God takes in the arena of history and involves ethical judgments and decisions having to do with liberation from racism, poverty, cultural and political domination and economic exploitation. Black people see the hand of God not only in personal salvation but in social and political deliverance.

Even if black people were to obtain complete freedom and justice throughout the world, new forms of injustice and oppression would demand their identification with those who suffer from man's perennial inhumanity to man. Black Theology seeks to interpret the world-wide revolution against inhumanity, exploitation and oppression in which Black people have played a major role and which is the work of Jesus Christ, and the mission of his church.

Black Theology affirms that the faiths and ideologies of the oppressed masses can be used by God as instrumentalities of their liberation. It teaches

Black people to be radically critical of both the American *status quo* and also of their own political strategies for change.

Because some forms of socialism which stress humanism and cooperation are more Christian and more contributive to justice and morality than American capitalism, Black Theology does not shrink from the exploration of socialistic alternatives to the idolatrous worship of the dollar, the chaotic individualism and corroding materialism of the American economic and political system. Black Theology affirms that "the earth is the Lord's" and opposes any politics which are based on a theory of adherence to absolute self-interest, the precedence of private to public ownership, and the ascendancy of the profit motive and property rights over the public good.

Black Theology, seeking to follow Jesus in his concern for the whole person in the whole community, presents a vision of the world in which all persons can find fulfillment in families and natural communities linked by bonds of love and affection. Such a vision includes the institution of governments of the people committed to peaceful coexistence and self-determination for all races and cultural groups, universal human rights—including the right of revolution for just cause, equal justice, the fair and equitable distribution of wealth, the protection of the weak and helpless, and the fostering of human fulfillment by the enhancement of culture and religion.

Black Theology as a political theology seeks to inculcate this vision in America and to equip the Black Church to be an agent of its realization. The specific content of political strategy for its actualization will evolve in the wrestling of the Black Church with the meaning of the gospel of liberation, the realities of each historical situation and the collective judgment of those who bear the greatest burden of suffering and deprivation.

Black Theology is a theology for political reconstruction under the Lordship of Jesus Christ. Within its prayerful reflection and praxis reverberates God's call to Black Christians to join the people of the Third World in the social revolutions of this century—to overthrow every structure of domination and injustice as a faithful response to the prophetic ministry of Jesus Christ who said, "The spirit of the Lord is upon me to set at liberty those who are oppressed."

34

MESSAGE TO THE
BLACK CHURCH AND COMMUNITY

National Conference of the Black Theology Project, 1977

Grace, liberation and peace in struggle be unto all who are in Jesus Christ and to all the world's suffering people.

Gathered here in the City of Atlanta from all parts of God's world to examine the meaning and implications of Black Theology for our day, we greet you in the name of that same Jesus Christ, the Black Messiah and Liberator.

Why We Have Come to Atlanta

We have come in quest of authentic liberation for ourselves and all people. We have come seeking God's will for our people in a time of crisis. We believe that the black church and community stand at a point of profound transition.

Together, we can go forward to a deeper understanding of present reality and a fuller measure of freedom. Or, forsaking the distinctive heritage of our faith and history, we can fall back into even greater oppression and exploitation. In North America and throughout the black world, our present situation demands that we master those processes of thought and action which can refine and enhance our theological understanding for practical application to every aspect of our common life.

We give thanks to God for the black church's witness to His creation, providence and redemption. Without our church, we would have ceased to be as a people. Thus, this assembly in Atlanta makes bold to speak the hard truth, in love, to both the black church and the black community, confessing

This statement was drafted and adopted by the National Conference of the Black Theology Project, of "Theology in the Americas," in session in Atlanta, Georgia, August 3–7, 1977.

our own part in whatever sins may be laid against both as we pray for God's gracious pardon and renewal.

By the power of the Holy Spirit, in this place, we have decided to embolden our stand with Jesus Christ for the preaching of good news to the poor, the healing of broken hearts, the releasing of captives, the recovering of sight to the blind, the setting at liberty of the oppressed—for proclamation of the acceptable year of our Lord.

The Message of Black Theology

We speak from the perspective we call Black Theology: *Black*—because our enslaved foreparents appropriated the Christian Gospel and articulated its relevance to our freedom struggle with incisive accents that black women and men have sounded ever since. *Theology*—because our people's perception of human life and history begins with God, who works in the person of Jesus Christ for liberation from every bondage.

Therefore, Black Theology is "God-talk" that reflects the black Christian experience of God's action and our grateful response. Black Theology understands the "good news" as freedom and Jesus Christ as the Liberator.

Black Theology is formulated from our reading the Bible as we experience our suffering as a people. Black Theology moves between our church and our community: the church proclaims the message and the message reverberates back upon the church, enhanced by the religious consciousness of black people, including those who stand outside of the institutional church but are not beyond God's grace and His revelation.

The God of Moses and Joshua, of sister Ruth and brother Amos, of our African ancestors and our slave forebearers, has revealed Himself in Jesus Christ, the Black Messiah. He has heard the cry of our people, captive to the racist structures of this land, and is come to deliver us as He came to Israel of old in Egypt-land. In our day, the blackness of Jesus is a religious symbol of oppression and deliverance from oppression; of His struggle and victory over principalities, powers and wickedness in the high places of this age.

The Failure of Traditional Christianity

We cannot affirm the present religious situation in the USA. One of the greatest tragedies of American Christianity has been its failure to comprehend the physical as well as spiritual nature of human beings. With few exceptions, the church has attempted to address the spiritual needs of people while negating their physical and material requirements. Traditional theology has failed to see that ultimate salvation and historical liberation are inseparable aspects of the indivisible gospel of Jesus.

We disassociate ourselves from such piecemeal Christianity. Any gospel that speaks the Truth of God in the black community must deal with the issues of life here and now as well as with the transcendent dimension of the proclamation. The gospel cannot surrender to blind tradition or emotional effusion that renders people insensible to the pain and conflict of earthly experience.

The church must come out from behind its stained-glass walls and dwell where mothers are crying, children are hungry, and fathers are jobless. The issue is survival in a society that has defined blackness as corruption and degradation. Jesus did not die in a sanctuary, nor did Martin Luther King, Jr. In those places where pain was the deepest and suffering the most severe, there Jesus lived and suffered, died and was resurrected.

As long as innocent children continue to die in tenement fires; as long as families have to live in winter without heat, hot water and food; as long as people are forced to live with rats and roaches, the gospel must be heard in judgment against the disorder of society and the church has a responsibility—not to point people to the future life when all troubles will cease, but to help them overcome their powerlessness, rise up and take charge of their lives.

The Power of the Black Church

We reject the notion that the black church has no power. Each and every week, black ministers interact with more people than do any other community leaders. Indeed, many black ministers have limited their roles to visiting the sick, burying the dead, marrying the lovers and presiding over institutional trivia, while leaving responsibility for real social change to politicians and social agencies whom they feel to be more qualified than themselves. But the black preacher is still the natural leader and the black church continues to be the richest source of ethically motivated leadership, lay and clergy, in our community.

The black church must re-assert its power to transform our neighborhoods into communities. Our church possesses gospel power which must be translated into community power, for there can be no authentic community in a condition of powerlessness.

The Desperation of the Black Middle Class

We are concerned also about people whose desperation is not abject material poverty but poverty of soul and spirit. We do not believe that better jobs and bigger houses, color televisions and latest model cars prove that people have attained the abundant life of which Jesus spoke. That abundant life cannot be experienced by a people captive to the idolatry of a sensate and materialistic culture.

We abhor the capitulation of some of our people to values based on the assumptions that things make for security and that distance from the distressed masses makes for a trustworthy barricade against the racism that holds us all in contempt. Commitment to physical gratification as the purpose of life and voidance of the gospel's moral, ethical standards provide false foundations for hard choices. Such false values divide and separate a people who would be free.

The identification of black liberation with the material success of a few, physically and mentally severed from the black masses, makes mockery of the unity essential for the salvation of us all. Even the material good fortune of that few is poisoned by emptiness and isolation from the people's struggle without which the mission of Jesus Christ can be neither understood nor undertaken.

The Roots of the Crisis

The issue for all of us is survival. The root problem is human sinfulness which nurtures monopolistic capitalism, aided by racism and abetted by sexism.

Our crisis is spiritual, material and moral. Black people seem unable to effectively counter disruptive forces that undermine our quality of life. We seem unable to collectively define our situation, discover the nature of our problems, and develop sustained coalitions that can resolve our dilemmas.

Exploitative, profit-oriented capitalism is a way of ordering life fundamentally alien to human value in general and to black humanity in particular. Racism and capitalism have set the stage for despoliation of natural and human resources all around the world. Yet those who seriously challenge these systems are often effectively silenced. We view racism as criminality and yet we are called the criminals. We view racism as a human aberration, yet we are called the freaks. The roots of our crisis are in social, economic, media and political power systems that prevent us from managing the reality of our everyday lives.

It is this intolerable, alien order that has driven us to Atlanta seeking a word from the Lord out of the wellsprings of black theological tradition.

The Inseparability of the
Black Church and Black Community

The black church tradition of service to its people is documented in our history books, our poetry, our drama and our worship. This tradition will not permit us to separate ourselves from our African heritage which is characterized by the sharing of resources and talents by all. Therefore, the black church and the community which it serves are one in the Spirit of God, Who does not differentiate between the secular and the sacred and Who binds us inseparably to one another.

Our victimization by the rich, the powerful, and the greedy makes it necessary for us to continually renew the tradition of our forebearers who stood in the foreground of the struggle for freedom. The black church is the only institution over which black people have total control. That church must remain in service among black people wherever they may reside.

That church must be one with and inseparable from our brothers and sisters around the world who fight for liberation in a variety of ways, including armed struggle. We affirm whatever methods they decide best in their particular situations and make no pious and hypocritical judgments which condemn those efforts to bring an end to their oppression, recognizing that we in this country have ourselves been compelled to make similar choices and may be so compelled again.

Because of racism and imperialism, domestic and foreign, we black people are an international community of outlaws and aliens in our respective homelands and in those communities where we have chosen or been forced to reside. The loving servanthood of the black church has been and is, today, an inescapable necessity. Therefore, we do not reject the disinherited, for they are us. We do not reject the disenfranchised, for they are us.

Rather we embrace all of God's children who hunger and thirst for justice and human dignity. We rededicate and recommit ourselves, and the black churches in whose leadership we participate, to the struggle for freedom from injustice, racism and oppression. This we declare to be the essential meaning of Black Theology as defined by those who conceive it, nurture it and affirm it as a source of inspiration and reflective action for all black people and for all the exploited and oppressed peoples of the world who are grasped by its truth for their situations.

The Witness of the Past, Hope of the Future

Here in Atlanta, as we have struggled over ideas and realities, as we have worshipped in the black tradition, we have felt ourselves surrounded by a great cloud of witnesses. Richard Allen, David Walker, Nat Turner, Henry McNeal Turner, Sojourner Truth, Harriet Tubman, Henry H. Garnet, Frederick Douglass, W.E.B. DuBois, Marcus Garvey, Malcolm X, Martin Luther King, Ralph Featherstone, Paul Robeson, Fannie Lou Hamer—the innumerable hosts of our ancestors, heroes unknown and unsung. Their blood cries out from the ground. They endured trials and tribulation; braved hate-crazed mobs; were attacked, beaten and lynched; watched loved ones killed before their eyes without surrendering their integrity or dignity as they took up the cross of struggle. Of them this world is not worthy.

In their company and in the company of generations yet unborn, whose life and liberty will be shaped by our deeds, we call upon our church and our community to join us in the warfare that shall know no end, until we shall be perfected together in that kingdom of justice, love and peace which moves relentlessly toward us by the dominion of Jesus the Christ, our Lord and Liberator. AMEN.

35

BLACK THEOLOGY AND
THE BLACK CHURCH:
WHERE DO WE GO FROM HERE?

James H. Cone

Since the appearance of black theology in the late 1960's, much has been written and said about the political involvement of the black church in black people's historical struggle for justice in North America. Black theologians and preachers have rejected the white church's attempt to separate love from justice and religion from politics because we are proud descendants of a black religious tradition that has always interpreted its confession of faith according to the people's commitment to the struggle for earthly freedom. Instead of turning to Reinhold Niebuhr and John Bennett for ethical guidance in those troubled times, we searched our past for insight, strength and the courage to speak and do the truth in an extreme situation of oppression. Richard Allen, James Varick, Harriet Tubman, Sojourner Truth, Henry McNeal Turner and Martin Luther King, Jr. became household names as we attempted to create new theological categories that would express our historical fight for justice.

It was in this context that the "Black Power" statement was written in July 1966 by an ad hoc National Committee of Negro Churchmen [now known as the National Conference of Black Churchmen.][1] The cry of Black Power by Willie Ricks and its political and intellectual development by Stokely Carmichael and others challenged the black church to move beyond the models of love defined in the context of white religion and theology. The black church was thus faced with a theological dilemma: either reject Black Power as a contradiction of Christian love (and thereby join the white church in its condemnation of Black Power advocates as un-American and unchristian), or

This essay, first presented as a lecture for the Black Theology Project of the Theology in the Americas Conference of August 1977, is reprinted from *Cross Currents*, Summer 1977, pp. 147-156.

accept Black Power as a socio-political expression of the truth of the gospel. These two possibilities were the only genuine alternatives before us, and we had to decide on whose side we would take our stand.

We knew that to define Black Power as the opposite of the Christian faith was to reject the central role that the black church has played in black people's historical struggle for freedom. Rejecting Black Power also meant that the black church would ignore its political responsibility to empower black people in their present struggle to make our children's future more humane than intended by the rulers in this society. Faced with these unavoidable consequences, it was not possible for any self-respecting church-person to desecrate the memories of our mothers and fathers in the faith by siding with white people who murdered and imprisoned black people simply because of our persistent audacity to assert our freedom. To side with white theologians and preachers who questioned the theological legitimacy of Black Power would have been similar to siding with St. George Methodist Church against Richard Allen and the Bethelites in their struggle for independence during the late 18th and early 19th centuries. We knew that we could not do that, and no amount of white theological reasoning would be allowed to blur our vision of the truth.

But to accept the second alternative and thereby locate Black Power in the Christian context was not easy. First, the acceptance of Black Power would appear to separate us from Martin Luther King, Jr., and we did not want to do that. King was our model, having creatively combined religion and politics, and black preachers and theologians respected his courage to concretize the political consequences of his confession of faith. Thus we hesitated to endorse the "Black Power" movement, since it was created in the context of the James Meredith March by Carmichael and others in order to express their dissatisfaction with King's continued emphasis on non-violence and Christian love.[2] As a result of this sharp confrontation between Carmichael and King, black theologians and preachers felt themselves caught in a terrible predicament of wanting to express their continued respect for and solidarity with King, but disagreeing with his rejection of Black Power.

Secondly, the concept of Black Power presented a problem for black theologians and preachers not only because of our loyalty to Martin Luther King, but also because many of us had been trained in white seminaries and had internalized much of white people's definition of Christianity. While the rise and growth of independent black churches suggested that black people had a different perception of the gospel than whites, yet there was no formal theological tradition to which we could turn in order to justify our definition of Black Power as an expression of the Christian gospel. Our intellectual ideas of God, Jesus, and the Church were derived from white European theologians and their textbooks. When we speak of Christianity in theological categories, using such terms as revelation, incarnation and reconciliation, we naturally turn to people like Barth, Tillich and Bultmann for guidance and direction. But these Europeans did not shape their ideas in the social context of white racism and thus could not help us out of our dilemma. But if we intended to fight on a theological and intellectual level as a way of empowering our historical and political struggle for justice, we had to create a new theological movement, one that was derived from and thus accountable to our people's fight for justice. To accept Black Power as Christian required that we thrust ourselves into our history in order to search for new ways to think and be black in this world. We felt the need to explain ourselves and to be understood from our own vantage point and not from the perspective and experiences of whites. When white liberals questioned this approach to theology, our response was very similar to the bluesman in Mississippi when told he was not singing his song correctly: "Look-a-heah, man, dis yere *mah song*, en I'll sing it howsoevah I pleases."[3]

Thus we sang our Black Power songs, knowing that the white church establishment would not smile upon our endeavors to define Christianity independently of their own definitions of the gospel. For the power of definition is a prerogative that oppressors never want to give up. Furthermore, to *say* that love is compatible with Black Power is one thing, but to demonstrate this compatibility in theology and the praxis of life is another. If the reality of a thing was no more than its verbalization in a written document, the black church since 1966 would be a model of the creative integration of theology and life, faith and the struggle for justice. But we know that the meaning of reality is found *only* in its historical embodiment in people as structured in societal arrangements. Love's meaning is not found in sermons or theological textbooks but rather in the creation of social structures that are not dehumanizing and oppressive. This insight impressed itself on our religious consciousness, and we were deeply troubled by the inadequacy of our historical obedience when measured by our faith claims. From 1966 to the present, black theologians and preachers, both in the church and on the streets, have been searching for new ways to confess and to live our faith in God so that the black church would not make religion the opiate of our people.

The term "Black Theology" was created in this social and religious context. It was initially understood as the theological arm of Black Power, and it enabled us to express our theological imagination in the struggle of freedom independently of white theologians. It was the one term that white ministers and theologians did not like, because, like Black Power in politics, black theology located the theological starting point in the black experience and not the particularity of the western theological tradition. We did not feel ourselves accountable to Aquinas, Luther or Calvin but to David Walker, Daniel Payne and W.E.B. DuBois. The depth and passion in which we express our solidarity with the black experience over against the western tradition led some black scholars in religion to reject theology itself as alien to the black culture.[4] Others, while not rejecting theology entirely, contended that black theologians should turn primarily to African religions and philosophy in order to develop a black theology consistent with and account-able to our historical roots.[5] But all of us agreed that we were living at the beginning of a new historical moment, and this required the development of a *black* frame of reference that many called "black theology."

The consequence of our affirmation of a black theology led to the creation of black caucuses in white churches, a permanent ecumenical church body under the title of the National Conference of Black Churchmen, and the endorsement of James Forman's "Black Manifesto." In June 1969 at the Interdenominational Theological Center in Atlanta and under the aegis of NCBC's Theological Commission, a group of black theologians met to write a policy statement on black theology. This statement, influenced by my book, *Black Theology and Black Power*, which had appeared two months earlier, defined black theology as a "theology of black liberation."[6]

Black theology, then, was not created in a vacuum and neither was it simply the intellectual enterprise of black professional theologians. Like our ser-mons and songs, black theology was born in the context of the black commu-nity as black people were attempting to make sense out of their struggle for freedom. In one sense, black theology is as old as when the first African refused to accept slavery as consistent with religion and as recent as when a black person intuitively recognizes that the confession of the Christian faith receives its meaning only in relation to political justice. Although black theology may be considered to have formally appeared only when the first book was published on it in 1969, informally, the reality that made the book possible was already present in the black experience and was found in our songs, prayers, and sermons. In these outpourings are expressed the black visions of truth, pre-eminently the certainty that we were created not for slavery but for freedom. Without this dream of freedom, so vividly expressed in the life, teachings, and death of Jesus, Malcolm, and Martin, there would be no black theology, and we would have no reason to be assembled in this place. We have come here today to plan our future and to map out our strategy because we have a dream that has not been realized.

To be sure, we have talked and written about this dream. Indeed, every Sunday morning black people gather in our churches, to find out where we are in relation to the actualization of our dream. The black church community really believes that where there is no vision the people perish. If people have no dreams they will accept the world as it is and will not seek to change it. To dream is to know what "is ain't suppose to be." No one in our time expressed this eschatological note more clearly than Martin Luther King, Jr. In his "March on Washington" address in 1963 he said: "I have a dream that one day my four children will live in a nation where they will not be judged by the color of their skin but by the content of their character." And the night before his death in 1968, he reiterated his eschatological vision: "I may not get there with you, but I want you to know tonight that we as a people will get to the promised land."

What visions do we have for the people in 1977? Do we still believe with

Martin King that "we as a people will get to the promised land"? If so, how will we get there? Will we get there simply by preaching sermons and singing songs about it? What is the black church doing in order to actualize the dreams that it talks about? These are hard questions, and they are not intended as a put-down of the black church. I was born in the black church in Bearden, Arkansas, and began my ministry in that church at the early age of sixteen. Everything I am as well as what I know that I ought to be was shaped in the context of the black church. Indeed, it is because I love the church that I am required, as one of its theologians and preachers, to ask: When do the black church's actions deny its faith? What are the activities in our churches that should not only be rejected as unchristian but also exposed as demonic? What are the evils in our church and community that we should commit ourselves to destroy?" Bishops, pastors, and church executives do not like to disclose the wrong-doings of their respective denominations. They are like doctors, lawyers, and other professionals who seem bound to keep silent, because to speak the truth is to guarantee one's exclusion from the inner dynamics of power in the profession. But I contend that the *faith* of the black church lays a claim upon all church people that transcends the social mores of a given profession. Therefore, to cover-up and to minimize the sins of the church is to guarantee its destruction as a community of faith, committed to the liberation of the oppressed. If we want the black church to live beyond our brief histories and thus to serve as the "Old Ship of Zion" that will carry the people home to freedom, then we had better examine the direction in which the ship is going. Who is the Captain of the Ship, and what are his economic and political interests? This question should not only be applied to bishops, but to pastors and theologians, deacons and stewards. Unless we are willing to apply the most severe scientific analysis to our church communities in terms of economics and politics and are willing to confess and repent of our sins in the struggle for liberation, then the black church, as we talk about it, will remain a relic of history and nothing more. God will have to raise up new instruments of freedom so that his faithfulness to liberate the poor and weak can be realized in history. We must not forget that God's Spirit will use us as her instrument only insofar as we remain agents of liberation by using our resources for the empowerment of the poor and weak. But if we, like Israel in the Old Testament, forget about our Exodus experience and the political responsibility it lays upon us to be the historical embodiment of freedom, then, again like Israel, we will become objects of God's judgment. It is very easy for us to expose the demonic and oppressive character of the white church, and I have done my share of that. But such exposure of the sins of the white church, without applying the same criticism to ourselves, is hypocritical and serves as a camouflage of our own shortcomings and sins. Either we mean what we say about liberation or we do not. If we mean it, the time has come for an inventory in terms of the authenticity of our faith as defined by the historical commitment of the black denominational churches toward liberation.

I have lectured and preached about the black church's involvement in our liberation struggle all over North America. I have told the stories of Richard Allen and James Varick, Adam Clayton Powell and Martin Luther King. I have talked about the double-meaning in the Spirituals, the passion of the sermon and prayer, the ecstasy of the shout and conversion experience in terms of an eschatological happening in the lives of people, empowering them to fight for earthly freedom. Black theology, I have contended, is a theology of liberation, because it has emerged out of and is accountable to a black church that has always been involved in our historical fight for justice. When black preachers and laypeople hear this message, they respond enthusiastically and with a sense of pride that they belong to a radical and creative tradition. But when I speak to young blacks in colleges and universities, most are surprised that such a radical black church tradition really exists. After hearing about David Walker's "Appeal" in 1829, Henry H. Garnet's "Address to the Slaves" in 1843, and Henry M. Turner's affirmation that "God is a Negro" in 1898, these young blacks are shocked. Invariably they ask, "Whatever happened to the black churches of today?" "Why don't we have the same radical spirit in our preachers and churches?" Young blacks contend that the black churches of today, with very few exceptions, are not involved in liberation but primarily concerned about how much money they raise for a new church building or the preacher's anniversary.

This critique of the black church is not limited to the young college students. Many black people view the church as a hindrance to black liberation, because black preachers and church members appear to be more concerned about their own institutional survival than the freedom of poor people in their communities. "Historically," many radical blacks say, "the black church *was* involved in the struggle but today it is not." They often turn the question back upon me, saying: "All right, granted what you say about the historical black church, but *where* is an institutional black church denomination that still embodies the vision that brought it into existence? Are you saying that the present day AME Church or AME Zion Church has the same historical commitment for justice that it had under the leadership of Allen and Payne or Rush and Varick?" Sensing that they have a point difficult to refute, these radicals then say that it is not only impossible to find a black church denomination committed to black liberation but also difficult to find a local congregation that defines its ministry in terms of the needs of the oppressed and their liberation.

Whatever we might think about the unfairness of this severe indictment, we would be foolish to ignore it. For connected with this black critique is our international image. In the African context, not to mention Asia and Latin America, the black church experiences a similar credibility problem. There is little in our theological expressions and church practice that rejects American capitalism or recognizes its oppressive character in Third World countries. The time has come for us to move beyond institutional survival in a capitalistic and racist society and begin to take more seriously our dreams about a new heaven and a new earth. Does this dream include capitalism or is it a radically new way of life more consistent with African socialism as expressed in the *Arusha Declaration* in Tanzania?[7]

Black theologians and church people must now move beyond a mere reaction to white racism in America and begin to extend our vision of a new socially constructed humanity for the whole inhabited world. We must be concerned with the quality of human life not only in the ghettos of American cities but also in Africa, Asia and Latin America. Since humanity is one, and cannot be isolated into racial and national groups, there will be no freedom for anyone until there is freedom for all. This means that we must enlarge our vision by connecting it with that of other oppressed peoples so that together all the victims of the world might take charge of their history for the creation of a new humanity. As Frantz Fanon taught us: if we wish to live up to our people's expectations, we must look beyond European and American capitalism. Indeed, "we must invent and we must make discoveries. . . . For Europe, for ourselves and for humanity, we must turn over a new leaf, we must work out new concepts, and try to set afoot a new [humanity]."[8]

New times require new concepts and methods. To dream is not enough. We must come down from the mountain top and experience the hurts and pain of the people in the valley. Our dreams need to be socially analyzed, for without scientific analysis they will vanish into the night. Furthermore, social analysis will test the nature of our commitment to the dreams we preach and sing about. This is one of the important principles we learned from Martin King and many black preachers who worked with him. Real substantial change in societal structures requires scientific analysis. King's commitment to social analysis not only characterized his involvement in the civil rights movement but also led him to take a radical stand against the war in Vietnam. Through scientific analysis, King saw the connection between the oppression of blacks in North America and the United States involvement in Vietnam. It is to his credit that he never allowed a pietistic faith in the other world to become a substitute for good judgment in this world. He not only preached sermons about the promised land but concretized his vision with a political attempt to actualize his hope.

I realize, with Merleau-Ponty, that "one does not become a revolutionary through science but through indignation."[9] Every revolution needs its Rosa Parks. This point has often been overlooked by Marxists and other sociologists who seem to think that all answers are found in scientific analysis. Mao Tse-tung responded to such an attitude with this comment: "There are people who think that Marxism is a kind of magic truth with which one can cure any disease. We should tell them that dogmas are more useless than cow dung. Dung can be used as fertilizer."[10]

But these comments do not disprove the truth of the Marxists' social analysis which focuses on economics and class and is intended as empowerment for the oppressed to radically change human social arrangements. Such an analysis will help us to understand the relation between economics and oppression not only in North America but throughout the world. Liberation is not a process limited to black-white relations in the United States; it is also something to be applied to the relations between rich and poor nations. If we are an African people, as some of the names of our churches suggest, in what way are we to understand the political meaning of that identity? In what way does the economic investment of our church resources reflect our commitment to Africa and other oppressed people in the world? For if an economic analysis of our material resources does not reveal our commitment to the process of liberation, how can we claim that the black church and its theology are concerned about the freedom of oppressed peoples? As an Argentine peasant poet said:

> They say that God cares for the poor
> Well this may be true or not,
> But I know for a fact
> That he dines with the mine-owner.[11]

Because the Christian church has supported the capitalists, many Marxists contend that "all revolutions have clashed with Christianity because *historically* Christianity has been structurally counter-revolutionary."[12] We may rightly question this assertion and appeal to the revolutionary expressions of Christianity in the black religious tradition, from Nat Turner to Martin Luther King. My concern, however, is not to debate the fine points of what constitutes revolution, but to open up the reality of the black church experience and its revolutionary potential to a world context. This means that we can learn from people in Africa, Asia and Latin America, and they can learn from us. Learning from others involves listening to creative criticism; to exclude such criticism is to isolate ourselves from world politics, and this exclusion makes our faith nothing but a reflection of our economic interests. If Jesus Christ is more than a religious expression of our economic and sexist interests, then there is no reason to resist the truth of the Marxist and feminist analyses.

I contend that black theology is not afraid of truth from any quarter. We simply reject the attempt of others to tell us what truth is without our participation in its definition. That is why dogmatic Marxists seldom succeed in the black community, especially when the dogma is filtered through a brand of white racism not unlike that of the capitalists. If our long history of struggle has taught us anything, it is that if we are to be free, we black people will have to do it. Freedom is not a gift but is a risk that must be taken. No one can tell us what liberation is and how we ought to struggle for it, as if liberation can be found in words. Liberation is a process to be located and understood only in an oppressed community struggling for freedom. If there are people in and outside our community who want to talk to us about this liberation process in global terms and from Marxist and other perspectives, we should be ready to talk. But *only* if they are prepared to listen to us and we to them will genuine dialog take place. For I will not listen to anybody who refuses to take racism seriously, especially when they themselves have not been victims of it. And they should listen to us *only* if we are prepared to listen to them in terms of the particularity of oppression in their historical context.

Therefore, I reject dogmatic Marxism that reduces every contradiction to class anlaysis and thus ignores racism as a legitimate point of departure in the process of liberation. There are racist Marxists as there are racist capitalists, and we must struggle against both. But we must be careful not to reject the Marxist's social analysis simply because we do not like the vessels that the message comes in. If we do that, then it is hard to explain how we can remain Christians in view of the white vessels in which the gospel was first introduced to black people.

The world is small. Both politically and economically, our freedom is connected with the struggles of oppressed peoples throughout the world. This is the truth of Pan-Africanism as represented in the life and thought of W. E. B. DuBois, George Padmore, and C. L. R. James. Liberation knows no color bar; the very nature of the gospel is universalism, i.e., a liberation that embraces the whole of humanity.

The need for a global perspective, which takes seriously the struggles of oppressed peoples in other parts of the world, has already been recognized in black theology, and small beginnings have been made with conferences on African and black theologies in Tanzania, New York, and Ghana. Another example of the recognition of this need is reflected in the dialogue between black theology in South Africa and North America. From the very beginning black theology has been influenced by a world perspective as defined by Henry M. Turner, Marcus Garvey, and the Pan-Africanism inaugurated in the life and work of W. E. B. DuBois. The importance of this Pan-African perspective in black religion and theology has been cogently defended in Gayraud Wilmore's *Black Religion and Black Radicalism*. Our active involvement in the "Theology in the Americas," under whose aegis this conference is held, is an attempt to enlarge our perspective in relation to Africa, Asia, and Latin America as well as to express our solidarity with other oppressed minorities in the United States.

This global perspective in black theology enlarges our vision regarding the process of liberation. What does black theology have to say about the fact that two-thirds of humanity is poor and that this poverty arises from the exploitation of the poor nations by rich nations? The people of the United States compose 6 percent of the world's population, but we consume 40 percent of the world resources. What, then, is the implication of the black demand for justice in the United States when related to justice for all the world's victims? The dependent status we experience in relation to white people, Third World countries experience in relation to the United States? Thus, in our attempt to liberate ourselves from white people in North America, it is important to be sensitive to the complexity of the world situation and the oppressive role of the United States in it African, Latin American, and Asian theologians, as well as sociologists and political scientists can aid us in the analysis of this complexity. In this analysis, our starting point in terms of racism is not negated but enhanced when connected with imperialism and sexism.

We must create a global vision of human liberation and include in it the distinctive contribution of the black experience. We have been struggling for nearly four hundred years! What has that experience taught us that would be useful in the creation of a new historical future for all oppressed peoples? And what can others teach us from their historical experience in the struggle for justice? This is the issue that black theology needs to address. "Theology in the Americas" provides a framework in which to address it. I hope that we will not back off from this important task but face it with courage, knowing that the future of humanity is in the hands of oppressed peoples, because God has said: "Those that hope in me shall not be put to shame" (Isa. 49:23).

Notes

1. This statement first appeared in the *New York Times*, July 31, 1966 and is reprinted here as Document 1.

2. For an account of the rise of the concept of Black Power in the civil rights movement, see Stokely Carmichael and Charles Hamilton, *Black Power: The Politics of Liberation in America* (New York: Random House, 1967). For Martin King's viewpoint, see his *Where Do We Go from Here: Chaos or Community?* (Boston: Beacon Press, 1967).

3. Cited in Lawrence W. Levine, *Black Culture and Black Consciousness* (New York: Oxford University Press, 1977), p. 207.

4. This is especially true of Charles Long, who has been a provocative discussant about black theology. Unfortunately, he has not written much about this viewpoint. The only article I know on this subject is his "Perspectives for a Study of Afro-American Religion in the United States," *History of Religions*, vol. 11, no. 1, August 1971.

5. The representatives of this perspective include Gayraud S. Wilmore, *Black Religion and Black Radicalism* (Garden City, N.Y.: Doubleday, 1972), and my brother, Cecil W. Cone, *Identity Crisis in Black Theology* (Nashville: AMEC, 1976).

6. This statement was issued on June 13, 1969, and is also reprinted here as Document 10.

7. See Julius Nyerere, *Ujamaa: Essays on Socialism* (Dar es Salaam: Oxford University Press, 1968).

8. Frantz Fanon, *The Wretched of the Earth* (New York: Grove Press, 1966), p. 255.

9. Cited in José Míguez Bonino, *Christians and Marxists* (Grand Rapids, Mich.: Wm. B. Eerdmans, 1976), p. 76.

10. Cited in George Padmore, *Pan-Africanism or Communism* (Garden City, N.Y.: Doubleday, Anchor Books, 1972), p. 323.

11. Cited in Míguez Bonino, *Christians and Marxists*, p. 71.

12. A quotation from Giulio Girardi, cited in Míguez Bonino, *Christians and Marxists*, p. 71.

PART V

BLACK THEOLOGY
AND BLACK WOMEN

INTRODUCTION

Although Black women represent more than one-half of the population in the Black community and 75 percent in the Black Church, their experience has not been visibly present in the development of Black Theology. For the most part, Black male theologians have remained conspicuously silent on feminist theology generally and Black women in particular. We have spoken of the Black religious experience as if it consisted only of our male experience with no distinctive contribution from Black women. Recently the emergence of a feminist consciousness in the Black community has made Black male theologians more sensitive to the contributions of such women as Harriet Tubman, Sojourner Truth, and Rosa Parks, but not in terms of their unique contributions as women. Do Black women, *as women*, have a distinctive contribution to make in our definition of Black religion that is as significant as we claim our Black experience is in the context of North American Christianity? Unfortunately the silence of Black male theologians on feminist issues seems to suggest a negative answer on their part. But the recent appearance of Black women theologians, with a Black and feminist consciousness, means that our silence will not go unchallenged.

There are various reasons for this silence on feminist issues among Black male theologians. Some Black male theologians are blatantly sexist and thus reflect the values of the dominant society regarding the place of women. Others regard the problem of racism as the basic injustice and say that feminism is a middle-class White woman's issue. Still others make the controversial claim that the Black woman is already liberated. This list could be extended. But whatever the reason for our silence on the unique oppression of Black women, we now must realize that our continued silence can only serve to alienate us further from our sisters. We have no other choice but to take a public stance for or against their liberation.

Since I have been involved in defining the meaning of Black Theology, it may be appropriate to say a word about my theological development in relation to feminism. When I first set myself to the task of developing a Black theology of liberation during the summer of 1968, the distinctive contribution of Black women was not a part of my theological consciousness. To be sure, I was aware of the women's movement, but considered it at best secondary to the Black struggle and at worst simply a White attempt to usurp the revolutionary significance of the Black liberation struggle. It was not until I was challenged by Black and other Third World women that I became aware that the significance of feminism was not exhausted by the White women's movement.

In the Third World context, two events helped to raise my consciousness of the significance of feminism for theology and the Church. The first event occurred in Asia. When I was invited by the Korean Christian Church in Japan (May 1975) to lead a discussion on the theme of "The Church Struggling for the Liberation of the People," one of the four workshops was held in Fukuoko.[1] There were approximately thirty persons present, including young and old, ministers and laypersons. I began this workshop by asking each person to comment on the question "What is it that most troubles you in the Church and the society?" After several persons had commented on racism in Japan, one Korean woman, to the surprise of all present, focused on the subordinate role of women and related it to other forms of oppression. She was not a university-trained person and spoke from the depth of her lived experience. I will never forget her quiet insistence that persons who do not experience a certain form of oppression often minimize its importance in human relations. She appealed to Korean men, rightly challenging the oppressive structures of Japanese society, to let their engagement in the liberation process make them more sensitive to the distinctive oppression of Korean women. I could not help but think that the truth of her comment was applicable to the often strained relations of Black men and women.

The second event happened at the conference on liberation theology in Mexico City (October 1977) entitled "Encounter of Theologians."[2] Of the nearly thirty professional theologians invited to participate, not one was a woman. The absence of this perspective was dramatically articulated by Dora E. Valentin from Cuba, who was present in the audience only because her husband, Sergio Arce Martínez of the Evangelical Seminary, had been invited. No one could question Valentin's commitment to class analysis, but she insisted that such an analysis was inadequate without combining it with racism and sexism. She asked her Latin American brothers why none of their sisters had been invited to participate in the discussion? After a few seconds of an embarrassing silence, someone apologized for the oversight and then invited Valentin to join the discussion. But she politely refused. Again, I could not help but ask myself, how long will men from oppressed communities continue to remain indifferent to the special oppression of their sisters?

It is one thing, however, to be challenged by women from a different cultural and political context, and quite another to hear the cry of pain from women in one's own community. In the Black North American context, the theological significance of the Black woman's experience has been dramatically expressed in conferences on Black women, sponsored both by seminaries and by churches. On such occasions, both formally and informally, the issue of the role of Black women in church and society inevitably arises as a topic of discussion. In most cases, Black women contend that Black men, inside and outside the church, are insensitive to experiences of sexism in the Black community. Black women's deep disappointment with the response of Black men to their oppression cannot be dismissed as a superficial inconvenience that will soon disappear.

When I observe many Black men's reaction to sexism in our community, then I can understand the significance of Sister Anna Cooper's comment that "while our [Black] men seem thoroughly abreast of the times on every subject, when they strike the women question they drop back into sixteenth century logic."[3] Among professional theologians and preachers as well as seminary and university students, few Black men seem to care about the pain our Black sisters claim that we inflict on them with our sexist behavior. If we expect to be taken seriously about our claim to love them, must not our love express itself in our capacity to hear their cry of pain and to experience with them their mental and physical suffering?

By suffering with our sisters and struggling with them to eliminate sexism in our community, we create a deeper solidarity in our common struggle against racism. When one examines the writings of Black women and listens to their testimonies, it is clear that most make the unity and liberation of Black people their starting point in an analysis of Black feminism. A significant example is the very important anthology, *The Black Woman,* edited by Toni Cade.[4] I have chosen Frances Beale's essay, "Double Jeopardy: To Be Black and Female" (Document 36) from that volume, because of the breadth of her analysis, and also because she renders incorrect the Black male's claim that feminism is a White woman's issue, and that Black women's concern for their liberation necessarily involves them in an interracial sexual alignment in lieu of racial unity. Frances Beale states clearly the complexity of the Black woman's situation, but includes in her analysis of the Black woman's particularity a universalism that embraces all people.

If Black women's liberation is a serious issue in the society at large, what then is the role of the Black Church in this struggle? Because the Black Church has a long history of struggle against racism, it should be in the vanguard of the struggle against Black women's oppression. But unfortunately the Black Church is one of the most sexist institutions in the Black community, and Black male ministers often appeal to the Bible to justify the subordinate role defined for women. While many Black male ministers have little difficulty rejecting Paul's command to slaves to be obedient to their masters as a valid justification of Black slavery, they seem incapable of taking a similar stance in relation to Paul's comments about women. Once again the social and political interests of the interpreter seem to control his exegetical conclusions.

In order to transcend the theological limitations that are often determined by political and social interests, Black churchmen will need to listen to Black feminist voices in the church. One such voice is Teressa Hoover, whose essay, "Black Women and the Churches: Triple Jeopardy" (Document 37), is a personal account of her experience in the Black Church. She shows the limitation of the Black Church in dealing with the oppression of the Black Woman in its own household.

When I first recognized the limitation of the Black Church and Black Theology in this area, I did not know what to say about it. My silence was broken when I was asked by Black women students at Garrett-Evangelical Seminary (October 1976) to address a Black women's conference on the theme, "New Roles in the Ministry: A Theological Appraisal" (Document 38). I have included this previously unpublished essay, because it represents (to my knowledge) the first attempt of a Black male theologian to address this issue directly. Since that time, I have tried to deepen my sensitivity and knowledge of this issue, because I firmly believe with Toni Cade that "a man cannot be politically correct and a chauvinist too."[5]

Being sensitive to Black feminism inevitably leads to the question of the relationship between feminist theology and Black Theology. While Rosemary Ruether[6] and Letty Russell[7] have touched on the relation between sexism and racism in theology, neither White feminist theologians nor Black male theologians have the experience that will enable them to do justice to this issue. Only Black feminist theologians have the experience necessary for the creation of intellectual tools that are needed in analyzing the complexity of this issue. Pauli Murray's article "Black Theology and Feminist Theology" (Document 39) indicates the need for a dialogue between Black and feminist theologians. However, before such a dialogue can take place, it is necessary to create a Black feminist theology. Jacquelyn Grant's essay, "Black Theology and the Black Woman" (Document 40), is an important contribution in this area.

While Jacquelyn Grant's perspective on Black feminist theology is derived primarily from the faith of the Christian Church, not all Black women will follow that line of thinking. Some Black women express the need to separate Black feminist theology from any dependence on White feminist and Black male theologies, on the one hand, and the Christian faith on the other. In this perspective, the distinctive experience of Black women, inside and outside the Black Church, becomes the primary norm in its analysis. Alice Walker's "In Search of Our Mothers' Gardens" (Document 41) is an important contribution for this perspective. She contends that there is something unique in Black women's spirituality that is "so intense, so deep, so *unconscious*, that they [are] themselves [often] unaware of the richness they [hold]." "Therefore we must fearlessly pull out of ourselves and look at and identify with our lives the living creativity some of our great-grandmothers were not allowed to know."

From the essays included in this part, it is clear that a variety of perspectives on Black feminist theology are in the process of development. The precise shape of these perspectives is still unclear. But what is clear is Black women's challenge to the dominant male perspective in the Black Church and its theology. I only hope that our love for the Black community is deep enough to enable us to hear and to respond to the pain of our sisters.

J.H.C.

Notes

1. For another discussion of the Korean Christian Church in Japan, see "Black Theology and Third World Theologies," p. 456 below.

2. For another reference to this event, see "Black Theology and Third World Theologies," p. 452 below.

3. Cited in Robert Staples, *The Black Woman in America: Sex, Marriage and the Family* (Chicago: Nelson-Hall, 1973), p. 69.

4. See also the excellent collection of essays in Toni Cade, ed., *The Black Woman* (New York: Signet Book, 1970). Another important collection is G. Lerner, *Black Women in White America: A Documentary History* (New York: Vintage Books, 1973). For book-length treatises on the Black woman, see Joyce Ladner, *Tomorrow's Tomorrow* (Garden City, N.Y.: Doubleday, 1971); Robert Staples, *The Black Woman*; Jeanne Noble, *Beautiful, Also, Are the Souls of My Black Sisters* (Englewood Cliffs, N.J.: Prentice-Hall, 1978). I regret that the much publicized and provocative book by Michele Wallace, *Black Macho and the Myths of the Superwoman* (New York: Dial Press, 1979), was not available in time to be included in this discussion.

5. "On the Issue of Roles," in Cade, ed., *The Black Woman*, p. 107.

6. See her *Liberation Theology* (New York: Paulist Press, 1972); *New Woman, New Earth* (New York: Seabury Press, 1975); "Crisis in Sex and Race," in *Christianity and Crisis*, vol. 34, no. 6, April 15, 1974.

7. See her *Human Liberation in a Feminist Perspective—A Theology* (Philadelphia: Westminster Press, 1974).

36

DOUBLE JEOPARDY:
TO BE BLACK AND FEMALE

Frances Beale

In attempting to analyze the situation of the Black woman in America, one crashes abruptly into a solid wall of grave misconceptions, outright distortions of fact, and defensive attitudes on the part of many. The system of capitalism (and its afterbirth—racism) under which we all live has attempted by many devious ways and means to destroy the humanity of all people, and particularly the humanity of Black people. This has meant an outrageous assault on every Black man, woman, and child who resides in the United States.

In keeping with its goal of destroying the Black race's will to resist its subjugation, capitalism found it necessary to create a situation where the Black man found it impossible to find meaningful or productive employment. More often than not, he couldn't find work of any kind. And the Black woman likewise was manipulated by the system, economically exploited and physically assaulted. She could often find work in the white man's kitchen, however, and sometimes became the sole breadwinner of the family. This predicament has led to many psychological problems on the part of both man and woman and has contributed to the turmoil that we find in the Black family structure.

Unfortunately, neither the Black man nor the Black woman understood the true nature of the forces working upon them. Many Black women tended to accept the capitalist evaluation of manhood and womanhood and believed, in fact, that Black men were shiftless and lazy, otherwise they would get a job and support their families as they ought to. Personal relationships between Black men and women were thus torn asunder and one result has been the separation of man from wife, mother from child, etc.

America has defined the roles to which each individual should subscribe. It

This article was first published in *The Black Woman,* ed. Toni Cade (New York Signet, 1970). Frances Beale is active in several Black Women's groups. She lives in New York City.

has defined "manhood" in terms of its own interests and "femininity" likewise. Therefore, an individual who has a good job, makes a lot of money, and drives a Cadillac is a real "man," and conversely, an individual who is lacking in these "qualities" is less of a man. The advertising media in this country continuously inform the American male of his need for indispensable signs of his virility—the brand of cigarettes that cowboys prefer, the whiskey that has a masculine tang, or the label of the jock strap that athletes wear.

The ideal model that is projected for a woman is to be surrounded by hypocritical homage and estranged from all real work, spending idle hours primping and preening, obsessed with conspicuous consumption, and limiting life's functions to simply a sex role. We unqualitatively reject these respective models. A woman who stays at home caring for children and the house often leads an extremely sterile existence. She must lead her entire life as a satellite to her mate. He goes out into society and brings back a little piece of the world for her. His interests and his understanding of the world become her own and she cannot develop herself as an individual having been reduced to only a biological function. This kind of woman leads a parasitic existence that can aptly be described as legalized prostitution.

Furthermore it is idle dreaming to think of Black women simply caring for their homes and children like the middle-class white model. Most Black women have to work to help house, feed, and clothe their families. Black women make up a substantial percentage of the Black working force, and this is true for the poorest Black family as well as the so-called "middle-class" family.

Black women were never afforded any such phony luxuries. Though we have been browbeaten with this white image, the reality of the degrading and dehumanizing jobs that were relegated to us quickly dissipated this mirage of womanhood. The following excerpts from a speech that Sojourner Truth made at a Women's Rights Convention in the nineteenth century show us how misleading and incomplete a life this model represents for us:

> ... Well, chilern, whar dar is so much racket dar must be something out o' kilter. I tink dat 'twixt de niggers of the Souf and de women at the Norf all a talkin' 'bout rights, de white men will be in a fix pretty soon. But what's all dis here talkin' bout? Dat man ober dar say dat women needs to be helped into carriages, and lifted ober ditches, and to have de best place every whar. Nobody ever help me into carriages, or ober mud puddles, or gives me any best places, ... and ar'nt I a woman? Look at me! Look at my arm! ... I have plowed, and planted, and gathered into barns, and no man could head me—and ar'nt I a woman? I could work as much as a man (when I could get it), and bear de lash as well—and ar'nt I a woman? I have borne five chilern and I seen 'em mos' all sold off into slavery, and when I cried out with a mother's grief, none but Jesus heard—and ar'nt I a woman?

Unfortunately, there seems to be some confusion in the Movement today as to who has been oppressing whom. Since the advent of Black power, the Black male has exerted a more prominent leadership role in our struggle for justice in this country. He sees the system for what it really is for the most part, but where he rejects its values and mores on many issues, when it comes to women, he seems to take his guidelines from the pages of the Ladies' Home Journal. Certain Black men are maintaining that they have been castrated by society but that Black women somehow escaped this persecution and even contributed to this emasculation.

Let me state here and now that the Black woman in America can justly be described as a "slave of a slave." By reducing the Black man in America to such abject oppression, the Black woman had no protector and was used, and is still being used in some cases, as the scapegoat for the evils that this horrendous system has perpetrated on Black men. Her physical image has been maliciously maligned; she has been sexually molested and abused by the white colonizer; she has suffered the worse kind of economic exploitation, having been forced to serve as the white woman's maid and wet nurse for white offspring while her own children were more often than not starving and neglected. It is the depth of degradation to be socially manipulated, physically raped, used to undermine your own household, and to be powerless to reverse this syndrome.

It is true that our husbands, fathers, brothers, and sons have been emasculated, lynched, and brutalized. They have suffered from the cruelest assault on mankind that the world has ever known. However, it is a gross distortion of fact to state that Black women have oppressed Black men. The capitalist system found it expedient to enslave and oppress them and proceeded to do so without consultation or the signing of any agreements with Black women.

It must also be pointed out at this time that Black women are not resentful of the rise to power of Black men. We welcome it. We see in it the eventual liberation of all Black people from this corrupt system of capitalism. Nevertheless, this does not mean that you have to negate one for the other. This kind of thinking is a product of miseducation; that it's either X or it's Y. It is fallacious reasoning that in order for the Black man to be strong, the Black woman has to be weak.

Those who are exerting their "manhood" by telling Black women to step back into a domestic, submissive role are assuming a counter-revolutionary position. Black women likewise have been abused by the system and we must begin talking about the elimination of all kinds of oppression. If we are talking about building a strong nation, capable of throwing off the yoke of capitalist oppression, then we are talking about the total involvement of every man, woman, and child, each with a highly developed political consciousness. We need our whole army out there dealing with the enemy and not half an army.

There are also some Black women who feel that there is no more productive role in life than having and raising children. This attitude often reflects the conditioning of the society in which we live and is adopted from a bourgeois white model. Some young sisters who have never had to maintain a household and accept the confining role which this entails tend to romanticize (along with the help of a few brothers) this role of housewife and mother. Black women who have had to endure this kind of function are less apt to have these utopian visions.

Those who project in an intellectual manner how great and rewarding this role will be and who feel that the most imporant thing that they can contribute to the Black nation is children are doing themselves a great injustice. This line of reasoning completely negates the contributions that Black women have historically made to our struggle for liberation. These Black women include Sojourner Truth, Harriet Tubman, Mary McLeod Bethune, and Fannie Lou Hamer, to name but a few.

We live in a highly industrialized society and every member of the Black nation must be as academically and technologically developed as possible. To wage a revolution, we need competent teachers, doctors, nurses, electronics experts, chemists, biologists, physicists, political scientists, and so on and so forth. Black women sitting at home reading bedtime stories to their children are just not going to make it.

Economic Exploitation of Black Women

The economic system of capitalism finds it expedient to reduce women to a state of enslavement. They oftentimes serve as a scapegoat for the evils of this system. Much in the same way that the poor white cracker of the South, who is equally victimized, looks down upon Blacks and contributes to the oppression of Blacks, so, by giving to men a false feeling of superiority (at least in their own home or in their relationships with women), the oppression of women acts as an escape valve for capitalism. Men may be cruelly exploited and subjected to all sorts of dehumanizing tactics on the part of the ruling class, but they have someone who is below them—at least they're not women.

Women also represent a surplus labor supply, the control of which is absolutely necessary to the profitable functioning of capitalism. Women are systematically exploited by the system. They are paid less for the same work that men do, and jobs that are specifically relegated to women are low-paying and without the possibility of advancement. Statistics from the Women's Bureau of the U.S. Department of Labor show that in 1967 the wage scale for white women was even below that of Black men; and the wage scale for non-white women was the lowest of all:

White Males	$6704
Non-White Males	$4277
White Females	$3991
Non-White Females	$2861

Those industries which employ mainly Black women are the most exploitive in the country. Domestic and hospital workers are good examples of this oppression; the garment workers in New York City provide us with another view of this economic slavery. The International Ladies Garment Workers Union (ILGWU), whose overwhelming membership consists of Black and Puerto Rican women, has a leadership that is nearly all lily-white and male. This leadership has been working in collusion with the ruling class and has completely sold its soul to the corporate structure.

To add insult to injury, the ILGWU has invested heavily in business enterprises in racist, apartheid South Africa—with union funds. Not only does this bought-off leadership contribute to our continued exploitation in this country by not truly representing the best interests of its membership, but it audaciously uses funds that Black and Puerto Rican women have provided to support the economy of a vicious government that is engaged in the economic rape and murder of our Black brothers and sisters in our *Motherland* Africa.

The entire labor movement in the United States has suffered as a result of the super-exploitation of Black workers and women. The unions have historically been racist and chauvinistic. They have upheld racism in this country and have failed to fight the white skin privileges of white workers. They have failed to fight or even make an issue against the inequities in the hiring and pay of women workers. There has been virtually no struggle against either the racism of the white worker or the economic exploitation of the working woman, two factors which have consistently impeded the advancement of the real struggle against the ruling class.

This racist, chauvinistic, and manipulative use of Black workers and women, especially Black women, has been a severe cancer on the American labor scene. It therefore becomes essential for those who understand the workings of capitalism and imperialism to realize that the exploitation of Black people and women works to everyone's disadvantage and that the liberation of these two groups is a steppingstone to the liberation of all oppressed people in this country and around the world.

Bedroom Politics

I have briefly discussed the economic and psychological manipulation of Black women, but perhaps the most outlandish act of oppression in modern times is the current campaign to promote sterilization of non-white women in an attempt to maintain the population and power imbalance between the white haves and the non-white have-nots.

These tactics are but another example of the many devious schemes that the ruling-class elite attempt to perpetrate on the Black population in order to keep itself in control. It has recently come to our attention that a massive campaign for so-called "birth control" is presently being promoted not only in the underdeveloped non-white areas of the world, but also in Black communities here in the United States. However, what the authorities in charge of these programs refer to as "birth control" is in fact nothing but a method of outright surgical genocide.

The United States has been sponsoring sterilization clinics in non-white countries, especially in India, where already some three million young men and boys in and around New Delhi have been sterilized in makeshift operating rooms set up by the American Peace Corps workers. Under these circumstances, it is understandable why certain countries view the Peace Corps not as a benevolent project, not as evidence of America's concern for underdeveloped areas, but rather as a threat to their very existence. This program could more aptly be named the Death Corps.

Vasectomy, which is performed on males and takes only six or seven minutes, is a relatively simple operation. The sterilization of a woman, on the other hand, is admittedly major surgery. This operation (salpingectomy)* must be performed in a hospital under general anesthesia. This method of "birth control" is a common procedure in Puerto Rico. Puerto Rico has long been used by the colonialist exploiter, the United States, as a huge experimental laboratory for medical research before allowing certain practices to be imported and used here. When the birth-control pill was first being perfected, it was tried on Puerto Rican women and selected Black women (poor), using them as human guinea pigs, to evaluate its effect and its efficiency.

Salpingectomy has now become the commonest operation in Puerto Rico, commoner than an appendectomy or a tonsillectomy. It is so widespread that it is referred to simply as *la operación. On the island, 10 percent of the women between the ages of 15 and 45 have already been sterilized.*

And now, as previously occurred with the pill, this method has been imported into the United States. These sterilization clinics are cropping up around the country in the Black and Puerto Rican communities. These so-called "maternity clinics" specifically outfitted to purge Black women or men of their reproductive possibilities are appearing more and more in hospitals and clinics across the country.

A number of organizations have been formed to popularize the idea of sterilization, such as the Association for Voluntary Sterilization and the Human Betterment (! ! ! ?) Association for Voluntary Sterilization, Inc., which has its headquarters in New York City.

Threatened with the cut-off of relief funds, some Black welfare women have been forced to accept this sterilization procedure in exchange for a continuation of welfare benefits. Black women are often afraid to permit any kind of necessary surgery because they know from bitter experience that they are more likely than not to come out of the hospital without their insides. (Both salpingectomies and hysterectomies are performed.)

We condemn this use of the Black woman as a medical testing ground for

*Salpingectomy: Through an abdominal incision, the surgeon cuts both fallopian tubes and ties off the separated ends, after which act there is no way for the egg to pass from the ovary to the womb.

the white middle class. Reports of the ill effects, including deaths, from the use of the birth control pill only started to come to light when the white privileged class began to be affected. These outrageous Nazi-like procedures on the part of medical researchers are but another manifestation of the totally amoral and dehumanizing brutality that the capitalist system perpetrates on Black women. The sterilization experiments carried on in concentration camps some twenty-five years ago have been denounced the world over, but no one seems to get upset by the repetition of these same racist tactics today in the United States of America—land of the free and home of the brave. This campaign is as nefarious a program as Germany's gas chambers, and in a long-term sense, as effective and with the same objective.

The rigid laws concerning abortions in this country are another vicious means of subjugation and, indirectly, of outright murder. Rich white women somehow manage to obtain these operations with little or no difficulty. It is the poor Black and Puerto Rican woman who is at the mercy of the local butcher. Statistics show us that the non-white death rate at the hands of the unqualified abortionist is substantially higher than for white women. Nearly half of the childbearing deaths in New York City are attributed to abortion alone and out of these, 79 percent are among non-whites and Puerto Rican women.

We are not saying that Black women should not practice birth control. *Black women have the right and the responsibility to determine when it is in the interest of the struggle to have children or not to have them, and this right must not be relinquished to anyone.* It is also her right and responsibility to determine when it is in her own best interests to have children, how many she will have, and how far apart. The lack of the availability of safe birth-control methods, the forced sterilization practices, and the inability to obtain legal abortions are all symptoms of a decadent society that jeopardizes the health of Black women (and thereby the entire Black race) in its attempts to control the very life processes of human beings. This is a symptom of a society that believes it has the right to bring political factors into the privacy of the bedchamber. The elimination of these horrendous conditions will free Black women for full participation in the revolution, and thereafter, in the building of the new society.

Relationship to White Movement

Much has been written recently about the white women's liberation movement in the United States, and the question arises whether there are any parallels between this struggle and the movement on the part of Black women for total emancipation. While there are certain comparisons that one can make, simply because we both live under the same exploitative system, there are certain differences, some of which are quite basic.

The white women's movement is far from being monolithic. Any white group that does not have an anti-imperialist and anti-racist ideology has absolutely nothing in common with the Black woman's struggle. In fact, some groups come to the incorrect conclusion that their oppression is due simply to male chauvinism. They therefore have an extremely anti-male tone to their dissertations. Black people are engaged in a life-and-death struggle and the main emphasis of Black women must be to combat the capitalist, racist exploitation of Black people. While it is true that male chauvinism has become institutionalized in American society, one must always look for the main enemy—the fundamental cause of the female condition.

Another major differentiation is that the white women's liberation movement is basically middle-class. Very few of these women suffer the extreme economic exploitation that most Black women are subjected to day by day. This is the factor that is most crucial for us. It is not an intellectual persecution alone; it is not an intellectual outburst for us; it is quite real. We as Black women have got to deal with the problems that the Black masses deal with, for our problems in reality are one and the same.

If the white groups do not realize that they are in fact fighting capitalism and racism, we do not have common bonds. If they do not realize that the reasons for their condition lie in the system and not simply that men get a vicarious pleasure out of "consuming their bodies for exploitative reasons" (this kind of reasoning seems to be quite prevalent in certain white women's groups), then we cannot unite with them around common grievances or even discuss these groups in a serious manner because they're completely irrelevant to the Black struggle.

The New World

The Black community and Black women especially must begin raising questions about the kind of society we wish to see established. We must note the ways in which capitalism oppresses us and then move to create institutions that will eliminate these destructive influences.

The new world that we are attempting to create must destroy oppression of any type. The value of this new system will be determined by the status of the person who was low man on the totem pole. Unless women in any enslaved nation are completely liberated, the change cannot really be called a revolution. If the Black woman has to retreat to the position she occupied before the armed struggle, the whole movement and the whole struggle will have retreated in terms of truly freeing the colonized population.

A people's revolution that engages the participation of every member of the community, including man, woman, and child, brings about a certain transformation in the participants as a result of this participation. Once you have caught a glimpse of freedom or experienced a bit of self-determination, you can't go back to old routines that were established under a racist, capitalist regime. We must begin to understand that a revolution entails not only the willingness to lay our lives on the firing line and get killed. In some ways, this is an easy commitment to make. To die for the revolution is a one-shot deal; to live for the revolution means taking on the more difficult commitment of changing our day-to-day life patterns.

This will mean changing the traditional routines that we have established as a result of living in a totally corrupting society. It means changing how you relate to your wife, your husband, your parents, and your co-workers. If we are going to liberate ourselves as a people, it must be recognized that Black women have very specific problems that have to be spoken to. We must be liberated along with the rest of the population. We cannot wait to start working on those problems until that great day in the future when the revolution somehow miraculously is accomplished.

To assign women the role of housekeeper and mother while men go forth into battle is a highly questionable doctrine for a revolutionary to maintain. Each individual must develop a high political consciousness in order to understand how this system enslaves us all and what actions we must take to bring about its total destruction. Those who consider themselves to be revolutionary must begin to deal with other revolutionaries as equals. And so far as I know, revolutionaries are not determined by sex.

Old people, young people, men and women, must take part in the struggle. To relegate women to purely supportive roles or to purely cultural considerations is dangerous doctrine to project. Unless Black men who are preparing themselves for armed struggle understand that the society which we are trying to create is one in which the oppression of all members of that society is eliminated, then the revolution will have failed in its avowed purpose.

Given the mutual commitment of Black men and Black women alike to the liberation of our people and other oppressed peoples around the world, the total involvement of each individual is necessary. A revolutionary has the responsibility not only of toppling those that are now in a position of power, but of creating new institutions that will eliminate all forms of oppression. We must begin to rewrite our understanding of traditional personal relationships between man and woman.

All the resources that the Black community can muster up must be channeled into the struggle. Black women must take an active part in bringing about the kind of society where our children, our loved ones, and each citizen can grow up and live as decent human beings, free from the pressures of racism and capitalist exploitation.

37

BLACK WOMEN AND THE CHURCHES: TRIPLE JEOPARDY

Theressa Hoover

To be a woman, black, and active in religious institutions in the American scene is to labor under triple jeopardy.

It is a well-accepted fact that women in America, though in the majority statistically, are generally in inferior positions. Economically they are at the bottom of the ladder in terms of those receiving high-paying salaries. Politically, although they have the possibility of more voters being women, they have not yet experienced the full potential of that vote. Women constitute a very small number of the persons in political office at all levels of the nation's life. Religiously, though they comprise more than 50 percent of the churches' membership, they are by no means at the higher levels of decision-making in the churches.

It has long been an established fact in American life that color is a deterrent to high achievement; not because there is inherent inferiority but because societal conditions predetermine lower achievement. Thus, while every woman in America faces economic and political discrimination, a woman who is black has an added barrier.

Religion in American society is often espoused, even in high places, but it is not yet the warp and woof of our actions. The woman who is vitally involved with religious institutions in our society must take on responsibilities often not accepted by others.

To confront the inequities of women and the inequities of blacks, and to have the responsibilities of a dedication to the church, is triple jeopardy for a

Theressa Hoover is Associate General Secretary, Women's Division, Board of Global Ministries of the United Methodist Church. This essay first appeared in Alice Hageman, ed., *Sexist Religion and Women in the Church* (New York: Association Press, 1974), pp. 63-76.

black woman. There is very little written which brings together these three elements. There is little or no mention of black women in accounts of any black church or black theology and in the *Ebony* special issue on "The Negro Woman" (August 1960) she is treated in every way except in the area of religion. *The Making of Black Revolutionaries* by James Forman and *Black Women in White America* by Gerda Lerner, both published in 1972, are the only books available which give a bit more dimension to the strength and courage of black Christian women now and in the past. Any thinking person cannot help wondering why so little has been written, since women are by far the largest supporting groups in our religious institutions, and, in the black church, are the very backbone.

We know too well the debates going on in the American religious institutions about women—their role, their access to all privileges and responsibilities in the priestly hierarchy, their representation in decision-making places, and their total condition in these institutions. Apparently no one has seen the plight of American black women in the religious institutions of our society. One might conclude that where something is written about women in general in these institutions black women are included. This may be true, but it is not the total picture. Even in the predominantly all-white denominations, the black woman commonly finds herself in black local congregations. Judged by what is written in the historic black denominations the black woman is invisible.

Black Women: The Backbone of the Black Churches

Some people hallow the black church, citing evidence of the hope such churches could give their communities if they had the financial support of a larger group. Others detract from the past and belittle the future potential of the black church in the black community, claiming these churches have become little more than middle-class social clubs, out of contact with the real hurts of people in their communities. The detractors use caricatures of a black preacher riding around town in his Cadillac purchased by gifts from welfare checks or chicken dinners sold by black women of his congregation. There is probably truth in both the compliment and the caricature: the black church which properly assesses the potential of its community, and applies its resources to that potential, can be the better servant of the community. The preacher in the black church *is* more directive, authoritarian, and singular in his administration. The degree to which he uses his position selfishly marks the amount of personal privilege and reward he enjoys at the expense of a "not so well endowed" membership—the majority of which are women.

This situation has sociological and psychological explanations. In the post-slavery period, the black church was the only place in the community where economic well-being was dependent on direct black giving. In many situations the preacher had to play the roles of social worker and political and religious adviser. To perform properly he had to have enough ability to get on with the powers at city hall or in the county courthouse. In town after town—even in the Deep South—he was the only black man not referred to as "George" or "boy." He was called "Rev." or "Preacher." Such courtesy did not necessarily concede he was a man, but that he was a little more than "boy."

Many of today's major black churches have their roots in protest. Richard Allen walked out of the Methodist Episcopal Church in Philadelphia rather than accept segregation at the communion table, and the African Methodist Episcopal Church is a monument to that protest. Countless hundreds of local Methodist and Baptist congregations across the country have kept alive that protest. They were the churches that provided succor to the slave family, that also helped them accommodate to earthly travail with the promise of a better life in the hereafter. Today many criticize this role of the past. Given a similar oppressive situation, however, would we have done otherwise? During the same period some churches were the places where insurrectionists gathered to plan strategies and attacks.

In the 1960s during the civil rights struggle there were black ministers in leadership in difficult places and situations. With them were women and men who had come under the teaching of the gospel in the churches and had believed. Churches were the targets of the racists' bombs and guns. In some ways, they were targets more than any other institutions, since the schools—probably the only other places in the community which could accommodate the crowds—were the property of the Establishment. The black church was of the black community, owned by it and sustained by it, and thus it became the target of the racists. Joseph R. Washington, Jr., illustrated the point well:

> In the beginning was the black church, and the black church was with the black community, and the black church was the black community. The black church was in the beginning with the black people; all things were made through the black church, and without the black church was not anything that was made. In the black church was life, and the life was the light of the black people. The black church still shines in the darkness and the darkness has not overcome it.[1]

Lest it be thought that this is a valid description of the black church in black Southern communities only, the experience of Cicely Tyson, who grew up in New York City, should be noted:

> We were in church Sunday morning to Saturday night. It was our whole life, our social life, our religious training, everything. My mother didn't believe in movies, so I didn't go to the movies. . . . But I enjoyed the church services. I sang in the choir and played the piano and the organ.

Sometimes when my mother worked late at night, Nana would take my sister and my brother and me to the Baptist church. It was that kind of thing that saved us. Church became a shelter for us. A lot of kids growing up with us are not here today because of drugs or alcohol, or they died some violent death. They weren't necessarily bad kids.[2]

During the period 1948 to 1958 I traveled eleven months out of each year, all across the United States. I spent those years in and out of every major city, in countless small towns, and on the back roads in open country. Needless to say, hospitality for me in those days was always arranged for in the home of some black Methodist family. The only able-bodied, employed male I observed at home during the weekdays was the pastor. For some it was an escape into a natural or acquired laziness. For others it was an opportunity to read, study, and join with other clergymen in talking of their dilemmas, boasting of last Sunday's offerings, or strategizing about some community need.

During those ten years of travel I discovered that black women were truly the glue that held the churches together. The women worked, yet found time to be the Sunday school teachers, sing in the choir, and support the church's program in every way. The women found the time and energy to be active in the women's missionary societies and to serve as counselors or sponsors for the youth group. They were the domestics of the community and the teachers in the black schools. The latter were often either hometown girls or ones who had grown up in a town similar to the one in which they now worked and boarded with a respectable family. The church was their "home away from home," the social orbit in which they met the right people.

The minister's wife deserves special mention. She often worked outside the home, too, depending on the financial status of the church her husband served. In many cases she gave piano lessons—or did sewing for a little change if she was lucky. She was sometimes a teacher in the nearby country school. On occasion she, too, joined the long line of domestics leaving her end of town to spend part of the day at work in homes on the other side of town. She was still expected to prepare her family's meals, clean the parsonage, and do the allotted amount of church work.

In most of these communities the blacks were either Methodists or Baptists. The Methodists were a mixture. Some belonged to a primarily white denomination even though they found the local expression in black congregations. Others belonged to one of the three primarily black Methodist denominations—African Methodist Episcopal, African Methodist Episcopal Zion, or Christian Methodist Episcopal. All, however, were related to a connectional system, meaning that they had a presiding elder who was their link to other churches in the denomination and to a bishop who linked them to a still larger judicatory of the denomination. The Baptists tended to belong to a fellowship of Baptists, but each local church was autonomous. History has produced many varieties: there were progressive and independent; there were Antioch and Shiloh.

In both Baptist and Methodist churches the women were the backbone, the "glue." They were present at the midweek prayer services, the Monday-afternoon women's missionary meetings, and the Sunday morning, afternoon, and evening preaching services. Rarely has there been in the black church a great distinction between men and women holding office or sharing in decision-making in the local churches.

Missions as Focus for Contact and Cooperation

In the 1950s, women in the various Methodist groups began to discover one another. While there had been a sharing of programs and other resources in many local communities, there had been no real coming-together nationally. The women of the basically white Methodist Church had a joint committee with the women of the basically black Christian Methodist Episcopal (CME) Church. The relationship was still in the realm of a "missionary project" on the part of the white denomination, for it was they who provided the staff help, the printed resources, and the money to assure leadership training for the women of the CME Church. The two groups have since moved into an era of more equitable contribution to the joint experiment. Coming together later as co-units in the World Federation of Methodist Women, they extended the fellowship to include women of the African Methodist Episcopal and the African Methodist Episcopal Zion churches.

Each of the four Methodist women's groups has a history of mission work in this country and overseas. They have supported their own programs even as they have aided the mission outreach of the denomination in which they were a part. These women's missionary groups developed out of the desire of women to be involved with the hurts, needs, and potential of women everywhere. The regular mission channels of the denominations were controlled by the clergy to the point of the deliberate exclusion of women. To give expression to the needs felt by women the women's missionary society was organized as a parallel or auxiliary group. That felt need and that exclusion from main church channels still exist. Today these groups of women are strong numerically and financially.

The nationally organized churchwomen's groups active today are: the African Methodist Episcopal Church Women's Missionary Society, the African Methodist Episcopal Zion Church Women's Home and Missionary Society, the Christian Methodist Episcopal Church Women's Missionary Council, the Women's Auxiliary of the National Baptist Convention, and the United Methodist Women's Division.

There are varying degrees of autonomy in these organizations. Each is a recognized body of the denomination which makes possible the functioning of the group at all levels of the church's life. The groups range in size from two thousand to thirty thousand local units in the United States with a combined membership in the millions.

United Methodist Women, part of a Board of Global Ministries, retains the constitutional right to enlist women as members, to provide program and educational materials, and to secure and expend funds. It is the largest remaining mainline churchwomen's group with that degree of autonomy. It has some thirty thousand local units.

Black Women and the Black Manifesto

In the late 1960s the religious institutions in America toward which the Black Manifesto was directed were in disarray. The legally achieved integration of the early sixties had been found wanting in quality and in practice. For the liberal white integrationists, the apparent move toward separatism, signaled by the Black Power movement and culminating in the Manifesto of 1969, was mind-blowing to say the least. To some, separatism represented a threat or a cop-out.

Not long after the Black Manifesto was made public I was called by the executive director of Church Women United to a conference to discuss what impact this move would have on black women in that organization. My counsel to her then, later borne out, was that it would produce no "break-off" though it might well call forth some soul searching as to the seriousness with which women honor our differences and pool our resources and resourcefulness on behalf of all.

Nevertheless, to test my counsel, Church Women United called a small consultation of black churchwomen in September, 1969, at Wainwright House, Rye, New York, to consider their role and expectations in the aftermath of the Black Manifesto. The group concluded that churchwomen—black and white—must function under the limitations of religious thought and practice. This fact alone was sufficiently limiting; there was no purpose to be served by further splintering ourselves along the lines of race.

We talked about the role women can play in the total life of the church, about the areas the church has not yet given evidence of serving, about the gap between mainline black churchwomen and their younger black sisters. Most of us represented the former category. We were the ones who attended the colleges set up by the churches to educate the recently freed slaves and had gone on to become teachers in them or staff in their national headquarters. We had little experience with overt assignment of women to second-class posts in churches, largely because we were so vitally needed if churches were even to exist. We were the ones who had been taught and had accepted a role on behalf of "our people" even if it meant foregoing a personal life exemplified in husband and children. We were the ones who, if married at all, had married "beneath us"—meaning that we had married men with less education who did manual labor. (Note the influence of white society's value system.) This was not true for the young black woman of the late 1960s.

These are some of the remarks heard at that weekend consulation:

"The young black's mistake is in not making enough of their American experience. We will never be Africans. In slavery only the strong and those with a will to live survived—those with spiritual resiliency."

"Black people once thought education was the answer; they found it wasn't. Now they think economics is the answer; we'll find it won't be, either. We have to find something else—we have to deal with the attitude of people on the top in order to solve this. As churchwomen and as black women, how can we do this?"

"Women have always taken care of everyone's problems and have been left behind. Women must be free before they can begin to make decisions."

"To accomplish a specific goal, an organized minority can bring about change. It is not necessary to have great numbers."

"Women must be accepted as persons. The black man wants to assert today his so-called masculinity, but it is really *personhood*—for both sexes."

"So far as young women versus men are concerned, let the men have their power and status; we organize the women's caucus; when the men are ready for our help, they will have to bargain for it."

Ethnic Caucuses in White Churches

Ethnic caucuses in white denominations sprang up in the aftermath of the civil rights struggle. The soil had been prepared for their advent. It took an act of national significance to release the simmering disenchantment of minority groups with their place in white denominations. What is interesting is the role and status of women within the ethnic caucuses.

Not unlike the role of women in the civil rights struggle of the sixties women in the caucuses have been assigned (and have accepted) a supportive role. Most of the decision-makers have been men, primarily clergymen. It might help to look closely at the "life and growth of caucuses" in a major mainline denomination whose membership is a replica of the nation at large. Let's take the United Methodist Church (which has 54 per cent women members) as a case study.

1. At the 1966 Special Session of General Conference of the Methodist Church, with the Evangelical United Brethren Church Conference in session across the hall, there was only one visible caucus, Methodists for Church Renewal. This caucus cut across race and sex lines, though the dominant group consisted of white male clergy.

2. At the regular Methodist General Conference in 1968 (with the Evangelical United Brethren Church holding a simultaneous Special Ses-

sion), a second caucus was present, Black Methodists for Church Renewal (BMCR). At this session the union of the two denominations was consummated and, with it, the official end of the Methodist all-Negro Central Jurisdiction. In February, 1968, just two months prior to the General Conference, over two hundred black Methodists had gathered in Cincinnati, Ohio. They came from the Far West and East, where structural segregation included only the local church; from the Middle West (Illinois to Colorado, Missouri to Kentucky), where conferences had already been merged with their white counterparts; and from the Southwest and Southeast, where no noticeable change was in the offing. While it was church renewal that brought them together, it was their blackness which made the gathering imperative.

Black clergymen were by far the majority of those attending, but a real effort was made to get lay men and women. Both were there. Strategically, many of them would be voting delegates in the upcoming General Conference. The national board of directors elected before the conference closed totaled forty-four, with nine women, a number not commensurate with black women's presence or support in black churches—but an action taken without recourse to pressure by women.

One directive to the board of directors says something about the group's awareness of the black woman. They were directed to "employ an assistant director which shall be a woman, *if* the executive director is a man." There was not the assumption, which is so often true, that the director would be a man. Instead, it was an assurance that the leadership of the staff would reflect the talents of both male and female.

Black women and men, lay and clerical, were visible at the luncheons, after-hours caucuses, and the on-floor debate at the General Conference. As a result, our denomination created and funded a Commission on Religion and Race. When the Commission was organized and staffed, however, there were no guarantees for the participation of women, and the Commission cannot be applauded for their involvement. In fact, it is fair to say that women have been generally disregarded in its life and work. So the struggle must go on.

3. At the 1970 Special General Conference, still another caucus, youthful United Methodists, secured the right to self-determination.

4. At the 1972 General Conference the youth caucus was the only caucus that included women in the warp and woof of its proceedings and decision-making. Black Methodists for Church Renewal, barely visible and still masculine and clerical, saw the rise of a women's caucus in its own ranks before it got the message that "coalition around common interests" was not only desirable but imperative.

The newest caucus—the women's caucus—was a great new fact. Black women were among its members and took active roles. Representatives of the BMCR women's caucus were a bridge so that BMCR, the women's caucus, and the Youth-Young Adult Caucus formed a working coalition to achieve common goals. As a result a Commission on the Status and Role of Women was created and funded, though not to the desired degree. The Commission has organized with a black woman as its chairperson. The effort brought together still another interesting phenomenon—the joint effort of young, unorganized women with the older, organized women's group in the denomination.

Judith Hole and Ellen Levine in their book *Rebirth of Feminism* say:

> Feminist activities within the Christian community most often fall into three categories: (1) challenging the theological view of women; (2) challenging the religious laws and/or customs which bar women from ordination; (3) demanding that the professional status and salaries of women in the church be upgraded.[3]

These categories may apply to the total feminist movement in the churches, but do not yet reflect the view of many black women. First, the economic necessity of the black woman's efforts on behalf of her church has not pressured her to the point of accepting the prevailing theological view of women. When she gets a little release from other church pressures, she will look beyond her local church and realize that such theological views and practices are operative both in her exclusion from doctrinal decision-making and in her absence from national representation.

Second, in the predominantly black churches women are not excluded from ordination by law, though they may be in practice. Third, most of the black denominations are not financially capable of maintaining even a minimal professional staff (outside the clerical hierarchy). Where there is staff, women already know the necessity of insisting on comparable salaries.

Most of the women in such staff positions—not unlike those in their more wealthy sister churches—tend to be related to the women's missionary groups and/or the church's educational agencies. Most of the national presidents receive a nominal cash stipend for the administrative work they do in the absence of a staff. The other most likely staff position is as the editor of the women's paper or the women's column in the denominational paper.

In 1967 the national Woman's Division (the Methodist Church) held a consultation of Negro women. The focus was on Negro women in merged situations. From the findings I have excerpted the following expectations the women brought: "What can be done in situations where there has been desegregation but no integration? How can we somehow deflate the superiority complex in the white woman and help to eliminate the inferiority complex in the nonwhite? What can we do to recognize good judgment, and respect it, in the noneducated woman?"

In 1968 a survey was made of Methodist leadership in merged structures.[4] Interpretive comments based on the response, elicited through a questionnaire distributed across the organization, speak to the dilemma of black leadership in white churches.

This inquiry (or survey) was planned as a broad-based, though focused, review of progress made toward integrating hitherto racially separated structures. It was not designed as a statistical inquiry. Generalizations made by the research team were:

1. It was not found that enlightenment regarding other ethnic groups is a product of geographical location.

2. It was not demonstrated that size of locality determines the nature and extent of "progress" toward successful integration.

3. It was not manifest that membership in any particular ethnic group controls or determines readiness for either "merger" or "integration."

"Merger" was an area of misconception. A number of replies indicate that this was commonly thought of as the process through which the racial or ethnic minorities were to give up their identities.

"Integrated merger" was a concept employed by a few who saw the previously separated groups as coming together in one "mix," to which each would contribute and for which each would yield some of its former prerogatives, comforts, and complacencies.

At this writing only one of the jurisdictional women's groups out of the five regional jurisdictions has a black president; two have black vice-presidents.

In February 1972, a National Black Women's Conference was called by Mrs. Elizabeth M. Scott, president of Black Women's Association. It met in Pittsburgh. In its section on "Role of Black Woman in the Community," there are conclusions and suggestions for actions that at least make some acknowledgement of the black woman in her church. One reads: "The church must be a meeting place for different people of the community, a place to listen to the problems of the community, a place for planning better opportunities for the people of the community." In its action section there are two references to black women as church women. "We, the black churchwomen, must move our churches to serve as a meeting place to provide the opportunity for volunteers, e.g., tutoring, detection of learning deficiencies, supervision, planning skills, leadership." And the following: "Black women must get on policy making boards (both secular and sacred) in the community and serve in executive positions. . . ."

Black Women—Strengthened by Faith

The black churchwoman must come to the point of challenging both her sisters in other denominations and the clerical-male hierarchy in her own. In many ways she has been the most oppressed and the least vocal. She has given the most and, in my judgment, gotten the least. She has shown tremendous faithfulness to the spirit of her church. Her foresight, ingenuity, and "stick-to-itiveness" have kept many black churches open, many black preachers fed, many parsonages livable.

She has borne her children in less than desirable conditions, managed her household often in the absence of a husband. She has gathered unto herself the children of the community, she has washed them, combed their hair, fed them and told them Bible stories—in short, she has been their missionary, their substitute mother, their teacher. Many leaders of the present-day black church owe their commitment to the early influence of just such a black woman.

You may have heard of the Church of the Black Madonna in Detroit, Michigan. While I do not know how it came to be so named, I would guess that it is not to be confused with the usual "pedestal placing" of woman—above the fray protected, adorned, and excluded! I choose to see it as homage to black women—their numbers, their strength, their faith, their sustaining and prophetic role in the black church.

In James Forman's book, referred to earlier, there is a chapter on "Strong Black Women." Forman speaks to the heart that women bring to the black church, indeed to the entire religious community, in references to women in the Albany, Georgia, protest of the 1960s.

> The strength of the women overwhelmed me. Here they were in jail, but their spirits seemed to rise each minute. They were yelling at the jailer, cursing, singing, ready to fight if someone came to their cell to mistreat them. Images of other strong black women resisting slavery and servitude flooded my mind. I thought of Georgia Mae Turner and Lucretia Collins and the young girls in the cell block next to me now as the modern-day Harriet Tubmans, Sojourner Truths, and all those proud black women who did not allow slavery to break their spirits. . . . As I thought about the women protesting their arrest, I knew that the black liberation movement would escalate, for too many young people were involved. Most of the women in the cells were very young, one of them only fourteen.[5]

With such a heritage of strength and faith, black women in the churches today must continue strong in character and in faith. They must reach other sisters and brothers with a sense of the commonality of their struggles on behalf of black people, and ultimately all humanity. They must continue to work within the "walls" of the church, challenging theological pacesetters and church bureaucrats; they also must continue to push outward the church "walls" so it may truly serve the black community. They must be ever aware of their infinite worth, their godliness in the midst of creatureliness, and their having been freed from the triple barriers of *sex, race,* and *church* into a community of believers.

Notes

1. Joseph R. Washington, Jr., "How Black Is Black Religion?" in *Quest for a Black Theology*, eds. James J. Gardiner, S.A., and J. Deotis Roberts, Sr. (Philadelphia: Pilgrim Press, 1970), p. 28.

2. Cicely Tyson, *The New York Times*, October 1, 1972.

3. Judith Hole and Ellen Levine, *Rebirth of Feminism* (New York: Quadrangle Books, 1971), p. 377.

4. A survey within Woman's Societies of Christian Service and Wesleyan Service Guilds (the Methodist Church) by Research and Action, Inc., New York City, 1968.

5. James Forman, *The Making of Black Revolutionaries* (New York: Macmillan Co., 1972), p. 200.

38

NEW ROLES IN THE MINISTRY: A THEOLOGICAL APPRAISAL

James H. Cone

Many problems arise concerning the church and its ministry, because we forget what these terms mean in the context of the gospel of Jesus. Aside from the customary verbal confessions of belief in Jesus Christ that we have been conditioned to say in prayers, sermons, and other religious situations, a large number of church people seldom reflect in their everyday lifestyle a faith commitment to the One who was crucified on Golgotha's hill. Our church is an impostor, because we no longer believe the gospel we proclaim. There is a credibility gap between what we say and what we do. While we may preach sermons that affirm the church's interests in the poor and the downtrodden, what we actually do shows that we are committed to the "American way of life," in which the rich are given privileged positions of power in shaping the life and activity of the church, and the poor are virtually ignored. As a rule, the church's behavior toward the poor is very similar to the society at large: the poor are charity cases. Our negligence of them is symbolized in the small offering taken in their name every Sunday morning in most Black churches. It is appalling to see some Black churches adopting this condescending attitude toward the victims, because these churches were created in order to fight against slavery and injustice. For many slaves, the Black Church was God's visible instrument for freedom and justice. Therefore, to have contemporary middle-class Black Christians treating the poor as second-class members of the church is a disgrace not only to the Scripture but also to our Black religious heritage.

Because our churches adopt their value system from the American capitalistic society and not from Jesus Christ, church offices are more often than not valued as indications that one has achieved a certain status in life. This partly accounts for the fact that women are not permitted in any

389

denomination to exercise power commensurate with their numbers, and in some denominations are even denied ordination. Although there is room for legitimate debate in these matters, it seems clear that no appeal to Scripture or church tradition can remove the suspicion that all who stand against the equality of women in every dimension of the church's life do so in the light of the political and social interests of men. Whatever the exegesis of Scripture and tradition one may advocate, one fact is certain: when a particular interpretation of Scripture benefits people who hold positions of power, it can never be the gospel of Jesus.

No amount of clever reasoning can camouflage the obvious social, economic, and political interests involved in the subordination of women in the church. Black women know that their ministry has been severely limited, and they also know why. That is, they know *who* benefits from their oppression. That is the reason they have called this conference and now openly speak of "new roles in the ministry." Such a theme is not only appropriate, but necessary, so that attention can be called to certain apostasies and heresies in the Black Church.

The need for a definition of new roles for women and men in the Black Church arises not from the fact that the gospel is new or is changing. The opposite is the case: there is a *constancy* about the gospel that is derived from the One who is the content of its message. Anyone who encounters the biblical God experiences the divine constancy. In the Scriptures, God's constancy is spoken of as divine faithfulness, that is, God's promise to be with and for the people in time of trouble. Theologians of the early church, paying more attention to Greek philosophy than to the Bible, spoke of the divine constancy in terms of the absence of suffering in the Being of God. But more than one thousand years later, Black slaves took the tradition *back* to the Scriptures by expressing their confidence in a divine constancy that was clearly derived from biblical roots.

> God is a God!
> God don't never change!
> God is a God
> An' He always will be God.

This constancy was the foundation of their faith and the source of black slaves' confidence that God had not left them alone in servitude. In this essay, I want to examine the idea of new roles in the ministry for Black men and women in the light of the constancy of the gospel of Jesus.

I. The Holy Spirit and Social Reality

One of the most important and perplexing questions in systematic theology is the relation between the gospel and culture. What is this gospel that does not change? What is it that we preach and sing about that is the same today as yesterday and will be the same tomorrow and forevermore? Unless we answer this question, then there is no way to identify the new roles that our ministry is required to take in our faithfulness to the gospel of Jesus. By failing to identify the universal dimension of the gospel and to subject it to the judgment of Scripture and the traditions of the church, we leave ourselves vulnerable to the charge of ideology, that is, allowing the gospel to be defined by our cultural and political interests. While I do not agree with Karl Barth's assertion that there is an "infinite qualitative distinction" between God and humanity, it is still true that we seek a Christian lifestyle and proclamation that are not simply the values of our society or community. This means that we must ask the critical question, "What is the gospel, and how is it different from my own social conditioning?"

However, before we can define the gospel and then develop new roles in the ministry on the basis of its proclamation, it is necessary to describe the theological and social context in which my perspective on the gospel has been shaped. I do not believe that it is possible to understand what the gospel is all about in terms of its demands on people in our world unless one encounters the Spirit, i.e., God's presence with the people. The Spirit refers to God's gift of the power of insight so that one can hear and do the truth as revealed in the biblical witness. Without an openness to the power and guidance of the divine Spirit and her presence in the world, we will not understand what the gospel is. One should not belittle the value of disciplined intellectual effort in the life of the church, but the gospel is more than intellectual study. Sometimes intellectual formulations give us a false confidence about our understanding of the truth. This has often been the case with the literary and historical criticism of the Bible. The truth of the Bible is simply not accessible apart from the Spirit.

To claim that the Spirit is needed to understand what the gospel is, is to say that our resources alone are not enough to know who Jesus is. To speak of Jesus and his gospel is to speak of his Spirit who opens up dimensions of reality that are not reducible to our intellectual capacity. The Spirit is the power to hear and do the truth as lived by the people. Without an openness to walk and talk with Jesus and to be led by a Spirit not of our own creation, there is no way to hear the gospel and to live out its meaning in our ministry.

But lest we think that God's Spirit is merely a pious feeling in our hearts, it is necessary to point out the relations between social reality and God's presence in the world. The only way to encounter God's Spirit is to have one's religious consciousness formed in a political context. The social and political context of the victims is indispensable for hearing our true calling, a vocation that is always bound up with the liberation of victims from servitude. It is not possible for anyone to hear the divine Spirit's call into the Christian ministry, and at the same time derive his or her perception of that ministry from an ecclesiastical structure that oppresses women.

One does not need a seminary education to know that oppression in any form is a contradiction of God's Spirit. Indeed, I firmly believe that the insight into the radical contradiction between the divine Spirit and human oppression is disclosed to people only when they find their consciousness being formed in a community of victims. There will be no new roles in the ministry for women and men unless they are created in the struggle of freedom for the victims of the land. We do not learn this insight in seminaries, because they are largely defined by the existing structures of power. We may hear about Marx, Fanon, and Gutiérrez in White seminaries, but we must not mistake revolutionary rhetoric for actual praxis in the community of victims. Rhetoric is learned in the classrooms by reading Marx's *Das Capital* and Fanon's *Wretched of the Earth*. But if we are to take Marx seriously when he says, "It is not consciousness that determines life but life that determines consciousness," then we must conclude that a true revolutionary consciousness is formed only in the social context of victims. Only as we join the poor in their struggle can we encounter the divine Spirit of liberation disclosed in their fight for justice.

II. The Gospel Defined

What is this gospel that can only be understood in the social and political context of victims and from which new styles of ministry must be shaped in the Black Church? I do not want to spend too much time repeating what I have written and said elsewhere. Yet I will say something about defining the gospel, partly to avoid being misunderstood, but more because I come from that tradition of Black preachers who contended that one should never pass up an opportunity to say a word about Jesus. Therefore I am compelled by the nature of my vocation to say a word about what we call the "gospel of Jesus."

To put it as clearly as I know how: *the Christian gospel is God's good news to the victims that their humanity is not determined by their victimization*. This means that the poor do not have to adjust to poverty; the oppressed do not have to reconcile themselves to humiliation and suffering. They can do something to change not only their perception of themselves, but also the existing structures of oppression. Indeed this is what the Exodus, the prophets, and the Incarnation are all about. These events and people are God's way of saying that injustice is a contradiction of the divine intention of humanity. Persons, therefore, who embark on a vocation in the Christian ministry and do not view their calling as a commitment to the victims of the land, are not really servants of the gospel of Jesus. We may be servants of the United Methodist or A.M.E. denominations, but not of the One whom the Lucan Evangelist reported as saying:

The Spirit of the Lord is upon me
because he has anointed me to preach good news to the poor.
He has sent me to proclaim release to the captives

and recovering of sight to the blind,
to set at liberty those who are oppressed,
to proclaim the acceptable year of the Lord. (Luke 4:18-19)

Jesus' consciousness was defined by his identity with the liberation of the weak and helpless. That is why the Lucan account tells us that he was born in a stable at Bethlehem. We are also told that Jesus defined his ministry for the poor and not the rich. Jesus' identity with the victims led to his condemnation as a criminal of the Roman state. If Jesus had been born in the emperor's court and had spent most of his life defending the interests of the rulers of that court, then what I am saying would have no validity at all. It is because the Scripture is so decisively clear on this matter that I insist on the liberation of the victim from social and economic oppression as the heart of the gospel. Anything less than this message is an ideological distortion of the biblical message.

Therefore, whatever new styles we create, they must never be allowed to camouflage the true meaning of the gospel. Our endeavor to "get with it," to be "up-to-date" or avant-garde must never deter us from our calling. I like being fashionable as much as anybody. There is nothing wrong with that, if it does not become a substitute for the substance of our faith. This faith is universal and is identical with God's will to liberate the victims of the land.

To go further, the new styles must not only not obscure the gospel, they must actually be derived from the gospel. Otherwise we run the risk of having our ministry controlled by another Lord. This is the danger of every theological movement. Whether one speaks of the old or new quest of the historical Jesus, liberalism or neo-orthodoxy, secular theology or liberation theologies among Latin Americans, White women or Black people, we must never forget the basic proclamation and praxis that make the gospel *the* gospel in our cultural and political settings.

Whatever we do at Garrett-Evangelical, or Union and Yale, we must not forget about the faith of our mothers and fathers. For it was this faith that enabled our grandparents to survive the slave ships and a lifetime of servitude in North America. Not much has been written about their faith, since they were not White and thus not privileged to learn to read and write theological discourses. Instead, we read about their enslavers and the theological justifications they made in defense of White supremacy and American domination. Of course, the validity of the faith of our mothers and fathers must not be determined by theological criteria devised by the descendants of slave masters. Rather, the authenticity of our parents' faith should be decided by whether or not that faith empowered them to live as they sang. They sang that Jesus is a "bridge over troubled water," that he is the "lily of the valley and the bright and morning star." Our grandparents' claimed that Jesus will "pick you up when you are falling" and "prop you up on every leaning side." To test the validity of these faith claims is to ask whether our parents gave up in despair in slavery and oppression or whether they continued to fight in the knowledge and hope that oppressors did not have the last word about their humanity. I think the historical record speaks for itself. We have been bequeathed a faith that brought our grandparents through hard trials and great tribulations. Therefore we should not abandon it in our search for new lifestyles in the ministry. Since this faith has survived the tests of slavery, lynchings, and ghettos and has sustained our parents in their struggle to be something other than what White people said they were, we Black heirs of this faith should not be too quick to discard the religion of our ancestors. I believe that we ought to follow unashamedly in their footsteps and sing as they once sang:

> Give me that old-time religion,
> Give me that old-time religion,
> Give me that old-time religion,
> It's good enough for me.

The epistemological reason for our confidence in that "old-time religion" is grounded in our claim that "it was good enough for our mothers," and "it was tried in the fiery furnace." Therefore, "it's good enough for you and me." Our parents also claimed that "it will make you love everybody," and "will do when you are dying."

This religion must be the source for our definition of new roles in the ministry.

III. New Roles in the Ministry: Black Women and Men

What are these new roles that are required for the church to remain faithful to the gospel of Jesus expressed in Black people's old-time religion? Since this is a conference called by Black women, I want to say a word about new roles in the Black Church for women and men.

For obvious reasons, this is not an easy subject for me to talk about in that I, like most, have been socially conditioned to accept what White culture has defined as the woman's place in the church and society. And even though I may assert the liberation of Black women, that public assertion alone is no guarantee that I truly share the commitment that Black women should not be oppressed by anybody, including Black male clergy. But regardless of the question that may remain about the validity of my conversion, the gospel is quite clear on this matter. The gospel bears witness to the God who is against oppression in any form, whether inflicted on an oppressed group from the outside or arising from within an oppressed community. The Exodus is the prime example of the first instance and the rise of prophecy is a prominent example of the second. But in both cases, Yahweh leaves no doubt that oppression is not to be tolerated. Therefore, people who claim to believe in the biblical God and also claim that this God supports the subordination of women to men have not really understood the Bible. They have distorted it and thus confused cultural limitations and errors with the message itself.

If the biblical message is one of liberation, then a ministry based on that message must be creative and liberating. There is no place for differences in the roles of men and women in the ministry. God has created man and woman as equals, that is, as co-partners in service of freedom. Therefore, whatever differences are found in present-day churches arise from human sin, that is, the will of men to dominate and control women. If we are to be true ministers of the gospel, then we must create new roles for everyone so that the distinctions between man and woman for the purpose of domination are no longer a reality for our churches. We must liberate our own community from its own internal destructiveness, so that we will be free to fight against oppression in the larger society.

It is a contradiction for Black men to protest against racism in the White church and society at large and then fail to apply the same critique to themselves in their relation to Black women. This contradiction led Sister Frances Beale to comment that the Black man "sees the system for what it is for the most part, but where he rejects its values on many issues, when it comes to women, he seems to take his guidelines from the pages of the *Ladies Home Journal*."[1]

If Black people are going to create new roles in the ministry, Black men will have to recognize that the present status of Black women in the ministry is not acceptable. Since the gospel is about liberation, it demands that we create structures of human relations that enhance freedom and not oppression.

I know that such affirmations are much easier said than done. Where then do we begin? This conference is already a beginning in that it has brought men and women together to discuss their hurts and pains in the ministry. Liberation is not an individual's agenda but, rather, the commitment of the Black community. If we Black men and women shall achieve freedom, we must do it together. Accordingly, the test of the authenticity of our commitment to freedom is found not only in what we say about freedom generally, but in what we do about the liberation of victims within our community. We cannot support a subordinate ministry for women and also claim to be for the liberation of the oppressed. How is Black men's insistence on the subordination of Black women in the church and society any different from White people's enforcement of Black subordination? No matter how much we wish the similarity to be nonexistent, it is unmistakably present. This point has been clearly stated by Anna Hedgman:

> We have had the extra burden of being women. But if you just review the problems that women face, you need only substitute the word Afro-American people for the word women and you have the same problems—job discrimination, want ads that discriminate and false stereotypes.[2]

Moreover, when the heat has cooled and the dust has cleared in the Black man and woman debate, the Black male's arguments against authentic female empowerment, as defined from the Black woman's perspective, are virtually the same as the White racist arguments against Black people. The similarity of the arguments should at least be enough to cause Black men to question heretofore accepted dogma about the secondary role that has been created for women in the Black Church.

I think the time has come for Black men and women to create new roles in the ministry so that the church can better serve as a liberating agent in the community. But the question is: Where do we look for role models in the ministry? Who will provide the resources that we will use for the definition of our ministry? Where will we turn for inspiration, that is, for images that will shape our perceptions of ourselves and what our ministry ought to be? We could say the gospel of Jesus, but that is too easy and consequently does not reflect sufficiently the ambiguity of the relation between culture and the gospel. There is no gospel that is not at the same time related to politics and culture. Therefore whatever we may say about the otherness in the gospel, we cannot avoid asking what cultural and historical resources we will use to organize our perceptions and images of the Christian ministry. Will we turn to Europe or Africa, to White American Christianity or to the Black religious tradition?

This question is especially applicable to Black men whose definition of ministry in relation to women appears to be derived from White church traditions. If our definitions of the ministry are uncritically derived from people who have systematically tried to oppress us, is it not reasonable to conclude that we ought to be suspicious of their models of the ministry? If our perceptions of the woman's place in the ministry is derived from beliefs and doctrines concocted by people who enslaved our grandparents, how do we know that their doctrines about the woman's place are not intimately connected with their beliefs concerning Black people's place? Is it not possible that the two doctrines are derived from the same root disease? This does not necessarily mean that the struggles of White women are identical with Black people's liberation. It does mean that oppressions are interconnected, and if Black men are incapable of self-criticism, we will be guilty of the same crimes against our women as White men are against theirs.

I believe that the resources for our creation of new roles must come from our own tradition. Whatever we may think about the difficulties of male-female relations in the Black community, we know that we have a common heritage, which reaches back to our African homeland. We are an African people; we cannot affirm that too often, because we live in a land where people try to make us believe that we have no identity except what is given by White oppressors. Both Black women and men were stolen from Africa and brought on ships in chains to the shores of the Americas. Both were made to work in the fields from sun-up to nightfall. No distinctions were made between Black men and women in relation to the brutality meted out in slavery. A Gullah woman's comment is graphic and to the point: "Ah done been in sorrow's kitchen and ah licked de pots clean."

But despite White brutality, we have not been destroyed or defeated. We still believe that "we shall overcome." This hope is not a "pie-in-the-sky" religion, but the religion of our grandparents who tested it in the cotton fields of Arkansas, Alabama, and Mississippi. If we create new roles in the ministry on the basis of this religion, there will be no place for those who want to oppress their sisters. We need all the strength, courage, and power that we can get in order to fight against the principalities and powers of this world.

Therefore we conclude with an appeal to Black sisters and brothers in the church: The time has come for us to deal honestly with our differences, our hurts, and our pains. We cannot pretend any longer that all is well and that the problem of male-female relations is limited to the White community. It is in the Black community as well; and it is time that we face up to the need to speak openly and frankly about what is right and wrong in our community in relation to Black men and women. This conference is an important beginning. We must continue the hard task of healing the wounds that we inflict on each other. For it is only as we build strong and healing relationships with each other that we are then given the strength and courage to "keep on keeping on" until freedom comes for all humankind.

Notes

1. "Double Jeopardy: To Be Black and Female," in Toni Cade, ed., *Black Woman* (New York: Signet Book, 1970), p. 92.

2. Cited by Renée Ferguson, "Women's Liberation Has a Different Meaning for Blacks," in Gerda Lerner, *Black Women in White America: A Documentary History* (New York: Random House, 1973), p. 588.

39

BLACK THEOLOGY AND FEMINIST THEOLOGY: A COMPARATIVE VIEW

Pauli Murray

Since the 1960's, contemporary theologians within the Christian tradition have responded to movements around the globe toward liberation of oppressed peoples with a growing body of literature variously called theology of liberation, political theology, theology of hope, or theology of revolution. Their common theme is the relation between Christian theology and social action. While much of this writing has come from Europe and Latin America, black theology and feminist theology are native to the United States and have emerged out of parallel movements for black liberation and women's liberation in this country. The purpose of this essay is to examine briefly the relationship between these two theologies, their common perspectives, their points of tension, and their potential to act as effective forces for liberation within the context of the Christian message.

Theologies of liberation are specific; they are usually written out of the concrete situations and experiences of particular groups. Black theology focuses upon the black experience under white racism; feminist theology is concerned with the revolt of women against male-chauvinist structures of society; Third World theologies develop out of the struggle for national liberation. Their common purpose is to commit Christians to radical political and social change, and to transform society in order to create a new and more humane world. This task is seen as the heart of the Gospel message. Gustavo Gutiérrez, a leading Latin American theologian, defines the purpose and method of this theological undertaking as follows:

Pauli Murray, former Professor of Law and Politics at Brandeis University, holds a J.S.D. degree from Yale Law School and a Master of Divinity from General Theological Seminary. In January 1977 she was ordained a priest in the Episcopal Church. This essay first appeared in the *Anglican Theological Review*, vol. 60, no. 1 (January 1978), pp. 3-24.

The theology of liberation attempts to reflect on the experience and meaning of the faith based on the commitment to abolish injustice and to build a new society; this theology must be verified by the practice of that commitment, by active, effective participation in the struggle which the exploited classes have undertaken against their oppressors. Liberation from every form of exploitation, the possibility of a more human and more dignified life, the creation of a new man—all pass through this struggle.[1]

These theologies are also strategic and contextual. They do not attempt to construct an overarching systematic theology. Their method is inductive, based upon *praxis*, which Letty M. Russell describes as "action that is concurrent with reflection or analysis and leads to new questions, actions and reflections. . . . The direction of thought flows, not 'downward' from 'theological experts' but also upward and outward from the collective experience of action and ministry."[2]

Gutiérrez, writing out of the Latin American experience, frankly acknowledges the influence of Marxist thought, "focusing upon praxis and geared to the transformation of the world." Pointing to the confrontation between contemporary theology and Marxism, he says, "it is to a large extent due to Marxism's influence that theological thought, searching for its own sources, has begun to reflect on the meaning of the transformation of this world and the action of man in history."[3] John C. Bennett sees Gutiérrez as a Marxist in his acceptance of the class struggle as a present reality and the source of revolutionary dynamism. He also notes that Gutiérrez sees the need for revolutionary violence in Latin America if the institutionalized violence of the established order is to be overcome.[4]

While these points of contact with Marxism appear in a Third World context, Marxist liberationist principles cannot be said to be a dominant influence in theologies of liberation. Bennett observes that Gutiérrez' basic theological method is a critical reflection on experience, always in the light of the normative sources of the Christian faith, and believes that he uses Marxism quite freely to illumine his situation in much the same way as Reinhold Niebuhr did in his *Moral Man and Immoral Society* in 1932.[5]

Among writers on black theology, James H. Cone has found Marxist analysis useful in his argument that theological ideas arise out of the social context of existence. However, he thinks that while Marxism may be helpful in providing a theoretical framework with respect to economic oppression any analysis which fails to deal with racism is inadequate.[6] Among feminists, Letty M. Russell acknowledges that groups involved in the struggle for liberation may use various ideologies as "conceptual tools for change," but holds that for Christians, "all ideologies must be subject to constant critique in the light of the gospel."[7]

It is apparent, however, that the theology of liberation goes beyond a particular theological tradition and draws upon many fields of knowledge to illuminate the human situation. Rosemary Ruether argues forcefully for a multidisciplinary integration of human sciences as the necessary foundation for a theology of liberation adequate to the present human condition. She contends that "in order to rise to the task of sketching the horizon of human liberation in its fully redemptive context," the theologian today must be willing to become "the generalist *par excellence* seeing as his context and data the whole range of human science and the whole history of human cultures of self-symbolization."[8]

Liberation theologies, according to Russell, share at least three common perspectives: biblical promises of God's liberation in the Old and New Testaments; viewing the world as history and therefore as a process of change; and strong emphasis upon salvation as a social or communal event which has its beginnings in the here and now.[9] The image of "Christ the Liberator" is part of the ideology of liberation theology and is intended to express the notion that salvation in Christ includes political and social as well as individual spiritual salvation. Christ the Savior liberates man from sin, which is the ultimate root of all injustice and oppression; the struggle for a just society is seen as a significant part of salvation history. In Gutiérrez' analysis, liberation and salvation are inseparably connected. He asserts that the term *liberation* has three distinct levels of meaning: (1) socio-political liberation; (2) a historical process of humanization and self-realization; and (3) liberation from sin and admission to communion with God. The work of Christ as the Liberator embraces all three levels of meaning which are part of an all-embracing process of salvation.[10]

Similarly, liberation theology points to the corporate nature of sin. Sin is not regarded as merely a private and individual transgression which can be cured by individual repentance, leaving unchallenged the social order in which we live. Rather, it is seen as a social, historical fact and is evident in oppressive institutional structures, in human exploitation, and in the domination of peoples, races, and classes.[11] Rosemary Ruether equates corporate evil with St. Paul's reference to "Powers and Principalities." She declares:

> The individualistic concept of sin ignores this social-cosmic dimension of evil. A concentration on individualistic repentance has led, in Christianity, to a petty and privatistic concept of sin which involves the person in obsessive compunction about individual (mostly sexual) immorality, while having no ethical handle at all on the great structures of evil which we raise up corporately to blot out the face of God's creation.[12]

Sin builds up corporate structures of alienation and oppression which man, individually, cannot overcome; salvation from corporate evil, therefore, requires participation in those political processes which seek to destroy injustice and misery. Conversion to Christ, whose saving work is seen as radical liberation from all forms of enslavement and alienation, implies conversion to the neighbor, or as Gutiérrez puts it, "the oppressed person, the exploited class, the despised race, the dominated country." "To place oneself in the perspective of the Kingdom means to participate in the struggle for the liberation of those oppressed by others."[13]

Theology of liberation also calls for a redefinition of the task of the Church in the world. Gutiérrez asserts that salvation is not limited to the action of the Church but is a reality which occurs in history and, therefore, the Church must cease looking upon itself as the exclusive place of salvation and orient itself to a new and radical service to the people. As a sacramental community and a sign of the liberation of humanity and history, the Church in its concrete existence should be a place of liberation and should signify in its own internal structure the salvation whose fulfillment it announces. True renewal of the Church must be on the basis of an effective awareness of the world and a commitment to it; "the Church must be the visible sign of the presence of the Lord within the aspiration for liberation and the struggle for a more human and just society. Only in this way will the message of love which the Church bears be made credible and efficacious."[14]

This method of doing theology is avowedly experimental, but Russell contends that this experiment in liberation is not done only on man's initiative. "It is a way of participating in the humanity of God; joining God's experiment in being together with us, so that we might be together with one another." She points out that while liberation theology looks toward the eschatological future, "the expectation of the full restoration of the groaning universe," it offers hope in the present. "It is *now* that liberation and new humanity have begun." It is now that we must risk the praxis of freedom so that God's will is done on *earth* as it is in heaven!"[15]

As we examine black theology and feminist theology in the light of these general perspectives, we will discover considerable variations in approach and emphasis. We will also find that perhaps the greatest danger to the effectiveness of specific theologies is a tendency to compete with one another in defining a particular form of oppression as the "source of all evil," and thus losing sight of the goal of universal liberation and salvation.[16]

I. Background of Racism and Sexism in the United States

Racism and sexism illustrate corporate evils which are built into the structures of the United States. There are striking similarities in their origins, ideologies, and practices. Race and sex are comparable to the extent that they form large permanent classes identifiable by indelible physical characteristics which fix one's status at birth. Blanche Crozier, a lawyer writing in 1935, pointed out that no other kind of class is as susceptible to implications of innate inferiority. "Only permanent and natural classes are open to those deep, traditional implications which become attached to classes regardless of the actual qualities of the members of the class."[17]

Feminist writers increasingly call attention to the oppression of women as the oldest form of subjugation in human history and suggest that it has served as a model for other kinds of oppression. Gunnar Myrdal's study of the racial problem in the United States, published in 1944, supports this view. He observed that the Negro problem and the women's problem in this country revealed parallels which were not accidental but were rooted in the paternalistic order of preindustrial society.

> In the earlier common law, women and children were placed under the jurisdiction of the paternal power. When a legal status had to be found for the imported Negro servants in the seventeenth century, the nearest and most natural analogy was the status of women and children. The ninth commandment—linking together women, servants, mules and other property—could be invoked as well as a great number of other passages of Holy Scripture.[18]

Thus, although tremendous differences existed between white women and black slaves in actual status and in their relations with the dominant class, the paternalistic idea placed the slave "beside women and children in the power of the *paterfamilias*."[19]

In the American South during the period before the Civil War, "woman was elevated as an ornament and looked upon with pride, while the Negro slave became increasingly a chattel and a ward." Nevertheless, defenders of slavery exploited paternalistic ideology and the inferior status of women in their arguments. George Fitzhugh asserted in *Sociology of the South*, published in 1854, "Wives and apprentices are slaves; not in theory only, but often in fact." He found moral support for slavery in the "instance of the Patriarch Abraham. His wives and his children, his men servants and his maid servants, his camels and his cattel, were all equally his property."[20] Another typical defense called attention to the fact that "the general good requires us to deprive the whole female sex of the right to self-government. They have no voice in the formation of the laws which dispose of their persons and properties."[21]

Women, like Negro slaves, were deprived of the right to vote, legal rights over their property and custody of their children, educational opportunities, and were virtually excluded from participation in government, business, and the professions. After emancipation and well into the twentieth century, similar ideologies were used to rationalize continued subordination of blacks and women—smaller brains, less intellectual capacity, weaker moral fibre, "the woman's place," the "Negro's place," the "contented woman," the "contented Negro," and so on.

These historical similarities have persisted into the present. Both groups continue to experience in varying degrees economic and social exploitation, limited access to educational and professional opportunities, and under-representation at the higher policy levels of the major institutions which shape and control society, all of which contribute to dependency and power-lessness. Members of both groups have internalized negative images projected upon them by the dominant class and absorbed attitudes of inadequacy and self-contempt. Historically, the Christian Church has been deeply implicated in perpetuating the alienation of both groups, and the strong patriarchal tradition in the Church has been especially damaging with respect to women. The context out of which black theology and feminist theology arise, then, is what Ruether characterizes as "the overarching system of racist elite patriarchalism."[22]

11. Black Theology and Feminist Theology Compared

For purposes of comparison, we will rely primarily upon the work of three academic theologians in each of the two fields.[23] Attempts to generalize are hazardous; significant differences in perspective and formulation appear among the writers within each field as well as between the two groups. Strong differences occur in how they perceive God in relation to their struggle and in how they relate to other movements for liberation.

Mary Daly and James H. Cone are ultraradical in their respective analyses and probably stand farthest apart in their theological perspectives. Michael Berenbaum has referred to them as "theologians of survival." He says their suffering has become for them a root experience which now alters their conception of God.[24] Cone places himself within the Gospel tradition, but uses language at times which is so sweeping as to seem foreign to Christian doctrine. A typical example: "Black theology refuses to accept a God who is not identified totally with the goals of the black community. If God is not for us and against white people, then he is a murderer, and we had better kill him."[25] Daly's analysis of sexism has led her, in her own words, to "a dramatic/traumatic change of consciousness from 'radical Catholic' to post-christian feminist" and to reject entirely patriarchal symbols of God.[26]

Black theologians have not successfully resolved the dilemma of specific theologies, that of maintaining a universal perspective within the context of particularization. In their understandable preoccupation with the phenomenon of white racism, they tend to forego a sharpened analysis which would reveal its interrelatedness with other structures of oppression and human exploitation. When Cone defines black theology as a theology of liberation because it believes that "the liberation of black people *is* God's liberation,"[27] he gives the impression that black people only are the instrument of salvation. J. Deotis Roberts disavows any duty of the black theologian to speak on behalf of other minorities although he has great empathy for them and would encourage them to speak for themselves. He argues: "The white oppressor must be confronted by the scandal of particularity. He must not be allowed the escape hatch of universality."[28] The weakness of Roberts' approach is not that he sees his primary task as an analysis of racism but that he appears to overlook the fact that an effective understanding of the black experience in the United States requires knowledge of what Ruether calls the "interstructuring" of racism with sexism and class exploitation. His general tone, however, is more restrained than that of Cone. He defines black theology as liberation theology in more traditional terms.

> Liberation is revolutionary—for blacks it points to *what ought to be*. Black Christians desire radical and rapid social change. . . . We believe that the Christian faith is avowedly revolutionary and, therefore, it may speak to this need with great force.[29]

The point of departure for Ruether and Russell, on the other hand, is the universal human condition to which they speak from a feminist perspective. Ruether keeps in mind the need "to bring together the full picture" of the "history of aberrant spirituality, expressed in self-alienation, world-alienation, and various kinds of social alienations in sexism, anti-Semitism, racism, alienation between classes, and finally colonialist imperialism."[30] Russell defines feminist theology as liberation theology "because it is concerned with the liberation of all people to become full participants in human society."[31]

Daly is closer to Roberts in her suspicion that "universalism" is used as a device to deflect attention from sexual caste. "One frequently hears 'But isn't the real problem human liberation?' The difficulty with this approach is that the words may be 'true,' but when used to avoid the specific problems of sexism they are radically untruthful."[32] While Daly gives priority to feminist liberation, she also claims for it a universal goal. The purpose of her work *Beyond God the Father*

> is to show that the women's revolution, insofar as it is true to its own essential dynamics, is an ontological, spiritual revolution, pointing beyond the idolatries of a sexist society and sparking creative action in and toward transcendence. The becoming of women implies universal becoming. It has everything to do with the search for ultimate meaning and reality, which some would call God.[33]

On the crucial questions of violence and reconciliation in the context of black-white confrontation in America, Cone's position is radically different from that of his colleagues in black theology. Cone appears to embrace revolutionary violence and argues that no one can be nonviolent in an unjust society.[34] Roberts rejects violence not only because he believes it is inconsistent with the Christian ethic but also because he thinks it is pragmatically and psychologically bad for blacks.

> The workability of violence as a means to a better position for blacks is in question. As one who has seen the stark face of racial violence in several major cities and observed up close the tragic aftermath for blacks (even at the hands of their own soul brothers), I have yet to be convinced of the pragmatic test of violence.[35]

Major J. Jones, whose work *Christian Ethics for Black Theology* examines the ethical implications of strategies for liberation, raises a number of questions about violence as a means of self-defense in the struggle for liberation. He poses the alternative of nonviolence as both a theology and a method of social action, and points to the thought of Dr. Martin Luther King, Jr.

> For him [King], nonviolence was not a capitulation to weakness and fear; rather nonviolence demanded that difficult kind of steadfastness which can endure indignation with dignity. For King, nonviolence always attempted to reconcile and establish a relationship rather than humiliate the opponent. For him nonviolence was always directed against the evil rather than against the person responsible for the evil.[36]

Roberts' perspective includes an abiding concern for reconciliation. He asserts that "liberation and reconciliation are the two main poles of black theology," and that "authentic existence for blacks and whites can only be realized finally in reconciliation as equals in the body of Christ." He believes there can be no liberation without reconciliation and no reconciliation without liberation, and says that the only Christian way in race relations is a liberating experience for white oppressor as well as black oppressed.[37] Jones also holds this view and believes that the black man "cannot find the way to liberation and a larger freedom for himself without also finding the way to liberation and freedom for his white brother."[38]

Cone is sharply critical of Roberts' view that black theology must work at the task of intercommunication between blacks and whites so that white Christians may be led to understand and work with blacks for liberation and reconciliation on an interracial basis. For Cone, "All talk about reconciliation with white oppressors, with mutual dialogue about its meaning, has no place in black power or Black Theology." He thinks such talk opens the door "not only for white people to be oppressors and Christians *at the same time*, but also for them to participate in black liberation and to set the *terms* of our reconciliation with them." He projects the black struggle as a closed circle to which white people may be admitted only by repentance and conversion on terms defined by black people.[39]

Both black theology and feminist theology express the goal of *wholeness* of the human being, of authentic selfhood, self-esteem, and dignity. They deal with questions of identity, the retrieval of lost history, the destruction of self-depreciation, and liberating self-affirmation. Letty Russell refers to this process as *conscientization*, a term borrowed from Latin American theology, through which people come to a self-awareness that helps them to shape their own personal and social history and learn their own potential for action in shaping the world.[40]

A crucial task for both theologies is what Russell calls "the search for a usable past."[41] Black theology sees its task as one of reclaiming a people from humiliation and achieving black consciousness, black pride, and black self-determination. Cone relates black theology to an identity crisis.

> There is more at stake in the struggle for survival than mere physical existence. You have to be *black* with a knowledge of the history of this country to know what America means to black people. You also have to know what it means to be a nonperson, a nothing, a person with no past to know what Black Power is all about. Survival as a person means not only food and shelter, but also belonging to a community that remembers and understands the meaning of its past. Black consciousness is an attempt to recover a past deliberately destroyed by slave masters, an attempt to revive old survival symbols and create new ones.[42]

For Roberts the task of black theology is to provide an understanding of black self-awareness and black pride and "at the same time, to give a helpful interpretation of the Christian faith to those who honestly seek to be their true black selves and Christians at the same time."[43] In seeking continuity of tradition with the African past, he finds linkages between the African world view and black religious tradition in the United States which he thinks are worthy of further exploration. He also argues that American blacks, being neither fully African nor fully American, but in a real sense participating in both worlds, "may yet be the most important bridge to humanize relations between the West and the Third World."[44]

From the feminist perspective, Ruether sees the first stage of women's liberation as the process of raising consciousness, of exorcizing debasing self-images which women have internalized. This "involves the exploration of the history of sexism and the reconstruction of its ideology in order to loosen its hold on the self and to permit the gradual growth of self-definition over against a world defined in male terms."[45] Russell observes that almost all existing historical records have been preserved by men who defined women's roles and functions for them and that for women as a group, awareness of their own history and struggles is frequently nonexistent. She notes that the attempt on the part of women "to recreate a usable past as *her-story* and not just *his-story* is part of a widespread development in the modern world," and sees it as a necessary effort in order for women to shape their future as partners in society.[46]

Both groups are also engaged in a critical reexamination of biblical tradition as well as Christian theology and anthropology. Roberts and Ruether call attention to the dualistic strain in Christianity absorbed from the Platonic view of the split in human existence between body and soul, which they find antagonistic to the principle of wholeness in human relations.[47] Ruether relates it explicitly to the subjugation of women. She finds that this dualistic view which Christianity inherited from classical civilization repressed the possibility of the liberation of women—a possibility clearly revealed in the teaching and action of Jesus and in the early Christian community—by "equating soul-body dualism with male-female dualism, and thus reestablishing the subordination of women in a new form."[48] She also shows how religious tradition has facilitated this subjugation.

> Traditional theological images of God as father have been the sanctification of sexism and hierarchalism precisely by defining this relationship of God as father to humanity in a domination-subordination model and by allowing ruling class males to identify themselves with this divine fatherhood in such a way as to establish themselves in the same kind of hierarchical relationship to women and lower classes.[49]

This analysis has implications for both blacks and women in their attempts to express images of God which will be meaningful to them in their struggle. Black theologians, however, seem to have no difficulty with patriarchal symbolism. For Cone and Roberts, at least, the concern is racial. Both reject a "white Americanized Christ" and have substituted the symbol of a Black Christ. According to Cone,

> To say that Christ is black means that black people are God's poor people whom Christ has come to liberate. . . . To say that Christ is black means that God, in his infinite wisdom and mercy, not only takes color seriously, he takes it upon himself and discloses his will to make us whole—new creatures born in the divine blackness and redeemed through the blood of the Black Christ. . . . The "blackness of Christ," therefore, is not simply a statement about skin color, but rather the transcendent affirmation that God has not ever, no not ever, left the oppressed alone in the struggle.[50]

Roberts wrestles with the implications of such particularism and offers the following explanation:

> In one sense Christ must be said to be universal and therefore colorless. Only in a symbolic or mythical sense, then, must we understand the black Messiah in the context of the black religious experience. . . . In other words the universal Christ is particularized for the black Christian in the black experience of the black Messiah, but the black Messiah is at

the same time universalized in the Christ of the Gospels who meets all men in their situation. The *black Messiah* liberates the black man. The universal Christ *reconciles* the black man with the rest of mankind.[51]

Ruether's comment on this symbolism is that since God is the God of all men, each in his own particular culture, "the Gospel rightfully comes to the black man in the form of a Black Messiah . . . in the sense of that historical contextualism, which gives to each people a salvation that encounters their situation."[52]

Jones, however, seems less certain about the usefulness of such imagery in the long run. He concedes that "when the oppressed is no longer willing to accept or adopt the God of his oppressor, especially his explicit or implicit color as it is expressed in art and literature, then the process of liberation has already begun." He also suggests that it is a sign of maturity when an oppressed people are no longer willing to adopt without question a religion or God who accepts the idea of inequality for any part of the human family. But he wonders "what this altering of God's color will do for the black man. Will it make him, as a mature religious person, any more responsible with the use of his newly acquired black power than the white man was with his white power? Will the black man, with his black God, be a better man than the white man was with his white God?" He observes that those who advocate black awareness and separation as a means to achieve the ultimate realization of black self-identity often ignore the fact that the humanity of man is much deeper than color.

> The deeper question is whether it is possible for God to acquire color without becoming identified with that which is too narrow to be fully representative of the total human family, much less that which is Divine. . . . This is the inherent danger in representing God in any human conception, either concrete or abstract.[53]

The question of theological symbolism arises in a more intensified form for women confronted with the weight of Judaeo-Christian tradition filled with imagery of an exclusively male, patriarchal God. Religion, as Ruether points out, "is undoubtedly the single most important shaper and enforcer of the image and role of women in society."[54] Joan Arnold Romero accurately describes how women are beginning to respond.

> In much the same way as blacks have experienced the white Jesus in a white church preaching an alienating message, a number of women, too, are becoming conscious of the alienation from a masculine God, a masculine Church, and a masculine theology. For women the situation has in many ways been worse, for they form the bulk of the population

of the Church, while in the structures of authority as represented both theologically and institutionally, it is men who have had the role of representing God to the people.[55]

The negative impact upon women of the "maleness" of God-language cannot be regarded lightly. In her study of sexist ideologies, Ruether points to language as the prime reflection of the power of the ruling group to define reality in its own terms and demote oppressed groups into invisibility. "Women, more than any other group, are overwhelmed by a linguistic form that excludes them from visible existence."[56] Nelle Morton has dramatized this issue by using reversed terminology. She asks what image is invoked in the reader:

> When one enrolls in a seminar on "The Doctrine of Woman" [and] the professor intends at least to deal with men also. When one sings of the Motherhood of God and the Sisterhood of Woman, one breathes a prayer that all men as well as women will come to experience true sisterhood.[57]

Daly speaks of liberation as retrieving the power to name.

> To exist humanly is to name the self, the world, and God. The "method" of the evolving spiritual consciousness of women is nothing less than this beginning to speak humanly—a reclaiming of the right to name. The liberation of language is rooted in the liberation of ourselves.[58]

She introduces the phrase "sisterhood of man," explaining:

> What "sisterhood of man" does is to give a generic weight to "sister-hood" which the term has never before been called upon to bear. At the same time it emasculates the pseudo-generic "man." The expression, then, raises the problem of a sexually oppressive world and it signals other possibilities.[59]
> Similarly, she speaks of "the death of God the Father in the rising woman-consciousness and the consequent breakthrough to conscious, communal participation in God the Verb."[60]

Thus, while a black theologian may find the Old Testament symbolism of the Chosen People "important for the unity of purpose among black people and the feeling that their group life has lasting salvific significance,"[61] a feminist theologian may look upon the Old Testament as "a man's 'book,' where women appear for the most part simply as adjuncts of men, significant only in the context of men's activities."[62] While Roberts finds the symbol of the black Christ "related to the affirmation of blackness and the antidote of self-hatred,"[63] Daly finds the patriarchal implications of Christology so overwhelming and "the functioning of the Christ image in Christianity to legitimate sexual hierarchy" so blatant that she would move beyond what she terms "Christolatry" to the "Second Coming of Women," the "new arrival of the female presence, once strong and powerful, but enchained since the dawn of patriarchy."[64]

The images "Black Messiah" and the "Second Coming of Women" are irreconcilable symbols to one who shares both the black experience and the experience of being a woman. Ruether thinks it impossible for the black movement to respond to Daly's sort of feminist theology because of her heavy stress on mariological symbols as symbols of feminine superiority and her judgmental symbol of castration. Ruether believes these symbols "are totally encapsulated in white racism through which black women and black men have been victimized" and, instead of being liberating, "such symbols seem simply expressions of white sexual pathology conducting business as usual."[65] Both the racial and the sexual symbols point to the danger of exclusivism.

Russell seeks to avoid both extremes. She believes that Christian women can see in Jesus one who helped both men and women to understand their total personhood, and that to think of Christ first in terms of his racial origin or his male sex "is to revert again to *biological determinism* which affirms that the most important thing about a person is her or his race or sex. The most important affirmation of ourselves and of Jesus is that we want to be accepted as subjects and persons, within whom biological differentiation is a secondary aspect."[66]

III. Areas of Tension

Although certain historical similarities and common motifs would suggest a basis for fruitful dialogue between black theology and feminist theology, so far this has not happened. Ruether has been deeply concerned about the tensions between the two groups. In a thoughtful analysis she has observed that although these are the two most important theologies of liberation to emerge in the United States, "an undeclared war is brewing between them." She notes that both groups are potential victims of typical efforts on the part of a ruling class to divide and rule.[67] She points to the historical parallel in the nineteenth century when women leaders who supported abolition of slavery became alienated after the Civil War as they saw their own concerns shunted aside by white male legislators who extended suffrage to black males only, and warns this can happen again in this century unless women and blacks can find ways to avoid the trap. The symptoms are already evident.

> Black caucuses, appearing a year or two earlier than women's caucuses, have generally denied reciprocal solidarity with the women's movement. . . . In the black power and black nationalist movements that

arose in the latter half of the 1960's the negative reactions toward women's liberation have come from many black males themselves. Far from being open to the question of female oppression, the model of black liberation has appeared to be modeled after the super-male chauvinist traditions.[68]

Analyzing the roots of this clash, Ruether focuses upon the results of plantation slavery in the American South which depended not only upon a debasing racist anthropology but also upon the destruction of black family life, sexual exploitation of the black woman, and suppression of the rights of the black male as husband, father, and householder. Postbellum white racism was a system which combined social and economic deprivation of the black group with direct terrorization of the black family, especially directed against the black male. Today, Ruether says, "the memory of that terrorization still forms the ultimate point of reference for black liberation." She notes that the movement for black liberation "has been overwhelmingly male-oriented in style and leadership."[69]

Differences in status and outlook contribute to misunderstandings and tensions. Blacks have been set apart through rigidly enforced segregation buttressed by institutionalized violence. Their apartness and the pervasiveness of their humiliation gave rise to a high degree of solidarity against racial oppression, the development of parallel institutions, notably the black Church, and to recurring periods of intense cultural nationalism. Thus, black theologians speak of a quest for a distinctive "peoplehood."

Women's status is more ambiguous. Ruether notes that sociologically, women are a caste within every class and race. As women, they share a common condition of dependency, secondary existence, domestic labor, sexual exploitation, and the projection of their role in procreation into a total definition of their existence. But this common condition is expressed in profoundly different forms, she says, as women are divided against each other by class and race.[70] In sum, women are distributed throughout every segment of the population and share the particular advantages or disadvantages of the race or class to which they belong. It is difficult for a black person to see a white upper-class woman as "oppressed." Her concerns seem trivial beside the stark struggle of existence. For many blacks, she represents the white "oppressor." Black males, especially, express the fear that the women's movement is a diversionary tactic to deflect attention from the more urgent struggle for black liberation.

Ruether suggests that racism and sexism should not be looked upon as exactly parallel but as "interstructural elements within the overarching system of white male domination." As she sees it,

> this interstructuring of oppression by sex, race, and also class creates intermediate tensions and alienations—between white women and black women, between black men and white women, and even between

black men and black women. Each group tends to suppress the experience of its racial and sexual counterparts. The black movement talks as though "blacks" mean black males. In doing so it conceals the tensions between black males and black females. The women's movement fails to integrate the experience of black and poor women, and so fails to see that much of what it means by female experience is confined to those women within the dominant class and race.[71]

She is critical of a tendency among radical feminists to make a monolithic analysis of sexism as the ultimate evil and believes it essential that the women's movement reach out and include in its struggle the interstructuring of sexism with all other kinds of oppression as well as recognize the pluralism of women's movements in the context of different groupings. Otherwise, she thinks, the women's movement will tend to remain a women's movement of the white upper class that can be misused to consolidate the power of that class against the poor and nonwhite of both sexes. She also believes that only as autonomous women's movements develop in the context of various kinds of race, ethnic, and class oppression will the missing links in the structure of oppression become visible.[72]

Black theology presently suffers from a similar tendency toward monolithic analysis. It reveals little understanding of the problems of black women as women and almost totally ignores feminist theology. Black women are torn between their loyalty to their racial community and growing consciousness of the need to struggle against sexism. Although they are now beginning to form their own feminist networks, there is a dearth of black women theologians—due in large part to the strong patriarchal tradition of the black Church—who can bring to bear their influence upon the development of black theology. The interlocking factors of racism and sexism within the black experience await analysis.

IV. Possibilities and Limitations

One can make only tentative assessments of theologies still in their embryonic stages, but it would seem that black theology and feminist theology have the potential to develop as strong forces for the renewal of Christian dynamism in the United States. They speak prophetically to the Church, confronting it with its own contradictions. Ruether says bluntly that the Church has allowed itself to become the cultural guardian of the symbols of domination and subjugation and this role is apostasy to the mission of the Church. The Church must exorcise these demonic symbols within its structure and must recover its own revolutionary heritage as liberating force in the world.

The gospel of the Church must again come to be the recognized social mandate of human history, not the means of setting up a new regime of domination or, on the other hand, of withdrawing into a private world of individual "salvation."[73]

For those who, by birth or circumstance, are necessarily involved in the struggle against racism, sexism, or both, these theologies present many liberating ideas, offer hope and a vision of new humanity. In doing so they help to give deeper meanings to the Christian faith and its relevance to their struggle.

On the other hand, as we have seen, there are certain limiting factors which seem to arise out of efforts to particularize the theology of liberation within different contexts. Carried to the extreme, particularization can stifle self-criticism, lead to isolation and ultimately frustration. It can develop into a myopia and obscure the vision of the wholeness of humanity which liberation theologians seek. We have already made reference to this danger in discussing the tensions between the black movement and the feminist movement. Here we call attention to the tendency to identify without qualification the suffering of a particular group with righteousness and redemption. This tendency appears in Third World theology[74] and is particularly strong in Cone's writings. He uses language which identifies "whiteness" with all that is evil and "blackness" with authentic personhood. His identification of blacks with ultimate righteousness is central to his theological perspective. A striking example is his assertion that "[t]he divine election of the oppressed means that black people are given the power of judgment over the high and mighty whites."[75]

Cone has drawn sharp criticism from his black colleagues for his extreme views. Jones wonders "whether Cone's God is big enough for the liberation struggle," and says "the black Christian can never dismiss the fact that the white oppressor is also God's child in need of a redemption of another kind."[76] Roberts is also concerned that blacks not fall into the danger of exchanging physical oppression for the bondage of race hate on the part of blacks themselves. Blacks should "be aware that their own togetherness is shot through with the possibility of exploitation of one another." Roberts warns that sin as self-centeredness is a disease which infects the black community as well as the white community. "Even the black church has not escaped the blight of self-centeredness."[77]

Ruether finds that liberation theologies which stress "the role of the 'oppressed community' as the primary locus of the power for repentance and judgment" have adopted this model from the literature of apocalypticism. This model has inherent limitations, she believes. The initial effort of self-affirmation on the part of an oppressed group becomes distorted at the point where all evil is projected upon an alien group, "so that judgment is merely a rejection of that 'other' group of persons, and salvation simply self-affirmation *per se*" without regard for the humanity of the oppressors. She is convinced that all theologies of liberation will abort both their power to liberate themselves and their possibilities as a liberating force for their oppressors "unless they finally go beyond the apocalyptic sectarian model of the oppressor and the oppressed" and "rise to a perspective that affirms a universal humanity as the ground of their own self-identity, and also to a power of self-criticism."[78]

To a great extent, the writings of Ruether and Russell, who stand within the Christian tradition, reveal an awareness of the need for broad social analysis, a sensitivity to other forms of oppression, a willingness to engage in dialogue with black theology, and to overcome the tensions. Despite the limitations of feminist analysis to which Ruether has referred, feminist theology indicates an inclusive approach and a capacity for self-critical reflection which, if taken seriously, can be a powerful force for humanizing the entire spectrum of liberation movements. As Ruether points out, no other definable group has such a broad range of historical tasks. "The woman's story must encompass the entire scope of the human condition. Moreover the issue of sexism crosses and includes every field of specialization."[79] Women, through coalitions on issues of common concern, can begin to transcend barriers of race, class, and nationality. They can provide a basis for intercommunication and interpenetration of all social structures and act as leaven within all groups.

Black theology has much to gain by recognizing this dynamic potential as a resource which can be tapped to strengthen rather than compete with the black liberation movement. It offers a vital link to broader insights and larger perspectives. It also offers the possibility of effective cooperation, especially at points where race, sex, and class intersect. Such interchange and cooperation within the Christian context make it possible to experience moments of liberation and reconciliation, however fleeting and fragmentary, in the course of the struggle. These glimpses of the "new creation" and the "new human being" provide the hope which is the wellspring of any meaningful theology of liberation in our time.

Notes

1. Gustavo Gutiérrez, *A Theology of Liberation*, tr. and ed. Caridad Inda and John Eagleson (Maryknoll, N.Y.: Orbis Books, 1973), p. 307.

2. Letty M. Russell, *Human Liberation in a Feminist Perspective–A Theology* (Philadelphia: Westminster Press, 1974), p. 55. The Oxford Universal Dictionary defines *praxis* as action, practice. Gutiérrez writes of "the importance of concrete behavior, of deeds, of action, of praxis in the Christian life." In liberation theology the term seems to carry the meaning *action-reflection* in a continuing process.

3. Gutiérrez, *Theology of Liberation*, p. 9.

4. John C. Bennett, *The Radical Imperative* (Philadelphia: Westminster Press, 1975), p. 136.

5. Bennett, *Radical Imperative*, p. 134. Gutiérrez writes, "Our purpose is not to elaborate an ideology to justify postures already taken. . . . It is rather to let ourselves be judged by the Word of the Lord, to think through our faith, to strengthen our love, and to give reason for our hope from within a commitment which seeks to become more radical, total and efficacious. It is to reconsider the great themes of Christian life within this radically changed perspective and with regard to the new questions posed by the commitment." *Theology of Liberation*, p. ix.

6. James H. Cone, *God of the Oppressed* (New York: Seabury Press, 1975), pp. 42-43, 155-156. J. Deotis Roberts says that "Black political theology is not cast in the mold of the

Marxist-Christian dialogue." *A Black Political Theology* (Philadelphia: Westminster Press, 1974), p. 218.

7. Russell, *Human Liberation*, p. 60.

8. Rosemary Radford Ruether, *Liberation Theology* (New York: Paulist Press, 1972), pp. 2-3.

9. Russell, *Human Liberation*, pp. 56-62. God is portrayed in both the Old Testament and New Testament as the Liberator, the one who sets people free. God is not the liberator of one small nation or group, but of all humankind, pp. 56-57.

10. Gutiérrez, *Theology of Liberation*, pp. 175-178.

11. Gutiérrez, *Theology of Liberation*, ch. 9.

12. Ruether, *Liberation Theology*, p. 8.

13. Gutiérrez, *Theology of Liberation*, pp. 203-205. See also Frederick Herzog, *Liberation Theology* (New York: Seabury Press, 1972), passim.

14. Gutiérrez, *Theology of Liberation*, pp. 256-261, 262.

15. Russell, *Human Liberation*, pp. 183-185.

16. "In order to qualify as true liberation movements, *black liberation* from the oppressors and *women's liberation* from the traditionally fixed set of feminine roles should regard themselves as steps on the road toward a *human liberation of all people*, becoming free in conformity with the authentic humanity of the Son of Man. . . . The time may have come to divest ourselves of the ideological fixations of our own peculiar concerns and to seek concrete cooperation with other liberation movements. It is impossible to eliminate racism without putting an end to economic exploitation by one part of the human family of their brothers and sisters. True human rights for women is a utopia as long as we refuse to eliminate racism and a competitive society." Elisabeth Moltmann-Wendel and Jürgen Moltmann, Foreword to *Human Liberation*, by Russell, pp. 13-14, 15.

17. Blanche Crozier, "Constitutionality of Discrimination Based on Sex," *Boston University Law Review* 15 (1935):723, 727-728.

18. Gunnar Myrdal, *An American Dilemma* (New York: Harper & Bros., 1944), Appendix 5, "A Parallel to the Negro Problem," pp. 1073-1078, 1073.

19. Myrdal, *American Dilemma*, p. 1073.

20. Cited and quoted in Myrdal, *American Dilemma*, pp. 1073-1074.

21. Charles Hodge, "The Bible Argument on Slavery" (1860), cited and quoted in Myrdal, *American Dilemma*, p. 1074.

22. Rosemary Ruether, *New Woman/New Earth: Sexist Ideologies and Human Liberation* (New York: Seabury Press, 1975), p. 116.

23. The writers selected for black theology are: James H. Cone (Union Theological Seminary); J. Deotis Roberts (Howard University School of Religion); and Major J. Jones (Gammon Theological Seminary in Atlanta). The writers on feminist theology are: Mary Daly (Boston College); Letty M. Russell (Yale Divinity School); and Rosemary Radford Ruether (Garrett Theological Seminary). The three black theologians are Protestant. Daly and Ruether are products of the Roman Catholic tradition; Letty Russell is an ordained Presbyterian minister.

24. Michael Berenbaum, "Women, Blacks, and Jews: Theologians of Survival," *Religion in Life: A Christian Quarterly of Opinion and Discussion* 45 (Spring 1976): 106-118.

25. James H. Cone, *A Black Theology of Liberation* (Philadelphia: J. B. Lippincott Co., 1970), pp. 59-60.

26. Mary Daly, *The Church and the Second Sex, With a New Feminist Post-Christian Introduction by the Author* (New York: Harper Colophon Books, 1975), p. 5. See also Mary Daly, *Beyond God the Father: Toward a Philosophy of Women's Liberation* (Boston: Beacon Press, 1973).

27. Cone, *Black Theology of Liberation*, p. 23.

28. Roberts, *Black Political Theology*, p. 16.

29. J. Deotis Roberts, *Liberation and Reconciliation: A Black Theology* (Philadelphia: Westminster Press, 1971), p. 27. Cf. Major J. Jones, *Black Awareness: A Theology of Hope* (Nashville: Abingdon Press, 1971), passim.

30. Ruether, *Liberation Theology*, p. 21.

31. Russell, *Human Liberation*, p. 20.

32. Daly, *Beyond God the Father*, pp. 4-5.

33. Daly, *Beyond God the Father*, p. 6.

34. James H. Cone, *Black Theology and Black Power* (New York: Seabury Press, 1969), pp. 138ff; and *God of the Oppressed*, pp. 217ff.

35. Roberts, *Liberation and Reconciliation*, p. 189.

36. Major J. Jones, *Christian Ethics for Black Theology* (Nashville: Abingdon Press, 1974), p. 142.

37. Roberts, *Liberation and Reconciliation*, pp. 25, 26; and *Black Political Theology*, p. 222.

38. Jones, *Christian Ethics*, p. 195.

39. Cone, *God of the Oppressed*, pp. 239, 241, 242. See footnote 75 *infra*.

40. Russell, *Human Liberation*, p. 66. Cf. Paulo Freire, *Pedagogy of the Oppressed* (New York: Seabury Press, 1973), passim.

41. Russell, *Human Liberation*, ch. 3.

42. Cone, *Black Theology of Liberation*, p. 37.

43. Roberts, *Liberation and Reconciliation*, p. 14.

44. Roberts, *Black Political Theology*, pp. 53, 55-56, 74ff.

45. Ruether, *New Woman/New Earth*, p. 29.

46. Russell, *Human Liberation*, p. 81.

47. Roberts, *Black Political Theology*, pp. 75, 84-85.

48. Ruether, *Liberation Theology*, p. 99.

49. Ruether, *New Woman/New Earth*, p. 65.

50. Cone, *God of the Oppressed*, pp. 136-137.

51. Roberts, *Liberation and Reconciliation*, pp. 139-140.

52. Ruether, *Liberation Theology*, p. 133.

53. Jones, *Black Awareness*, pp. 115, 116.

54. Rosemary R. Ruether, ed. *Religion and Sexism* (New York: Simon & Schuster, 1974), p. 9.

55. Joan Arnold Romero, "The Protestant Principle: A Woman's-Eye View of Barth and Tillich," in *Religion and Sexism*, ed. Ruether, p. 319.

56. Ruether, *New Woman/New Earth*, p. xiii.

57. Nelle Morton, "Preaching the Word," in *Sexist Religion and Women in the Church*, ed. Alice L. Hageman (New York: Association Press, 1974), p. 29.

58. Daly, *Beyond God the Father*, p. 8.

59. Daly, *Beyond God the Father*, p. 9.

60. Daly, *Beyond God the Father*, p. 12.

61. Roberts, *Liberation and Reconciliation*, p. 58.

62. Phyllis Bird, "Images of Women in the Old Testament," in *Religion and Sexism*, ed. Ruether, p. 41.

63. Roberts, *Black Political Theology*, p. 137.

64. Daly, *Beyond God the Father*, pp. 79, 96.

65. Ruether, *New Woman/New Earth*, p. 121.

66. Russell, *Human Liberation*, pp. 138-139.

67. Ruether, *New Woman/New Earth*, p. 115.

68. Ruether, *New Woman/New Earth*, p. 116.

69. Ruether, *New Woman/New Earth*, pp. 117-121.

70. Ruether, *New Woman/New Earth*, p. 125.

71. Ruether, *New Woman/New Earth*, p. 116. For a discussion of the analogous position of race and sex in the process of social control and of social change, and of the differences, see William H. Chafe, *Women and Equality* (New York: Oxford University Press, 1977), chaps. 3, 4.

72. Ruether, *New Woman/New Earth*, pp. 121-125, 131-132.

73. Ruether, *New Woman/New Earth*, p. 82.

74. "The future of history belongs to the poor and exploited. True liberation will be the work of the oppressed themselves; in them, the Lord saves history." Gutiérrez, *Theology of Liberation*, p. 208.

75. Cone, *God of the Oppressed*, p. 225. "When the whites undergo the true experience of conversion wherein they die to whiteness and are reborn anew in order to struggle *against* white oppression and *for* the liberation of the oppressed, there is a place for them in the black struggle of freedom. Here reconciliation becomes God's gift of blackness through the oppressed of the land. But it must be made absolutely clear that the black community decides both the *authenticity* of white conversion and also the place these converts will play in the black struggle of freedom. The converts can have nothing to say about the validity of their conversion experience or what is best for the community or their place in it, *except* as permitted by the oppressed community itself." Ibid., p. 242.

76. Jones, *Christian Ethics*, pp. 69-74.

77. Roberts, *Liberation and Reconciliation*, pp. 112-113.

78. Ruether, *Liberation Theology*, pp. 10-16. Elsewhere Ruether speaks of "the tendency of both the black movement and the women's movement to ignore the structures of oppression within their own groups and to attempt to reduce 'oppression' to a single-factored analysis. . . . To recognize structures of oppression within our own group would break up this model of ultimate righteousness and projection of guilt upon the 'others.' It would force us to deal with ourselves, not as simply oppressed or oppressors, but as people who are sometimes one and sometimes the other in different contexts. A more mature and chastened analysis of the capacities of human beings for good and evil would flow from this perception. The flood gates of righteous anger must then be tempered by critical self-knowledge." *New Woman/New Earth,* p. 132.

79. Ruether, *New Woman/New Earth*, p. 12.

40

BLACK THEOLOGY AND
THE BLACK WOMAN

Jacquelyn Grant

Liberation theologies have arisen out of the contexts of the liberation struggles of Black Americans, Latin Americans, American women, Black South Africans and Asians. These theologies represent a departure from traditional Christian theology. As a collective critique, liberation theologies raise serious questions about the normative use of Scripture, tradition and experience in Christian theology. Liberation theologians assert that the reigning theologies of the West have been used to legitimate the established order. Those to whom the church has entrusted the task of interpreting the meaning of God's activity in the world have been too content to represent the ruling classes. For this reason, say the liberation theologians, theology has generally not spoken to those who are oppressed by the political establishment.

Ironically, the criticism that liberation theology makes against classical theology has been turned against liberation theology itself. Just as most European and American theologians have acquiesced in the oppression of the West, for which they have been taken to task by liberation theologians, some liberation theologians have acquiesced in one or more oppressive aspects of the liberation struggle itself. Where racism is rejected, sexism has been embraced. Where classism is called into question, racism and sexism have been tolerated. And where sexism is repudiated racism and classism are often ignored.

Although there is a certain validity to the argument that any one analysis—race, class or sex—is not sufficiently universal to embrace the needs of all oppressed peoples, these particular analyses, nonetheless, have all been well

Jacquelyn Grant, a graduate student at Union Theological Seminary, New York City, is a lecturer at Harvard Divinity School. Her essay is published here for the first time.

presented and are crucial for a comprehensive and authentic liberation theology. In order for liberation theology to be faithful to itself it must hear the critique coming to it from the perspective of the Black woman—perhaps the most oppressed of all the oppressed.

I am concerned in this essay with how the experience of the Black woman calls into question certain assumptions in Liberation Theology in general, and Black Theology in particular. In the Latin American context this has already been done by women such as Beatriz Melano Couch and Consuelo Urquiza. A few Latin American theologians have begun to respond. Beatriz Couch, for example, accepts the starting point of Latin American theologians, but criticizes them for their exclusivism with respect to race and sex. She says:

> . . . we in Latin America stress the importance of the starting point, the praxis, and the use of social science to analyze our political, historical situation. In this I am in full agreement with my male colleagues . . . with one qualitative difference. I stress the need to give importance to the different cultural forms that express oppression; to the ideology that divides people not only according to class, but to race and sex. Racism and sexism are oppressive ideologies which deserve a specific treatment in the theology of liberation.[1]

More recently, Consuelo Urquiza called for the unification of Hispanic-American women in struggling against their oppression in the church and society. In commenting on the contradiction in the Pauline Epistles which undergird the oppression of the Hispanic-American woman, Urquiza said: "At the present time all Christians will agree with Paul in the first part of [Galatians 3:28] about freedom and slavery that there should not be slaves. . . . However, the next part of this verse . . . has been ignored and the equality between man and woman is not accepted. They would rather skip that line and go to the epistle to Timothy [2:9-15]."[2] Women theologians of Latin background are beginning to do theology and to sensitize other women to the necessity of participating in decisions which affect their lives and the life of their communities. Latin American theology will gain from these inputs which women are making to the theological process.

Third World and Black women[3] in the United States will soon collaborate in an attack on another aspect of Liberation Theology—Feminist Theology. Black and Third World women have begun to articulate their differences and similiarities with the Feminist Movement, which is dominated by White American women who until now have been the chief authors of Feminist Theology. It is my contention that the theological perspectives of Black and Third World women should reflect these differences and similarities with Feminist Theology. It is my purpose, however, to look critically at Black Theology as a Black woman in an effort to determine how adequate is its conception of liberation for the total Black community. Pauli Murray and Theressa Hoover have in their own ways challenged Black Theology. Because their articles appear in this section (Documents 39 and 37), it is unnecessary for me to explain their point of view. They have spoken for themselves.

I want to begin with the question: "Where are Black women in Black Theology?" They are, in fact, invisible in Black Theology and we need to know why this is the case. Because the Black church experience and Black experience in general are important sources for doing Black Theology, we need to look at the Black woman in relation to both in order to understand the way Black Theology has applied its conception of liberation. Finally, in view of the status of the Black woman vis-à-vis Black Theology, the Black Church and the Black experience, a challenge needs to be presented to Black Theology. This is how I propose to discuss this important question.

The Invisibility of Black Women in Black Theology

In examining Black Theology it is necessary to make one of two assumptions: *(1)* either Black women have no place in the enterprise, or *(2)* Black men are capable of speaking for us. Both of these assumptions are false and need to be discarded. They arise out of a male-dominated culture which restricts women to certain areas of the society. In such a culture, men are given the warrant to speak for women on all matters of significance. It is no accident that all of the recognized Black theologians are men. This is what might be expected given the status and power accorded the discipline of theology. Professional theology is done by those who are highly trained. It requires, moreover, mastery of that power most accepted in the definition of manhood, the power or ability to "reason." This is supposedly what opens the door to participation in logical, philosophical debates and discussions presupposing rigorous intellectual training, for most of history, outside the "woman's sphere." Whereas the nature of men has been defined in terms of reason and the intellect, that of women has to do with intuition and emotionalism. Women were limited to matters related to the home while men carried out the more important work, involving use of the rational faculties.[4] These distinctions were not as clear in the slave community.[5] Slaves and women were thought to share the characteristics of emotionality and irrationality. As we move further away from the slave culture, however, a dualism between Black men and women increasingly emerges. This means that Black males have gradually increased their power and participation in the male-dominated society, while Black females have continued to endure the stereotypes and oppressions of an earlier period.

When sexual dualism has fully run its course in the Black community (and I believe that it has), it will not be difficult to see why Black women are invisible in Black Theology. Just as White women formerly had no place in

White Theology—except as the receptors of White men's theological interpretations—Black women have had no place in the development of Black Theology. By self-appointment, or by the sinecure of a male dominated society, Black men have deemed it proper to speak for the entire Black community, male and female.

In a sense, Black men's acceptance of the patriarchal model is logical and to be expected. Black male slaves were unable to reap the benefits of patriarchy. Before emancipation they were not given the opportunity to serve as protector and provider for Black women and children, as White men were able to do for their women and children. Much of what was considered "manhood" had to do with how well one could perform these functions. It seems only natural that the post-emancipation Black men would view as primary importance the reclaiming of their property—their women and their children. Moreover, it is natural that Black men would claim their "natural" right to the "man's world." But it should be emphasized that this is logical and natural only if one has accepted without question the terms and values of patriarchy—the concept of male control and supremacy.

Black men must ask themselves a difficult question. How can a White society characterized by Black enslavement, colonialism, and imperialism provide the normative conception of women for Black society? How can the sphere of the woman, as defined by White men, be free from the evils and oppressions that are found in the White society? The important point is that in matters relative to the relationship between the sexes, Black men have accepted without question the patriarchal structures of the White society as normative for the Black community. How can a Black minister preach in a way which advocates St. Paul's dictum concerning women while ignoring or repudiating his dictum concerning slaves? Many Black women are enraged as they listen to "liberated" Black men speak about the "place of women" in words and phrases similar to those of the very White oppressors they condemn.

Black women have been invisible in theology because theological scholarship has not been a part of the woman's sphere. The first of the above two assumptions results, therefore, from the historical orientation of the dominant culture. The second follows from the first. If women have no place in theology it becomes the natural prerogative of men to monopolize theological concerns, including those relating specifically to women. Inasmuch as Black men have accepted the sexual dualisms of the dominant culture they presume to speak for Black women.

Before finally dismissing the two assumptions a pertinent question should be raised. Does the absence of Black women in the circles producing Black Theology necessarily mean that the resultant theology cannot be in the best interest of Black women? The answer is obvious. Feminist theologians during the past few years have shown how theology done by men in male-dominated cultures has served to undergird patriarchal structures in society.[6] If Black men have accepted those structures, is there any reason to believe that the theology written by Black men would be any more liberating of Black women than White Theology was for White women? It would seem that in view of the oppression that Black people have suffered Black men would be particularly sensitive to the oppression of others.[7]

James Cone has stated that the task of Black Theology "is to analyze the nature of the gospel of Jesus Christ in the light of oppressed Black people so they will see the gospel as inseparable from their humiliated condition, bestowing on them the necessary power to break the chains of oppression. This means that it is a theology of and for the Black community, seeking to interpret the religious dimensions of the forces of liberation in that community."[8] What are the forces of liberation in the Black community and the Black Church? Are they to be exclusively defined by the struggle against racism? My answer to that question is No. There are oppressive realities in the Black community which are related to, but independent of, the fact of racism. Sexism is one such reality. Black men seek to liberate themselves from racial stereotypes and the conditions of oppression without giving due attention to the stereotypes and oppressions against women which parallel those against Blacks. Blacks fight to be free of the stereotype that all Blacks are dirty and ugly, or that Black represents evil and darkness.[9] The slogan "Black is Beautiful" was a counterattack on these stereotypes. The parallel for women is the history of women as "unclean" especially during menstruation and after childbirth. Because the model of beauty in the White male-dominated society is the "long-haired blonde," with all that goes along with that mystique, Black women have an additional problem with the Western idea of "ugliness," particularly as they encounter Black men who have adopted this White model of beauty. Similarly, the Christian teaching that woman is responsible for the fall of *mankind* and is, therefore, the source of evil has had a detrimental effect in the experience of Black women.

Like all oppressed peoples the self-image of Blacks has suffered damage. In addition they have not been in control of their own destiny. It is the goal of the Black liberation struggle to change radically the socioeconomic and political conditions of Black people by inculcating self-love, self-control, self-reliance, and political power. The concepts of self-love, self-control, self-reliance, and political participation certainly have broad significance for Black women, even though they were taught that, by virtue of their sex, they had to be completely dependent on *man*; yet while their historical situation reflected the need for dependence, the powerlessness of Black men made it necessary for them to seek those values for themselves.

Racism and sexism are interrelated just as all forms of oppression are interrelated. Sexism, however, has a reality and significance of its own because it represents that peculiar form of oppression suffered by Black women at the hands of Black men. It is important to examine this reality of sexism as it operated in both the Black community and the Black Church. We will consider first the Black Church and secondly the Black community to determine to what extent Black Theology has measured up to its defined task with respect to the liberation of Black women [10]

The Black Church and the Black Woman

I can agree with Karl Barth as he describes the peculiar function of theology as the church's "subjecting herself to a self-test." "She [the church] faces herself with the question of truth, i.e., she measures her action, her language about God, against her existence as a Church."[11]

On the one hand, Black Theology must continue to criticize classical theology and the White Church. But on the other hand, Black Theology must subject the Black Church to a "self-test." The task of the church according to James Cone is threefold: *(1)* "It proclaims the reality of divine liberation. . . . It is not possible to receive the good news of freedom and also keep it to ourselves; it must be told to the whole world. . . ." *(2)* "It actively shares in the liberation struggle." *(3)* It "is a visible manifestation that the gospel is a reality. . . . If it [the church] lives according to the old order (as it usually has), then no one will believe its message."[12] It is clear that Black Theology must ask whether or not the Black Church is faithful to this task. Moreover, the language of the Black Church about God must be consistent with its action.[13] These requirements of the church's faithfulness in the struggle for liberation have not been met as far as the issue of women is concerned.

If the liberation of women is not proclaimed, the church's proclamation cannot be about divine liberation. If the church does not share in the liberation struggle of Black women, its liberation struggle is not authentic. If women are oppressed, the church cannot possibly be "a visible manifestation that the gospel is a reality"—for the gospel cannot be real in that context. One can see the contradictions between the church's language or proclamation of liberation and its action by looking both at the status of Black women in the church as laity and Black women in the ordained ministry of the church.

It is often said that women are the "backbone" of the church. On the surface this may appear to be a compliment, especially when one considers the function of the backbone in the human anatomy. Theressa Hoover prefers to use the term "glue" to describe the function of women in the Black Church. In any case, the telling portion of the word backbone is "back." It has become apparent to me that most of the ministers who use this term have reference to location rather than function. What they really mean is that women are in the "background" and should be kept there. They are merely support workers. This is borne out by my observation that in many churches women are consistently given responsibilities in the kitchen, while men are elected or appointed to the important boards and leadership positions. While decisions and policies may be discussed in the kitchen, they are certainly not made there. Recently I conducted a study in one conference of the African

Methodist Episcopal Church which indicated that women are accorded greater participation on the decision-making boards of smaller rather than larger churches.[14] This political maneuver helps to keep women "in their place" in the denomination as well as in the local congregations. The conspiracy to keep women relegated to the background is also aided by the continuous psychological and political strategizing that keeps women from realizing their own potential power in the church. Not only are they rewarded for performance in "backbone" or supportive positions, but they are penalized for trying to move from the backbone to the head position—the leadership of the church. It is by considering the distinction between prescribed support positions and the policy-making, leadership positions that the oppression of Black women in the Black Church can be seen more clearly.

For the most part, men have monopolized the ministry as a profession. The ministry of women as fully ordained clergypersons has always been controversial. The Black church fathers were unable to see the injustices of their own practices, even when they paralleled the injustices in the White Church against which they rebelled.

In the early nineteenth century, the Rev. Richard Allen perceived that it was unjust for Blacks, free and slaves, to be relegated to the balcony and restricted to a special time to pray and kneel at the communion table; for this he should be praised. Yet because of his acceptance of the patriarchal system Allen was unable to see the injustice in relegating women to one area of the church—the pews—by withholding ordination from women as he did in the case of Mrs. Jarena Lee.[15] Lee recorded Allen's response when she informed him of her call to "go preach the Gospel":

> He replied by asking in what sphere I wished to move in? I said, among the Methodists. He then replied, that a Mrs. Cook, a Methodist lady, had also some time before requested the same privilege; who it was believed, had done much good in the way of *exhortation*, and *holding prayer meetings*; and who had been permitted to do so by the *verbal license* of the preacher in charge at the time. But as to women preaching, he said that our Discipline knew nothing at all about it—that *it did not call* for women preachers.[16]

Because of this response Jarena Lee's preaching ministry was delayed for eight years. She was not unaware of the sexist injustice in Allen's response.

> Oh how careful ought we be, lest through our by-laws of church government and discipline, we bring into disrepute even the word of life. For as unseemly as it may appear nowadays for a women to preach,

it should be remembered that nothing is impossible with God. And why should it be thought impossible, heterodox, or improper for a woman to preach, seeing the Saviour died for the woman as well as the man?[17]

Another "colored minister of the gospel," Elizabeth, was greatly troubled over her call to preach, or more accurately, over the response of men to her call to preach. She said:

> I often felt that I was unfit to assemble with the congregation with whom I had gathered. . . . I felt that I was despised on account of this gracious calling, and was looked upon as a speckled bird by the ministers to whom I looked for instruction . . . some [of the ministers] would cry out, "you are an enthusiast," and others said, "the Discipline did not allow of any such division of work."[18]

Sometime later when questioned about her authority to preach against slavery and her ordination status, she responded that she preached "not by the commission of men's hands: if the Lord had ordained me, I needed nothing better."[19] With this commitment to God rather than to a male-dominated church structure she led a fruitful ministry.

Mrs. Amanda Berry Smith, like Mrs. Jarena Lee, had to conduct her ministry outside the structure of the A.M.E. Church. Smith described herself as a "plain Christian woman" with "no money" and "no prominence."[20] But she was intrigued with the idea of attending the General Conference of 1872 in Nashville, Tennessee. Her inquiry into the cost of going to Nashville brought the following comments from some of the A.M.E. brethren:

> "I tell you, Sister, it will cost money to go down there; and if you ain't got plenty of it, it's no use to go"; . . . another said:
> "What does she want to go for?"
> "Woman preacher; they want to be ordained," was the reply.
> "I mean to fight that thing," said the other.
> "Yes, indeed, so will I," said another.[21]

The oppression of women in the ministry took many forms. In addition to not being granted ordination, the authenticity of "the call" of women was frequently put to the test. Lee, Elizabeth, and Smith spoke of the many souls they had brought to Christ through their preaching and singing in local Black congregations, as well as in White and mixed congregations. It was not until Bishop Richard Allen heard Jarena Lee preach that he was convinced that she was of the Spirit. He, however, still refused to ordain her. The "brethren," including some bishops of the 1872 General Conference of the A.M.E. Church were convinced that Amanda Berry Smith was blessed with the Spirit of God after hearing her sing at a session held at Fisk University. Smith tells us that ". . . the Spirit of the Lord seemed to fall on all the people. The preachers got happy. . . ." This experience brought invitations for her to preach at several churches, but it did not bring an appointment to a local congregation as pastor or the right of ordination. She summed up the experience in this way: ". . . after that many of my brethren believed in me, especially as the question of ordination of women never was mooted in the Conference."[22]

Several Black denominations have since begun to ordain women.[23] But this matter of women preachers having the extra burden of proving their call to an extent not required of men still prevails in the Black Church today. A study in which I participated at Union Theological Seminary in New York City bears this out. Interviews with Black ministers of different denominations revealed that their prejudices against women, and especially women in the ministry, resulted in unfair expectations and unjust treatment of women ministers whom they encountered.[24]

It is the unfair expectations placed upon women and blatant discrimination that keeps them "in the pew" and "out of the pulpit." This matter of keeping women in the pew has been carried to ridiculous extremes. At the 1971 Annual Convocation of the National Conference of Black Churchmen,[25] held at the Liberty Baptist Church in Chicago, I was slightly amused when, as I approached the pulpit to place my cassette tape recorder near the speaker, Walter Fauntroy, as several brothers had already done, I was stopped by a man who informed me that I could not enter the pulpit area. When I asked why not, he directed me to the pastor who told me that women were not permitted in the pulpit, but that he would have a man place the recorder there for me. Although I could not believe that explanation a serious one, I agreed to have a man place it on the pulpit for me and returned to my seat in the sanctuary for the continuation of the convocation. The seriousness of the pastor's statement became clear to me later at that meeting when Mary Jane Patterson, a Presbyterian Church executive, was refused the right to speak from the pulpit.[26] This was clearly a case of sex discrimination in a Black church—keeping women "in the pew" and "out of the pulpit."

As far as the issue of women is concerned it is obvious that the Black Church described by C. Eric Lincoln has not fared much better than the Negro Church of E. Franklin Frazier.[27] The failure of the Black Church and Black Theology to proclaim explicitly the liberation of Black women indicates that they cannot claim to be agents of divine liberation. If the theology, like the church, has no word for Black women, its conception of liberation is inauthentic.

The Black Experience and the Black Woman

For the most part, Black churchmen have not dealt with the oppression of Black women in either the Black Church or the Black community. Frederick Douglass was one notable exception in the 19th century. His active advocacy for women's rights was a demonstration against the contradiction between preaching "justice for all" and practicing the continued oppression of women. He, therefore, "dared not claim a right [for himself] which he would not concede to women."[28] These words describe the convictions of a man who was active both in the church and in the larger Black community. This is significant because there is usually a direct relationship between what goes on in the Black Church and the Black secular community.

The status of Black women in the community parallels that of Black women in the church. Black Theology considers the Black experience to be the context out of which its questions about God and human existence are formulated. This is assumed to be the context in which God's revelation is received and interpreted. Only from the perspective of the poor and the oppressed can theology be adequately done. Arising out of the Black Power Movement of the 1960s, Black Theology purports to take seriously the experience of the larger community's struggle for liberation. But if this is, indeed, the case, Black Theology must function in the secular community in the same way as it should function in the church community. It must serve as a "self-test" to see whether the rhetoric or proclamation of the Black community's struggle for liberation is consistent with its practices. How does the "self-test" principle operate among the poor and the oppressed? Certainly Black Theology has spoken to some of the forms of oppression which exist within the community of the oppressed. Many of the injustices it has attacked are the same as those which gave rise to the prophets of the Old Testament. But the fact that Black Theology does not include sexism specifically as one of those injustices is all too evident. It suggests that the theologians do not understand sexism to be one of the oppressive realities of the Black community. Silence on this specific issue can only mean conformity with the status quo. The most prominent Black theologian, James Cone, has recently broken this silence.

> The Black church, like all other churches, is a male dominated church. The difficulty that Black male ministers have in supporting the equality of women in the church and society stems partly from the lack of a clear liberation-criterion rooted in the gospel and in the present struggles of oppressed peoples. . . . It is truly amazing that many black male ministers, young and old, can hear the message of liberation in the gospel

when related to racism but remain deaf to a similar message in the
context of sexism. . . .[29]

It is difficult to understand how Black men manage to exclude the liberation
of Black women from their interpretation of the liberating gospel. Any
correct analysis of the poor and oppressed would reveal some interesting and
inescapable facts about the situation of women within oppressed groups.
Without succumbing to the long and fruitless debate of "who is more oppressed than whom?" I want to make some pointed suggestions to Black male
theologians.

It would not be very difficult to argue that since Black women are the
poorest of the poor, the most oppressed of the oppressed, their experience
provides a most fruitful context for doing Black Theology. The research of
Jacquelyne Jackson attests to the extreme deprivation of Black women.
Jackson supports her claim with statistical data that "in comparison with black
males and white males and females, black women yet constitute the most
disadvantaged group in the US, as evidenced especially by their largely
unenviable educational, occupational, employment and income levels, and
availability of marital partners."[30] In other words, in spite of the "quite
insignificant" educational advantage that Black women have over Black men,
they have "had the greatest access to the worst jobs at the lowest earnings."[31]
It is important to emphasize this fact in order to elevate to its rightful level of
concern the condition of Black women, not only in the world at large, but in
the Black community and the Black Church. It is my contention that if Black
Theology speaks of the Black community as if the special problems of Black
women do not exist, it is no different from the White Theology it claims to
reject precisely because of its inability to take account of the existence of
Black people in its theological formulations.

It is instructive to note that the experience of Black women working in the
Black Power movement further accented the problem of the oppression of
women in the Black community. Because of their invisibility in the leadership of the movement they, like women of the church, provided the "support" segment of the movement. They filled the streets when numbers were
needed for demonstrations. They stuffed the envelopes in the offices and
performed other menial tasks. Kathleen Cleaver, in a *Black Scholar* interview,
revealed some of the problems in the movement which caused her to become
involved in women's liberation issues. While underscoring the crucial role
played by women as Black Power activists, Kathleen Cleaver, nonetheless,
acknowledged the presence of sex discrimination.

> I viewed myself as assisting everything that was done. . . . The form
> of assistance that women give in political movements to men is just as
> crucial as the leadership that men give to those movements. And this is

something that is never recognized and never dealt with. *Because women are always relegated to assistance* and this is where I became interested in the liberation of women. Conflicts, constant conflicts came up, conflicts that would rise as a result of the fact that I was married to a member of the Central Committee and I was also an officer in the Party. Things that I would have suggested myself would be implemented. But if I suggested them the suggestion might be rejected. If they were suggested by a man the suggestion would be implemented.

It seemed throughout the history of my working with the Party, I always had to struggle with this. The suggestion itself was never viewed objectively. *The fact that the suggestion came from a women gave it some lesser value.* And it seemed that it had something to do with the egos of the men involved. I know that the first demonstration that we had at the courthouse for Huey Newton I was very instrumental in organizing; the first time we went out on the soundtrucks, I was on the soundtrucks; the first leaflet we put out, I wrote; the first demonstration, I made up the pamphlets. And the members of that demonstration for the most part were women. I've noticed that throughout my dealings in the black movement in the United States, that the *most anxious, the most eager, the most active, the most quick to understand the problem and quick to move are women.*[32]

Cleaver exposed the fact that even when leadership was given to women, sexism lurked in the wings. As executive secretary of the Student Nonviolent Coordinating Committee (SNCC), Ruby Doris Robinson was described as the "heart beat of SNCC." Yet there were "the constant conflicts, the constant struggles that she was subjected to because she was a woman."[33]

Notwithstanding all the evidence to the contrary, some might want to argue that the central problem of Black women is related to their race and not their sex. Such an argument then presumes that the problem cannot be resolved apart from the Black struggle. I contend that as long as the Black struggle refuses to recognize and deal with its sexism, the idea that women will receive justice from that struggle alone will never work. It will not work because Black women will no longer allow Black men to ignore their unique problems and needs in the name of some distorted view of the "liberation of the total community." I would bring to the minds of the proponents of this argument the words of President Sekou Toure as he wrote about the role of African women in the revolution. He said, "if African women cannot possibly conduct their struggle in isolation from the struggle that our people wage for African liberation, African freedom, conversely, is not effective unless it brings about the liberation of African women."[34] Black men who have an investment in the patriarchal structure of White America and who intend to do Christian theology have yet to realize that if Jesus is liberator of the oppressed, all of the oppressed must be liberated. Perhaps the proponents of the argument that the cause of Black women must be subsumed under a larger cause should look to South African theologians Sabelo Ntwasa and Basil Moore. They affirm that "Black theology, as it struggles to formulate a theology of liberation relevant to South Africa, cannot afford to perpetuate any form of domination, not even male domination. If its liberation is not human enough to include the liberation of women, it will not be liberation."[35]

A Challenge to Black Theology

My central argument is this: Black Theology cannot continue to treat Black women as if they were invisible creatures who are on the outside looking into the Black experience, the Black Church, and the Black theological enterprise. It will have to deal with the community of believers in all aspects as integral parts of the whole community. Black Theology, therefore, must speak to the bishops who hide behind the statement "Women don't want women pastors." It must speak to the pastors who say, "My church isn't ready for women preachers yet." It must teach the seminarians who feel that "women have no place in seminary." It must address the women in the church and community who are content and complacent with their oppression. It must challenge the educators who would reeducate the people on every issue except the issue of the dignity and equality of women.

Black women represent more than 50 percent of the Black community and more than 70 percent of the Black Church. How then can an authentic theology of liberation arise out of these communities without specifically addressing the liberation of the women in both places? Does the fact that certain questions are raised by Black women make them any less Black concerns? If, as I contend, the liberation of Black men and women is inseparable, then a radical split cannot be made between racism and sexism. Black women are oppressed by racism *and* sexism. It is therefore necessary that Black men and women be actively involved in combating both evils.

Only as Black women in greater numbers make their way from the background to the forefront will the true strength of the Black community be fully realized. There is already a heritage of strong Black women and men upon which a stronger nation can be built. There is a tradition which declares that God is at work in the experience of the Black woman. This tradition, in the context of the total Black experience, can provide data for the development of a wholistic Black Theology. Such a theology will repudiate the God of classical theology who is presented as an absolute Patriarch, a deserting father who created Black men and women and then "walked out" in the face of responsibility. Such a theology will look at the meaning of the total Jesus Christ Event; it will consider not only how God through Jesus Christ is related to the oppressed men, but to women as well. Such a theology will "allow" God through the Holy Spirit to work through persons without regard to race, sex, or class. This theology will exercise its prophetic function, and serve as a "self-test" in a church characterized by the sins of racism, sexism, and other forms of oppression. Until Black women theologians are fully participating in the theological enterprise, it is important to keep Black male theologians and Black leaders cognizant of their dereliction. They must be made aware of the fact that Black women are needed not only as Christian educators, but as theologians and church leaders. It is only when Black women and men share jointly the leadership in theology and in the church and community that the Black nation will become strong and liberated. Only then will there be the possibility that Black Theology can become a theology of divine liberation.

One final word for those who argue that the issues of racism and sexism are too complicated and should not be confused. I agree that the issues should not be "confused." But the elimination of both racism and sexism is so crucial for the liberation of Black persons that we cannot shrink from facing them together. Sojourner Truth tells us why this is so. In 1867 she spoke out on the issue of suffrage and what she said at that time is still relevant to us as we deal with the liberation of Black women today.

> I feel that if I have to answer for the deeds done in my body just as much as a man, I have a right to have just as much as a man. There is a great stir about colored men getting their rights, but not a word about the colored women; and if colored men get their rights, and not colored women theirs, you see the colored men will be masters over the women, and it will be just as bad as it was before. So I am for keeping the thing going while things are stirring: because if we wait till it is still, it will take a great while to get it going again. . . .[36]

Black women have to keep the issue of sexism "going" in the Black community, in the Black Church, and in Black Theology until it has been eliminated. To do otherwise means that they will be pushed aside until eternity. Therefore, with Sojourner Truth, I'm for "keeping things going while things are stirring. . . ."

Notes

1. Beatriz Melano Couch, remarks on the feminist panel of Theology in the Americas Conference in Detroit in August 1975, printed in *Theology in the Americas*, ed. Sergio Torres and John Eagleson (Maryknoll, N.Y.: Orbis Books, 1976), p. 375.

2. Consuelo Urquiza, "A Message from a Hispanic-American Woman," *The Fifth Commission: A Monitor for Third World Concerns* IV (June-July 1978), insert. The Fifth Commission is a commission of the National Council of the Churches of Christ in the USA (NCC), 475 Riverside Drive, New York, N.Y.

3. I agree with the Fifth Commission that "the Third World is not a geographical entity, but rather the world of oppressed peoples in their struggle for liberation." In this sense, Black

women are included in the term "Third World." However, in order to accent the peculiar identity, problems, and needs of Black women in the First World or the Third World contexts, I choose to make the distinction between Black and other Third World women.

4. For a discussion of sexual dualisms in our society, see Rosemary Ruether, *New Woman/New Earth* (New York: Seabury Press, 1975), chap. 1; and *Liberation Theology* (New York: Paulist Press, 1972), pp. 16ff. Also for a discussion of sexual (social) dualisms as related to the brain hemispheres, see Sheila Collins, *A Different Heaven and Earth* (Valley Forge: Judson Press, 1974), pp. 169-170.

5. Angela Davis, "Reflections on the Black Woman's Role in the Community of Slaves," *The Black Scholar,* vol. 4 no. 3 (December 1971), pp. 3-15. I do take issue with Davis's point, however. The Black community may have experienced "equality in inequality," but this was forced on them from the dominant or enslaving community. She does not deal with the inequality within the community itself.

6. See Sheila Collins, op. cit., Rosemary Ruether, op. cit., Letty Russell, *Human Liberation in the Feminist Perspective* (Philadelphia: Westminster Press, 1974); and Mary Daly, *Beyond God the Father* (Boston: Beacon Press, 1973).

7. Surely the factor of race would be absent, but one would have to do an in-depth analysis to determine the possible effect on the status of Black women.

8. James Cone, *A Black Theology of Liberation* (Philadelphia: J.B. Lippincott, 1970), p. 23.

9. Eulalio Baltazar discusses color symbolism (white is good; black is evil) as a reflection of racism in the White Theology which perpetuates it. *The Dark Center: A Process Theology of Blackness* (New York: Paulist Press, 1973).

10. One may want to argue that Black Theology is not concerned with sexism but with racism. I will argue in this essay that such a theology could speak only half the truth, if truth at all.

11. Karl Barth, *Church Dogmatics*, vol. 1, part 1, p. 2.

12. Cone, op. cit., pp. 230-232.

13. James Cone and Albert Cleage do make this observation of the contemporary Black Church and its response to the struggles against racism. See Cleage, *The Black Messiah* (New York: Sheed and Ward, 1969), passim; and Cone, op. cit., passim.

14. A study that I conducted in the Philadelphia Conference of the African Methodist Episcopal Church, May 1976. It also included sporadic samplings of churches in other conferences in the First Episcopal District. As for example, a church of 1,660 members (500 men and 1,160 women) had a trustee board of 8 men and 1 woman and a steward board of 13 men and 6 women. A church of 100 members (35 men and 65 women) had a trustee board of 5 men and 4 women and a steward board of 5 men and 4 women.

15. Jarena Lee, *The Life and Religious Experience of Jarena Lee: A Colored Lady Giving an Account of Her Call to Preach the Gospel* (Philadelphia, 1836), printed in Dorothy Porter, ed., *Early Negro Writing 1760–1837* (Boston: Beacon Press, 1971), pp. 494-514.

16. Ibid., p. 503 (italics added). Carol George in *Segregated Sabbaths* (New York: Oxford University Press, 1973), presents a very positive picture of the relationship between Jarena Lee and Bishop Richard Allen. She feels that by the time Lee approached Allen, he had "modified his views on woman's rights" (p. 129). She contends that since Allen was free from the Methodist Church he was able to "determine his own policy" with respect to women under the auspices of the A.M.E. Church. It should be noted that Bishop Allen accepted the Rev. Jarena Lee as a woman preacher and not as an ordained preacher with full rights and privileges thereof. Even Carol George admitted that Lee traveled with Bishop Allen only "as an unofficial member of their delegation to conference sessions in New York and Baltimore," "to attend," not to participate in them. I agree that this does represent progress in Bishop Allen's view as compared to Lee's first approach; on the second approach, he was at least encouraging. Then he began "to promote her interests" (p. 129)—But he did not ordain her.

17. Ibid.

18. "Elizabeth: A Colored Minister of the Gospel," printed in Bert James Loewenberg and Ruth Bogin, ed., *Black Women in Nineteenth-Century American Life* (University Park, Pa.: The Pennsylvania State University Press, 1976), p. 132. The denomination of Elizabeth is not known to this writer. Her parents were Methodists, but she was separated from her parents at the age of eleven. However, the master from which she gained her freedom was Presbyterian. Her autobiography was published by the Philadelphia Quakers.

19. Ibid., p. 133.

20. Amanda Berry Smith, *An Autobiography: The Story of the Lord's Dealings with Mrs.*

Amanda Berry Smith, the Colored Evangelist (Chicago, 1893); printed in Loewenberg and Bogin, op.cit., p. 157.

21. Ibid.

22. Ibid., p. 159.

23. The African Methodist Episcopal Church started ordaining women in 1948, according to the Rev. William P. Foley of Bridgestreet A.M.E. Church in Brooklyn, New York. The first ordained woman was Martha J. Keys.

The African Methodist Episcopal Zion Church ordained women as early as 1884. At that time, Mrs. Julia A. Foote was ordained Deacon in the New York Annual Conference. In 1894 Mrs. Mary J. Small was ordained Deacon and in 1898, she was ordained Elder. See David Henry Bradley, Sr., *A History of the A.M.E. Zion Church,* vol. (part) II, 1872–1968 (Nashville: The Parthenon Press, 1970), pp. 384, 393.

The Christian Methodist Episcopal Church enacted legislation to ordain women in the 1970 General Conference. Since then approximately 75 women have been ordained. See the Rev. N. Charles Thomas, general secretary of the C.M.E. Church and director of the Department of Ministry, Memphis, Tennessee.

Many Baptist churches still do not ordain women. Some churches in the Pentecostal tradition do not ordain women. However, in some other Pentecostal churches, women are founders, pastors, elders, and bishops.

In the case of the A.M.E.Z. Church, where women were ordained as early as 1884, the important question would be, what happened to the women who were ordained? In addition, all of these churches (except for those which do give leadership to women) should answer the following questions: Have women been assigned to pastor "class A" churches? Have women been appointed as presiding elders? (There is currently one woman presiding elder in the A.M.E. Church.) Have women been elected to serve as bishop of any of these churches? Have women served as presidents of conventions?

24. Yolande Herron, Jacquelyn Grant, Gwendolyn Johnson, and Samuel Roberts, "Black Women and the Field Education Experience at Union Theological Seminary: Problems and Prospects" (New York: Union Theological Seminary, May 1978).

25. This organization continues to call itself the National Conference of Black Churchmen despite the protests of women members.

26. NCBC has since made the decision to examine the policies of its host institutions (churches) to avoid the reoccurrence of such incidents.

27. E. Franklin Frazier, *The Negro Church in America*; C. Eric Lincoln, *The Black Church Since Frazier* (New York: Schocken Books, 1974), passim.

28. Printed in Philip S. Foner, ed., *Frederick Douglass on Women's Rights* (Westport, Conn.: Greenwood Press), p. 51.

29. Cone, "Black Ecumenism and the Liberation Struggle," delivered at Yale University, February 16-17, 1978, and Quinn Chapel A.M.E. Church, May 22, 1978. In two other recent papers he has voiced concern on women's issues, relating them to the larger question of liberation. These papers are: "New Roles in the Ministry: A Theological Appraisal" and "Black Theology and the Black Church: Where Do We Go from Here?" Both papers appear in this volume.

30. Jacquelyne Jackson, "But Where Are the Men?" *The Black Scholar,* op. cit., p. 30.

31. Ibid., p. 32.

32. Kathleen Cleaver was interviewed by Sister Julia Herve. Ibid., pp. 55-56.

33. Ibid., p. 55.

34. Sedkou Toure, "The Role of Women in the Revolution," *The Black Scholar,* vol. 6, no. 6 (March 1975), p. 32.

35. Sabelo Ntwasa and Basil Moore, "The Concept of God in Black Theology," in *The Challenge of Black Theology in South Africa*, ed. Basil Moore (Atlanta, Ga.: John Knox Press, 1974), pp. 25-26.

36. Sojourner Truth, "Keeping the Things Going While Things Are Stirring," printed in Miriam Schneir, ed., *Feminism: The Essential Historical Writings* (New York: Random House, 1972), pp. 129-130.

41

IN SEARCH OF OUR
MOTHERS' GARDENS

Alice Walker

I described her own nature and temperament. Told how they needed a
larger life for their expression. . . . I pointed out that in lieu of proper
channels, her emotions had overflowed into paths that dissipated them.
I talked, beautifully I thought, about an art that would be born, an art
that would open the way for women the likes of her. I asked her to
hope, and build up an inner life against the coming of that day. . . . I
sang, with a strange quiver in my voice, a promise song.

"Avey," Jean Toomer, *Cane*
The poet speaking to a prostitute who falls asleep while he's talking—

When the poet Jean Toomer walked through the South in the early
twenties, he discovered a curious thing: Black women whose spirituality was
so intense, so deep, so *unconscious,* that they were themselves unaware of the
richness they held. They stumbled blindly through their lives: creatures so
abused and mutilated in body, so dimmed and confused by pain, that they
considered themselves unworthy even of hope. In the selfless abstractions
their bodies became to the men who used them, they became more than
"sexual objects," more even then mere women: they became Saints. Instead
of being perceived as whole persons, their bodies became shrines: what was
thought to be their minds became temples suitable for worship. These crazy
"Saints" stared out at the world, wildly, like lunatics—or quietly, like
suicides; and the "God" that was in their gaze was as mute as a great stone.

This article was first published in *Ms.,* vol. 2, no. 11 (May 1974). Alice Walker, poet and
novelist, is the author of *In Love and Trouble: Stories of Black Women,* among other books.

Who were these "Saints"? These crazy, loony, pitiful women?

Some of them, without a doubt, were our mothers and grandmothers.

In the still heat of the Post-Reconstruction South, this is how they seemed to Jean Toomer: exquisite butterflies trapped in an evil honey, toiling away their lives in an era, a century, that did not acknowledge them, except as "the *mule* of the world." They dreamed dreams that no one knew—not even themselves; in any coherent fashion—and saw visions no one could understand. They wandered or sat about the countryside crooning lullabies to ghosts, and drawing the mother of Christ in charcoal on courthouse walls.

They forced their minds to desert their bodies and their striving spirits sought to rise, like frail whirlwinds from the hard red clay. And when those frail whirlwinds fell, in scattered particles, upon the ground, no one mourned. Instead, men lit candles to celebrate the emptiness that remained, as people do who enter a beautiful but vacant space to resurrect a God.

Our mothers and grandmothers, some of them: moving to music not yet written. And they waited.

They waited for a day when the unknown thing that was in them would be made known; but guessed, somehow in their darkness, that on the day of their revelation they would be long dead. Therefore to Toomer they walked, and even ran, in slow motion. For they were going nowhere immediate, and the future was not yet within their grasp. And men took our mothers and grandmothers, "but got no pleasure from it." So complex was their passion and their calm.

To Toomer, they lay vacant and fallow as autumn fields, with harvest time never in sight: and he saw them enter loveless marriages, without joy; and become prostitutes, without resistance; and become mothers of children, without fulfillment.

For these grandmothers and mothers of ours were not "Saints," but Artists; driven to a numb and bleeding madness by the springs of creativity in them for which there was no release. They were Creators, who lived lives of spiritual waste, because they were so rich in spirituality—which is the basis of Art—that the strain of enduring their unused and unwanted talent drove them insane. Throwing away this spirituality was their pathetic attempt to lighten the soul to a weight their work-worn, sexually abused bodies could bear.

What did it mean for a Black woman to be an artist in our grandmothers' time? In our great-grandmothers' day? It is a question with an answer cruel enough to stop the blood.

Did you have a genius of a great-great-grandmother who died under some ignorant and depraved white overseer's lash? Or was she required to bake biscuits for a lazy backwater tramp, when she cried out in her soul to paint watercolors of sunsets, or the rain falling on the green and peaceful pasturelands? Or was her body broken and forced to bear children (who were more often than not sold away from her)—eight, ten, fifteen, twenty children—

when her one joy was the thought of modeling heroic figures of Rebellion, in stone or clay?

How was the creativity of the Black woman kept alive, year after year and century after century, when for most of the years Black people have been in America, it was a punishable crime for a Black person to read or write? And the freedom to paint, to sculpt, to expand the mind with action, did not exist. Consider, if you can bear to imagine it, what might have been the result if singing, too, had been forbidden by law. Listen to the voices of Bessie Smith, Billie Holiday, Nina Simone, Roberta Flack, and Aretha Franklin, among others, and imagine those voices muzzled for life. Then you may begin to comprehend the lives of our "crazy," "Sainted" mothers and grandmothers. The agony of the lives of women who might have been Poets, Novelists, Essayists, and Short Story Writers (over a period of centuries), who died with their real gifts stifled within them.

And, if this were the end of the story, we would have cause to cry out in my paraphrase of Okot p'Bitek's great poem:

> O, my clanswomen
> Let us all cry together!
> Come,
> Let us mourn the death of our mother,
> The death of a Queen
> The ash that was produced
> By a great fire!
> O this homestead is utterly dead
> Close the gates
> With *lacari* thorns,
> For our mother
> The creator of the Stool is lost!
> And all the young women
> Have perished in the wilderness!

But this is not the end of the story, for all the young women—our mothers and grandmothers, *ourselves*—have not perished in the wilderness. And if we ask ourselves why, and search for and find the answer, we will know beyond all efforts to erase it from our minds, just exactly who, and of what, we Black American women are.

One example, perhaps the most pathetic, most misunderstood one, can provide a backdrop for our mothers' work: Phillis Wheatley, a slave in the 1700s.

Virginia Woolf, in her book, *A Room of One's Own*, wrote that in order for a woman to write fiction she must have two things, certainly: a room of her own (with key and lock) and enough money to support herself.

What then are we to make of Phillis Wheatley, a slave, who owned not even herself? This sickly, frail, Black girl who required a servant of her own at times—her health was so precarious—and who, had she been white, would have been easily considered the intellectual superior of all the women and most of the men in the society of her day.

Virginia Woolf wrote further, speaking of course not of our Phillis, that "any woman born with a great gift in the sixteenth century [insert *eighteenth century,* insert *Black woman,* insert *born or made a slave*] would certainly have gone crazed, shot herself, or ended her days in some lonely cottage outside the village, half witch, half wizard [insert *Saint*], feared and mocked at. For it needs little skill and psychology to be sure that a highly gifted girl who had tried to use her gift for poetry would have been so thwarted and hindered by contrary instincts [*add chains, guns, the lash, the ownership of one's body by someone else, submission to an alien religion*], that she must have lost her health and sanity to a certainty."

The key words, as they relate to Phillis, are "contrary instincts." For when we read the poetry of Phillis Wheatley—as when we read the novels of Nella Larsen or the oddly false-sounding autobiography of that freest of all Black women writers, Zora Hurston—evidence of "contrary instincts" is everywhere. Her loyalties were completely divided, as was, without question, her mind.

But how could this be otherwise? Captured at seven, a slave of wealthy, doting whites who instilled in her the "savagery" of the Africa they "rescued" her from . . . one wonders if she was even able to remember her homeland as she had known it, or as it really was.

Yet, because she did try to use her gift for poetry in a world that made her a slave, she was "so thwarted and hindered by . . . contrary instincts, that she . . . lost her health. . . ." In the last years of her brief life, burdened not only with the need to express her gift but also with a penniless, friendless "freedom" and several small children for whom she was forced to do strenuous work to feed, she lost her health, certainly. Suffering from malnutrition and neglect and who knows what mental agonies, Phillis Wheatley died.

So torn by "contrary instincts" was Black, kidnapped, enslaved Phillis that her description of "the Goddess"—as she poetically called the Liberty she did not have—is ironically, cruelly humorous. And, in fact, has held Phillis up to ridicule for more than a century. It is usually read prior to hanging Phillis's memory as that of a fool. She wrote:

> The Goddess comes, she moves divinely fair,
> Olive and laurel binds her *golden* hair:
> Wherever shines this native of the skies,
> Unnumber'd charms and recent graces rise.
> (Emphasis added.)

It is obvious that Phillis, the slave, combed the "Goddess's" hair every morning; prior, perhaps, to bringing in the milk, or fixing her mistress's lunch. She took her imagery from the one thing she saw elevated above all others.

With the benefit of hindsight we ask, "How could she?"

But at last, Phillis, we understand. No more snickering when your stiff, struggling, ambivalent lines are forced on us. We know now that you were not an idiot or a traitor; only a sickly little Black girl, snatched from your home and country and made a slave; a woman who still struggled to sing the song that was your gift, although in a land of barbarians who praised you for your bewildered tongue. It is not so much what you sang, as that you kept alive, in so many of our ancestors, *the notion of song.*

II

Black women are called, in the folklore that so aptly identifies one's status in society, "the *mule* of the world," because we have been handed the burdens that everyone else—*everyone* else—refused to carry. We have also been called "Matriarchs," "Superwomen," and "Mean and Evil Bitches." Not to mention "Castraters" and "Sapphire's Mama." When we have pleaded for understanding, our character has been distorted; when we have asked for simple caring, we have been handed empty inspirational appellations, then stuck in the farthest corner. When we have asked for love, we have been given children. In short, even our plainer gifts, our labors of fidelity and love, have been knocked down our throats. To be an artist and a Black woman, even today, lowers our status in many respects, rather than raises it: and yet, artists we will be.

Therefore we must fearlessly pull out of ourselves and look at and identify with our lives the living creativity some of our great-grandmothers were not allowed to know. I stress *some* of them because it is well known that the majority of our great-grandmothers knew, even without "knowing" it, the reality of their spirituality, even if they didn't recognize it beyond what happened in the singing at church—and they never had any intention of giving it up.

How they did it: those millions of Black women who were not Phillis Wheatley, or Lucy Terry or Frances Harper or Zora Hurston or Nella Larsen or Bessie Smith—nor Elizabeth Catlett, nor Katherine Dunham, either— bring me to the title of this essay, "In Search of Our Mothers' Gardens," which is a personal account that is yet shared, in its theme and its meaning, by all of us. I found, while thinking about the far-reaching world of the creative Black woman, that often the truest answer to a question that really matters can be found very close. So I was not surprised when my own mother popped into my mind.

In the late 1920s my mother ran away from home to marry my father.

Marriage, if not running away, was expected of 17-year-old girls. By the time she was 20, she had two children and was pregnant with a third. Five children later, I was born. And this is how I came to know my mother: she seemed a large, soft, loving-eyed woman who was rarely impatient in our home. Her quick, violent temper was on view only a few times a year, when she battled with the white landlord who had the misfortune to suggest to her that her children did not need to go to school.

She made all the clothes we wore, even my brothers' overalls. She made all the towels and sheets we used. She spent the summers canning vegetables and fruits. She spent the winter evenings making quilts enough to cover all our beds.

During the "working" day, she labored beside—not behind—my father in the fields. Her day began before sunup, and did not end until late at night. There was never a moment for her to sit down, undisturbed, to unravel her own private thoughts; never a time free from interruption—by work or the noisy inquiries of her many children. And yet, it is to my mother—and all our mothers who were not famous—that I went in search of the secret of what has fed that muzzled and often mutilated, but vibrant, creative spirit that the Black woman has inherited, and that pops out in wild and unlikely places to this day.

But when, you will ask, did my overworked mother have time to know or care about feeding the creative spirit?

The answer is so simple that many of us have spent years discovering it. We have constantly looked high, when we should have looked high—and low.

For example: in the Smithsonian Institution in Washington, D.C., there hangs a quilt unlike any other in the world. In fanciful, inspired, and yet simple and identifiable figures, it portrays the story of the Crucifixion. It is considered rare, beyond price. Though it follows no known pattern of quiltmaking, and though it is made of bits and pieces of worthless rags, it is obviously the work of a person of powerful imagination and deep spiritual feeling. Below this quilt I saw a note that says it was made by "an anonymous Black woman in Alabama, a hundred years ago."

If we could locate this "anonymous" Black woman from Alabama, she would turn out to be one of our grandmothers—an artist who left her mark in the only materials she could afford, and in the only medium her position in society allowed her to use.

As Virginia Woolf wrote further, in *A Room of One's Own:*

"Yet genius of a sort must have existed among women as it must have existed among the working class. [Change this to *slaves* and *the wives and daughters of sharecroppers.*] Now and again an Emily Brontë or a Robert Burns [change this to *a Zora Hurston or a Richard Wright*] blazes out and proves its presence. But certainly it never got itself on to paper. When, however, one reads of a witch being ducked, of a woman possessed by devils [or *Sainthood*], of a wise woman selling herbs [our rootworkers], or even a very remarkable man who had a mother, then I think we are on the track of a lost novelist, a suppressed poet, of some mute and inglorious Jane Austen. . . . Indeed, I would venture to guess that Anon, who wrote so many poems without signing them, was often a woman. . . .

And so our mothers and grandmothers have, more often than not anonymously, handed on the creative spark, the seed of the flower they themselves never hoped to see: or like a sealed letter they could not plainly read.

And so it is, certainly, with my own mother. Unlike "Ma" Rainey's songs, which retained their creator's name even while blasting forth from Bessie Smith's mouth, no song or poem will bear my mother's name. Yet so many of the stories that I write, that we all write, are my mother's stories. Only recently did I fully realize this: that through years of listening to my mother's stories of her life, I have absorbed not only the stories themselves, but something of the manner in which she spoke, something of the urgency that involves the knowledge that her stories—like her life—must be recorded. It is probably for this reason that so much of what I have written is about characters whose counterparts in real life are so much older than I am.

But the telling of these stories, which came from my mother's lips as naturally as breathing, was not the only way my mother showed herself as an artist. For stories, too, were subject to being distracted, to dying without conclusion. Dinners must be started, and cotton must be gathered before the big rains. The artist that was and is my mother showed itself to me only after many years. This is what I finally noticed:

Like Mem, a character in *The Third Life of Grange Copeland,* my mother adorned with flowers whatever shabby house we were forced to live in. And not just your typical straggly country stand of zinnias, either. She planted ambitious gardens—and still does—with over 50 different varieties of plants that bloom profusely from early March until late November. Before she left home for the fields, she watered her flowers, chopped up the grass, and laid out new beds. When she returned from the fields she might divide clumps of bulbs, dig a cold pit, uproot and replant roses, or prune branches from her taller bushes or trees—until night came and it was too dark to see.

Whatever she planted grew as if by magic, and her fame as a grower of flowers spread over three counties. Because of her creativity with her flowers, even my memories of poverty are seen through a screen of blooms—sunflowers, petunias, roses, dahlias, forsythia, spirea, delphiniums, verbena . . . and on and on.

And I remember people coming to my mother's yard to be given cuttings from her flowers; I hear again the praise showered on her because whatever rocky soil she landed on, she turned into a garden. A garden so brilliant with colors, so original in its design, so magnificent with life and creativity, that to this day people drive by our house in Georgia—perfect strangers and imperfect strangers—and ask to stand or walk among my mother's art.

I notice that it is only when my mother is working in her flowers that she is radiant, almost to the point of being invisible—except as Creator: hand and eye. She is involved in work her soul must have. Ordering the universe in the image of her personal conception of Beauty.

Her face, as she prepares the Art that is her gift, is a legacy of respect she leaves to me, for all that illuminates and cherishes life. She had handed down respect for the possibilities—and the will to grasp them.

For her, so hindered and intruded upon in so many ways, being an artist has still been a daily part of her life. This ability to hold on, even in very simple ways, is work Black women have done for a very long time.

This poem is not enough, but it is something, for the woman who literally covered the holes in our walls with sunflowers:

> They were women then
> My mama's generation
> Husky of voice—Stout of
> Step
> With fists as well as
> Hands
> How they battered down
> Doors
> And ironed
> Starched white
> Shirts
> How they led
> Armies
> Headragged Generals
> Across mined
> Fields
> Booby-trapped
> Ditches
> To discover books
> Desks
> A place for us
> How they knew what we
> *Must* know
> Without knowing a page
> Of it
> Themselves.

Guided by my heritage of a love of beauty and a respect for strength—in search of my mother's garden, I found my own.

And perhaps in Africa over 200 years ago, there was just such a mother; perhaps she painted vivid and daring decorations in oranges and yellows and greens on the walls of her hut; perhaps she sang—in a voice like Roberta

Flack's—*sweetly* over the compounds of her village; perhaps she wove the most stunning mats or told the most ingenious stories of all the village storytellers. Perhaps she was herself a poet—though only her daughter's name is signed to the poems that we know.

Perhaps Phillis Wheatley's mother was also an artist.

Perhaps in more than Phillis Wheatley's biological life is her mother's signature made clear.

PART VI

BLACK THEOLOGY AND
THIRD WORLD THEOLOGIES

INTRODUCTION

Black theologians' dialogue with other Third World theologians has been limited. Aside from the historical independent Black churches' mission in Africa, the Caribbean, and their very limited work with the Black community in Britain, the North American Black Christian's encounter with poor Christians in other countries is almost nonexistent. The reason for this is obvious. Poor people seldom have the economic and political resources to enable them to come together for conversation regarding their common plight.

One of the unhappy results of this situation is that what poor people in one country know about poor people in another country is usually limited to what their oppressors permit them to know. Because what we think we know about each other has been communicated to us by a common White capitalist oppressor (through the news media and White missionaries), we often share the stereotypes of each other that have been created by oppressors in order to control us more effectively. "Divide and rule" is the motto of all oppressors, and they have successfully applied it in politics and theology. While most oppressed groups can easily recognize stereotypes applied to themselves, they often thoughtlessly accept similar contemptuous stereotypes applied to other oppressed groups. Consequently, when representatives of oppressed groups do meet, usually in ecumenical settings controlled by White Christians from Europe and North America, their conversations are often poisoned by misunderstanding, distrust, and contempt.

The antidote is *independent* dialogue among the poor. An indispensable aspect of the process of liberation is the people's responsibility to seize control of their history so that their identity as a people can be defined by themselves. When a people engage themselves in this process of historical self-definition, they also begin to reject all the stereotypes about their community created by their oppressors. The rise of Third World theologies (in Africa, Asia, Latin America, and the Caribbean) and theologies of the poor in rich countries is a theological witness to a global liberation process of self-definition. The distinguishing mark in all these theologies of the poor is the opportunity for the poor to define themselves and to reject all definitions about their communities created and promoted by their oppressors. Such theologies open new possibilities for transcending petty differences and establishing an effective coalition against the common enemy. But, of course, theologians of the poor have themselves been caught in networks of mutual misunderstanding. Failing on some crucial occasions to seize control of our talks, we have found ourselves manipulated by our oppressors.

445

When the meaning of the poor is placed in a global context, with Africa, Asia, Latin America, and the Caribbean as focal points, the complexity of the problem is enhanced. There is, of course, the cultural barrier, with language being a major problem to surmount, especially in Asia and Africa. Even if poor people could manage to travel to each other's setting, how are they going to talk with each other if they do not know each other's language? Language is not simply a technical tool but is the mirror that reflects a people's culture. Without the proper sensitivity to a people's cultural definition of themselves, it is not possible to talk with them. Culture is the source of a people's spiritual empowerment. Without the spiritual resources that are mediated through culture, there is no way for a people to sustain itself in the midst of extreme forms of economic and political oppression. That is why it is important to recognize that an economic and political analysis of a people's oppression is not enough. Culture is also important. If oppressed groups are going to converse with each other and thereby establish an effective coalition, it will be necessary to show a mutual respect for each other's cultural identity.

I think that Black theologians' dialogue with other oppressed peoples should begin with people in Africa and its diaspora and then move to other oppressed minorities in North America. Our cultural continuity with Black people in Africa, the Caribbean, and Latin America should enable us to talk with each other about common hopes and dreams in politics and economics. A similar political and economic oppression of racial minorities in the United States should enable Black people to share their cultural identities with each other so as to achieve a mutual recognition of the value of each culture in a common historical project of liberation. On the basis of Black people's solidarity with other oppressed minorities in the United States, they would be in a better position to create a coalition with oppressed people in other parts of the world.

Unfortunately there has not been much formal dialogue between Black theologians and other minorities in the United States: Chicanos, Asian-Americans, Puerto Ricans, and Native Americans. To be sure, there have been informal conversations between individual theologians but no planned conversations such as might be arranged through the National Conference of Black Churchmen or the Society for the Study of Black Religion. This fact makes it especially important to note the one instance of dialogue between Black theologians and theologians of other United States minorities. The occasion was the Theology in the Americas Conference in Detroit (1975), which was planned and dominated by White North Americans. The dialogue between minorities was definitely *not* planned. Rather, it was the result of the reaction of United States minority delegates against some White North Americans who tried to dominate the conference by verbally expressing their solidarity with oppressed people in Latin America. If these White North American so-called liberation theologians had not been able to establish a genuine solidarity with oppressed people in their own country, what right had they to address the oppressed of other lands? As Jean-Paul Sartre puts it: "The only way of helping the enslaved out there is to take sides with those who are here." We wanted to caution our Latin American brothers and sisters about North American White theologians' solidarity with suffering humanity, which usually extends no further than a conference speech on behalf of the poor. As a result, North American minorities formed a caucus within the conference and issued a brief statement (see Document 49). Following the Detroit conference, various projects were created under the auspices of Theology in the Americas, representing the various minority groups in the United States. At present, dialogue between minorities is beginning to take place but no written documents have emerged from these conversations.

The remainder of this introductory essay will be devoted to Black theologians' dialogue with African, Latin American, and Asian theologians.

A. Black Theology and African Theology

Black theologians' dialogue with African theologians began when the Board of Directors of the National Conference of Black Churchmen decided in May 1969 to take steps that would enhance relations between the two groups. NCBC representatives went to the All-Africa Conference of Churches (AACC) in Abidjan, Ivory Coast, in September 1969. Numerous meetings together followed this conference as well as the creation of NCBC of a Pan-African Skills Project devoted to the recruitment of "technically skilled Afro-Americans who have a sense of commitment toward the development of truly independent, progressive African nations. . . ."[1] Because of the effectiveness of this project in Tanzania, some church people in that country grew eager to hold a consultation with the National Conference of Black Churchmen. The first formal consultation between Black theologians and African theologians (about forty participants equally divided) occurred in Dar es Salaam, August 22-28, 1971, under the joint sponsorship of the Tanzanian Council of Churches and the newly established African Commission of NCBC.

The papers and other documents prepared for this conference were published under the title *Black Faith and Black Solidarity*. An excellent discussion of this dialogue between Africans and Black Americans is found in Cornish Rogers's *Christian Century* article, "Pan-Africanism and the Black Church: A Search for Solidarity."[2] The major issues discussed were economic development, education, and theology. These issues were perceived and discussed in relation to each other. As we expected, there were both agreement and disagreement reflected in our discussions, but all of us firmly agreed on the necessity for independent dialogue among ourselves. On the subject of "Black Theology and African Theology," a great deal of discussion happened around a paper jointly written by Gayraud Wilmore and me (see Document 42). This paper identified *liberation* and *Africanization* as the respective chief themes of the two theologies. These two themes, liberation and Africanization, have remained at the center of our discussions, with Black Theology emphasizing politics and African Theology focusing on culture. Neither theology has denied the importance of the other's emphasis, and that alone has enabled us to learn from each other's experiences of oppression.

One of the participants at the Dar es Salaam consultation was Charles S. Spivey, Jr., a Black American who was then working with the World Council of Churches Program to Combat Racism. At his suggestion and with support from the Program to Combat Racism, a second consultation was held at Union Theological Seminary, New York (June 7-9, 1973), under the sponsorship of the All-Africa Conference of Churches and the Society for the Study of Black Religion. There were twelve Black Americans and six Africans in attendance. Unlike the Dar es Salaam consultation (which covered a wide range of subjects and included persons from many backgrounds and fields of study), the Union consultation included only professional theologians, and they limited their concern to African and Black religions, with special reference to Christian theological expressions in Africa and North America. The explicit purpose was to explore the meaning of African and Black theologies as they are articulated in seminaries and universities and preached in churches on both continents.

We decided to limit the Union consultation to a small group discussion, because we felt that we were not ready for carefully structured papers. We needed to sit down and talk about our political and religious situations and the theological responsibility we perceived in them. No one denied the influence of the situation on theological formulation. But how much should a particular sociopolitical situation define theological expression? Rather than try to answer this question in the abstract, we talked about its concrete implications for Africa and North America. Our conversation lasted for three days, touching on themes ranging from Jesus and violence to the idea of sacrifice in the Old Testament and African Traditional Religions.

We became convinced of the worth of our discussion and decided to meet again in Ghana to probe more deeply some of the questions raised at the Union consultation. However, before our next meeting in Ghana, John Mbiti, who was present at the Union consultation, published an article entitled "An African Views American Black Theology" (*Worldview*, August 1974). In this article (see Document 43), he makes a sharp distinction between African Theology and Black Theology, identifying the latter with bitterness, anger, and hatred and the former with "joy in the experience of the Christian faith." Needless to say, many North American Black theologians were deeply disturbed by Mbiti's analysis, because they felt that it did not represent fairly their theological perspectives.

John Mbiti's article also disturbed South African Black theologians. For the Ghana consultation (December 29-31, 1974), Desmond Tutu wrote a paper entitled "Black Theology/African Theology—Soul Mates or Antagonists?" (see Document 44). It was obviously written as a reply to Mbiti's *Worldview* article and caused a great deal of discussion in Ghana. Unfortunately, neither Mbiti nor Tutu was present at the Ghana meeting, which also included other papers.[3] By the time we met in Ghana, we were beginning to move beyond a certain politeness toward each other to a discussion of serious differences. Again the critical difference focused at the point of Africanization and liberation, but this difference could not be defined simply *between* African and Black Americans but also *among* Africans and *among* Black Americans. The consultation ended with the realization that our conversations must continue.

Our next consultation occurred in Accra, Ghana (December 17-23, 1977) in connection with the Pan-African Conference of Third World Theologians, sponsored by the Ecumenical Association of Third World Theologians. There were about 100 participants from Africa, Latin America, and Asia, with the largest number from Africa. A small number of Black Americans were invited, including Wilmore and me.[4] I had been asked by Africans who planned this conference to present a paper on "A Black American Perspective on the Future of African Theology" (Document 45). I took the occasion to respond to Mbiti's *Worldview* article and to try to move the dialogue between African and Black theologians to a deeper level by placing it in the larger context of the Third World. The account of the conference, as well as the reactions to my presentation, is found in Wilmore's *Christian Century* article, "Theological Ferment in the Third World."[5]

The discussion following my presentation was provocative and intense. As expected, not everyone agreed with my analysis and emphasis, but the paper created a context for discussing seriously our agreements and disagreements. Our agreement is reflected in the Communiqué coming out of this conference (Document 46).

There have been many other discussions between Africans and Black theologians in Africa, the Caribbean, and North America. The Society for the Study of Black Religion held one of its annual meetings in Kingston, Jamaica (November 1976), and heard papers on various themes in relation to Black religion in Jamaica and the United States. Also a Seminar on Liberation Theology was held in the Caribbean at St. Andrew's Theological College, San Fernando, Trinidad, under the sponsorship of the Caribbean Conference of Churches, in which I was invited to make presentations on Black Theology (December 8-11, 1976).[6] African and Black theologians have also met each other in the context of the World Council of Churches and its Bossey Institute in Celigny near Geneva, Switzerland, but none of these proceedings has been published.

The influence of North American Black Theology on Black Theology in South Africa has been pointed out many times.[7] Black theologians from both continents have met each other in the context of dialogues on Black and African theologies, and other ecumenical contexts in Africa, Europe, and

North America. But we have not been able to get together for a conference among ourselves. I was invited to a conference in South Africa on the theme "The Role of the Black Clergy in South Africa Today," in August 1976. I applied for my visa and, to my surprise, received it in July. But before I could reach South Africa, F. D. Tothill, the South African Consul-General in Geneva, informed me by telephone (at the World Council of Churches) of the following, and later hand-delivered the same message, which read:

> Inasmuch as the Chief Magistrate of Pretoria has declined to give his permission for the holding of the Hammanskraal seminar, scheduled for 9 to 13 August 1976, the Department of the Interior desired you to be informed that your visa to visit South Africa, which was issued solely for the purpose of enabling you to attend the seminar, is no longer valid and should be regarded as withdrawn. If you should in any event decide to come to South Africa, it would unfortunately not be possible to admit you.

I found out later that the meeting was held as scheduled, and the reason for the withdrawal of my visa was obviously related to my theological perspective. I certainly hope that the dialogue between South African Black theologians and North American Black theologians can take place soon on the subject of their mutual interest in Black Theology. There are obvious similarities and some differences that need to be explored.

B. Black Theology and Latin American Liberation Theology

The first encounter of Black Theology with Latin American Liberation Theology took place at a symposium in Geneva at the World Council of Churches in May 1973 (Document 47).[8] This event was not for the purpose of discussions between these theologians but, rather, to introduce them both on the agenda of the WCC, whose theological focus was so decidedly European. Therefore the dialogue was essentially between traditional European theologians and Black and Latin theologians. Only in a small part of the symposium, and in the context of speaking to Europeans, did we raise the question about our mutual relations. In connection with our mutual condemnation of European theology, we began to ask about the differences and similarities among Black theologians and Latin American theologians. The matter was touched on in a comment by Paulo Freire and then addressed pointedly by Hugo Assmann, who suggested that we needed to discuss among ourselves the issues of *color* and *class*. My response touched on the issue he raised, but the presence of the Europeans prevented its exploration. I am including this brief exchange in this volume because it represents the beginning of fruitful dialogue, and the issues raised here (especially by Assmann) have remained central in our conversations.

The next occasion for dialogue occurred at the Detroit Conference on Theology in the Americas: 1975.[9] The conference began with presentations from Latin American theologians, José Míguez Bonino, Juan L. Segundo, Javier Iguíñiz, Enrique Dussel, José P. Miranda, Leonardo Boff, Hugo Assmann, and Beatriz M. Couch. Gustavo Gutiérrez arrived later in the week and also made a statement. The first day was devoted to an explication of Latin American Liberation Theology and its relation to social analysis as defined by Marxism. The class contradiction was emphasized by Latin theologians. Some persons felt that Latin theologians were too antagonistic toward any other contradiction (i.e., race and sex). Since the conference was held in the midst of an oppressed Black community in Detroit at the White Roman Catholic Sacred Heart Seminary, which obviously had little relation to the Black community, many Black theologians strongly resented the Latin theologians' dogmatic position on class, as if Black people have no creative contribution to make in the liberation process.

Even before the Detroit conference, the tension between Black Theology and Latin American Liberation Theology began to take place early in the planning process when Black theologians were first invited to the conference about nine months before its occurrence. The announced statement of the conference read:

> The intention of the planners of the "Theology in the Americas: 1975" conference is to invite a group of Latin American theologians, representing the theology of liberation, to dialogue with North American theologians concerning the context and methodology of this new theological current. It is hoped that such a dialogue would help both groups: the Latin Americans to understand the complex reality of the U.S.; the North American theologians to initiate a process of evaluation of the American reality from the viewpoint of the poor and the oppressed.

When Black theologians were confronted with this plan, we protested the assumption that North American theologians do not do theology from the perspective of the poor. This assumption is true *only* if by North American theologians one means White theologians exclusively, which is apparently what some persons had in mind. Thus Black theologians and other minorities felt that the invitation to them was more of an afterthought. Some expressed their opinions sharply to Sergio Torres, the chief organizer and executive secretary of the Theology in the Americas. Black theologians contended that if Latin Americans are really interested in a global understanding of the theological enterprise as it relates to the liberation of victims, then why not talk with the victims in other countries and not with the oppressors, especially since the expressed assumption of Liberation Theology in Latin America is directly connected with what Hugo Assmann has called "the epistemological privilege of the poor."[10] This controversy inspired the coalition statement (Document 49).

Prior to the presentation of the coalition statement Herbert O. Edwards presented a paper on "Black Theology and Liberation Theology" (Document 48), which was followed by a panel of Black theologians for the purpose of answering questions on Black Theology. Both the paper and the panel discussion created heated exchanges between Latin and Black participants and led to a private meeting between the two groups. The exchanges in this meeting were even more heated, the differences centering on the significance of color and class in social analysis. Most Black theologians felt that Latin theologians were completely insensitive to racism, and many Latin Americans contended that we needed to be awakened to the global oppression of international capitalism. But all of us left this Detroit meeting understanding each other better and with the resolution to continue our dialogue.

Because of the sensitivity of Sergio Torres to the concerns of oppressed minorities in the United States, Theology in the Americas has radically redirected its concerns toward the oppressed in North America, with projects representing each group.[11] The Black Theology Project held its first major event in Atlanta, Georgia (August 1977).[12] The influence of Latin American Liberation Theology was openly affirmed and the significance of class in the struggle for liberation was strongly emphasized.

The following October (1977) Latin American theologians held a conference in Mexico City on the Encounter of Theologians, and invited me as a representative of Black Theology. Other theologies were represented by Harvey Cox, Jürgen Moltmann, and David Griffin. At this meeting, it was clear that we had come a long way since Geneva 1973 and thus expressed our willingness to listen and learn from each other in a common struggle for liberation. The same openness was expressed in our meeting together in the context of the Pan-African Conference of Third World Theologians at Ghana in December 1977.[13] Gustavo Gutiérrez, Sergio Torres, Gayraud Wilmore, George Thomas, other Blacks and Latin Americans, and I worked smoothly together with Africans and Asians. The experience of a common struggle became a reality for us all. While we still recognized our differences in emphasis, the experience of working together on a common project tended to bring all of us closer together rather than to separate us as had happened in earlier meetings.

I think that the most significant and fruitful dialogue between Latin and Black theologians occured in Matanzas, Cuba, February 25 to March 2, 1979. This conference focused on the theme of "Evangelization and Politics" and was sponsored by the Evangelical Theological Seminary of Matanzas and the Christian Peace Conference for Latin America and the Caribbean. Seventy-eight theologians from Christian Churches of Europe, Asia, Africa, the United States, the Caribbean, and Latin America dialogued on the general theme of "Evangelization and Politics."

The focus of my paper, "Evangelization and Politics: A Black Perspective" (Document 50) was intended to address Black Theology's interpretation of this general theme as defined in the context of its dialogue with Latin American theologians. The response to my paper was provocative, and the discussion continued in a group session under the heading of "Evangelization, Racism, and Sexism." For the first time the question of racism was faced head-on by Latin American liberation theologians. The progress we have made on this issue since 1973 is reflected in the "Final Document" (Document 51) emerging from our conversations.

Our ability to move the dialogue to a much deeper level was undoubtedly due to a large extent to our presence in Cuba and to the significant role that Cuban theologians played in our discussions. Cuban theologians have developed a slightly different methodological approach to both theology and race, an approach open, if not similar, to Black theologians. They take the Bible seriously as the point of departure for doing theology, and their approach to the Scripture clearly shows the continued influence of Karl Barth. Sergio Arce, perhaps the most influential theologian in Cuba, has referred to Barth as the greatest theologian of all time, a judgment that no Latin American liberation theologian is likely to make.

Cuban theologians also take the race question seriously, and this is due to the fact that black people are taken seriously in the context of the larger society. The Cuban Revolution affected deeply the relations between Blacks and Whites, and the positive consequences are found in the openness of Cuban people to face head-on the race question in their society. I met no Cuban people who attempted to minimize the sickness of racism or who attempted to reduce it to a category under the class issue.

Because other Latin American liberation theologians look to Cuba as a concrete symbol to which their sociological and theological analyses refer, they are naturally open to hearing what Cubans have to say, even on the question of race. And Cubans have much to say on that subject which supported many of the concerns of Black theologians. I think Black and Cuban theologians have much to learn from each other, because our respective histories have prepared us for an openness for genuine dialogue.

However, even before our meeting in Cuba, the impact of Latin and Black theologians' dialogue since 1973 was reflected in the document emerging from the Third General Conference of the Latin American Episcopate in Puebla, for they spoke of having seen the "faces of Indians" and of "Afro-Americans who live marginalized and in sub-human conditions and can be considered to be the poor among the poor." A special session on Puebla was held at the Cuba conference, and it enabled us to deal openly with racism, sexism, and classism.

Most Latin American liberation theologians now take seriously the issue of race, and this new-found theological consciousness is beginning to appear in their public writings and speeches. I have been informed that the forthcom-

ing Latin American Conference of the Ecumenical Association of Third
World Theologians (February 1980 in Brazil) plans to take seriously the issue
of race. (How could it be avoided in Brazil, where more Blacks live than in
the United States?) As a preparation for the Brazil Conference, a pre-
conference meeting will be held in order to focus directly on the special
problems of Indians and Blacks in Latin America.

An account of the dialogue between Latin and Black theologians would not
be complete without a special reference to the contributions of Sergio Torres
of Chile and Gustavo Gutiérrez of Peru. The former deserves much
credit for the breakdown of the tension between Latin and Black theologians.
He has helped to keep us together with his patience and his leadership in
creating contexts for dialogue. In addition to Torres, Gustavo Gutiérrez has
made an important contribution to our dialogue in his teaching at Union
Theological Seminary and his lecturing in the United States. We taught a
joint course on the theme of "Theology from the Reversal of History." This
course enabled us both to understand each other better, which has been
reflected in an enlargement of our theological perspectives. His openness to
the importance of racism and popular religion is genuine. With a similar
openness from other Latin theologians and with more Black theologians
becoming open to the significance of the Marxist class analysis in theology, I
am sure that we can mutually enrich each other's theology and thereby help to
create a common Christian theology that will take seriously oppression in its
global manifestations.

The essay "Black Theology and Marxist Thought" by Cornel West (a Black
philosopher) is an important contribution for our dialogue (Document 52).
He has not only shown the importance of both class and race analyses in
uncovering the structures of domination but has also demonstrated the
weakness of either emphasis without an appropriate stress on the other.
According to West, the Latin Americans are correct in their contention that
"class position contributes more than racial status to the basic form of
powerlessness in America." Therefore, without the focus on class as the
primary contradiction, no analysis can claim to be adequate. However, on the
other hand, West contends that Black theologians are correct with their
emphasis on race and culture (even though it is not the primary contradiction), because without culture no oppressed people can be expected to
participate creatively in their own struggle for freedom. His essay moves the
debate to a deeper level and thus enables both Latin American and Black
theologians to learn from each other's historical struggles for freedom.

Some of the similarities and differences have already become clear.

1. We have already mentioned the emphasis on class and color. This means
that Marxism as a tool of analysis is more important for Latin American
theologians. However, some Black theologians are beginning to introduce
Marxism into Black Theology, while others remain resistant to it. The same is
true of Latin theologians in relation to the importance of racism. It is clear

from our dialogue that some Latin theologians are open to the problem of racism. In fact, we pointed out to them that there are more Blacks and Indians in Latin America than in North America, and that they should therefore be suspicious of their silence on racism. With the exception of Gutiérrez (part Indian), why is it that there are no people of color among the theologians of liberation in Latin America? Some Latin theologians understood the significance of this question and others did not.

2. Latin American Theology of Liberation is recent in origin, and it is often connected with the revolutionary struggle of the Colombian priest Camilo Torres, who said: "I discovered Christianity as a life centered totally on love of neighbor. . . . It was later that I understood that in Colombia you can't bring about this love simply by beneficence. There was needed a whole change of political, economic, and social structures. These changes demanded revolution. That love was intimately bound up with revolution." There was little involvement of the church in radical change or of theologians interpreting the gospel in the context of revolution before the 1960s in Latin America.

The opposite is the case with Black Theology in North America. Black Theology interprets itself in the context of Nat Turner, Henry Highland Garnet, and the independent Black Church movement. It views itself as part of the realization of a revolutionary past in the context of the Black Church. Therefore, Black theologians do not regard God-talk to be as alien to the liberation struggle as do some Latin Americans. In view of their church history, Latin Americans are suspicious of any talk that seems to usurp the human responsibility to transform the world.

3. Most of the representatives of Black Theology are Protestant, and most of the Latin American representatives of Liberation Theology are Roman Catholic. Although we have not discussed too much the significance of this difference, it perhaps does explain some of our sensitivities in theology.

4. Both theologies agree that the content of Christian theology is liberation and that it is inseparably connected with the struggle of the victims. But the methodology of its explication is different in both theologies. Latin American Liberation Theology begins with Marxism and the analysis of social reality and then moves to the Bible for secondary support. Black Theology begins with the Bible and the culture of Blacks extending back to Africa. The exodus, prophets, and Jesus as interpreted by Black history and culture are central for Black Theology, and it gets only secondary support from social philosophy. It is obvious that both approaches can learn from each other.

C. Black Theology and Asian Theology

If Black Theology's dialogue with African Theology and Latin American Liberation Theology has been limited, the dialogue with Asian Theology has been almost nonexistent. To my knowledge we have not had a formal face-to-face dialogue, and there has been very little informal conversation between us. In such ecumenical contexts as the World Council of Churches, especially in the Faith and Order Commission, we have met each other, but have seldom talked about our theologies.[14] In the absence of formal dialogues, my comments must be limited to personal reflections on the possibility of dialogue in the future.

My first contact with Asia occurred in May 1975 when I was invited by the Korean Christian Church in Japan (KCCJ) in cooperation with the Japan-North American Commission on Cooperative Mission to initiate a three-year leadership training program for church laity. There was also an opportunity to visit several Japanese universities and churches and to visit with struggling Christians in South Korea. During my three-week visit in Asia, I was impressed by the historical commitment of Korean Christians in Japan and South Korea to struggle against injustice and oppression. For Koreans in Japan, oppression was expressed in the racism of the Japanese who created societal structures that excluded them. That was why the KCCJ chose as the theme of its four workshops "The Church Struggling for the Liberation of the People." They asked me to speak on this theme in the light of the role of the Christian faith and the church in Black people's struggle for freedom in the United States. My living together with Korean Christians in Japan, listening to their stories of pain and suffering in a racist Japanese society, enabled me to see the close relation between the Black struggle in the United States and the Korean struggle in Japan. For Koreans, also, the church is an important instrument in the struggle for justice, and the gospel it preaches becomes the Word which empowers the people to take charge of their history.

It is significant that Asian theologians in the context of the Christian Conference of Asia have chosen to focus their distinctive theological reflections on *suffering* and *hope*.[15] This is certainly an accurate way to define the mood of Korean Christians in Japan. They experience racial suffering and discrimination in life and work.[16] This suffering arises because the Koreans have *chosen* to struggle (refusing the option of assimilation into Japanese culture). Having the option but refusing it gives the Korean struggle a certain strength, integrity, and freedom—qualities which can make a deep impression on movements of oppressed people throughout the world. I pointed out to the Korean Christians the importance of the option that they had freely chosen. Black people in the United States do not have the choice of assimilation because we cannot escape our blackness in a White society. Thus we are *forced* to struggle or accept the place defined for us by White society. But Koreans could assimilate; they could deny their identity and become Japanese because the physical differences are not clearly visible. I was deeply impressed by their refusal to assimilate, and they grounded it in their faith in the God of the Exodus and Jesus Christ. I was encouraged by their expressions of hope in the midst of suffering. On several occasions in church worship, they expressed their hope with such songs as "Were you there when they crucified my Lord" and "Lord, I want to be a Christian in my heart." When I first heard these songs, they were sung, of course, in the Korean language but I recognized the melody and turned to my interpreter (Dr. In Ha Lee) for a translation. Suddenly the cultural and language barriers were temporarily broken and we were one in spirit and the struggle of freedom. I realized that the spirit and meaning of Black Theology was already present among Koreans in song. But from their own experiences of hope in struggle, the Korean people are creating a Theology of Liberation, grounded in the universal hope that God has not left the little ones alone in the fight for justice. Therefore when they tell their stories of suffering, they are not expressions of despair but of their faith that God is still keeping the divine promise to liberate the oppressed from the shackles of bondage. I left Koreans in Japan with the knowledge that we have much to learn and share with each other in the struggle of freedom.

In contrast to Koreans in Japan, Japanese Christians reminded me very much of the White Christians whom I have met so often in the United States and Europe. With rare exceptions, the theologians I met at their universities seemed more concerned with the dialogue with Euro-American theologians of the West than addressing the oppression of Koreans or of the poor generally. The laypeople and ministers of the Japanese churches seemed especially bothered when the gospel was identified with the liberation of the poor. In fact, I could easily distinguish between the composition of my audience in terms of Korean or Japanese people by the kind of reaction they gave to my analysis of the gospel in terms of liberation. Koreans without exception heard the message of liberation as good news. In presenting this message in sermons, talks, and discussions to Koreans in Tokyo, Nagoya, Osaka, Kyoto, and Fukuoka, I experienced no resistance but was received gladly. By contrast, most Japanese audiences had difficulty with my interpretation of the gospel as liberation and asked all of the questions I had already been so accustomed to hearing from White people in the United States. Once again, I realized that one's social location in a given society will determine, at least partly, one's theological interest.

From Japan I flew to South Korea. I will never forget that experience. Again the theme of suffering and hope is appropriate. In South Korea, the suffering is obviously political and is directly connected with South Korean Christians who have refused to accept the oppression of the poor as consistent with the gospel. Their theological stand is found in the "Theological Declaration of Korean Christians of 1973"[17] and it has been compared with the "Barmen Declaration" of 1934. I have read it in the light of several NCBC statements included in this volume.

During my brief stay, I encountered Christians whose friends and loved ones had been put in jail because of their resistance to the Park dictatorship. I met many others who had been in jail for similar reasons and others who expected to be arrested soon. The government had made it clear that anyone attending my lectures would be subject to arrest. I met university and seminary professors who had been fired and others who expected to be released soon. In the context of such blatant expressions of political oppression and with little leverage for resistance without the risk of imprisonment and death, how could people still struggle when the odds seemed so much against them? Again I thought of the struggles of my people in Mississippi, Arkansas, and Alabama, and in Harlem and Watts. It is hope in the midst of suffering that sustains people for struggle. When people no longer hope, suffering destroys them. To hope is to know that one's humanity cannot be defined by oppression. This knowledge is God's gift to the weak so that they will be led to struggle for the realization of their hopes and dreams.

In reading the documents on suffering and hope published by the Christian Conference of Asia, it is clear that Black theologians have much to learn from Asian Theology. That Asians have something to learn from Black theologians has already been demonstrated by their openness to Black Theology.[18] Gayraud Wilmore (with Choan-Seng Song) delivered the Cook Memorial Lectures, which were published by the Christian Conference of Asia under the title *Asians and Blacks.* While the lectures do not deal with a proposed dialogue between Asian and Blacks, they do lay the foundation for such a dialogue. And in a recent publication, Song has made an initial step in this direction when he writes on the theme of "The Black Experience of the Exodus." I have included this essay (Document 53) because it is important in starting the exchange between Black Theology and Asian Theology.

My first opportunity to dialogue with a cross-section of Asian theologians occurred at the Asian Theological Conference, sponsored by the Ecumenical Association of Third World Theologians which was held at Wennappuwa, Sri Lanka, January 7–20, 1979. I found out more about the Asian reality and the theology arising from it than I could ever learn by reading textbooks on the subject. This conference affected me deeply, and I am still struggling to assimilate its impact upon my theological consciousness. I have included the "Final Statement" (Document 54) arising from the conference and my report on it (Document 55), because I believe that this conference lays a foundation for the formal beginning of Black Theology's dialogue with Asian Theology.

As a concluding comment for this introductory essay, what can be said about the distinctive elements of Black Theology's dialogue with other Third World theologies? With reference to African Theology, our concerns have focused almost exclusively on *Africanization* and *liberation,* as well as how we can bridge the gap created by colonization and slavery. There have been some tensions, but they are clearly of a different sort in character and depth when compared with our relation to Euro-American theologians or even Latin American theologians. Our common racial origin has undoubtedly contributed to the ease with which our dialogues have taken place.

More tensions have occurred between Black and Latin theologians than with theologians from either Africa or Asia. This is unquestionably due to the issues of *race* and *class* and *which* should define our priority. Since Black theologians have said so little about class, it is easy for Latin Americans to conclude that they must be capitalists, and thus indifferent to the global context of oppression. This is the opinion of many Latin theologians. Since, on the other hand, Latin theologians have said so little about color and have no Blacks among their theologians, it is easy for Black Americans to conclude that they are racists. Many Black theologians share this opinion. I am hopeful that this account of the growth of our dialogue will help to create less tensions and more fruitful conversations.

Because Black Theologians' dialogue with Asian Theology has been so limited, the tensions present between Blacks and Latins or even between U.S. Blacks and Africans are not found in our dialogue with Asians. Because there has been little historical contact between us, there is hardly any reason to be suspicious of each other. Asians are certainly open to the issue of racism, as the Final Statement of the Asian Theological Conference clearly indicates. I was on the writing committee that produced the statement and experienced first-hand the openness of Asian theologians to Black Theology. This openness is found not only in what the Final Statement says about racism but especially in what it says about theology and culture and their mutual relation. Black theologians have much to learn from Asians on the relation of religion and culture to the struggle for political freedom. A symbolic expression of Asia's openness to the Black reality happened to me in Ratmalana, Sri Lanka, when I met a young Buddhist industrial worker. She did not know English very well, and I did not know her language. We were frustrated because of this language barrier. But we knew that we had a commonality, and she managed to express it by putting her arm next to mine, saying: "Same color, same struggle!" This phrase symbolized the fruitful dialogue that is certain to occur among Asians and Blacks in the future.

Black Theology's relation to Third World theologies is one of the largest sections in this volume, because we believe that Black Theology's future will be determined, to a large degree, by this international dialogue. The importance of this international context of Black Theology is clearly emphasized in a concluding essay, "The New Context of Black Theology in the United States," by Gayraud Wilmore published in the *Occasional Bulletin of Missionary Research,* vol. 2, no. 4, October 1978 (Document 56). Whether Black theologians like it or not, it is no longer possible to limit one's theological concern to white racism in North America or to the ecclesiastical issues arising out of Black church politics. Racism is an international phenomenon, and it is connected with classism, sexism, and imperialism. Therefore our analysis of it in North America must reflect the global perspective of human oppression. I believe that the future of Black Theology will be determined by Black theologians' ability to reflect this international awareness in their theological practice in the Black Church and community. When black theologians and church people are able to articulate in word and practice the international dimension of human oppression, the Third World poor and those who have expressed their solidarity with them will perceive that the Black struggle in North America is not an isolated, bourgeois Black attempt to gain a larger share of the capitalistic pie. Our struggle is global and is connected with Black and poor people throughout the world. We are a Third World people in the First World, and thus our fight for justice is in solidarity with the poor of this earth. If what I am saying is true, then we Black theologians must begin to relate the particularity of our concern about racism to Africa, Asia, Latin America, and the poor wherever they may be found. I only hope that we Black theologians can implement this international concern in the Black church and community, for the realization of Black humanity in North America is intimately connected with the humanization of all peoples.

J.H.C.

Notes

1. *Black Faith and Black Solidarity*, ed. Priscilla Massie (New York: Friendship Press, 1973), p. 134.

2. November 17, 1971, pp. 1345-1347.

3. The essays, with an Introduction by Charles S. Rooks, Jr., and Summary Reports by G. S. Wilmore and J. N. K. Nugambi, are published in *The Journal of Religious Thought*, vol. 32, no. 2, (Fall-Winter 1975). See also James Cone, "Black and African Theologies: A Consultation," in *Christianity and Crisis*, vol. 35, no. 3 (March 3, 1975); G. S. Wilmore, "To Speak with One Voice?: The Ghana Consultation on African and Black Theology," *Christian Century*, February 19, 1975.

4. The first conference of the Ecumenical Association of Third World Theologians was held in Dar es Salaam, Tanzania (August 1976). See *The Emergent Gospel*, ed. S. Torres and V. Fabella (Maryknoll, N.Y.: Orbis Books, 1978).

5. *Christian Century*, February 17, 1978.

6. Black theologians' dialogue with theologians in the Caribbean is at its beginning stage on the subject of theology. While our social, economic, and political situations are similar, there are important differences. These differences will necessitate a different theological approach, and Caribbean theologians are already in the process of developing such a theology. See, for example, Idris Hamid, *In Search of New Perspectives* (Barbados: CADEC); "Theology and Caribbean Development," in David I. Mitchell, ed., *With Eyes Wide Open* (Barbados: CADEC, 1973); Idris Hamid, ed., *Troubling of the Waters* (Trinidad: Rahaman Printery Limited, 1973); Idris Hamid, ed., *Out of the Depths* (Trinidad: Rahaman Printery Limited, 1977); K. Davis, ed., *Moving into Freedom* (Bridgetown, Barbados: Cedar Press, 1977); Leonard Barrett, *Soul-Force* (Garden City, N.Y.: Doubleday, 1974); Leonard Barrett, *The Rastafarians* (Boston: Beacon Press, 1977).

7. See Basil Moore, ed., *The Challenge of Black Theology in South Africa* (Atlanta: John Knox Press, 1974); Alan Boesak, *Farewell to Innocence: A Socio-Ethical Study on Black Theology and Black Power* (Maryknoll, N.Y.: Orbis Books, 1977); David J. Bosch, "Currents and Crosscurrents in South African Black Theology," *Journal of Religion in Africa*, vol. 6, no. 1 (Leiden: Brill, 1974), which is also reprinted here, see Document 19 above.

8. The papers and proceedings of this symposium were published in *Risk*, vol. 9, no. 2 (1973).

9. The papers and proceedings of the conference were published under the title *Theology in the Americas*, eds. S. Torres and J. Eagleson (Maryknoll, N.Y.: Orbis Books, 1976).

10. "Statement by Hugo Assmann," in *ibid.*, pp. 299-303.

11. Theology in the Americas is a five-year program for doing theology (1975–1980) which has divided itself into affinity groups. According to its brochure "the affinity groups, organized

around a specifically felt injustice, create a *project* within the Theology in the Americas program. The projects grapple theologically and analytically with the particular oppression of each group. While focusing on its own context of exploitation, each affinity group seeks to enrich and be enriched by the action/reflection process of the others so that a holistic U.S. theology might develop from the perspective of the society's poor and powerless." The projects include. The Black Project, The Hispanic Project, The Women's Project, Quest for Liberation in the White Church, The Task Force of Professional Theologians, Labor and Church Dialogue, Asian-Americans in the U.S. Context, and Land: Native Americans and Red Theology. This approach is far more creative and responsible than the earlier one, which tended to exclude oppressed United States minorites. This major change in focus is undoubtedly due to the united voices of United States minorities in rejecting White domination, together with the capacity of Sergio Torres and others to hear them.

12. See the "Message to the Black Church and Community" and James Cone's "Black Theology and the Black Church: Where Do We Go From Here?" Documents 34 and 35 of this volume. See also "The Atlanta Statement: Some Background and Commentary," by Shawn Copeland in *Cross Currents*, vol. 27, no. 2 (Summer 1977), pp. 144-146.

13. It is significant to note that during the first meeting of the Ecumenical Association of Third World Theologians in Dar es Salaam, Tanzania (August 1976) only *one* Black North American was present (the Rev. C. T. Vivian). But largely due to the protests of Africans, a significant number were invited to their second meeting in Ghana and are now a part of this important association. Sergio Torres reported the tensions regarding exclusion of North American Blacks with this comment: "One point was discussed at length in Dar es Salaam. Some of the participants felt that North American blacks did not belong to the Third World, so they should not be included in the process. However, the Africans claimed that for them, there was only one black world, whether in Africa, in North America, or in the Caribbean. The future will show whether this statement proves true or not" (*The Emergent Gospel*, eds. S. Torres and V. Fabella [Maryknoll, N.Y.: Orbis Books, 1978], p. x; this book is an account of the conference). Although not explicitly stated by Torres, most Black North Americans contend that it was primarily the Latin Americans who attempted to exclude us, and that such an attempt was motivated by our heated discussions on racism versus class oppression. This conclusion is partly supported by D. S. Amalorpavadass's account of the conference. On the "areas of disagreement," he writes: "The Latin Americans were the whole time harping on socio-economic-political dimensions as the major or only reality, and applied rigorously the Marxian tool of analysis. All the other realities were so insignificant for them that they could be integrated into the economic-political domination or its consequences. This was questioned strongly by Asians and Africans though they agreed with the analysis and results of socio-economic-political reality" ("News and Comments: Ecumenical dialogue of Third World Theologians," *Indian Theological Studies*, vol. 14, no. 4, December 1977). The difficulty of Black theologians with Latin Americans was precisely at this point. Most Black theologians have never questioned the importance of class analysis and did not do so with Latin Americans. Our conflicts emerged when Latin Americans reduced to insignificance the issue of race. That our exclusion from the Dar es Salaam Conference is related to a difference on class and race also seems supported by Sergio Torres's definition of the Third World: "The concept of Third World is, in the first place, not limited to geographical space. It is not enough to live in Africa or Asia to share what we understand by theology of the Third World. There are people who live in Hong Kong or Bolivia who do not identify ideologically with the Third World. Their hearts, their interests, their futures are linked with the dominant classes of the world. . . . It is not enough for [theologians] to live in or come from poor countries for their theology to differ basically from the theology of the rich countries. Herein lies the originality of this book and the emergent theology it represents. It proposes to develop scientifically a theology that speaks with the voice of the poor and the marginated in history" (*Emergent Gospel*, p. ix). If what Sergio Torres says here represented the consciousness of the participants, why then should there be such a lengthy discussion on the inclusion or exclusion of Black North Americans? The only issue (on the basis of the above description of the Third World) should be whether Black North Americans or any people represent "the poor and the marginated in history."

14. One significant context for dialogue has been the Ecumenical Institute Bossey Colloquiums with African and Asian theologians, in which a small number of Black North Americans have been present. There have been three colloquiums, two of which have been published. See John S. Mbiti, ed., *African and Asian Contributions to Contemporary Theology* (Geneva: World

Council of Churches, 1976); J. S. Mbiti, ed., *Confessing Christ in Different Cultures* (Geneva: World Council of Churches, 1977). All of these proceedings are expected to be made available in print.

15. See especially *Asia Focus*, no. 661 (January 1977), ed. Yap Kim Hoa, on the theme "Asian Theological Reflections on Suffering and Hope," Christian Conference of Asia, Singapore; *Towards a Theology of People: I*, published by Urban Rural Mission and Christian Conference of Asia, 1977; *Testimony Amid Asian Suffering*, ed. T. K. Thomas, CCA, 1977; *Jesus Christ in Asian Suffering and Hope*, ed. J. M. Colaco (Madras: The Christian Literature Society, 1977); *Christian Action in the Asian Struggle* (Singapore: CCA, 1973).

16. See "Race and Minority Issues in Theological Perspective" by In Ha Lee in *Towards a Theology of People: I*. See also the report of the Consultation on Minority Issues in Japan and Mission Strategy, May 6-10, 1974, Kyoto, Japan, *IDOC*, no. 65, September 1974.

17. This Declaration is included in *Towards a Theology of People:I*, pp. 28-32; it is also included in the important publication *Documents on the Struggle for Democracy in Korea*, ed. The Emergency Christian Conference on Korean Problems (Tokyo: Shinkyo Shuppansha, 1975), pp. 37-43. It is also found in Kim Chi Ha, *The Gold Crowned Jesus and Other Writings* (Maryknoll, N.Y.: Orbis Books, 1978). See also the excellent article by Y. Kim, "Christian Koinonia in the Struggle and Aspirations of the People of Korea," in *Asia Focus*, January 1977.

18. I found this openness to be clearly present among Korean theologians in Japan and South Korea. The famous poet Kim Chi Ha, who is currently in prison on charges of subversion, referred to Black Theology in his "Declaration of Conscience"; and Steve Moon of Hankuk Theological Seminary calls for a dialogue of Korean Theology with Black Theologies of Liberation and Latin American Theologies of Liberation. (See Y. Kim's reference to Moon's "Theology of Liberation and Korean Christianity" in his "Christian Koinonia in the Struggle and Aspirations of the People of Korea," in *Asia Focus*, January 1977, p. 46.)

42

BLACK THEOLOGY AND AFRICAN THEOLOGY: CONSIDERATIONS FOR DIALOGUE, CRITIQUE, AND INTEGRATION

James H. Cone and Gayraud S. Wilmore

A young Ghanaian scholar of the University of Ghana at Legon remarked recently: "You Afro-Americans are very concerned about Africa these days. As we say in Ghana: *'Akwaaba'*—'You are welcome.' You are, after all, our brothers and sisters and we have missed you. But why do you speak of Black Theology? Why don't you call the theology you are doing today an *African Theology?*"

That question uncovers a historic anomaly which points to a vast and largely unexplored wilderness of other questions about political, social, and intellectual developments on both sides of the Atlantic between peoples of African descent who, in one way or another, received the message about Jesus Christ from the hands of White men. We cannot hope in this consultation to reconnoitre the full expanse of this overgrown and almost trackless wilderness. But upon its rough terrain lay the most difficult problems and promising opportunities of our encounter and we cannot hope to find one another unless we make a beginning of blazing some trails and erecting some guideposts along the way.

I

H. R. Mackintosh begins his well-known book *Types of Modern Theology* with a discussion of what he understands to be important differences between

This essay was first published in *Pro Veritate,* January 15 and February 15, 1972 under the title "The Future and . . . African Theology." Later this article was published in P. Massie, ed., *Black Faith and Black Solidarity* (New York: Friendship Press, 1973).

German and Anglo-Saxon styles of theological scholarship. For many years these two races dominated the theological scene, with the ponderous scholarship of Teutonic philosophers and theologians holding, perhaps, a slight edge. But neither German nor British theologians have occupied the field exclusively. Over the past two centuries or more we have had a French Catholic theology, a Swedish Lutheran theology, an American evangelical theology or "Fundamentalism," and more recently that peculiarly American "God-is-dead" theology. Since the end of the Second World War theological thinking in India has been stamped with a British-influenced, but distinctive Indian or Ceylonese flavor by such men as D. T. Niles and M. M. Thomas. Dutch Catholic theologians have led certain nationalistic developments within contemporary Roman Catholicism and a politically self-conscious Latin American theology is emerging among both Protestant and Roman Catholic churchmen in Brazil, Chile, Colombia, and elsewhere south of the Rio Grande.

With all these distinctive emphases and schools of thought centering around particular national or regional identities, why has it seemed so outlandish and so threatening to some of our White Christian friends to find Afro-Americans talking about *Black* Theology and Africans beginning to shape an *African* Theology? Does it not have to do with the residual influence of the age-old assumption that African culture and intellectuality is and always has been inferior to that of Europe and the accepted adage of American liberals that "the Negro is nothing but a chocolate-covered White American"?

What we are experiencing among Black people in the United States, the Caribbean, and Africa is an outright rejection of both of these assumptions and a new consciousness of racial, national, and cultural identity which asserts a certain discontinuity with Euro-American values and perceives Black people to have, by virtue of historical circumstances if not innate characteristics, a distinctive and independent contribution to make to world civilization. This assumption is, by no means, something new. Long before Africa had extricated itself from European colonial domination or the slogan "Black Power" was bandied about on the civil rights march through Mississippi, Black preachers in Africa and in the United States were proclaiming the prophecy of Psalm 68:31: "Princes shall come out of Egypt; Ethiopia shall soon stretch out her hands unto God."

Our fathers fervently believed that God had a grand and glorious plan for Black people and that the redemption of the African race—both in Africa and in the diaspora—would begin an outpouring upon the world of gifts of inestimable worth from a despised and rejected race. Whatever our poets, writers, and statesmen have said about the sources of African nationalism and Pan-Africanism, it was from religious men in Africa and the United States— from Paul Cuffee, Daniel Coker, Bishop Turner, Mangena Mokone, James M. Dwane, John Chilembwe, Edward Blyden, and a host of others—that the religious vision of Africa's great destiny first arose and the initial call went out for the elevation and solidarity, under God, of all peoples of African descent.

These were the first Black or African Christian theologians south of the Sahara and in the New World and all that we have today that can be termed Black Theology or African Theology, all that we can justly interpret as Black Consciousness or Pan-Africanism, had its origin in their thoughts and actions. It remains for young scholars on both sides of the Atlantic to reopen the neglected pages of history and trace the development of African nationalism and Black Power back through these men of faith who believed that God had revealed something for the Black race beyond that which it had received from Europe and Africa and that in good time he would bring it to fulfillment for the benefit of all mankind.

Black consciousness did not come into being with Stokely Carmichael or Leopold Senghor. It began with the plunder of Africa by the Portuguese, the Dutch, and the English. It began with the slave ships, the auction blocks, and the insurrections. It began with the experience of and resistance to White domination and it was shaped and honed and given its most profound statement by the preaching of the gospel by Black men to Black men in the cotton fields of the South, on the plantations of the Caribbean, among the freedmen of Philadelphia and New York, in Cape Colony and Nyasaland. All along, it was more than simply color consciousness. It was the consciousness of God's liberation. It was the consciousness that White was not always right and Black always wrong. It was saying Yes to what the White man regarded as evil, and No to his definition of good. It was, as Delany would say, *thanking* God for making us *Black* men and women and believing that implicit in what he had led us through was a gift and a blessing which the White world could neither give nor take away.

II

Despite their common relationship to the experience of Black suffering, the preaching of the gospel of liberation and resistance to White political and ecclesiastical domination, what we are calling Black Theology in the United States and African Theology in Africa have, since the independence of most of sub-Saharan Africa and the rise of the Black Power movement in the 1960s, proceeded along somewhat different lines. The Black experience in Africa and the Black experience in the United States and the Caribbean have not been the same. In the United States it has been a minority experience, separated, for the most part, from the ownership of land, from a discrete tribal language and culture, and from a living, historical memory. In Africa it has been a majority experience which has never been wholly disjoined from the land, the tribe, and the ancestors. White oppression in Africa did not show the same face as it did in the United States. Even where Direct Rule was administered, as in the French and Portuguese colonies, and under brutally repressive systems, such as the former Belgian Congo and the Republic of South Africa, there was for the White man always the pervasive, overwhelming reality of the vast and alien land and the conspicuousness of an indigenous people who had latent power to resist foreign acculturation and swallow up the transplanted White civilization in the bowels of blackness. Africa and the African people had to be reckoned with—their existence was bound to be acknowledged and respected, if grudgingly.

Such was not the case in the Americas. The Black man had never been known as anything but a slave, a species without an authentic racial or national identity, a beast of burden. While his power to rise up and overthrow his masters was recognized, that possibility decreased each passing year as the total White majority increased and the controls were tightened. Thus the peculiar form of White oppression and racism which developed in the United States did not simply exploit the Black man, it denied his right to exist except by sufferance of the White man. Christian America has known a virulent disease of hatred against the Black man and against blackness as a symbol of the very evil the White man knew to be in his own heart. In both Africa and America, "dark skin came to symbolize the voluntary and stubborn abandonment of a race in sin" (Roger Bastide), but in Calvinistic, Protestant America that symbolic association became rooted in a pathological hatred and fear of what Laurens van der Post has called "the dark brother within."

Blackness, for the White American, has been something that needed to be expunged from reality, blotted out before the face of God. There was, therefore, an ontological basis for White racism in America and a corresponding ontological ground for Black pride and the Black man's struggle against a latent but frighteningly real possibility of genocide. This is why it is correct to say that the Black American's struggle is against the threat of nonbeing, the ever present possibility of the inability to affirm one's own existence. The structure of White society in America attempts to make "Black being" into "nonbeing" or "nothingness." Black Power, therefore, whatever else it may be, is a humanizing force by which we Black Americans have attempted to affirm our being over against the White power which seeks to dehumanize us.

Without understanding this difference between White racism in the United States and White racism in colonial Africa, one cannot understand why there has to be a Black Theology or the differences between Black Theology in America and African Theology in Africa.

III

What does Black consciousness in America have to do with theology? This question forces us to consider the relationship between Black self-identity and the biblical faith. White American theology has never inquired into this relationship because it has pursued the theological task from the perspective of the oppressor rather than the oppressed. White religious thinkers have been blind to the theological significance of Black presence in America and no White American theologian or church historian has bothered to discover what Black religious thinkers have been saying for almost two hundred years.

The theological perspective that defines God as unquestionably identified with the liberation of the oppressed from earthly bondage arises out of the biblical view of divine revelation. According to the Bible, the knowledge of God is neither mystical communion nor abstract rational thought. Rather, it is recognizing divine activity in human history through faith. The biblical God is the God who is involved in the historical process for the purpose of human liberation. To know him is to know what he is doing in historical events as they relate to the liberation of the oppressed. Faith is the divine-human encounter in the historical situation of oppression, wherein the enslaved community recognizes that its deliverance from bondage is the Divine himself at work in history. To know God, therefore, is to know the actuality of oppression and the certainty of liberation.

The liberation theme stands at the center of the Hebrew view of God in the Old Testament. Throughout Israelite history, God is known as the one who acts in history for the purpose of Israel's liberation from oppression. This is the meaning of the Exodus, the Covenant at Sinai, the conquest and settlement of Palestine, the United Kingdom and its division, and the rise of the great prophets and the emancipation from Babylonian captivity. This is also why salvation in the Old Testament basically refers to "victory in battle" (I Sam. 14:45). "He who needs salvation," writes F. J. Taylor, "is one who has been threatened or oppressed, and his salvation consists in deliverance from danger and tyranny or rescue from imminent peril (I Sam. 4:3, 7:8; 9:16). To save another is to communicate to him one's prevailing strength (Job 26:2), to give him the power to maintain the necessary sovereign rule in guiding the course of human history, setting right that which is unrighteous, liberating the oppressed."

In the New Testament the same theme is carried forward by the appearance of Jesus Christ the Incarnation of God, born of common parentage under highly suspicious circumstances, in a lowly stable, during the Roman occupation of Palestine. This Jesus takes upon himself the oppressed condition, so that all men may be what God created them to be. He is the Liberator par excellence, who reveals not only who God is and what he is doing, but also who we are and what we are called to do about human degradation and oppression. It is not possible to encounter Jesus Christ and acquiesce in oppression—either of oneself or of others. Human captivity of every sort is ruled out by the coming of Jesus. That is why Paul writes, "For freedom, Christ has set us free" (Gal. 5:1). The free man in Christ is the man who rebels against false authorities by reducing them to their proper status. The Christian gospel is the good news of liberation.

If the gospel is preeminently the gospel of the liberation of the oppressed, then the theological assessment of divine presence in America must begin with the Black condition as its point of departure. It is only through an analysis of God as he is revealed in the struggle for Black liberation that we can come to know the God who made himself known through Jesus Christ.

The presence of Black people in America, then, is the symbolic presence of God and his righteousness for *all* the oppressed of the land. To practice theology is to take the radical Black perspective wherein all religious and nonreligious forms of thought are redefined in the light of the liberation of the oppressed. This is what we call "Black Theology."

Black Theology, therefore, is that theology which arises out of the need to articulate the religious significance of Black presence in a hostile White world. It is Black people reflecting on the Black experience under the guidance of the Holy Spirit, attempting to redefine the relevance of the Christian gospel for their lives. It is a mood, a feeling that grips the soul of a people when they realize that the world is not what God wills it to be—with respect to the defining reality of their lives—Black subjugation under White oppression. To practice theology from the perspective of Black Theology means casting one's intellectual and emotional faculties with the lot of the oppressed so that they may hear the gospel in terms of the cause and cure of their humiliation.

In the words of the official statement on Black Theology of the National Conference of Black Churchmen:

> Black Theology is a theology of black liberation. It seeks to plumb the black condition in the light of God's revelation in Jesus Christ, so that the black community can see that the gospel is commensurate with the achievement of black humanity. Black theology is a theology of "blackness." It is the affirmation of black humanity that emancipates black people from white racism, thus providing authentic freedom for both white and black people. It affirms the humanity of white people in that it says No to the encroachment of white oppression.

As we have seen, the seminal Black Theology was the theology that secretly taught that God wanted Black people to be free. Our greatest fighters for freedom were religious leaders—Denmark Vesey, Nat Turner, David Walker, Henry Highland Garnet, and others. Our spirituals and slave songs echoed a theology of liberation and laid the groundwork for a faith that reflected the essential meaning of the biblical revelation in a way that broke radically with conventional White Christianity. As the young Black professor Sterling Stuckey, of the University of Massachusetts, writes:

> There was theological tension here, loudly proclaimed, a tension which emanated from and was perpetuated by American slavery and race prejudice. This dimension of ambiguity must be kept in mind, if for no

other reason than to place in bolder relief the possibility that a great many slaves and free Afro-Americans could have interpreted Christianity in a way quite different from white Christians.

Today some Black theologians are seeking the original source of this unique form of Christianity in the New World, not only in the experience of the slaves and freedmen, but even further back—in the traditional religions of Nigeria, Dahomey, Ghana, and other areas of Africa from which our ancestors came. Until very recently, and in some cases (such as in the Sea Islands off the coast of South Carolina) survivals of African religiosity could be found in Black religion in the United States. For example: the deep sense of the pervasive reality of the spirit world; the blotting out of the line between the sacred and the profane; the practical use of religion in all of daily life; reverence for the ancestors and their presence with us; the corporate-ness of social life; locating evil in the consequences of an act rather than in the act itself; and using drums, singing, and dancing in the worship of God.

The search for a Black Theology takes us not only into the survivals of African religions and the syncretistic religion of the slaves yearning for freedom, but also into the Black experience in the Black ghetto today. Black theologians cannot ignore the words of Langston Hughes about the living religion of the Black poor:

> But then there are the low-down folks, the so-called common element, and they are the majority—may the Lord be praised! The people who have their nip of gin on Saturday nights and are not too important to themselves or the community, or too well fed, or too learned to watch the lazy world go round. They live on 7th Street in Washington, or State Street in Chicago and they do not particularly care whether they are like white folks or anybody else. Their joy runs, bang! into ecstasy. Their religion soars to a shout. Work maybe a little today, rest a little tomorrow. Play awhile. Sing awhile. O, let's dance! These common people are not afraid of spirituals, as for a long time their more intellectual brethren were, and jazz is their child. They furnish a wealth of colorful, distinctive material for any artist because they still hold their own individuality in the face of American standardization.

It is from this reservoir of Black culture—of which religion has always been an inseparable part—that Black Theology seeks the genius of what Professor Joseph Washington called "Negro Folk Religion—the religion of protest and relief." It was this Folk Religion that Marcus Garvey, Elijah Muhammad, Malcolm X, Maulana Ron Karenga, and Albert Cleage tapped when they began to build their Black nationalist movements. It was this same Folk Religion which came into its own in the Southern civil rights movement under Martin Luther King, Jr., and has found its most profound expression in the Black Power and Black Theology movements of the 1960s and 1970s. In the final analysis, Black Theology is concerned with the ultimate questions which arise from the Black folk of the ghetto—from their suffering, their joy, their perception of themselves and of American reality. Black Theology is saying that the God who spoke to us out of our African past and out of the religion of the slaves, is speaking to us today in the accents of the contemporary Black community—and his message is Liberation.

IV

It is clear that there are areas of convergence and dissimilarity between what we are calling Black Theology in the United States and what is termed African Theology in Africa. Both of these theologies are rooted in the experience of Black people who received a highly attenuated form of Christianity from the White churches of Europe and America. Both are, in part, religious reactions to White ecclesiastical domination and political and economic oppression. Both are in quest for a base in the authentic milieu of an indigenous people—in one case, in the environment of the postcolonial African state; in the other, in the environment of the contemporary Afro-American ghetto. In both instances we are dealing with self-conscious African or Afro-American churches (or the Black constituencies of White-controlled European or American churches and missionary societies) which are emerging from a period of emulating White standards and are seeking a distinctive style of life and relevance to the culture of the people to whom they minister. But in terms of theological renewal there are important differences that we must consider—differences which are inevitable in light of the different situations in which these churches exist, but which may be used to enrich the life of each other.

It would be presumptuous for the authors of this paper to attempt to commend what follows here as an accurate interpretation of African Theology. That task belongs to African theologians themselves. What we will present is what some African theologians are saying and what, rightly or wrongly, is communicated to us about the theological program implicit in the work now in process.

Professor Idowu of Nigeria, in one of his first published works on indigenization describes the "shock of recognition" he experienced when he first realized that the Christ he worshiped as an African had been presented to him in the context of a language and culture not his own, and that he had assumed that it was impossible to understand Christ and Christianity in any other way. Idowu was only one of several African theologians for whom it has become increasingly and disturbingly clear that the Church in Africa could not attain selfhood and maturity until it possessed a knowledge of Jesus Christ in

African terms and could communicate that knowledge in the languages and thought-forms of Africa. For many years it had been assumed that God did not come to Africa until the first European missionaries landed on these shores and that, lying in the darkness of a primitive and pagan faith, Africa had nothing to offer as a cultural or spiritual basis for the gospel.

In his *African Ideas of God*, Edwin Smith reports his conversation with Emil Ludwig, an eminent biographer, in which he told Ludwig about the progress of Christian missions in Africa, how the Africans were being taught about the Christian God. Ludwig was perplexed. "How," he exclaimed, "can the untutored African conceive God? . . . How can this be? . . . Deity is a philosophical concept which savages are incapable of framing." Thus have the traditional religions of Africa and African spirituality, as such, been regarded by both Africans and Europeans in the not distant past. We understand that one of the first tasks of African Theology is to put an end to this nonsense, for which White missionaries and anthropologists must bear no little responsibility, and begin a reconstruction of the Christian faith in Africa which takes seriously the fact that God had revealed himself in the traditional religions and that by a selective process African theologians can use this revelatory content to throw light on the message and meaning of Jesus Christ. Thus the consultation of African theologians held in Ibadan in 1965 could conclude:

> We recognize the radical quality of God's self-revelation in Jesus Christ; and yet it is because of this revelation we can discern what is truly of God in our pre-Christian heritage: this knowledge of God is not totally discontinuous with our people's previous traditional knowledge of him.

In the now standard work by Kwesi Dickson and Paul Ellingworth, *Biblical Revelation and African Beliefs* (London: Lutterworth Press, 1969; Maryknoll, N.Y., Orbis Books), Idowu, Mbiti, Kibongi, Adegbola, and other distinguished African theologians deal with such themes as the African image of man, concepts of God and the spirit world, priesthood, sacrifice, and ideas of morality in such a way as to demonstrate the linkages between African and Christian religious knowledge. This cataloguing of African beliefs and comparing them with similar beliefs in biblical religion, particularly in the Old Testament, was evidently an early stage in the development of African theological thinking and indicates the extent to which African theologians, most of whom were educated in European and American seminaries, have sought, first of all, a deepening of Christian orthodoxy by bringing to it insights and discernments which lie outside the Judeo-Christian tradition. In an unpublished paper presented at the 1969 AACC [All Africa Conference of Churches] meeting in Abidjan, Professor Dickson of Ghana clarifies the significance of this tendency in the theological work being done in Africa:

Of course, whatever help that may come from sources outside the Judeo-Christian traditions are most likely to lie within the realm of the explicatory rather than the foundational; nevertheless, it could fill out a hitherto western expression of Christian theological concepts. One might hazard the example that the doctrine of Justification by Faith, which is the most missionary of doctrines, is usually expounded in terms of the salvation of the individual, to the exclusion of all ideas of corporate salvation, through the body of Christ. . . . We have only to allude to the metaphors of the Body and the Vine and its Branches to show that the African sense of corporateness . . . could be a reminder that the traditional western interpretation of the doctrine of Justification does not pre-empt the implications of that doctrine.

According to Dickson this approach to the African theological task is complemented by a second line of approach, which is represented by the work of Professor Mbiti, who, "recognizing the essential limitation of certain aspects of African thought by comparison with Christian teachings . . . suggests that Christian views should be imported into African thought to the enrichment of the latter." In this he refers to Mbiti's comment that the African cyclical view of history must be invaded by the Christian concept of the *eschaton* because, while Africa has an eschatology, it has no teleology and it is in this area that Christian eschatology can contribute to natural revelation in Africa.

With the publication of *African Religions and Philosophy* (New York: Praeger, 1969) Professor Mbiti of Uganda became widely acknowledged as the leading scholar of religion in Africa and his recent published works lay down some of the new directions for an indigenous African theology. As indicated by the above reference to African eschatology, Mbiti's work on the concept of Time in African religions has major significance for a fuller understanding of traditional values and how Christian theology, properly integrated with what he calls "transfused Religion" in the culture, can help shape the future of modern Africa. Thus, having exonerated African traditional religions from the charge of "primitivism" and given them the dignity they deserve, African Theology seems now to be taking up the task of bringing to traditionalism the insights of the Christian faith which are able to renovate the total life and culture of the new African nations.

In a lecture delivered at St. Paul's Theological College in Kenya, Mbiti said: "I believe that this is one of the most exciting principles in the whole relationship between Christianity and Traditional Religions. It calls for a theological articulation of the fulfillment not only as an academic exercise, but to guide the church in its life, work and mission in Africa. . . . The Lord God may have spoken Hebrew to the children of Israel: He now speaks the Christ-language. This is the language of the Gospel; and the Gospel comes to fulfill, not to destroy."

From the perspective of many of the younger Afro-American theologians, the "Africanization" of theology in Africa seems more academic, more bound to orthodoxy and more conservative than Black Theology in the United States and the Caribbean. It is, however, among the burgeoning phenomenon of African Independent or "spiritual" churches that one sees another side of this picture, with increasing significance for African Theology. Thousands of Independent Churches now exist in all parts of Africa alongside the older churches; and their evangelistic fervor, their appeal to the poor and uneducated masses, and their utilization of traditional elements in music and liturgy give them a vitality and relevance to African Christianity which cannot be ignored by African theologians. The problem that African Theology has in helping to relate Christianity to the new social and political realities cannot be solved without reference to the spiritual churches. The influence of these churches, as they become more institutionalized and led by trained clergy, is inestimable. Because of the role that they now and will increasingly play in the urbanization process, family life, social education and action, etc., they offer to African theologians the same exciting prospects for the indigenization of theology and the renewal of the church that the Black Consciousness churches of the ghettos offer to Black theologians in the United States. It is clear that the AACC is prepared to make a more energetic approach to the African Independent Churches, and at Abidjan it was proposed that a secretariat be set up for that purpose, with broad implications for theological study, dialogue, and collaboration, as well as affiliation.

We conclude this part of the paper with reference to the significant fact that at Abidjan the discussion of African Theology was held in the section dealing with the topic "Working with Christ in the Cultural Revolution." The group recognized that since African Theology was in an early stage of development, an exhaustive definition was impossible. An attempt was, however, made and seems to gather up all of the emphases, nuances, and problems we have noted in this brief discussion:

> By African Theology we mean a theology which is based on the Biblical Faith and speaks to the African "soul" (or is relevant to Africa). It is expressed in categories of thought which arise out of the philosophy of the African people. This does not mean that it is narrow in outlook. To speak of African theology involves formulating clearly a Christian attitude to other religions. It must be pointed out that the emphasis is basically on *Christian* theology, which could be expressed through African thinking and culture.

V

One of the peculiar features of our present situation is that Black Theology is reaching out to African Theology, but the reverse is not necessarily true. In a sense Black American theologians are more isolated, more suspect of heretical inclinations, and more embattled than African theologians. Therefore we are in greater need of dialogue and collaboration with those with whom we believe we have something in common. This is so not only because of forces within the American churches which define the canons of theological respectability, but also because, paradoxically, Black people in the United States are probably the most religious *and* the most secular of all American ethnic minorities (with the possible exception of the Jews). It is not an exaggeration to say that the hostility of the present generation of young Blacks outside the church to what they understood to be the subservience of Black Christianity to the status quo, played an important part in forcing Black Theology and Black churchmen generally into a more independent and militant posture vis-à-vis White Christianity. On the other hand, African theologians and the African churches, because of the recent paternalistic relationship in which they stood to European churches, enjoy a certain popularity among White Christians outside Africa, both Protestants and Roman Catholics, and feel less insecure about their status within the ecumenical Church.

This does not mean that African theologians feel no need to "reason together" with their Afro-American brethren. Quite the contrary, for many of them recognize a certain tokenism in ecumenical circles, and some of the same pressures we feel from our young people are experienced increasingly by African churchmen. It does mean that in the nature of the situation Afro-American theologians are and will be taking the initiative for dialogue. Black Theology needs African legitimation, for strategic reasons if for no other. But the situation is a delicate one. No one should expect African Theology, as yet so tentative in its disengagement from the categories of Western thought, to permit itself to fall into what could become the suffocating embrace of another style of theological reflection—even that of black brothers from across the sea. There is an amiability and gentleness about African religion, which is not true today about religion in Black America. In any dialogue between Black Theology and African Theology, care needs to be taken that the aggressiveness and "hardnosedness" of Black Theology does not mount such an assault on African religious sensibilities that the situation turns out to be one side shouting and the other closing its ears in pained indifference. On the other hand, African Theology cannot be so impressed with its good reputation in WCC circles, and so convinced that theological reflection is something that properly takes place in a setting resembling a sequestered English vicarage, that it cannot bring itself to converse with its tough, boisterous counterpart from the urban ghettos of America. We must talk to one another, for we have much to talk about. But we must hear one another with sympathy and understanding.

Dialogue first requires getting acquainted, but any dialogue between Black Theology and African Theology should, in due course, lead to mutually constructive critique and correction. The criterion of judgment is, of course, the Word of God and the testimony of the Holy Spirit. But there is also the action of God in history and the discernment of faithful men of how God is moving in their world to plant and build, and to root out and tear down. "Now we see through a glass darkly" and neither the church in Africa nor the church in Black America has the full truth about what God is saying today to people of African descent and what he is doing in the world to make them fulfill their calling among the races of mankind.

African Theology is concerned with Africanization. Black Theology is concerned with liberation. But Africanization must also involve liberation from centuries of poverty, humiliation, and exploitation. A truly African Theology cannot escape the requirement of helping the indigenous churches to become relevant to the social and political ills of Africa, which are not unrelated to Euro-American imperialism and racism. Similarly, liberation has to do with more than political oppression and social justice. It is Jesus Christ who is the Liberator; the justified man is also liberated from "the lust of the flesh and the pride of life." The liberated man is no longer under the unqualified power of sin and the Devil. How can these two theologies correct the excesses and deficiencies of one another? What can African Theology learn from Black Theology about the demonic power of White racism in the world today and what God is doing about it? What can Black Theology learn from African Theology about faithfulness to the Word of God in a situation of rapid secularization out of a traditional ethos, about Christian morality and the devotional life? What can the older churches of Africa learn from the Black churches of the United States about the assimilation of quasi-Christian ideologies and secular cults which can help them in rapprochement with the Independent Churches? What can the Black churches of America learn from the African churches about reconciliation between tribal groups and between Black and White in a multiracial society? Does African Theology depend too much upon the modalities of European theology in discriminating between what traditional religion offers as "preparation for the gospel" and what it does not? Is Black Theology so obsessed with concepts of negritude, "Black Consciousness," and revolution that it is in danger of becoming so localized and so self-interested that it loses the universal message of love, peace, and redemption for the whole world?

These are a few of the critical questions which will arise in any serious and candid encounter between Black Theology and African Theology. There are many more that can be instructive to both sides if we believe that mutual critique and reformation, under the judgment and the grace of God, are the true functions of theological reflection.

To what end will this long-frustrated and belated encounter between African and Afro-American theologians lead our churches in Africa and the United States? The answer to that question is not given to us today. We can only say that there exists between us a mysterious bond of blood brotherhood, a common past and a common experience of suffering and subjugation which God can use to his own good purposes as we come closer together in faith and life. The old Black theologians (and we have used that term broadly to encompass all reflective Christian churchmen) used to talk about the destiny of the Black race and how the sons of Ham would be a blessing to the world. Surely Fanon and others have taught us that the star of Euro-American civilization is in decline and a new humanity must arise and point the way to a future of justice and equality for all peoples. In these days of revolutionary Black Power and African Socialism those themes are being sounded again. It is not racist madness to believe that Africa shall again have one of the greatest civilizations the world has known and that long-separated brethren, weary of bruising their fists upon doors that will not fully open, will come home by the millions to contribute to and share in the building of that greatness. It is not too much to believe that God wills to use the churches of Africa and Black America to give the sublimity and spiritual depth to that historical process that will make it minister to the humanization and redemption of the world. If some future integration of the truths and insights of Black Theology and African Theology can accelerate the fulfillment of that lofty vision of our destiny, then we need to be about the task that has brought us together.

The young theologian at Legon wanted to know why we cannot speak of an *African* Theology which encompasses the theological work we are doing on both sides of the Atlantic. That felicitous possibility is not available to us today, but by meeting and critically examining one another's views and working together in the world, that day may come. Let the Church say, "Amen."

43

AN AFRICAN VIEWS
AMERICAN BLACK THEOLOGY

John Mbiti

Black Theology is a painful phenomenon in the history of the Church. Painful not because of what it says—although it certainly does not deal in soft phrases—but because it has emerged in an America that, since the arrival of the Pilgrims in the seventeenth century, has claimed to be a Christian country. Black Theology is a judgment on American Christianity in particular and Christianity in general. Ideally there would be no reason for Black Theology. It was forced into existence by the particularities of American history.

Black Theology as an academic concern can be dated from July 31, 1966, when the National Conference of Black Churchmen issued a statement asking for power and freedom from the leaders of America, for power and love from white churchmen, for power and justice from Negro citizens, and for power and truth from the American mass media [see Document 1]. Three years later the Black Manifesto [see Document 7] demanded, inter alia, reparations to Negroes by the white churches because of the latter's complicity in the exploitation of Negroes (blacks, as they now prefer to call themselves). In the same year Professor James H. Cone published *Black Theology and Black Power*, which marked the formal inauguration of Black Theology as a serious academic concern with which the whole of Christian theology must reckon. Other publications appeared earlier, but Cone's is the one that formally incorporated Black Theology into the stream of Christian theology at large.

The roots of Black Theology must in fact be traced to a much earlier period

John Mbiti, a leading African theologian, is Director of the Ecumenical Institute, World Council of Churches, Geneva. His books include *African Religions and Philosophy*. This essay first appeared in *Worldview*, August 1974.

of American history, the arrival of the first African slaves in the seventeenth century. The subsequent history of Americans of African origin— of exploitation, segregation and general injustice—is the raw material of what we now call Black Theology. Insofar as Black Theology is a response to this history of humiliation and oppression it is a severe judgment and an embarrassment to Christianity, especially in America. Black Theology was born from pain and communicates pain and sorrow to those who study it. It is a cry of protest against conditions that have persisted for nearly four hundred years in a land which otherwise takes pride in being free and Christian, or at least in having Christian institutions.

One would hope that theology arises out of spontaneous joy in being a Christian, responding to life and ideas as one redeemed. Black Theology, however, is full of sorrow, bitterness, anger and hatred. Little wonder Black Theology is asking for what black Americans should have had from the start—freedom, justice, a fair share in the riches of their country, equal opportunities in social, economic and political life. The wonder is that it has taken all these years for the anger of Black Theology to surface. It draws from the peculiar history of the Negroes in America: from the "Black Experience," which is "a life of humiliation and suffering . . . existence in a system of white racism"; from the Black History of "the way Black people were brought to this land and the way they have been treated in this land"; from Black Culture with its "creative forms of expressions as one reflects on the history, endures the pain, and experiences the joy"; and in a more general way from the Scriptures, Christian tradition and African religious heritage (see Cone's *A Black Theology of Liberation* and Gayraud S. Wilmore's *Black Religion and Black Radicalism*). Professor Cone defines Black Theology as "that theology which arises out of the need to articulate the significance of Black presence in a hostile white world. . . . Black Theology is revolutionary in its perspective. It believes that Black people will be liberated from oppression" ("Black Consciousness and the Black Church" in *Christianity and Crisis*, November 2 and 16, 1970).

The main concerns of Black Theology are directly related to the circumstances that brought it into being. One such concern is "blackness" itself. It wants to see "blackness" in everything. It speaks of a Black God, Black Church, Black Liberation, Black this and Black that. While some theologians, notably James Cone, try to give a wider ontological meaning to "blackness," it is nevertheless a color terminology arising out of the color consciousness of American society. Indeed Professor Cone goes so far as to say that "white theology is not Christian theology." In reading Black Theology one becomes sated by color consciousness. It is necessary to remind oneself that racial color is not a theological concept in the Scriptures. A few black theologians are becoming aware of the dangers in excessive emphasis upon color. Professor Miles J. Jones has written (*The Christian Century*, September 16, 1970): "Color is merely a vehicle; experience is the concern. . . . Changing our concept of Christ's color is no acceptable substitute for interpreting our experience as black people in what God did and is doing through the Christ. Moreover, such 'coloring' is dangerously idolatrous. We need not color God or the Christ black in order to appreciate blackness as an instrument of the Divine."

Nonetheless, for Black Theology blackness has become an ideology embracing much of the life and thinking of Negroes in America, whether their skin color is black, dark brown, light brown, khaki or coffee, or even if they have a remote African ancestry and most of their biological heritage is actually French, English, Scottish, American Indian or other. All are "black."

Next to blackness the main concern of Black Theology is liberation. It is also, of course, the concern of Black Power and of the Negro community as a whole. Black Theology simply provides a theological dimension to the concept of liberation, a dimension for which there is a great deal of biblical support. Black Theology speaks of liberation in all spheres of the Negro's experience in America—social, economic, political, ecclesiastical, educational and cultural. Black Theology is a response to an American past and to an American present. It is a highly politicized theology designed to shape, advance and protect a popular ideology within the American scene. Without the American history of slavery, racism and domination by whites (pinks) over blacks (browns) and without the present realities of an America shaken by the Vietnam war, student protest, the civil rights movement and continued poverty among large numbers of whites and Negroes there could be no Black Theology.

Black Theology's preoccupation with liberation is brought out powerfully in James Cone's *Black Theology and Black Power:* "Black Power and Christianity have this in common: the liberation of man!" "Jesus' work is essentially one of liberation"; "Black rebellion is a manifestation of God himself actively involved in the present-day affairs of men for the purpose of liberating people"; and so forth. His subsequent book, *A Black Theology of Liberation*, opens with the assertion that "Christian theology is a theology of liberation," and that "liberation [is] the content of theology."

On the question of liberation there is a near absolute unanimity among the theologians of Black Theology. They find ample grounds for it in the Old Testament, in the story of the Exodus and the history of Israel, and in the life and work of Jesus Christ. As a theology of the oppressed, every concern in Black Theology has some bearing on the question of liberation. What I view as an excessive preoccupation with liberation may well be the chief limitation of Black Theology. When the immediate concerns of liberation are realized, it is not at all clear where Black Theology is supposed to go. Black Theology is deeply "eschatological," yet its eschatological hopes are not clearly defined. There is no clue as to when one arrives at the paradise of "liberation." One gets the feeling that Black Theology has created a semi-mythological urgency for liberation that it must at all costs keep alive. As a result it seems that Black

Theology is avoiding other major theological issues not directly related to "liberation."

Black Theology presents Jesus Christ variously as the liberator, the Black Messiah, the Black Christ, and so on. We are told that Negroes are tired of a Jesus seen through the eyes of white or pink Americans. The Negroes in the Black Power movement are said to cry: " 'Give us no pink, two-faced Jesus who counsels love for you and flaming death for the children of Vietnam. Give us no bloodsucking savior who condemns brick-throwing rioters and praises dive-bombing killers. That Christ stinks. We want no black men to follow in *his steps* . . .' " (see "Black Power and the American Christ" by V. Harding in *The Christian Century*, January 4, 1967). So in Black Theology Jesus has to be "the liberator par excellence" who sets free the oppressed and identifies himself with the poor; there is no salvation apart from identification with this Black Christ. Some see the Negroes as the Old Testament children of Israel, enslaved, delivered, led to the Promised Land, promised the Messiah and finally welcoming the Black Messiah who leads them to the Kingdom of God. The most explicit statement along these lines is *The Black Messiah* by Albert B. Cleage, Jr. (New York, 1968). Similar sentiments are variously expressed in the Negro Sprituals and, undoubtedly, from many a pulpit in Negro churches.

A further theme in Black Theology is that "God himself must be known only as he reveals himself in his blackness. The blackness of God, and everything implied by it in a racist society, is the heart of Black Theology's doctrine of God. There is no place in Black Theology for a colorless God in a society when people suffer precisely because of their color. . . . The blackness of God means that God has made the oppressed condition his own condition . . . [and] that the essence of the nature of God is to be found in the concept of liberation. . . . It is Black Theology's emphasis on the blackness of God that distinguishes it sharply from contemporary white views of God" (James H. Cone in *A Black Theology of Liberation*). Cone declares categorically, "We must become black with God!"

Of course Black Theology addresses itself also to other themes, such as the Church, the Community, the Bible, the World, Man, Violence and Ethics. But the treatment of these topics is subservient to the overriding emphasis on blackness and liberation as they relate to Jesus Christ and God. At least this is my impression of Black Theology as I have tried to read it sympathetically and have discussed it extensively with such leading Black Theologians as James Cone of Union Theological Seminary in New York, Charles Long of the Divinity School at Chicago, Preston Williams of Harvard, Vincent Harding and George Thomas at Atlanta, Gayraud Wilmore of Boston University and many others. A number of questions keep coming up as one views Black Theology from the perspective of an African theologian. It is impossible to offer anything but provisional comments, for I am still digesting Black Theology and admiring it as a specifically American phenomenon. I admire the boldness with which it is presented. I admire the commitment Black Theologians have shown to this theological movement. I admire the zeal, the enthusiasm, even the joviality with which these Americans are going about their work. I understand the reasons for their bitterness, their anger, their hatred, all of which comes through in their Black Theology. Standing as I do at a distance, I am impressed with this sudden eruption of theological liveliness in America. Black Theology has been made necessary by the American past and present; the wonder is that it did not erupt sooner. It is long overdue.

But Black Theology cannot and will not become African Theology. Black Theology and African Theology emerge from quite different historical and contemporary stiuations. To a limited extent the situation in Southern Africa is similar to that which produced Black Theology in America. African peoples in Southern Africa are oppressed, exploited and unjustly governed by minority regimes; they have been robbed of their land and dignity and are denied even a minimum of human rights. For them Black Theology strikes a responsive chord and perhaps offers some hope, if that be any consolation. In Southern Africa Black Theology deserves a hearing, though it is impossible to see how that hearing could be translated into practical action. But even in Southern Africa the people want and need liberation, not a theology of liberation. America can afford to talk loud about liberation, for people are free enough to do that in America. But in Southern Africa people are not even free enough to talk about the theology of liberation. Thus when *Essays on Black Theology* (edited by Mokgethi Motlhabi) was published in Johannesburg in 1972, the government banned it before it reached the bookstores. (The same work has since been republished, edited by B. Moore, in London under the title *Black Theology: The South African Voice*.) This book, however, is no more than an echo of American Black Theology; it even includes a contribution by James Cone. But the fact that it was banned so readily clearly indicates that Black Theology has a measure of relevance in Southern Africa.

Apart from Southern Africa the concerns of Black Theology differ considerably from those of African Theology. The latter grows out of our joy in the experience of the Christian faith, whereas Black Theology emerges from the pains of oppression. African Theology is not so restricted in its concerns, nor does it have any ideology to propagate. Black Theology hardly knows the situation of Christian living in Africa, and therefore its direct relevance for Africa is either nonexistent or only accidental. Of course there is no reason why Black Theology should have meaning for Africa; it is not aimed at speaking for or about Africa. As an African one has an academic interest in Black Theology, just as one is interested in the "water buffalo theology" of Southeast Asia or the theology of hope advocated by Jürgen Moltmann. But to try and push much more than the academic relevance of Black Theology for the African scene is to do injustice to both sides. In America and Europe, and to a lesser extent in Africa, there is an obvious temptation to make a connection that should not be made.

It would seem healthier if Black Theology and African Theology were each left to its own internal and external forces to grow in a natural way without artificial pressure and engineering. African Theology is concerned with many more issues, including all the classical theological themes, plus localized topics, such as religious dialogue between Christianity and African Religion and between Christianity and Islam. Relations between Christianity and African culture, between Church and State, together with innumerable pastoral and liturgical problems, give African Theology a very full agenda for the years ahead. African Theology is not something that can be done in a decade or covered in one volume. It is a living phenomenon that will continue as long as the Church exists in our continent. African Theology has no interest in coloring God or Christ black, no interest in reading liberation into every text, no interest in telling people to think or act "black." These are interests of Black Theology across the Atlantic, and they are admirable on the American scene.

Similarly, African theologians have no business trying to tell other Christians how to solve their theological problems, or what theology to use for their situations. We (I) wish only for dialogue, fellowship, sharing of ideas and insights, and learning from one another as equal partners in the universal Body of Christ, even if we Africans may still speak the theological language of Christianity with a stammering voice, since most of us are so new to it. We appreciate what others are saying according to their peculiar circumstances and the inspiration of the Holy Spirit, but what they say reaches us only in whispers because they are speaking primarily to themselves and for themselves, just as we speak first and foremost to ourselves and for ourselves. We must recognize simultaneously our indebtedness to one another as fellow Christians and the dangers of encroaching upon one another's theological territories.

Black Theology and African Theology have each a variety of theological concerns, talents and opportunities. Insofar as each contributes something new and old to Christian theology as such, it will serve its immediate communities and also serve the universal Church.

44

BLACK THEOLOGY/AFRICAN THEOLOGY—
SOUL MATES OR ANTAGONISTS?

Desmond M. Tutu

This consultation being held at this time at the University of Ghana, Accra, between black American theologians and churchmen and their African counterparts is a welcome sequel to a similar consultation on African and Black Theology which was held in New York in June, 1973, under the auspices of the All Africa Conference of Churches and the Society for the Study of Black Religion. But already in August, 1971, a meeting between a similar group of black Americans and East Africans had taken place sponsored by the National Conference of Black Churchmen and the Council of Churches of Tanzania in Dar es Salaam. The papers delivered at that first consultation are available in paperback.[1]

I have referred to these past occasions because the series of consultations reflects a noteworthy phenomenon—a new and deep desire for black men to find each other, to know one another as brothers and sisters because we belong to one another. We are bound together by close bonds on three levels at least.

We are united willy nilly by our blackness (of all shades). Now some may feel squeamish about this apparently excessive awareness of our skin color. But are we not in fact so bound? If anyone of us assembled here today goes into a situation where racial discrimination is practiced would he ever escape the humiliation and indignity that are heaped on us simply because he was black no matter whether he was native to that situation or not? Our blackness is an intractable ontological surd. You cannot will it away. It is a brute fact of existence and it conditions that existence as surely as being male or female,

Desmond M. Tutu, a leading South African theologian, is head of the South African Council of Churches. This essay first appeared in the *Journal of Religious Thought*, vol. 32, no. 2 (Fall-Winter 1975), pp. 25-33.

only more so. But would we have it otherwise? For it is not a lamentable fact. No, far from it. It is not a lamentable fact because I believe that it affords us the glorious privilege and opportunity to further the gospel of love, forgiveness and reconciliation—the gospel of Jesus Christ in a way that is possible to no other group, as I hope to show later.

The second level of unity between us is this. All of us are bound to mother Africa by invisible but tenacious bonds. She has nurtured the deepest things in us as blacks. All of us have roots that go deep in the warm soil of Africa; so that no matter how long and traumatic our separation from our ancestral home has been, there are things we are often unable to articulate, but which we feel in our very bones, things which make us, who are different from others who have not suckled the breasts of our mother, Africa. Don't most of us, for instance, find the classical arguments for the existence of God just an interesting cerebral game because Africa taught us long ago that life without belief in a supreme divine being was just too absurd to contemplate? And don't most of us thrill as we approach the awesomeness of the transcendent when many other of our contemporaries find even the word God an embarrassment? How do you explain our shared sense of the corporateness of life, of our rejection of hellenistic dichotomies in our insistence that life, material and spiritual, secular and sacred, that it is all of a piece? Many characteristics of our music, our religion, our culture and so on, today in Africa and America can be explained adequately only by reference to a common heritage and common source in the past. We cannot deny too that most of us have had an identical history of exploitation through colonialism and neo-colonialism, that when we were first evangelized often we came through the process having learned to despise things black and African because these were usually condemned by others. The worst crime that can be laid at the door of the white man (who, it must be said, has done many a worthwhile and praiseworthy thing for which we are always thankful) is not our economic, social and political exploitation, however reprehensible that might be; no, it is that his policy succeeded in filling most of us with a self-disgust and self-hatred. This has been the most violent form of colonialism, our spiritual and mental enslavement when we have suffered from what can only be called a religious or spiritual schizophrenia. What I said in an unpublished paper, titled "Whither African Theology?" of the African is largely true too of the black American.

> Up to fairly recently, the African Christian has suffered from a form of religious schizophrenia. With part of himself he has been compelled first to play lip service to Christianity as understood, expressed and preached by the white man. But with an ever greater part of himself, a part he has been ashamed to acknowledge openly and which he has struggled to repress, he has felt that his Africanness has been violated. The white man's largely cerebral religion was hardly touching

the depths of his African soul; he was being given answers, and often splendid answers to questions he had not asked.

Speaking about this split in the African soul, J. C. Thomas writes:

The African in fact seems to find himself living at two levels in every aspect of his life. First, there is the western influence on him from two different quarters: there is the influence inherited from the period of colonial rule; but also the inevitable influence of post colonial industrialization and education. Secondly, there is the influence of his traditional culture and upbringing that gives many Africans the sense that they have a unique culture of their own which gives them an identity as Africans. Yet it appears inevitable that in some areas traditional culture will be abandoned if African states are to become self-sufficient economically and so free of dependence on foreign aid and trade.[2]

The third level of unity comes through our baptism and through our membership in the Body of Christ which makes us all His ambassadors and partakers in the ministry of reconciliation. As a consequence of our imperatives of the Gospel and being constrained by the love of God in Jesus Christ, we cannot but be concerned to declare the whole counsel of God as much to the white man as to our own black communities. We are compelled to help the white man to correct many of the distortions that have happened to the gospel to the detriment of all. To paraphrase what Manas Buthelezi from South Africa once said: God will say to the blackmen: "Where were you when the white man did this to my Gospel?" We are together involved in a common task and we are engaged in a single quest. After this preamble let us return to the subject of this paper.

Black Theology/African Theology—Are They Compatible?

Are black theology and African theology related or are they quite distinct and even incompatible entities? John Mbiti, an outstanding theologian, is quite clear in his own mind about the answer to the question. In a recent article, Mbiti has this to say:[3] "But Black Theology cannot and will not become African Theology." He can be so categorical because, to quote from the article again: "the concerns of Black Theology differ considerably from those of African Theology. The latter grows out of our joy and experience of the Christian faith, whereas Black Theology emerges from the pains of oppression." He seems to imply at an earlier point without being explicit that black theology is perhaps not quite Christian: "One would hope that theology arises out of spontaneous joy in being a Christian responding to life and ideas as one redeemed. Black Theology, however is full of sorrow, bitterness, anger and hatred."[4] But is this borne out by a study of the history of Christian doctrine? Most New Testament commentators appear to agree that the Epistle to the Galatians was written when Paul was very angry and yet in the Galatians he develops the theology of justification by faith. And what would we make of the theology that occurs in the Christian Apocalypse of St. John the Divine? There was no oppression, no anger and not even hatred of the oppressor, and yet this book has found its way, admittedly after a long struggle, into the Christian canon. Professor Mbiti is unhappy with Black Theology, mainly because it is concerned too much with blackness and liberation. To quote again:

> Of course Black Theology addresses itself also to other themes, such as the Church, the Community, the Bible, the World, Man, Violence and Ethics. But the treatment of these topics is subservient to the overriding emphasis on blackness and liberation as they relate to Jesus Christ and God.[5]

Another African, this time a young theologian, J. Ndwiga Mugambi, writes concerning liberation and theology as follows:

> Liberation is the objective task of a contemporary African Christian theology. It is not just one of the issues, but rather, all issues are aimed at liberating Africans from all forces that hinder them from living fully as human beings.
>
> In the African context, and in the Bible, SALVATION as theological concept cannot be complete without LIBERATION as a social/political concept.[6]

I will have something to say on this issue later. I contend that there are very close similarities between African Theology and Black Theology:

(a) Both to my way of thinking have arisen as reactions against an unacceptable state of affairs. Most people would agree that the most potent impetus for the development of an African Christian theology has come because Christianity came swathed in Western garb. Most Western missionaries in the early days found it difficult if not virtually impossible to distinguish between the Christian faith and Western civilization. No less a person than Robert Moffat could say:

> Satan has employed his agency with fatal success, in erasing every vestige of religious impression from the minds of the Bechuana, Hottentots and Bushmen; leaving them without a single ray to guide them from the dark and drab futurity, or a single link to unite them to the skies.[7]

And if this was how you felt then it was logical to pursue a policy of the root and branch condemnation of things African, which had to be supplanted by their obviously superior Western counterpart. It was as if Robertson Smith had never written as he did in his *Religion of the Semites:*

> No positive religion that has moved man has been able to start with a *tabula rasa* to express itself as if religion was beginning for the first time; in form if not in substance, the new system must be in contact along the line with the old ideas and practices which it finds in possession. A new scheme of faith can find a hearing only by appealing to a religious instinct and susceptibility that already exists in its audience and it cannot reach these without taking account of the traditional forms in which religious feeling is embodied, and without speaking a language which men accustomed to these forms can understand.

The African religious consciousness and Weltanschauung were not acknowledged as possessing much validity or value. Much the same comment could be made of the Black American experience. The blacks in America had their humanity defined in the terms of the white man. To be really human he had to see himself and be seen as a chocolate-colored white man. His humanity was stunted. It is against this deplorable condition that both African and Black Theology have reacted. They stake the claim for the personhood and humanity of the African and Afro-American, for anything less than this is blasphemy against God who created us as we are in His own image, not to be carbon copies of others of His creatures no matter how advanced or prosperous they might conceive themselves to be. Some might feel ashamed that the most serious enterprise in which they have engaged should be characterized as a reaction rather than resulting from their own initiative. But there is no need for such a negative response. Much of the development of Christian dogma may be shown to resemble the oscillations of a pendulum. When Hegelian idealism was the philosophy of the day, Christian theology, not remaining unaffected, moved very far in the direction of immanentism. Against this trend a reaction set in exemplified by the stress on transcendence as in the theology of Karl Barth. In its turn, this emphasis on transcendence provoked the reaction that spoke about "a beyond in our midst" as in John Robinson's *Honest to God*. Perhaps today we are beginning to discern a tentative groping towards a renewed sense of awe and mystery. And this would be as yet another reaction.

More positively we could say that African theology and Black Theology are an assertion that we should take the Incarnation seriously. Christianity to be truly African must be incarnated in Africa. It must speak in tones that strike a responsive chord in the African breast and must convict the African of his peculiar African sinfulness. It must not provide him with answers to questions he has never asked. It must speak out of and to his own context. Christ came to fulfill, not to destroy. Christianity should be seen as fulfilling the highest and best in the spiritual and religious aspirations of the black and yet stand in judgement of all that diminishes him and makes him less than what God intended him to be.

African and Black theology provide a sharp critique of the way in which theology has been done mostly in the North Atlantic world. Westerners usually call for an ecumenical, a universal theology which they often identify with their brand of theologizing. Now this is thoroughly erroneous. Western theology is no more universal than other brands of theology can ever hope to be. For theology can never properly claim a universality which rightly belongs only to the eternal Gospel of Jesus Christ. Theology is a human activity possessing the limitations and the particularities of those who are theologizing. It can speak relevantly only when it speaks to a particular historically and spatio-temporally conditioned Christian community: and it must have the humility to accept the scandal of its particularity as well as its transcience. Theology is not eternal nor can it ever hope to be perfect. There is no final theology. Of course the true insights of each theology must have universal relevance, but theology gets distorted if it sets out from the very beginning to speak or attempt to speak universally. Christ is the Universal Man only because He is first and foremost a real and therefore a particular Man. There must therefore of necessity be a diversity of theologies and our unity arises because ultimately we all are reflecting on the one divine activity to set man free from all that enslaves him. There must be a plurality of theologies because we don't all apprehend the transcendent in exactly the same way nor can we be expected to express our experience in the same way. On this point, Maurice Wiles writes:

> Theology today is inductive and empirical in approach. It is the ever changing struggle to give expression to man's response to God. It is always inadequate and provisional. Variety is to be welcomed because no one approach can ever do justice to the transcendent reality of God; our partial expressions need to be complemented by the different apprehensions of those whose traditions are other than our own. There are no fixed criteria for the determination of theological truth and error. We ought therefore to be ready to tolerate a considerable measure even of what seems to us to be error, for we cannot be certain that it is we who are right. On this view a wide range of theological difference (even including what we regard as error) is not in itself a barrier to unity.[8]

African theology has given the lie to the belief that worthwhile religion in Africa had to await the advent of the white man. Similar to African history,

African theology has done a wonderful service in rehabilitating the African religious consciousness. Both African and Black theology have been firm repudiations of the tacit claim that white is right, white is best. In their own ways these theologies are giving the black man a proper pride in things black and African. Only thus can we ever be able to make our distinctive contributions to the kingdom of God. We must love and serve God in our own way. We cannot do it as honorary whites. And so Black and African theology have contributed to those exhilarating movements of our day, Black and African consciousness. Both say we must provide our source for theologizing. They seek to be effective instruments in bringing about change not merely as academic exercises. I may be wrong, but at these levels, I see remarkable similarities between African theology and Black Theology and I contend that they have a great deal to learn from one another and to give to each other. But there are obvious differences.

(b) There must be differences because the two theologies arise in a sense from different contexts. African theology on the whole can probably afford to be a little more leisurely (I am not convinced of this) because Africa by and large is politically independent (but is it really free?). There is not the same kind of oppression which is the result of white racism except in Southern Africa (soon it may only be South Africa the way things seem to be developing in the sub-continent, and God let the day soon come when all of Africa will be truly free). Black Theology arises in context of black suffering at the hands of rampant white racism. And consequently Black Theology is much concerned to make sense theologically out of the black experience whose main ingredient is the suffering in and the light of God's revelation of Himself in the man, Jesus Christ. It is concerned with the significance of black existence, with liberation, with a meaning of reconciliation, with humanization, with forgiveness. It is much more aggressive and abrasive in its assertions because of a burning and evangelistic zeal necessary to convert the black man out of the stupor of his subservience and obsequiousness to acceptance of the thrilling but demanding responsibility of full human personhood—to make him reach out to the glorious liberty of the sons of God. It burns to awake the white man to the degradation into which he has fallen by dehumanizing the black man and so is concerned for the liberation of the oppressor equally with that of the oppressed. I am not quite sure that I understand what Professor Mbiti in the article I have referred to means when he says that people in Southern Africa "want and need liberation, not a theology of liberation." Could we not say the same thing about a theology of hope, that what people want is hope, not a theology of hope?

Black Theology is more thoroughly and explicitly political than African theology is. It cannot be lulled into complacency by a doctrine of pie in the sky which is reprehensible travesty of the gospel of the Incarnation. It has an existential urgency which African theology has so far appeared to lack.

African theology has tended to be more placid; to be interested still too much with what I call anthropological concerns. This has been its most important achievement in the quest for indigenization.

Conclusion

I myself believe I am an exponent of Black Theology coming as I do from South Africa. I also believe I am an exponent of African theology coming as I do from Africa. I contend that Black Theology is like the inner and smaller circle in a series of concentric circles. I would not care to cross swords with such a formidable person as John Mbiti, but I and others from South Africa *do* Black Theology, which is for us, at this point, African theology.

But I fear that African theology has failed to produce a sufficiently sharp cutting edge. It has indeed performed a good job by addressing the split in the African soul and yet it has by and large failed to speak meaningfully in the face of a plethora of contemporary problems which assail the modern African. It has seemed to advocate disengagement from the hectic business of life because very little has been offered that is pertinent, say, about the theology of power in the face of the epidemic of coups and military rule, about development, about poverty and disease and other equally urgent present-day issues. I believe this is where the abrasive Black Theology may have a few lessons for African theology. It may help to recall African theology to its vocation to be concerned for the poor and the oppressed, about men's need for liberation from all kinds of bondage to enter into an authentic person-hood which is constantly undermined by a pathological religiosity and by political authority which has whittled away much personal freedom without too much opposition from the church. In short, African theology will have to recover its prophetic calling. It can happen only when a radical spiritual decolonization occurs within each exponent of African theology. Too many of us have been brainwashed effectively to think that the Westerners' value system and categories are of universal validity. We are too much concerned to maintain standards which Cambridge or Harvard or Montpelier have set even when these are utterly inappropriate for our situations. We are still too docile and look to the metropolis for approval to do our theology, for instance, in a way that would meet with the approval of the West. We are still too much concerned to play the game according to the white man's rules when he often is the referee as well. Why should we feel that something is amiss if our theology is too dramatic for verbalization but can express itself adequately only in the joyous song and movement of Africa's dance in the liturgy? Let us develop our insights about the corporateness of human existence in the face of excessive Western individualism, about the wholeness of the person when others are concerned for hellenistic dichotomies of soul and body, about the reality of the spiritual when others are made desolate with the poverty of the material. Let African theology enthuse about the awesomeness of the transcendent when others are embarrassed to speak about the king, high and lifted up, whose train fills the temple. It is only when African theology is true to itself that it will go on to speak relevantly to the contemporary African— surely its primary task and also, incidentally, make its valuable contribution to the rich Christian heritage which belongs to all of us.

Notes

1. *Black Faith and Black Solidarity: Pan Africanism and Faith in Christ,* ed. Priscilla Massie (New York: Friendship Press, 1973).
2. "What Is African Theology?" *Ghana Bulletin of Theology,* vol. 4, no. 4 (June 1973), p. 15.
3. "An African Views American Black Theology," *Worldview,* vol. 17, no. 8 (August 1974), p. 43; see also Document 43, above, for reprint of Mbiti article.
4. Mbiti, op.cit.
5. Ibid.
6. *World Student Christian Federation Dossier,* no. 5 (June 1974), pp. 41-42.
7. E. W. Smith, *African Ideas of God* (London: Edinburgh House, 1966), p. 83.
8. "Theology and Unity," *Theology,* vol. 77, no. 643 (January 1974), p. 4.

45

A BLACK AMERICAN PERSPECTIVE
ON THE FUTURE OF AFRICAN THEOLOGY

James H. Cone

Because I am a Black North American, whose theological consciousness was shaped in the historical context of the civil rights movement of the 1950s[1] and the subsequent rise of Black Power during the 1960s,[2] it is difficult for me to speak about the future of African Theology without relating it to the social and political context of Black people's struggle for freedom in the United States of America. The effect of this social reality upon my theological perspective could blind me to the uniqueness of the African situation. The concern to accent the distinctiveness of the African context has led many African theologians to separate African Theology not only from traditional European theology but also from American Black Theology. In an article entitled "An African Views American Black Theology," John Mbiti is emphatic on this issue.

> . . . the concerns of Black Theology differ considerably from those of African Theology. [African Theology] grows out of our joy in the experience of the Christian faith, whereas Black Theology emerges from the pains of oppression. African Theology is not so restricted in its concerns, nor does it have an ideology to propagate. Black Theology hardly knows the situation of Christian living in Africa, and therefore its direct relevance for Africa is either nonexistent or only accidental.[3]

In order to appreciate the seriousness and depth of Mbiti's concern, it is necessary to point out that his perspective is not based upon a superficial encounter with Black Theology. On the contrary, Mbiti made these remarks *after* he and I had had many conversations on the subject in the context of our

This paper was presented at the Pan-African Conference of Third World Theologians, held December 17–24, 1977, in Accra, Ghana.

jointly taught year-long course on African and Black theologies at Union Theological Seminary.[4] Nevertheless, it seems to me that he misrepresented Black Theology.[5] More important, however, was Mbiti's contention that African and Black American theologians should have no more than an indirect or accidental interest in each other. This perspective on African Theology not only makes substantive dialogue difficult but also excludes Black American theologians from a creative participation in the future development of African Theology.

John Mbiti is not alone in making a sharp distinction between Black Theology and African Theology. Similar views are found in the writings of Harry Sawyerr,[6] E. W. Fashole-Luke,[7] and (to a lesser extent) Kwesi Dickson.[8] While there are significant exceptions to this perspective among theologians in Southern Africa and also among certain African church-people associated with the All Africa Conference of Churches,[9] these exceptions do not remove the risks inherent in any attempt by a North American to speak about the future of African Theology. For there is much truth in the widespread belief that the future of African Theology belongs to Africans alone.

There is a second difficulty in approaching this topic, in addition to existential and intellectual sensitivities of African theologians. That other problem is the existential conflict inherent in my double identity as American *and* African. This identity conflict is widespread among Black Americans, and it is a prominent theme in Black literature and theology. This theme is found in Ralph Ellison's *Invisible Man* and in James Baldwin's claim that "nobody knows my name." In a theological context, Cecil Cone has addressed this problem in his book entitled *The Identity Crisis in Black Theology*.[10] But one of the earliest and most classic statements on this problem is found in the writings of W. E. B. DuBois:

> It is a peculiar sensation, this double-consciousness, this sense of always looking at one's self through the eyes of others, of measuring one's soul by the tape of a world that looks on in amused contempt and pity. One ever feels his twoness—an American, a Negro; two souls, two thoughts, two unreconciled strivings; two warring ideals in one dark body, whose dogged strength alone keeps it from being torn asunder.[11]

The significance of the problem of Black identity in the context of African Theology may be clarified by asking: How can I speak about the future of African Theology when my Black identity is so inextricably tied to North America? Aside from the technicality of my genetic origin and its relation to the African continent, what right do I have to participate in the future development of African Theology? Unless these questions are honestly faced, then the relations between African Theology and Black Theology will remain superficial. The purpose of this essay is to attempt to move our dialogue beyond the phase of theological politeness to a serious encounter of each other's historical options. What is the relation between our different historical contexts and our common faith in God's power to make us all one in Jesus Christ? How do we translate the universal claim of our faith into a common historical practice? These are the issues that define the focus of this paper.

In order to protect against a possible misunderstanding of my concern, an additional word of clarification is necessary. If by African Theology we mean an interpretation of the Christian gospel in the light of the political and cultural situation in Africa, then it is obvious that the future of this enterprise belongs primarily to Africans alone. Persons who have little or no knowledge of Africa or whose theological consciousness was shaped elsewhere should not expect to play a decisive role in the future development of theology on the African continent. This point is applicable not only to White Europeans but to Black Americans as well. I want to emphasize this point, because my disagreement with Mbiti and other African theologians who separate radically African Theology and Black Theology does not mean that I believe that Black Americans should play a major role in the formulation of the meaning of African Theology. My contention is that Black and African theologies are not as different as has been suggested and that their common concerns require a dialogue that is important to both. I want to suggest two reasons why we ought to engage in a substantive dialogue, and then use the third section of this paper to say a word about the future of African Theology.

I

The history of American Blacks cannot be completely separated from the history of Africa. Therefore, whatever may be said about the significant distinctions between Africans and Black people of the American diaspora, there was once a time when these distinctions did not exist. The significance of this point extends beyond a mere academic interest in historical origins. The recognition of the interrelation of our histories is also important for assessing our present realities and the shaping of our future hopes and dreams. Whether we live in Africa or the Americas, there is some sense in which the Black World is one, and this oneness lays the foundation and establishes our need for serious dialogue. Marcus Garvey expressed this point in his ill-fated "back to Africa" movement. With a similar philosophical ideal but a radically different political vision, W.E.B. DuBois, George Padmore, and Kwame Nkrumah expressed the unity of the Black World in their development of Pan-Africanism. But we do not need to accept Garveyism or the Pan-African philosophy of DuBois in order to realize that the future of Africa and Black people in the Americas is inextricably bound together. International economic and political arrangements require a certain kind of African and Black nationalism if we are to liberate ourselves from European and White American domination. This economic and political domination, sharply enhanced and defined by racism, will not cease simply through an appeal to reason or the religious piety of those who hold us in captivity. Oppression ceases only when the victims accumulate enough power to stop it.

The oneness that I refer to is made possible by a common historical option available to both Africans and Black Americans in their different social contexts. Each of us can make a choice that establishes our solidarity with the liberation of the Black World from European and American domination. This domination is not only revealed in the particularity of American White racism or European colonialism in Africa, but also in Euro-American imperialism in Asia, Latin America, and the Caribbean. World history has been written by "white hands" (to borrow a graphic expression from Leonardo Boff), and the time has come to recover the memory of the victims of this world. The need to reinterpret history and theology in the light of the hopes and struggles of the oppressed peoples of the world establishes not only a oneness between Africans and Black Americans, but also makes possible our common solidarity with the liberation of the poor in Asia and Latin America. This global perspective requires that we enlarge the oneness of the Black World to include our solidarity with the world's poor. It was this assumption that defined the "Final Statement" of the Ecumenical Dialogue of Third World Theologians that met in Tanzania (August 1976),[12] and it continues to shape our dialogue in Ghana. To be sure, we must recognize that we live in quite different historical and contemporary situations, which will naturally influence certain emphases in our theologies. But we should guard against the tendency of allowing our various particularities to blind us to the significance of our commonality. It is a oneness grounded in a common historical option for the poor and against societal structures that oppress them. This "poor perspective" (to use an apt phrase from Gustavo Gutiérrez) makes us one and establishes the possibility of our mutual sharing in the creation of one humanity.

II

The possibility of substantive dialogue between African Theology and other Third World theologies is created not only on the basis of our common historical option, but also on the basis of our common faith in Jesus Christ. Because we confess Jesus as Lord, we are required to work out the meaning of that confession in a common historical project. Faith and practice belong together. If we are one in Christ Jesus, then this oneness should be seen in our struggle together to create societal structures that bear witness to our vision of humanity. If our common confession of faith is in no way related to a common historical commitment, how do we know that what we call the universal Church is not the figment of our theological imagination? I contend that the unity of the Church can only be found in a common historical commitment.

Anyone acquainted with my theological perspective knows that I have placed much emphasis on the social context of theology. And I have no intention of relinquishing this point in this paper. But it is important to recognize the limitation of our particularity so that we will not ignore the universal claims that the gospel lays upon all of us. Whether Christians live in Africa, Asia, Latin America, or Europe, we have been called by God to bear witness to the gospel of Jesus to all peoples. Therefore, we must ask not only what does the gospel mean for me in Africa or North America, but also for Christians in the whole inhabited world. And our explication of the gospel must be universal enough to include the material conditions in which people are forced to live. There is only one history, one Creator, and one Lord and Savior Jesus Christ. It is the centrality of this faith claim that brings us together and requires us to have dialogue with each other about its meaning in society. Our cultural limitations do not render us silent but open us up to share with others our perspective about the historical possibility for the creation of a new humanity.

What is the universal dimension of the gospel that transcends culture and thus lays a claim upon all Christians no matter what situation they find themselves in?[13] This is the question that every theology must seek to answer. Because our various theologies are so decidedly determined by our historical option in a given context, different answers have been given to this question. Because dominant European and American theologies have chosen an option that establishes their solidarity with western imperialism and capitalism, they usually define the universality of the gospel in terms that do not challenge the White western monopoly of the world's resources. There have been many debates in traditional theology about the precise content of the essence of the gospel, but seldom has the debate included political and economic realities that separate the rich nations from the poor ones. This is not an accident, and our meeting together in Ghana means that we recognize the danger of defining the universal aspect of the gospel in the light of western culture.

We meet here today because we are in search for other theological options than the ones found in traditional theology. I believe that we will find our common vision of the gospel through a serious encounter of the biblical message as defined by our common historical commitment in our various social contexts. We must be prepared to listen to each other, and to learn what it means to be historically involved in the realization of the gospel. Our dialogue is only beginning, and it is thus too early to expect unanimous agreement on various issues. But if we take seriously our common faith in the crucified Christ, as encountered in the struggle for freedom, then I believe that God's Spirit will break down the barriers that separate us. For Christian "unity only becomes a reality to the extent that we partake of Christ [who] is hidden in those who suffer."[14] It is within this ecumenical context that I will venture to say a word about the future of African Theology.

III

The future of African Theology is found in its creative interpretation of the gospel for the African situation and in relation to the theologies of the poor throughout the world. This emphasis does not exclude the legitimacy of African Theology's concern with indigenization and selfhood[15] in its attempt to relate the biblical message to the African cultural and religious situation. But selfhood and indigenization should not be limited to cultural changes alone. There is a *political* ingredient in the gospel that cannot be ignored if one is to remain faithful to biblical revelation. The recognition of this political ingredient in the gospel is clearly implied in the All-Africa Conference of Churches' call for a moratorium and in its continued support of the liberation movements in Southern Africa. It is within this context that we should understand Canon Burgess Carr's highly publicized distinction between the "selective violence employed by the Liberation Movement" and the " 'collective vengeance' perpetrated by the South African, Rhodesian and Portuguese regimes in Africa. Thus, any outright rejection of violence is an untenable alternative for African Christians."[16] These words caused a great deal of unrest. He drew a radical theological conclusion from the liberation struggles of African people, and the churches of Africa and Europe are still trying to assimilate its significance.

> If for no other reason, we must give our unequivocal support to the Liberation Movements because they have helped the Church to rediscover a new and radical appreciation of the cross. In accepting the violence of the cross, God, in Jesus Christ, sanctified violence into a redemptive instrument for bringing into being a fuller human life.[17]

Burgess Carr is not alone among African theologians and church people who define liberation as a common theme in the gospel. "Liberation," writes Jesse Mugambi, "is the objective task of contemporary African Christian Theology. It is not just one of the issues, but rather, all issues are aimed at liberating Africans from all forces that hinder them from living fully as a human being." According to Mugambi, the idea of liberation is inherent in the concept of salvation. "In the African context, and in the Bible, *salvation* as a theological concept cannot be complete without *liberation* as a social/political concept."[18] A similar point is also made by Eliewaha Mshana: "Africanization must involve liberation from centuries of poverty, humiliation and exploitation. A truly African Theology cannot escape the requirement of helping the indigenous churches to become relevant to the spiritual, social, and political ills of Africa."[19] Kofi Appiah-Kubi also includes liberation as an important ingredient of African Theology. He not only uses liberation as an important christological theme in Africa,[20] but locates liberation in his definition of African Theology. African Theology, he contends, "should be a liberating theology, liberating us from the chains of social, economic, political and even at times traditional and cultural dominations and oppressions."[21]

No African theologians, however, have expressed the theme of liberation more dramatically than South African theologians. Desmond Tutu[22] and Manas Buthelezi[23] are prominent examples of this new theological perspective emerging from behind the apartheid walls of the Republic of South Africa. Both have challenged African theologians to take seriously the political ingredient of the gospel as related to the contemporary problems of Africa. Desmond Tutu is emphatic:

> . . . African theology has failed to produce a sufficiently sharp cutting edge. . . . It has seemed to advocate disengagement from the hectic business of life because very little has been offered that is pertinent, say, about the theology of power in the face of the epidemic of coups and military rule, about development, about poverty and disease and other equally urgent present-day issues. I believe this is where the abrasive Black Theology may have a few lessons for African theology. It may help to recall African theology to its vocation to be concerned for the poor and the oppressed, about [people's] need for liberation from all kinds of bondage to enter into an authentic personhood which is constantly undermined by pathological religiosity and by political authority which has whittled away much personal freedom without too much opposition from the church.[24]

These are strong words and they remind us all of the prophetic calling of the Church and theology.

Additional examples of this African perspective in theology are found in a collection of essays entitled *Essays on Black Theology*. This book was banned by the Republic of South Africa and was later published in Britain under the title *Black Theology: The South African Voice*.[25] More recently Allan Boesak has added his contribution to South African Black Theology with his publication of *Farewell to Innocence*.[26] The central theme among these new theological voices from South Africa is their focus on liberation in relation to politics and blackness. They insist that blackness is an important ingredient in their view of African Theology.

Unfortunately, John Mbiti and Edward Fashole-Luke have been very critical of this South African Black Theology as being too narrowly focused on blackness, liberation, and politics. Both contend that Christian theology must transcend race and politics.[27] I believe that their criticisms are misplaced because the theme of liberation, as interpreted by the particularity of the African economic and political situation, provides the most creative direction for the future development of African Theology. If God came to us in the human presence of Jesus, then no theology can transcend the material conditions of humanity and still retain its Christian identity. Jesus did not die on the cross in order to transcend human suffering, but rather, so that it might be overcome. Therefore, any theology whose distinctive perspective is defined by Jesus is required to find its creative expression in the practice of overcoming suffering.

The need for African Theology to focus on politics and liberation arises not only out of a christological necessity. It is also a necessity that arises out of the ecumenical context of contemporary theology. By locating the definition of African Theology in the context of the political and economic conditions of Africa, African theologians can easily separate their theological enterprise from the prefabricated theologies of Europe and establish their solidarity with other Third World theologies. This point is suggested by Canon Burgess Carr.

> The forthrightness of Black Theology and the theology of liberation canvassed today presents a dual challenge to our Christian style of life. In a profound way, it challenges the preoccupation with African Theology to advance beyond academic phenomenological analysis to a deeper appropriation of the ethical sanctions inherent in our traditional religious experience. It also forces Christians to come to grips with the radical character of the gospel of Jesus as an ideological framework for their engagement in the struggle for cultural authenticity, human development, justice and reconciliation.[28]

If Black Theology's focus on liberation is its challenge to African Theology, what then is the challenge of African Theology to Black Theology, Latin American Liberation Theology, and theology in Asia? Unless the challenge is mutual, then there is no way for substantive dialogue to take place. I believe that African Theology's challenge to us is found by rejecting prefabricated theology, liturgies, and traditions and focusing the theological task on the selfhood of the Church and the incarnation of Christianity in the life and thought of Africa. African theologians challenge all Christians in the Third World to take seriously popular religion and unestablished expressions of Christianity. Perhaps more than any other Third World theological expression, African Theology takes seriously the symbols and beliefs of the people whom all liberation theologians claim to represent. If liberation theology in any form is to represent the hopes and dreams of the poor, must not that representation be found in its creative appropriation of the language and culture of the people? If the poor we claim to represent do not recognize themselves in our theologies, how then will they know that we speak for them? From their earliest attempt to create an African Theology, African theologians are agreed that their theology must take seriously three sources: the Bible, African traditional religion, and the African Independent Churches. The appropriation of these sources structurally locates the theological task among the poor people of Africa. Until recently Latin American Liberation Theology has tended to overlook the importance of this cultural ingredient in theology. The same is true to some extent of American Black Theology and perhaps, to a lesser degree, of theology in Asia.[29]

The relation between indigenization and liberation does not have to be antagonistic. In fact, we need both emphases. Without the indigenization of theology, liberation theology's claim to be derived from and accountable to oppressed peoples is a farce. Indigenization opens the door for the people's creative participation in the interpretation of the gospel for their life situation. But indigenization without liberation limits a given theological expression to the particularity of its cultural context. It fails to recognize the universal dimension of the gospel and the global context of theology. It is simply not enough to indigenize Christianity or to Africanize theology. The people also want to be liberated from racism, sexism, and classism. If theology is to be truly indigenized, its indigenization must include in it a social analysis that takes seriously the human struggles against race, sex, and class oppression. I contend therefore that indigenization and liberation belong together. The future of African Theology, and all Third World theologies, is found in the attempt to interpret the Christian gospel in the historical context of the people's struggle to liberate themselves from all forms of human oppression.

Notes

1. The beginning of the contemporary civil rights movement of American Blacks is usually identified with the bus boycott in Montgomery, Alabama, led by Martin Luther King, Jr., in December 1955. For an account of this event, see Martin Luther King, Jr., *Stride Toward Freedom* (New York: Harper & Row, 1958). For more information about the later development of this movement in the 1960s and Martin King's reaction to the rise of Black Power, see his *Why We Can't Wait* (New York: Harper & Row, 1963) and *Where Do We Go From Here: Chaos or Community* (New York: Harper & Row, 1967).

2. For an account of the rise of Black Power, see Stokely Carmichael and Charles Hamilton, *Black Power: The Politics of Black Liberation* (New York: Random House, 1967).

3. John Mbiti, "An African Views American Black Theology," reprinted in this volume (quotation found on p. 481).

4. John Mbiti was the Harry Emerson Fosdick Visiting Professor at Union Theological Seminary, New York, during the academic year 1972–1973.

5. I was especially disturbed by Mbiti's assertion that "Black Theology . . . is full of sorrow, bitterness, anger and hatred." I know of no Black American theologian who would accept this description of Black Theology.

6. See his "What Is African Theology?" *Africa Theological Journal*, no. 4, August 1971.

7. See his "The Quest for African Christian Theology," *The Journal of Religious Thought*, vol. 32, no. 2 (Fall–Winter 1975). This issue is devoted to essays presented at the Consultation on African and Black Theology, Accra, Ghana, December 1974. See also an earlier article in which Fashole-Luke questions the possibility of the development of an African Theology, "An African Indigenous Theology: Fact or Fiction?" *The Sierra Leone Bulletin of Religion*, 1969.

8. While Kwesi Dickson is not as emphatic about the distinction between Black and African Theology, as suggested by Mbiti, Sawyerr, and Fashole-Luke, the sharp separation of African Theology from Black Theology is clearly implied in his writings. See his contribution at the Ghana Consultation, "African Theology: Origin, Methodology and Content," *The Journal of Religious Thought*, Fall–Winter 1975. See also his "Towards a Theologia Africana," in M. E. Glasswell and E. W. Fashole-Luke, eds., *New Testament Christianity for Africa and the World* (London: S.P.C.K., 1974); "The Old Testament and African Theology," *The Ghana Bulletin of Theology*, vol. 4, no. 4 (June 1973); "The African Theological Task" in *The Emergent Gospel* edited by Sergio Torres and Virginia Fabella (Maryknoll, N.Y.: Orbis Books, 1978).

9. A partial account of these exceptions is treated in the third section of this paper.

10. Nashville: AMEC, 1975.

11. *The Souls of Black Folk* (Greenwich, Conn.: Fawcett, 1961). Originally published in 1903, pp. 16-17.

12. See *The Emergent Gospel*, ed. S. Torres and V. Fabella, pp. 259ff.

13. This question involves the problem of ideology in theological discourse. I have discussed the implications of this problem in my *God of the Oppressed* (New York: Seabury Press, 1975).

14. Rubem Alves, "Protestantism in Latin America: Its Ideological Function and Utopian Possibilities," *The Ecumenical Review*, January 1970, p. 15.

15. The themes of selfhood and indigenization are very prominent in African Theology. On indigenization, see the important book by Bolaji Idowu, *Towards an Indigenous Church* (London: Oxford University Press, 1965); Kwesi Dickson and Paul Ellingworth, eds., *Biblical Revelation and African Beliefs* (London: Lutterworth Press, Maryknoll, New York: Orbis Books, 1969). On the theme of selfhood, see Kwesi Dickson, "African Theology: Origin, Methodology and Content," *The Journal of Religious Thought; The Struggle Continues*, official report, Third Assembly of the All-Africa Conference of Churches, Lusaka, May 1974. This theme is also found in the report of the First Assembly of the AACC in Kampala, 1963. See *Drumbeats from Kampala* (London: Lutterworth Press, 1963).

16. "The Engagement of Lusaka," in *The Struggle Continues*, p. 78.

17. Ibid., p. 78.

18. "Liberation and Theology," in WSCF Dossier no. 5, June 1974, pp. 41-42.

19. "The Challenge of Black Theology and African Theology," *Africa Theological Journal*, no. 5, 1972.

20. See his "Jesus Christ—Some Christological Aspects from African Perspectives," in *African and Asian Contributions to Contemporary Theology*, ed. John Mbiti (Celigny: WCC Ecumenical Institute, Bossey, 1977).

21. "Why African Theology?" *AACC Bulletin*, vol. 7, no. 4 (July–August 1974), p. 6.

22. See his contribution at the Ghana Consultation on African and Black Theology, "Black Theology/African Theology: Soul Mates or Antagonists?" (reprinted above, Document 44); see also his "Black Theology," *Frontier*, Summer 1974; "African and Black Theologies," an interview in the *AACC Bulletin*, vol. 7, no. 4 (July–August 1974).

23. See his contribution "Toward Indigenous Theology in South Africa," in *The Emergent Gospel*; see also his important essay "An African Theology or a Black Theology," in *Essays on Black Theology*, ed. George Mokgethi Motlhabi (Johannesburg, 1972). Other essays by Buthelezi include "Apartheid in the Church Is Damnable Heresy," *AACC Bulletin*, vol. 9, no. 2; "Daring to Live for Christ," in *Mission Trends No. 3: Third World Theologies*, ed. G. H. Anderson and T. F. Stransky (New York: Paulist Press, 1976).

24. "Black Theology/African Theology: Soul Mates or Antagonists?" see above, Document 44.

25. Edited by Basil Moore (London: Hurst, 1973). This book was later published in the United States by John Knox Press under the title *The Challenge of Black Theology in South Africa*. The original book, *Essays on Black Theology*, was edited by Mokgethi Motlhabi.

26. Maryknoll, N.Y.: Orbis Books, 1977.

27. See John Mbiti, "African Theology," *Worldview*, August 1973, pp. 37f.; see also his "Some Current Concerns of African Theology," *The Expository Times*, March 1976, p. 166. See E. W. Fashole-Luke, "The Quest for an African Christian Theology," *The Journal of Religious Thought*, pp. 87f. Fashole-Luke writes: "In the Republic of South Africa, African Theology is equated with Black Theology and the emphasis on Blackness indicates the ethnic implications of the task; considerable attention is given there to the exposition of the Gospel in terms of liberation from political, social and economic injustice, and the creation of a new sense of dignity and equality in the face of white oppression and discrimination. It is surely at this critical point

that African theologians are challenged by the Gospel to raise African Christian theologies above the level of ethnic or racial categories and emphasis, so that Christians everywhere will see that Christianity is greater and richer than any of its cultural manifestations, and that the Gospel of liberation is for the oppressed and oppressor alike" (ibid., pp. 87-88).

28. "The Engagement of Lusaka," p. 78.

29. African Theology's concern to use the thought forms for the people is not a slogan. The extensive research that African theologians have done on indigenous African religions and unestablished forms of Christianity does not have its counterpart among Latin American liberation theologians or even among Black theologians in the United States. John Mbiti has been one of the most prolific in this area. His books include *New Testament Eschatology in an African Background* (London: Oxford University Press, 1971); *African Religions and Philosophy* (London: Heinemann, 1969); *Concepts of God in Africa* (London: S.P.C.K., 1970). Some of his articles that are particularly appropriate in this discussion are "The Growing Respectability of African Traditional Religion," *Lutheran World*, Geneva, vol. 49, no. 236 (October 1970); "The Ways and Means of Communicating the Gospel," in C. G. Baëta, ed. *Christianity in Tropical Africa* (London, 1968).

Other African theologians' work in this area include Harry Sawyerr, *Creative Evangelism: Towards a New Christian Encounter with Africa* (London: Lutterworth Press, 1968); *God: Ancestor or Creator* (London: Longmans, 1970); Bolaji Idowu, *Olódùmarè* (London: Longmans, 1962); *African Traditional Religion: A Definition* (Maryknoll, N.Y.: Orbis Books, 1973).

46

COMMUNIQUÉ,
PAN-AFRICAN CONFERENCE
OF THIRD WORLD THEOLOGIANS,
ACCRA, GHANA, DECEMBER 17-23, 1977

Introduction

We are African Christians who met in Accra, Ghana, from December 17 to 23, 1977, as part of the Ecumenical Dialogue of Third World Theologians to discuss emerging themes in African theology. We address ourselves and the rest of the Christian community in Africa and in other parts of the world in this statement.

We came together because of our deep concern for faith in Jesus Christ in Africa. It is this faith in the Lord of history that speaks to us concretely today. As we joyfully praise the saving Lord and share our problems, we are aware of the very real presence of the incarnate Jesus, who comforts us and gives us hope.

Our meeting here was filled with experiences of a new life. We were able to move beyond denominational barriers and even beyond the usual rules of formal representation. Among us were Protestants, Orthodox, and Roman Catholics who have shared each other's concerns as we moved beyond the limitations of officiality. We have also experienced living together as a community of God's people with our brothers and sisters from the black American world, from Asia, Latin America, the Caribbean, and the Pacific Islands. We have shared the warmth of togetherness as captives in this world full of oppression and injustices that are more than often not of our own making. And above all we have shared the same hope.

The Communiqué was issued by the Ecumenical Association of Third World Theologians. It was published in Kofi Appiah-Kubi and Sergio Torres, eds., *African Theology en Route* (Maryknoll, N.Y.: Orbis Books, 1979), pp. 189-95, containing papers from the conference.

The saving Word of the Lord which provides freedom to captives has been our guiding stick. This was manifested not only in our daily worship and singing, but also in drama, plenary presentations, and group discussions. We affirm emphatically that it is the message of the Old and the New Testaments which gives boldness and power to our dialogue as African Christians with other Third World theologians.

The African Reality

The Living Word of the Lord has led us to consider the realities of Africa today.

We thank God for the dynamism and vitality of African Christian communities and churches. The rapid growth of the people of God in Africa, the uniqueness of the African experience in original African liturgy, Bible reading, and Christian community life, are for all of us a matter of hope and confidence.

We realize that African unity is the unity of spirit and soul, an indivisible historical unity that may even transcend geographical differences. Our unity contributes to the total community of God without being blown away in the wind of unspecified universalism. We also realize that there are threats to this unity of our people. We deplore anything that seeks to shake the solidness of our deep-rooted unity, whether economic isolation, power manipulation, or even styles of life.

Colonialism has hampered our unity throughout the history of our relations with the western world. Although we are in a post-colonial era in most of Africa, colonialism continues to be perpetuated in Southern Africa. The white regimes in Zimbabwe, Namibia, and South Africa are nothing but disguised colonial occupations, a white minority's domination of the African majority through military force. In South Africa, the colonial domination is perpetuated through the Bantustans; the minority regime's program of independence for the so-called Homelands is nothing but a fraud aimed at deceiving the world into thinking that the black majority have accepted white domination. The ends of this colonial occupation are served by institutionalized white racism in South Africa, Namibia, and Zimbabwe. Africans deplore the fact that white racists from Zimbabwe and South Africa are now being exported to Latin American countries.

Ethnicity in Africa, as anywhere in the world must not be confused with racism. Ethnicity is a positive element in any society. It can, however, be misused by outside powers to serve the ends of racism and cause disunity, wars, and human suffering.

We have no intention of underrating the internal misuse of power, but we also realize that often structures of internal oppression are perpetuated by questionable alliances under the disguise of friendship treaties or development aid. We affirm that our history is both sacred and secular. We see God's movement in our hope for a free and just society in Africa. Any destruction of this hope, be it in the misuse of power and authority or in the exploitation of resources by national institutions or by multinational corpora tions, is a direct and damnable violation of the destiny of God's people. God's demand is that human beings be subordinate to God's will for the total human community, making true Christ's command to love our neighbors as we love ourselves. Love for us signifies a communal act of obedience to God who is eternally with us. In Africa today this love is being destroyed by the ill effects of some national institutions and multinational corporations. Moreover, these ill effects cause great disunity, often perpetuated through militarism. The resultant suffering has led to thousands of deaths, detentions, and painful refugee situations. It is our belief that God's demand of the churches in Africa is that they not only oppose any form of oppression and suffering but also sever any alliances, direct or indirect, with the forces of oppression, e.g., by reviewing their stock portfolios in multinational corporations which facilitate the systematic militarization of governments that suppress human rights and violate human dignity.

The Presence of Christianity in Africa

The methodology of studying the presence of Christianity in Africa must shift from hagiography of yesterdays to a more critical approach that starts from African worldviews, examines the impact of Christianity, and evaluates the varieties of African responses. Old strategies in mission are no longer relevant. It is not sufficient simply to maintain inherited church structures. Moreover, there is a gap between the rhetoric of church officials, adminis- trators, and theologians and the reality in the villages. This has made the African masses passive. Limited funds to run institutions and the confused concept of stewardship make it impossible to realize self-reliance and moratorium.

The missionary church in Africa has used education as a means of domesti- cation. This has led to misunderstandings with our colleagues in the wider dialogue, as was evident during the Christian-Muslim conference in Cham- besy, 1976. This education has also produced an elite class in our countries.

We are therefore impelled to rethink the relevant strategies for the future of God's people in Africa. Efforts are being taken to contextualize the Gospel and to take full responsibility for the maintenance of the church. We proclaim the basis of the church in Africa is the vitality of the African Christian communities. Beyond the missionary structures and power, our Christian communities in poverty, humility, and faith continue to witness to the Gospel of Jesus Christ, creating their own Christian way of life and their own language to express the originality of their Christian experience.

In the traditional setting there was no dichotomy between the sacred and the secular. On the contrary, the sacred was experienced in the context of the secular. This healthy way of understanding our African society must be taken seriously by the church.

The Emergence of African Theologies

Context of African Theology

Despite the colonial experience of depersonalization and cultural invasion, the African cultures have kept their vitality. This vitality is expressed in the revival of African language, dances, music, and literature and in Africa's contribution to human sciences and to the human experience. This cultural vitality is the support of the African people in their struggle for complete liberation and for the construction of a human society.

Nevertheless, we must recognize the persistence of the domination that resulted from colonialism. This domination also exists in the churches. The organizational model imported from the West is still proposed and accepted. The life of our churches has been dominated by a theology developed with a methodology, a worldview, and a conception of humanity using western categories.

Present Trends in Theology

African theology has already emerged and is alive. Among the various approaches in African theology are:

1. one which, while admitting the inherent values in the traditional religions, sees in them a preparation for the Gospel;

2. a critical theology which comes from contact with the Bible, openness to African realities, and dialogue with non-African theologies;

3. black theology in South Africa, which takes into consideration the experiences of oppression and the struggle for liberation and gets its inspiration from the biblical faith as expressed in African language and categories as well as from the experience and reflections of black North Americans.

This list of approaches is not exhaustive, but it reveals the dynamism of the theological movement on the continent.

Sources of Theology

1. *The Bible and Christian heritage:* The Bible is the basic source of African theology, because it is the primary witness of God's revelation in Jesus Christ. No theology can retain its Christian identity apart from Scripture. The Bible is not simply a historical book about the people of Israel; through a re-reading of this Scripture in the social context of our struggle for our humanity, God

speaks to us in the midst of our troublesome situation. This divine Word is not an abstract proposition but an event in our lives, empowering us to continue in the fight for our full humanity.

The Christian heritage is also important for African theology. This is the heritage of the life and history of the church since the time of our Lord, with a long tradition of scholarship, liturgies, experiences, etc. African Christianity is a part of worldwide Christianity.

2. *African anthropology:* For Africans there is unity and continuity between the destiny of human persons and the destiny of the cosmos. African anthropology and cosmology are optimistic. The victory of life in the human person is also the victory of life in the cosmos. The salvation of the human person in African theology is the salvation of the universe. In the mystery of incarnation Christ assumes the totality of the human and the totality of the cosmos.

3. *African traditional religions:* The God of history speaks to all peoples in particular ways. In Africa the traditional religions are a major source for the study of the African experience of God. The beliefs and practices of the traditional religions in Africa can enrich Christian theology and spirituality.

4. *African Independent churches:* The Independent churches have developed through their long history a type of worship, organization, and community life rooted in African culture and touching the daily life of the people.

5. *Other African realities:* The experiences of cultural forms of life and arts, extended family, hospitality, and communal life are the expression of deep feelings of love and care. The struggles for the transformation of socio-economic systems, the struggles against racism, sexism, and other forms of economic, political, social, and cultural oppressions, are all to be taken seriously as sources for theology.

Perspectives for the Future

We believe that African theology must be understood in the context of African life and culture and the creative attempt of African peoples to shape a new future that is different from the colonial past and the neo-colonial present. The African situation requires a new theological methodology that is different from the approaches of the dominant theologies of the West. African theology must reject, therefore, the prefabricated ideas of North Atlantic theology by defining itself according to the struggles of the people in their resistance against the structures of domination. Our task as theologians is to create a theology that arises from and is accountable to African people.

We feel called to proclaim the love of God for all people within the dynamics of a conflictual history. We are committed to the struggles of our people to be free and we believe that the theology that arises from that commitment will have three characteristics.

1. African theology must be *contextual* theology, accountable to the context

people live in. In drama, novels, and poetry, Africans demonstrate the importance of contextual expression. Contextualization will mean that theology will deal with the liberation of our people from cultural captivity.

2. Because oppression is found not only in culture but also in political and economic structures and the dominant mass media, African theology must also be *liberation* theology. The focus on liberation in African theology connects it with other Third World theologies. Like black theologians in North America, we cannot ignore racism as a distortion of the human person. Like Latin American and Asian theologians, we see the need to be liberated from socio-economic exploitation. A related but different form of oppression is often found in the roles set aside for women in the churches. There is the oppression of Africans by white colonialism, but there is also the oppression of blacks by blacks. We stand against oppression in any form because the Gospel of Jesus Christ demands our participation in the struggle to free people from all forms of dehumanization. African theology concerns itself with bringing about the solidarity of Africans with black Americans, Asians, and Latin Americans who are also struggling for the realization of human communities in which the men and women of our time become the architects of their own destiny.

3. Throughout this document, we have referred to the need to struggle against *sexism*. If that struggle is to be taken seriously by the church, then our seriousness will be reflected in the way we do theology. We recognize that African women have taken an active role in the church and in the shaping of our history. They have shown themselves to be an integral part of the liberation struggle. But we cannot ignore their exclusion from our past theological endeavors. The future of African theology must take seriously the role of women in the church as equals in the doing of theology.

Conclusion

In post-independent Africa and in Southern Africa, theology confronts new challenges, hopes, and opportunities. The vigor of the traditional African religions and cultures and the renewal of the churches, thanks principally to a return to the Scriptures, present us with the resources for our tasks.

Our belief in Jesus Christ Liberator convinces us that there is a noble future for our countries, if the processes of nation-building are geared to providing the urgent basic needs of all instead of the privileges of a few. We are confident that the creative vitality of our own traditional religions and cultures can provide the inspiration for a free and just form of community organization and national development.

In order to serve the people, the Gospel, and the churches in these tasks we pledge to renew ourselves according to the needs of today discerned by us under the light of the Spirit of God present among us. For this we need an interdisciplinary methodology of social analysis, biblical reflection, and active commitment to be with the peoples in their endeavors to build a better society. Toward this end we have formed today an Ecumenical Association of African Theologians. Conscious of our deficiencies and weaknesses, yet encouraged by the nobility of the task before us, we undertake this journey of service through theology so that all the women, men, and children of our lands may be able "to have life and live abundantly."

47

BLACK THEOLOGY
AND LATIN AMERICAN
LIBERATION THEOLOGY

Excerpts from a Symposium of the World Council of Churches

Paulo Freire* In this meeting I have again seen something which has become clear to me from my experiences in Europe and the United States. First of all, we who call ourselves educated and civilized people, the academics, the intellectuals—and I mean *we*, I don't want to exclude myself—, we are so alienated, so domesticated, so ideologically conditioned in our existential and intellectual experience that we have created a terrible dichotomy between manual and intellectual work. Education, instead of being an act of knowing, is an act of transference of knowledge. We think knowledge is something we can possess. We divide the world into those who know and those who do not know . . . those who work manually and those who do not. In this way, instead of touching the reality, we touch the concepts. And the concepts become empty and lose their dialectical relationship with the facts.

We come to a meeting like this previously conditioned ideologically by this false concept of knowledge. And so instead of trying to look at the complete context in which we live and experience, we come looking for answers and prescriptions and transference of knowledge. That is my first observation.

My second observation is a challenge. There is a dialectical relationship between thinking and acting. We think and act in context: no language

This symposium was held in May 1973, at the Geneva headquarters of the World Council of Churches, and the material was later published in *Risk*, vol. 9, no. 2 (1973).

*Paulo Freire, a staff member of the Office of Education, World Council of Churches, is the author of *Pedagogy of the Oppressed*.

without context; no text without context. I look at my friend James Cone, whom I admire, as a Third World man—it does not matter that he was born in the United States—it's an accident. He is a Third World man because he was born in the world of dependence—of exploitation—within the First World. So our way of thinking is absolutely conditioned by our existential experience in your context. This does not mean that because I am a Latin American I cannot use Marx because Marx was a German. No. But I am conditioned not only by my physical context but by the ideology which is being developed in my concrete situation. Many times we say something and the question is not tongue but language. We can speak the same tongue using a different language, and many times we cannot understand.

For example, one of the participants could not at first understand when I said that the oppressors hate the flowers. He said, "It's a myth about the oppressors." No, it is not a myth, and by using the word *myth* he is using a different language. There is no time to begin the process of unveiling ourselves so that we can become equals, to discover ways to improve our communication by analyzing some texts within our contexts.

Another thing that I have perceived on different occasions in Europe is that when we are explaining our position the Europeans are really curious to understand what we are trying to do, what we are trying to say. But there is a background of ideology which means that behind much curiosity there is a certain paternalistic attitude. For example, many Europeans listen to us in the same style in which some parents—not good parents—listen to their children. *"Oh, yes, let's listen to what little John can tell us."* It is not conscious, it is because of your historical experience: you have commanded the world, you have imposed on Africa, Latin America and Asia your way of thinking, your technology, your values, your civilization, your goods, your humanism . . . and so on.

I would like to die like I am now, without systematizing things. I love to live, to exist, to love the flowers, but when people whose experience has been developed in the culture of silence—the culture of dependent people, oppressed people—come to talk within the spoken culture there is a tendency towards estrangement. You are very curious about what we are saying, but because of your ideological background you see our wish to say something as an attempt to impose our point of view on you. No, my friends, we are not trying to impose anything on you. We don't really want to receive anything from you. We want to exchange some things with you. It is not impossible to have dialogue. I was told in the United States: "Now the Latin Americans are trying to colonize us." I said, "No, we did not come here to impose our point of view, but we have something to say." This is what we are trying to do here.

It is a myth that Europeans have to teach the ignorant people of Africa and Latin America how to be civilized: the myth of the superiority of whites vis-à-vis blacks. This myth is reinforced by white science, which says that blacks are inferior. It is myth, it is not science; it is ideology and not science; it is the myth of the superiority of the colonizers vis-à-vis the colonized. It is a myth which is fundamental to the preservation of exploitation. Take, for example, the myth of the superiority of language. The language of the colonizers is language; the language of the colonized is dialect. The cultural productions of the colonizers are art; the cultural productions of the colonized are folklore. This is ideology, not science. The myth of the *conciliation des inconciliables* is the same myth. A Brazilian philosopher said, "Myth is the attribution of absolute value to something which is relative."

A last word. If you ask me if I think we have wasted our time here, I would say, "No, I learned a lot of things here. I was challenged." It was not the intention of the symposium to arrive at final conclusions or to define Black Theology or the Theology of Liberation. The intention was to provoke a step towards dialogue, and I think it has been achieved.

*Hugo Assmann** I would like to say something to the representatives of Black Theology. My biggest mistake in the first days of the symposium was that I was speaking to the participants and not to my friends who represent Black Theology. In my group there was a problem. . . . It was a dialogue between Latin American Theology of Liberation and European questions and problems. I would like to enter into dialogue with Black Theology. Let me say openly, though, that a very positive aspect of this symposium has been the experience of "incommunication" between us, because this "incommunication" is a dialectic part of our communication—the starting point. It would be terrible to remain in "incommunication" with Black Theology.

I ask myself: What is Latin American Theology of Liberation? Is it a new theology for the Western part of Latin America? In the name of what part of Latin America can we theologians of the Theology of Liberation in Latin America speak? In the name of Latin Americans? In the name of the Western part of Latin America? An important element of the Latin American reality is Western.

There is another problem: the non-Western part of Latin America—the Brazilian Africans, the people of the Caribbean Islands, the mysterious Mexicans. In Latin America there are whole countries where up to 80% of the people do not speak Spanish. Travelling in Latin America, I have had the experience of terrible "incommunication" with these people.

Until now the Latin American Theology of Liberation has used mostly Western and European theories and this poses a great question. We are trying now in Christian revolutionary groups to find a new communicative language. The Christians for Socialism movement in Chile is attempting to reinterpret in Marxist popular language the history, the revolution, the

---

*Hugo Assmann, Brazilian theologian and author of *Theology for a Nomad Church*, is now serving as Professor of Communications at the University in San José, Costa Rica.

struggles and the processes of the proletarian movement in Chile. This strikes a somewhat false note, I must say, in an effort to communicate with Black Theology. It is false, because *who* is making this effort of communication in a popular language, a popular translation? Western people—Latin Americans, but Western people. There is another language—a grass-roots language. They have a language; we don't want to give them one. Perhaps it is impossible to wait until they "say their word," as Freire says. It is necessary to have a dialectic relationship between our Western, colonized, dependent language and their language. Both ISAL and the Christians for Socialism are trying to make them speak *their* language, not translations of our versions.

I am a Marxist and I can't see the reality of Latin America in any other category. But what is Marxism in Latin America? What would a Marx born in Latin America be like? A Quechua Christ? An Aymara Christ? Until now I have had very little communication with black people in the United States because when as a Westernized Latin American I read books and articles about the problem of black people in the United States, I am tempted to introduce Western Marxism. What must I do in order to have a better dialogue with you?

Perhaps we have something to give you—our experiences, our struggle, our difficulties in our theology of liberation—but we have much to learn from you. This is not an attempt at Christian reconciliation, it's a Latin American problem. In my country [Brazil], for example, there is a serious lack of communication between black people and half-black people. I think that when we make progress in this direction with people in Latin America, we will find another language, a different language, a third language. Also, if there is more communication with Black Theology and theologies from other countries of the Third World, there will be less "incommunication" between us.

In my opening address I was sometimes aggressive because, as a Westernized Latin American, I don't feel at ease with my color, my "gringo" face, my German origin. I don't feel happy with the fact that my theological dissertation was written in German. I have a psychological necessity to say to you in Western language that I am not Western. We Latin Americans are still in the early stages of our search for a Latin American identity. If you look in my library you will find books by German authors, French authors, Italian authors, Marx, Moltmann, etc. There is something false in this. . . . Something which is not Latin American. I would like to say to my friends in Black Theology: I don't know how this dialogue with you can be improved, but it is more important than European theology for us Latin Americans. I don't want to destroy the connection with you. But I do want to reach a state of tension with you—a third kind of tension which is found more and more in the Third World.

In my group it was said that the contradictions of the world are not between

the United States and Moscow, or between Europe and the United States—
the fundamental contradiction is between the rich world and the oppressed
world. I think a lot of things will be different when we come to an alliance
with our real friends—the people of the Third World. In the United States
and Europe, there are people of the Third World—the poor and oppressed
world. If I believe as a Marxist in the necessity of the conflict in history, can it
change the world? If I believe that the class struggle is really necessary in
order to change the world, can it change the world?

People who are not the allies of the Third World are our enemies, and we
will struggle against them. This class struggle inside the churches will be the
biggest opportunity to transform the Church.

James Cone In the last four days, one important issue has emerged, and it has
to do with what I have called the social context of theological language. That
phrase is related to my conviction that thinking, or thought, can never be
separated from our socio-political existence. If one is a slave, then one's
thinking about God will have a different character than if one is a slave
master. This conviction has been illustrated again in this conference, and in
one way, the relation between thought and social existence is the source of
our communication with each other.

I have sensed this both as a black person from the United States trying to
speak to Europeans, and also in the relationship between Black Theology and
Latin American Theology. How do we communicate when we live in different worlds?

The question arises from the very moment of our presentations. What is
Black Theology? Or, again, what is Liberation Theology in Latin America?
The Europeans want to understand. When I am in America, white people
want to understand. They want to know what we are talking about. What do
we mean when we say: God is black? What do we mean when we say: Jesus is
black? The more the question is explained, the more you realize that communication is not possible . . . because we live in two worlds: the world of the
oppressed and the world of the oppressors; the world of the black and the
world of the white. These separate worlds, in part, define our language, our
communication. This issue is illustrated by the way in which liberation
theology in Latin America takes *class* as its point of departure and people in
the black world take *color* as a point of departure for theological analysis. One
of the reasons for the separate starting points are the separate ways in which
people make an *entrée* into their language about God, politics, economics,
etc., because of the historical context in which they live; and language and
symbols—whether they be about politics or God or religion—are created in
this historical context.

As long as we live in a world in which we may be defined as the oppressed
and the oppressors, I do not believe that communication is possible. I do not

believe that the oppressed and the oppressors can communicate at levels where it really makes a difference, because they have different realities to which the symbols and the language refer. I am pleased to hear you describe your world in order to see how that world is radically different from mine.

I will stop at this point because I sense on your faces an anxious desire to respond to the four of us—not only in terms of what we have said here but in terms of what we have said in our groups. If I wanted to be an oppressor, I would talk until one o'clock. But I will stop, in a gracious attempt to be— quote—"a Christian."

48

BLACK THEOLOGY
AND LIBERATION THEOLOGY

Herbert O. Edwards

Historical and structural analysis are essential to understanding where we are and what is required of us if our vision of where we ought to go is to be radically different from where we are. We have to realize the interdependent character of the unfolding events of history and the formation of societal structures.

Unless we are willing to be honest about our history, we will be hampered in our attempts to understand the structures which stand over against us and are in us at the same time.

The historical experiences of different groups tend to create within them different perspectives, both on their history and the history of other groups, and in regard to the structural arrangements of the political and socioeconomic orders. The black experience in America differs from the white experience; the black experience in America differs from the Latin American experience. We must address some of these differences momentarily. Suffice it to say at the moment that some of the issues as well as the options facing black theology differ in many ways from those facing liberation theology in Latin America.

Rising Expectations in the Third World

Levels of expectation are informed by a fusion of one's perception of the present circumstances, including the power and will of the enemy, the resources available to alter those circumstances, the will to use these re-

Herbert O. Edwards is Associate Professor of Black Church Studies, Divinity School of Duke University. This essay first appeared in Sergio Torres and John Eagleson, eds., *Theology in the Americas* (Maryknoll, N.Y.: Orbis Books, 1976), pp. 177-91.

sources, and one's view of the world, including one's understanding of the "politics of God."

When slavery in the South became identified and synonymous with black-ness; when state after state altered their laws, making manumission of any slave for whatever reason more difficult; when one's black body was not one's own; when family joys and possibilities were destroyed by law, religion, and custom; when memory of the ancient homeland—Africa—was no longer strong enough to evoke even the remotest hope of returning; what could one really expect, at best, but flight to the North or to Canada, where one might at least have something to say about one's own individual destiny.

When the awareness of the reality of the limited freedom and dignity afforded blackness in the North dawned upon the escaped or freed slave; when he realized that there was not, in actuality, any Red Sea in America for blackness; when he realized that the spirit that informed slavery in the South also informed and shaped the ethos of the North in its response to his blackness: what could one really hope in except the remote possibility that North and South might go to war and occasion the destruction of the institution, if not the spirit, of slavery?

When war finally came and required such a tremendous expenditure of treasure and blood for the North to emerge physically victorious, with the elimination of slavery as a penalty imposed upon the South for its failure on the battlefield, the hopes and expectations of blackness seemed justly to soar and know no bound. The Day of Jubilee is just around the corner! Patient trust in God and struggle for freedom will be rewarded, not only with forty acres and a mule, but also with the right to freely participate in the decision-making processess of the country, to become, at last, a participant in history.

At last a historical congruence has been effected between one's percep-tions of the former "unreality of the then objectionable present," one's fondest dreams and hopes, the resources of oneself and allies, and the view of the world as being indeed in the hands of a just God. The historical nightmare is over. The Four Horsemen of the Apocalypse rode, in succeeding order, from 1861 to 1865. The blindfold has been snatched from the eyes of justice; now she can see to set things right. Did not Lincoln himself, that paragon of racist ideology, proclaim that he saw the hand of God in it all?

> The Almighty has His own purposes. Woe unto the world because of offences for it must needs be that offences come; but woe to that man by whom the offence cometh. If we shall suppose that American slavery is one of those offences which, in the providence of God, must needs come, but which, having continued through His appointed time, He now wills to remove, and that He gives to both North and South, this terrible war, as the woe due to those by whom the offence came, shall we discern therein any departure from those divine attributes which the believers in a Living God always ascribe to Him? Fondly do we hope—

fervently do we pray—that this mighty scourge of war may speedily pass away. Yet, if God wills that it continue, until all the wealth piled by the bondman's two hundred and fifty years of unrequited toil shall be sunk, and until every drop of blood drawn with the lash, shall be paid by another drawn with the sword, as was said three thousand years ago, so still it must be said "the judgments of the Lord, are true and righteous altogether".[1]

Lincoln was not alone in seeing the hand of God in the crisis-filled events of the Civil War. Some saw the hand of God threatening before the terrible events began to unfold; some stood within the eye of the hurricane and loudly proclaimed it; some, with the benefit of hindsight, interpreted it all as the work of God in some measure.

Gayraud Wilmore quotes a letter from Theodore Weld to Angelina Weld, dated February 6, 1842, which read:

> The slaveholders of the present generation, if cloven down by God's judgment, cannot plead that they were unwarned. . . . Well may the God of the oppressed cry out against them, "because I have called and ye have refused, . . . therefore will I laugh at your calamity and mock when your fear cometh. When your fear cometh like desolation and destruction like a whirlwind, then shall ye call but I will not answer."[2]

In 1827, the Reverend Nathaniel Paul, pastor of the First African Baptist Society in Albany, New York, declared at the celebration of the abolition of slavery in that state:

> The progress of emancipation, though slow, is nevertheless certain. It is certain because that God who has made of one blood all nations of men . . . has so decreed. . . . Slavery . . . is so contrary to the laws which the God of nature has laid down as the rule of action by which the conduct of man is to be regulated towards his fellow man, which binds him to love his neighbor as himself, that it ever has, and ever will meet the decided disapprobation of heaven.[3]

During the later afternoon and early evening of January 1, 1863, Negroes throughout the country held meetings to celebrate the promised signing of the Emancipation Proclamation. Frederick Douglass spoke at such a meeting in Boston at Tremont Temple. In his autobiography, Douglass described the meeting:

> Every moment of waiting chilled our hopes, and strengthened our fears. . . . A visible shadow seemed falling on the expecting throng. . . . At last. . . . "It is coming. It is on the wires." The effect of this an-

nouncement was startling beyond description, and the scene was wild and grand. Joy and gladness exhausted all forms of expression, from shouts of praise to sobs and tears. My old friend Rue, a colored preacher, . . . expressed the heartfelt emotion of the hour, when he led all voices in the anthem, "Sound the loud timbrel o'er Egypt's dark sea, Jehovah hath triumphed, his people are free."[4]

But the joy and exultation were short-lived. With the cessation of hostilities came the passing of stringent black codes in the South to "regulate" the relationships between white society and the newly freed slaves. However, the North reacted vigorously at first, seemingly determined not to lose in peace what had been purchased so dearly on the field of battle.

So for a brief period of time the nation again, as once before at its beginning, toyed with the idea of trying to shore up the defenses around every inalienable right to life, liberty, and the pursuit of happiness/property. The Reconstruction period was even more propitious than the revolutionary one, because in the latter no one any longer had legal title to another person's being as property. Nonetheless, after a short, dizzying period of flirting with justice and equality of opportunity, the North and the South "came to its senses" and returned to their father's house, a house of oppressive and racist bondage.

As the Cotton Curtain had fallen in 1789, so now in 1877, the wall of racism, supported by fledgling science, an apostate religion, and political expediency, was raised to shut out the light of hope and to place impenetrable ceilings on the aspirations and expectations of five millions. Violence and injustice had kissed each other; the union resulted in an unforgettable harvest of slaughter.

For fully two generations, black religious and social institutions scaled down the level of hope and expectation in the black community to fit the limited possibilities occasioned by the oppressive power of the white community to destroy blackness coupled with an almost sadistic will to use that power.

World War I caused hope to soar again. Surely if the world is made "safe for democracy," black people can expect better things. But it was not to be. Wilson, like the Founding Fathers before him, knew how to use universal language with particularistic application.

When World War II came, accompanied as it was with the openly declared racist ideology of Nazi Germany, the country had to be a bit more subtle and ingenious in proclaiming its hatred of a system which was simply carrying to its logical conclusion the philosophy which both lived by.

By this time the social scientists and theologians had "come of age" and proved more than equal to the task. The *soul* of white America was really different from that of Nazi Germany. Whereas Nazi Germany's problem lay in being consistent, America's problem really was occasioned by an "uneasy conscience" which was caused by the awareness of the gap between creed and deed. However, the dilemma could and would be resolved because America's commitment to justice and equality of opportunity was real. Also, the victims of injustice were growing in numbers, ability, and determination.

The theologians, sometimes following the lead of the social scientists, sometimes not, set out to show how "different" America really was from Nazi Germany, and how this country had been placed by God in a peculiar position in history for a special, if limited, destiny.

In *Christian Realism* (1941), Professor John C. Bennett confesses: "No one can say that in America we live according to a high standard of *interracial justice*, but we know in our hearts that every institution that perpetuates racial discrimination is wrong. We are on the defensive when we consent to such a wrong."[5]

We are better than Nazi Germany, however, for Dr. Bennett continues: ". . . Contrast that situation with what happens when discrimination is taught as a good, when anti-Semitism is an officially recognized policy, supported by the agencies that mould public opinon as a higher form of morality than interracial justice."[6]

Could one possibly say, in 1941, that racist policies were not officially supported by the opinion-moulding institutions in the United States? Was not racial discrimination taught as a higher form of morality than interracial justice?

Federal aid to housing was officially based on a philosophy of white racism. All branches of the Armed Forces were completely segregated along racial lines. The New Deal programs were operating in a manner respectful of racist principles. The Supreme Court was continuing to interpret the exercise of citizenship rights along racial lines.

The stepped-up defense industries excluded black employees. Almost all educational institutions, from nursery schools to universities, including especially theological seminaries and Bible colleges, operated so as to give aid and comfort to white racism. White political primaries were the order of the day in our southern states. Hospitals, prisons, churches, cemeteries—all were guided by racist policies in their practices.

Restrictive covenants were respectable and legal methods for keeping undesirable racial and other groups out of certain areas and neighborhoods; lynching was not an uncommon occurrence; and more than a third of the states had laws on their books which denied to clergymen the right to join persons together in holy matrimony without using race as the most determinative factor.

In Professor Bennett's American society of 1941, there was not nearly as much of a difference as he would have us believe, if there was any, between America's commitment to racism as a "positive good," and the racist beliefs of Nazi Germany. At least in Germany, according to Paul Tillich, the "Nordic blood theory" was artificially imposed upon and reluctantly accepted by the

German people. Racism has had no such difficult time in America. It has been a part of the moral ethos from the very beginning of the country's national existence.

In an article in the October 4, 1943, issue of *Christianity and Crisis*, entitled "Anglo-Saxon Destiny and Responsibility," Reinhold Niebuhr responded to the critical situation in which the Western world found itself by reminding the Ango-Saxon peoples that the crucial and strategic point at which they found themselves in the building of world community was of such significance as to require that it be apprehended in religious terms. "Without a religious sense of the meaning of destiny, such a position as Britain and America now hold is inevitably corrupted by pride and the lust of power."

Although Niebuhr felt that it would serve no good purpose to try to compare the special destiny of the Anglo-Saxon peoples with that of Israel in olden times, "nevertheless," he said, "only those who have no sense of the profundities of history would deny that various social groups and races are at various times placed in such a position that a special measure of the divine mission in history falls upon them." In that sense God has chosen us in this fateful period of world history.

World War II created the possibility—even as it was proclaimed by our spokesmen to be the occasion—for extending freedom throughout the world. However, God was apparently not choosing the Anglo-Saxon peoples to help remove the yoke of bondage from those who suffered under their oppression. As Winston Churchill made clear, he was not prime minister to preside over the dismemberment of "Her Majesty's Empire."

The problem for the theologians during this period was how to justify fighting for the "Four Freedoms" against Hitler, and denying the extension of those freedoms to non-Anglo-Saxon peoples. However, as in times past in their responses to the black presence in America they proved equal to the task.

Albert C. Knudson believed that one of the conditioning factors in the application of the law of love is that due to the "orders of creation"; the "orders of creation" are all but synonymous with the various divisions that exist in the world. People are divided into different families, different economic and cultural groups, different nations, and different *races*.

Professor Knudson makes a great deal of freedom, and of the free relations of men to each other, as does Christian ethics generally. But this freedom is not and cannot be absolute. There are two important limitations upon the exercise of freedom.

One is in the case of children, and the other limitation is in the case of *undeveloped* peoples or races. "Children require restraint and discipline for their proper training. They need to have their wills to some degree subjected to the wills of their superiors. . . . In a similar way, *undeveloped* tribes and races may to their own advantage and that of the world be kept in tutelage by more highly civilized peoples."[7]

It is clear that the Third World, including black Americans, could find very little in the writings of Christian theologians during the period of World War II to give them any reason for hope. White theology, drawing upon psychology and a biased cultural anthropology, could justify the West's hegemony over the rest of the world.

So the rising expectations in the Third World generally, and among black Americans particularly, were once again proved to be unfounded. Nonetheless, following World War II, neither the United Nations nor the Western plea for realism and patience was sufficient to still the voices calling for freedom in Asia, Africa, and the Americas.

The Cold War between East and West led the United States to pridefully assume the role of "leader of the Free World." Translated into geo-political terms that meant that this country would support every regime, however oppressive, in every country, so long as it was willing to mouth the ideological rantings of the West.

The war-torn and economically weakened countries of Western Europe turned to America to gain support and assistance to enable them to hold on to their colonies which were "undeveloped" and "not ready for independence." Much to the dismay of revolutionaries in Asia, Africa, and Latin America— many of whom thought, like Ho Chi Minh, that the adoption of the American Revolution as a model would be a clear signal to America and the rest of the world that they were not enemies of the "Free World," but oppressed people longing for and determined to gain freedom—the United States generally entered the struggles against them.

So we attempted to bail out France in Indochina, and only after sacrificing thousands of our own youth, visiting unprecedented devastation on the Indochinese, killing thousands and thousands, wasting as much of the area as we could, and spending billions of dollars, were we forced to give up the struggle.

In Africa, for the most part we have settled for neocolonialism, since we could not preserve the colonial situation intact for most of the European countries. And in Latin America we have alternated between "dollar diplomacy," "gunboat and marine diplomacy," "CIA diplomacy," and "plans for progress."

There is little question that economics has played a significant role in shaping this country's responses to the aspirations of Third World peoples. However, it would be shortsighted indeed to ignore the social, political, and racial factors that have played and continue to play an important role in this area.

There is little question that the racial factor has been the most important single determinant in the responses of the religious, educational, political, economic and social forces in this country to the black American's demand for justice.

The civil rights movement served to raise the hopes of black Americans. For a time, during the early sixties, it appeared that white theology was changing its stance toward the oppression of blacks and entering the lists, at long last, on the side of an interpretation of the gospel that saw freedom as being at least not incompatible with the gospel.

However, the Black Power movement, the Black Manifesto, the rise of black caucuses in the white denominations, and the early attempts at black theological formulations resulted in theologico-ethical appeals for order as necessarily prior to justice. It did not seem to matter that the "order" which was being given theological support was really "ordered injustice."

How was it that the inspiring and encouraging fifties gave way to the rising expectations of the sixties, only to eventuate into the despairing seventies? In all probability, Martin L. King, Jr., analyzed it correctly in 1967:

> Throughout our history, laws affirming Negro rights have consistently been circumvented by ingenious evasions which render them void in practice. Laws that affect the whole population—draft laws, income tax laws, traffic laws—manage to work even though they may be unpopular; but laws passed for the Negro's benefit are so widely unenforced that it is a mockery to call them laws.[8]

Black Theology: View from the Bottom

White theological interpretations of American history often remind one of the drunken man who was stumbling around under a lamppost. When asked what he was doing, he replied that he was looking for some money that he had lost. When asked if he thought that he had lost it near or under the lamppost, he replied, "No, I lost it over there but it is dark and I can't see over there. I am looking where the light is."

The historical truth about America, a truth which includes what America has done to Indians, blacks, and women, in the name of God, has been and remains covered by a self-imposed blanket of preferred darkness and silence. And so as we approach the bicentennial observances, an increasing number of historical and analytical, moral, and theological treatises and monographs are being produced, calling us once again to remember, to appeal to, to transmit the values of the Founding Fathers in order to revitalize America and recall it to its original noble foundational purposes.[9]

One sometimes gets the feeling that many Americans have convinced themselves that Vietnam, Watergate, and all its attendant White House horrors did something to our national heritage. But the view from the bottom is that these were all consistent with our national heritage.[10]

Some want to elevate Watergate to the status of a Fall. Why? Because for the first time in the history of the country, the White House consciously tried to subvert our ideals (?), destroy our tradition of fair election (?), used agencies and departments of government to violate the constitutional privileges and guarantees of our citizens (?).

Therefore, some spokesmen for black and women's liberation have been very proudly pointing to the fact that neither group was represented among those who were at the center of the Watergate disaster.[11]

The view from the bottom, as articulated by black theology, does not see Watergate as a Fall in any sense of the word. Black theology must remain conscious of the vast gap that has always existed between the religion and religious interpretations of the white, Western world, and the religion and religious interpretations in the historical black community.

At the center of the religious life of the black community has been the application of the promises of God to those who are not only among the dispossessed and the disinherited, but also to those who have not been considered human and worthy of participation in the Western processes of history.

James Cone's claim: "We were not created for humiliation!" does not and has not led to its obverse in the black community: "We were created to humiliate!" But it is this latter claim that white religion has supported even when it has not proclaimed it as such.

Consequently, we have had a religiously divergent history in this country. The black churches have been the churches of the oppressed; the white churches have been the churches of the oppressor. These differences can be spelled out in much greater detail. However, for our purposes in this context, we are concerned about the implications of these differences for our understanding of some of the differing concerns and options between white North American theology, women's liberation theology, Latin American liberation theology, and black theology.

Let it be clearly understood that I believe that women's liberation theology has a very real and a very long list of grievances against white theology (and perhaps no less so against Latin American theology).

It is also true that Latin American theology, concerned with all of the problems facing their countries, must inevitably challenge the patriotic stance of North American theology, which has too long been too supportive of the expansive, imperialistic policies of this country. Some would also say that black theology's very reason for being is related to the failures of white theology.

So, at first glance, it may appear that women's, Latin American, and black theology, having a mutual enemy, are, therefore, very much alike and are operating on the same theologico-liberation wavelength. There are, however, some very compelling reasons why this may not be so.

More is required than the fact that we may have a mutual enemy to make us allies. If we can discover a way for our varying experiences and perspectives, viewed through the prism of every person's relationship to God, to lead us through our theological wrestling to a shared vision of a different future, under God, then we may be able to move from being nonenemies, perhaps to shared membership in a liberated community.

Women's liberation theology and Latin American theology are presently both more acceptable to the enemy than is black theology. Both are primarily white and whatever their concern for liberation and justice—and it is real—they speak out of a context of shared power with the enemy in a way that black theology never has and cannot.

Both the women's liberation movement and the Latin American movement are spearheaded by those who are *concerned about* the suffering of the powerless and the poor; but all of black theology's spokesmen are *among* the powerless and the oppressed. They do not have to *assume* identification with the struggle, for their blackness makes them one with the despised whether they will it or no.

Neither the history of the base of the Latin American spokesmen's church, nor that of white middle-class women, forces them to identify with those who are "outside the camp." Granted, there may be some instances of individual awareness of powerlessness in both groups; it is not the same as the history and, therefore, the perspective of the black theologian.

It should be remembered, for example, that when Frederick Douglass, Sojourner Truth, and other black men and women joined in and supported the struggle for women's suffrage, the struggle was successfully concluded at a time when black men were being systematically and "legally" denied the right to vote, I have yet to uncover any significant protest being made by the women suffragettes for the enfranchisement of black women, or for the "re-enfranchisement" of black men.

The willingness to listen to, to learn from, Latin American theology by U.S. theologians must not blind the former to the past history of the United States in its totality of effects on Latin American life and thought, theory and praxis. Latin American liberation theology, in its dialogic encounter with North American theology, must not be unaware of the ease with which one can speak universal language with the understanding that it is not really inclusive of all in the society.

How much racism, Western, North American style, has entered the veins of Latin American thought is difficult to say; that it is not absent from it is almost a certainty. For my part, I have discovered all too little attention being given to it in the literature that I have read. There is no question that the U.S. ethos of racism has followed its dollar and military power wherever it has gone.

In this context, the statement by Gustavo Gutiérrez gives us both pause and hope. "Although until recently the Church was closely linked to the established order, it is beginning to take a different attitude regarding the exploitation, oppression, and alienation which prevails in Latin America."[12]

What Is Liberation?

Black theology is committed to the prosecution of a theological task which must hold in creative tension the need of the oppressed for dual liberation—

from sin and guilt and from physical oppression in all its varied forms in a racist society. Black religious experience has always been conscious of and sensitive to the eschatological and the historical.

During the days of slavery, liberation was conceived of as the antithesis of human bondage. It was not difficult to provide content to the term "liberation." To be free meant no more auction block, no more being owned and used by another, no more denial of one's right to go and come, to hope and dream. It meant being able to project marriage and family life, to be paid for one's labor, to be able to defend oneself and family when attacked, and to worship God without humiliation.

Following the wholesale, explicit institutional capitulation to discriminatory practices based on racism, liberation seems clearly less complex than now. The removal of all discriminatory legislation, the passage of laws guaranteeing equal access to the institutional resources of the community, and the judicial invalidation of those laws which denied equality of treatment and opportunity represented liberation.

The Civil Rights movement did succeed in large measure, in the legislative and judicial arenas, in effecting the passage of laws and having other laws declared illegal. But liberation did not follow; Black Power did.

Black Power was the needed corrective to the major thrusts of the Civil Rights movement because the movement raised primarily the question about the access to resources, but did not raise the issue of power redistribution.

Throughout the historical struggles involved in the black experience in America, black theology, whether articulated in sermon, song, testimony, or essay, has always been cognizant of the celebrative aspect of life. Black religion talked about the caring and the acting God who was working to set the captives free. Consequently, in the midst of historical oppression, degradation, and exploitation, participation in the earnest expectation of their liberation led to what has been ineptly defined as "otherworldliness."

However, when the slave experienced the liberating power of the gospel, he was also made free to acknowledge the "unreality of the present" and to project a new and different future. Some may call it "escapism," but who could have foreseen, in 1793, except through the "eyes of faith," that seventy years later black slaves would be standing on the threshold of "freedom"? So one works and prays, wearing loosely the mantle of loyalty to any oppressive system and structures, knowing that God is not captive to American history, but is working through and in it to set the oppressed free.

Further, who could have foreseen, in 1972, considering the massive landslide won by Mr. Nixon for his platform and program of "keeping blacks in their places," that less than two years later a chagrined, though not chastened, country would conclude that they were indeed paying too large a price for the ceilings placed on black aspirations?

Liberation is not yet, to be sure, but God is still at work in the affairs of this world, and it may not be quite as incredible as some think to project the liberation of the oppressed and the destruction of white racism.

Marxism

The attractiveness of Marxism, whether appealed to for critical analysis of capitalist society, or for its vision of a new society void of the evils attendant upon capitalism, may very well be due to its distance from the Christianity which the churches preached and practiced in Latin America. When people are caught up in an apparently hopeless situation and their hopelessness seems informed and occasioned by their powerlessness, only a different analysis and a different vision seem to hold any promise of real and meaningful change.

The black theologian, whether North or South, however, knows that ideological changes have not made any significant difference in the black situation in America. This country has evidenced a tremendous capacity and versatility in shifting ideological stances while holding on to the basic fundament in ethos—creating, namely, racism. Consequently, whether Adam Smith or Karl Marx, whether Herbert Hoover or Franklin D. Roosevelt, whether Richard M. Nixon or Lyndon B. Johnson prevails, racism continues to be the one overarching and informing principle of action.

When it is suggested that a "peculiar American" brand of socialism is what is needed or desired, we are too consciously aware that what has in the past made almost any economic, political, or social policy or practice peculiarly "American" is the same racist spirit that informed and supported its "Peculiar Institution" for two and one half centuries.

Civil Religion

Black theology, viewing the historical development of civil religion in America, views the content of the "convenant concept" that informed it differently from some interpreters.[13]

The faith that bound together Protestant, Catholic, Jew, rich and poor, educated and illiterate, liberal and conservative, laissez-faire capitalist and New Dealer, high churchmen and low, pious and irreverent, Republican and Democrat, was white racism. Racism has been the only ecumenical faith that America has consistently subscribed to.

Civil religion began to unravel and to come apart at the mythic seams not because the myths were no longer possessed of symbolic value, but because the victims of the mythic and symbolic interpretations of America's history were raised to a new level of consciousness and action.

Black theology, then, does not envision that a future in the restoration of civil religion holds any hope; neither does it place much confidence in an American brand of socialism. We are too conscious of British socialism and its racism. Rather we envision a future which is brought about by the liberating activities of God and the struggles of the oppressed, toward which we must move without a blueprint or a utopian scenario spelled out in detail.

However, those policies and practices which prevail today must give way to the new. The task at this time involves the destruction of the myths that have supported the old way and a calling to all who can will the destruction of the old, and who under the aegis of the Holy Spirit can go forth to a land which God will show us.

Notes

1. Second Inaugural Address, March 4, 1865, in Don E. Fehrenbacher, ed., *Abraham Lincoln: A Documentary Portrait Through His Speeches and Writings* (New York: New American Library, 1964), p. 278.

2. Gayraud S. Wilmore, *Black Religion and Black Radicalism* (Garden City, N.Y: Doubleday & Company, Inc., 1972), p. 40.

3. Quoted in Benjamin E. Mays, *The Negro's God* (New York: Atheneum, 1968 [1938]), p. 42.

4. Frederick Douglass, *Life and Times of Frederick Douglass* (New York: Collier Books, 1962 [reprint rev. ed. 1892]), p. 353.

5. John C. Bennett, *Christian Realism* (New York: Scribner's, 1941).

6. Ibid.

7. Albert C. Knudson, *The Principles of Christian Ethics* (Nashville: Abingdon Press, 1943), p. 190; italics added.

8. Martin L. King, Jr., *Where Do We Go From Here: Chaos or Community?* (Boston: Beacon Press, 1967), p. 82.

9. Cf. special 1776 issue *Time* magazine; Harry Jewell, *The Bicentennial–A New Look* (Detroit: Stress American League, 1973).

10. Cf. Charles H. Long, "The Ambiguities of Innocence": " . . . innocence of the American is not a natural innocence, that innocence which is prior to experience: rather, this innocence is gained only through an intense suppression of the deeper and more subtle dimensions of American experience. Americans never had or took the time to contemplate the depths of their deeds. America's . . . future lies in its ability to live with, support, and understand the new world of Asia and Africa" (in William A. Beardslee, ed., *America and the Future of Theology* [Philadelphia: Westminster Press, 1967], p. 50).

11. I am not sure how the women view Rose Mary Woods and her role in Watergate.

12. Gustavo Gutiérrez, *A Theology of Liberation*, trans. Sister Caridad Inda and John Eagleson (Maryknoll, N.Y.: Orbis Books, 1973), p. 133.

13. Robert Bellah, *The Broken Covenant: American Civil Religion in Time of Trial* (New York: Seabury Press, 1974).

49

STATEMENT FROM THE COALITION
OF U.S. NONWHITE RACIAL
AND NATIONAL MINORITIES

We would like to express our appreciation to Sergio Torres and the planning committee for convening a conference on liberation theology, thereby making it possible for us to be in conversation with our brothers and sisters from Latin America. We know that they are dedicated and committed to the struggle of the oppressed. We have become aware of their persecution and suffering due to their fight for justice.

Because we believe that the struggles of oppressed peoples are interconnected, we are deeply pained that the programming of this conference prevented us from sharing our similar experiences with out Latin American brothers and sisters.

We noted the following:

1. The North American section did not express the conditions, experiences, and theological reflections of the nonwhite racial and national minorities living within the United States.

2. The way the conference was structured perpetuated a tone of divisiveness among us nonwhites. We feel that the section on "Emerging Theology" was a token one. We were forced into a situation which objectively appeared that we were competing with each other.

3. We have noticed that there has been a tendency to look at the Latin American liberation struggles in a way where the real essence of this struggle and the solidarity it should evoke from everyone is not really grasped.

4. This lack of understanding results in insufficient will, sensitivity, and understanding to embrace the oppressed U.S. racial and national minorities and their liberation struggles. But we believe that liberation theology in the U.S. must be written in the struggle of the oppressed and by the oppressed. Liberation theology written in any other way could be easily interpreted as being elitist, co-optive, and presumptuous.

This statement was first published in Sergio Torres and John Eagleson, eds., *Theology in the Americas* (Maryknoll, N.Y.: Orbis Books, 1976), pp. 359-360.

We express our solidarity and support with all oppressed peoples of the world. We, the people of color in this conference, expect and demand recognition of our existence and contributions in the area of liberation theology. We expect and demand an expression of the concrete reality of what was put forward as the goals of this conference.

In the spirit of solidarity and being able to correct these very shortcomings of the conference, we submit that the following are indispensable:

1. For future planning, representation of North American minority peoples on planning committees.

2. Participation of a significant and substantial representation of minority peoples in the conference, or any process.

3. A serious examination in the process of the conference of oppressive structures and situations of the black people, the Asian people, the Hispanics, and native Americans in North America.

Sister Jamie Phelps, O.P.
Preston N. Williams
Willie J. Dell
Roberto Peña
Nelson Trout
Jun Atienza
Dominga Zapata
Joaquina Carrion
Maria Antonia Esquerra
Dr. J. Deotis Roberts
Gilberto Marrero
Walden Bello
Clarence G. Newsome

Margarita Jiménez
Toinette Eugene
Geline Avila
José Luis Velazco
Rafael Jiménez
Sister Mario Barron
Miriam Cherry
Sister Juana Clare José
Violet Masuda
Ricardo Parra
Herb Barnes
James H. Cone
Joseph B. Bethea
Herbert O. Edwards, Sr.

50

EVANGELIZATION AND POLITICS:
A BLACK PERSPECTIVE

James H. Cone

What is the relationship between evangelization and politics, the propagation of the faith and the building of a just society? This is the question that defines the focus of this essay. Unfortunately many Christians believe that there is a sharp distinction between evangelization and politics. They claim that evangelization refers to the preaching of the gospel of Jesus to unbelievers so they can through faith receive the gift of eternal life. Politics has to do with the creation of laws that will govern people in society so that they can live together in peace in this world. According to this view, evangelization is the primary task of the church with its priests, preachers, and missionaries. But politics is the job of politicians and lawyers, that is, persons who are trained in political science and the legal statutes of a given nation.

The separation of evangelization and politics is based on the assumption that they refer to different realities. For example, politics is limited to this world. It is a human affair that is concerned with the creation of a social contract among people that will enhance justice and minimize injustice. Therefore most politicians claim to base their political platform upon their capacity to create social structures that will make this world a more humane place to live for everyone.

While politics is concerned with the affairs of this world, many Christians believe that evangelization is concerned with the next world. It focuses on the salvation of the soul, the proclamation of the gospel to sinners, the unsaved, the lost. Preachers, priests, and missionaries, therefore, should not concern themselves with politics because salvation has nothing to do with the material conditions of people. Their task is derived exclusively from the kerygma of the early church, concretized in Jesus' command: "Go forth therefore and make all nations my disciples; baptize men everywhere in the name of the

Father and the Son and the Holy Spirit, and teach them to observe all that I have commanded you. And be assured, I am with you always, to the end of time" (Mt. 28:19–20 NEB). On the basis of this saying European Christians have invaded Asia, Africa, and the Americas enslaving and colonizing the "pagans" so that their souls might be saved and their society civilized.

> From the very beginning of the Atlantic slave trade, conversion of the slaves to Christianity was viewed by the emerging nations of Western Christendom as a justification for enslavement of Africans. When Portuguese caravels returned from the coast of West Africa with human booty in the fifteenth century, Gomes Eannes De Azurara, a chronicler of their achievements, observed that "the greater benefit" belonged not to the Portuguese adventurers but to captive Africans, "for though their bodies were now brought into some subjection, that was a small matter in comparison of their souls, which would now possess true freedom for evermore."[1]

This same "evangelistic" motive gave rise to the missionary movement during the eighteenth and nineteenth centuries and continues today to define the North American and European churches' involvement in the Third World.

Recently the divorce of evangelization and politics has been seriously questioned by Christians in Africa, Asia, and Latin America. On each continent, there is the increasing recognition that missionaries from Europe and North America identify the gospel of Jesus with western culture, thereby giving credence to the contention that missionary work is primarily an instrument of neo-colonial penetration. In response to the European and North American missionaries' distortion of the faith by identifying it with western culture, Third World Christians have begun to think about the gospel in the historical context of their own struggle to liberate themselves from the relation of dependence and domination. What does it mean to preach the gospel in the context of poverty and oppression? And how is this gospel related to the human struggle to create a just social order? These are some of the questions that inform the Third World perspective on evangelization and politics. In an attempt to answer these questions the All-Africa Conference of Churches, in its historic Third Assembly, called for a moratorium on all western missionaries,[2] and the Christian Conference of Asia and many Latin American Christians supported them.[3]

Naturally the struggle to relate evangelization to politics has necessitated a new theological approach defined not by Europe and North America but by Asia, Africa, and Latin America. These theologies are shaped by the particularity of the political situation on their continent. That is why the name of the continent rather than a particular confession of faith has been chosen as a description of their theological starting point: *African* theology, *Asian* theology, and *Latin American* liberation theology. Each theology is characterized by its struggle against the dominance of Europe and North America and by its creative attempt to fashion a perspective on the gospel that arises out of the people's struggle to liberate themselves from oppression.

In addition to Christians in Asia, Africa, and Latin America, there are also oppressed Christians in North America who have rejected the Euro-American divorce of evangelization and politics. They include Women, Native, Hispanic, Asian, and Black Americans. Each of these communities recognizes the need to develop a theology out of their historical struggle for freedom. For Black Americans, this recognition shaped our religious consciousness. Our perception of the connection between evangelization and politics was defined on the slave ships, the auction block, and the Underground Railroad. In the historical context of oppression and our struggle against it, we realize that the good news of the gospel could only mean our political liberation from the chains of slavery. While the white missionaries introduced Christianity to African slaves, "the meaning which the missionaries wished the slave to receive and the meaning which the slave actually . . . made . . . were not the same."[4] Because the reality of the freedom they encountered in the gospel involved its implementation in society, African slaves found white churches socially unacceptable as places of worship. Therefore they created their own church structures that would more accurately represent their affirmation of faith in their struggle for freedom. In the northern section of the United States, Blacks created radically independent church structures. This independent church movement began when Richard Allen and other blacks walked out of St. George Methodist Church at Philadelphia in 1787, because they refused to accommodate themselves to racial barriers erected by the white members of that church. From this incident emerged the African Methodist Episcopal Church which was officially organized in 1816. Later other Blacks followed suit in New York and organized the African Methodist Episcopal Zion Church in 1821. Similar events occurred among Black Baptists.

However, even Blacks who remained in white denominational structures often refused to accept the divorce between preaching the gospel and the establishment of justice in the land. Such persons as David Walker, Nathaniel Paul, and Henry Garnet are prominent examples. No one expressed this point any clearer or more radically than Garnet. In a famous address to the slaves in 1843, he said:

> If . . . a band of Christians should attempt to enslave a race of heathen men, . . . the God of heaven would smile on every effort which the injured might make to disenthrall themselves. Brethen, it is as wrong for your lordly oppressors to keep you in slavery as it was for the man thief to steal our ancestors from the coast of Africa. You should therefore use the same manner of resistance as would have been just in our ancestors when the bloody footprints of the first remorseless

soul-thief were placed upon the shores of our fatherland. . . . Liberty is
a spirit sent from God and like its great Author is no respector of
persons.[5]

For Garnet, evangelization was not only preaching in words but also the
undertaking of action to release and to liberate. This is the ethos that shaped
the Black church's involvement in the abolition of slavery.

African slaves' refusal to separate evangelization and politics forced them
to create an invisible institution in the South, because it was illegal for them to
assemble without the presence of a white person to monitor the meeting.
Therefore African slaves organized secret worship services in the slave cabins
and woods at night in order to fashion a perspective on evangelization that
transcended white interpretation of the gospel. Carey Davenport, a former
slave, remembered those meetings: "Sometimes the cullud folks go down in
dugouts and hollows and hold their own service and they used to sing songs
that come a-gushing from the heart."[6] Another ex-slave from Texas, Adeline
Cunningham, made a similar report: "No suh, we never goes to church.
Times we sneaks in the woods and prays de Lawd to make us free and times
one of the slaves got happy and made a noise dat they heered at de big house
and den de overseer come and whip us 'cause we prayed de Lawd to set us
free."[7]

Unlike white missionaries and preachers who identified evangelization
with the proclamation of the gospel to unbelievers and heathens, African
slaves identified it with the proclamation of freedom. That was why they sang:

> Oh Freedom! Oh Freedom!
> Oh Freedom! I love thee!
> And before I'll be a slave,
> I'll be buried in my grave,
> And go home to my Lord and be free.

Other slave songs such as "Go Down Moses," "Steal Away," and "Oh
Mary, Don't You Weep" express the same liberation theme. This theme not
only defined the rise of the Black church in the eighteenth and nineteenth
centuries but continues today to give political direction to the Black church's
involvement in Black people's struggle for justice. The refusal to divorce
evangelization from politics is the chief reason why the Black struggle for
justice has taken place primarily in the church. As most of the slave insurrections were organized in the Black church and were led by preachers, also the
contemporary movement of Black liberation in the 1950s and '60s took place
in the context of the proclamation of the gospel in the Black church. Martin
Luther King, Jr., is an international symbol of a pervasive reality in the Black
Christian community.

It is within the context of the Black church's participation in Black people's struggle for political justice that Black Theology's origin must be understood. Black Theology was not created in seminaries and universities but on the streets of Harlem and Watts and in the context of the rise of Black Power, as Black people attempted to fashion a political project consistent with their knowledge of themselves as creative, free human beings. When Willie Ricks sounded the cry of Black Power during the James Meredith March in Mississippi (1966), it was a clarion call for Black people to take charge of their history. Once again we Blacks realized that if we are to be free, we must ourselves create the revolutionary structures for the implementation of that freedom. Expecting white oppressors to participate in the creation of political structures that will liberate us is like expecting Pharaoh in Egypt to respond affirmatively to God's demand to "Let my people go!"

The contemporary appearance of Black theology happened as Black people attempted to give theological structure to a political commitment they had already made. Black theology became the theological arm of Black Power by defining Black people's political struggle as identical with the gospel of Jesus. The title of my first book in 1969 reflects this political stance: *Black Theology and Black Power.*[8] My second book followed a year later (1970). Its title, *A Black Theology of Liberation,* reflected the fact that it identified *liberation* as the central motif of the gospel.[9] Since the publication of these two books, other Black theologians have supported me in joining the gospel with political struggle, even though they have not always agreed with the way I have done it. They include J. Deotis Roberts,[10] Major Jones,[11] Gayraud S. Wilmore,[12] and Cecil Cone.[13]

White North American theologians' response to Black theology has been interesting but consistent with their usual failure to take seriously Black people's struggle for freedom. Often without even reading the literature on the subject, some say that Black theology is nothing but racism in reverse. Others, still refusing to immerse themselves in the social history out of which Black theology comes, reply by accusing Black theologians of reducing Christianity to a political ideology and thereby failing to recognize revelation as the starting point of the gospel. But the great majority of white theologians, who feel uncomfortable remaining silent on the theme of liberation, ignore Black theology by dealing exclusively with Latin American liberation theology. These theologians turn liberation theology into a new theological fad, a commodity in that what they say about Latin America does not require of them a revolutionary act in their own social context. Much of their talk remains in the seminaries and universities, and it often appears that all that is necessary to demonstrate their commitment to the poor is to write a book or to attend a conference on the subject.

Although Union Theological Seminary in New York has done far more for Black liberation than any other North American white seminary, it is nevertheless an excellent model of the danger about which I speak. For example, we have many white liberation-oriented professors and students but their preoccupation is primarily with Latin American liberation theology, and there are many courses on that subject in the Union catalogue. Also students and professors take field trips to Latin America, and Union presently is trying to establish a structural relationship with seminaries on that continent. Now I am not against all this, because I firmly believe that we need a global perspective in theology. But as I have said to my Union colleagues, there is no way, absolutely no way, for them to demonstrate a real solidarity with the poor in Latin America without taking sides with poor people in North America. Union is located on the edge of Harlem, the largest and perhaps the most oppressed Black community in the U.S.A., but it is difficult to get Union Seminary faculty and students as a community to make a political commitment in solidarity with Black people in that community. I have raised this concern many times but their reply is that Black people have many able spokespersons. But my reply is: So do Latin Americans! The issue is not whether Blacks, Latins, or Africans have able spokespersons but whether we have genuine allies in the North American white community.

After much reflection, I have come to the conclusion that most of the North American Whites who talk about liberation theology do nothing more than talk. For the only way that I can know that any person means more than talk is for him or her to make a political decision for poor people in their own historical context. And I know what decision you have made by the company you keep, by whom you regard as your friends, and essentially Whites still remain exclusively within the framework of their own racial group. Whatever we say about class, which I firmly believe is central and perhaps the primary contradiction, I do not believe that the race problem in North America or the world will be solved by focusing exclusively on the economic problem. I know that many white North Americans use the class issue as a way of ignoring their own racism.

However, I am very pleased to say that there are a few white theologians who have taken the time to read, listen, and participate with an openness to encounter the truth inherent in the black struggle, and I have found dialogue with them enriching and creative. When I meet white persons who want to discuss not because of guilt or some other condescending motive, but because their own humanity is at stake in Black people's struggle, then I know that I have a genuine dialogical situation in which much mutual learning is possible.

While this genuine mutuality is hard to find among white persons in North America and Europe, such is not the case in Asia, Africa, and Latin America. I have sought to deepen and to enlarge the political focus of Black theology by entering into dialogue with theologians who have a Third World consciousness. That is why I gladly accepted the invitation to come to this conference in Cuba. It is also why I have attended similar conferences in Asia, Africa, Latin America, and the Caribbean.[14] My experience on these continents has disclosed more clearly the global context of oppression, and I feel compelled to reflect that reality in my theological project.

The Black Theology Conference in Atlanta, August 1977, may be dated as the beginning of Black theologians' attempt to take seriously the international context of oppression. This global perspective is found not only in my lecture entitled "Black Theology and the Black Church: Where Do We Go From Here?",[15] but more importantly in the "Message to the Black Church and Community"[16] that was written as the official statement of the conference. Since the Atlanta meeting, I have attended conferences in Mexico,[17] Ghana,[18] and Sri Lanka,[19] each of which focused on ways that Third World theologians can meaningfully share a common theological project that will be beneficial in the struggles of oppressed peoples from which we come.

Here in Cuba also I am hopeful that our being together will contribute to a further clarification of the theological task, so that we can return to our respective communities with a clearer vision of our responsibility in the struggle for freedom. Within the context of dialogue it is my belief that we have much to learn from each other that motivates me to say a further word about evangelization and politics. I want to examine briefly (1) evangelization and salvation; (2) evangelization and politics; and (3) salvation and eschatology.

Evangelization and Salvation

If we are to understand correctly the relation between evangelization and politics, I believe that it is necessary to state clearly the content of salvation we have been entrusted to proclaim. How can we evangelize if we do not know what salvation means? Without a clear perspective on salvation, we will remain confused about whether politics has anything to do with preaching the gospel.

The place to begin is with the Bible. In the Old Testament, salvation is grounded in history and is identical with God's righteousness to deliver people from bondage. Literally, the root meaning of the word salvation is "to be wide or spacious, to develop without hindrance, and thus ultimately to have victory in battle."[20] The Savior is the one who has power to gain victory, and the saved are the oppressed who have been set free. For Israel, it is Yahweh who is the Savior because "the Lord *saved* Israel that day from the hand of the Egyptians; and Israel saw the Egyptians dead upon the seashore" (Exodus 14:30 RSV). That is why the people sang:

> The Lord is my strength and my song,
> and he has become my salvation;
> This is my God, and I will exalt him,
> The Lord is a man of war;
> the Lord is his name (Ex. 15:2–3 RSV).

Here salvation is God's deliverance of the people from political danger. It is his divine righteousness to liberate the weak and the oppressed. Salvation therefore is a historical event of rescue, an event of freedom.

There are several terms which describe God's saving activity, and they include "deliverance," "redemption," and "healing." Almost without exception, in the Old Testament, the Deliverer, Redeemer, and Healer is God, and the delivered, the redeemed, and the healed are oppressed people. It is impossible to understand the Old Testament view of salvation without recognizing it is God's deliverance of helpless victims from physical suffering or political menace.

In the New Testament, the Old Testament emphasis on God as the One who effects salvation, and salvation as historical liberation is not denied but reinforced and carried through to its most radical consequences. In the New Testament as in the Old, God is the Savior par excellence, and his salvation is the revolutionary historical liberation for the oppressed of the land. That is why it is reported that Jesus was born in a stable at Bethlehem, and why Mary describes the divine meaning of his coming presence with these words:

> My soul magnifies the Lord,
> and my spirit rejoices in God my Savior.
> For . . . he has shown strength with his arm,
> he has scattered the proud in the imagination of their hearts,
> he has put down the mighty from their thrones,
> and exalted those of low degree;
> he has filled the hungry with good things,
> and the rich he has sent empty away (Luke 1:47, 51–53 RSV).

The identification of salvation with freedom from bondage in history is revealed in the New Testament through Jesus' identity with the poor. He came to and for the poor; he ate with the outcasts, the "bad characters" of his day, the ones whom the Pharisees called sinners. He healed the sick, bestowed the blind their sight, and restored health to the lame and the crippled. When John sent his disciples to Jesus asking, "Are you he who is to come, or shall we look for another?" Jesus replied: "Go and tell John what you have seen and heard: the blind receive their sight, the lame walk, lepers are cleansed, and the deaf hear, the dead are raised up, the poor have good news preached to them" (Lk. 7:20f, RSV). These acts locate salvation in history, the concreteness of human existence. If the kingdom of God (God's rule) is identical with Jesus' person, and if his person is inseparable from his work, then there is little doubt what salvation means. It is the bringing of wholeness and health in the conditions of brokenness, peace, and justice where oppression exists. In a word, it is the restoration of people to their true humanity. Salvation is the bestowal of freedom for the unfree, redemption for the slave, acquittal for the convicted, and deliverance for the captives.

As people who have encountered this event of liberation in Jesus Christ, the church has been called into being to spread the good news of salvation to all humankind. The church's task is to be the embodiment of salvation that it has encountered in Jesus' death and resurrection. Evangelism, therefore, arises from a natural ingredient inherent in the church's being. For if the church does not spread salvation, it denies the one who makes its identity as a Christian community possible. Therefore it is not evangelistic for any selfish reason of its own but because of a theological necessity that arises from its own identity in Jesus Christ. Because all people belong to him, through the salvation he has wrought for them, the church excludes itself from that salvation if it tries to possess it as a property of its own. It is out of this biblical understanding of salvation as liberation that we must understand the relationship between evangelism and politics.

Evangelization and Politics

Because salvation is grounded in history, there is no way to separate the preaching of the gospel from a political commitment on behalf of the oppressed of the land. If there is no salvation independent of the struggle for liberation in history, independent of the emancipation of people from the chains of slavery, then there can be no Christian proclamation apart from the political commitment to fight against injustice, slavery, and oppression. Evangelization, then, is not only the proclamation of thoughts about freedom found in the Bible or in my head. Rather it is primarily *participation* in the socio-historical movement of a people from oppression to liberation. Anything less than a political commitment that expresses one's solidarity with the poor in the struggle for freedom is not Christian evangelization. For the word "Christian" connects evangelization with politics and thus requires that the one who dares to claim that identity must necessarily make a historical commitment identical with the struggle of the poor for freedom.

When Christians recognize the demands that their faith places upon them, they then began the search for tools that will help them actualize it in society. It is because faith does not have within its own confession the social tools necessary for its implementation that we are required to look elsewhere. If evangelization is inseparably connected with the political demand to liberate the poor, what resources do we need in order to accomplish that task? It is at this point that we realize that justification by faith alone is not enough. In order for the poor to experience a justification in which the Lutheran emphasis on the forensic declaration is transformed into liberating social structures, then faith must connect itself with a social theory of change. How can the poor liberate themselves if they do not know why they exist in poverty? How can the oppressed free themselves from bondage if they do not understand the world that enslaves them? It is because Latin American theologians take seriously the structures of economic oppression that they have turned to Marx as the primary resource for their liberation theology. Black theologians have similar resources for an analysis of racism. The same is true for feminist theologians in relation to sexism. Anyone who claims that evangelization is connected with politics but ignores the need to develop a social theory of change does not intend to be taken seriously.

However, liberation theologians, whether Black, Latin, African, or Feminist, need to stay in constant dialogue with each other lest they become too narrow in their approach to liberation. We need each other because there can be no genuine freedom for anyone until all are free. If we do not remain open to each other, then we will simply negate the truth not only as it arises out of another social context but also as we have encountered it in our own. For Blacks to ignore class oppression or sexism simply turns the Black struggle into a male middle-class preoccupation, without any real change in the capitalistic structures that oppress us all. But a similar middle-class and racism emphasis is possible among Marxists and women. The only way we can help to protect ourselves from this fallacy is to have the persons in our struggle represent the revolutionary consciousness reflected in the complexity of our historical situation. Therefore Blacks, women, and poor persons who have a revolutionary consciousness must be present as we attempt to create a social theory of change. For without their presence, there is no way to guarantee that their unique interests, defined by their color, sex, and class, will play a significant role in shaping the social structures of the new, revolutionary society.

Salvation and Eschatology

Although evangelization is connected with politics because the biblical view of salvation is grounded in history, we must not fail to say a concluding word about an even more radical dimension of the New Testament view of salvation. The radical character of the New Testament view of salvation is not the rejection of history. To reject history in salvation leads to passivity and makes religion the opiate of the people. The New Testament, while accepting history, does not limit salvation to history. As long as people are bound to history, they are bound to law and thus death. If death is the ultimate power and life has no future beyond this world, then the rulers of the state who control the military are in the place of God. They have the future in their hands and the oppressed can be made to obey the law of injustice. But if the oppressed, while living in history, can see beyond it, if they can visualize an eschatological future beyond this world, then the "sigh of oppressed creatures," to use Marx's phrase, can become a revolutionary cry of rebellion against the established order. It is this revolutionary cry that is granted in the resurrection of Jesus. Salvation then is not simply freedom in history; it is freedom to affirm that future which is beyond history. Indeed, because we know that death has been conquered, we are truly free to be human in history, knowing that we have a "home over yonder."

"The home over yonder," vividly and artistically described in the slave songs, is the gift of salvation granted in the resurrection of Jesus. If this "otherness" in salvation is not taken with utmost seriousness, then there is no way to be sustained in the struggle against injustice. The oppressed will get tired and also afraid of the risks of freedom. They will say as the Israelites said to Moses when they found themselves between Pharaoh's army and the Red Sea: "Is it because there are no graves in Egypt that you have taken us away to die in the wilderness? What have you done to us, in bringing us out of Egypt?" (Ex. 14:11 RSV). The fear of freedom and the risks contained in struggle are an ever-present reality. But the "otherness" of salvation, its transcendence beyond history, introduces a *factor* that makes a difference. The difference is not that we are taken out of history while living on earth—that would be an opiate. Rather it is a *difference* that plants our being firmly in history because we know that death is not the goal of history. The transcendence-factor in salvation helps us to realize that our fight for justice is God's fight too; and his presence in Jesus' resurrection has already defined what the ultimate outcome will be. It was this knowledge that enabled black slaves to live in history but not to be defeated by their limitations in history. To be sure, they sang about the fear of "sinking down" and the dread of being a "motherless child." They encountered trouble and the agony of being alone where "I couldn't hear nobody pray." They encountered death and expressed it in song:

> Soon one mornin',' death comes a creepin' in my room.
> O my Lawd, O my Lawd, what shall I do?

Death was a terrible reality for black slaves, and it visited the slave quarters leaving orphans behind.

> Death done been here, took my mother an' gone,
> O my Lawd, what shall I do?
> Death done been here, left me a motherless child,
> O my Lawd, what shall I do?

In these songs are expressed the harsh realities of history and the deep sense of dread at the very thought of death. But because the slaves knew or believed that death had been conquered in Jesus' resurrection, they could also transcend death and interpret salvation as a heavenly, eschatological reality. That is why they also sang:

> You needn't mind my dying,
> Jesus' goin' to make up my dying bed.
> In my room I know,
> Somebody is going to cry,
> All I ask you to do for me,
> Just close my dying eyes.

Notes

1. Albert J. Raboteau, *Slave Religion: The "Invisible Institution" in the Antebellum South* (New York: Oxford University Press, 1978), p. 96.

2. For a report on the May 12–24, 1974, Lusaka Assembly, see *The Struggle Continues* (Nairobi, Kenya: All-Africa Conference of Churches, 1975).

3. See *International Review of Mission*, a special issue on "Moratorium," Volume LXIV, No. 254, April 1975. For a response of the Christian Conference of Asia, see "Let My People Go" by Harvey Perkins, Harry Daniel, and Asal Simandjuntak in *Mission Trends No. 3: Third World Theologies*, eds., Gerald H. Anderson and Thomas F. Stransky, C.S.P. (New York: Paulist Press, 1976).

4. Raboteau, *Slave Religion*, p. 126.

5. Henry H. Garnet, *An Address to the Slaves of the United States of America* (New York: Arno Press, 1969), p. 93

6. Cited in George P. Rawick, *From Sundown to Sunup* (Westport, Conn.: Greenwood Publishing Co., 1972), p. 40.

7. Ibid., p. 35.

8. New York: Seabury Press, 1969.

9. Philadelphia: Lippincott, 1970. My other books are *The Spirituals and the Blues* (New York: Seabury Press, 1972) and *God of the Oppressed* (New York: Seabury Press, 1975).

10. *Liberation and Reconciliation: A Black Theology* (Philadelphia: Westminster, 1974).

11. *Black Awareness: A Theology of Hope* (Nashville: Abingdon, 1971) and *Christian Ethics for Black Theology* (Nashville: Abingdon, 1974).

12. *Black Religion and Black Radicalism* (Philadelphia: Lippincott, 1972).

13. *The Identity Crisis in Black Theology* (Nashville: A.M.E. Church, 1975).

14. A very significant organization that brings Third World theologians together for dialogue is The Ecumenical Association of Third World Theologians. J. Russell Chandran is president (South India) and Sergio Torres is the executive secretary. For an account of the organization, see *Voices of the Third World*, Vol. 1, No. 1, December, 1978. This association has held three major conferences—two in Africa (August 1976 in Tanzania and December 1977 in Ghana), one in Asia (January 1979 in Sri Lanka); another is to be held in Latin America (February 1980 in Brazil). Two books have been published from the Africa Conferences: Sergio Torres and Virginia Fabella, eds., *The Emergent Gospel* (Maryknoll, New York: Orbis Books, 1978), and Kofi Appiah-Kubi and Sergio Torres, eds., *African Theology en Route* (Maryknoll, New York: Orbis Books, 1979). *The Emergent Gospel* is an account of the organizing conference of the association in Tanzania and also a collection of background papers. A balanced representation from Africa, Asia, and Latin America were present but only one person from Black America and one from the Caribbean. It was agreed that conferences would be held on the three continents with the major focus and representation being controlled by persons from the particular continent itself. *African Theology en Route* is an account of the Association meeting in Ghana which focused on African Theology. A book is in preparation that deals with the Sri Lanka Conference.

15. See *Cross Currents*, Vol. XXVII, No. 2, Summer 1977.

16. See Ibid.

17. This was a conference called primarily by Latin American theologians in Mexico City, October 7–10, 1977. It was called "Encounter of Theologies." The encounter included Black Theology, Process Theology, Political and Secular Theologies from North America and Europe, and of course Latin American Liberation Theology.

18. See *African Theology en Route*.

19. See the reference in note 14.

20. F. J. Taylor, "Salvation," in Alan Richardson, ed., *A Theological Word Book of the Bible* (New York: Macmillan, 1960), p. 219.

51

FINAL DOCUMENT
OF THE CUBA CONFERENCE
ON "EVANGELIZATION AND POLITICS"

We, a group of theologians (78 in all) from Christian churches of Europe, Asia, Africa, the United States, the Caribbean, and Latin America, invited by the Evangelical Theological Seminary of Matanzas and the Christian Peace Conference for Latin America and the Caribbean, met from February 25 to March 2, 1979, in the Seminary in Matanzas, Cuba, to reflect on the theme "Evangelization and Politics."

The Encounter was marked by a climate of frankness, freedom of criticism, and fellowship which permitted the confrontation of different positions and points of view. We also feel stimulated by the successful efforts being made in Cuba in the construction of the Socialist Society.

The climate of search for unity in solidarity with the poor who are fighting for their liberation marked this dimension of Christian ecumenism, namely, our unity with each other and with Christ in the liberation of the oppressed.

Two important recent Christian events were a part of the Encounter: the Assembly of Protestant Churches of Latin America in Oaxtepec [Mexico] in September, 1978, and the recent III General Conference of the Latin American Episcopate in Puebla.

We are happy to see a convergence, centering on a rediscovery that the fundamental evangelizing option of liberation of the poor unites us and frees us from the many confessional barriers we have constructed. As Oaxtepec says: "The historic Subject of the unity of Christians is people, the poor of Yahweh to whom Jesus Christ announced their liberation through his death and resurrection" (Preparatory report No. 2, The Role of the Church in Latin America, I, 5).

We are stimulated to deepen our commitment to the poor and dispossessed of the earth by the affirmation of Puebla that "for Jesus, the evangelization of the poor was one of the messianic signs. For us, too, it will be a sign of evangelical authenticity" (no. 1130) and the recognition that "human promotion and its aspects of development and liberation" are an "integral part of evangelization" (no. 355).

Our faith in Jesus Christ teaches us that we are evangelized and we evangelize in the measure in which we are capable of saying truly and with deeds that the poor and meek are blessed because they possess the earth (Psalm 37:8–9, Matthew 5:3–4). Evangelization for us is centered on making this struggle come true in the name of Christ in order that the poor and dispossessed might, soon, possess the inheritance of the earth. They are the Subject of this process: "the historical overcoming of the existing power structures corresponds to the organized people, who design and struggle for new and different styles" (Oaxtepec, I, 10).

Today the dispossessed of the earth are, in a special way, that immense multitude of peoples of the dependent and underdeveloped periphery of Asia, Africa, Latin America, and the South Pacific. We have developed our theological reflection during these days from the situation and aspirations of those peoples and from their struggle to be co-participants in the evangelical promise of inheriting the earth. In the light of the contributions of the social sciences we have, "in prayer and in spiritual discernment" (Puebla, Presentation), gone deeper into the meaning of the relation between Evangelization and Politics, between the poor and their liberation through developing a power of their own.

The presence, in our encounter, of theologians from Europe and the United States brings alive the universal character of evangelization. We join Christians of all times in Jesus' prayer for the coming of his Kingdom, and so affirm the eschatological and eternal horizon of our hope. We believe that in the social-political juncture of the present, the concretion of the signs of the Kingdom are manifested in the struggles of the poor for their liberation.

The specific theme of Christian reflection on politics does not mean either the negation or the under-evaluation of other central aspects of the announcement of the good news of Jesus Christ to all peoples.

If Puebla makes "every effort to understand and denounce the mechanisms that generate poverty" (no. 1160) and combines its efforts "with those of people of good will in order to uproot poverty and create a more just and fraternal world" (no. 1161), we find ourselves in this joint effort and in the clarification of our tasks, and we offer some of the reflections out of our time together.

Biblical Meaning of the Poor

As Christians we cannot come near to the massive reality of the misery of our times—especially in the periphery—without looking for help in the Bible to understand and overcome it.

In Latin America, the new reality of a Church in solidarity with the oppressed turns us back to the Bible, but requires of us a reading from the perspective of solidarity with the poor. In the past, the dominant reading of Biblical texts—with some exceptions—was satisfied with trying to find space for the Church in a world that produced misery for others. We need a fresh, communitarian and people's reading of the Holy Scripture which generates faith in the possibility of a new world.

Our reading is focussed on the observation of the privileged place of the poor in the Bible. This springs from the two life-giving themes: Exodus and Incarnation. In the first God sends Moses to liberate the slaves from their oppressors (Ex. 3:7–10); in the second, Jesus announces through powerful works the Kingdom of God to the blind, the lame, the lepers, the harlots, the hungry and those possessed by demons (Matthew 11:2–6; Acts 10:38).

According to different Bible texts (for example, Ex. 22:20–23, Dt. 10:16–19), God manifests his justice taking the side of the orphan, of the widow, of the foreigner against their exploiters. The Bible speaks of the power of the poor saying that the God of Gods is with them. In this affirmation of the power of the poor we find a clear convergence with revolutionary theory today.

The New Testament defines solidarity as the presence and power of God with the poor. (We find a synthesis of this idea in II Cor. 8:9—"We know well the grace of our Lord Jesus Christ who, being rich, became poor for us in order that you might be enriched with his poverty.") This corrects a possible misinterpretation that would see the God of Exodus as a benefactor of the poor from a place outside history, an interpretation that raises problems of paternalism. God, according to the gospels, is one who walks with the poor, so that, together, poverty can be overcome.

This walking with the poor is also a source of conflict since the poor are exploited and have enemies who deny them power (and with it, the powerful presence of God). We discover every day that the class struggles are a reality and that the exploiters are the ones who initiate them. So we are not surprised that solidarity with the poor involves conflict as we enter the class struggle. In the gospel we read that Jesus and his disciples fought with demons, priests, and even with pious and paternalistic Pharisees.

In this situation, to accept the good news of God means to be converted—converted to God and to solidarity with the exploited in their struggle. There are some who protest: Is the gospel not for all? Is the love of God not universal? To which we respond: Yes, but as an invitation to conversion. The rich persons without paternalism will have to cast their lots with the exploited, as the Son of God did. The poor persons will have to be converted from their dreams of becoming better off without their brothers and sisters and affirm participation with the people who struggle and walk with God toward the Kingdom.

When we say that God is with the exploited in their struggles, we proclaim our faith in the fact that the decisive power of history is the power of the people ("the divine weakness is stronger than the strength of men," I Cor. 1:25). The reality of the cross reminds us that this cannot be a triumphalistic faith. Rather God struggles along with us, which means that together we will make our analyses, together we will formulate our strategies, and together we will struggle, with the confidence that the Principalities and Powers cannot prevail against us, because God is with us (Rom. 8:31–39).

Today Evangelization Comes from the Periphery

Within our societies, the poor and the oppressed are the indigenous populations, the peasants, the workers in industries and services, the collective victims of racist and sexist discrimination, the unemployed, the underemployed, and the marginalized. But all of them are thrust within societies subjected to centuries of international domination. This domination keeps the countries under forms of dependent and underdeveloped capitalism. The task of developing the power of the poor of the earth should be understood in the light of this reality.

In the last decade an increasing awareness of this situation has taken place, and the ties between the oppressed peoples have been strengthened around what the Africans have called a "terrible option": liberty at any price.

Only from the perspective of human negation caused by capitalist imperialism can one see the terrible sin hidden by affluence. Only from the perspective of the poor is it possible to see, enclosed in the wealth coming from exploitation, the negation of God in the negation of the brother. Therefore the dominated countries of the periphery are the evangelizers of the countries of the imperial centers.

Peoples in Asia, Africa, and Latin America emerge today in the global context as a peripheric force closely united in a single project of emancipation; the particularities of each continent and each country strengthen the common struggle of the oppressed peoples in terms of history, race, and culture.

Paradoxically, this periphery is now not only the protagonist of its own historic project, but also a challenge to the centers of world power and to Christians in those centers.

The exploited themselves—those privileged people to whom the gospel is addressed—are those who now socially appropriate the gospel, liberating it from the captivity and manipulation of the powerful. And now the exploited are those who are organized in small communities or organizations which are wider, and project over the country the liberating force of the original message of the gospel and show that when the poor begin to live the gospel in all its radicalness, the gospel is necessarily dangerous and subversive for the centers of domination.

Today the poor of the peoples and countries of the periphery are confronting, questioning and denouncing the Churches of the center for their accommodating themselves within the *status quo* and for their power, and they announce a future of authentic freedom for all people. This Christian experience is shared by all Christians who, from inside the powerful countries of the center, show their solidarity with the periphery, because they all experience a similar oppression and all have the same commitment to liberty.

New authentic experiences of faith have emerged out of this solidarity with the countries of the periphery, particularly as they have let the countries of the periphery evangelize them. Actions of denunciation of the economic exploitation which the underdeveloped countries suffer, actions of solidarity with the economic and political refugees and exiles, contributions to the creation of world opinion against dictators, boycotts against transnationals which exploit countries of the periphery, the struggle against attempts to revive the cold war and the spread of the arms race, efforts to eradicate racism and sexism: these and many other kinds of actions carried out in capitalist countries in favor of disarmament, justice, and peace for the oppressed peoples are other expressions of how Christians carry out evangelical tasks in all of public life. At the same time these struggles have wide possibilities of transforming and converting the very life of the Church.

Evangelization, Racism, and Sexism

Oppression and domination among human beings appear also in the form of racism and sexism. Both are expressed in a sense of superiority resulting in scorn and subordination to the other race or sex. On the American continent, within which this Encounter takes place, millions of Afro-Americans, Indians and Hispanics, especially in the United States, suffer from socio-economic conditions of exploitation reinforced by the discrimination that results from racial prejudice. Puebla saw faces of Indians and it also saw faces of Afro-Americans who live "marginalized lives in inhuman situations" and "can be considered the poorest of the poor" (no. 34).

In the origin and the foundation of the racist subordination and discrimination, there is economic exploitation. Slaves were brought to the American continent as a captive labor force. Slave traffic was one of the main sources of capitalist accumulation and slave labor was the base of the plantation economy.

Something similar happened with the conquest and submission of the Indians, and it happens today with Asiatics, Chicanos, Puerto Ricans, and other Latins in the United States. Similar actions and situations exist in other continents, for example, the treatment of foreign laborers in the rich countries of Occidental Europe.

The discrimination against women within the different societies is one of the most generalized forms of human domination. This reality cuts across the whole society but has its most dramatic expression in the dispossessed classes because of their doubly oppressed and doubly marginalized condition, as Puebla says (no. 1135). Thus women are the object of the greatest labor exploitation since they are treated as especially cheap labor hands. Women, victimized by financial need and forced by family poverty, are sexually exploited under the form of prostitution. Women, due to the "machista" cultural peculiarities which we have inherited, are frequently reduced to simple objects of sexual pleasure, decorative objects, or a means of capitalist advertising. At the same time, they are denied a presence in various spheres of life where they might fulfill their personalities.

The construction of a new society will be deeply inhuman without the presence and specific contribution of women in equality of opportunity.

Each mode of exploitation requires a legitimation. Thus the racist and sexist prejudice of the oppressors is an ideological elaboration, a false consciousness that justifies and maintains the barriers of domination. The false presuppositions of inferiority because of race or sex assimilated by the exploiters, and also by the exploited, are gradually taken for granted and perpetuate the barriers of domination artificially established. The racial and sexist ideological elaboration thus adds elements to the original social and economic factors and these elements strengthen the situation so that the false awareness is even internalized by the discriminated groups.

There is a growing awareness of this situation and the mechanisms of its perpetuation on the part of oppressed ethnic groups. At the same time they are finding a new identity through their specific struggles and their particular cultures, which have nourished resistance for long periods, and have thus continued to feed the hope of liberation denied by their socio-economic reality. This sense of racial and sexual identity among the dominated is a vigorous liberating force.

The liberating struggle to which we as Christians commit ourselves must assume as its own these forms and nuances of class exploitation. As theologians we lack the necessary understanding of this reality of which we are undeniably a part. Therefore, an intensive dialogical effort to understand the reality of racist and sexist discrimination and the importance of the cultural ethnic identities of the oppressed races is necessary.

At the same time, this understanding of the peculiarity of racist and sexist domination ought to contribute to the articulation of particularities of a common global struggle and of support for one another in the creation of an effective power for those who are dispossessed and oppressed. In this manner they will assume specific roles in one common task. The construction of a socialist society as an economic organization without exploiters or exploited, and with a culture of equality and solidarity, will underline the danger of the survival of racist and sexist pockets of discrimination, at the same time it will stimulate the cultural particularities of the ethnic groups.

As Christians we are committed to this fight, illuminating our action with the Word of God, which from the first paragraphs of Genesis until the New Testament presents an anthropological vision in which all beings are radically equal in the creative project of God. But this contribution of the churches will be neither sincere nor Christian if forms of racist or sexist domination, however subtle, endure within the churches. In this sense it is important to take seriously what was affirmed in Oaxtepec: "We should encourage the Churches of Latin America to undertake action for the training of native leaders for the administration of the Church at all levels, taking into consideration the cultural values of each ethnic group based on a cultural, social, and religious reality of the indigenous population" (Oaxtepec, VI, VIII).

On our part, we commit ourselves to this integration in the Encounters and in the reflection of the Theology of Liberation where increasingly we must perceive the presence and contribution of races and ethnic groups and women in order to find together the roots of global exploitation and build the roads towards the power of the people.

Evangelization, Power, and the State

The Christian does not accept any form of domination of persons by persons. [Translator's note: "man by man" in *Spanish* text!] In the political sphere such domination takes place precisely because the people have no power. Political power in the dominant classes is organized to ensure lack of power among the people. Political power, which is based on economic power, is one of the most complex and difficult realities to humanize. Nevertheless we must attempt to describe the evangelical orientation stemming from Jesus himself, which is to make a service out of power, and not convert it into a domination of others (Mark 10:42).

The State is the most efficient instrument of power and through it the perpetuation of existing order is sought. In the capitalist societies, the dominant classes seek to maintain an ability to plunder the people. The State has the exclusive right to the use of "legitimate violence," and presents and enforces laws in the name of the "common good." But those laws and orders fundamentally express the specific interests of the exploiting class. In order to conceal this fact, the State generates an ideology that obscures its true meaning and refuses to let us see the reality of class struggle by denying a truly human life to the oppressed. That is why the State develops welfare policies that soften the class struggle.

The economic power of the capitalist class, an all-pervading reality of social and political life, transforms the religion that accepts this alliance into a legitimizing ideological apparatus of domination, while offering in exchange a number of social privileges and support in its proselytizing task. Thus, those religions allied with the established power and the State become organs which bless and sacralize the established disorder.

In this situation, the liberating struggle continues through the creation of the people's power, consisting of the increase of their capacities, their critical consciousness, and their organization, until action on behalf of the whole society has taken place.

The alternative to this reality is the construction of a State identified with the masses and is an institutional expression of the people's movement. This means the transformation of the economic organizations and of the different aspects of societal life where workers can be generators of their own life. Although the task is complex and permanent, it is an area where Christians must commit themselves.

Christians have, in the name of the gospel, the very special task of de-legitimizing all religion—especially if it is Christian—that is identified with the oppressive State.

On the other hand we must contribute to those actions in civil life and in the churches that bring about growth of the capacity, of the consciousness, and of the alternative organization of the people and give our support to political expressions which look for such an alternative.

Likewise we must contribute to the linking of theological reflection and the social sciences with the people's causes and collaborate in this way in the developing of people's power.

Challenges and Perspectives of Evangelization

In conclusion we wish to show our global concern over the relation of evangelization with politics in the coming years. How can evangelization in relation with politics be made a reality in the different national contexts in which we find ourselves and where we have made out commitment? How can we make a real contribution to world politics?

In the first place, Christians are peace-builders in justice. The first great challenge for all persons and Churches is their contribution in an effective way to world peace in this dramatic moment in which the brutal aggression of China against Vietnam reminds us that the world is sitting on an arsenal of destructive long-range weapons, fed by ambitions of preeminence or by fear. The development and proliferation of nuclear weapons puts all life on the planet in danger. The arms race is no longer just a military and political matter, but it is essentially an economic one, which leads to the economy of the developed countries depending more and more on arms production. These industries assure a good number of jobs, and the exporting of weapons contributes to the balancing of the trade deficit. On the other hand, this commercial interest stirs up rivalries and local wars in the underdeveloped countries, and ruins their economies. This reality cannot be dismissed by any rhetoric, but it is evident that it must stimulate the imagination and initiative of Church people to contribute to the development of a world consciousness capable of translating this into concrete actions against armaments.

At the same time, the transnational corporations with the planetization of their economic decisions tend to make the peoples and even their governments into simple instruments of economic decisions ordered to assure profit. Only an alliance of political action by people and government officials can put an end to this threat.

Especially in countries of the periphery, the fundamental challenge is deep economic, social, and political impoverishment experienced by the poor who are the majority. The opulence of the countries of the center is a consequence of this poverty. Hence, when the poor gain consciousness and organize themselves, the established national and transnational powers react by enforcing "national security," which is really the security of the empire, in whose name the brutal repression by military forces is legitimized. This policy of "national security" also has its manifestations in the countries of the center.

Faced with the inability of military solutions to guarantee the stability of systems of domination, and after military governments have destroyed popular organizations, exiled some leaders, and killed or imprisoned others, the oppressors launch a policy of a "more human face." This is the direction of the trilateral policy and its encouragement of "controlled democracies" and of human rights understood only as liberal political rights that set aside the more serious and widespread violation of basic social human rights of the oppressed.

The evangelical significance of politics requires us to identify with peoples and classes subjected to this sort of manipulation and to contribute to the increase of their power.

In the developed capitalist countries, Christians must also seek to find political tasks oriented toward world peace and the dismantling of the immense capitalist economic and political apparatus erected by terrible and inhuman rationality. In countries where Socialism is being built, the Church has the permanent task of contributing to the building of the socialist society where the economics and politics are always in the hands of the people without any deviation.

Christians in these situations express their condition as children of God, their radical solidarity with men and women, and their poverty, so as not to be possessed by anything other than the love of God and of humanity. In this way their worship, their prayer, and their hope in eschatological fullness will not be alienating or justify a social disorder, but will be the expression of their genuine Christian life in the construction of the Kingdom of God, of a new heaven and a new earth where justice, unity, and peace shall reign. The concrete manifestations, historically achievable, manifest the truth of a God who is always greater, toward whom we walk insofar as we construct a new vision for the human family.

52

BLACK THEOLOGY
AND MARXIST THOUGHT*

Cornel West

Black theologians and Marxist thinkers are strangers. They steer clear of one another, each content to express concerns to their respective audiences. Needless to say, their concerns overlap. Both focus on the plight of the exploited, oppressed and degraded peoples of the world, their relative powerlessness and possible empowerment. I believe this common focus warrants a serious dialogue between Black theologians and Marxist thinkers. This dialogue should not be a mere academic chat that separates religionists and secularists, theists and atheists. Instead it ought to be an earnest encounter that specifies clearly the different sources of their praxis of faith, yet accents the possibility of mutually arrived-at political action.

The aim of this encounter is to change the world, not each other's faith; to put both groups on the offensive for structural social change, not put Black Christians on the defensive; and to enhance the quality of life of the dispossessed, not expose the empty Marxist meaning of death. In short, Black theologians and Marxist thinkers must preserve their own existential and intellectual integrity and explore the possibility of promoting fundamental social amelioration together.

Black theology and Marxist thought are not monolithic bodies of thought; each contains different perspectives, distinct viewpoints and diverse conclusions. Therefore it is necessary to identify the particular claims put forward by Black Theology and Marxist thought, those claims that distinguish both as

*I would like to extend my gratitude to my close colleagues at Union Theological Seminary, Professors James Cone and James Washington, for our provocative and fruitful discussions and conversations which bear directly on the subject matter of this essay. C.W.

Cornel West is Assistant Professor of Philosophy of Religion at Union Theological Seminary, New York City. His essay is published here for the first time.

discernible schools of thought. Black Theology claims that *(1)* the historical experience of Black people and the readings of the biblical texts that emerge from there are the centers around which reflection about God evolves; and that *(2)* this reflection is related, in some way, to the liberation of Black people, to the creation of a more abundant life definable in existential, economic, social and political terms.

Marxist thought contains two specific elements: a theory of history and an understanding of capitalism. Both are inextricably interlinked, but it may be helpful to characterize them separately.

The *Marxist theory of history* claims: *(1)* The history of human societies is the history of their transitional stages. *(2)* The transitional stages of human societies are discernible owing to their systems of production, or their organizational arrangements in which people produce goods and services for their survival. *(3)* Conflict within systems of production of human societies ultimately results in fundamental social change, or transitions from one historical stage to another. *(4)* Conflict within systems of production of human societies consists of cleavages between social classes (in those systems of production). *(5)* Social classes are historically transient, rooted in a particular set of socioeconomic conditions. *(6)* Therefore, the history of all hitherto existing society is the history of class struggles.

The *Marxist theory of capitalist society* claims: Capitalism is a historically transient system of production which requires human beings to produce commodities for the purpose of maximizing surplus value (profits). This production presupposes a fundamental social relation between the purchasers and sellers of a particular commodity, namely the labor-power (time, skill and expertise) of producers. This crucial commodity is bought by capitalists who own the land, instruments and capital necessary for production; it is sold by producers, whose labor-power is needed for production. The aim of the former is to maximize profits; that of the latter, to insure their own survival.

I shall claim that Black Theology and Marxist thought share three characteristics. *(1)* Both adhere to a similar methodology, the same way of approaching their respective subject matter and arriving at conclusions. *(2)* Both link some notion of liberation to the future socioeconomic conditions of the downtrodden. *(3)* And this is most important, both attempt to put forward trenchant critiques of liberal capitalist America. I will try to show that these three traits provide a springboard for a meaningful dialogue between Black theologians and Marxist thinkers and possibly spearhead a unifying effort for structural social change in liberal capitalist America.

Dialectical Methodology: Unmasking Falsehoods

Black theologians have either consciously or unconsciously employed a dialectical methodology in approaching their subject matter. This methodology consists of a three-step procedure of negation, preservation, and transformation; their subject matter, of White interpretations of the Christian gospel and their own circumstances. Dialectical methodology is critical in character and hermeneutic in content.[1] For Black theologians it is highly critical of dogmatic viewpoints of the gospel, questioning whether certain unjustifiable prejudgments are operative. It is hermeneutic in that it is concerned with unearthing assumptions of particular interpretations and presenting an understanding of the gospel that extends and expands its ever unfolding truth.

Black theologians have, for the most part, been compelled to adopt a dialectical methodology. They have refused to accept what has been given to them by White theologians: they have claimed that all reflection about God by Whites must be digested, decoded and deciphered. The first theological formulations by Afro-Americans based on biblical texts tried to come to terms with their White owners' viewpoints and their own servitude. Since its inception, Black theologians have been forced to reduce White deception and distortion of the gospel and make the Christian story meaningful in light of their oppressive conditions.

Black theological reflection begins by negating White interpretations of the gospel, continues by preserving its own perceived truths of the biblical texts, and ends by transforming past understandings of the gospel into new and novel ones. These three steps embody an awareness of the social context of theologizing, the need to accent the historical experience of Black people and the insights of the Bible, and the ever evolving task of recovering, regaining and repeating the gospel.

Black theologians underscore the importance of the social context of theological reflection.[2] Their dialectical methodology makes them sensitive to the hidden agendas of theological formulations they negate, agendas often guided by social interests. Their penchant for revealing distortions leads them to adopt a sociology of knowledge-approach that stresses the way in which particular viewpoints endorse and encourage ulterior aims.

An interpretation of the Black historical experience and the readings of the biblical texts that emerge out of this experience constitute the raw ingredients for the second step of Black theological reflection. By trying to understand the plight of Black people in light of the Bible, Black theologians claim to preserve the biblical truth that God sides with the oppressed and acts on their behalf.[3] Subsequently, the Black historical experience and the biblical texts form a symbiotic relationship, each illuminating the other.

Since Black theologians believe in the living presence of God and the work of the Holy Spirit, they acknowledge the constant unfolding process of the gospel. Paradoxically, the gospel is unchanging, yet it is deepened by embracing and encompassing new human realities and experiences. The gospel must speak to every age. Therefore it must be recovered and repeated, often sounding different, but, in substance, remaining the same. For Black theologians, it sounds different because it addresses various contexts of oppression; it remains the same because it is essentially a gospel of liberation.

Marxist thinkers, like Black theologians, employ a dialectical methodology in approaching their subject matter. But they do so consciously and their subject matter is bourgeois theories about capitalist society. The primary theoretical task of Marxist thinkers is to uncover the systematic misunderstanding of capitalist society by bourgeois thinkers; to show how this misunderstanding, whether deliberate or not, supports and sanctions exploitation and oppression in this society; and to put forward the correct understanding of this society in order to change it.

Marxist social theory is first and foremost a critique of inadequate theories of capitalist society and subsequently a critique of capitalist society itself. The subtitle of Marx's magnum opus, *Capital*, is "A Critique of Political Economy," not "A Critique of Capitalism." This work takes bourgeois economists to task for perpetuating falsehoods, and results in revealing the internal dynamics of capitalism and their inhumane consequences. For Marx, a correct understanding of capitalist society is possible only by overcoming present mystifications of it; and this correct understanding is requisite for a propitious political praxis.

Marxist thought stresses the conflict-laden unfolding of history, the conflict-producing nature of social processes. Therefore it is not surprising that Marxist thinkers employ a dialectical methodology, a methodology deeply suspicious of stasis and stability, and highly skeptical of equilibrium and equipoise. This methodology, like that of Black theologians, is critical in character and hermeneutic in content. It is critical of perspectives presented by bourgeois social scientists, questioning whether certain ideological biases are operative. It is hermeneutic in that it is obsessed with discovering correct understanding underneath wrong interpretations, disclosing latent truths behind manifest distortions. For Marx, to be scientific is to be dialectical and to be dialectical is to unmask, unearth, bring to light.[4]

This conception of science, derived from Hegel, attempts to discern the hidden kernel of an evolving truth becoming manifest by bursting through a visible husk. The husk, once a hidden kernel, dissolves, leaving its indelible imprint upon the new emerging kernel. This idea of inquiry highlights the moments of negation, preservation and transformation. By presenting his theory of history and society from this perspective, Marx provided the most powerful and penetrating social criticism in modern times. Dialectical methodology enabled him to create a whole mode of inquiry distinctively his own, though often appearing hermetic and rigid to the untutored and fanatic.

Despite the similar procedure Black theologians and Marxist thinkers share, there has been little discussion about it between them. This is so primarily because a dialectical methodology is implicit, undeveloped and often unnoticed in Black Theology. This failure to examine the methodological stance embodied in Black theological reflection obscures its similarity with that of Marxist thought.

Liberation: Its Constitutive Elements

Black theologians all agree that Black liberation has something to do with ameliorating the socioeconomic conditions of Black people. But it is not clear what this amelioration amounts to. There is little discussion in their writings about what the liberating society will look like. The notion and process of liberation is often mentioned, but, surprisingly, one is hard put to find a sketch of what liberation would actually mean in the everyday lives of Black people, what power they would possess, and what resources they would have access to.

There are two main reasons for this neglect among Black theologians. First, a dialectical methodology discourages discussions about the ideal society and simply what ought to be. Instead, it encourages criticizing and overcoming existing society, negating and opposing what is.

The second reason, the one with which we shall be concerned in this section, is the failure of Black theologians to talk specifically about the way in which the existing system of production and social structure relates to Black oppression and exploitation. Without focusing on this relation, it becomes extremely difficult to present an idea of liberation with socioeconomic content. In short, the lack of a clear-cut social theory prevents the emergence of any substantive political program or social vision.

Except for the latest writings of James Cone, Black theologians remain uncritical of America's imperialist presence in Third World countries, its capitalist system of production, and its grossly unequal distribution of wealth. Therefore we may assume they find this acceptable. If this is so, then the political and socioeconomic components of Black liberation amount to racial equality before the law; equal opportunities in employment, education and business; and economic parity with Whites in median income.

Surely this situation would be better than the current dismal one. But it hardly can be viewed as Black liberation. It roughly equates liberation with American middle-class status, leaving the unequal distribution of wealth relatively untouched and the capitalist system of production, along with its imperialist ventures, intact. Liberation would consist of including Black people within the mainstream of liberal capitalist America. If this is the social vision of Black theologians, they should drop the meretricious and flamboyant term "liberation" and adopt the more accurate and sober word "inclusion."

Marxist thought, like Black Theology, does not elaborate on the ideal society. As we noted earlier, a dialectical methodology does not permit this elaboration. But the brief sketch Marxist thinkers provide requires a particular system of production and political arrangement: namely, participatory democracy in each. Human liberation occurs only when people participate substantively in the decision-making processes in the major institutions that regulate their lives. Democratic control over the institutions in the productive and political processes in order for them to satisfy human needs and protect personal liberties of the populace constitutes human liberation.

Marxist thinkers are able to present this sketch of human liberation primarily because they stress what people must liberate themselves *from*. They suggest what liberation is for only after understanding the internal dynamics of the society people must be liberated from. Without this clear-cut social theory about what *is*, it is difficult to say anything significant about what *can be*. The possibility of liberation is found only within the depths of the actuality of oppression. Without an adequate social theory, this possibility is precluded.

Social Criticism: Class, Race, and Culture

Black Theology puts forward a vehement, often vociferous, critique of liberal capitalist America. One of its most attractive and alluring characteristics is its theological indictment of racist American society. An undisputable claim of Black Theology is America's unfair treatment of Black people. What is less apparent is the way in which Black theologians understand the internal dynamics of liberal capitalist America, how it functions, why it operates the way it does, who possesses substantive power, and where it is headed. As noted earlier, Black theologians do not utilize a social theory that relates the oppression of Black people to the overall make-up of America's system of production, foreign policy, political arrangement, and cultural practices.

Black theologians hardly mention the wealth, power, and influence of multinational corporations that monopolize production in the marketplace and prosper partially owing to their dependence on public support in the form of government subsidies, free technological equipment, lucrative contracts and sometimes even direct-transfer payments. Black theologians do not stress the way in which corporate interests and the government intermesh, usually resulting in policies favorable to the former. Black theologians fail to highlight the fact that in liberal capitalist America one-half of 1 percent own 22 percent of the wealth, 1 percent own 33 percent of the wealth, the lower 61 percent own only 7 percent of the wealth, and the bottom 45 percent own only 2 percent of the wealth.[5] Lastly, Black theologians do not emphasize sufficiently the way in which the racist interpretations of the gospel they reject encourage and support the capitalist system of production, its grossly unequal distribution of wealth and its closely connected political arrangements.

Instead of focusing on these matters, Black theologians draw attention to the racist practices in American society. Since these practices constitute the most visible and vicious form of oppression in America, Black theologians justifiably do so. Like the Black Power proponents of the sixties, they call for the empowerment of Black people, the need for Black people to gain significant control over their lives. But neither Black Power proponents nor Black theologians have made it sufficiently clear as to what constitutes this Black control, the real power to direct institutions such that Black people can live free of excessive exploitation and oppression. The tendency is to assume that middle-class status is equivalent to such control, that a well-paying job amounts to such power. And surely this assumption is fallacious.

The important point here is not that racist practices should be stressed less by Black theologians, for such practices deeply affect Black people and shape their perceptions of American society. What is crucial is that these practices must be linked to the role they play in buttressing the current mode of production, concealing the unequal distribution of wealth, and portraying the lethargy of the political system. Black theologians are correct to relate racist practices to degrees of Black powerlessness, but they obscure this relation by failing to provide a lucid definition of what power is in American society. Subsequently, they often fall into the trap of assuming power in American society to be synonymous with receiving high wages.

Marxist social criticism can be quite helpful at this point. For Marx, power in modern industrial society consists of a group's participation in the decision-making processes of the major institutions that affect their destinies. Since institutions of production, such as multinational corporations, play an important role in people's lives, these institutions should be significantly accountable to the populace. In short, they should be democratically controlled by the citizenry; people should participate in their decision-making processes. Only collective control over the major institutions of society constitutes genuine power on behalf of the people.

For Marx, power in modern industrial society is closely related to a group's say over what happens to products produced in the work situation, to a group's input into decisions that direct the production flow of goods and services. The most powerful group in society has the most say and input into decisions over this production flow; the least powerful group does not participate at all in such decisions. In liberal capitalist America, the former consists of multiple corporate owners who dictate policies concerning the mass production of a variety of products produced by white- and blue-collar workers who receive wages in return. The latter consists of the so-called underclass, the perennially unemployed, who are totally removed from the work situation, precluded from any kind of input affecting the production flow, including negotiation and strikes available to white- and blue-collar workers.

Racist practices intensify the degree of powerlessness among Black people. This is illustrated by the high rates of Black unemployment, the heavy Black concentration in low-paying jobs, and inferior housing, education, police protection and health care. But it is important to note that this powerlessness differs from that of white- and blue-collar workers in degree, not in kind. In human terms, this difference is immense, incalculable; in structural terms, this difference is negligible, trifling. In other words, most

Americans are, to a significant degree, powerless. They have no substantive control over their lives, little participation in the decision-making process of the major institutions that regulate their lives. Among Afro-Americans, this powerlessness is exacerbated, creating an apparent qualitative difference in oppression.

This contrast of the social criticism of Black theologians and Marxist thinkers raises the age-old question as to whether class position or racial status is the major determinant of Black oppression in America. This question should be formulated in the following way: Does class position or racial status contribute more to the fundamental form of powerlessness in America?

Racial status contributes greatly to Black oppression. But Black middle-class people are essentially well-paid white- or blue-collar workers who have little control over their lives primarily owing to their class position, not racial status. This is so because the same limited control is held by White middle-class people, despite the fact that a higher percentage of whites are well-paid white- and blue-collar workers than Blacks. Significant degrees of powerlessness pertain to most Americans and this could be so only if class position determines such powerlessness. Therefore, class position contributes more than racial status to the basic form of powerlessness in America.

I am suggesting that the more Black theologians discard or overlook Marxist social criticism, the further they distance themselves from the fundamental determinant of Black oppression and any effective strategy to alleviate it.[6] This distancing also obscures the direct relation of Black oppression in America to Black and Brown oppression in Third World countries. The most powerful group in America, those multiple corporate owners who dictate crucial corporate policies over a variety of production flows, are intimately and inextricably linked (through their highly paid American and Third World white-collar workers and grossly underpaid Third World blue-collar workers) to the economies and governments of Third World countries, including the most repressive ones. Marxist social criticism permits this relation to come to light in an extremely clear and convincing way.

The social criticism of Black theologians reflects the peculiar phenomenon of American liberal and radical criticism. This criticism rarely has viewed class position as a major determinant of oppression primarily owing to America's lack of a feudal past, the heterogeneity of its population, the many and disparate regions of its geography, and the ever increasing levels of productivity and growth. These facts make it difficult to see class divisions; indeed, along with other forms of oppression, they make it almost impossible to see the divisions. But, like protons leaving vapor trails in a cloud chamber, one is forced to posit these class divisions in light of the overwhelming evidence for their existence. Only class divisions can explain the gross disparity between rich and poor, the immense benefits accruing to the former and the depravity of the latter.

Region, sex, age, ethnicity, and race often have been considered the only worthy candidates as determinants of oppression. This has been so primarily because American liberal and radical criticism usually has presupposed the existing system of production, assumed class divisions and attempted to include only marginal groups in the mainstream of liberal capitalist America. This criticism has fostered a petit-bourgeois viewpoint that clamors for a bigger piece of the ever growing American pie, rarely asking fundamental questions such as why it never gets recut more equally or how it gets baked in the first place. In short, this criticism remains silent about class divisions, the crucial role they play in maintaining the unequal distribution of goods and services, and how they undergird discrimination against regions, impose ceilings on upward social mobility and foster racism, sexism and ageism. With the exception of the most recent writings of James Cone, contemporary Black theologians suffer from this general myopia of American liberal and radical criticism.

Despite this shortsightedness, Black theologians have performed an important service for Marxist thinkers, namely emphasizing the ways in which culture and religion resist oppression. They have been admirably sensitive to the Black cultural buffers against oppression, especially the Black religious sources of struggle and strength, vitality and vigor. They also have stressed the indispensable contribution the Black churches have made toward the survival, dignity and self-worth of Black people.

Contrary to Marxist thinkers, Black theologians recognize that cultural and religious attitudes, values, and sensibilities have a life and logic of their own, not fully accountable in terms of a class analysis. Subsequently, racist practices are not reducible to a mere clever and successful strategy of divide-and-conquer promoted by the ruling class to prevent proletarian unity. Rather, racism is an integral element within the very fabric of American culture and society. It is embedded in the country's first collective self-definition; enunciated in its subsequent laws; and imbued in its dominant way of life.

The orthodox Marxist analysis of culture and religion that simply relates racist practices to misconceived material interests is only partially true, hence deceptive and misleading. These practices are fully comprehensible only if one conceives of culture, not as a mere hoax played by the ruling class on workers, but as the tradition that informs one's conception of tradition, as social practices that shape one's idea of social practice.

The major objection to the orthodox Marxist analysis of culture and religion is not that it is wrong, but that it is too narrow, rigid and dogmatic. It views popular culture and religion only as instruments of domination, vehicles of pacification. It sees only their negative and repressive elements. On this view, only enlightenment, reason, or clarity imposed from the outside can break through the cultural layers of popular false consciousness.[7] Therefore, the orthodox Marxist anlaysis refuses to acknowledge the positive, liberating aspects of popular culture and religion, and their potential for fostering structural social change.

This issue is at the heart of the heated debate over the adequacy of a

Marxist analysis between Black theologians and Latin American liberation theologians. The latter tend to adopt the orthodox Marxist view, paying little attention to the positive, liberating aspects of popular culture and religion.[8] They display a contempt for popular culture and religion, a kind of tacit condescension that reeks of paternalism and elitism. They often speak of the poor possessing a privileged access to truth and reality, but rarely do they take seriously the prevailing beliefs, values or outlooks of the poor. Instead, Latin American liberation theologians stress the discontinuity and radical rupture of progressive consciousness with popular culture and religion, suggesting a desire to wipe the cultural slate clean and begin anew.

To the contrary, Black theologians recognize the positive and negative elements, the liberating and repressive possibilities, of popular culture and religion. To no one's surprise, they devote much attention to the armors of survival, forms of reaction, and products of response created by Black people in order to preserve their dignity and self-respect.[9] Black theologians view themselves as working within a tradition of political struggle and cultural and religious resistance to oppression. They emphasize their continuity with this tradition.

It is possible to account for this important difference between Black theologians and Latin American liberation theologians by appealing to the different histories of the particular countries about which they theorize. But there is possibly a deeper reason for this disagreement. It relates directly to the composition of the two groups of theologians.

For the most part, Latin American liberation theologians belong to the dominant cultural group in their respective countries. As intellectuals educated in either European schools or Europeanized Latin American universities and seminaries, they adopt cosmopolitan habits and outlooks.[10] Like their theoretical master, Karl Marx, a true cosmopolitan far removed from his indigenous Jewish culture, they tend to see popular culture and religion as provincial and parochial. It is something to be shed and ultimately discarded, replaced by something qualitatively different and better. They do not seem to have encountered frequently situations in which they were forced to rely on their own indigenous cultural and religious resources in an alien and hostile environment. So their own experiences often limit their capacity to see the existential richness and radical potential of popular culture and religion.

In contrast to this, Black theologians belong to the degraded cultural group in the United States. As intellectuals trained in American colleges, universities and seminaries, they have first-hand experiences of cultural condescension, arrogance and haughtiness. They know what it is like to be a part of a culture considered to be provincial and parochial. Hence they view Black culture and religion as something to be preserved and promoted, improved and enhanced, not erased and replaced. In short, Black theologians acknowledge their personal debts to Black culture and religion, and incorporate its fecundity and fertility in their understanding of American society.

Latin American liberation theologians and Black theologians can learn from each other on this matter. The former must be more sensitive to the complexities and ambiguities of popular culture and religion; the latter should more closely relate their view of Black culture and religion to a sophisticated notion of power in liberal capitalist America. And both can learn from the most penetrating Marxist theorist of culture in this century, Antonio Gramsci.[11]

Gramsci provides a valuable framework in which to understand culture, its autonomous activity and status, while preserving its indirect yet crucial link with power in society. Unlike the Latin American liberation theologians, he does not downplay the importance of popular culture; unlike the Black theologians, he does not minimize the significance of class. Instead, he views the systems of production and culture in a symbiotic relationship with one another, each containing intense tension, struggle and even warfare. Class struggle is not simply the battle between capitalists and proletariat, owners and producers, in the work situation. It also takes the form of cultural and religious conflict over which attitudes, values and beliefs will dominate the thought and behavior of people. For Gramsci, this incessant conflict is crucial. It contains the key to structural social change; it is the springboard for a revolutionary political praxis.

According to Gramsci, no state and society can be sustained by force alone. It must put forward convincing and persuasive reasons, arguments, ideologies or propaganda for its continued existence. A state and society require not only military protection, but also principled legitimation. This legitimation takes place in the cultural and religious spheres, in those arenas where the immediacy of everyday life is felt, outlooks are formed, and self-images adopted.

Gramsci deepens Marx's understanding of the legitimation process by replacing the notion of ideology with his central concept of hegemony. For Marx, ideology is the set of formal ideas and beliefs promoted by the ruling class for the purpose of preserving its privileged position in society; for Gramsci, hegemony is the set of formal ideas and beliefs and informal modes of behavior, habits, manners, sensibilities and outlooks that support and sanction the existing order.

In Gramsci's view, culture is both tradition and current practices. Tradition is understood, not as the mere remnants of the past or the lingering, inert elements in the present but, rather, as active formative and transformative modalities of a society. Current practices are viewed as actualizations of particular modalities, creating new habits, sensibilities and world-views against the pressures and limits of the dominant ones.

A hegemonic culture subtly and effectively encourages people to identify themselves with the habits, sensibilities, and world-views supportive of the status quo and the class interests that dominate it. It is a culture successful in persuading people to "consent" to their oppression and exploitation. A hegemonic culture survives and thrives as long as it convinces people to adopt its preferred formative modality, its favored socialization process. It begins to crumble when people start to opt for a transformative modality, a socialization process that opposes the dominant one. The latter constitutes a counter-hegemonic culture, the deeply embedded oppositional elements within a society. It is these elements that the hegemonic culture seeks to contain and control.

Based on the insights of Gramsci, along with those of the distinguished English cultural critic Raymond Williams, I shall present a theoretical framework that may be quite serviceable to Black theologians, Latin American liberation theologians, and Marxist thinkers.[12] Cultural processes can be understood in light of four categories: hegemonic, pre-hegemonic, neo-hegemonic, and counter-hegemonic.

Hegemonic culture is to be viewed as the effectively operative dominant world-views, sensibilities, and habits that sanction the established order. Pre-hegemonic culture consists of those residual elements of the past which continue to shape and mold thought and behavior in the present; it often criticizes hegemonic culture, harking back to a golden age in the pristine past. Neo-hegemonic culture constitutes a new phase of hegemonic culture; it postures as an oppositional force, but, in substance, is a new manifestation of people's allegiance and loyalty to the status quo. Counter-hegemonic culture represents genuine opposition to hegemonic culture; it fosters an alternative set of habits, sensibilities, and world-views that cannot possibly be realized within the perimeters of the established order.

This framework presupposes three major points. First, it accents the equivocal character of culture and religion, their capacity to be instruments of freedom or domination, vehicles of liberation or pacification. Second, it focuses on the ideological function of culture and religion, the necessity of their being either forces for freedom or forces for domination, for liberation or for pacification. Third, it views the struggle between these two forces as open-ended. The only guarantee of freedom rests upon the contingencies of human practice; the only assurance of liberation relies on the transformative modalities of a society. No matter how wide the scope of hegemonic culture may be, it never encompasses or exhausts all human practice or every transformative modality in a society. Human struggle is always a possibility in any society and culture.

In order to clarify further my four categories, I shall identify them crudely with particular elements in contemporary American society. Hegemonic culture can be seen as the prevailing Horatio Alger mystique, the widespread hopes and dreams for social upward mobility among Americans. This mystique nourishes the values, outlooks, and lifestyles of achievement, careerism, leisurism, and consumerism that pervade American culture. Pre-hegemonic culture is negligible owing to the country's peculiar inception, namely, that it was "born liberal." Subsequently, American conservatives and reactionaries find themselves in the ironic position of quarreling with liberals by defending early versions of liberalism. Neo-hegemonic culture is best illustrated by the counter-cultural movement of the sixties, specifically the protests of White middle-class youth (spin-offs of the Black political struggles) which, with few exceptions, was effectively absorbed by the mainstream of liberal capitalist America. The continuous creation of a counter-hegemonic culture is manifest in the multifarious, though disparate, radical grass-roots organizations; elements of the socialist feminist groups; and aspects of Afro-American culture and religion.

A present challenge confronting Black theologians is to discover and discern what aspects of Afro-American culture and religion can contribute to a counter-hegemonic culture in American society. They may find Gramsci's conception of organic intellectuals helpful on this matter.[13] Gramsci views organic intellectuals as leaders and thinkers directly tied to a particular cultural group primarily by means of institutional affiliations. Organic intellectuals combine theory and action, and relate popular culture and religion to structural social change.

Black religious leadership can make an enormous contribution to a counter-hegemonic culture and structural social change in American society. Black preachers and pastors are in charge of the most numerous and continuous gatherings of Black people, those who are the worst victims of liberal capitalist America and whose churches are financially, culturally and politically independent of corporate influence.[14] This freedom of Black preachers and pastors, unlike that of most Black professionals, is immense. They are the leaders of the only major institutions in the Black community that are not accountable to the status quo. Needless to say, many abuse this freedom. But what is important to note is that the contribution of Black religious leaders can be prodigious, as exemplified by the great luminaries of the past, including Nat Turner, Martin Delany, Martin Luther King, Jr., and Malcolm X.

An Alliance of Black Theology and Marxist Thought: The Case of Reverend George Washington Woodbey

The best example of a Black religious thinker and leader who combined the insights of Black theological reflection and Marxist social theory was the Rev. George Washington Woodbey.[15] He devoted his life to promoting structural social change and creating a counter-hegemonic culture in liberal capitalist America.

Rev. Mr. Woodbey was a Baptist preacher, for many years pastor of Mt. Zion Baptist Church in San Diego, California, and a major socialist leader in the first few decades of this century. He was uncompromising in his religious faith, unyielding in his confidence in the radical potential of Black culture and religion, and unrelenting in his devotion to fundamental social change. Widely known in California during his day as "The Great Negro Socialist Orator," Woodbey delivered poignant yet incisive lectures across the country, including his famous reply to Booker T. Washington's "Capitalist Argument for the Negro." Woodbey also wrote books such as *The Bible and Socialism: A Conversation between Two Preachers* (1904) and *The Distribution of Wealth* (1910), and such essays as "Why the Negro Should Vote the Socialist Ticket" (1908) and "Why the Socialists Must Reach the Churches with Their Message" (1915).[16]

Woodbey's most influential work, *What to Do and How to Do It or Socialism vs. Capitalism* (1903) was translated into three languages. It was often compared to Robert Blatchford's *Merrie England*, the most widely read Socialist educational publication at the turn of the century.

Woodbey's important work consists of a conversation between himself and his mother, taking place after a long separation. She begins with the question, "Have you given up the Bible and the ministry and gone into politics?" He replies that he became a Socialist precisely because of his strict adherence to principles put forward in the Bible. She then points out that many of his comrades do not believe in God or in biblical truths. He reminds her that other political parties, such as the Republican and Democratic parties, have their equal portion of nonbelievers. He assures her that he does not fully agree with some of his comrades on religious matters, but since Socialism is "a scheme for bettering things here first," he can be a Socialist without giving up his religious beliefs. He then states that, under Socialism, religious freedom will be guaranteed.

Later on, the mother asks, "Like all other women, I want to know where are we to come in?" He answers that it is in the interest of "the women, more than the men, if possible, to be Socialists because they suffer more from capitalism than anyone else." Under Socialism, each woman will receive her own income and be an equal shareholder in the industries of the country. Under these conditions, there will be no need for a woman to "sell herself through a so-called marriage to someone she did not love, in order to get a living"; instead, she could marry for genuine love. In capitalist society, a working man is a slave, "and his wife is the slave of a slave." Therefore liberation of both would enhance the position of women more than that of men. This conversation ends with the mother's conversion to Socialism, and she comments,

> Well, you have convinced me that I am about as much a slave now as I was in the south, and I am ready to accept any way out of this drudgery.

Rev. Mr. Woodbey was the only Black delegate to the Socialist Party conventions of 1904 and 1908. In the latter convention, he was nominated as Eugene Debs's running mate in the presidential election of 1908. He was once described as "the greatest living negro in America. . . . his style is simple and his logic invincible. He knows the race question, and one of his most popular lectures relates to the settlement of this vexed question under Socialism."

Jailed frequently, hospitalized more than once owing to police brutality, barely escaping murder during the famous 1912 Free Speech fight in San Diego, Rev. Mr. Woodbey was a devoted Christian who sacrificed greatly for fostering a counter-hegemonic culture and promoting structural social change in liberal capitalist America. He was a man of inexorable Christian faith, anchored deep in the best of Black culture and religion, and of intransigent Socialist conviction. His life and writings best exemplify the point at which Black theologians and Marxist thinkers are no longer strangers.

Notes

1. Dialectical methodology is a complex procedure useful for grasping, comprehending, interpreting, explaining or predicting phenomena. Aside from the foundation laid by Plato, this procedure was first fully developed by Hegel and deepened by Marx. Hegel's most succinct discussions of this approach can be found in his *Logic* (Part 1, *Encyclopedia of Philosophical Sciences*), trans. William Wallace (Oxford, 1975), no. 81, pp. 115-119, and *The Phenomenology of Mind*, trans. J. B. Baillie (New York, 1967), pp. 80ff. For Marx's brief formal presentation of this approach as it relates to his social theory, see *The Grundrisse*, trans. Martin Nicolaus (New York, 1973), pp. 83-111.

2. The most explicit and extensive treatment of this matter by a Black theologian is found in James Cone's *God of the Oppressed* (New York, 1975), chap. 3, pp. 39-61.

3. The most sophisticated dialogue among Black theologians has focused on the status of this biblical truth. William Jones has claimed that Black theologians do not provide sufficient empirical evidence to warrant this truth. He suggests that Black theologians have not taken seriously the possibility of a malevolent deity. For Jones, an acceptable Black Theology must deal adequately with the problem of theodicy. James Cone has responded to Jones's argument by claiming that Jesus' victory over suffering and death constitutes the necessary and sufficient evidence for the belief that God sides with the oppressed and acts on their behalf. In short, Cone holds that empirical evidence is never a reliable basis of a biblical truth; the problem of theodicy is never solved in a theoretical manner, only defeated by one's faith in Jesus Christ. For Jones's incisive and insightful discussion, see his *Is God a White Racist?* (Garden City, N.Y., 1973). For Cone's reply, see his *God of the Oppressed*, op. cit., pp. 187-194.

4. This conception of science pervades Marx's mature writings. For example, he states, "But all science would be superfluous if the outward appearance and the essence of things directly coincided." *Capital*, ed. Friedrich Engels (New York, 1967), vol. 3, p. 817. Notice also the demystifying aim of theory in the first few paragraphs of the famous section 4, entitled, "The Fetishism of Commodities and the Secret Thereof" of chap. 1 in *Capital*, vol. 1, pp. 71ff.

5. These figures come from the nearest thing to an official survey on the maldistribution of wealth in America, conducted by the Federal Reserve Board in 1962. As one of its authors, Herman Miller, noted, "the figures were so striking as to obviate the need to search for trends." For further exposition and elaboration on this study, see "The Other Economy: America's Working Poor," Gus Tyler, *The New Leader* (Special Issue), May 8, 1978, pp. 20-24.

6. I have tried to give persuasive reasons as to why this is so for any viewpoint which overlooks class oppression, in my paper, "Institutional Racism, Liberalism, and Self-Determination" (to be published in the Fall 1979 issue of *The Journal of Religious Ethics*).

7. This point illustrates the undeniable link of the orthodox Marxist view to the Enlightenment. More specifically, it portrays the inherent elitism and paternalism of such a view. We need only recall Lenin's well-known claim (in *What Is to Be Done?*) that the working class can achieve only trade-union consciousness on its own, thereby requiring a vanguard party to elevate it to revolutionary consciousness. For Lenin, this party brings enlightenment to the benighted proletariat.

8. This view is illustrated clearly in an essay by José Míguez Bonino, a leading Latin American liberation theologian, entitled "Popular Piety in Latin America," in which he states, "From a theological as well as a political perspective the popular piety that used to exist and that still predominates in Latin America can only be considered as a profoundly alienated and alienating

piety, a manifestation of an enslaved consciousness and, at the same time, a ready instrument for the continuation and consolidation of oppression. The intent to transform the mobilizing power of that piety to goals of transformation without radically altering the very content of the religious consciousness seems psychologically impossible and theologically unacceptable." This essay appeared in *Cristianismo y Sociedad* (Buenos Aires), no. 47 (first issue, 1976), pp. 31-38, trans. James and Margaret Goff. Gustavo Gutiérrez, another prominent Latin American liberation theologian, understands popular culture and religion in a more subtle and sophisticated way. I base this judgment on my cordial and provocative discussions with him during his visiting professorship at Union Theological Seminary in the fall of 1977. It seems to me his own cultural roots and his serious study of cultural Marxist thinkers, especially Antonio Gramsci and José Carlos Mariátegui (the father of Latin American Marxism) principally account for his sensitivity to popular culture and religion.

9. This serious concern of Black theologians and religious scholars is exemplifed best by Charles H. Long's highly suggestive essay, "Perspectives for a Study of Afro-American Religion in the United States," *History of Religions*, vol. 2, no. 1 (August 1977), pp. 54-66; Gayraud S. Wilmore's solid study, *Black Religion and Black Radicalism* (Garden City, N.Y., 1972), esp. pp. 298-306; and James Cone's speculative work, *The Spirituals and the Blues* (New York, 1972). The "armors, forms, and products" of Afro-American culture I have in mind here are the spirituals, blues, gospels, jazz, folktales and sermons. What is not sufficiently emphasized by Black theologians, religious scholars or cultural critics is the radical potential embedded within the style of these art-forms. The most important aspect of them is not what is conveyed, but *how* this "what" is conveyed. It is this "how" which bears the imprint of struggle and constitutes the distinctive imposition of order on chaos by Black people. It is this "how," or style, that contains the real message or genuine content of these works of art. To my knowledge, only the essays of Ralph Ellison and Albert Murray explore this frontier of Afro-American art-forms.

10. This point is best illustrated by the words of Hugo Assmann, one of the most radical Latin American theologians. "In my opening address I was sometimes aggressive because, as a Westernized Latin American, I don't feel at ease with my colour, my 'gringo' face, my German origin. I don't feel happy with the fact that my theological dissertation was written in German. I have a psychological necessity to say to you in Western language that I am not Western. We Latin Americans are still in the early stages of our search for a Latin American identity. If you look in my library you will find books by German authors, French authors, Italian authors, Marx, Moltmann, etc. There is something false in this, . . . something which is not Latin American." This quote is from the publication *Risk*, which is based on the Symposium on Black Theology and Latin American Theology of Liberation, May 1973 at the Ecumenical Center in Geneva, Switzerland, p. 62; see Document 47 above.

11. It is not surprising that Gramsci comes from a degraded cultural region in Italy, namely Sardinia, and had intense experiences of ostracism owing to his hunchback, poor health and short height (he was barely five feet tall). A sample of his writings can be found in *Selections from the Prison Notebooks*, trans. and ed. Quintin Hoare and Geoffrey Nowell Smith (New York, 1971).

12. The book by Raymond Williams I have in mind is his *Marxism and Literature* (London, 1977), esp. chap. 2, pp. 75-141.

13. Gramsci discusses this conception in his seminal essay, "The Intellectuals," *Selections from the Prison Notebooks*, op. cit., pp. 5-23. Although he completely misunderstands the nature of the radical potential of Afro-American culture and Afro-American intellectuals, this does not harm his theoretical formulation of the notion of organic intellectuals.

14. I should add that this also holds to an important degree for White poor and Hispanic Pentecostal churches.

15. My information about this fascinating Black preacher comes directly from Philip Foner's timely essay, "Reverend George Washington Woodbey: Early Twentieth Century California Black Socialist," *The Journal of Negro History*, vol. 61, no. 2 (April 1976). For Foner's treatment of Woodbey along with other Black Socialist preachers in the United States, including the Reverends George W. Slater, Jr., S. C. Garrison and George Frazier Miller, see his monumental work, *American Socialism and Black Americans: From the Age of Jackson to World War II* (Westport, Conn., 1977), chap. 7, pp. 151-181.

16. It is interesting to note that the first book mentioned here was dedicated to "the Preachers and Members of the Churches, and all others who are interested in knowing what the Bible teaches on the question at issue between the Socialists and the Capitalists, by one who began preaching twenty-nine years ago, and still continues."

53

THE BLACK EXPERIENCE OF THE EXODUS

Choan-Seng Song

The experience of the exodus does become alive and real for the black people in the United States. In order to bring this experience to the level of articulate consciousness for the black people in general, black theologians have exploited the biblical theme of the exodus to the full. To many of them, the exodus is the greatest event in the whole message of the Bible which has closest and most relevant bearings on their situation today in America. They, therefore, not only attempt to interpret the Bible in the light of the theme of the exodus but also to weave it into the texture of black consciousness. For them, God is the God of the exodus from the house of bondage in Egypt in the historical sense. At the same time, God is the God who stands on their side in their struggle to be liberated from white oppression. Hence, they see a remarkable parallel between the people of Israel in ancient days and the black people in twentieth century America. It is very seldom that we see a biblical theme so closely linked with an existential situation as this one. For those who are interested in the problem of theological hermeneutics, black theology provides a case study. But this is not our principal concern here. Our chief interest here is to examine the meaning of the black experience of liberation on the basis of the mission of the exodus. . . .

The black theologian most articulate in relating the biblical experience of the exodus to the experience of the black people in America is James Cone. For him, theology is "that discipline which seeks to analyze the nature of the Christian faith in the light of the oppressed."[1] Such a definition of theology is quite a departure from the traditional approach to the exposition of the contents of Christian faith. In traditional theology the condition of man to

Choan-Seng Song is Associate Director, Commission on Faith and Order, World Council of Churches.

This essay is an excerpt from Song's book *Christian Mission in Reconstruction: An Asian Attempt* (Madras: Christian Literature Society, 1975 and Maryknoll, N.Y.: Orbis Books, 1977).

which Christian faith addresses itself is that of sin. It is the sinful nature of man that constitutes the main burden of the message of salvation. Consequently, the doctrine of sin occupies a central place in the Christian understanding of man. When such a theological understanding of the nature of man is translated into the practical aspect of religious life, asceticism, moralism or puritanism becomes a predominant feature in the practice of Christian faith. The history of the Christian church gives us ample examples of how one-sided emphasis on the sinful state of man may be carried to the extremes of legalism. Instead of enjoying new found freedom in the love of God, man becomes a captive to the self-imposed bondage of the law. Martin Luther's experience of justification by faith is a dramatic example of how man needs to be emancipated or liberated from the bondage of religion. In this aspect, Christianity shares much in common with other world religions.

Christian mission is thus considered and carried out almost solely as the mission effecting conversion from the darkness of sin. People are challenged to repent of their sins, sins conceived morally. The Christian community made up of such converts cannot but become a spiritually introverted community. When they venture into the outside world, it is for the purpose of snatching repentant sinners away from this sinful world to join the community of saints. Thus, Christian mission tends to become uprooted from its messianic foundation and to take root in moral teachings. The challenge of faith becomes a demand of moral codes. Needless to say, such a tendency completely obscures other equally important, or perhaps more important, dimensions of the message of the Bible.

By relating the particular experience of being black in white America to the biblical experience of the exodus, black theology does succeed in becoming liberated from morbid preoccupation with sin and thus opens up a new dimension for theology and mission. To quote Cone again:

> ... God's call of this people (Israel) is related to their oppressed condition and to his own liberating activity already seen in the exodus. *You have seen what I did!* By delivering this people from Egyptian bondage and inaugurating the convenant on the basis of that historical event, God reveals that He is the God of the oppressed, involved in their history, liberating them from human bondage.[2]

As in the ancient days when God was on the side of the people under Moses, enabling them to leave the land of oppression, so black thinkers such as Cone believe that God stands beside the black minority over against the white majority in their struggle for liberation from white oppression.

Cone pursues relentlessly and singlemindedly the black interpretation of the Christian faith based on the theme of the exodus. With his characteristic pungent language he declares:

If God has made the world in which black people *must* suffer, and if he is a God who rules, guides and sanctifies the world, then he is a murderer. To be the God of black people, he must be against the oppression of white people.[3]

Here is an existential issue which, to black people, is a matter of life and death. If we believe that faith is a response to God who acts in concrete historical situations, we then have in black theology a very genuine expression of that faith. That is why black theology is radically different, in style at least, in the form represented by people like James Cone. It is a missionary theology because it takes its rise not in the quiet sanctuary of the church but in real concrete situations which black people in America are facing today.

But liberation from oppression does not constitute the whole experience of the exodus. The people of Israel, after having won liberation from the land of bondage, had to press towards the land of promise through the agonizing journey in the desert. As Gayraud Wilmore has put it: "The Egyptian captivity of the Jews, the miraculous deliverance from the hands of the Pharaohs, and their eventual possession of the land promised by God to their fathers— this was the inspiration to which the black religionist so often turned in the dark night of his soul."[4] In other words, redemption is not complete until the promised land is reached and won. For this reason, theological language of black theologians must be translated into practical actions which will make manifest the freedom which black people in principle have won.

Thus, we have had to witness the fact that both blacks and whites in the United States have no alternative but to face the reality of power squarely. Sentimentalism, charity and favoritism must be cast aside in order that the cause of justice for the oppressed may not be compromised. The Civil Rights Movement under the leadership of Martin Luther King engulfed this nation with cries for freedom, justice and equality. It was a radical form of Christian mission which the black church leaders undertook toward white America. The black experience of the exodus becomes inevitably embodied in black revolution. The pain of revolution experienced by both blacks and whites is in reality the pain of the cross. It is deeply religious and spiritual, and it has its aim in the redemption of both blacks and whites from the sin of racism—the sin of abusively treating a certain group of mankind by another group, thus desecrating the creation of God. How true it is to say:

Reconciliation must pass through the revolution of the cross. . . . Reconciliation in the race issue has simply been translated as integration. Whereas the church should have recognized that integration which bypasses "Black Power" demands means a resurrection without a cross.[5]

The church in America must bear the cross of black power before she may emerge out of the darkness of death as the church triumphant.

One of the dramatic expressions of black revolution was the appearance of James Forman in a number of white churches, claiming retribution money. He was armed with the Black Manifesto issued by the National Black Economic Development Conference in Detroit, Michigan, on April 26, 1969. The Manifesto in part says:

> . . . we have been forced to come together because racist white America has exploited our resources, our minds, our bodies, our labour. For centuries we have been forced to live as colonized people inside the United States, victimized by the most vicious, racist sytem in the world. We have helped to build the most industrialized country in the world. We are, therefore, demanding of the white Christian churches and Jewish synagogues that they begin to pay reparation to Black people in this country. We are demanding $500,000,000—This total comes to fifteen dollars per nigger.[6]

This sounds all very monetary, but the intention of the Manifesto was to formulate "a comprehensive strategy for the development of pride, unity and self-determination as the first step toward the orderly and intelligent control of the Black Community, its institutions, resources and skills."[7]

What was the reaction of the white churches to the demands of the Manifesto? Was it viewed as the cross to bear in order to reach reconciliation and resurrection? Or was it regarded as a disturbance disrupting the worship service? William Stringfellow, attorney and lay theologian, remarks as follows:

> There is dismay [in the White churches and synagogues] because the direct implication of the reparations Manifesto is a challenge to the integrity of White worship and an exposé of those who still attend such worship while countenancing the inherited and continuing alienation of the races in this land and in most of its churches.[8]

How dreadful it is to realize that Christians can lie at the very heart of the practice of their faith, namely, worship. Worship should be the visible expression of the relation between God's love and man's response to that love. It should be a witness to the reconciliation that takes place between God and man and between man and man. For this reason, Jesus wants us to be reconciled to our brothers and sisters before coming to lay our gifts at the foot of the altar.[9] A Christian worship which denies anyone on the grounds of his race, religion or profession is no longer Christian. It amounts to a slap in the face of God who loved the world so much that He sent His only Son to redeem it.

This is, in fact, one of the chief burdens of the prophets in the Old Testament. Their vehement contentions are often directed at the worship in the temple because it has become the height of hypocrisy and lies. The religious activities of Israel have actually become a burden to Yahweh. Listen to these words of Isaiah:

> Your new moons and your appointed feasts
> my soul hates;
> They have become a burden to me,
> I am weary of bearing them.[10]

The piety that we show at worship services is no guarantee of our acceptance by God. In good prophetic tradition, Jesus Christ tried to demonstrate this again and again in his dealings with the Pharisees and scribes. If a worship service is held with all sorts of false pretensions, it can become our own condemnation. Indeed, the judgment of God begins with the Christian church. God judges the Christian churches through racial crises in the States, in South Africa and elsewhere. God judges the Christian churches in the communist-dominated countries, especially in China, because of their other-worldly oriented religion. God also judges the Christian churches in Asia through the resurgence of old religions and the emergence of new religions. And when the churches in Asia tenaciously cling to the out-dated contents and forms of missionary Christianity representing a particular period in the history of the Western church, God judges them by the invasion of secularism. The church, the Christian mission, which loses its sacramental nature and is thus entrenched in the dichotomy between word and act, is a dead church, a dead mission. It becomes the church and mission which perpetuates human interests alone and thus bears the name of Christ in vain.

It will not be incorrect to say that blacks in the States not only challenge the integrity of the white church but actually become the latter's conscience. Furthermore, this black revolution has a third world connotation, for it also challenges the integrity of the mission carried out overseas by the white church in the States. All in all, it is a challenge to the church and mission which shows more interest in updating statistics, conducting body counts, indoctrinating converts with dogmatical formulae than in really coming to grips with human problems. It is against this kind of church and mission that Bonhoeffer spoke in 1936:

> Because the church is concerned with God, the Holy Spirit and His Word, it is, therefore, not specially concerned with religion, but with obedience to the Word, with the work of the Father, i.e., with the completion of the new creation in the Spirit. It is not religious question

or religious concern of any form which constitutes the church—from a human point of view—but obedience to the Word of the new creation of grace. In other words, the church is constituted not by religious formulae, by dogma, but by the practical doing of what is commanded.[11]

The plea of this martyred theologian is that the church must not allow herself to be undermined by the divorce of word and act. As soon as the divorce of word and act takes place in the church, the world ceases to take her seriously. The reason is simple. The church, whose words are not accompanied by deeds, becomes innocuous. Her mission becomes words without substance. It is a *religious* undertaking without existential meaning. Bonhoeffer wants the church to go beyond a mere religious institution.

It is true to say that Black Power in the United States has exposed the weakest point of the church which is primarily oriented to the needs and aspirations of white Christians. And together with this, there is the most vulnerable aspect of Western Christian mission. Thus, the Black Manifesto pointedly relates black oppression to colonization with military power. "We are not threatening the churches," says the Manifesto:

> We are saying that we know the churches came with the military might of the colonizers and have been sustained by the military might of the colonizers. Hence, if the churches in colonial territories were established by military might, we know how deep within our hearts that we must be prepared to use force to get our demands. We are not saying that this is the road we want to take. It is not, but let us be very clear that we are not opposed to force and we are not opposed to violence. We were captured in Africa by violence. We were kept in bondage and political servitude and forced to work as slaves by the military machinery and the Christian church working hand in hand.[12]

This is a forceful and candid statement. Violence, which is negative use of power, is not glorified but acknowledged as a means of achieving liberation after other means have proved ineffectual and unfruitful. Here is a tragedy which repeats itself again and again in the history of mankind. There is, therefore, no use in just condemning violence. The church has to inquire why blacks are driven to violence and proceed to eliminate one by one those conditions which generate violence. In fact, violence is a desperate expression of those who feel that no ordinary means will bring back to them the integrity of being human.

Thus, the oppressed groups have to take fate into their own hands in order to be their own masters. This is a deeply spiritual problem involving life and death for those who find themselves in the midst of struggle for liberation. Very often the Christian church does not fully understand what is going on in such struggles. She fails to discern the spiritual forces at work to give birth to liberated men and women. The spiritual dimension of revolution often eludes her. Because of this, she tends to find excuses to continue her alliance with the *status quo*, to hold on to the security she has built up over the years and centuries, and to be the tacit collaborator of the powers that be. This is too easy a way out in a most difficult and demanding situation. Not only has the church in America often tended to take such an easy way out in her dealings with blacks, but her mission overseas has more often than not had recourse to it. Just to give an example, we may quote Paul A. Cohen who, in the cause of tracing the causes of Chinese anti-foreignism way back in 1860-1870, observes:

> . . . the missionary made his power felt on the local scene by abusing his treaty rights or by using them with a minimum of discretion. Catholic and Protestant missionaries accepted, at times with considerable delight, the application of force to obtain redress.[13]

It may not, therefore, be totally unjustifiable to say that the seed of Chinese anti-foreignism with its culmination in the period of the communist takeover was partly sown by missionaries themselves. It has to be stressed that the integrity of Christian mission, and that of the church for that matter, cannot be maintained if Christian mission forms alliance with the powers that be. Once again, we must remind ourselves of the prophetic spirit in the Old Testament which never loses its critical function in relation to the political and social establishments. When Christian mission departs from this prophetic spirit, it becomes less Christian. Although there is a danger of it becoming a cliché, it is still true to say that the communist rise to power in China is the judgment of God on Western Christian mission. Can we not also say that black power is the judgment of God on the white church in America?

Stride Toward Self-Determination

The exodus, both that of Israel and of blacks in America, is a gigantic stride toward self-determination. It is a resolute rejection of an outward authority imposing its will on those without power and incarcerating them in bondage and servitude. It is a declaration of No to the power that exercises control over them and determines their fate. The courage to say No to those who hold power over one's life and death is the courage to assert one's humanity. By saying No, one comes to realize one's individuality over against others. As long as one shrinks back from saying No, one is still not a full person. And insofar as one is conscious of being a person, one is able to become a responsible member of society.

The exodus of Israel from Egypt is such a No to the Pharaoh and the Egyptian taskmasters. Under the leadership of Moses, the Israelites took the first step towards growing into full humanity. The exodus itself, namely, the departure from Egypt in defiance of the Pharaoh's objections, was a mere beginning. Athough the subsequent long treks in the wilderness were to prove that the stride toward self-determination was far more difficult than anticipated by both Moses and those who followed him, nonetheless it was the course they had to take in order to become responsible members of humanity. Faced with heat, thirst, hunger and enemies, their courage to say No faded and their determination to march toward the land of promise wavered. They challenged Moses and said: "if only we had died at the Lord's hand in Egypt, where we sat round the fleshpots and had plenty of bread to eat! But you have brought us out into this wilderness to let this whole assembly starve to death."[14] But they had already reached the point of no return to the fleshpots of Egypt. They had no choice but to continue their long journey toward self-determination. It was in the course of this long tortuous journey that they grew into a coherent group of men and women with a vision of a common future. The foundation for the birth of a new nation was thus laid.

Furthermore, self-determination leads to self-fulfilment. We may put it differently and say, self-determination is a prerequisite of self-fulfilment. As long as a man is deprived of the right to determine his own destiny, there will be no self-fulfilment for him. He fulfils himself as he decides what to do and what not to do. He can speak of self-fulfilment only insofar as he can choose what to be and what not to be. Of course, this choice or this determination may not come easily. It has to be won, often with great difficulty and much struggle. A price has to be paid for the right of self-determination. The Israelites had to pay the price to win self-determination. They had to leave behind them the security of fleshpots, the security of a slave, nonetheless a security. They had to put up with extreme hardships in the wilderness. The threat of death was never far from them. But without paying these prices, there was no way for them to reach their destination, enabling them to enjoy self-fulfilment.

For the Israelites who took part in the exciting drama of the exodus, this self-determination/self-fulfilment component is expressed in their desire to worship God away from Egypt, the house of bondage. In his demands to the Pharaoh, Moses repeatedly said: "Let my people go in order to worship the Lord." For them self-determination/self-fulfilment is a religious act. It is a profoundly spiritual event which culminates in the act of worship. Worshipping God in the land of freedom is the integral part of the political and social struggle for liberation.

Self-fulfilment means, in part, bringing out the best in a man in order to put it to the best possible use for which it is originally intended by God. Described in this way, self-fulfilment becomes extremely difficult, if not impossible, if a person lives in the state of bondage or oppression. His sense of justice has to be suppressed. His sensitivity towards basic human needs and aspirations is expected to go blunt. His love for his fellowmen is not allowed a free expression. In a word, he is expected to behave as less than a full person. That is why the oppression in a totalitarian state tends to bring out the worst in man. It thrives on the dark side of human nature. It is self-fulfilment in an absolutely reverse sense.

We may side-track a little, but it has to be mentioned that here we seem to touch upon a very essential element in Christian worship. We would like to affirm that worship service should be the occasion to celebrate the self-fulfilment of believers in the love and grace of God. In the worship service the fact that we are children of God, that we are His own creatures, is affirmed and confessed. This is the basic element in human self-fulfilment. We can fulfil the meaning of our being precisely because we are created by God. We can see hope and future in our lives only because God has given it to us through Jesus Christ. There should be confession of our sins, repenting our failures in responding to the love of God. But the worship service cannot stop short at confession of sins and repentance of our failures. Worship service can become oppressive if it does not go beyond this. Indulgence in sins is bad, of course; but indulgence in exploiting sins, which is often done from the pulpit, is even worse. The church tends to turn inward toward herself when worship service is conducted in this way. She becomes an introverted church, busy fending off sins, both real and imaginary, coming from the outside world.

Evangelism, especially in its narrow sense of converting people into the fold of the fellowship of the repentant, often proves to be the opposite of the self-fulfilment just described. The way in which the evangelist pounces upon the audience by giving gruesome pictures of sin and hell becomes almost a threat to the integrity of man as God's creature. His assault on the sin of the world leaves little room for goodness, truth and beauty in God's creation. To make the matter worse, the sin that he attacks so vehemently is invariably related to the moral aspect. There is little attack on social injustice, the abuse of power by those in political power and the exploitation of the powerless, and so on. Thus, the picture or image of an evangelist in Asia, and perhaps in other parts of the world as well, is that of a moralist and not of a prophet in the Old Testament sense of the word. It goes without saying that this kind of evangelistic approach is the seed-bed of narrow sectarianism. It not only thwarts ecumenical cooperation among Christians of differing backgrounds, but also obstructs any meaningful contacts with men and women of other faiths. It also adopts a defensive attitude towards secularization. It responds negatively to the social changes brought about by the process of technological developments. It is no wonder that those who have close association with sectarian Christianity do not show much interest in the struggle for self-determination in which their fellowman is involved.

For the church and the Christian mission to break out of this self-imposed sectarian restriction, what is needed is an articulate theological expression with regard to the subject of self-determination and self-fulfilment as an essential part of God's design for man. In the contemporary scene, this kind of theological articulation is provided most unequivocally by black theology. This we have already shown in the previous pages as we dealt with the black experience of the exodus. Let us bring to a sharper focus at this point the attempt of black theology to probe into the basic problem of human destiny.

For some black theologians the very first step in coming to grips with self-determination and self-fulfilment is the acceptance of what one is as a black person. This is a very legitimate and logical step. If one denies the very self which constitutes one's own being, it will be contradictory to speak of the determination of this self or the fulfilment of this self. As the center of consciousness and being, the self must be the starting point. Deotis Roberts, another black theologian is thus right when he says:

> Blackness is a fact of life for the Negro. It is a given. It must be accepted—it cannot be ignored, escaped or overcome. Acceptance of blackness is the only healthy stance for the black man. In Tillichian language, "he must have the courage to be black."[15]

Basically this statement has its grounds in the theological understanding of the relation between God and man in and through Jesus Christ. God's dealing with man in Christ begins with the acceptance of man by God; and in accepting man, God wants him to accept himself. Jesus Christ is the most radical expression of what takes place between God and man. Jesus Christ, though representing God, though being of the divine nature, becomes and is one of us, literally one of us. Without his acceptance of man, there will be no salvation, no restoration of relationship between God and man, and between man and man.

But acceptance can mean for some people resignation, the rationale being that since this is the fact of life, you have to accept it. There is not much that you can do about it. But this is not the theological meaning of the word acceptance. Nor does Roberts advise his fellowman to accept blackness as a fact of life and resign himself to it. That is why he goes on to say:

> One of the most wholesome and positive aspects of the black revolution is the assertion that "black is beautiful" and that we should seek "black pride."[16]

This is the acceptance of life with meaning for the present and hope for the future. The quality of beauty and pride here is not to be simply understood aesthetically or ethically. It is a quality that gives black men and women confidence of being equal partners with others in the human community. Lacking this confidence, it will probably be difficult for them even to accept the love of God. There would always be nagging questions in their minds:

Does God truly love me as He does others such as the White man? What kind of place do I have in the providence of God? But perhaps the most depressing question will be this: Why has God made me so?

Herein consists the essence of black Christian mission, if we may coin a term in line with terms such as black theology or black power. The primary task of black Christian mission is to be actively engaged in the effort to make beauty and pride as an integral part of black consciousness. It would be irrelevant and harmful even for evangelists addressing themselves to a black audience to dwell on the subject of sin as the one single important issue. The morbid fear of sin especially in its moral aspect only serves to make one retreat farther into the secret corner of one's heart where anxiety and uncertainty are harboured. This does not mean that the word "sin" should be dropped from the vocabulary of Christian theologians. It does mean, however, that the concept of sin must be redefined in the light of the Bible and of the existential situations in which the concept is to be understood and communicated.[17]

Having taken the first step in accepting oneself as one really is, black theologians go farther in asserting the fulfilment of one's being as the goal of their endeavours. Thus, we are told:

> . . . freedom is not doing what I will but becoming what I should. A man is free when he sees clearly the fulfilment of his being and is thus capable of making the envisioned self a reality.[18]

For black theologians such as Cone, the self thus envisioned is not an abstract concept without reality. Nor is it a utopian picture of a man of perfect virtues. There is no actual counterpart of such a man in the real world. What black theologians are after is a black man who is fully conscious of humanity and who demands the white man to recognize his full humanity. Therefore, Cone continues to tell us that:

> As long as man is a slave to another power, he is not free to serve God with mature responsibility. He is not free to become what he is—human.[19]

In other words, the givenness called blackness provides the framework of meaning for black people to be human. It is through his blackness that a black person may come to grips with his own humanity and come into touch with humanity as a whole. Consequently, to accept blackness as the givenness in God's creation and to be human amounts to one and the same thing for him. If he refuses to accept his blackness and escapes it, he will be in fact refusing his own humanity and escaping it.

It is on these grounds that the mission carried out among the black people must be criticized and appraised. For instance, it is said of missions in the inner city: " . . . When one looks into the work which was performed, one sees, until the very recent past, no concern for or appreciation of the religious background of the people of the inner city and no development of relationships with the black churches of the ghetto. Black religion was to be upgraded; that is, made to conform to mainstream white Christianity and the models had more of a relationship to Greenwich Village than Harlem or Georgia."[20] This is exactly what happened also in Asia and elsewhere in the Third World. The uniformity thus created was to give rise to the problem of identity for Christians surrounded by non-white culture. It has also made it necessary for the church in the Third World to be dependent on the Western church for her well-being. It is of interest to realize that the black church in the States had to agonize over the same problem besetting the church in Asia.

In view of this situation, the mission of the black church must be quite different from that of the Western church. It consists of

> the task of making black life more human, of getting black people to accept their acceptance, and of helping to bring into existence mature, authentic black persons.[21]

We cannot agree more with this statement. It will be utterly wrong to criticize it as being humanistic and therefore contradicting the main thrust of Christian mission. Such a criticism is entirely beside the point. For one thing, the concept of Christian mission under which Western missions operated, especially that of conservative trends, has no normative claim over the form and content of Christian mission in the contexts of the Third World, including the black church in the United States. In fact, conscious effort is now being made to come up with a different concept and practice of Christian mission which will depart essentially from the traditional one. In the light of this, the concept of the task of the church implied in the statement just quoted is a viable one in the life and historical contexts of the black people.

The statement is not only existentially viable. It can also be defended theologically. Humanity is the basis on which the relation between God and man becomes possible. This seems to be one of the implications of the biblical insight which sees man as created in the image of God. It is a well-known fact that Karl Barth speaks of the humanity of God in his later theology. Although he insists that this is by no means a diversion from his Christocentric theology, it does indicate that he has come a long way from his earlier theological career in which the qualitative difference between God and man was his major theological emphasis. Applied to our discussion here, the humanity of God seems no other than the image according to which God created man. Man, therefore, differs from other animals in that he is endowed with this humanity. And it is by means of this humanity that he is able to communicate with God. The communion between God and man becomes possible on the basis of this humanity.

Does it not follow that the most essential task of Christian mission consists in helping people to regain their humanity and to become human? Does this not mean that for Christian mission to become actively involved in redressing the conditions which deny full humanity to certain people because of their race, colour, or social status is part and parcel of the ministry of the church? Is it not obvious that as long as oppression exists, there are people who are deprived of the basis on which they can be in communion with God?

In addition, humanity is the bridge which relates not only man to God but also man to man. Interpersonal relationship is not possible without this humanity. The political power and social system which uses coercion and oppression to control people poses a serious threat to the humanity of man. That is why interpersonal relationships are most easily disrupted in a dictatorial country. Under such circumstances, suspicion takes the place of trust, faithfulness is replaced by treachery and truth is confused with falsehood. This reinforces our belief that the Christian mission must begin by removing obstacles to humanity such as this.

This analysis has shown beyond the possibility of doubt that the traditional concept of Christian mission is no longer relevant. Perhaps we may go so far as to say that it has misrepresented the basic understanding of the task of the church. Thus, there is every justification for saying that

> Christianity cannot rob the black man of his blackness unless it desires him to be something less than a man. The black church and black theology thus seeks to permit the black man to be both black and Christian.[22]

It is self-evident that this blackness of the black man, namely, his humanity, does not merely mean the colour of his skin. In blackness is embodied the whole past history of the slavery a black man went through individually and corporately. It stands for the whole of culture built on the basis of that history. Furthermore, blackness represents the future hope of the black man and his community. Christianity must speak to this blackness. Any form of the work of the church which belittles this blackness becomes irrelevant. It betrays the soul of the black man.

The same quest for identity has been going on in Asia and in other parts of the Third World for quite some time already. Only it has not come out in forceful and blunt statements such as the ones we have been quoting from black theologians. The basic issue is the same, although historical circumstances and existential situations differ greatly. It amounts to this: Christian mission must seek to permit the Asian to be both Asian and Christian. This requires the church in Asia to give up all her heritages, precious though they may be, that hinder her search for identity. She must seriously question the validity of her relationships with the Western churches maintained through Western personnel and financial assistance. These relationships are becoming more fragile than before. This is all to the good both for the church in Asia and the church in the West. They must make every possible resistance to strengthening these relationships on the old basis. In fact, in order for new relationships to come into existence, the old relationships must be broken. This is precisely what black Christians try to do through their theological effort. Theirs is a resolute No to the Christian heritage thrust upon them by the white church. They rightly insist that they cannot build the new structure of faith and life on the basis of the old. The new wine needs new wineskins.

However, this critical approach to the Christian heritages is only one aspect of the task in the quest for identity. Another important, and perhaps more important, aspect of the question is that of the culture into which one is born. Thus, the black Christian's search for identity plunges him into black culture. The black Christian's identity can be genuine only if it comes out of his deep experience of what it means to be black in the white society. Not only this, it can be found only when he permits himself to be involved in struggles that may usher in a new day for his own people. Black theology, therefore, cannot but take on a revolutionary tone. It will be a mistake to think that the revolutionary and militant tone of black theology is the result of the black theologian's frustration with the black man's situation in America. Let us quote Moltmann just to show that such judgment on black theology is not true. He says:

> . . . the missionary proclamation of the cross of the Resurrected One is not an opium of the people which intoxicates and incapacitates, but the ferment of new freedom. It leads to the awakening of that revolt which, in the "power of the resurrection" . . . follows the categorical imperative to overthrow all conditions in which man is a being who labours and is heavily laden.[23]

We cannot lightly speak of "overthrowing all conditions in which man is a being who labours and is heavily laden," for this is a highly revolutionary statement. We just cannot empty it of all social and political implications and fill it with a harmless spiritual interpretation. Let us face it. The cross is a revolutionary event. It literally seeks to overthrow those conditions which enslave man. How can the theology which seeks to interpret the meaning of the cross be anything but revolutionary?

The quest for identity has, needless to say, its fertile field in arts also. Consequently, black theologians endeavor to read theological meaning in cultural expressions of black consciousness. What Preston Williams says about the phenomenon of "soul"[24] is very revealing:

> Soul is the constant feeling of one's two-ness, of being a part yet not being a part. It is a warring of two thoughts, two ideals, two unreconciled strings within one dark body. Soul is the expression of both the

black man's freedom and his bondage. It is a spontaneous and free response to life. Yet also the stolid-stoical response to a fate one can barely endure and from which one can never fully escape. Soul catches up both the heroism and the pathos of black life, its frenzies of joy and its sullen dark sorrow.

Soul is elusive and vague, it is contradictory and confusing: it is the heart and marrow of black existence. When then the black church/black theology phenomenon gave expression to soul, it was affirming the black man's right to be himself.[25]

Does this interest of black theology in soul not indicate that any cultural expression can be the subject of theological reflection? Can we not draw a conclusion here that the richer one's cultural creation is, the fuller the content of theology would be? Therefore, theology done outside a particular cultural context is a poor theology. It is an abstraction separated from the dramas of the real life. For the church in Asia, as well as for the black church in America, we need to bring into existence the kind of theology firmly rooted in a particular culture. Christian mission not predicated on theological reflection on culture often becomes anti-cultural. The divorce of Christian faith from culture has been the result of such Christian mission. In this event, faith has little implication beyond individual men and women. They are peremptorily torn away from their living contexts and placed in a domain which has no vital relation to the reality of this world. The strength of black theology consists in its effort to reflect on the meaning of Christian faith in the living contexts of black people. If black theologians persevere in this effort, they will be able to come up with creative alternatives not only in doing theology but also in applying Christian faith to their social and cultural situations.

Notes

1. James H. Cone, *A Black Theology of Liberation* (Philadelphia and New York: J. B. Lippincott Company, 1970), p. 18.

2. Ibid., pp. 18-19.

3. James Cone, *Black Theology and Black Power* (New York: The Seabury Press, 1969), pp. 124-125.

4. Gayraud S. Wilmore, *Black Religions and Black Radicalism* (Garden City, N.Y.: Doubleday and Company, 1972), p. 52.

5. J. Christian Beker, "Biblical Theology Today," in *New Theology*, No. 6, edited by Martin E. Marty and Dean G. Peerman (London: The Macmillan Company, 1969), p. 31.

6. *Black Manifesto*, edited by Robert S. Lecky and H. Elliot Wright (New York: Sheed and Ward, 1969), p. 119; see also Document 7, above.

7. Gayraud S. Wilmore, op. cit., p. 280.

8. William Stringfellow, "Reparations: Repentance as a Necessity to Reconciliation," in *Black Manifesto*, p. 52.

9. Matthew 5:23-24.

10. Isaiah 1:14.

11. Dietrich Bonhoeffer, *The Way to Freedom*, letters, lectures and notes 1935-1939, translated by Edwin H. Robertson and John Bowden (New York: Harper & Row, 1966), p. 48.

12. *Black Manifesto*, pp. 125f.

13. Paul A. Cohen, *China and Christianity*, the Missionary Movement and the Growth of Chinese Anti-foreignism 1860-1870 (Harvard University Press, 1963), p. 128.

14. Exodus 16:23.

15. J. Deotis Roberts, "Black Consciousness in Theological Perspective," in *Quest for a Black Theology*, edited by James J. Gardiner and J. Deotis Roberts (Philadelphia: Pilgrim Press, 1971), p. 64.

16. Ibid.

17. James Cone has attempted a redefinition as follows: "If we are to understand sin and what it means to black people, it is necessary to be black and also a participant in the black liberation struggle. Because sin represents the condition of estrangement from the source of one's being, for black people this means a desire to be white and not black. It is the refusal to be what we are. Sin then for black people is the loss of identity" (*A Black Theology of Liberation*, p. 190).

18. James Cone, *Black Theology and Black Power* (New York: The Seabury Press, 1969), p. 39.

19. Ibid.

20. Preston N. Williams, "The Ethics of Black Power," in *Quest for a Black Theology*, p. 86.

21. Ibid., p. 87.

22. Ibid., p. 88.

23. Jürgen Moltmann, "Toward a Political Hermeneutics of the Gospel," *Union Seminary Quarterly Review*, vol. 23, no. 4 (Summer, 1968), pp. 313-314. Quoted by James Cone in *Black Theology and Black Power*, p. 37.

24. "Soul, as expressed in Afro-American music, is hardly definable in any clear, literal sense. To be sure the complexity of this concept is as complex as the Afro-American life-experience itself. Soul music is reflective of that complex experience. And as evasive as it may be, it is easily identified in all the musical forms which blacks have generated. It resides in so-called jazz, gospel, rhythm and blues, rock and roll. Soul is by its nature, a reality manifested in visceral experience and continues to defy rational containment"—M. William Howard, Executive Director, Black Council, Reformed Church in America.

25. Preston N. Williams, op. cit., p. 84.

54

FINAL STATEMENT,
ASIAN THEOLOGICAL CONFERENCE,
SRI LANKA, JANUARY 7–20, 1979

Preamble

We, Christians from Asia, along with fraternal delegates from other continents, gathered in Wennappuwa, Sri Lanka, from January 7 to 20, 1979, motivated by our solidarity with our people in the struggle for full humanity and by our common faith in Jesus Christ, bringing with us the experience of the struggle in our own countries, we came to share in the life and situations of the masses striving for justice in Sri Lanka, through our four-day "live-ins."

During the days that followed, we became more aware of the commonalities and divergences in our background, which sharpened our understanding both of the richness and the anguish of our people in Asia.

As Asians, we recognize the important task before us. Our reflections, already begun in our local realities, helped us to enrich the process of interaction and sharing among us who have committed ourselves to the struggle of the poor in Asia. At the same time, we realize that these reflections are only part of the beginning of a collective and continuous search for a relevant theology in Asia.

The Asian Context

Asia suffers under the heels of a forced poverty. Its life has been truncated by centuries of colonialism and a more recent neocolonialism. Its cultures are marginalized, its social relations distorted. The cities, with their miserable slums, swollen with the poor peasants driven off the land, constitute a picture of wanton affluence side by side with abject poverty that is common to the majority of Asia's countries. This extreme disparity is the result of a class contradiction, a continuous domination of Asia by internal and external forces. The consequence of this type of capitalist domination is that all things,

The Asian Theological Conference was sponsored by the Ecumenical Association of Third World Theologians.

time and life itself, have become marketable commodities. A small minority of owners dictates the quality of life for the producers (workers, peasants, and others) in determining the price of their energy, skills, intelligence, as well as the material benefits needed to sustain these. What is produced, how and where it is produced, for whom it is produced, are the decisions of transna tional corporations in collusion with the national elites and with the overt or covert support of political and military forces.

The struggle against these forces has been courageously taken up by the advocates of socialism. This socio-political order corresponds to the aspirations of the Asian masses both in the rural and urban areas since it promises to them the right to take their life into their own hands, to determine both the social and economic conditions that govern their well-being. A very large part of Asia has succeeded, after long struggles, in establishing this socialist order. However, it must be added that the socialist transformation in these countries is not yet complete and that these countries must continue to liberate themselves from all distortions in an on-going self-criticism.

Neither will socialist movements in Asia be thorough in their struggle for full humanity without an inner liberation from self-seeking and exploitative instincts. The rich traditions of the major religions of Asia (Hinduism, Buddhism, Islam, and Christianity) offer many inspirations. The richness is expressed not only in philosophical formulations but also in various art forms such as dance and drama, poems and songs, as well as in myths and rites, parables and legends. It is only when we immerse ourselves in the "peoples' cultures" that our struggle acquires an indigenous dimension.

However it is equally true that the social function of religions or cultural systems is ambiguous. In the past religions and cultural systems have played the role of legitimizing feudal relationships, yet the self-critical principle inherent in them can be a source of liberation today from the domination of capitalist values and ideologies.

Hence we feel that the Asian context which dictates the terms of an Asian theology consists of a struggle for fuller humanity in socio-political as well as psycho-spiritual aspects. The liberation of all human beings is both societal and personal.

The Issues

We realize that if large numbers of men and women find themselves socially deprived and progressively thrown further and further away from the center of life and meaning, it is not a mere accident or the effect of a national catastrophe. In fact, from Pakistan to Korea, passing through the subcontinent and Southeast Asia, practically all parliamentary governments, with the exception of Japan, have at some time given way to military governments or authoritarian regimes of one form or the other. In these countries not only political rights are suppressed, but also the rights of workers to strike in the cities and the rights of peasants to organize themselves in the countryside.

Many leaders and people holding political views contrary to the ruling group are condemned to spend several years in prison, often without due process of trial.

Behind the facade of "law and order" are Asia's cheap and docile labor and laws that leave the country open to unrestricted exploitation by foreign capital with the profit going to a small elite. A deeper logic is to be found in the dual economies of these countries. The industrial sector, monopolized by the national elite, has developed along the lines of an export economy that does not correspond to the needs of the local population. It also depends heavily on foreign capital and technology. And as a result of unequal trade relations and the weakness of these countries, their indebtedness and dependence grew to an extent beyond their control. International banks and transnational corporations have become the new masters of Asia's politics and economics.

At the same time the rural sector in these countries has remained stagnant. The so-called agrarian reforms did not change the unequal social relations of production in the rural areas. The benefit of the "Green Revolution" went only to the middle and big landowners who could afford its technology. A great number of peasants were driven off the land in the process and ended in the slums of the swollen cities of Asia. On the other hand, the rural surplus thus accumulated is often re-invested in crops for export or chanelled into urban industries, preventing the growth of production of food. As a result, Asia, which is potentially rich in agriculture, is importing food and the amount is increasing continually at an alarming rate. Hunger and poverty will be the fate of Asian masses for many years to come.

A hopeful sign is the growing awareness among the oppressed peoples that leads to the growth and increase of peoples' organizations in both the cities and the rural areas. The majority of Asian countries have witnessed peasant uprisings and urban disturbances. Put down by bloody oppression and intimidated by imprisonment and torture, many of these movements have gone underground and turned to a protracted struggle as the only means of changing their societies. While not necessarily condoning the use of violence, which is most often unavoidable, we question and object to the enforcement of "law and order," which consolidates the control of the power elites while thwarting the organized conscientious objections of the deprived majorities. When legalized violence leaves no room for peoples to free themselves from their misery, are we surprised that they are so compelled to resort to violence? Have the Christian churches sufficiently understood the message of revolutionary violence in the Asian struggles for political independence, social emancipation, and liberation from the built-in violence of the present economic and political structures?

The youth in Asia, who form a large segment of the Asian population, are continuously victimized. They constitute the growing number of unemployed and underemployed labor force. A lack of proper educational facilities and decreasing employment opportunities in the rural areas where the majority of youth come from lead to the irreversible process of migration to urban centers; in the urban areas, the youth are the targets of consumer culture and in turn become vehicles of deculturation. We emphasize also that some students, youth, and workers have been playing the important role of a critical and committed force in the struggle for the basic rights of the oppressed people. At the same time, they are also made pawns in the power politics of politicians and other interest groups, thus losing their genuine relevance and are even sacrificed in abrupt physical violence.

The educational system, linked to the established centers of power, is geared to perpetuate the domination of youth. It serves as a mere channel for the transfer of technical skills and alienated knowledge without reference to humanistic values. The pyramidal elitist structure of education is used to fabricate losers, who are continuously exploited.

We recognize deeply that women are also victims of the same structures of domination and exploitation. In the context of the Asiatic religions and cultures, the relationship between men and women is still one of domination. This situation is worse in the poorer classes of society. Thus women face an unforgivable double oppression.

In the economic sphere, a male-dominated society reduces the "price" of woman-labor and limits the scope of women's participation in the process of production at all levels—the local, national, regional, and consequently the international levels. In the political sphere, women are aware of the political situation in their countries, but here too their competence and activity are greatly stifled.

Women are sexually and intellectually vulnerable in a society where an interaction of traditional and modern forces (especially tourism) compels them to compromise with consumeristic values of capitalist society. It also compels them to prostitution. Instead of condemning the system that forces women into prostitution, the men who exploit the women also condemn them.

We recognize the existence of ethnic minorities in every Asian country. They are among the most deprived sectors at all levels, including the economic, political, and cultural. They are struggling for self-determination against heavy odds, yet their authentic struggle is often utilized by the centers of power in playing up racial antagonism to camouflage themselves and disrupt the unity among the marginalized.

Mass media, including the printed word, films, and television, are controlled by the ruling elite to propagate their dominant value systems and myths, providing a dehumanizing, individualistic, consumerist culture. Despite this domination, we also witness the emergence of a more creative micro-media that portrays realistically the struggle of the dominated people.

We need to mention also the increasing impact of urbanization and irrational industrialization. Women, children, and men together face narrowing opportunities for education, housing, and health services as these social needs are determined by market forces. With the transfer of the platforms of production and mechanization from industrialized countries, environmental pollution surfaces in most of the Asian countries, causing ecological imbalances. Here we join with our fishermen in their struggle against the unscrupulous practices in certain countries like Japan, Taiwan, and South Korea.

We realize also the legitimizing role of religion in the course of history within the Asian context. Religions form an integral part of the total social reality, inseparable from all spheres of action. Much interaction has taken place between religion and politics in Asia down through the ages, and today there are significant movements of social renewal inspired by religions outside the traditional institutions. We need to stress the critical and transforming element in religion and culture. A serious socio-political analysis of realities and involvement in political and ideological struggles should be seen as vital elements of religion in its role as a critic. Here we realize the creative force of culture in bringing people together and giving them an identity within their struggles. Critical cultural action would destroy old myths and create new symbols in continuity with the cultural treasures of the past.

Toward a Relevant Theology

We are conscious of the fact that the vital issues of the realities of Asia indicate the ambivalent role of the major religions in Asia and pose serious questions to us, hence challenging the dehumanizing status quo of theology. To be relevant, theology must undergo a radical transformation.

Liberation: Area of Concern

In the context of the poverty of the teeming millions of Asia and their situation of domination and exploitation, our theology must have a very definite liberational thrust.

The first act of theology, its very heart, is commitment. This commitment is a response to the challenge of the poor in their struggle for full humanity. We affirm that the poor and the oppressed of Asia are called by God to be the architects and builders of their own destiny. Thus theology starts with the aspirations of the oppressed toward full humanity and counts on their growing consciousness of, and their ever-expanding efforts to overcome, all obstacles to the truth of their history.

Subject of Theology

To be truly liberating, this theology must arise from the Asian poor with a liberated consciousness. It is articulated and expressed by the oppressed community using the technical skills of Biblical scholars, social scientists, psychologists, anthropologists, and others. It can be expressed in many ways, in art forms, drama, literature, folk stories, and native wisdom, as well as in doctrinal-pastoral statements.

Most participants asserted that every theology is conditioned by the class position and class consciousness of the theologian. Hence a truly liberating theology must ultimately be the work of the Asian poor, who are struggling for full humanity. It is they who must reflect on and say what their faith-life experience in the struggle for liberation is. This does not exclude the so-called specialists in theology. With their knowledge they can complement the theologizing of the grassroots people. But their theologizing becomes authentic only when rooted in the history and struggle of the poor and the oppressed.

Liberation, Culture, and Religion

To be authentically Asian, theology must be immersed in our historico-cultural situation and grow out of it. A theology that emerged from the people's struggle for liberation would spontaneously formulate itself in religio-cultural idioms of the people.

In many parts of Asia, we must integrate into our theology the insights and values of the major religions, but this integration must take place at the level of action and commitment to the people's struggle and not be merely intellectual or elitist. These traditions of Asia's great religions seem to understand liberation in two senses: liberation from selfishness both within each person and in society. These religious traditions also contain a strong motivation for personal conversion of life. These religions, together with our indigenous cultures, can provide the Asian sense in our task of generating the new person and the new community. We view them as a potential source of a permanent critique of any established order and a pointer toward the building of a truly human society. We are conscious, however, of the domesticating role religions have often played in the past, so we need to subject both our religion and culture to sustained self-criticism. In this context, we question the academic preoccupation to work toward the so-called "indigenization" or "inculturation" of theology divorced from participation in the liberational struggle in history. In our countries today, there can be no truly indigenized theology that is not liberational. Involvement in the history and struggle of the oppressed is the guarantee that our theology is both liberating and indigenous.

Social Analysis

Theology working for the liberation of the poor must approach its task with the tools of social analysis of the realities of Asia. How can it participate in the liberation of the poor if it does not understand the socio-political, economic, and cultural structures that enslave the poor? The vision of full humanity and the complexity of the struggle leading to its achievement are continually challenged and distorted by the meshing of mixed motives and interests and by the interweaving of the apparent and the real. This analysis must extend to the whole length and breadth, height and depth of Asian reality, from the family to the village, the city, the nation, the continent, and the globe. Economic and socio-political interdependence has shrunk the earth to a global village. The analysis must keep pace with the ongoing historical process to ensure a continuing self-criticism and evaluation of religions, ideologies, institutions, groups, and classes of people that by their very nature run the hazard of a dehumanizing bureaucracy.

Biblical Perspective

Because theology takes the total human situation seriously, it can be regarded as the articulated reflection, in faith, on the encounter of God by people in their historical situations. For us, Christians, the Bible becomes an important source in the doing of theology. The God encountered in the history of the people is none other than the God who revealed himself in the events of Jesus' life, death, and resurrection. We believe that God and Christ continue to be present in the struggles of the people to achieve full humanity as we look forward in hope to the consummation of all things when God will be all in all.

When theology is liberated from its present race, class, and sex prejudices, it can place itself at the service of the people and become a powerful motivating force for the mobilization of believers in Jesus to participate in Asia's ongoing struggle for self-identity and human dignity. For this, we need to develop whole new areas of theology such as understanding the revolutionary challenge of the life of Jesus, seeing in Mary the truly liberated woman who participated in the struggle of Jesus and her people, bridging the gaps of our denominational separation, and rewriting the history of the Asian churches from the perspective of the Asian poor.

Spirituality and Formation

The formation for Christian living and ministry has to be in and through participation in the struggle of the masses of our people. This requires the development of a corresponding spirituality, of opting out of the exploitative system in some way, of being marginalized in the process, of persevering in our commitment, of risk-bearing, of reaching deeper inner peace in the midst of active involvement with the struggling people (Shanti).

Our fellow Christians who have become regular inmates of the Asian prisons bring us new elements of fidelity to our people inspired by Jesus. To them we too send a message of humble solidarity and prayerful hope. May the suffering of today's prisoners in the Asian jails give birth to a genuine renewal of ourselves and our communities of believers.

Future Tasks

Coming to the end of this conference, we feel the need to continue the search we have initiated here. To keep alive our efforts toward a theology that speaks to our Asian peoples, we see the following tasks before us.

1. We need to continue deepening our understanding of the Asian reality through *active involvement* in our people's struggle for full humanity. This means struggling side by side with our peasants, fishermen, workers, slum dwellers, marginalized and minority groups, oppressed youth, and women so that together we can discover the Asian face of Christ.
2. Our theology must lead us to transform the society in which we live so that it may increasingly allow the Asian person to experience what it means to be fully alive. This task included the transformation of our church structures and institutions as well as ourselves.
3. We shall continue to assist in the development of a relevant theology for Asia through constant interaction and mutual respect for the different roles we have in the struggle, as professional theologians, grassroots workers, and church people.
4. We seek to build a strong network of alliance by linking groups who are struggling for full humanity nationally and internationally. The following concrete actions taken in the course of the conference show the beginnings of this network:
   a. A letter of solidarity with seventy-six boat people in Hong Kong who were arrested on their way to petition for better housing.
   b. A public statement by the Sri Lankan delegation pledging to support the Tamil-speaking people in their struggle for their just rights.
   c. A message to Bishop Tji of Korea, supporting the Korean struggle and regretting the absence of the entire Korean delegation at the conference.
   d. A letter to Kawasaki Steel Corporation, Japan, protesting the export of pollution to other Asian countries.
   e. A telegram to the Latin American Bishops as well as to Pope John Paul II, expressing deep concern for the CELAM conference in Puebla, Mexico.
   f. Solidarity with the Filipino participants in their protest against the pollution caused by the transfer of high pollutant industries and the erection of nuclear power plants.
5. We are concerned about formation programs in our training institutions and the lifestyle of our pastoral leaders. The experiences of the conference

make it clear that there must be new emphases in our theological and
pastoral policy. We need to evaluate our parish and diocesan structures to
assess where they alienate us from the poor masses of Asia and give us the
image of might and power. We urge that necessary adjustments be made so
that our religious personnel may be more deeply in touch with the problems of our people.

6. In order to facilitate the implementation of our tasks, we have formed the
Ecumenical Theological Fellowship of Asia.

For two weeks eighty of us, participants at this Asian Theological Conference, have tried to grapple with the contemporary call of the Asian poor and
oppressed.

The prayerful silence in worship and the unity in faith helped to keep our
communion in dialectical and creative tension.

As Christians we see the urgent tasks of renewing ourselves and the
churches in order to serve our people.

To this sacred and historic task we humbly commit ourselves and invite all
Christians and people of good will everywhere to participate in this ongoing
search.

55

"ASIA'S STRUGGLE
FOR A FULL HUMANITY:
TOWARD A RELEVANT THEOLOGY"
(AN ASIAN THEOLOGICAL CONFERENCE)

James H. Cone

The Asian Theological Conference (ATC), sponsored by the Ecumenical Association of Third World Theologians (EATWOT), was held at Wennappuwa, Sri Lanka, January 7–20, 1979. About seventy-five Asian delegates (including Protestants and Roman Catholics but mostly the latter) were present, with a small representation of fraternal delegates from Africa (2), Latin America (2), the Caribbean (1), and the United States (2).

The ATC was the second of a series of conferences planned by EATWOT in its attempt to promote dialogues among Third World theologians. After the organizing conference in August 1976, at Dar-es-Salaam, Tanzania (see S. Torres and V. Fabella, eds., *The Emergent Gospel,* Maryknoll, New York: Orbis, 1978), the first conference was held at Accra, Ghana, December 1977, and it focused on the future development of an African Theology (see Kofi Appiah-Kubi and S. Torres, eds., *African Theology en Route,* Maryknoll, New York: Orbis, 1979). The third conference will be held in Latin America with an agenda determined mainly by liberation-oriented theologians on that continent. There has been some discussion about a 1981 conference with equal representation from the three continents and a significant number from the Black community in the United States and the Caribbean and some white guests from Europe and North America. Some conversations also have taken place about a conference the following year (1982) with delegates from the First, Second, and Third World continents. All of this is still in the planning stage.

The ecumenical composition of the Sri Lanka conference was impressive. Delegates came from eleven Asian countries—Bangladesh, Hong Kong,

India, Indonesia, Japan, Pakistan, Philippines, Thailand, Taiwan, Fiji Islands, and Sri Lanka. They included Justinus Cardinal Darmojuwono of Indonesia, several Catholic and Protestant bishops, church officials and seminary professors, nuns and priests, Moslems and Buddhists, young workers and persons engaged in alternative ministries. The several contexts in Asia from which these persons came reinforced the multifaceted character of the Asian reality and thus created a spirited and dynamic exchange of ideas among the delegates that exceeded the limits of the "ecumenical etiquette" characteristic of most church conferences. Some persons were troubled by the obvious tensions generated, especially among young workers from Hong Kong and some defenders of the theological tradition of the churches. But I think the exchange was healthy, because it prevented theologians and church officials from camouflaging the past and present failures of the churches with theological jargon.

Like African theology, Latin American liberation theology, and theologies of the oppressed in North America, the search for an Asian theology has its origin with the recognition that Euro-American theology is totally inadequate as a creative response to the Asian reality. The theme of the ATC reflects this recognition: "Asia's Struggle for a Full Humanity: Toward a Relevant Theology." The focus on the need to develop a relevant theology out of the historical context of Asia's struggle for a full humanity connected the ATC with previous conferences devoted to the theme of suffering and hope. The Christian Conference of Asia (CCA) has been at the center of this theological ferment. Such publications as *Towards a Theology of People: I, Asian Theological Reflections on Suffering, Jesus Christ in Asian Suffering and Hope, Testimony Amid Asian Suffering and Hope,* and "Let My People Go" (1974 CCA study document) reflect the creative theological work the CCA has generated.

In order to concretize the theological significance of the Asian context and also to separate the search for an Asian theology from what many called the "traditional deductive method," the conference planners opted for the "inductive method" and implemented that decision by having a three-day live-in at the beginning of the conference. The intention was to develop an Asian theology based on Asian realities and not theological ideas imported from Europe and North America. This meant that persons who wanted to participate in the creation of a distinctive Asian theology must immerse themselves in the religio-cultural and the socio-political realities of Asia.

Because the Sri Lanka situation was chosen as a point of departure for the conference proper, all the live-in sites were located in that country. Six groups were identified for case studies: peasants, industrial workers and the city marginalized, plantation laborers, women and children, minorities, youth and students. Instead of choosing the minorities (race relations) live-in site, as many persons expected me to do, I chose the industrial workers at Ratmalana, and it proved to be a revealing experience. For any sensitive person inclined to import theology to Asia from Europe and North America or even Latin America and Africa, the live-in experience served as a significant check against that temptation. Although the three-day experience was quite limited, in no way serving as a substitute for a scientific analysis of the Asian context, it could and did serve as a way of introducing and sensitizing people to the uniqueness of the Asian reality. After that experience, I found it difficult to approach the Asian situation with theological categories I had grown accustomed to in North America and Europe.

A similar point can be said about Asia's relation to Africa and Latin America. While the latter's socio-political situations are similar to Asia's, their religio-cultural contexts are quite different and thus require theological categories defined by each continent. For people who are convinced that Christian theology begins and ends with God's revelation in Jesus Christ (a point I have often expressed), a sensitive encounter with the Asian context will necessitate some uneasiness with the western formulation of that theological starting point. It is not possible to remain open to learn from the Asian reality and also to hold firmly to a christological perspective that precludes the creative contribution of that culture to humanity. I am referring especially to those aspects of Asia's culture that are expressed in and through the living faiths of that continent. How is it possible to hold to a christological expression of Christianity defined by the West and still claim to remain open to the Asian reality whose continent has been colonized and oppressed by western missionaries and other Christians? For a non-liberation-oriented theologian, this question may not present a serious problem. But for one who has made the liberation of the oppressed from bondage the central motif of the gospel, such a question cannot be dismissed easily.

The minority status of Christianity is one thing that distinguishes Asia not only from Europe and North America but also from Latin America and Africa. This fact is so obvious in Sri Lanka that no one can ignore it. I had read about Christianity's minority status in books, but it was more revealing for me theologically to experience it in Ratmalana among ordinary working people. During the day and early evening, the industrial workers live-in group (about ten persons) met and talked with urban workers and their trade union leaders, nearly all of whom were Buddhists. They were also Marxists or at least influenced by that ideology. It was fascinating to encounter people who combined their devotion to the Buddha with their commitment to Marx and not experience any apparent contradictions. During the night, I slept at a worker's home who earned less than two dollars per week for the support of a family of four adults and two children. They freely shared their space with Sergio Torres (Executive Secretary of EATWOT) and me without asking about our religious persuasion. They were devout Buddhists.

After the three-day live-in, we traveled to the Holy Family Convent in Wennappuwa for the formal opening of the conference itself. As a "fraternal" delegate, I did not know what my status or role in the conference would be. The ambiguity of the status of the fraternal delegates disturbed many of them. When we were arbitrarily given two evenings to make presentations about the theology on our respective continents, without notice before the conference, we decided as a group to request an opportunity to discuss this matter with the Organizing Committee. At that meeting, we expressed our resentment about the arbitrary request and also our concern about the meaning of the term "fraternal" delegates. The Organizing Committee was frank in their reply to us. They admitted that they recognized the ambiguity of our status and expressed their disappointment about it. But they assured us that we were full participants, and that this information would be formally conveyed to the conference delegates. In addition, they invited us to play a critical role by evaluating the work of the conference from our particular viewpoints. They wanted us to help to ensure that the Asian reality would not be divorced from the global reality. Since we accepted their invitation to become full participants, we then informed the Organizing Committee that we had no desire to devote two evenings to theological movements on our continents but wanted to make our contribution during the natural development of the conference itself.

The Organizing Committee provided background on the reason for the small number of fraternal delegates and why this unique name was given to non-Asians. They were determined to make the ATC an *Asian* conference. They did not want any theological importations coming from Latin America, Africa, or any other continent. This concern was deeply felt and is the reason the CCA did not sponsor the ATC but only supported it. The CCA was particularly concerned about EATWOT's Latin American influence, and Preman Niles, Secretary for Theological Concerns, expressed it sharply:

> Asian theologians have usually been co-opted into theological agendas and theological positions which originate elsewhere. This is a constant danger, and is in many ways why clear Asian theological positions are either slow to emerge or do not emerge at all. The danger of co-option is particularly evident when an organization [EATWOT] seeks to speak for the whole of the Third World while taking its basic theological impetus from one section of the Third World, namely, Latin America. This is not to say that insights from Latin American theologies have no significance for Asia. They do; and many Asian theologians owe much to the breakthroughs accomplished on that continent. Also, many of these themes were already being explored in Asia before the so-called Latin American Liberation Theology hit the theological market. Taking this whole rather complex situation into account the CTC Commission on Theological Concerns of the CCA felt that it should support [*not sponsor*] this consultation in a discriminating and critical way so that the motif of liberation is explored in relation to Asian contexts and situations (cf. *HAYYIM,* vol. 1, no. 1, January 1979, p. 5).

The tensions between Asians and the fraternal delegates were greatly reduced during the course of the development of the conference. I felt completely free to make whatever contribution I thought appropriate and did not once feel that because I was not Asian that I had to be cautious about what I said. This feeling of freedom was reinforced when I was selected by the conference to serve on several committees, including the committee that would write the official document of the conference.

The conference proper began with an auspicious grand opening, with many welcoming addresses from the Sri Lanka government and the religious establishment. Following that event, the work of the ATC started with reports (oral and written) by the live-in groups. Most of the oral reports were exciting, because several groups chose to make that aspect of the presentation in dramatic form.

The most controversial group report dealt with the minorities (race relations). While other reports dealt with the harsh realities of the people's suffering, no report generated such intense emotional reactions as did the race issue. The excitement centered around a song which the live-in group created in order to express the feelings they encountered among the Tamils (minority) and Sinhalese (majority). The audience was requested to sing the lines of the Sinhalese majority and the live-in group itself would sing the demands of the Tamil minority. When the song sheet was distributed and some native Sinhalese delegates saw that for every demand of the Tamils was the Sinhalese response, "We shall not be moved," they strongly objected to the song, because they claimed that it increased the racial tensions already present in their country and also did not represent correctly the feelings of many Sinhalese people.

Of course I felt at home in the context of this heated debate, but to everyone's surprise, I chose not to participate. Unfortunately the song was not sung, but everyone knew that it touched on human issues that could not be avoided. Thus at the end of this debate, someone took the mike and appropriately announced: "The conference has *now* begun!" Before this debate, there was a tendency to treat human problems in a detached manner as if the Marxist ideology would provide all the answers. While Marxism as a science will help us to understand the world, it will not necessarily cause people to join the struggle for freedom. It is not until people experience a sense of indignation (which arises when they realize that their suffering is unnecessary) that they are then aroused not only to take Marxism seriously but also to join together in a common struggle against the enemies of freedom. To ask people to regard their suffering as secondary, as some Marxists ask the victims of racism to do, only serves to alienate them from the truth of the Marxist analysis. No oppressed minority group is going to join with the majority in a common fight for justice while the latter insist on ignoring the racism in its own group. For the validity of any appeal for solidarity against a common enemy is found when each group commits itself to struggle against oppression in any form. The main reason why the oppressed masses seldom unite against a mutual enemy is because a majority race in the masses often oppresses the minority, thereby destroying the trust that would normally arise in a common struggle. This is especially true among poor whites and blacks in the United States as well as among the Sinhalese and Tamils in Sri Lanka. But people (particularly intellectuals) who are identified with the culture and ideas of the majority seldom can see the importance of this point. Instead of using their efforts in destroying the racism of the majority, they usually exhort the minority to regard the race problem as secondary to class analysis.

Following the reports of the live-in groups, several major presentations were made by sociologists, theologians, and other resource people. Also, groups continued to meet around their live-in experiences, national issues, and other social, political, and religious issues that emerged from the conference itself. One weakness of the ATC was the failure to coordinate most of the group meetings and presentations. Thus many persons felt that there was little relation between the long plenary sessions and the small group meetings.

But despite this lack of coordination, several important issues emerged that captured the attention of the delegates. One such issue was identified by Aloysius Pieris's provocative presentation, "Toward an Asian Theology of Liberation: Some Religio-Cultural Guidelines." Everyone agreed with his contention that "the common denominator between Asia and the rest of the Third World is its overwhelming *poverty*," and that "the specific character which defines Asia within the other poor countries is its multifaceted *religiosity*. These two inseparable realities in their interpenetration constitute what might be designated as the *Asian context* and are the matrix of any theology that is truly Asian."

Pieris's presentation served to define the theological axis of much of our deliberations, and it also served as the focal point of the tensions and sharp disagreements in the conference. Some delegates (especially from the Philippines and Hong Kong) felt that Pieris's approach placed too much emphasis on the religio-cultural aspects and not enough on the social, political, and economic aspects of Asia. In order to challenge his emphasis on the religio-cultural and thereby clarify the debate, the delegates from the Philippines issued a National Group Report on Asian theology. They agreed with Pieris on the two essential characteristics of Asian theology: its "third-worldness" (socio-political liberation of the poor) and its "Asianness" (the religio-cultural dimensions). But they separated themselves from him with the assertion that "the main and principal characteristic of a truly Asian theology . . . is its 'third-worldness': this is the *substantive,* while the 'Asian' is the *adjective.*" Therefore "the primary thrust and concern . . . of the Asian third world theology is *liberation* (which to be authentic must be indigenized or inculturated); *inculturation,* though an essential and unavoidable task, takes second place." The concern of the delegates from the Philippines was to emphasize the class character of theology in contrast to Pieris's emphasis on the religio-cultural. "Every theology is conditioned by the class position and class consciousness of the theologian. Are we aware, in this consultation, of the petty bourgeois character of our theologizing?" These and other sharp comments served to join the issue between Pieris and his supporters and the delegates from the Philippines and their sympathizers.

My own view was to treat each emphasis with the same weight, because it is not necessary to decide which is the most important. Furthermore, the decision about which is most important (the religio-cultural or the socio-political) seems to be too much determined by the social location of the advocates. In Asian countries where intense political oppression exists along with the near elimination of indigenized religions (Philippines), the delegates tended to play down the role of native culture and accent the social and political struggle as defined by Marxism. In Asian countries where Christianity was a small minority among other faiths (Sri Lanka), the delegates tended to emphasize the primary role of the religio-cultural in the creation of a distinctive Asian theology.

A similar debate has occurred among black theologians in North America and also among African theologians in Africa. Latin American liberation theologians are also beginning to discuss the same issue in their attempt to assess the importance of popular religion in doing theology. While I think that both the religio-cultural and the socio-political factors are important in the development of any theology of liberation, the decision about which is the *most* important ought to be made in the context of struggle and with an openness to learn from both emphases. On the one hand, to ignore the religion and culture of a people only serves to alienate them from the liberation struggle that is being waged on their behalf. How can a people participate in their struggle for freedom if they do not understand the language in which it is being articulated? But on the other hand, to ignore the socio-political factors in order to accent religion and culture only serves to make the latter the opiate of the people. There are so many examples of this danger that no further comment is needed.

In the context of small group discussions and plenary sessions, several guidelines began to emerge about the character of Asian theology. The guidelines were articulated in several group reports as well as in the official ATC document that was written to express the theological convictions of the delegates. A section of the ATC document, under the heading of "Toward a Relevant Asian Theology," began with an emphasis on *liberation* as the chief motif of Asian theology. While the liberation theme connects Asian theology with other Third World theologies, the delegates were firm in their conviction that the meaning of liberation for Asian theology must be derived from the struggles of people on that continent. To be sure, many ATC delegates were advocates of the Marxist analysis of the class struggle, and several delegates readily admitted that Latin American liberation theologies have made an important contribution in this area. But they strongly resisted any pre-fabricated definition of liberation from Latin America or any other continent. To know what liberation must mean for Asian theology, they contended, it is necessary to be sensitive to the uniqueness of the Asian context. This context includes the socio-political and the religio-cultural, both of which are important for a definition of liberation.

Because Asian theology focuses on liberation, it must also be a *servant* theology, that is, a theology that arises out of a commitment to serve the poor and the oppressed. Some persons spoke of this commitment as a personal conversion. All agreed that no theology is neutral, but must take sides in the struggle for freedom. As the National Group Report of the Philippines expressed it: "The basic question here is: *for whom* are we theologizing?"

In order to serve the poor in terms of their liberation struggle, it is necessary for theology to have included in its methodology a critical component, that is, *social analysis.* How can theology serve the poor in their liberation struggle if it does not understand why they exist in poverty? It is not enough for theology to proclaim freedom, it also must participate in the production of freedom.

The liberation of the poor in society is real only when the poor themselves participate in their struggle for freedom. This participation happens in an authentic manner when the concepts used to analyze the struggle of the oppressed are derived from their history and culture. Hence Asian theology cannot ignore the *culture* of its people that is expressed in the living faiths of Asia. To quote the National Group Report of the Philippines again: "We need to affirm strongly that the formulation of an Asian theology, which is really liberating to the masses of the poor and oppressed of Asia, is the work of the Asian poor with liberated consciousness. It is they who must reflect on and say what their faith-life experience in the struggle for liberation is. This trust of the people and belief that they can theologize and are the real theologians is *central* to our position."

Liberation, service, social analysis, and culture lead to a focus on the *Bible* and *Jesus Christ.* To be sure, the presence of other faiths means that the biblical Christ does not dominate the emerging shape of Asian theology as might be found among other Third World theologies. However, it would be incorrect to suggest that Christ has been excluded from Asian theology. On the contrary, Jesus Christ occupies a central place in Asian Christianity. Asian theologies are simply re-interpreting Christology in the contexts of the living faiths of Asia. A theology group expressed it this way: "As we do theology in Asia, we move in a context of other faiths as a small, diaspora community. This littleness of the Asian Christian flock is providential and formative of our own theology. One of the places of God's action in and through Christ is the living faiths. In the history and present teaching and praxis of these faiths, we must learn to discern the presence of God and his message to us."

From Christ and Scripture followed the emphasis on the *church,* which was identified both with ecclesiastical institutions and emerging communities committed to the struggle for freedom. The main point here was the emphasis that theology is done for and within the context of a particular community.

The ATC ended with a worship service in which prayers were offered for each country represented at the meeting. While everyone was not pleased with everything that happened, no one could claim that the vital issues were ignored. If conferences have any worth at all (which is open to serious doubt), then I would contend that the ATC ranks among the very best that I have attended.

56

THE NEW CONTEXT OF BLACK THEOLOGY IN THE UNITED STATES

Gayraud S. Wilmore

Most Black American scholars in the field of religion and theology contend that Black Theology, as critical reflection about God and religious faith from the perspective of racial oppression and African cultural adaptation in America, began with the first Black American "Independent Churches" in the eighteenth century.[1] The 1960s, however, brought the first attempts since Garveyism to produce a more or less systematic Black Christian Theology.[2] In the immediate post-civil-rights period, the focus was reparations and Black Power considered in the light of the gospel. The flood of books and articles has diminished during the last three years, but interest in Black Theology continues, with the international scene and the renewal of the Black Church providing a new basis for contextualization.[3]

When the Society for the Study of Black Religion (SSBR) was organized in 1970, a second phase of Black theological formation in the United States became evident.[4] The earlier work of the Theological Commission of the National Conference of Black Churchmen (NCBC) was largely in response to current political developments and had an ad hoc quality. Under the SSBR, Black Theology took on greater credibility as an academic discipline. But it was the participation of black scholars in the Detroit conference on Theology in the Americas, in August 1975, which sensitized certain key leaders to issues that Black Theology could address only by broadening its context in an engagement with other ethnic minority and Third World theologians.

Two hundred Latin American and North American Christians met in Detroit during the week of August 17-24, 1975. The purpose was an extended analysis of the theology of liberation in Latin America, but the conference also dealt with the new theological winds blowing through the Black, Native American, Chicano, Puerto Rican, Asian American, and White working-class churches in the United States. The issues of feminist theology and traditional Protestant and Catholic liberal theology were faced in subsequent meetings. Keyed to the vitality of Latin American liberation theology, much of the Detroit conference focused on the socioeconomic exploitation of minorities, the repression of human rights, and the class struggle within both the internal and external colonies of North and South America. Theologians, church leaders, and grass-roots Christians wrestled together over the meaning of God's action in history, and the need for radical transformation, the tensions between Marxism and Christianity, and the task of the churches in the praxis of liberation.

Out of this meeting came the decision to organize several projects to continue study and move toward greater collaboration in an attack upon the structures of injustice and domination at a second hemispheric conference to be convened in 1980. The Black Theology Project, chaired by Dr. Charles Spivey, former president of Payne Theological Seminary (A.M.E.) and pastor of Quinn Memorial Chapel in Chicago, rapidly arose as the most successful of the several continuation projects sponsored by Theology in the Americas.[5]

The Detroit conference made a decisive impact on Black theologians. Since 1975, a network of small groups of pastors, professors, church people, and social activists has been developed and nurtured by the staff of the Black Theology Project. In the summer of 1977, the project sponsored in Atlanta what is probably the most significant conference ever held on the subject of Black Theology and its relation to the Black Church and community.[6]

What have been some of the consequences of the transcultural and interracial encounters with Black theologians orchestrated by Theology in the Americas? Recent statements and activities seem to point in the direction of a less exclusive introspective obsession with the American race problem than was characteristic of the earliest development of Black Theology. The Black-White dichotomy shows signs of breaking up, yielding to a widening perspective on human oppression which recognizes the importance of the class and cultural analyses of other theologians—especially the Latin Americans. But there should be no misunderstanding here. Black theologians are still concerned with racist oppression. Despite the insistence of the Latinos that they exaggerate race and color and give too little attention to the class factor, Blacks continue to argue that as far as the North American experience is involved, the contradictions within American Christianity are closely related to and aggravated by its historic connection with color prejudice.

The basic problem addressed by Black Theology is the ideological role that racism plays in the culture of the North Atlantic Christian community, a culture which equated the authority and omnipotence of Euroamerican White men with the authority and omnipotence of God himself, a culture which for almost two thousand years created deity in the image of the White man and gave to God the attributes of Caucasian idealization. That is essentially the religious basis of the ideology of the Christian West and the cause of much of the oppression that Blacks and other non-White minorities have experienced. Black Theology, therefore, is about the disestablishment of this ideology, the dismantling of the old order based upon it, the liberation from ideology to reality by disengaging the Black religious experience and its theological interpretation from the appropriation of an imposed unreality. Its purpose is the development of an inner-directed, self-determined theology grounded in the praxis of liberation from White domination in all areas of faith and life.

What Black Theology affirms is the opposite of the ideology that distorts the Christian faith to make God identical with the culture of White domination. It is, rather, that God has identified himself with the oppressed of every race and nation, and is present in their suffering, humiliation, and death. The violence perpetrated upon the oppressed is violence against God. Their death is God's assassination. But God raised Jesus from death and because we see in him the faces of the poor, oppressed peoples of the world—and particularly Black people denigrated by both Jewish and Christian biblical interpretation—Black theologians speak unabashedly of the Black Messiah, this oppressed and assassinated God who is risen to give life and hope to all who are oppressed. This Black Messiah who is the Oppressed Man of God, who is seen in the faces of the poor, oppressed Black people, and whose death and resurrection is their rising to new life and power, is the meaning of the gospel of liberation that stands opposite to the ideology of domination by which the God of the Christian culture of Europe and America was fabricated before and after the Enlightenment.[7]

The failure of Enlightenment optimism to purge the West of the idea of White supremacy means that the seminal Black Theology of Afro-American Christians in the nineteenth and twentieth centuries was the first self-conscious and consistent attempt to break with the ideological foundation of Euroamerican culture. It is possible to identify, as a consequence of this critical discontinuity between Black and White theology, three specific contributions that Black theologians have made to the theological enterprise in Europe and North America since the mid-1960s.

First, Black Theology discovered on indisputable biblical grounds that the liberation of the poor and oppressed, of which Blacks are a prominent example in western civilization, is at the heart of the Christian faith. It is not that this truth had not been known before, but it had been either suppressed or ignored whenever it surfaced over the millennia of Judeo-Christian history. Black Theology has helped us to rediscover that this is what our faith is about—the liberation of human beings from every form of oppression.

Second, Black Theology demonstrates that Jesus Christ can be de-Americanized without losing his essential meaning as the incarnate Son of God who takes away the sin of the world by his cross and resurrection. Black Theology authenticated an apprehension of Jesus of Nazareth in cultural symbols and contexts other than those of White American society. In so doing, it provides an example or model for the indigenization of theology in other societies and cultures. Subsequent developments in the United States within Hispanic, Native American, and Asian-American theologies show that this do Americanization, de-westernization of Christ opened the way for other ethnic groups to identify with him in the depths of their own historical experience. We now see the oppressed and assassinated Messiah rising in cultural symbols other than those of the White people of the West.

Third, Black Theology has legitimated a return to the religious genius of the ancestors who came from places other than Europe. It discovered traces of God's visitation in the primal non-Christian traditions of the past. Because of the work Black historians and theologians have done on the African inheritance in Black religion in the New World, the beliefs, insights, and religious imagination of "primitive" Blacks can be appropriated as correctives to the deficiencies of the western version of the Christian faith.

All of this is not to suggest that Black Theology does not have excesses and deficiencies of its own. Black theologians regarded American reality almost excusively in terms of Black and White. The attempt to understand Scripture and God's action in history in a way that made sense to oppressed Blacks makes it too easy to invest skin color with ontological significance. Certainly the Black-White dualism dramatically symbolizes a basic aspect of western experience without which much of it cannot be decoded. But the Black-White dichotomy leaves out other important areas of church and societal experience—particularly those reflecting the experience of Red, Brown, and Yellow people. Moreover, the oppression of women, Appalachian Whites, homosexuals, and other groups in American life must qualify dualistic analysis.

All theology, Black Theology included, is contextual and situational. We do not know of any school of Christian theology that is universal. The claim of some White theologians that what they call theology is the universal understanding of the faith for modern people is not only ridiculous, but an arrogant falsification of the nature of all theological reflection. Since 1975, Black theologians are less tempted to fall into this way of thinking about their work than formerly. Of course, they continue to make the interpretation of the gospel to the poor and oppressed Blacks of North America their primary vocation. But Black Theology today makes room in its formulations for an understanding of liberation that includes the contributions of Native American, Hispanic, Asian, and White brothers and sisters in struggle for the humanity made possible for all by the cross of Christ. Most Black theologians are now prepared to enter into the "pentangular" discussion of American theology proposed by Benjamin A. Reist.[8]

One problem is that Blacks have too often had the experience of seeing other non-White ethnic groups break ranks with them to trade on a preferred status with Whites. Bitter memories counsel caution in the opinion of those who continue to contend that a broadly inclusive program on liberation theology is still premature.

There are also other problems. A pluralistic theology, like ecumenism, ought not mean a democratization of thought in the sense that the lowest common denominator becomes the norm of truth. The desire for consensus should not be permitted to adulterate the distinctive gifts which each group has to bring from its own history and cultural inheritance. Moreover, the issue is complicated by the fact that if theological pluralism leads to a more faithful praxis of liberation, it must not only present the implications of the gospel for American minorities, but also the texture of the faith when it is filtered through the cultures and experiences of the people of Africa, Asia, Latin America, and the Pacific.

This means that the task of theology leading to authentic pluralism in a world context is fraught with enormous dangers and difficulties. It can, nevertheless, begin in the United States with its unique racial and cultural composition. The work of Black theologians over the last ten years provides American churches with foundational resources. Theology in the Americas, as the first research group to promote the idea that collaborative theological work on liberation should be the next item on the American theological agenda, deserves much greater support from the churches than it has received thus far.

Judging by their silence, many White American theologians do not seem to be enthusiastic about the possibility of a renewal of theology along these lines. Baffled by the demise of neo-orthodoxy since the Black revolution of the 1960s, they tend to see only confusion, fragmentation, and an exaggerated religious pluralism that produces theological fads unlikely to stand the test of time and the enormous new challenges of the twenty-first century. Those who find in process philosophy the only acceptable basis for a new systemization speak of an emerging Gestalt that will reject all dualism and view the reality of God, people, and nature as an organic whole, interdependent congeries connected in ways that verify the bio-spiritual analysis of modern psychology and the expanding, open-ended process conceptions of the physicists. These theologians have much to contribute in the areas of science and technology, particularly as they apply to bioethics and ecology, and their suggestions of an evolving, androgynous God makes contact with a central emphasis in some feminist theology.

But for all its interest in futurism and relevance to the difficult and pressing problems of the age of robots and computers—the science of the First World—many White theologians seem, to the theologians of liberation among the non-White minorities, to be one step removed from the immediate and monotonously routine problems of economic exploitation, political oppression, and cultural domination. These problems call for the conscientization and mobilization of the submerged masses of the United States and the Third World. The revival of conservative evangelicalism, the pop religion and mystification inundating the middle-class White churches, which are in retreat from social action, renders them not only unresponsive to process theology but oblivious to its existence. Black Theology and the other ethnic theologies of liberation may frighten the White churchgoing public, but the truth they speak about the meaning of the gospel and the judgment and grace of God cannot be evaded. Process theology does not attack the soft underbelly of American religion—its hedonism, its racism, and its worship of a privatistic, domesticated God.

There is no guarantee that the new context of Black Theology will provide an acceptable basis for wider collaboration or even that the God of the Black, Hispanic, and Native American theologians will turn out to be the God of the Bible who is no respecter of persons and races. The folk-religious base of the ethnic theologies spells certain dangers as well as an opportunity for a revolution of the oppressed masses. It is nevertheless true that these theologies open the way for American churches better to understand indigenous theologies in the Third World and make an important contribution to the internationalization of the mission of American Christianity. The convergence of non-White ethnicity and theology in the United States, to the extent that it avoids trivialization and the suburban captivity of the mainline churches, can recall neglected themes in biblical religion and can tap into subterranean streams which flow together at the deepest levels of our common humanity and need. Robert N. Bellah, a perceptive critic of the current American religious pluralism, is correct in his observation that

> the survival of ethnic identities seems to me only meaningful in the context of the survival of religious identities. Religion provides an essential mediation between the ethnic group and the larger culture of the modern world. Not only does religion often preserve the deepest symbols of ethnic identity, it also exerts a pull away from ethnic particularity to that which is morally and religiously universal.[9]

Notes

1. This is one of the basic discoveries of ethnohistorical research since 1964 and is elaborated in my *Black Religion and Black Radicalism* (New York: Doubleday, 1972). Further work is needed to show how the study of the present-day African Independent Churches, if important differences are respected, throws light on the theological development of Black religious institutions in the United States and the Caribbean, which began to break away from the White churches in the 1700s.

2. Randal K. Burkett has done valuable work on Garveyism as a Black religious movement of the 1920s. See his *Black Redemption: Churchmen Speak for the Garvey Movement* (Philadelphia: Temple University Press, 1978).

3. For a survey of most of the literature, see J. Deotis Roberts, Sr., "Black Theological Ethics: A Bibliographical Essay," *Journal of Religious Ethics* 3/1 (1975): 69–109. The most important recent book is James H. Cone, *God of the Oppressed* (New York: Seabury Press, 1975), although several Ph.D. dissertations by younger Black scholars should be published. One that has been published is Allan A. Boesak, *Farewell to Innocence: A Socio-Ethical Study on Black Theology and Power* (Maryknoll, N.Y.: Orbis Books, 1977). Two recent paperbacks on Black Theology published abroad are Bruno Chenu, *Dieu est Noir: Histoire, Religion et Théologie des Noirs Américains* (Paris: Le Centurion, 1977), and Rosino Gibellini, ed., *Theologia Nera* (Brescia, Italy: Queriniana, 1978).

4. The SSBR's chief architect was C. Shelby Rooks, president of Chicago Theological Seminary. Its founding was related to the increased attention given to the academic study of Black religion since 1968 by the Association of Theological Schools (ATS). See the issue of *Theological Education* on the theme "The Black Religious Experience and Theological Education" (Spring 1970). The SSBR includes most of the 158 Black scholars teaching (full- and part-time in 1976) in ATS-related seminaries. It has a working group of theologians, many of whom are also members of the Theological Commission of the National Conference of Black Churchmen. Within the last few years, the SSBR sponsored two consultations on Black Theology in dialogue with African and Caribbean theologians: Accra, Ghana, 1974, and Kingston, Jamaica, 1976. The papers of the Accra meeting were published in the *Journal of Religious Thought* 22/2 (1975).

5. Theology in the Americas has its office at the Interchurch Center, 475 Riverside Drive, New York City, and is headed by Sergio Torres, an exiled priest-theologian who also staffs the new Ecumenical Association of Third World Theologians.

6. The "Message to the Black Church and Community" with commentary by Shawn Copeland, adopted by the Atlanta conference, and the keynote address by James H. Cone appeared in *Cross Currents* 27/2 (1977):140–156.

7. Although the Enlightenment intellectuals opposed slavery, their argument that Blacks were a separate species did considerable damage. In the end, the polygenist theorists "frequently denied that the nonwhite races were people at all and maintained that the missionary efforts among them were wholly wasted." Thomas F. Gossett, *Race: The History of an Idea in America* (Dallas: S.M.U. Press, 1963), p. 54.

8. Benjamin A. Reist, *Theology in Red, White and Black* (Philadelphia: Westminster Press, 1975).

9. Robert N. Bellah, *The Broken Covenant* (New York: Seabury Press, 1975), pp. 108–109.

EPILOGUE:
AN INTERPRETATION OF THE
DEBATE AMONG BLACK THEOLOGIANS

James H. Cone

The purpose of this bibliographical essay is to evaluate the literature of Black Theology in the light of the internal debates of Black theologians among themselves in the academy and in the church. (The context for the latter was located in the Theological Commission of the National Conference of Black Churchmen and the former in the Society for the Study of Black Religion.) Few outside persons realize how seriously and vigorously the various theological perspectives in the Black community have been debated, and the effect these debates have had in defining the issues to which Black theologians have addressed themselves in their writings. To be sure, there has been much discussion about the imperialistic and racist character of Euro-American theology and the need to develop an alternative Black liberation theology. But because we generally agree on that point, we have seldom debated it among ourselves. Our discussions have involved much more than simply reacting to the racism of White theologians and church people. More important has been our concern to develop a Black theological perspective that takes seriously the *total* needs of the Black community, here and abroad. Needless to say, we have not been in total agreement about our needs, and our differences are partly reflected in the published writings on Black Theology.

The place to begin is with Joseph R. Washington, Jr., *Black Religion: The Negro and Christianity in the United States*. Before the publication of this book in 1964, most interpreters viewed Black religion as an aspect of North American Protestantism as defined by the traditions of the Reformation and contrasted with Catholicism and Judaism.[1] Washington was one of the first scholars to challenge this thesis and insisted that Black religion was a distinctive phenomenon in North American religious life. However, he viewed that distinction negatively. He contended that the unique quality of Black religion, namely, its emphasis on the quest for freedom, justice and equality in this world, prevented Blacks from developing a genuine Christian theology.

Indeed, Washington questioned whether the Black religious community itself was a genuine *Christian* community (i.e., a church), since the distinctive identity of a Christian community in North America would involve participation in the Western theological tradition. According to Washington:

> Concern with the ultimate in the Christian faith and what God requires of those who are called to live responsibly in His world may easily be less than primary for a segregated minority without a theology. It is evident that a crass materialism pervades Negro congregations, overlaid with a few theological generalizations, a terminology, and a feeling for religion which when anlayzed may now be more this-worldly than other-worldly. But a firm theological basis for a responsible perspective is missing, and Negro congregations are finally forced to seek purpose from the twin stimuli of social dictates and class values.[2]

Washington located the problem almost exclusively at the point of the lack of a theology in Black religious communities. In a bold assertion, which did not win him many admirers among religiously oriented Blacks, he wrote:

> Negro congregations are not churches but religious societies—religion can choose to worship whatever gods are pleasing. But a church without a theology, the interpretation of a response to the will of God for the faithful, is a contradiction in terms.[3]

The only solution to this problem in Black religious societies is for the White church to integrate them into the mainstream of American religion.

Although seldom referred to in Black scholars' critiques of Washington's book, one of its chief purposes was to criticize the White churches for excluding Black religious societies from the mainstream of American Protestantism. But his assault on the authenticity of the Black Church was so grave that no Black theologian could afford to ignore his interpretation. What precisely was at stake in Washington's interpretation of Black religion?

By defining Black religion as an instrument of social protest and excluding it as a genuine historical manifestation of Christianity, Washington undermined the connection between the Christian faith and political struggle as found in the history of the Black Church. The discipline of Black theology was developed partly to correct this distortion.[4] In view of the continuity of the secular and sacred in our African heritage and the biblical location of God's revelation in history, many of us believed that it would be a serious mistake to sever the connection between theology and politics. If we were going to protect the Black community from Washington's promotion of this widely held White thesis that the Black Church had no theology, then we needed to give some intellectual structure to the implicit Black Theology that we claimed was already present in the history of the Black Church.

The issues at stake were not simply intellectual or theoretical. They involved the identity and survival of the Black community. If it is true that the Black Church has no theology, because it has not produced professional theologians like Karl Barth or Paul Tillich, then are not White theologians and preachers correct in their almost universal tendency to separate Christianity from the political struggle of an oppressed people for freedom? If there is an inseparable connection between the Christian confession of faith and the struggle of poor people for justice, as the songs and sermons of Black Christians had suggested, then there was the need to demonstrate that connection in formal theological discourse.

The so-called riots in the cities, the cry of Black Power (Spring 1966), and James Forman's Black Manifesto (Spring 1969) made the situation even more acute. In response to White theologians and church people who demanded that their Black constituency denounce Black Power as unchristian, an ad hoc group of Black church people wrote a statement entitled "Black Power,"[5] which, to the surprise of the White church establishment, provided a theological defense of this emotionally charged phrase. But as Black church people themselves realized, they could not afford for the Black perspective on religion and politics to be limited to a "Black Power" statement or to other topical statements, such as those later produced by the National Conference of Black Churchmen. Such statements are too severely limited by the particularity of the historical events that occasioned them and by the lack of a clear theological structure upon which they were based. What was needed was the development of a theological methodology derived from and accountable to the Black community in the struggle for freedom.

Some of the vacuum was filled with the publication of Albert Cleage's *The Black Messiah* (Sheed and Ward, 1968). Cleage also insisted on the uniqueness of Black religion. But unlike Washington he gloried in it, claiming that Black Christianity is the only true expression of the religion of the Old Testament Israel and the New Testament Jesus, both of whom were African in their origins. Cleage's concern was to provide a Black nationalist interpretation of biblical religion and the Black Church, so that young Black Power advocates could view the church as an important agent in our struggle for justice and freedom. But Cleage's book did not have much impact in the Black church community, because it was seriously limited by its rhetorical and sermonic style, the historical and theological problems associated with his use of the terms "Black Nation" and "Black Messiah," and the absence of an ecumenical vision in his theological perspective. If Black Theology were to have any impact beyond the particularity of the American Black community, then there was a need to broaden the dialogue to include the ecumenical church. If we were going to liberate the Black church community from a mental enslavement to White definitions of the Christian gospel, then there was the need to challenge White North American theology in a larger world context.

My *Black Theology and Black Power* (Seabury, 1969) was the first book to be published on the subject of Black Theology. Its central thesis was that Black Power, contrary to dominant White theological opinion, is an authentic historical embodiment of the Christian faith in our time. This was so because Christianity is essentially a religion of liberation. Any theology, therefore, that takes this religion as its starting point must also be accountable to an oppressed community in its struggle for freedom. It was in this theological and political context that the task of Black Theology was defined as that of analyzing "black [people's] condition in the light of God's revelation in Jesus Christ with the purpose of creating a new understanding of black dignity among black people, and providing the necessary soul in that people to destroy white racism."[6]

The publication of *Black Theology and Black Power* caused a great deal of unrest in the White theological and church community. Immediately following its April 1969 appearance in seminary and college bookstores, James Forman presented the Black Manifesto at Riverside Church in New York (May 4) and NCBC's Theological Commission, in its first public statement on "Black Theology" (June 13, 1969), endorsed both Forman's concept of reparations and my view of Black Theology as liberation theology.[7] Black theologians and church people were determined not to let the White church and theological establishment escape the intellectual and political impact of Black Theology.

The following year, in *A Black Theology of Liberation* (Lippincott, 1970), I developed further the theological structure already present in *Black Theology and Black Power*, taking the theme of liberation as the organizing principle for my theological program. With the publication of this book, it was clear to some persons that Black Theology would not pass too quickly from the scene, and that what was needed was more discussion among Black theologians about the scope of their task, so that it would not be merely a reaction against errors of White theology.

My first two books on Black Theology defined several issues around which the subsequent debates among Black theologians would occur; especially *(1)* liberation, reconciliation, and violence; *(2)* Black religion and Black Theology; and *(3)* Black Theology and Black suffering.

1. Liberation, Reconciliation, and Violence

With the publication of J. Deotis Roberts's *Liberation and Reconciliation: A Black Theology* (Westminster, 1971), the assumption that all black theologians agreed with my perspective on Black Theology was laid to rest. There is little doubt that Roberts was writing in response to my earlier works, and our previous discussions in the Theological Commission of NCBC and the Society for the Study of Black Religion had already prepared me for his book on Black Theology.

Roberts did not deny that liberation is as important as I would claim. Indeed he would insist with me that liberation precedes reconciliation. "Liberation," he writes, "is a proper precondition for reconciliation in the area of race relations."[8] Roberts's difficulty with my perspective is that I, according to him, have overlooked reconciliation. A Christian perspective must include both liberation *and* reconciliation. "Christians are called to be agents of liberation. We have been able to love and forgive. . . . The assertion that all are 'one in Christ Jesus' must henceforth mean that all slave-master, servant-boss, inferior-superior frames of reference between blacks and whites have been abolished."[9] For Roberts, this means that we should begin to act as if these relations do not exist by being always open to the reconciling love in Christ Jesus. He therefore insists that Black people "must hold up at all times the possibility for black-white interracial fellowship and cooperation."[10]

In order to understand the debate between Roberts and me on this issue, it is necessary to note that there is a significant difference in what the terms "liberation" and "reconciliation" mean for both persons and the social context that defines them. Contrary to Roberts's implications, it is not true that I have overlooked love and reconciliation. In *Black Theology and Black Power*, there is a discussion of "Christian Love and Black Power" (pp. 47-56), and also a section on "Reconciliation" in the last chapter (pp. 143-152). The problem is that his view of love and reconciliation is different from mine, and it would have been more accurate if he had pointed that out rather than suggest that I have omitted them. I reject any view of love and reconciliation that would imply that oppressed people ought to be passive in the face of the oppressor's brutality. The weight of my perspective on love and reconciliation is located therefore at the point of guarding against any interpretation of the gospel that would render Black people powerless when confronted with White violence. I still do not see any reason why Black theologians should assure White oppressors that we want to be reconciled with them while they are brutalizing our communities.

Roberts obviously has a different concern, even though he also rejects any theology that supports Black passivity in the context of injustice. Indeed it is here that I am often confused regarding the emphasis of Roberts's theological perspective. Sometimes he seems to advocate seeking reconciliation with Whites while the latter are still in power, but at other times he explicitly makes liberation a precondition of reconciliation. How is it possible to say that "liberation is a proper precondition of reconciliation" and then also say that

> a black theology that takes reconciliation seriously must work at the task of intercommunication between blacks and whites under the assumption that for those who are open to the truth, there may be

communication from the inside out, but at the same time there may be communication from the outside in. In the latter sense, white Christians may be led to understand and work with blacks for liberation and reconciliation on an interracial basis.[11]

If liberation comes before reconciliation, then that assumption seems to negate the view that White oppressors can participate creatively in the liberation of the oppressed Blacks. Sociologically and theologically, I do not think that there is any reason to believe that oppressors can participate in the liberation of the people they hold in bondage.

Roberts takes up similar themes in a later book, *A Black Political Theology* (Westminster, 1974). But the discussion does not appear to be any further advanced than that found in his earlier book. It seems that part of our differences on this issue is related to the different political periods in which our theological consciousness was developed. Roberts belongs to the "integration period," and I belong to the era of "Black Power." This difference in the social and political formation of our theological perspectives affects how we treat the themes of love, reconciliation, and violence. Roberts seems to make the integration of Black people into White society the primary goal of his theological endeavors, and I do not regard that as a desirable goal. I believe that Black theologians need to move beyond "civil rights" (i.e., integration of Black people into a capitalistic, oppressive White society) to a political commitment that seeks to restructure society along the lines of creative socialism.[12]

A similar point can be made also about Major Jones, whose two books on the subject of Black Theology should be mentioned, even though they have not been discussed as much as they perhaps deserve. In fact, the third volume to appear on Black Theology was Jones's *Black Awareness: A Theology of Hope* (Abingdon, 1971). He was undoubtedly borrowing from the current popularity of Jürgen Moltmann's theology of hope, and the lack of an original approach to the theme probably accounted for the absence of much serious discussion of this book in the Black theological and church community. In 1974 Jones published a second book under the title of *Christian Ethics for Black Theology* (Abingdon).

It is clear that, in both books, Jones is addressing himself to what he regards as inadequacies in my theological program. Like Roberts, he questions my view of love, reconciliation, and violence. There is no need to discuss the details of Jones's argument, because they are not significantly different from Roberts's, especially at the point of his theological perspective reflecting the "integration period" rather than the "Black Power" era. Again, like Roberts, he appears to be more concerned with presenting a theological perspective acceptable to the White church establishment than about the Black community he claims to represent.

2. Black Religion and Black Theology

No issue has generated more discussion among Black theologians than the twin questions of "What is the essence of Black religion, and what is its relation to the development of a Black Theology?" I have learned much from these discussions and regard them as having made a critical difference in the development of my theological perspective. Even a superficial reading of my writings on Black Theology will reveal a significant difference in my first two books and the last two, *The Spirituals and the Blues* (Seabury, 1972) and *God of the Oppressed* (Seabury, 1975). What precisely is at stake in the discussion, and who are some of the chief participants?

The issue of the relation between Black religion and Black Theology was first sharply defined by Charles Long, and he received much oral support from the late Carlton Lee. This debate has been subsequently taken up by Gayraud S. Wilmore (*Black Religion and Black Radicalism*, Doubleday, 1972) and my brother, Cecil Cone (*Identity Crisis in Black Theology*, AMEC, 1975).

The debate itself is not easy to describe. The issues are complex, and the participants do not agree on the theological consequences of their assumptions, even though there is general agreement on the limitation of my theological perspective. The place to begin is with Charles Long, whose viewpoint is perhaps the most influential, despite his failure to publish a long-awaited book on the subject. He has written, however, an important article, "Perspectives for a Study of Afro-American Religion in the United States" (1971),[13] that emerged out of the context of our discussions. A similar article appeared under the title "Structural Similarities and Dissimilarities in Black and African Theologies" (1975).[14]

Charles Long was one of the first persons to raise the question about the legitimacy of a Black Theology, and he did it at a time when most Black scholars took Black Theology for granted. Long did not share Joseph Washington's reduction of Black religion to the quest for freedom and equality, and he also rejected my tendency to identify Black Theology with Black Power based on a theological program whose christological structure was derived from the Western theological tradition.[15] Whether the political liberation theme was treated negatively (Washington) or positively (Cone), neither view is adequate for describing the essence of Black religion. Long is a provocative and persuasive discussant, and has won many adherents to his viewpoint, which was largely directed against my theological program.

Long's concern is to make a sharp contrast between Europe and Africa, with the latter serving as the decisive ingredient in the definition of Black religion. While being keenly aware of the scholarly difficulties in deciding the question about the persistence of African cultural elements in the North American Black communities, he is convinced that there is "a characteristic mode of orienting and perceiving reality."[16] There are the "image of Africa" and "the involuntary presence and orientation as a religious meaning."[17] Here Long introduces what he calls the "historical and present experiences of opacity,"[18] the meaning of which is not altogether clear, but definitely related to "the otherness of Blackness."

> This Black reality took us down, down, way down yonder where we saw only another deeper Blackness, down where prayer is hardly more than a moan, down there where life and death seem equitable. We descended into hell, into the deepest bowels of despair, and we were becoming blacker all the time. We cried like a Job or we laughed to keep from crying and we wanted to curse God and die.[19]

According to Long, this is the reality that any serious student of Black religion cannot ignore, and it is not reducible to Christianity. Indeed this experience of blackness as Other cannot be analyzed theologically, because it is an African way of experiencing the world.

Long's radical departure on Black religion led him to question the legitimacy of a Black Theology, because theology itself is a Western theological construct, especially useful as a language of domination. Referring to Paul Tillich's Christology, Long writes: "Now Tillich's theology is a theology that presupposes the 'will to power' of modern Western civilization and it is addressed to those who have been imbued with the cultural form of inordinate and unrestrained use of power."[20] Those who are the victims of this power are the colonized and oppressed peoples.

The practical implication of Long's theoretical analysis was not entirely clear, and that partly accounts for the limitation of its influence in the Black Church and theological community. The Black community confronts a situation of oppression, and it must choose political options that will enlist participation in the struggle to transform the world. A simple call to a return to our African cultural heritage is not enough. What is the political import in our return to African culture? There is no clear answer in any of Long's published writings. While I do not minimize the need for culture if a people are going to survive in an alien society, cultural survival alone is not enough. We must survive politically with dignity by creating a social theory that will help us to transform the world according to our peoplehood.

An important contribution of Charles Long's scholarship has been its emphasis on Africa, the Caribbean, and Latin America. Thus in the early development of Black Theology, a Third World element was present. We began to realize that we could not develop a Black Theology in isolation from Blacks in other parts of the world. This global perspective that began with Africa and its diaspora would be extended to other Third World peoples.[21]

Gayraud Wilmore and Cecil Cone represent perspectives on Black religion similar to Charles Long's, but unlike Long, neither rejects theology itself. When the question is asked, "What is the proper subject matter of Black Theology?," their answer is, "Black religion." Cone and Wilmore agree with Joseph Washington in his contention that Black religion is unique and therefore cannot be subsumed under the categories of Protestant, Catholic, and Jew. They differ with Washington when the latter defines this uniqueness in terms of politics alone, instead of faith. Like Charles Long, they do not think that Black religion is reducible to political struggle even when it is related to Christianity. While Black religion has elements of Christianity and political resistance in it, neither of these elements can be elevated to the exclusion of the other. Their critique of my theological program begins precisely at this point. They claim that I have proposed a Black Theology that is based on White Western theological doctrine and the politics of Black Power, neither of which can really explain the complex phenomena of Black religion.

Since there are differences between Cone and Wilmore, it is necessary to look briefly at each theological proposal separately. The weight of Wilmore's critique is that I have simply blackened White Theology, failing to develop a unique Black Theology based on Black religion. "Is Black theology simply the blackenization of the whole spectrum of traditional Christian theology, with particular emphasis on the liberation of the oppressed, or does it find in the experience of the oppression of black people, as *black*, a single religiosity, identified not only as Christianity, but with other religions as well?"[22] While J. Deotis Roberts and Major Jones claim that I am too exclusive and not universal enough to include White people, Wilmore claims that I am too universal and not exclusive enough. Wilmore says that I am too oriented toward Christian categories as defined by White theology and have not paid sufficient attention to the complete uniqueness of Black religion.

Cecil Cone's perspective is similar to Wilmore's. He contends that since Black religion is unique and should be the foundation of Black Theology, the error of Black theologians has been their failure to recognize this uniqueness (Roberts and me) or of having located it in the wrong place (Washington). The failure to use Black religion as the foundation of Black Theology has produced an identity crisis in this discipline. This identity crisis is located at two points First, the tools which Black theologians use to do Black Theology are derived from White seminaries and are therefore inadequate for understanding Black religion and thus for developing a Black Theology. Second, while Black religion is related to Black Power, it is not identical with it or with any political program.

According to Cecil Cone, these two chief characteristics of Black Theology have produced an identity crisis, because they separate Black Theology from the essence of Black religion. The essence of Black religion is found in its distinctive origin in Africa with the focus on the Almighty Sovereign God. Both Wilmore and Cecil Cone agree with Melville Herskovits in his debate with E. Franklin Frazier on the issue of African survivals.[23] Both also contend that Black religion in North America is not reducible to Christian doctrine. And Cecil Cone, with Charles Long, would add that it is not identical with the politics of Black Power.

Wilmore is interested in a definition of Black Theology that will speak to Black "street people," the non-Christian, and the cult-oriented religions of the Americas, the Caribbean, and Africa. Therefore his list of sources for Black Theology includes the following: *(1)* "the existing Black community, where the tradition of Black folk religion is still extant and continues to stand over and against the insitutional church . . . "; *(2)* "the writings and addresses of the Black preacher and the public men of the past . . . "; and *(3)* "the traditional religions of Africa."[24] There is no reference to Scripture or Jesus Christ in the sources. Because of Wilmore's failure to use the Scripture and Jesus Christ as theological sources, his approach to Black Theology will be more acceptable among non-Christian Blacks (especially nationalists) than among Black Christians in the institutional Church, for whom Jesus Christ is the most important religious symbol.

Cecil Cone's perspective is closer to the Black institutional Church than Wilmore's. Wilmore is a member of the predominantly White Presbyterian Church and has spent much of his time making that church and other White churches take seriously the political demands of Black nationalists and other radical Black non-Christians.[25] Cecil Cone, on the other hand, wants to rehabilitate the institutional Black Church, because he believes it to be the primary instrument of Black liberation. Therefore he is critical of Black Theology's allegiance to Black Power, while Wilmore is not. Both are critical of Black Theology's dependence on White theological categories, but for different reasons. Wilmore wants a Black Theology that is accountable to the non-Christian Blacks, and Cecil Cone is concerned about the absolute integrity of the Black institutional Church.

As I suggested earlier, I have learned much from this discussion on Black religion and Black Theology, because there is a basic truth in the critiques of Long, Cone, and Wilmore. I have endeavored to incorporate this basic truth into *The Spirituals and the Blues* (1972) and *God of the Oppressed* (1975). If the struggle of the victims is the only context for the development of a genuine Christian theology, then should not theology itself reflect in its speech the language of the people about whom it claims to speak? This is the critical issue. When this assumption is applied to Black Theology, I think that Black religion or the Black religious experience must become one of the important ingredients in the development of a Black Theology. In his critical interpretations of Joseph Washington, J. Deotis Roberts, and my theological viewpoint, Cecil Cone has demonstrated the limitations of our perspectives at this point, even though he overstated his case and tended to be too superficial in his analysis of Black religion.

However, my concession on the importance of Black religion does not mean that I agree with their various interpretations of Black religion or the theological programs they seek to develop. Aside from the historical problems in the recovery of our African past, which only Charles Long seems to realize, all three appear to be unaware of the theological import of their historical suggestions. Long even makes the absurd contention that there can be no Black Theology based on Black religion. If he expects this point to be taken seriously, he will need to develop it much less in his sermonic oral style and much more comprehensively and systematically.

Cecil Cone and Gayraud Wilmore have a similar theological problem. While they do not reject the possibility of a Black Theology, both fail to say what Black Theology would look like if their suggestions about Black religion were taken seriously. There are several important questions which they need to answer. Is there anything in Black Theology that criticizes Black religion? If not, what is there in Black Theology that will prevent it from becoming ideology? It is interesting that neither raises this question. If Black religion is the *only* source for Black Theology, and if Black religion is identical with the *only* possible interpretation of the Bible for Black people, then what is the universality implied in the particularity of Black religion? Without this universalism, I do not see how we can make any Christian or human claims about Black religion. (The Christian identity of Black religion seems still to be important for Cecil Cone, and its human outreach is significant for Wilmore.) To be Christian and human means developing a perspective on life that includes all peoples.

Both Cecil Cone and Gayraud Wilmore's books end where I think they need to begin. They only devote a few pages to the future directions of Black Theology, and neither has proceeded to develop Black Theology according to their suggestions. Wilmore claims to be a social ethicist and Cecil Cone is deeply involved in the life of the institution he seeks to rehabilitate (African Methodist Episcopal Church). It would appear that Cecil Cone's existential involvement in the A.M.E. Church prevents his creative criticism of Black religion and thereby limits his theological imagination. The same is true of Wilmore in his concern for Black nationalists, especially non-Christians. But my question to both is this: What is the critical principle that should be used in the theological assessment of the Black Church or Black nationalism? This is the hard question which both appear to avoid but which desperately needs to be addressed. I have tried to answer this question by appealing to the biblical Christ who is present in the Black experience but not limited to it.[26]

Cecil Cone appears to equate the testimonies of Black people's experiences of God and Jesus with the biblical portrayal of them, without even asking whether the two (Bible and Black experience) are identical. If it makes no difference what the Scripture says and the only thing that matters is what Black religion says, then he should say that. He should not only assert it but be prepared to make a reasonable theological argument on its behalf. This same point is applicable to Wilmore in relation to Black nationalism. We Black theologians should not only be prepared to answer what a certain *segment* of the Black community thinks about the ultimate, but also the question, "What is the truth as applied to humanity?" I do not believe that we should limit our analysis of the truth to a certain ethnic manifestation of it in the Black community. This means that our development of a Black Theology must start with the particularity of the Black experience but cannot be limited to it. Therefore, we should create a perspective on Black Theology that invites other oppressed peoples to share with us in the search for the truth that defines us all. We must not allow Black Theology to reduce itself to an ethnic particularism.

As I suggested in an earlier comment about Charles Long, I am bothered by the lack of political vision inherent in Cecil Cone's analysis of Black religion. His analysis of Black religion is so "spiritual" and thus separated from politics that what he says about Black religion appears to be no different from conservative White evangelical Protestantism. What is the difference between Black religion and White evangelical Protestantism if the former must be radically distinguished from politics? Again it is revealing that Cecil Cone does not raise this question. It is a question that needs to be answered because most interpreters who appeal to the distinctiveness of Black religion and also insist on its *Christian* identity locate the uniqueness at the point of Black religion's focus on politics. The other possibility is to insist on Black religion's uniqueness but reject its primary Christian identity, a perspective represented by Long and Wilmore. But Cecil Cone appears to insist on Black religion's uniqueness without connecting it with politics or denying its primary Christian identity. Since he simply asserts his views about Black religion and Christianity without asking critical questions that seem to contradict his viewpoint, his analysis is often more confusing than clarifying.

We Black theologians cannot afford to ignore our political responsibility. For example, when the Black Church becomes politically conservative and defends that conservatism with a theological terminology similar to White evangelical Protestantism, what is the task of Black Theology? When Black Church preachers, bishops, and church executives begin to define the Black Church in the light of their own personal interests, is there anything in Cecil Cone's perspective on Black Theology that could critique them? When Black nationalists become so narrow in their view of Black reality, is there anything in Wilmore's perspective on Black Theology that could stand in judgment upon them? Of all the things we may say about our needs in Black Theology, we cannot ignore the need for creative criticism of Black religion and the Black Church, lest both become instruments of Black enslavement.

3. Black Theology and Black Suffering

Another important discussion among Black theologians has centered around the writings of William Jones, and it has focused on the problem of Black suffering generally and theodicy in particular. Although Roy Morrison has not written extensively on this issue, he also shares Jones's concern.[27] Both approach the themes in Black Theology from the perspective of philosophers of religion with no particular commitment to the Christian faith or the Black Church. I will limit my comments to Jones because he has been the most active and provocative discussant and also the most widely published.

In his book, *Is God a White Racist?* (1973) Jones uses Albert Camus and Jean-Paul Sartre in order to raise the problem of suffering in a fashion similar to what is found in the history of Western theology. If God is good and all-powerful, why is there so much evil? He takes this philosophical understanding of the problem and applies it to the writings of Albert Cleage, J. Deotis Roberts, Joseph Washington, Major Jones, and myself. He presents an argument from a Black humanist perspective, and no Black theologian should ignore the cogency of his analysis. Since Jones first raised this issue in an article in the *Harvard Theological Review*, it has received much discussion among Black theologians.

It is important to note that Jones claims to make an *internal* critique of Black theologians' various programs of Black Theology in the light of their own assumptions about the liberating activity of God in the world. He contends that in view of what Black theologians claim about God and Black people *and* the continued presence of Black suffering, each of their versions of Black Theology has an internal logical contradiction that cannot be tolerated. His critique of my perspective can be stated in this manner: If God is the liberator of Black victims, as you claim he delivered Israel from Egypt, where then is the empirical evidence that warrants that assertion of faith? If I claim that there is no empirical evidence, then Jones would say that that assertion contradicts what I say about God's liberating action in history. If God is involved in history, then there should be some empirical evidence of that involvement. Where then is the proof of your assertion that God is the God of oppressed Blacks, liberating them from bondage? Without an exaltation-liberation event, there is no basis for the theological claim.

The substance of my response to Jones is found in *God of the Oppressed*, chapter 8, "Divine Liberation and Black Suffering." I will not rehearse the details of my argument here, but the main point is that the Christ-event is the exaltation-liberation event to which Christians turn in order to answer the question that Jones raises. Because Jones does not refer to my Christology as the internal answer to the theodicy question in Black Theology, his claim to be doing only internal criticism is questionable.

However, as an *external* critique from the vantage point of Black humanism, Jones's analysis remains as a challenge to Black theological proposals and will continue to require the serious attention of Black theologians. We cannot remain satisfied with an easy *internal* solution, because what we say about God and suffering should be publicly defensible outside the confessional contexts from which they emerge. If we do not test the credibility of our theological judgments in a public arena, without resource to confessional narrowness, then we should not complain if what we say about God is ignored by those outside of our confession of faith. It is because Christians claim to have a universal message that they are required to speak its truth in a language publicly accessible to all. What then do Christians have to say about the continued presence of evil when we claim that God is both all-good and all-powerful? The historical character of divine revelation makes this question critically important.

I do not think that there is a definitive answer to the problem of suffering. Every generation of Christians must continue to try to give a response to the question of how one can believe in God in the context of human suffering. Two points can be made.

First, suffering is the source of faith. That is, without human suffering, there would be no need for the Christian gospel in particular or religion generally. Ludwig Feuerbach was right: "Thought is preceded by suffering." There would be no need for a Christian doctrine of salvation if there were no evil in the world. Therefore the gospel is the Christian answer to human misery.

Second, while the Christian faith arises out of suffering, suffering is the most serious contradiction of faith. This is the paradox. If the gospel of God is the answer to human misery, why do people still continue to suffer? There is no easy answer to this question.

I think that the only appropriate Christian and human answer is located at the point of what it causes people to do who are victimized by oppression. There is no way to answer to everyone's satisfaction the question of the objective status of God in relation to suffering, but we can ask about the political implications of our theological and philosophical claims. The problem with Jones's analysis and with many other philosophical treatments of suffering is that they are unlikely to engage the victims of injustice in the fight against those who enslave them. Jones's analysis can easily lead to despair, whereas belief in the presence of God in an oppressed community *can* lead to the empowerment of that community to struggle even though the odds may be against them. The task of Black Theology is to make sure that Black faith remains critical of itself so that Black religion can continue to function as a creative revolutionary challenge to the structures of injustice. If Jones can provide an interpretation of humanity and divinity that captures the imagination of poor people and enlists them in the struggle against oppression, at a deeper level than found in Black religion, then I would support his theological program. But I do not think that such an alternative is found in Black humanism.

Notes

1. See Will Herberg, *Protestant, Catholic, and Jew* (Garden City, N.Y.: Doubleday, Anchor Books, 1960).

2. *Black Religion: The Negro and Christianity in the United States* (Boston: Beacon Press, 1964), p. 141.

3. Ibid., pp. 142–143.

4. A similar comment on the rise of Black Theology in relation to Washington's interpretation of Black religion is found in Gayraud S. Wilmore, "Black Theology: Its Significance for

Christian Mission Today," *International Review of Mission,* vol. 63, no. 250 (April 1974).

    5. See Document 2 of this volume.

    6. *Black Theology and Black Power* (New York: Seabury Press, 1969), p. 117.

    7. James Forman's "Black Manifesto" and NCBC's first "Black Theology" statement are found in this volume as Documents 7 and 10 respectively.

    8. *Liberation and Reconciliation· A Black Theology* (Philadelphia: Westminster Press, 1971), p. 117.

    9. Ibid., p. 72.

    10. Ibid.

    11. Ibid., p. 23.

    12. For more information of my critique of Roberts, see my *God of the Oppressed* (New York: Seabury, 1975), chap. 10. See also our reviews of each other's books in the *Journal of the Interdenominational Theological Center,* vol. 3 no. 1 (Fall 1975).

    13. *History of Religion,* vol. 11, no. 1 (August 1971).

    14. *The Journal of Religious Thought,* vol. 32, no. 2 (Fall–Winter 1975). Other articles that make a similar point are "Civil Rights—Civil Religion: Visible People and Invisible Religion," in R. E. Richey and D. G. Jones, *American Civil Religion* (New York: Harper Forum Books, 1974); "The Oppressive Elements in Religion and the Religions of the Oppressed," *Harvard Theological Review,* vol. 69, no. 3–4 (1976).

    15. See his references to Washington and me in "Perspectives for a Study of Afro-American Religion in the United States." His critique of Washington and me is directly influenced by his dialogue with Carlton L. Lee. See the latter's review of Joseph Washington's "Black Religion" in *The Christian Scholar,* Fall 1965. See also Jerome Long's review in *Foundation,* October 1964.

    16. "Structural Similarities and Dissimilarities in Black and African Theologies," p. 10.

    17. Ibid., p. 13.

    18. Ibid., p. 21.

    19. Ibid.

    20. Ibid., p. 19.

    21. On the issue of the Third World, note the gradual development of this concern for Third World people in the various statements of the National Conference of Black Churchmen. In "Black Power" and "Racism and the Elections" (both issued in 1966), there is no reference to the Third World. But in "A Message to the Churches from Oakland" (1969, Document 11), there are specific references to the Third World (especially Africa and the Caribbean), a condemnation of racism, capitalism, and imperialism. This same concern is continued in its subsequent statements to its most recent Atlanta statement: "Message to the Black Church and Community" (1977, Document 34).

    22. *Black Religion and Black Radicalism* (Garden City, N.Y.: Doubleday, 1972), p. 296.

    23. See Melville Herskovits, *Myth of the Negro Past* (Boston: Beacon, 1969); E. Franklin Frazier, *The Negro Church in America* (New York: Schocken, 1962).

    24. Wilmore, *Black Religion and Black Radicalism,* pp. 298, 300.

    25. Before Wilmore's recent tenure as the Martin Luther King, Jr., Professor at Boston University and now Colgate Rochester/Bexley Hall/Crozer, he was the Chairperson of the Division of Church and Race of the United Presbyterian Church in the United States of America. On the issues of getting his church in particular and the White church generally to respond creatively to the Black struggle of freedom in the 1960s and 1970s, few persons made a greater contribution than Wilmore. His challenge to his church involved support for Angela Davis, for James Forman's "Black Manifesto," and for Black Theology. See his "Reparations: Don't Get Hung Up on a Word," *Theology Today,* vol. 26, no. 3 (October 1969), and an early essay introducing Black Theology entitled "Stalking the Wild Black Theologian," in *Social Progress,* vol. 60, no. 1 (October 1969).

    26. I have discussed this issue directly in *A Black Theology of Liberation* (Philadelphia: Lippincott, 1970), chap. 2; and in *God of the Oppressed,* chap. 2.

    27. William Jones's earliest article on this theme appeared in the *Harvard Theological Review,* vol. 64, no. 4 (October 1971): "Theodicy and Methodology in Black Theology: A Critique of Washington, Cone and Cleage." See also Roy D. Morrison II, "Black Philosophy: An Instrument for Cultural and Religious Liberation," *Journal of Religious Thought,* vol. 33, no. 1 (Spring–Summer 1976).

AN ANNOTATED BIBLIOGRAPHY
OF BLACK THEOLOGY

Vaughn T. Eason

The books and articles included here have been selected from a growing collection of literature on the subject of Black Theology. The sources of Black Theology are many and varied, not the least of which is the Black religious tradition. However, no attempt has been made to compile all the publications in the field, but rather to specialize in a selection representative of contemporary Black Theology in the United States. While Black people have done and continue to do theology from a variety of perspectives and hermeneutical principles, this listing primarily reflects a Black Theology whose point of departure and interpretative norm is liberation.

Included in this collection are a limited number of writings, which, while not themselves representative of contemporary Black Theology, are reflective of its source material. Such works include the writings of Thurman, Mays, King, and Frazier. It is hoped that the reader will find this listing to be a helpful introduction to the current corpus of Black Theology.

Books

Balthazar, Eulalio R. *The Dark Center*. New York: Paulist Press, 1973. An examination which locates the philosophic and religious roots of racism in western rational theology and seeks to demonstrate by a processive theology of blackness that theology as mystery, rather than reason, symbolizes the Supreme Reality as Divine Darkness and faith as a saving darkness.

Barrett, Leonard E. *Soul Force*. Garden City, N.Y.: Anchor Press/Doubleday, 1974. An examination of religious cults developed by Africans of the Diaspora, asserting that the religio-racial inheritance has been the sustaining force for Africans in America.

Boesak, Allan A. *Farewell to Innocence*. Maryknoll: Orbis Books, 1977. A socio-ethical study on Black Theology and Power, pointing out that Black Theology exposes the realities of the oppressed so that the church can no longer move "innocently" through history with no accountability for it.

Vaughn T. Eason is a Ph.D. student in Systematic Theology at Union Theological Seminary in New York.

Brown, Hubert L. *Black and Mennonite.* Scottdale: Herald Press, 1976. The conflict of being Black in a White church is examined with analyses of both traditions and the hope that mutual understanding will accord mutual freedom. Includes an analysis of Black Theology and a Black Theology bibliography.

Bruce, Calvin E., and William R. Jones, eds. *Black Theology II: Essays on Formation and Outreach of Contemporary Black Theology.* Lewisburg: Bucknell University Press, 1978. This book makes a distinction between Black Theology I and II by suggesting that the earlier exponents of Black Theology were engaged in "apologetic rage" but the latter stage is more constructive.

Carter, Harold A. *The Prayer Tradition of Black People.* Valley Forge: Judson Press, 1976. An examination of the tradition of prayer among Black people from Africa to the present. The author seeks to describe how prayer life in the Black tradition has brought together personal religion and social struggle.

Cleage, Albert B., Jr. *The Black Messiah.* New York: Sheed and Ward, 1969. A collection of sermons preached at the Shrine of the Black Madonna in Detroit, Michigan, which expresses the author's view that blackness is more than a symbol, because Jesus and the Jews of the Old Testament must be considered Black.

————. *Black Christian Nationalism.* New York: William Morrow and Co., 1972. This is the definitive text of the Black Christian Nationalist movement, setting forth its belief system, political perception, and program.

Cone, Cecil Wayne. *The Identity Crisis in Black Theology.* Nashville: AMEC, 1975. A critique of the work of three major Black theologians from the point of view of traditional experiential religion. The author argues that the crisis in Black Theology is its inability to reconcile Black Power with academic theology and both with traditional Black religion.

Cone, James H. *Black Theology and Black Power.* New York: Seabury Press, 1969. This first book published on Black Theology is the author's theological manifesto that Black Power is the central message of Christ to twentieth-century America. An analysis of the meaning of Black Power, the gospel, the church, and other theological and political themes from the Black perspective.

————. *A Black Theology of Liberation.* Philadelphia: Lippincott Co., 1970. A systematic treatment of the content of theology and traditional Christian doctrines from the perspective of the Black struggle for liberation.

————. *The Spirituals and the Blues.* New York: Seabury Press, 1972. A theological interpretation of the slave songs based on the socio-historical experience of Black people, and a comparison with the Blues from a theological and historical point of view.

————. *God of the Oppressed.* New York: Seabury Press, 1975. A measured treatment of the theme through an analysis of the social context of theology and biblical revelation. The author seeks to demonstrate that a Black Theology of liberation is the necessary imperative of the sermons, songs, and stories produced by the Black experience and its relationship with the Bible.

Dickson, Kwesi, and Paul Ellingworth, eds. *Biblical Revelation and African Beliefs.* Maryknoll: Orbis Books, 1969. This is a collection of essays by several African scholars published under the auspices of the All-Africa Conference of Churches. The theological methodology of relating traditional beliefs with biblical revelation is akin to that of Black Theology in America.

Dunston, Alfred G., Jr. *The Black Man in the Old Testament and Its World*. Philadelphia: Dorrance and Co., 1974. This work is written as a textbook, with questions at the end of each chapter. It treats the African presence in the Old Testament, offering a view of the Old Testament Jews as interrelated and interdependent with other people and cultures. The author seeks to dispel myths about Black people and biblical misinterpretations. An example of Black biblical theology.

Frazier, E. Franklin. *The Negro Church in America*. New York: Schocken Books, 1964. Published posthumously, this classic work on the Black Church, done from a sociological perspective, made many claims against which reaction has been directed. Aside from claiming that the Black Church in America has not transplanted any of its former African culture, the author coins and makes popular the phrase, "The Invisible Institution."

Gardiner, James J., and J. Deotis Roberts, eds. *Quest for a Black Theology*. Philadelphia: United Church Press, 1971. Six essays on an approach to Black Theology from different perspectives, resulting from an interdenominational conference devoted to an exploration of the Black Church/Black Theology.

Hamilton, Charles V. *The Black Preacher in America*. New York: William Morrow and Co., 1972. A socio-political study of the Black preacher, including the preacher's historic relationship to the people and the variety of roles assumed by the preacher from slavery to the present. Several interviews with contemporary preachers are the basis for a significant portion of the book. However, the author concedes that his types are not to be taken as "typical," for there is no "typical" Black preacher. Black Theology is given special attention in the chapter on "Preachers and Political Action."

Herzog, Frederick. *Liberation Theology: Liberation in the Light of the Fourth Gospel*. New York: Seabury Press, 1972. A systematic examination of the Gospel of John, which seeks to demonstrate that the principles of liberation are at the heart of the Gospel. A White theologian's response to Black Theology.

Hodgson, Peter C. *Children of Freedom*. Philadelphia: Fortress Press, 1974. A significant attempt by a White theologian to do Black Theology. Included is a provocative foreword by Gayraud Wilmore.

Johnson, Joseph A., Jr. *The Soul of the Black Preacher*. Philadelphia: United Church Press, 1971. A collection of sermons and lectures delivered at various times by the author. Seeks to explicate the meaning of the Christian faith for the Black struggle for freedom.

―――. *Proclamation Theology*. Shreveport: Fourth District Press, 1978. This work is the second of a projected three-volume publication, the first of which has already appeared. The author is a bishop in the Christian Methodist Episcopal Church, whose written works demonstrate that Black Theology is not alien to the Black Church.

Jones, Major J. *Black Awareness*. Nashville: Abingdon Press, 1971. An analysis of the historic Black experience and the church, Black and White, up to the contemporary period of Black awareness. The author suggests that the specifically Christian message of Black Theology must go beyond the immediate social context and affirm a theology of hope as the means to radical social change.

————. *Christian Ethics for Black Theology.* Nashville: Abingdon Press, 1974. An attempt to explicate the ethics of the Bible and Christian tradition and to apply the same to the situation of the Black liberation struggle.

Jones, William R. *Is God a White Racist?* Garden City, N.Y.: Anchor Press/Doubleday, 1973. A philosophical critique of major Black theologians from a Black humanist perspective, with theodicy serving as the point of departure. The author intends to do an internal critique of contemporary Black Theology and finds it unable to answer adequately the question of Black suffering because of its classical theism.

King, Martin L., Jr. *Where Do We Go from Here: Chaos or Community?* New York: Harper & Row, 1967. An analysis of the racial situation in America, with a look at Black Power, racism, and the dilemma facing Black Americans. The author seeks to demonstrate that community may still be possible, in spite of apparent chaos. While there has been debate as to King's relationship to Black Theology as it has emerged since his death, it is clear that he is treated by it with considerable regard. Indeed, his life and thought often serve as a paradigm for the political emphasis of Black Theology.

Lincoln, C. Eric. *The Black Church since Frazier.* New York: Schocken Books, 1974. An update of Frazier's work reflecting a more contemporary understanding of the Black Church in light of Black Theology.

————, ed. *The Black Experience in Religion.* Garden City, N.Y.: Anchor Press/Doubleday, 1974. A collection of essays by various authors on the Black Church, preaching, theology and protest, as well as religious alternatives to traditional Black churches, and a look at religion in Africa and the Caribbean.

Massie, Priscilla, ed. *Black Faith and Black Solidarity.* New York: Friendship Press, 1973. Addresses emerging from the 1971 consultation of Africans and Afro-Americans in Dar es Salaam, Tanzania, on "The Role of the Church as a Mechanism for Social Change."

Mays, Benjamin E. *The Negro's God.* New York: Atheneum, 1968. The republication of the 1938 classic study of the Black concept of God as reflected in Black literature, with a new preface by Vincent Harding.

Mitchell, Henry H. *Black Belief.* New York: Harper & Row, 1975. Seeks to demonstrate that American Black religion is derived from African beliefs and adapted to the needs of the people. An attempt to find a Black hermeneutic in folk religion. Foreword by Gayraud S. Wilmore.

Moore, Basil, ed. *The Challenge of Black Theology in South Africa.* Atlanta: John Knox Press, 1974. A collection of essays by several South African scholars and James H. Cone on the place of Black Theology in South Africa. The first publication in 1972 was banned by the South African government as a threat to the security of the state.

Moyd, Olin P. *Redemption in Black Theology.* Valley Forge: Judson Press, 1979. An examination by a Black Baptist theologian of redemption as liberation and confederation in Black religious experience. Foreword by J. Deotis Roberts.

Reist, Benjamin A. *Theology in Red, White and Black.* Philadelphia: Westminster Press, 1975. An attempt to open theological dialogue in a pluralistic society. An attempt to develop an American Theology from Black, Native American, and White perspectives.

Roberts, J. Deotis. *Liberation and Reconciliation: A Black Theology.* Philadelphia: Westminster Press, 1971. A Black Theology that necessitates a simultaneous consideration of liberation and reconciliation. The author argues that the two are inseparable in light of the Christian faith. The first full-length book reflecting a different perspective in Black Theology from that offered by James Cone.

————. *A Black Political Theology.* Philadelphia: Westminster Press, 1974. A discussion of human nature and destiny from a Black perspective. The author views the Black Church as the primary institution charged to implement the gospel of liberation by teaching that love of God includes love of others.

Skinner, Tom. *How Black Is the Gospel?* Philadelphia: J. B. Lippincott, 1970. An interpretation of the Gospel and the struggle of Black liberation from a Black evangelical perspective. The author suggests a third category exists in the midst of racial strife between revolutionary Blacks and reactionary Whites, namely, an interracial evangelicalism.

Thurman, Howard. *Jesus and the Disinherited.* Nashville: Abingdon-Cokesbury Press, 1949. Before the term "Black Theology" came into vogue, this author addressed its content, treating the significance of the religion of Jesus to the oppressed.

Traynham, Warner R. *Christian Faith in Black and White.* Wakefield, Mass.: Parameter Press, 1973. A primer in theology from the Black perspective. A number of traditional theological and political themes are explored, as the author argues that all theology has its peculiar perspective. This little book is important particularly for its Appendices, which include several original documents on Black Theology.

Washington, Joseph R., Jr. *Black Religion.* Boston: Beacon Press, 1964. A critical evaluation of the Black Church, which concludes that it is a fraternity of socio-political actions and not a church with a theology. Ironically, this claim is affirmed positively a few years later as the content of Black Theology. This work was published before the Black Power/Black Theology era, yet it offers a serious critique of White Christianity.

————. *The Politics of God.* Boston: Beacon Press, 1967. A significant reconsideration of the position taken in *Black Religion*; here the author sees the necessity of joining political struggle with religion in the Black Church as its only hope for survival.

————. *Black Sects and Cults.* Garden City, N.Y.: Doubleday, 1972. An analysis of the meaning of Black sectarianism and cults as they have developed from African roots through American revivalism. A new program for Black Theology is set forth in the chapter "A Measure of Black Sectarianism."

Wilmore, Gayraud S. *Black Religion and Black Radicalism.* Garden City, N.Y.: Anchor Press/Doubleday, 1973. A historical-theological analysis of the Black Church from slave religion to Black Power.

Articles

Bennett, Robert A. "Black Experience and the Bible." *Theology Today,* vol. 27 (January 1971), pp. 422–433. Argues that the Black experience offers a message consistent with the biblical witness though not itself found in that witness.

Brown, Charles S. "Present Trends in Black Theology." *Journal of Religious Thought,* vol. 33 (Fall-Winter 1975), pp. 60–68. An examination of the thought and methods of published Black theologians.

Bruce, Calvin. "Black Spirituality and Theological Method." *Journal of the Inter-denominational Theological Center,* vol. 32 (Spring 1976), pp. 65–76. An argument for the recognition of Black spirituality as the liberating quality of Black Theology.

Bucher, Glenn R. "Liberation in the Church: Black and White." *Union Seminary Quarterly Review,* vol. 29, no. 2 (Winter 1974), pp. 91–105. An attempt to explicate a theology of White liberation from the Black theology of James Cone.

Caldwell, Gilbert H. "Black Folk in White Churches." *Christian Century,* vol. 86 (February 12, 1969), pp. 209–211. Reflects the struggles and ambiguities of being Black in a White institution during the height of the Black Power era.

Campen, H. C. "Black Theology: The Concept and Its Development." *Lutheran Quarterly,* vol. 23 (November 1971), pp. 388–399. An examination of the meaning of Black theological thought through historical overview.

Carey, J. J. "What Can We Learn from Black Theology?" *Theological Studies,* vol. 35 (Summer 1974), pp. 518–528. An attempt to explicate the implications of Black Theology for White theologians.

Chapman, G. Clarke, Jr. "Black Theology and Theology of Hope: What Have They to Say to Each Other?" *Union Seminary Quarterly Review,* vol. 29, no. 2 (Winter 1974), pp. 107–129. Also included in this volume as Document 18. A critical comparison of the theology of Jürgen Moltmann and James H. Cone.

Cone, Cecil W. "The Black Religious Experience." *Journal of the Interdenominational Theological Center,* vol. 2 (Spring 1975) pp. 137–139. An argument for considering the Black religious experience as based on an encounter with God as opposed to political imperatives.

Cone, James H. "Christianity and Black Power," in *Is Anybody Listening to Black America,* ed. C. Eric Lincoln (New York: Seabury Press, 1968), pp. 3–9. This is James Cone's first published essay and served as the basis for his first book, *Black Theology and Black Power* (1969).

———. "Toward a Constructive Definition of Black Power." *Student World,* vol. 62, no. 3–4 (1969), pp. 314–333. An understanding of Black Power as the corrective to White racism and the assertion of Black dignity.

———. "Black Consciousness and the Black Church: A Historical-Theological Interpretation." *Annals of the American Academy of Political and Social Science,* vol. 387 (January 1970), pp. 49–55; *Frontier,* vol. 13 (June 1970), pp. 82–90; *Christianity and Crisis* (Nov. 2 and 16, 1970), pp. 244–250. An examination of the effect of Black awareness on the theology and action of the historic churches of liberation.

———. "Black Power, Black Theology and the Study of Theology and Ethics." *Theological Ethics,* vol. 6 (Spring 1970), pp. 202–215. An analysis of traditional theology and ethics reflecting its inadequacy in addressing the urgent concerns of Black people, thereby making imperative the development of Black Power and Black Theology.

———. "Christian Theology and the Afro-American Revolution." *Christianity and Crisis,* vol. 30 (June 8, 1970), pp. 123–125. Criticizes the White church as supporting racism and promulgates the notion that Blackness is indispensable to doing theology.

———. "Toward a Black Theology." *Ebony* (August 1970). An analysis of the meaning of Black Theology in terms of liberation with special reference to the Black Church.

———. "Black Theology and Black Liberation." *Christian Century,* vol. 87 (September 16, 1970), pp. 1084–1088. An analysis of Black Theology in relation to Black History, Black Power, and the biblical message.

———. "An Introduction to Black Theology." *Enquiry* (March–May 1971), pp. 51–80. An extensive interview on the meaning of Black Theology.

———. "Theological Reflections on Reconciliation." *Christianity and Crisis,* vol. 32 (January 22, 1973), pp. 303–306. An evaluation of the Christian doctrine of reconciliation in light of the suffering of Black people as it relates to biblical history.

———. "Black Theology on Revolution, Violence and Reconciliation." *Dialogue,* vol. 12 (Spring 1973), pp. 127–133. An apologetic on Black Theology's reinterpretation of contemporary issues in light of the biblical and Black historical witness.

———. "Freedom, History and Hope." *Journal of the Interdenominational Theological Center,* vol. 1 (Fall 1973), pp. 55–64. A theological assessment of freedom and hope in the light of the Black historical context.

———. "Negro Churches (in the United States)." *Encyclopaedia Britannica,* 15th ed. (1974), pp. 936–942. An examination of the nature and significance of Black churches from early slave religion to the present emergence of Black Theology.

———. "White and Black." *The Other Side* (May–June 1974). An interview on the meaning of Black and White theologies.

———. "The Dialectic of Theology and Life or Speaking the Truth." *Union Seminary Quarterly Review,* vol. 29, no. 2 (Winter 1974), pp. 75–89. An argument that the life experience of a people, reflected in their literature, must inform theology.

———. "Black and African Theologies: A Consultation." *Christianity and Crisis,* vol. 35 (March 3, 1975), pp. 50–52. A report on the similarities and differences of the two theologies as reflected in two consultations sponsored by the All-Africa Conference of Churches and the Society for the Study of Black Religion.

———. "Who Is Jesus Christ for Us Today?" *Christianity and Crisis,* vol. 35 (April 14, 1975), pp. 81–85. An examination of the Christology of Black Theology, informed by the interaction of Scripture, tradition and social context.

———. "The Story Context of Black Theology." *Theology Today,* vol. 32 (July 1975) pp. 144–150. Sets forth a case for understanding Black Theology through the story form out of which it emerges, with an analysis of the reasons for such a form.

———. "The Content and Method of Black Theology." *Journal of Religious Thought,* vol. 33 (Fall–Winter 1975), pp. 90–103. An examination of the socio-political context of Black religion and the development of Black Theology therefrom.

————. "Black Theology and the Black College Student." *Journal of Afro-American Issues*, vol. 4, no. 3–4 (Summer–Fall 1976), pp. 420–431. An examination of the place of Black Christianity on the college campus and in the Black community.

————. " 'God Our Father, Christ Our Redeemer, Man Our Brother': A Theological Interpretation of the A.M.E. Church." *Journal of the Interdenominational Theological Center*, vol. 4, no. 1 (Fall 1976). A theological interpretation of the meaning of the African Methodist Episcopal Church.

————. "Black Theology: Tears, Anguish and Salvation." *The Circuit Rider* (May 1978), pp. 3–6. An examination of the meaning of the biblical doctrine of salvation.

————. "Sanctification, Liberation and Black Worship." *Theology Today* (July 1978). A theological interpretation of the meaning of Black worship with special reference to the function of the Holy Spirit in sermon, prayer, song, conversion, shouting and testimony.

————, and William Hordern. "Dialogue on Black Theology." *Christian Century*, vol. 88 (September 15, 1971), pp. 1079–1080. A conversation on the nature and content of Black Theology between its foremost spokesperson and his former professor.

Delk, Yvonne. "Insights: A Discussion." *Andover Newton Quarterly Review*, vol. 14 (November 1973), pp. 135–142. A report of the responses of a group of Black seminarians on the relevance and meaning of theological education.

Duke, Robert W. "Black Theology and the Experience of Blackness." *Journal of Religious Thought*, vol. 29, no. 1 (Spring–Summer 1972), pp. 28–42. A White person seeks to analyze blackness in light of Black Theology.

Edwards, Herbert O. "Race Relations and Reformation-Oriented Theological Ethics." *Journal of the Interdenominational Theological Center*, vol. 2, no. 2 (Spring 1975), pp. 125–136. An examination of the effect of Protestant theological and ethical doctrines on White America's response to the historic plight of Blacks in America.

————. "Toward a Black Christian Social Ethic." *Journal of the Interdenominational Theological Center*, vol. 40, no. 2 (Spring 1975), pp. 97–108. An examination of the meaning of Black Christian social ethics in light of White establishment ethics.

————. "Black Theology: Retrospect and Prospect." *Journal of Religious Thought*, vol. 33 (Fall–Winter 1975), pp. 46–59. An assessment of the use of Black Theology and a prognosis for its future.

Eichelberger, William L. "A Mytho-Historical Approach to the Black Messiah." *Journal of Religious Thought*, vol. 33 (Spring–Summer 1976), pp. 63–74. An elucidation of the meaning of the symbols of Blackness and the Black Messiah.

Garber, Paul R. "King Was a Black Theologian." *Journal of Religious Thought*, vol. 31 (Fall–Winter 1974–75), pp. 16–32. An argument that Martin L. King's life and writings measure up to the content of contemporary Black theologians.

————. "Black Theology: The Latter Day Legacy of Martin Luther King, Jr." *Journal of the Interdenominational Theological Center*, vol. 2 (Spring 1975), pp. 100–113. An assessment of King in light of Black Theology reflecting mutual roots in the liberation struggle.

Gelzer, David G. "Random Notes on Black Theology and African Theology." *Christian Century,* vol. 87 (September 16, 1970), pp. 1091–1093. A comparison of the two theologies, indicating significant differences.

Grigsby, Marshall. "The Black Religious Experience and Theological Education." *Theological Education,* vol. 13 (Winter 1977), pp. 73–84. A statistical assessment of Black involvement in the academic theological enterprise for the period 1970–1976.

Hanson, Geddes. "Black Theology and Protestant Thought." *Social Progress,* vol. 60 (September–October 1969), pp. 5–12. An examination of Black Theology which presents a new hermeneutical principle to the Protestant tradition.

Herzfeld, Will. "Black Theology and White Theology." *Lutheran Quarterly,* vol. 27 (August 1975), pp. 230–233. Brief personal notes on the differences in the two theologies.

James, R. B. "Tillichian Analysis of James Cone's Black Theology." *Perspectives in Religious Studies,* vol. 1 (Spring 1974), pp. 15–28. An attempt to critique Cone's theology from within the structure of his system, treating especially the symbol of Blackness and the theme of reconciliation.

Jeffers, R. A. "Poor of God and the Black Christian in America." *Catholic World,* vol. 213 (June 1971), pp. 126–129. An examination of Black Theology as the first specifically American theology.

Johnson, Joseph. "The Need for a Black Christian Theology." *Journal of the Interdenominational Theological Center,* vol. 2 (Fall 1974), pp. 19–29. Demonstrates that Black Theology is grounded in the Christian witnessing community because God's revelation in Jesus Christ is its point of departure.

Jones, Lawrence. "Black Churches in Historical Perspective." *Christianity and Crisis,* vol. 30 (November 16, 1970), pp. 226–228. Reflects the notion that the Black Church was born in reaction to racism and as a positive assertion of Black humanity as a vehicle for racial salvation.

Jones, Miles J. "Toward a Theology of the Black Experience." *Christian Century,* vol. 87 (September 16, 1979), pp. 1088–1091. An argument for a Black Theology based on an ontological rather than an existential approach.

Jones, William R. "Theodicy and Methodology in Black Theology: A Critique of Washington, Cone and Cleage." *Harvard Theological Review,* vol. 64 (October 1971), pp. 541–557. A critique of Black Theology from the starting point of Black suffering, which raises the question of the possible malevolence of God.

———. "Theodicy: The Controlling Category for Black Theology." *Journal of Religious Thought,* vol. 30, no. 1 (Spring–Summer 1973), pp. 28–38. An analysis of Black Theology, with suffering as the hermeneutical principle.

———. "Toward an Interim Assessment of Black Theology." *Christian Century,* vol. 89 (May 3, 1972), pp. 513–517. Sets forth guidelines for an assessment of Black Theology through descriptive analysis and internal criticism.

Kameeta, Zephania. "Black Theology of Liberation." *Lutheran World,* vol. 22, no. 4 (1975), pp. 276–278. A Namibian theologian explores the nature and meaning of Black Theology.

LeMone, Archie. "When Traditional Theology Meets Black and Liberation Theology." *Christianity and Crisis,* vol. 33 (September 17, 1973), pp. 177–178. A report on a symposium at the World Council of Churches Ecumenical Center in Geneva, Switzerland.

Long, Charles. "The Black Reality: Toward a Theology of Freedom." *Criterion* (Spring–Summer 1969), pp. 2–7. An argument suggesting that the Black presence in America makes possible an American theology of freedom.

———. "Perspectives for a Study of Afro-American Religion in the U.S." *History of Religions,* vol. 2 (August 1971), pp. 54–66. A presentation of a methodology for the study of Black religion contrary to the traditional social science approach, and the new apologetic approach of Black Theology.

———. "Structural Similarities and Dissimilarities in Black and African Theologies." *Journal of Religious Thought,* vol. 33 (Fall–Winter 1975), pp. 9–24. An analysis of the principles underlying Black and African theologies which determine their common qualities and their differences.

Maultsby, Hubert. "Paul, Black Theology and Hermeneutics." *Journal of the Interdenominational Theological Center,* vol. 32 (Spring 1976), pp. 49–64. An examination of Black Theology from the vantage point of the Pauline corpus.

Mbiti, J. S. "An African Views American Black Theology." *Worldview,* vol. 17 (August 1974), pp. 41–44. An assessment of Black Theology which clearly differentiates it from African Theology.

McCall, Emmanuel. "Black Liberation Theology: A Politics of Freedom." *Review and Expositor,* vol. 23 (Summer 1976), pp. 323–333. An examination of Black Liberation Theology out of the context of larger historic theologies of liberation.

McClain, William B. "The Genius of the Black Church." *Christianity and Crisis,* vol. 30 (November 2 and 16, 1970), pp. 250–252. An apologetic stressing the historical and contemporary uniqueness of the Black Church.

McGraw, James R. ed. "NCBC Speaks." *Renewal,* vol. 10 (October–November 1970). The entire issue of this periodical is devoted to the National Conference of Black Churchmen. Included are the following: Leon Watts, "Caucuses and Caucasians"; Vincent Harding, "No Turning Back"; NCBC Statements on "Black Power"; "Racism and the Elections: 1966"; "Message to the Churches from Oakland, 1969"; and "Black Declaration of Independence." Harding's article is an in-depth analysis of the NCBC statements.

McKinney, Richard I. "The Black Church." *Harvard Theological Review,* vol. 64 (October 1971), pp. 452–481. An assessment of the history and present impact of the Black Church, suggesting that having been the most significant institution among Black people, the Black Church may prove to be a major factor in the renewal of Christianity in America.

Opocensky, M. "Afro-American Revolution and Black Theology." *Communio Viatorum,* vol. 15, no. 1 (1972), pp. 67–70. An examination of the necessary relationship between the Black struggle for freedom and the liberation content of Black Theology.

————. "Lessons from Black Theology." *Communio Viatorum*, vol. 17, no. 1–2 (1974), pp. 41–45. Reflections on the Consultation on Black Theology and Theology of Liberation held in May 1974.

Roberts, J. Deotis. "Folklore and Religion: The Black Experience." *Journal of Religious Thought*, vol. 27, no. 2 (Summer Supplement, 1970), pp. 5–15. Contrasting folklore and religion, the author seeks to demonstrate that Black people made little differentiation between the two and their faith has been grounded in both.

————. "Black Theology and the Theological Revolution." *Journal of Religious Thought*, vol. 28, no. 1 (Spring–Summer 1971), pp. 5–20. A dual analysis of Black Theology and the contemporary revolution in theology in general as they relate to each other.

————. "Africanisms and Spiritual Strivings." *Journal of Religious Thought*, vol. 30, no. 1 (Spring–Summer 1973), pp.16–27. An examination of several views by Black scholars on the subject.

————. "Black Theology in the Making." *Review and Expositor*, vol. 70 (Summer 1973), pp. 321–330. An examination of the development of Black Theology.

————. "Black Theological Ethics." *Journal of Religious Ethics*, vol. 3 (Spring 1975), pp. 69–109. A bibliographical essay discussing critically the literature in theological ethics by and about Black people.

————. "A Black Ecclesiology of Involvement." *Journal of Religious Thought*, vol. 32 (Spring–Summer 1975), pp. 36–46. An analysis of the Black church as family, socializing and political agent, a chosen people.

————. "Contextual Theology: Liberation and Indigenization." *Christian Century*, vol. 93 (January 28, 1976), pp. 64–68. An argument that theology from any context must have liberation as its content.

————. "Black Liberation Theism." *Journal of Religious Thought*, vol. 33 (Spring–Summer 1976), pp. 25–35. An examination of the understanding of the "God-idea" in Black Theology.

————, ed. "Black Theology in 1976." *Journal of Religious Thought*, vol. 33 (Spring–Summer 1976), pp. 3–100. A statement on major themes of Black Theology by the Theological Commission of the National Conference of Black Christians.

Rooks, C. Shelby. "Theological Education and the Black Church." *Christian Century*, vol. 86 (February 12, 1969), pp. 212–216. An assessment of the special needs of Black seminary education and a proposed methodology for meeting those needs.

Ruether, Rosemary. "The Black Theology of James Cone." *Catholic World*, vol. 214 (October 1971), pp. 18–20. A critique of Cone's theology by a White theologian teaching at a Black school.

————. "Crisis in Sex and Race: Black Theology vs. Feminist Theology." *Christianity and Crisis*, vol. 34 (April 15, 1974), pp. 67–73. A White theologian analyzes the conflict between these two theologies and points toward the need for an independent Black feminism.

Sheares, Reuben A., II. "Beyond White Theology." *Christianity and Crisis,* vol. 30 (November 2 and 16, 1970), pp. 229–235. Asserts that the Black Church has always been beyond White theology in its quest for survival, and now continues beyond in its quest for liberation.

Soulen, Richard N. "Black Worship and Hermeneutic." *Christian Century,* vol. 87 (February 11, 1970), pp. 168–171. An examination of style and interpretive methods in Black worship as the basis of any rapprochement with the White church.

Thomas, George B. "Black Theology: Vanguard of Pan-African Christianity in America." *Journal of the Interdenominational Theological Center,* vol. 1 (Spring 1974), pp. 69–77. An assessment of Black Theology which links it to African Theology as a reflection of Pan-African Christianity.

Tutu, Desmond. "Black Theology." *Frontier,* vol. 17 (Summer 1974), pp. 73–76. An examination of the meaning of Black Theology and the contribution it may make to African Theology.

———. "Black Theology/African Theology—Soul Mates or Antagonists?" *Journal of Religious Thought,* vol. 33 (Fall–Winter 1975), pp. 25–33. Also included in this volume as Document 44. A reflection on Black and African theologies by a South African who recognizes their differences but appropriates both.

Washington, Joseph R. "Are American Negro Churches Christian?" *Theology Today,* vol. 20 (April 1963), pp. 76–86. The precursor to the author's book *Black Religion,* where the theme of the Black Church's irrelevance to the Christian faith is more fully developed. This article, like the book, may well mark the end of an era in Black thought and the beginning of Black Theology.

———. "The Roots and Fruits of Black Theology." *Theology Today,* vol. 30 (July 1973), pp. 121–129. An examination of the religious history that has given rise to contemporary Black Theology.

———. "The Black Religious Crisis." *Christian Century,* vol. 91 (May 1, 1974), pp. 472–475. An analysis of the decline of participation in the Black Church.

———. "Shafts of Light in Black Religious Awakening." *Religion in Life,* vol. 43 (Summer 1974), pp. 150–160. A reflection on the various forms of Black religion in contemporary times.

Watts, Leon W., II. "The Black Church Yes! COCU No!" *Renewal,* vol. 10 (March 1970), pp. 10–11. An affirmation of the Black Church as an agent for Black liberation, and a rejection of the Consultation on Church Union as an impediment to liberation.

———. "The National Committee of Black Churchmen." *Christianity and Crisis,* vol. 30 (November 2 and 16, 1970), pp. 237–243. An analytical overview of the late 1960s with an explanation of the rise, function and goals of NCBC, including a statement on Black Theology and the Black Manifesto.

———. "Transcendence and Mystery in Black Theology." *IDOC International Documentation,* vol. 71 (March–April 1976), pp. 60–75. An examination of the varied sources of Black Theology and their expressions of the same transcendent revelation.

West, Cornel. "Philosophy and the Afro-American Experience." *Philosophical Forum,* March 1979. The article explores the possibility of a black philosophy.

White, Willie. "Separate unto God." *Christian Century,* vol. 91 (February 13, 1974), pp. 179–181. An argument calling for unity among Black Christians as the content of ecumenicity, excluding the White Church until it makes a clear and conscious commitment to liberation.

Williams, A. R. "A Black Pastor Looks at Black Theology." *Harvard Theological Review,* vol. 64 (October 1971), pp. 559–567. A critique of the theology of James Cone by one who is struggling to reconcile the revolutionary language of Black Theology to the traditional concepts of the church.

———. "Black Theology: Past, Present and Future." *Journal of the Interdenominational Theological Center,* vol. 40, no. 2 (Spring 1975), pp. 75–86. A Black pastor examines the development of Black Theology.

Williams, Preston N. "The Black Experience and Black Religion." *Theology Today,* vol. 26 (October 1969), pp. 246–261. A historical-cultural analysis seeking to demonstrate the mutually supportive relationship of religion and the struggle of life among Black people.

———. "James Cone and the Problem of a Black Ethic." *Harvard Theological Review,* vol. 65 (October 1972), pp. 483–484. An analysis of the ethic implicit in Black Theology.

Williams, Robert C. "Moral Suasion and Militant Aggression in the Theological Perspective of Black Religion." *Journal of Religious Thought,* vol. 30, no. 2 (Fall–Winter, 1973–1974), pp. 27–50. A historical-philosophical analysis of the theologies of James Cone and Albert Cleage.

Wilmore, Gayraud S. "Stalking the Wild Black Theologians." *Social Progress,* vol. 60 (September–October 1969), pp. 3–4. An introduction to an issue of *Social Progress* devoted to an examination of Black Theology.

———. "Ethics in Black and White." *Christian Century,* vol. 90 (September 1973), pp. 877–888. A report on a survey of Black ethicists highlighting the Black ethical dialectic.

———. "Black Theology: Its Significance for Christian Mission Today." *International Review of Missions,* vol. 63 (April 1974), pp. 211–231. An explication of the issues in contemporary Black Theology with a recognition that it represents a new way of describing an old phenomenon, i.e., the way Black people have thought about God. The claim is made that Black Theology may set the Christian world free for service wherever there is oppression.

———. "Black Messiah: Revising the Color Symbolism of Western Christology." *Journal of the Interdenominational Theological Center,* vol. 2 (Fall 1974), pp. 8–18. A Christology built upon the ontological symbol of Blackness as a point of departure.

———. "The Religion and Philosophy of Black America." *The World Encyclopedia of Black Peoples,* Conspectus volume (St. Clair Shores, Mich.: Scholarly Press, 1975), pp. 290–305. A general survey of the development of religion and philosophy in Black America during the nineteenth and twentieth centuries.

————. "To Speak with One Voice?" *Christian Century*, vol. 92 (February 1975), pp. 167–169. A report on the Ghana Consultation (December 1974) on African and Black Theology.

————. "Black Theology: Raising the Questions." *Christian Century*, vol. 94 (July 20–27, 1977), pp. 645–646. A prospectus of the Conference on Black Church and Black Community, sponsored by the Black Theology Project of Theology in the Americas.

Young, Henry J. "Black Theology and the Work of William A. Jones." *Religion in Life*, vol. 44 (Spring 1975), pp. 14–28. An exposition and critique of Black humanism by a Black theist.

————. "Black Theology: Providence and Evil." *Journal of the Interdenominational Theological Center*, vol. 40, no. 2 (Spring 1975), pp. 87–96. A critique of traditional ways of treating the justice and omnipotence of God in regard to Black suffering.

Ziegler, Jesse H., ed. "The Black Religious Experience and Theological Education." *Theological Education*, vol. 6 (Spring 1970), plus supplement. This entire issue is given over to Black religion and theological education. It contains nine essays, plus workshop reports by Black theologians and educators seeking to find meaning in the Black religious experience and theological education.

INDEX